THE ROAD TO PARADOX

Truth, provability, necessity, and other concepts are fundamental to many branches of philosophy, mathematics, computer science, and linguistics. Their study has led to some of the most celebrated achievements in logic, such as Gödel's incompleteness theorems, Tarski's theorem on the undefinability of truth, and numerous accounts of the paradoxes associated with these concepts. This book provides a clear and direct introduction to the theory of paradoxes and the Gödel incompleteness theorems. It offers new analyses of the ideas of self-reference, circularity, and the semantic paradoxes, and helps readers to see both how paradoxes arise and what their common features are. It will be valuable for students and researchers with a minimal background in logic and will equip them to understand and discuss a wide variety of topics in philosophical logic.

VOLKER HALBACH is Professor of Philosophy at the University of Oxford and a fellow of New College, Oxford. He is the author of *The Logic Manual* (2010) and *Axiomatic Theories of Truth* (Cambridge, 2011).

GRAHAM E. LEIGH is Associate Professor of Logic at the University of Gothenburg, Sweden. He has published a number of influential articles on the concepts of truth, reflection, and computation.

THE ROAD TO PARADOX

A Guide to Syntax, Truth, and Modality

VOLKER HALBACH
University of Oxford

GRAHAM E. LEIGH
University of Gothenburg

CAMBRIDGE
UNIVERSITY PRESS

CAMBRIDGE
UNIVERSITY PRESS

Shaftesbury Road, Cambridge CB2 8EA, United Kingdom

One Liberty Plaza, 20th Floor, New York, NY 10006, USA

477 Williamstown Road, Port Melbourne, VIC 3207, Australia

314–321, 3rd Floor, Plot 3, Splendor Forum, Jasola District Centre, New Delhi – 110025, India

103 Penang Road, #05–06/07, Visioncrest Commercial, Singapore 238467

Cambridge University Press is part of Cambridge University Press & Assessment, a department of the University of Cambridge.

We share the University's mission to contribute to society through the pursuit of education, learning and research at the highest international levels of excellence.

www.cambridge.org
Information on this title: www.cambridge.org/9781108841016

DOI: 10.1017/9781108888400

First published 2024

A catalogue record for this publication is available from the British Library

A Cataloging-in-Publication data record for this book is available from the Library of Congress

ISBN 978-1-108-84101-6 Hardback

In the beginning was the Word.

John 1:1

Contents

Preface

This book has its origin in attempts to teach to philosophers the theory of the semantic paradoxes, formal theories of truth, and at least some ideas behind the Gödel incompleteness theorems. These are central topics in philosophical logic with many ramifications in other areas of philosophy and beyond. However, many texts on the paradoxes require an acquaintance with the theory of computation, the coding of syntax, and the representability of certain functions and relations in arithmetical theories. Teaching these techniques in class or covering them in an elementary text leaves little space for the actual topics, that is, the analysis of the paradoxes, formal theories of truth and other modalities, and the formalization of various metamathematical notions such as provability in a formal theory.

It is not necessary to learn about the theory of computation in order to understand even fairly subtle points about the semantic paradoxes, nor should it be. The paradoxes do not conceptually presuppose a coding of syntax in the natural numbers. In fact, the coding of syntax in the natural numbers can create artefacts that add an additional layer of complication, as we argue in the final chapter 12 of this book. Occasionally, logicians acknowledge this and precede their paper with the promise that their reasoning is not essentially based on arithmetic and could, or perhaps even should, be carried out directly in a theory of syntax without the detour through the coding of syntax. The authors of this book are among them. We honour our promise with this monograph. We show how arithmetic can be replaced in sophisticated theories of truth and parts of metamathematics; we even prove the Gödel incompleteness theorems in a syntax theory. Of course, for some applications the traditional arithmetized versions are required, but for others it is desirable to bypass the vagaries of coding and proceed in a more direct way. In this book we show that using a syntax theory does not impose limitations on the study of the paradoxes, formal theories of truth, and even some incompleteness phenomena.

We also fill a gap among the existing introductory texts in philosophical logic. The semantic paradoxes, self-reference, theories of truth and of modal predicates such as necessity, and issues related to the Gödel incompleteness theorems are at the centre of many discussions in philosophical logic. Yet these topics are shunned by many introductory texts in philosophical logic; and one might easily get the impression that philosophical logic is mainly concerned with nonclassical and intensional logics, including modal logic and its offspring such as deontic, dynamic, and epistemic logic. We provide an introduction to the theory of paradoxes that allows one to reach central results such as the diagonal lemma, Tarski's theory on the undefinability of truth, and the Yablo–Visser paradoxes relatively quickly. To provide precise proofs of both Gödel incompleteness theorems requires more effort, but we do this without going through coding and its mathematical details.

Intended Readership

We have written this book with a wide variety of readers in mind. It is aimed at an audience ranging from experts to less experienced readers who have covered only the basics of first-order predicate logic. The reader should be familiar at least with the material covered in an elementary logic textbook such as (Halbach 2010). For readers with a minimal background we have provided auxiliary material in chapter 2 which explains the notation and some topics such as function symbols that will be familiar to all readers with a more extensive background in logic.

In particular, the reader is not assumed to have seen proofs of the Gödel incompleteness theorems or to be at all familiar with the techniques involved in the proofs such as arithmetization and the theory of computability. Occasionally we establish connections with known logical and philosophical theories and results that are usually not covered in a basic logic course. For instance, in chapter 7 we look at a possible-worlds semantics that is modelled on possible-worlds semantics for modal logic; and in section 9.3 we show how theories of arithmetic can be recovered in a theory of expressions. These parts do not presuppose an acquaintance with modal logic or systems of arithmetic; but to appreciate their significance, a background in modal logic and formal systems of arithmetic is helpful. These parts are not built on in later sections of the book.

How to read this book

The book need not be read in a linear way. The following diagram displays the technical dependencies of the chapters. We hope that it is helpful especially when teaching from the book. For instance, the technical background required for the central chapter 6 on the paradoxes is covered in chapters 2 and 5. In particular, for a course on the formal theory of paradoxes and basic applications of diagonalization, students can be sent straight from chapter 2 to chapters 5 and 6. There is also a short path to the chapter on the Gödel incompleteness theorem, that is, chapter 10. An arrow from one chapter to another indicates that the chapter at the tip presupposes material from the chapter at the origin of the arrow.

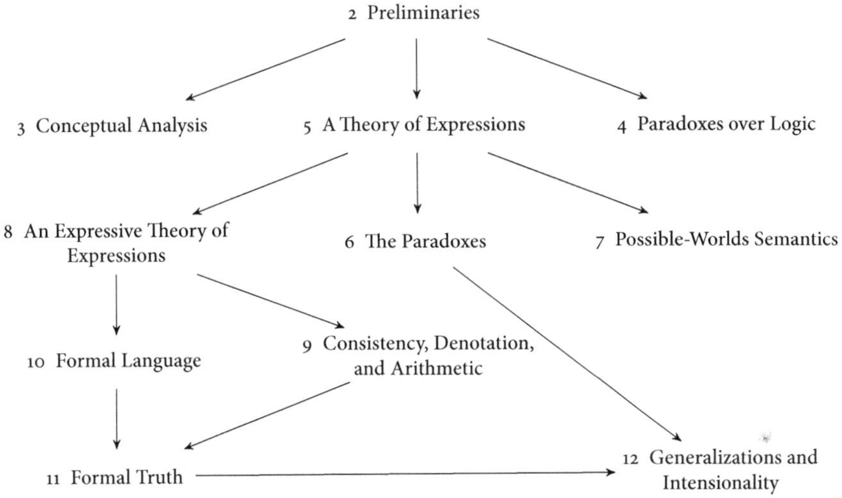

Acknowledgements

We would like to thank our friends and colleagues for conversations and discussions related to the topics in this book, especially Balthasar Grabmayr, Leon Horsten, Ming Hsiung, Boaz Laan, Beau Mount, Carlo Nicolai, Lavinia Picollo, Wim Vanrie, Albert Visser, Philip Welch, Tim Williamson, Luke Wojtalik, Johanna Wolff, Lingyuan Ye, and an anonymous referee. The second author is forever grateful to Bahareh whose encouragement and support through stressful times helped bring this project to fruition. Both authors are indebted to Christopher von Bülow for careful proofreading and eliminating many mistakes.

The New College Ludwig Fund for Humanities Research made it possible for Graham Leigh to visit Oxford in Trinity Term 2016 and to collaborate with Volker Halbach. Both authors would like to thank the New College Ludwig Fund, and Eugene Ludwig personally, for making this trip possible. We gratefully acknowledge support by the Arts & Humanities Research Council AH/H039791/1, the Leverhulme Trust, the Knut and Alice Wallenberg Foundation 2015.0179 and the Swedish Research Council 2017-05111.

1 Aims and Ends

Philosophers wonder whether some truths are not verifiable and whether there are things that are synthetic but a priori. They discuss whether all mathematical truths are logically valid and whether moral claims can be true. Many agree that whatever is known is true, that there are unknown justified true beliefs, and that whatever is logically provable is analytic. Logicians maintain that there are unprovable truths and that the claim that no contradiction is provable is not provable.

The reader will recognize some of the most famous problems in philosophy in this list. They are often existential or universal claims involving truth, necessity, logical validity, formal or absolute provability, analyticity, verifiability, apriority, knowability, and so on. Of course, one would expect that the respective discussions require arguments specific to the claim in question. However, all these discussions are threatened by what are usually called the *semantic paradoxes*.[1] The best known of these paradoxes is the liar paradox. It has many versions; here is one of them:

> *The sentence in italics on this page is not true.*

The reader will be familiar with the reasoning that leads to a contradiction. Assuming that the sentence is true leads to a contradiction, because it says that it is not true. Therefore, it is *not* true. This is what the sentence is saying, and thus the sentence *is* true. But that has been ruled out already. This is the liar paradox in a nutshell.

There are many other paradoxes involving truth, each with its own variants, refinements and formalizations. Notions other than truth are affected as well.

[1]The label 'semantic paradox' is problematic for various reasons, and we just use it for the kind of paradoxes that are introduced in this chapter by example. This distinction between semantic and logical paradoxes goes back at least to Ramsey (1926). In chapter 4 we show how closely they are related and that Russell's paradox can easily be converted into a semantic paradox. We have no ambition to provide a classification of paradoxes here, and for our purposes there is no need to be more precise.

As an example we choose, somewhat randomly, verifiability and a paradox very close to the liar paradox:

(V) (V) is not verifiable.

The point of labelling the sentence with '(V)' is that we have the following identity:

$$\text{(V)} = \text{'(V) is not verifiable'.}$$

Verifiability can be understood in different ways here, for instance, in the sense of 'can be demonstrated to be true', as 'can be known', or as 'is provable'. For this paradox we give the steps leading to a contradiction:

1. Assume (V) is verifiable.
2. Then '(V) is not verifiable' is verifiable (by the identity above).
3. Therefore, (V) is not verifiable (because this can be verified).
4. Hence, (V) is not verifiable (because the first line and the previous line, derived from it, contradict each other, and thus the assumption in the first line is refuted).
5. That is, we have just verified (V) (because the preceding sentence is just (V)).

The last two claims are contradictory.

The reasoning is by any means not unassailable, and various steps are questionable. However, the argument shows that it is easy to become entangled in the paradoxes. If we are not careful, we can, without very extravagant assumptions about truth or verifiability, arrive at contradictions. Any further agonizing about realism in the form of the claim that there may be truths that are not verifiable is pointless, if basic assumptions about the fundamental concepts in the debate can be used to derive a contradiction.

The reader may object at this point that we should have reasoned in a logic which does not support one of the steps, that we should not have ascribed verifiability to sentences but rather propositions, that some assumption on verifiability implicit in the reasoning ought to be rejected, or that something is wrong with labelling a sentence with a label that is already used in the sentence. For the time being, we only claim that the threat of the paradoxes should be taken seriously. If one of the mentioned objections is justified, it does have consequences for the further discussion of all the philosophical claims. If classical logic is to be rejected, we have to do metaphysics, epistemology, and so on in a nonclassical logic. If sentences cannot be verified, but, say, only propositions conceived as sets of possible worlds, then we need to reject as verifications proofs as lists of sentences. If we give up some fundamental assumption about verifiability, for instance, the assumption implicit in the transition from 2. to 3., we need to purge this assumption, as plausible and unproblematic as it may look, from all later reasoning about verifiability. If we disallow the use of labels such as (V) and try to block the derivation of the paradox in this way, still other assumptions that have a similar effect as our way of labelling (V) need to be revised; we have to give up basic reasoning about strings of symbols.

At any rate, philosophers need to think about the semantic paradoxes. As long as they have no strategy for blocking the derivation of the contradiction (or defusing it), all discussions about the claims above are up in the air.

1.1 The Quick Road to Paradox

Instead of using descriptions such as 'the sentence in italics', other constructions can be employed to obtain a liar sentence. For instance, we can use labels:

(L) (L) is not true.

Other versions, such as the following liar sentence, rely on pronouns:

This sentence is not true.

The first reaction to these and similar versions of the liar paradoxes is often a suspicion that something has gone wrong with the labelling of the sentence and the use of the pronoun 'this'. Thus, the blame for the paradox would go to the strange use of the label '(L)' and the pronoun, not to the truth predicate 'is true' or assumptions about the behaviour of the truth predicate. Avoiding this kind of use of labels and pronouns may be possible.

However, the liar paradox can be generated using purely syntactic means, without any pronouns or labels as in the mentioned examples. We use a variant of an example by Quine (1976b). The quotation of an expression is the expression enclosed in quotation marks. Now a liar sentence can be stated in the following way:

> 'preceded by its own quotation is not true' preceded by its own quotation is not true.

The means used in this variant of the liar paradox are far less dispensable. Enclosing an expression in quotation marks and appending an expression to another expression are very basic syntactic operations. Thus, trying to solve the paradoxes by restricting the means used in this version of the liar paradox is much harder; it would mean to sacrifice our ability to talk about expressions in any meaningful way.

However, we will not employ Quine's elegant trick, but a more versatile method due to Gödel. His fundamental result which permits to construct a sentence that is equivalent to the claim that it itself is not true (or provable or verifiable) is the so-called diagonal lemma.[2]

Our way to the paradoxes is quick in the sense that it permits a proof of the diagonal lemma and thus the formulation of the liar paradox in a very simple formal theory of syntax. The theory is versatile enough to permit the formulation of more sophisticated paradoxes such as Visser's and Yablo's. The theory can be used as a general framework for studying semantic paradoxes. In chapter 6 a collection of paradoxes will be presented, and a unified analysis of them is given in chapter 7. In this way we provide the reader with an access to the theory of the paradoxes that is quick and easy, uses only the means of syntax, and is formally precise. We use syntax theory – rather than labels such as '(L)' or pronouns as above – because the methods used in syntax theory are also those used (for good reason) in the more technical literature. The more sophisticated ones are best presented in syntax theory, as are the offspring of the paradoxes, such as Tarski's theorem on the undefinability of truth and Gödel's incompleteness theorems.

Our way of presenting the paradoxes can bridge the gap to the more technical literature on them. We hope that this is useful, because the technical apparatus that is applied to understand, solve, or analyze the paradoxes has become so sophisticated that only a relatively small group of logicians and technically versed philosophers have followed the rapid development of the theory of paradoxes.

It is an unfortunate consequence of this development that philosophers have often opted to leave the difficulties caused by the paradoxes aside and to concentrate exclusively on the 'philosophical' problems of the modal notions. We

[2]The diagonal lemma is actually a family of results with several variants and generalizations. We ascribe the diagonal lemma to Gödel, although he did not state it in its general form in his 1931.

think that it is not a promising strategy to devise theories of truth, necessity, and other modal notions while ignoring the paradoxes and hoping that they can be solved independently from the chosen philosophical account of the modal notions. Paradoxes are not just a nuisance that gets in the way of philosophical theorizing. They can also be the engine behind progress. In almost any area of philosophy, paradoxes of some kind have prompted new approaches. Paradoxes that arise from purely syntactic considerations can, and actually did, prompt philosophers of truth to rethink their theories. The situation may be compared to set theory, where Russell's and related paradoxes led to the formulation of modern axiomatic theories of sets; it may even be compared to the paradoxes that led Einstein to devise the theory of special relativity.

One reason why the literature on the paradoxes has become difficult to access is that they are often not studied before the background of a syntax theory. Instead they are studied before the background of a mathematical theory, usually arithmetic. The syntactic objects, that is, strings of symbols, including sentences, are then assigned numbers as codes. Syntactic operations, such as concatenation, substitution of symbols, etc., are then mimicked in the arithmetical language, using operations on these codes. That the theory of syntax can be simulated in arithmetic is one of Gödel's (1931) central insights. We think it is fair to say that, before Gödel, logicians assumed that this could be done in some way. However, it took Gödel to work out a precise mathematical account, which involves some results from number and computability theory. If one aims to show that some system of arithmetic is incomplete, as Gödel did, these results are hard to avoid. However, if one is interested in the analysis of the paradoxes and in a logical framework for studying modal notions, then it is not clear why the theory of syntax has to be transposed into arithmetic. In fact, for many applications in philosophy it is far more natural to study the paradoxes before the background of a theory of syntax and to bypass arithmetic entirely.

In this book, we present formal theories of syntax which capture our informal reasoning about syntax. This will greatly simplify the presentation of the paradoxes, but also of Gödel's incompleteness theorems. We hope that this will make the material more accessible and attractive to readers without a mathematical background.

Of course, for some goals there are very good reasons for taking the detour via arithmetic. For the purposes of an article in a logic journal it is much easier to state at the beginning that some system of arithmetic will be used as a proxy for a syntax theory, usually without specifying any specific coding. The specialist reader does not need reminding of the underlying assumptions about coding. Moreover, using arithmetic as framework permits one to tap into the wealth of existing results about such theories.

Many axiomatizations of the theory of syntax have been given in the literature. Some are intended to be theories of syntax for some object language, not necessarily the language of syntax theory itself. Some obey nominalistic constraints that are compatible with the assumption that there are only finitely many expressions. Others axiomatize a theory of syntax for a language with only two symbols, so that coding is required for languages in normal notation. As far as we know, Tarski (1935, § 2) was the first to axiomatize syntax theory. He used concatenation as a primitive operator and formulated his theory in second-order logic. Our system in this chapter employs some axioms found in Tarski's paper. His system has been developed, expanded, and analyzed by Corcoran, Frank, and Maloney (1974) and other logicians. Another classic in the field is Quine's (1940, chapter 7) protosyntax. He also developed a strictly nominalistic theory in (Goodman and Quine 1947). Smullyan (1957) provided a proof of the diagonal lemma in a very simple and elegant axiomatic theory. Grzegorczyk's (2005) proof of the undecidability of predicate logic in syntax theory (see also Visser 2009) contains many ideas that are mainly used in our more expressive theory in chapter 8. However, it differs significantly from our approach in axiomatizing the syntax of a language that has only two distinct symbols, so that, as mentioned above, coding is still required for languages in a normal notation. Blau (2008) uses a theory of quotation as his basis for analyzing the paradoxes. Perlis (1988) presents the paradoxes in a style similar to ours.

These approaches have influenced ours, which may well not contain any fundamentally new ideas. We have not tried to trace back our axioms and proofs to earlier versions in the literature. Many are straightforward formalizations of metatheoretic principles frequently used in reasoning about formal languages; the metatheoretic versions are commonly considered obvious, and the contribution of the logicians just mentioned is mainly to have made these principles formally explicit. It is not unlikely that many authors have arrived at similar principles independently. In many cases axioms and claims differ between various accounts in details; for instance, the empty string can be admitted or not. All this often makes it hard to identify a particular statement or observation in the literature as the original source of an axiom or theorem in syntax theory.

In contrast to many other authors, we do not aim at an *elegant* theory of syntax; our theory is aimed at capturing more directly our informal theory of syntax, even if that proves to be more clumsy than streamlined theories such as Grzegorczyk's. Our austere notion of quotation is that used in logical metatheory. In our syntax theories we do not attempt to capture the general phenomenon of quotation outside this confined range of application. For puzzles and observations arising from quotation elsewhere we refer the reader to (Cappelen and Lepore 2007).

1.2 The Direct Way to Paradox

This may sound as if our theories of syntax served merely the purpose to provide an easier route to theories of truth and the incompleteness theorems, avoiding coding and arithmetization. However, it also serves an important theoretical purpose.

A theory of syntax is always required, even in the usual proofs of the incompleteness theorems, which proceed via coding. In order to theorize about the relation between syntactic and arithmetical notions, we need a sufficiently precise theory of syntax. When we claim that the concept of being a sentence of the chosen language or of being provable in a specific system can be expressed in arithmetic, we should better be clear about these concepts.

Usually, the theory of syntax is not fully formalized in proofs of the incompleteness theorems. We do not think that something is wrong about this approach, but having a formal theory of syntax makes assumptions explicit that are usually left implicit in the metatheory. The reader familiar with one of the traditional proofs of the second incompleteness theorem or even the discussions about intensionality in metamathematics, as discussed by Feferman (1960) and many subsequent authors, will have seen claims that a certain formula of an arithmetical theory 'naturally expresses' provability. It is notoriously difficult to spell out what this means, but it must be some structural similarity between a formula in arithmetic and the definition of provability in informal metatheoretic syntax theory. If one aims to make the notion of natural expression (and similar concepts) precise, it would be useful to have a fully explicit and formal syntax theory like our theory E^*. Some observations about problems of intensionality in metamathematics and the use of syntax theories in their analysis will be discussed in the final chapter 12.

2 Technical Preliminaries

In this chapter we briefly review some basics of first-order predicate logic, which will be familiar to the expert reader. In particular, we fix our notation and review some topics, including function symbols and many-sorted languages, that are not always covered in introductory textbooks such as (Halbach 2010).

2.1 Languages of First-Order Predicate Logic

We describe the formation rules for the formulæ and sentences of our languages. All the languages we consider have an infinite stock of variables: $\mathsf{v}_0, \mathsf{v}_1, \mathsf{v}_2, \mathsf{v}_3, \ldots$ Some contain also function symbols. Each function symbol has an arity assigned, which is some natural number 0, 1, ...

All variables are terms. If f is a function symbol of arity n and $t_1, \ldots, t_n$ are terms, then $ft_1 \ldots t_n$ is a term. For some binary function symbols, that is, function symbols f of arity 2, we often write (t_1ft_2) for ft_1t_2, that is, we write the function symbol between terms and use brackets around this expression; but this is only our notation for the official ft_1t_2. In mathematics the symbols for addition and multiplication are binary function symbols. They correspond to the English phrases 'the sum of ... and ...' and 'the product of ... and ...' In mathematics we write $+$ and $\times$ between terms, for instance, $a+b$ rather than $+ab$; and this is why we adopt our notation for binary function symbols. It is also clear that in our notation brackets are required: $(a \times b) + c$ and $a \times (b+c)$, for instance, are clearly not equivalent. In the official notation brackets are not needed.

Unary function symbols correspond to expressions such as 'the mass of ...' in English. The expression 'the mass of ...' has arity 1. It takes a term, for instance, 'the Earth', and yields a new term, 'the mass of the Earth'. An example of a binary function expression is 'the border between ... and ...'

We also allow function symbols with arity 0. They are individual constants. Since individual constants are 0-place function symbols, they need to be combined with 0 many terms to yield a term, that is, they are terms already by themselves.

A language may have no function symbols at all or only individual constants, that is, function symbols of arity 0. All the languages we consider will have only finitely many function symbols.

In contrast, all our languages have at least one predicate symbol. As is the case with function symbols, each of the languages we consider will feature only a finite number of predicate symbols. Predicate symbols also come with an arity. If P is a predicate symbol with arity n and $t_1, \ldots, t_n$ are terms, then $Pt_1 \ldots t_n$ is an atomic formula. An exception is the binary predicate symbol $=$ for identity, which is written between terms. We use $=$ as a predicate symbol in our formal languages, but also as the usual identity symbol in the language we use, the 'metalanguage'. The identity symbol will be a predicate symbol in all of the languages we consider.

As in the case with function symbols, the predicate symbols will be specified for each language we discuss. In many elementary logic textbooks such as (Halbach 2010) a single language with infinitely many predicate symbols of arbitrary arities is considered. This ascertains that we never run out of predicate symbols when formalizing arguments in natural language. But once we consider a specific set of assumptions, that is, a theory, this will often be formulated with very few predicate symbols. Set theory, for instance, in which all (or perhaps almost all) of mathematics can be carried out, has only a single, binary predicate symbol.

All atomic formulæ are formulæ. If φ, ψ are formulæ and x is a variable, then $\neg\varphi$, $(\varphi \rightarrow \psi)$, and $\forall x\varphi$ are formulæ. We use $(\varphi \wedge \psi)$ as an abbreviation for $\neg(\varphi \rightarrow \neg\psi)$, $(\varphi \vee \psi)$ as an abbreviation for $(\neg\varphi \rightarrow \psi)$, $(\varphi \leftrightarrow \psi)$ as an abbreviation for $\neg((\varphi \rightarrow \psi) \rightarrow \neg(\psi \rightarrow \varphi))$, and finally $\exists x\varphi$ as an abbreviation for $\neg\forall x\neg\varphi$. These abbreviations are metalinguistic abbreviations. That is, we do not introduce new symbols $\wedge$, $\vee$, $\leftrightarrow$, and $\exists$ into our formal object language; rather, we use $\wedge$, $\vee$, $\leftrightarrow$, and $\exists$ in our informal metalanguage in order to save some space and make our text more readable. As we have already done here, we use lower-case Greek letters as metavariables for formulæ. Predicates of arity 0 are also admissible and called sentence parameters.

The notion of free and bound occurrences is defined in the usual way: In an atomic formula all occurrences of variables are free. All occurrences of variables that are free in φ and in ψ are also free in $\neg\varphi$ and $(\varphi \rightarrow \psi)$. Every free occurrence of a variable y in φ different from x itself is also free in $\forall x\varphi$; all occurrences of x in $\forall x\varphi$ are bound. An occurrence of a variable is bound iff it is not free.[1] Formulæ without any free occurrences of variables are sentences.

[1]As usual, 'iff' abbreviates 'if and only if'.

We use metatheoretic rules for omitting brackets: Our formulæ are always the formulæ with all the brackets. If we omit brackets, we obtain abbreviations of formulæ. The rules for omitting brackets are specific to the particular occurrence of a formula; so they should be formulated for occurrences of formulæ. We can omit the outer brackets in an occurrence of a formula $(\varphi \to \psi)$, as long as this occurrence is not within an occurrence of another formula. That is, we can drop the 'outermost' set of brackets. The expression $(\varphi \wedge \psi \wedge \chi)$ is short for $\big((\varphi \wedge \psi) \wedge \chi)\big)$. An analogous rule applies to $\vee$. Of course, here we are already using the abbreviations $\wedge$ and $\vee$. Moreover, in abbreviated formulæ with $\wedge$ and $\vee$, $\wedge$ and $\vee$ bind more strongly than $\to$ and $\leftrightarrow$. Thus, $\varphi \wedge \psi \to \chi$, for instance, is short for $(\varphi \wedge \psi) \to \chi$, which abbreviates $\big((\varphi \wedge \psi) \to \chi\big)$.

Above we have already used x and y as metavariables for variables in the object language. This means that x could be any of the variables $\mathsf{v}_0, \mathsf{v}_1, \mathsf{v}_2, \ldots$ As in the case of the metavariables for formulæ, we employed metavariables for variables in order to make our definitions sufficiently general. For instance, we stipulated that $\forall x \varphi$ is a formula if x is a variable and φ is a formula. It would not suffice to say that $\forall \mathsf{v}_0 \varphi$ is a formula if φ is, because this would not imply that $\forall \mathsf{v}_1 \varphi$ is a formula. In what follows we continue to use x, y, and so on as metavariables for variables.

Writing 'v_0', 'v_1', and so on makes the notation somewhat cluttered. To avoid the indices, we write x for v_0, y for v_1, z for v_2, and w for v_3. So sans-serif letters stand for specific variables, while letters in italics are metavariables for variables. In logic it usually does not matter which variable is used, as long as the variables employed in a formula are pairwise distinct. But in a theory of expressions and in proving results such as the diagonal theorem, we have to be very specific and will use sans-serif letters, that is, specific variables.

2.2 Logical Calculi

There are numerous ways to generate the logically valid sentences of the languages described in the previous section. In many textbooks some variant of the system of natural deduction is used, while tableaux systems are used in many others. There are also sequent and axiomatic systems, and calculi less likely to be seen in introductory texts for philosophers. For most parts of this book it does not matter which logical calculus is used. However, the reader should be familiar with at least one such calculus. When we prove a sentence of our formal language, we do not provide a proof in some specific calculus, but we rather outline the crucial steps that should allow the reader versed in a particular calculus to convert our informal proof into a fully formal proof in their preferred logical calculus.

For many logical calculi an infinite stock of individual constants is needed for the quantifier rules. However, we consider languages with only finitely many constants (or 0-place function symbols). We can simply add constants for the sake of proofs, so that these constants never appear in the premisses and the conclusion of the proof, but only in the intermediate steps. Alternatively, free variables can be used instead of the constants.

For the identity symbol =, the chosen logical calculus should contain suitable rules and/or axioms. For function symbols usually additional specific axioms or rules are not required, as long as the rules for identity apply. However, compared to calculi for languages without function symbols, the rules and axioms must cover not only free variables and/or constants as terms but also complex terms involving function symbols. In section 2.3 we show that function symbols are dispensable.

When a sentence φ is provable in some fixed logical calculus, for instance, in natural deduction, from sentences in a set Γ of sentences, we write $\Gamma \vdash \varphi$. We read $\Gamma \vdash \varphi$ as 'φ is (logically) provable from Γ' or 'φ is (logically) derivable from Γ.' The set Γ can be empty. In that case we write $\vdash \varphi$. For instance, sentences φ and ψ are logically equivalent iff $\vdash \varphi \leftrightarrow \psi$. Occasionally we will write $\Gamma \vdash \varphi$ for a formula φ containing free variables. We can take this to be shorthand for the claim that the universal closure of φ is provable from Γ. A universal closure of a formula φ is any result of prefixing to φ universal quantifiers for all free variables in φ. For instance, if $\varphi(\mathrm{v}_0, \mathrm{v}_3)$ has free occurrences of the variables v_0 and v_3 but of no other variables, then $\forall \mathrm{v}_0 \forall \mathrm{v}_3\, \varphi(\mathrm{v}_0, \mathrm{v}_3)$ and $\forall \mathrm{v}_3 \forall \mathrm{v}_0\, \varphi(\mathrm{v}_0, \mathrm{v}_3)$ are both universal closures of $\varphi(\mathrm{v}_0, \mathrm{v}_3)$. As the universal closures of a formula are logically equivalent to one another we will usually talk of *the* universal closure of a formula.

We use the deduction theorem without mentioning it explicitly, that is, we assume the following:

$$\Gamma \cup \{\varphi\} \vdash \psi \quad \text{iff} \quad \Gamma \vdash \varphi \rightarrow \psi.$$

The proof of the deduction theorem varies from calculus to calculus. For natural deduction it is trivial: ψ is provable with the undischarged assumption φ iff $\varphi \rightarrow \psi$ is provable without φ as undischarged assumption. This follows from the introduction and elimination rules for the material conditional $\rightarrow$.

We will often talk about theories. A theory is just a deductively closed set of sentences. A set of sentences is deductively closed iff the set contains all sentences logically derivable from it. The elements of a theory are called the *theorems of* the theory. Frequently we say that a theory is given by certain axioms and rules. This means that the theory is the set of all sentences that follow logically from these axioms and by applications of the inference rules. Of course, for each theory there are infinitely many sets of axioms that give rise to this theory. Usually we specify a particular theory by listing axioms and occasionally inference rules, and then we call these axioms and rules *the* axioms and rules of the theory. Therefore, the axioms and rules of a theory are the axioms and rules that have been used to describe the theory.

A theory Γ is *inconsistent* iff $\Gamma \vdash \varphi$ for all sentences φ of the language. It is not hard to show that Γ is inconsistent iff there is a sentence φ such that $\Gamma \vdash \varphi$ and $\Gamma \vdash \neg\varphi$. A theory is *consistent* iff it is not inconsistent.

2.3 Function Symbols

Because many introductory logic textbooks do not cover function symbols, we sketch some basics about them. Unary functions (not function *symbols*) can be understood as binary relations with certain properties. We write Rde to express that d and e stand in the relation R. If relations are conceived as sets of ordered pairs $\langle x, y\rangle$, this means that $\langle d, e\rangle \in R$.

A binary relation is a unary function on a set S iff it satisfies the following two conditions:

(i) For all $d \in S$ there is an e such that Rde.

(ii) If $d \in S$, Rde_1, and Rde_2, then $e_1 = e_2$.

We call (i) the *existence condition* and (ii) the *uniqueness condition.*

Binary functions are defined in an analogous way as special ternary relations: A ternary relation is a binary function on a set S iff the following two conditions are satisfied:

(i) For all $d_1, d_2 \in S$ there is an e such that Rd_1d_2e.

(ii) If $d_1, d_2 \in S$, $Rd_1d_2e_1$, and $Rd_1d_2e_2$, then $e_1 = e_2$.

In mathematics addition is a binary function on the natural numbers. For any numbers d_1 and d_2 there is exactly one number that is the sum of d_1 and d_2. Similarly, if d_1 and d_2 are strings of symbols, then there is exactly one string of symbols that is the result of writing d_2 after d_1 or, in other words, of concatenating d_1 with d_2.

This is generalized in the obvious way to functions of arbitrary arity: an $n+1$-ary relation R is an n-ary function on a set S iff the following two conditions are satisfied:

(i) For all $d_1, \ldots, d_n \in S$ there is an e such that $Rd_1 \ldots d_n e$.

(ii) If $d_1, \ldots, d_n \in S$, $Rd_1 \ldots d_n e_1$, and $Rd_1 \ldots d_n e_2$, then $e_1 = e_2$.

When we formulate our theories about expressions later, we will use function symbols, for instance, for the concatenation of expressions, that is, for the result of appending an expression to another expression. We hope that it makes our formulæ easier to comprehend. We could dispense with the function symbols and use suitable relation symbols instead. How function symbols can be eliminated using suitable predicate symbols is described in many textbooks, including (Boolos, Burgess, and Jeffrey 2007). Here we show how to eliminate function symbols of arity 1 or higher by means of predicate symbols. We do not eliminate individual constants, although this can be done as well.

Before describing the method of elimination in more detail, we give a sketch of the strategy, using a binary function symbol f as an example. Assume we have a formula of the form $fab = c$ where a, b, and c are individual constants and f is a binary function symbol. We introduce a new ternary predicate symbol P that corresponds to the function symbol f. The sentence $fab = c$ is replaced everywhere with $Pabc$. But $Pabc$ carries less information than fab, because $Pabc$ is consistent with $Pabd \wedge \neg c = d$, while $fab = c$ and $fab = d$ imply $c = d$ by the logical rules for identity. Thus, we will have to add an additional assumption about P to our theory, namely $\forall \mathrm{x} \forall \mathrm{y} \forall \mathrm{z} \forall \mathrm{w} (P\mathrm{xyz} \wedge P\mathrm{xyw} \rightarrow \mathrm{z} = \mathrm{w})$. This expresses the uniqueness condition. We also have to add an axiom corresponding to the existence condition. We can prove $\forall \mathrm{x} \forall \mathrm{y} \exists \mathrm{z}\, f\mathrm{xy} = \mathrm{z}$ in our logical calculus, that is, in logic (with identity), because we have $\forall \mathrm{x} \forall \mathrm{y}\, f\mathrm{xy} = f\mathrm{xy}$ and thus, by existential weakening, $\forall \mathrm{x} \forall \mathrm{y} \exists \mathrm{z}\, f\mathrm{xy} = \mathrm{z}$. However, the corresponding sentence $\forall \mathrm{x} \forall \mathrm{y} \exists \mathrm{z}\, P\mathrm{xyz}$ with the predicate symbol is not logically true. Therefore, we add $\forall \mathrm{x} \forall \mathrm{y} \exists \mathrm{z}\, P\mathrm{xyz}$ as an additional axiom. After replacing the binary function symbol f with the ternary predicate symbol P (in the way described in what follows) and adding the uniqueness and existence axioms to our theory, the new theory with the predicate symbol P and without the function symbol f will prove exactly the translations into our new theory with P of the theorems of the original theory with f.

Of course, there remain some details that need to be filled in. In particular, a binary function symbol f may not only occur in formulæ of the form $ft_1t_2 = t_3$ where t_1 and t_2 are constants or variables and t_3 is a term without an occurrence of f. Function symbols can be iterated. For instance $fxfxfxy$ is a term if f is a binary function symbol and x and y variables. Moreover, the function symbol can occur not only in atomic formulæ with identity, but also in atomic formulæ built from other predicate symbols. We sketch the method of elimination only for a binary function symbol f. The method works for function symbols of other arities in an analogous way. If more than one function symbol is present in the language, they can be eliminated by the same method.

First we show that any formula φ in the language with the binary function symbol f is logically equivalent to a formula in which all occurrences of f in atomic formulæ are in atomic formulæ of the form $ft_1t_2 = t_3$ where each of t_1, t_2, and t_3 is either a constant or a variable. This is shown by induction on the complexity of φ. Assuming the formula is not in the desired form, starting from the left of the formula there must be a first occurrence of f that is part of a term ft_1t_2 with t_1 and t_2 a variable or constant that is not on the left-hand side of an identity symbol (such an occurrence will be left alone). Replace ft_1t_2 with the first variable x not occurring in φ to obtain $\varphi(x)$. Let $\psi(x)$ be the (single) atomic subformula of $\varphi(x)$ containing x. In φ, replace $\psi(x)$ with the formula $\exists x\big(ft_1t_2 = x \wedge \psi(x)\big)$ and call this new formula φ'. The formula φ' is logically equivalent to φ. Iterate this procedure, always using the first variable not already used. The resulting formula $\varphi'^{\cdots\prime}$ is called φ^*. In φ^* there are only occurrences of f left that are in atomic formulæ of the form $ft_1t_2 = \ldots$ with t_1 and t_2 variables or constants. Finally we define φ^P as the result of replacing all atomic subformulæ $ft_1t_2 = t_3$ of φ^* with $Pt_1t_2t_3$.

Let a theory Γ and a sentence φ in the language with f but without P be given. Let Γ^P be the result of replacing all sentences γ in Γ with γ^* and adding the two axioms

(i) $\forall x \forall y \exists z\, Pxyz$,

(ii) $\forall x \forall y \forall z \forall w (Pxyz \wedge Pxyw \rightarrow z = w)$.

Then it is not hard to prove the following equivalence:

$$\Gamma \vdash \varphi \quad \text{iff} \quad \Gamma^* \vdash \varphi^*.$$

A detailed proof depends on the logical calculus chosen. Thus, we can dispense with the use of f and employ a predicate symbol instead. As the elimination procedure indicates, the formulation with the predicate symbol tends to produce less legible formulæ.

2.4 Semantics

In this section we sketch some fundamental notions of the semantics of predicate logic and fix our terminology. Large parts of our book do not presuppose any familiarity with formal semantics. However, especially in chapter 7 we employ basic semantic notions. Proper model-theoretic techniques are not used anywhere in the book.

This is not to say that model-theoretic methods are irrelevant. Given a language of first-order predicate logic, a model for this language specifies a non-empty set D as domain of discourse as well as interpretations for the non-logical vocabulary. The domain can itself contain linguistic items. Since our theories are about linguistic objects, such as predicate symbols, formulæ, and sentences, models with sets of expressions as their domains are of particular relevance. The interpretation of an n-ary function symbol is an n-ary function on D. In particular, constants are function symbols of arity 0 and interpreted as specific elements of the domain. The interpretation of an n-ary predicate symbol is an n-ary relation on D. In particular, unary relations are conceived as sets; and 0-place relations, which interpret sentence parameters, are either the truth value *true* or *false*.

The relation of satisfaction between models, variable assignments, and formulæ as well as the truth of a sentence in a model are defined in the usual way. Usually we are interested only in sentences, not in formulæ with free variables. We write $\mathbb{M} \models \varphi$ to express that the sentence φ is true in the model $\mathbb{M}$. We also say that φ *holds* or *is valid in* $\mathbb{M}$. If Γ is a set of sentences, we write $\mathbb{M} \models \Gamma$ iff $\mathbb{M} \models \gamma$ for all $\gamma \in \Gamma$. If Γ is a set of sentences (or only a single sentence) we say that Γ *has a model* iff there is a model $\mathbb{M}$ such that $\mathbb{M} \models \Gamma$. When we write $\mathbb{M} \models \gamma$ and the like, we always assume that $\mathbb{M}$ is a model for the appropriate language.

Occasionally, we will expand a language by one or more new non-logical symbols. The expansion of a language by these new symbols is, of course, the language obtained by adding them to the old symbols and expanding the notions of term and formula to include these additional symbols. Assume we have a model $\mathbb{M}$ for the language L and we expand the language by a new predicate symbol, which gives the language L'. Then an expansion of $\mathbb{M}$ to the language L' is a model for the language L' with the same domain as $\mathbb{M}$ and the same interpretations for all symbols in L, that is, an expansion of $\mathbb{M}$ to L' only adds an interpretation for the new predicate symbol.

The usual model-theoretic notion of logical consequence is defined as follows, if φ and all elements of Γ are sentences:

$$\Gamma \vDash \varphi \quad \text{iff} \quad \text{for all models } \mathbb{M}\text{: if } \mathbb{M} \vDash \Gamma, \text{ then } \mathbb{M} \vDash \varphi.$$

$\Gamma \vDash \varphi$ is also expressed by saying that φ *follows* (*logically*) *from* Γ, and similar phrases.

The following lemma is the main content of the completeness proof for predicate logic:

2.1 LEMMA *If a set Γ of sentences is consistent, then there is a model $\mathbb{M} \vDash \Gamma$.*

The proof obviously depends on the chosen calculus. The proof, which is the main ingredient of the proof of the following adequacy theorem, can be found in many textbooks.

2.2 THEOREM · ADEQUACY *Assume that φ and all elements of Γ are sentences. Then the following equivalence holds:*

$$\Gamma \vDash \varphi \quad \textit{iff} \quad \Gamma \vdash \varphi.$$

The right-to-left direction, also known as the soundness theorem, is proved by an induction on the length of proofs. The details depend on the proof system, of course. The other direction, the completeness theorem, follows from the previous lemma by contraposition: assume $\Gamma \nvdash \varphi$; then $\Gamma \cup \{\neg\varphi\}$ is consistent (this needs to be proved for the specific calculus), and therefore there is an $\mathbb{M}$ such that $\mathbb{M} \vDash \Gamma \cup \{\neg\varphi\}$; and consequently $\mathbb{M} \vDash \Gamma$ but $\mathbb{M} \nvDash \varphi$, that is, $\Gamma \nvDash \varphi$.

2.5 Many-Sorted Languages

In the following chapter we will present theories of expressions and of certain modal notions such as truth, necessity, and knowledge. Some of the main arguments are inconsistency proofs, that is, demonstrations of the inconsistency of certain axiom sets. Many of the inconsistent systems we consider have surprisingly simple axioms. They are designed to be just strong enough to yield the inconsistency. The significance of these inconsistency results lies in the fact that they are supposed to show that straightforward formalizations of certain informal assumptions or theories lead to inconsistency. However, there is an obstacle to applying our inconsistency results to comprehensive philosophical theories. A typical example of an axiom we will employ is the following:

(A4) $$\forall x \forall y \forall z \left((x^\frown y)^\frown z \right) = \left(x^\frown (y^\frown z) \right).$$

The function symbol $^\frown$ stands for concatenation. In words the axiom says that concatenating x with y first and then appending z gives the same string as first concatenating y and z and then putting x in front. The axiom states this for all x, y, and z. In philosophical theories we do not only deal with expressions, but also with persons, universals, brain states, chairs, and many other objects. Since the axiom A4 applies to all objects, it tells us something about the result of first concatenating Volker Halbach's present brain state with the chair he is sitting on and then concatenating their concatenation with himself. Of course, concatenating these objects does not make much sense. We might doubt that there is a result of concatenating the chair with a brain state. We might stipulate that the result of concatenating any object that is not an expression always results in a dummy object, say, Volker Halbach's chair. But that may not always be a viable solution. We will consider an axiom saying that an object is true iff the result of concatenating the negation symbol with that thing is not true. Thus, if Volker Halbach's pen is not true, then its negation (the result of concatenating the negation symbol with it) is true. This seems at least odd; and it can lead to inconsistency with other possible axioms.

To avoid any decision about what the result of concatenating Volker Halbach's present brain state with the chair he is sitting on may be, we could say that the quantifiers in A4 range only over expressions and not over other objects. There are different ways to implement this restriction in a formal setting. We could employ a predicate for restricting quantifiers to expressions. For instance, assuming that E stands for 'is an expression', A4 is replaced with the following axiom:

(A4) $$\forall x \forall y \forall z \Big(Ex \land Ey \land Ez \rightarrow \left((x^\frown y)^\frown z \right) = \left(x^\frown (y^\frown z) \right) \Big).$$

This axiom does not commit us to any view concerning the result of concatenating objects that are not expressions. However, the use of a function symbol $^\frown$ still commits us to the existence of the result of concatenating arbitrary objects, including objects that are not expressions. This is because the existence condition comes with the use of a function symbol. To avoid this commitment we could use a predicate instead of a function symbol.

Another, neater way to reformulate axioms such as A4 is the use of a many-sorted language. In our case we could employ a two-sorted language. In this language there are two sorts of variables, namely our variables $\mathsf{v}_0, \mathsf{v}_1, \ldots$ ranging over expressions and new variables $\mathsf{o}_0, \mathsf{o}_1, \ldots$ that range either over all objects or over all objects that are not expressions. Then predicate and function symbols have to be sorted. For instance, $(\mathsf{v}_1{}^\frown\mathsf{v}_1)$ would be a term, while $(\mathsf{o}_1{}^\frown\mathsf{o}_1)$ is not. The function symbol $^\frown$ can only be combined with expression variables. The identity predicate, in contrast, would be applicable to all sorts of variables. Still other predicates may allow only variables of the general-object sort.

Many-sorted languages and those with restricting predicates are intertranslatable under certain conditions, and the effects of using them would be similar.[2] Generally, the approach based on restricting predicates is expressively stronger, because predicate symbols can be combined with any kind of variable. This way formulæ can be formed that do not have an obvious counterpart in the many-sorted language. However, the reduction of a many-sorted language to a language with restricting predicates is straightforward, as long as suitable relativizing predicates are available. Assume that we have a language with two sorts of variables, say $\mathsf{v}_0, \mathsf{v}_1, \ldots$ and $\mathsf{o}_0, \mathsf{o}_1, \ldots$ We sketch a translation of all formulæ of this language into a language that has only $\mathsf{v}_0, \mathsf{v}_1, \ldots$ as variables and that features E and O as symbols for restricting predicates. In a given formula of the two-sorted language every occurrence of a variable v_n is replaced with an occurrence of the variable v_{2n} and every occurrence of a variable o_n is replaced with an occurrence of the variable v_{2n+1}. Moreover, every occurrence of a quantifier is suitably restricted, that is, a second kind of substitution is performed: a quantifier $\forall \mathsf{v}_{2n} \ldots$ is replaced with $\forall \mathsf{v}_{2n}(E\mathsf{v}_{2n} \rightarrow \ldots)$ and $\forall \mathsf{v}_{2n+1} \ldots$ is replaced with $\forall \mathsf{v}_{2n+1}(O\mathsf{v}_{2n+1} \rightarrow \ldots)$.

Our axioms can then be understood as being expressed with sorted expression variables. The theories based on these axioms can then be conjoined with theories about all kinds of things; but finally everything can be reduced to a single-

[2] One has to be careful about the notion of intertranslatability in this statement. Barrett and Halvorson (2017), for instance, have very different expectations of the reduction of a multisorted to a single-sorted language.

sorted language. Consequently our results can be applied to other, more comprehensive theories that are not only about expressions, but also about other objects.

3 Predicates and Conceptual Analysis

In this chapter we provide the philosophical motivation and some of the non-technical background for later chapters. We are aware that we touch upon many topics that deserve a much more careful discussion, and we only skim larger debates in the literature, omitting some influential views and arguments. Our excuse is that the main purpose of this book is the development of a formal framework that can be fruitfully applied to many questions and problems. If we tried to settle all philosophical questions before embarking on a formal analysis of syntax and the paradoxes, we would never get started with our main project. Results on syntax and the paradoxes can and should shape and inform the answers to philosophical questions. Only once the formal framework has been developed to a certain level can we go more deeply into its application. Thus, this chapter is not intended to provide a conclusive and exhaustive discussion of the topics mentioned in it.

Our target throughout the book is to provide a formal framework for analyzing modal notions. We are less interested in providing an analysis of how these notions are used in everyday talk, just as most epistemologists are not so much interested in how exactly the average speaker of English uses the word 'knows'. The analysandum is already a highly theoretical notion. There is a lot of regimentation required to carve out the target notion of the analysis of knowledge. In the same way, we aim at uses of modal notions in philosophical discourse. What we have in mind are discussions in modern analytic philosophy. While the speaker who uses modal notions in everyday talk can shrug their shoulders at paradoxes such as the liar paradox, Montague's paradox, and similar paradoxes involving knowledge, the philosopher should ignore them as little as he or she ignores other puzzles in epistemology, metaphysics, metaethics, and so on. Moreover, philosophical discourse abounds with quantified claims such as Kant's famous claim that there are synthetic a priori judgements. Hence, our formal framework must be able to deal with such quantified statements.

This does not mean that we do not pay attention to natural language. After all, philosophers use natural language for their theorizing. However, we are happy to make some regimentations in Quine's sense and exclude stylistic variants and simplify our language. Expressive strength, though, needs to/must be preserved. Paraphrasing certain constructions of natural language in a systematic way is permissible and often desirable, but declaring them illegitimate requires very good reasons.

3.1 Modal Predicates

In contrast to the dominating approach in philosophical logic, we analyze all modal notions, including necessity, apriority, analyticity, truth, future truth, and provability, as predicates in languages of first-order predicate logic. In philosophical logic, necessity, knowledge, and future truth, for instance, are commonly studied as sentential operators of modal logic, while truth is treated as a predicate.

In order to explain the difference between the predicate and the operator conception of a modality, we look at natural language. Without claiming that other notions behave in exactly the same way, we choose necessity as our example. The sentence

It is necessary that water is H_2O

can be parsed in at least two different ways. According to the first option, 'it is necessary that' is combined with the sentence 'Water is H_2O':

$$\underbrace{\text{It is necessary that}}_{\text{operator, adverb}}\ \underbrace{\text{water is } \mathrm{H_2O}.}_{\text{sentence}}$$

In this sentence the phrase 'it is necessary that' serves the same purpose as the adverb 'necessarily' in the following sentence:

$$\underbrace{\text{Necessarily}}_{\text{operator}}\ \underbrace{\text{water is } \mathrm{H_2O}.}_{\text{sentence}}$$

Adverbs serve various purposes in natural language. Only some behave like 'necessarily' by modifying an entire sentence. Therefore, we prefer the term 'sentential operator'. A sentential operator is an expression that, combined with a sentence, yields a new sentence. In the simple case here, the sentential operator 'necessarily' is prefixed to the sentence.

We turn to the second way of parsing the sentence. On this approach, necessity is conceived as a predicate:

$$\underbrace{\text{It is necessary}}_{\text{predicate}}\ \underbrace{\text{that water is H}_2\text{O.}}_{\text{singular term}}$$

In this form the predicate approach looks somewhat awkward, but by reversing the order of singular term and predicate it can be made more convincing:

$$\underbrace{\text{That water is H}_2\text{O}}_{\text{singular term}}\ \underbrace{\text{is necessary.}}_{\text{predicate}}$$

We can go even further and force the reading of the that-clause as a singular term by adding a noun, although reformulations of this kind are somewhat questionable because they add information about the kind of object that is denoted by the that-clause:

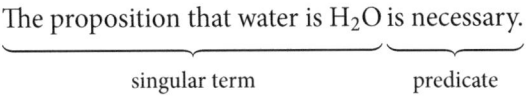

$$\underbrace{\text{The proposition that water is H}_2\text{O}}_{\text{singular term}}\ \underbrace{\text{is necessary.}}_{\text{predicate}}$$

Instead of 'proposition', also 'statement', 'belief', or the like could be used, while 'sentence' is at least very awkward.

Both approaches have been implemented in formal systems. Each of the modal operators $\Box$ for necessity and $\Diamond$ for possibility yield a formula when they are written in front of a formula. Thus, if φ is a formula, then $\Box\varphi$ and $\Diamond\varphi$ are formulæ as well. This means that the operators $\Box$ and $\Diamond$ behave syntactically like the negation symbol. Modal logic can be based on propositional logic. In this case the language contains sentence parameters and connectives (besides auxiliary symbols such as brackets). It can also be based on more sophisticated languages such as first-order predicate logic.

On the predicate approach, usually first-order languages are used. The symbol $\Box$ for necessity is then only another predicate symbol. In English the word 'that' can be used to form a singular term from a sentence: 'that' followed by a sentence such as 'water is H_2O' yields a singular term. In a formal language we may have an analogous device that gives, applied to a sentence φ, a singular term $\overline{\varphi}$.[1] Then the sentence 'It is necessary that water is H_2O' formalizes as $\Box\overline{\varphi}$, if φ formalizes 'water is H_2O'.

So far we have considered necessity as an example of a modal notion that can be conceived as either an operator or a predicate. Other notions behave differently and have been treated differently. For instance, some intentional-attitude predicates cannot so easily be combined with certain singular terms.[2] The problems of substituting 'that *A*' with 'the proposition that *A*' have been discussed in some detail (see, for instance, Moltmann 2003 and Prior 1971). In the case of necessity the substitution seems acceptable, but not in other cases. In the sentence

> Nigel fears that there will be more immigrants next year,

the substitution yields the sentence

> Nigel fears the proposition that there will be more immigrants next year.

But clearly Nigel is afraid of immigration and not propositions. Even with notions such as knowledge, analogous substitutions are at least problematic. Examples of this kind have been used to argue against the conception of that-clauses as singular terms.

Other somewhat tricky kinds of modality are future and past truth. Traditionally they have been treated as operators and studied in temporal logic. In English they are commonly expressed neither with an operator nor with a predicate, but rather with the help of tensed predicates. For instance, the sentence

> Nigel is in Norway

can be put in the future tense:

> Nigel will be in Norway.

[1] In other languages the rules for generating these singular terms are more complicated, even in closely related languages such as German. The predicate conception can be traced back to medieval logic, long before modern English came into existence. In the Latin texts, *accusativus cum infinitivo* constructions were used instead of that-clauses.

[2] Usually intentional attitudes are known as *propositional attitude* predicates, but we are going to construe them as relations between subjects and *sentences* rather than propositions understood in a language-independent way; therefore, we prefer the term *intentional attitude*, which leaves open what the objects of those attitudes are (if any).

It can be argued that changing the tense of a sentence is a modification of the original sentence similar to adding an adverb, just that no adverb is added but rather the verb itself is modified. A corresponding predicate is hard to come by. One could use 'will be the case' or 'will be true', but that is just a tensed truth predicate. There does not seem to be a simple primitive predicate for future truth, unless one resorts to awkward phrases such as

It is future that Nigel is in Norway.

While necessity, knowledge, belief, future truth, and many other notions have traditionally been formalized as modal operators, truth has hardly ever been treated as a sentential operator. Logicians usually decide in favour of one approach and discard the other, presumably because they expect that the chosen approach covers all aspects of the modality and the other approach can be reduced to their preferred conception. Now one could argue that it may be less controversial to keep both, a modal operator $\underline{\Box}$ and a predicate $\Box$. After all, there is an adverb 'necessarily' and a predicate phrase 'is necessary', and both coexist in English. So why should we not be liberal and admit both a predicate and an operator in a formal language? First, the predicate and the operator would have to be related in some way. The strongest relation would be a reduction of either the operator to the corresponding predicate or vice versa.

The reduction of a modal operator $\underline{\Box}$ to a corresponding predicate $\Box$ is technically straightforward under suitable assumptions. The idea is that a sentence $\underline{\Box}\varphi$ is taken as equivalent to $\Box\overline{\varphi}$ where φ does not contain a modal operator, and then the same kind of substitution is defined recursively for sentences with nested occurrences of $\underline{\Box}$ and $\underline{\Diamond}$. We sketch how to define the reduction. We assume that in the language with the predicate we also have a name or some singular term $\overline{\varphi}$ for each formula φ. The choice of the singular term is not without problems. We prefer the quotation of the sentence or some other term from which the structure of the named sentence can be read off. The translation O from the language with the operator to the one with the predicate is then defined recursively as follows:[3]

(i) If the formula φ is atomic, then $O(\varphi) = \varphi$;

(ii) If the formula φ is of the form $\neg\psi$, then $O(\varphi) = \neg O(\psi)$;

[3]The idea for this embedding can be traced back at least to Carnap 1934, IV.B.e. Carnap's translation is still very different and there are several variations. What caused problems especially in early variants were problems with the iteration of N.

(iii) If the formula φ is of the form $\psi \to \chi$, then $O(\varphi) = O(\psi) \to O(\chi)$;

(iv) If the formula φ is of the form $\forall x \psi$, then $O(\varphi) = \forall x\, O(\psi)$;

(v) If the formula φ is of the form $\Box\psi$, then $O(\varphi) = \Box\overline{O(\psi)}$.

The notation $\Box\overline{O(\psi)}$ may require some explanation. It denotes the application of the predicate symbol $\Box$ to the singular term $\overline{O(\psi)}$, which can be thought of as the quotation of the translation of ψ. The symbol O is not a symbol of the object language; it is a symbol for a function defined in the metalanguage. The expression $\overline{O(\psi)}$ is again a singular term of the object language.

Of course, in order to show that this reduction is successful, we have to prove that the translation preserves provability, truth, or even meaning. This task may be far from trivial and may require further tweaks and assumptions. However, if the reduction is successful, there is no need for a further operator for the modality, if the predicate is available. Conversely, if the predicate can be defined in terms of the operator (and perhaps other devices), then it is not required any longer. Such a definition is, as we shall see, more difficult.

Both the operator and the predicate approach have their problems. Deciding in favour of one or the other reading has deep ramifications for many philosophical areas such as metaphysics, epistemology, and philosophy of mind. For instance, if we adopt the predicate approach for intentional attitudes, it is plausible to conceive belief, knowledge, and various kinds of perception as relations between a subject and a belief. This rules out so-called adverbialist theories of these notions. They have been advocated specifically for perceptual notions by Chisholm (1957), Tye (1989), and others. Adverbialists deny that there are belief and perceptual contents. Adverbialism can be applied to other modal notions, although some applications may be implausible, for instance in the case of truth.

We do not even try to summarize these discussions about the predicate and operator conceptions of modalities and refer the reader to (Stern 2016) and (Nicolai and Stern 2021). One problem is that many philosophers have focused on a specific kind of modality, such as truth, necessity, or some intentional attitude. But presumably a general decision is needed, as we will try to show in what follows.

3.2 Problems of the Predicate Approach

Up to the 1960s, both predicate and operator approaches had been pursued, but then the operator view and modal logic ousted their rival. There were two main factors that led to the triumph of the operator over the predicate approach. The predicate approach is prone to paradox. Montague (1963) observed that a version of the liar paradox, namely the paradox now named after him, can be derived for modal predicates with axioms and rules analogous to those of the modal system T. His attack on the predicate approach, based on this observation, was widely seen as very successful (see theorem 6.5, page 80). Even more importantly, Saul Kripke, Stig Kanger, Jaakko Hintikka, and others developed possible-worlds semantics for modal logics.[4] Possible-worlds semantics offered a vast playground for philosophical and mathematical theorizing, and the number of papers on modal logic grew rapidly. No comparable semantics was available for the predicate approach. These are the two main factors that led to the dominance of the operator approach.

Besides the paradoxes and the lack of a neat semantics in the literature, there are more problems with the predicate account of modalities. In the rest of this section we concentrate on some ontological questions. If modalities are conceived as predicates, they apply to objects, according to standard referential semantics. But what kind of objects? In our paraphrase of 'It is necessary that water is H_2O' on page 27 we used propositions. This is presumably the most popular but by no means the only choice among philosophers. If propositions are conceived as abstract objects, nominalists will already see an advantage for the operator approach. An ontological commitment to abstract objects does not worry us, but there is another problem with propositions. Propositions may have to be individuated in different ways for different modalities. Propositions as objects of beliefs would have to be very fine-grained. One can believe that Cicero is a Roman orator without believing that Tully is a Roman orator. Hence, the proposition that Tully is a Roman orator and the proposition that Cicero is a Roman orator must be different. Kripke (1979) provided an example of a person who affirms the French sentence 'Londres est jolie' but disagrees with its English translation 'London is pretty.' So the two sentences should express different propositions. The puzzle threatens the conception of propositions as entities independent from language: it should not matter in which language a proposition is expressed, especially if only rigid designators such as 'London' are used. For necessity, these puzzles do not arise in the same way and coarse-grained propositions can be used.

---

[4]Copeland (2002) sketched the history of possible-worlds semantics for modal operators. See there for further details.

These problems have been discussed in some detail in the literature, and we do not enter the debate here. There is a much bigger problem that is not so frequently mentioned: some modalities do not apply to propositions but rather to other objects. Usually a sentence is said to be analytic if and only if it is true in virtue of the meanings of the expressions in the sentence. It does not make much sense to ascribe analyticity to propositions conceived as language-independent objects, because analyticity is standardly seen as defined in terms of the meanings of the linguistic items in a sentence. Similarly, provability in a formal system is a property of sentences, according to the standard view. If we go along with the usual assumptions, it becomes hard to compare analyticity and necessity. If we ask whether everything that is necessary is also analytic, the answer is trivially negative, because some propositions, but no sentences, are necessary. So the proposition that water is water is necessary, but not analytic, because only the *sentence* 'Water is water' is analytic, not the proposition. Similarly, if we ask whether provability in a certain formal system such as Peano arithmetic implies truth and assume that only propositions can be true, we have to conclude that no provable sentence is true, simply because sentences are never true; only propositions are.

These examples show that it is difficult to come up with one single kind of object of which all the modalities can be predicated. Among the candidates are sentences (conceived as types or tokens of sounds, graphical objects, or something else), propositions (with various granularities), statements, beliefs, utterances, judgements, and so on. It is not clear how they are related to propositions and sentences. We call the problem of finding a single class of objects to which all the modalities can sensibly be ascribed the *category problem*.

Various solutions to the category problem have been tested in the literature. The truth predicate has been used in some of them. Very often claims about the relation between analyticity, necessity, apriority, knowledge, and so on are couched in terms of truths. So instead of saying, 'There are synthetic a priori propositions' or 'All analytic sentences are necessary', philosophers write, 'There are synthetic truths that are a priori' or 'All analytic truths are necessary'. The use of the term 'truth' elegantly hides the problem, but does not solve it. Presumably the most natural way to understand these reformulations is the following:

> There is something that is synthetic, true, and a priori

and

Everything that is analytic and true is necessary.

But the category problem remains. If only sentences are analytic, and only propositions – conceived as language-independent entities – are necessary, then the last sentence is false.

One way to dodge the category problem could lie in a partial departure from the predicate approach. Halbach and Welch (2009) considered the option of retaining a predicate for truth and treating other modalities as sentential operators.[5] The two sentences can then be reformulated in the following ways:

There is something that is synthetically true and a priori true

and

Everything that is analytically true is necessarily true.

Thus, only adverbs or sentential operators for syntheticity, apriority, and analyticity are needed. Objects that can be true are still required, but we do not have to worry whether they can also be analytic or necessary, because these other modal notions are not conceived as predicates any longer. This mixed approach means that, with the exception of the truth predicate, the predicate approach is abandoned.

3.3 The Quantification Problem

By adopting the operator view of modalities we can avoid the drawbacks of modal predicates: there are no analogues to Montague's paradox in operator modal logic (unless diagonalization is added artificially); modal operators are adverbial modifiers of sentences or perhaps formulæ, but they do not apply to anything, and thus the category problem vanishes; we finally have mathematically and philosophically successful semantics for modal operators.

However, there is a steep price to pay for dodging the problems of modal predicates and settling for modal operators. The price is a lack of expressive power. If

[5] There have been other attempts to enhance the expressive power of modal operators with a truth predicate. Kripke (1975, p. 713) mentioned a reduction of the kind considered here, based on his truth predicate. Fine (1980) also considered a language with a truth predicate and a modal operator. However, his truth predicate applies to propositions, and thereby the problems with the paradoxes are largely avoided.

modalities are treated as sentential operators, many philosophical claims cannot be expressed. Earlier we considered the following example: 'There are synthetic a priori propositions.' This sentence cannot easily be reformulated if only modal operators are available. Assume we have a modal operator Syn for syntheticity and an operator Ap for apriority; then we can write $\mathrm{Syn}\,\varphi \wedge \mathrm{Ap}\,\varphi$ to express that φ is synthetic and a priori. With the sentence 'There are synthetic a priori propositions' we do not intend to claim this for a specific φ, but rather only make an existential claim. However, in a first-order language the expression $\exists \mathsf{x}(\mathrm{Syn}\,\mathsf{x} \wedge \mathrm{Ap}\,\mathsf{x})$ is only a well-formed formula if Syn and Ap are *predicates* and not sentential operators. On the operator view, $\mathrm{Syn}\,\mathsf{x}$ fails to be well formed in the same way $\neg\mathsf{x}$ fails to be well formed; the operators Syn and Ap need to be combined with formulæ, not singular terms such as the individual variable x. When we form quantified claims of this kind in English, we also resort to predicate phrases and not to adverbs.

There are many more philosophically important quantified statements. In particular, there are also many universally quantified claims, for instance, the claim that necessity implies truth (in the sense that whatever is necessary is also true), that what is known is true, that analyticity implies necessity, and that whatever is true can be known. Hence, as we mentioned above, the quantification problem is especially pertinent to philosophical discourse. For the purposes of a linguistic analysis of everyday language it may be less pressing, but, as mentioned before, philosophers are interested in general statements about modalities and their relations. If modal logic does not allow us to state that there are synthetic a priori judgements (or propositions), we are unable to discuss claims which are at the very centre of philosophy.

Defenders of the operator account have tried in various ways to show that the quantified statements can be expressed with operators. A first defence is obtained by claiming that universal statements can be expressed by schemas. According to this suggestion, the empiricist claim that apriority implies non-syntheticity would be expressed by all sentences of the form $\mathrm{Ap}\,\varphi \rightarrow \neg\mathrm{Syn}\,\varphi$. This strategy is not very promising. First, empiricism cannot be stated as a single sentence but only by employing infinitely many sentences. The opponent of empiricism would be in an even worse position, as they have to negate a schema. It is unclear how to do this. We know how to negate formulæ in the object language, but not how to negate schemas. The sentence $\neg(\mathrm{Ap}\,\varphi \rightarrow \neg\mathrm{Syn}\,\varphi)$ expresses the negation of each instance of $\mathrm{Ap}\,\varphi \rightarrow \neg\mathrm{Syn}\,\varphi$ instead of the failure of at least one instance. Also, quantifiers and connectives can be iterated and combined. If a claim involves alternating quantifiers embedded in sentences, then schemas are useless.

Propositional quantifiers have been used to boost the expressive power of a language with operators. The claim that apriority implies non-syntheticity would be expressed as $\forall P(\mathrm{Ap}\, P \rightarrow \neg \mathrm{Syn}\, P)$ on this strategy. Here, the letter P is a propositional variable. It can stand in the place of a formula as in $\mathrm{Ap}\, P$. The negation of this claim can be expressed as $\neg\forall P(\mathrm{Ap}\, P \rightarrow \neg \mathrm{Syn}\, P)$ or simply as $\exists P(\mathrm{Ap}\, P \wedge \mathrm{Syn}\, P)$. Usually modal operators and propositional quantifiers can be freely combined.[6]

At this point a thorough discussion of higher-order modal logic would be needed for a fair comparison with the predicate approach. We mention only a few general reasons why we prefer the predicate approach, which may not apply to all variants of propositional quantification or higher-order modal logic more generally.

Without explicitly specified semantics, it is not straightforward to distinguish between a multi-sorted first-order (in the sense of section 2.5) and a higher-order language. Propositional variables could be understood as a sort of first-order variables, and Ap and Syn as predicates that are combined with them. Formulæ of the form $\Box\varphi$ could be understood as the combination of a predicate and a singular term for φ. The same effect could be achieved, or so one could argue, by using a single sort of variable, introducing two new predicate symbols, and relativizing all quantifiers with one of the two predicates. So $\forall P$ would become $\forall \mathrm{x}\,(\mathrm{Pro}\,\mathrm{x} \rightarrow \dots)$, where Pro is a predicate symbol for restricting the quantifier to propositions. Here we will not make this reduction precise, because it depends on many further decisions and assumptions; but the general strategy should be clear.

There is one point where the reduction of modal operators with propositional quantifiers to modal predicates runs into problems. Presumably expressions of the kind $\forall P(\mathrm{Ap}\, P \rightarrow P)$ count as well formed. Replacing the last occurrence of

[6] Quantification into sentence position is as old as modal logic and was considered already by C. I. Lewis and Langford (1932). There are numerous accounts of propositional quantification, with subtle differences. They can be understood as quantifiers ranging over sets of possible worlds, as suggested already by Kripke (1959). Bull (1969), Fine (1970), and Kaplan (1970) elaborated on Kripke's suggestion. These accounts are commonly based on propositional logic, which is sufficient for expressing quantified claims such as $\exists P(\mathrm{Ap}\, P \wedge \mathrm{Syn}\, P)$, if suitable modal operators are available. Extending this to predicate logic is not trivial, and there is a vast literature on higher-order modal logic based on predicate logic.

the variable P with a first-order variable will give an ill-formed expression. The reduction could be saved, however, by using truth. The sentence $\forall P(\mathrm{Ap}\,P \to P)$ could be expressed with predicates Ap for apriority and $\Box$ for truth as $\forall \mathsf{x}\big(\mathrm{Pro}\,\mathsf{x} \to (Ap\,\mathsf{x} \to \Box \mathsf{x})\big)$. Actually, the first-order version with a truth predicate is closer to English. For propositional quantification there is no obvious equivalent in English: the sentence 'All a priori beliefs are true' is well formed.

To make the reduction more precise, we would have to spell out the assumptions in much more detail. In particular, we would have to make precise the syntax or semantics of the propositional quantifiers. We expect, however, that the problems of this kind of quantifier are very similar to those of adding a truth predicate. Kripke (1976) provided an account of such quantifiers that is very much based on his theory of truth in (Kripke 1975).

There are reasons to reject both propositional quantification and the multi-sorted approach. On both, the propositions and other objects are separated and cannot be related in a straightforward way. Sentences of the following kind mix propositions and other objects:

(3.1) Only propositions are necessary.

(3.2) The things that are necessary are not located in space.

(3.3) All sentences provable in PA are a priori and necessary.

We assume that 'is a proposition', 'is located in space', 'is provable in PA', and 'is a logical truth' should be treated as normal first-order predicates. With a modal operator $\underline{\Box}$ for necessity and a predicate Prop, $\forall P\,(\underline{\Box} P \to \mathrm{Prop}\,P)$ is not well formed, because Prop requires a first-order variable, not a propositional one. Equally, $\forall \mathsf{x}\,(\underline{\Box}\mathsf{x} \to \mathrm{Prop}\,\mathsf{x})$ is not well formed, because $\underline{\Box}$ requires a propositional variable.

The point is general: if we treat some notions as predicates and others as operators, then it will be difficult to relate them. The treatment of metaphysical necessity, knowledge, and belief as operators has become standard in philosophical logic. Truth, in contrast, is almost always conceived as a predicate. Similarly, provability in a fixed formal system is conceived as a predicate in the tradition of Gödel (1931). In provability logic the properties of these predicates are analyzed using modal operator languages; but the primary analysis of provability is always as a predicate. Surprisingly, absolutely general mathematical provability is then often treated as an operator. In limited contexts, where we focus only on one modality, it does not matter how the different theories fit together. But philosophical logicians should be able to provide a formal framework in which the various notions can be related and compared. The most obvious way to do so is a uniform treatment of all modalities and all notions to which they are related. As we have seen in the previous paragraph, even 'normal' notions such as being located in space may be related to a modality. So unless we treat them as operators as well, we are pushed towards the predicate conception. The predicate approach to modalities offers the most general uniform framework for studying modal notions as well as their interaction among each other and with other notions.

The proponent of the operator approach with propositional quantifiers has still further options to deal with examples such as (3.3): they can try to defend the account by using additional devices to boost the expressive strength of the language. It could be argued that provability in PA should be analyzed as a first-order predicate applying to sentences, and apriority and necessity as operators on, or predicates of, propositions (understood as objects distinct from sentences). The claim (3.3) would then be understood as an abbreviation of 'All sentences provable in PA express a priori and necessary propositions'. That is, one would invoke a bridging particle 'expresses', taking a sentence as first argument and a proposition as second. Also, truth would become an operator on, or predicate of, propositions. We suspect that a language with propositional quantification in conjunction with operators can be intertranslatable with a language that has only the corresponding predicates. But then the problems of the predicate approach will also affect such an elaborate account.[7]

3.4 The Category Problem

The predicate conception of modalities offers the most powerful, flexible, and straightforward way to theorize about modalities. However, if we opt for modal predicates, we have to pay a price for their expressive strength and the uniform treatment of quantified statements: we need to address the paradoxes of modal predicates, such as Montague's paradox. These will be the topic of subsequent chapters. Moreover, we need to equip our object theory with resources to reason about the things to which modalities can be ascribed. At least we need to build some assumptions about the ontology of these things into our object theory. These assumptions will depend on whether we think of them as beliefs, sen-

[7] For an attempt to formalize 'expresses' in such contexts, see (Mount 2019). His approach is a formalization of Ramsey's informal theorizing.

tences of a natural or mental language, structured or unstructured propositions, fine- or coarse-grained propositions, or yet something else.

We do not think that there is a definite solution to the category problem that can be unearthed by looking at linguistic data in English or other languages. By paying selective attention to certain examples, one can force an answer in one or the other direction.[8] We do not assume that there is a coherent underlying ontology to be found in the linguistic data. We take the protracted discussions in the literature about the objects of necessity, truth, belief, knowledge, and other modalities as an indication that there is not enough evidence from linguistic data to prefer one category of objects over the other. In the end some regimentation in Quine's (1960) sense may be required.

For our purposes here, no full solution to the category problem is required. We consider highly regimented formal languages, which lack many elements, such as indexicals, which cause trouble in natural languages for the category problem. In this section we give only a few reasons why we think an approach with sentences as the bearers of modal properties is a promising answer to the category problem.

Whatever the objects may be that can be true, analytic, necessary, known, a priori, and so on, our main access to them are sentences and in some cases also formulæ. Therefore, we focus on predicates applying to sentences and formulæ. We look at the truth predicate as an example.

If the predicate symbol $\Box$ expresses truth, a sentence such as $\Box\overline{\varphi}$, where $\overline{\varphi}$ is a name for φ, can be read as '"φ" is true' or as 'The proposition expressed by the sentence "φ" is true', as Quine (1970, p. 10), suggested. In the latter case the analysandum would be 'expresses a true proposition'. This is compatible with viewing propositions as the primary objects of truth.

Quine's predicate 'expresses a true proposition' can be taken to be primitive. Which elements are taken to be primitive is a methodological question, and one might have to explore different options. Even if propositions are employed as primary bearers of truth, one does not have to start with a unary predicate 'is true' applying to propositions, a unary predicate for 'is a proposition', and a binary relation *expresses*. Treating 'expresses a true proposition' as primitive does not rule out a later analysis from other notions.

Whether we read $\Box\overline{\varphi}$ as '"φ" is true' or as 'The proposition expressed by the sentence "φ" is true', we seem to have lost a very important device: neither of the two readings gives us an obvious formal counterpart of 'It is true that φ', and it

[8]Moltmann (2018) provides many examples.

is not clear how we can express that-sentences in our framework. Often, that-clauses are taken to be singular terms denoting propositions. It is here where our approach of viewing modalities as predicates of sentences seems to fall short.

An obvious reply would be that these that-clauses are (or can be constructed to be) coreferential with quotations, and that therefore nothing is lost by conceiving modalities as syntactic predicates. There are various reasons why philosophers have thought that neither of the two readings mentioned earlier are equivalent to 'It is true that φ'. In 'It is true that φ' or 'The proposition that φ is true', the sentence φ is *used*, while it is only *mentioned* in ' "φ" is true' and 'The proposition expressed by the sentence "φ" is true.' Sometimes the following observation is given as evidence for the claim that they are not equivalent: ' "Snow is white" is true' is about the sentence 'Snow is white', while 'It is true that snow is white' is about snow. We do not think that this is sufficient to establish the non-equivalence of the two sentences, because the notion of aboutness is so unclear. What is needed are examples that show that they are not substitutable *salva veritate*. And indeed, in certain modal contexts they seem to come apart. We give an example.

Whether 'It is true that snow is white' obtains depends only on the colour of snow. Whether ' "Snow is white" is true' obtains depends also on what 'Snow is white' means. If 'Snow is white' had meant 'Coal is white', then ' "Snow is white" is true' would be false, while snow would still be white. The meanings of sentences are contingent. Therefore, the truth conditions of ' "Snow is white" is true' and 'It is true that snow is white' are different. The origins of these arguments can be traced back at least to Plato's *Cratylus*. This kind of argument has been used to show that a truth predicate applied to sentences only is insufficient.

The claim that the usual 'snow' T-sentence is necessary provides an example of a sentence whose truth value changes if 'The proposition that φ is true' is replaced with ' "φ" is true' in the sentence. That is, the equivalence

(T) The proposition that snow is white is true iff snow is white

is necessary, according to this view, while

The sentence 'Snow is white' is true iff snow is white

is only contingently true: if 'Snow is white' had meant 'Coal is white,' the second equivalence would fail, while the first would still hold. Similarly, the equivalence

The proposition expressed by the sentence 'Snow is white' is true iff snow is white is only contingently true, because the sentence 'Snow is white' could have expressed some other proposition.

To capture (T), it may be argued, a predicate applying directly to propositions is required, probably in addition to some term-forming device (corresponding to *that*); predicates of sentences are insufficient to analyze (T), it could be claimed.[9]

The example of the T-sentences involves iterated modalities: (T) contains the truth predicate and then we ask whether (T) is necessary. There are variants of this argument. The sentence

(Log) ' "All logicians are logicians" is necessary' is necessary

is false under the following assumption: the expression 'All logicians are logicians' could have been used to express that snow is black; hence the sentence 'All logicians are logicians' is only contingently necessary, because its necessity depends on our contingent linguistic conventions.

We do not think that these arguments, purported to show that truth and necessity should primarily be understood as predicates of propositions, are convincing. The truth predicate can be read in different ways. We could focus on a reading of the truth predicate as 'is a true sentence now in my actual idiolect from my perspective'. Some deflationists about truth, including Field (1994), understand the truth predicate in this way. On this reading, 'Snow is white' would still be true even if 'Snow is white' had meant 'Snow is black': it would still be true in my idiolect. In the same way (Log) has a true reading if 'is necessary' is understood as 'is necessary now in my actual idiolect from my perspective'. If the necessity predicate is understood in this sense, propositions are not required for the reasons outlined above; and T-sentences such as (T) are necessary.

These readings are not completely unnatural. When ascribing truth to particular utterances and sentences we usually mean 'true in our language'. 'Is a true sentence now in my actual idiolect from my perspective' is taken as primitive, not as a truth predicate that takes additional arguments such as parameters for the language, the context, and so on. One could then hope to define truth predicates

[9]One of the first to make an argument along these lines on the status of such equivalences was Lewy (1947). G. E. Moore (1966, p. 142) mentioned a similar argument already in lectures 1925–26 (edited by Lewy). We thank Graham Solomon for making us aware of this passage in Moore's lectures. The argument, including a variant with translations by Lewy (1947), is a precursor to the Church–Langford argument by Church (1950), which concerns intentional attitudes rather than truth.

applied to sentences in other languages from this predicate via translations or interpretations. Starting with such readings of 'is true' and 'is necessary' would be our preferred methodological starting point. Of course, there are many problems. In particular, we do not claim that all other philosophically relevant uses of truth and necessity can be reduced to such primitive predicates. Even if one is sceptical about the possibility of such a reduction, we can still theorize about those predicates. They still go a long way in providing a formal framework for the use of truth, necessity, and other predicates in philosophical discourse.

Even though we call our formal systems 'theories of syntax', one may try to reinterpret them as theories of propositions, properties, and relations in some way. We like to call this kind of reinterpretation of our theories the 'Henry Ford theory of universals'. Ford allegedly pronounced that his customers could purchase his model T in any colour as long as it was black. Readers may take our formal theories as theories of universals as long as they are content to believe that there are operations on universals and their constituents that correspond to our syntactic operations. Universals would then truly be mere shadows of syntactic objects, to use Quine's phrase.

Ultimately we prefer to think of our predicates as syntactic predicates, that is, as predicates applying to sentences. Analyticity, provability (in some formal system), logical validity, and so on will have to be understood as predicates of sentences; and in order to make all predicates comparable we rather see truth and necessity as predicates of sentences than provability and analyticity as predicates of propositions.

We have said little about intentional attitudes such as believing or knowing. As mentioned above, Lewy's argument in its form with translations has a counterpart for intentional attitudes in the form of the Church–Langford argument, which is also known as the *argument from translation*. There is an extensive literature on this argument and its refinements. As intentional attitudes are not at the centre of our account, we only refer the reader to the relevant literature by Leeds (1979), Salmon (2001), Felappi (2014), Sackris (2016), and many others.

3.5 *De Re* Modality

Our conception of modalities as predicates of objects – whether they are sentences or propositions – faces another challenge. So far we have considered only *de dicto* modalities, but no *de re* modalities. If we cannot incorporate the latter into our account, large parts of modern philosophy of language and metaphysics would be incompatible with our predicate conception of modalities.

We begin by explaining the distinction and the problems of 'quantifying-in' from the perspective of modal logic and the operator approach. We start with the following situation:

> The people at the table in a Gothenburg restaurant are Mary's three best friends. Mary believes of each of them that they are in England.

We can conclude from this that Mary believes of every person at the table in Gothenburg that she is in England. Of course, this does not mean that she believes that every person at the table in Gothenburg is in England. The distinction can be made in modal logic with an operator $\underline{\Box}$ for 'Mary believes that ....' The claim that Mary believes of every person at the table in Gothenburg that they are in England can be formalized as follows:

$$\forall \mathsf{x}(P\mathsf{x} \rightarrow \underline{\Box}Q\mathsf{x}). \tag{3.4}$$

Here $P\mathsf{x}$ expresses that x is a person at the table in Gothenburg and $Q\mathsf{x}$ expresses that x is in England. In the formalization of the claim that Mary believes that every person at the table in Gothenburg is in England, the modal operator takes a wider scope: $\underline{\Box}\forall \mathsf{x}(P\mathsf{x} \rightarrow Q\mathsf{x})$.

In sentence (3.4) the quantifier $\forall \mathsf{x}$ binds all occurrences of x, including the last one, which is in the scope of the belief operator $\underline{\Box}$. Thus, in (3.4) we quantify into a modal context, more precisely a belief context.

Analogous examples can be given for other modalities. Kripke (1980) provided many examples for what he called metaphysical necessity. Assume we have a glass with pure water. It is necessary for each of the molecules in the glass that it contain a hydrogen atom. If it did not contain a hydrogen atom, it would not be a water molecule and thus a different molecule. The claim that it is necessary of every molecule in the glass that it contain a hydrogen atom can be formalized as $\forall \mathsf{x}(P\mathsf{x} \rightarrow \Box Q\mathsf{x})$ again. Now $\Box$ stands for metaphysical necessity, and the predicate symbols have to be understood in the obvious way. Clearly, we cannot move the modal operator out and write $\Box\forall x(Px \rightarrow Qx)$, as this would be the incorrect claim that it is necessary that every molecule in the glass contains a hydrogen atom – the glass could be empty.

Beyond necessity and intentional attitudes such as belief and knowledge, truth provides further examples of this kind. We can use the above example and replace necessity with truth: it is true for each of the molecules in the glass that it contains a hydrogen atom. However, as we have seen, truth has hardly ever been treated as an operator. But, at least on the surface, it seems to behave syntactically in a similar way. If we were to formalize truth as an operator, we would quantify into the scope of the truth operator.

In many places, among them his papers (1943) and (1976), Quine argued that quantifying into certain modal contexts is incomprehensible. How problematic quantifying-in is depends on the modality. Quine focused on a much smaller class of modalities than we do. For many modalities quantifying-in does not pose any problem. In the case of truth, for instance, there seems little reason to worry about the comprehensibility of quantifying-in; in other cases non-trivial *de re* conceptions make little sense, as in the case of analyticity.

Important objections against quantifying-in arise from puzzles about *de re* modality in general. A sentence such as

> Jana believes that the greatest sane logician was born in Poland

does not imply that Jana believes that the author of *The Concept of Truth* was born in Poland, even if it so happens that he and the greatest sane logician are the same person. Modal contexts are intensional, and identicals may not be substitutable *salva veritate*. The displayed sentence and the analogous sentence with 'the author of *The Concept of Truth*' ascribe *de dicto* beliefs to Jana. Whether the sentence is true depends on the specific singular term that is used. Using a different singular term, even if it refers to the same person or object, can affect the truth value of the entire sentence. In the case of a *de re* belief, roughly, the belief is about the person or the thing, independently of any specific singular term used to specify them. For instance, we could talk about a person and say even things about that person Jana does not know and then say that she believes of this person that he or she were born in Poland. Quantifying-in seems to presuppose that *de re* modality is comprehensible. If we have a variable in the scope of a modal operator, then we do not have any specific singular term for the corresponding object(s) but rather just an unspecific pronoun or a variable. Thus, the modality is *de re*.

There are many puzzles that arise from *de re* modalities. *De re* modalities have also been at the heart of the modern revival of metaphysics, as *de re* necessity is closely tied to essential properties. Here we do not intend to go any deeper into the analysis of *de re* necessity or take a specific stance. We are only interested in the question whether we can deal with such modalities and quantifying-in if modalities are conceived as predicates rather than sentential operators. Whatever our specific stance on *de re* modality and quantifying-in may be, our adoption of the predicate approach should not bar us from developing a theory of *de re* modality as it has been done for the operator approach. Here possible-worlds semantics has been used to sharpen and refine informal accounts of *de re* modality, and metaphysicians and philosophers of language have availed themselves of the methods of modal logic.

The transition from a modal operator that allows for quantifying-in to a predicate is not straightforward. If we replace the operator in $\forall \mathsf{x}(P\mathsf{x} \to \underline{\Box} Q\mathsf{x})$ with a predicate, we obtain the sentence $\forall \mathsf{x}(P\mathsf{x} \to \Box \overline{Q\mathsf{x}})$, where $\overline{Q\mathsf{x}}$ is a name for the formula $Q\mathsf{x}$ or for an object corresponding to $Q\mathsf{x}$, such as the property expressed by Q. This substitution does not achieve the desired effect. It cannot express what it is supposed to express, because the variable x is not free in $\Box \overline{Q\mathsf{x}}$; it is only mentioned, not used. Of course, we have not provided an axiomatic system or a semantics for the language with the predicate $\Box$, but in any reasonable axiomatization and under every reasonable semantics, $\forall \mathsf{x}(P\mathsf{x} \to \Box \overline{Q\mathsf{x}})$ will never be an adequate rendering of the above English sentences with quantifying-in. Only variables that are used can be bound; variables that are merely mentioned cannot. In $\overline{Q\mathsf{x}}$ the x is merely part of a name for the formula $Q\mathsf{x}$. It is a feature of our notation that the variable x shows up within the name $\overline{Q\mathsf{x}}$ for the formula $Q\mathsf{x}$. For instance, in the English singular term 'the letter Q followed by the antepenultimate letter of the alphabet' the variable x does not occur in any way.

There have been various attempts to address the problem (see Bealer 1982 for a detailed treatment). Our preferred method is a technique that is well known from the theory of truth. As mentioned above, the grammar of the truth predicate is very similar to that of the necessity and other modal predicates. In particular, we can form sentences with the truth predicate that involve quantifying-in. The sentence

> It is true for each of the molecules in the glass that it contains a hydrogen atom

displays the same grammatical structure as

> It is necessary for each of the molecules in the glass that it contains a hydrogen atom.

In the case of the first sentence a common way to deal with quantifying-in would rely on a binary predicate for satisfaction Sat $x\ y$, which is read as 'x is satisfied by y' or 'x is true of y'. The sentence could be formalized as

$$\forall \mathsf{x}\,(P\mathsf{x} \to \mathsf{Sat}\,\overline{Q\mathsf{x}}\,\mathsf{x}). \tag{3.5}$$

Here Sat is a binary predicate symbol that is applied to the two terms $\overline{Q\mathsf{x}}$ and x. As before, $\overline{Q\mathsf{x}}$ is a name for the formula $Q\mathsf{x}$. It is important that we use the specific variable x rather than the metavariable (see page 15), because now it really matters which variable is used. In predicate logic renaming a bound variable cannot transform a provable into an unprovable sentence, as long as the new variable does not occur in the original sentence; also the truth or falsity of a sentence does not depend on such a renaming. In the present case this means that, concerning provability or truth in any given model, there is no difference between $\forall \mathsf{x}\,(P\mathsf{x} \to \mathsf{Sat}\,\overline{Q\mathsf{x}}\,\mathsf{x})$ and, say, $\forall \mathsf{v}_{27}\,(P\mathsf{v}_{27} \to \mathsf{Sat}\,\overline{Q\mathsf{x}}\,\mathsf{v}_{27})$. Of course, when we rename bound variables, the name $\overline{Q\mathsf{x}}$ for the formula $Q\mathsf{x}$ is not replaced with the name of another formula; in particular, it is not replaced with a name of $Q\mathsf{v}_{27}$. Thus, in (3.5), there is no connection between the variable x that occurs as a symbol in (3.5) and the letter x, which is used in a way to communicate the name of $Q\mathsf{x}$.

There are different ways to understand Sat $x\,y$, where x and y are variables. It could be read as 'y satisfies x if the free variable v_0 (that is, x) of x is interpreted by y'. In this case Sat would be tied to the first variable v_0. Alternatively, we could read Sat $x\,y$ as 'y satisfies x if the free variable of x (whatever that free variable may be) is interpreted by y'. At any rate such a reading of Sat always confines us to a predicate expressing a relation between a formula with a single free variable and a single object. However, there are examples where we quantify into modal contexts with two variables:

> If *A* and *B* are distinct, then they are necessarily distinct.

We could employ a ternary predicate Sat to formalize claims of this kind, with the additional intricacies of determining which variables are interpreted by which object. Moreover, the binary and the ternary predicate would have to be related in some way.

The obvious solution is to follow Tarski's lead for truth and to conceive the necessity predicate as a binary predicate applying to formulæ and variable assignments. Variable assignments are lists of objects associating these with some or all variables. If variable assignments are finite, then we have to make sure that the variable assignment matches the free variables in the formula. Here we do not go deeper into the details. Whatever the details are, the operator and the predicate accounts of quantifying-in will diverge in some important aspects. On the predicate approach we will need a theory of variable assignments, usually a theory of sequences of objects. These sequences may be finite and their theory can be developed in weak systems of arithmetic already, but they still require more than pure logic. On the operator account nothing comparable is needed.

The predicate conception of *de re* modalities has also advantages over the operator conception. First, as with unary predicates, we can express quantification and generalizations as explained in section 3.3. With a binary necessity predicate applying to formulæ and variable assignments we gain even more expressive power, which is not easily matched by a language with an operator. With such a predicate we can express, for instance, that a formula is necessary of some objects. We can also use such a predicate to formulate the *ab necesse ad esse* or factivity of *de re* necessity as a universally quantified principle. In English the principle may be expressed as follows:

> If a formula is necessary of some objects, then the formula is true of these objects.

This principle can be expressed using the binary necessity predicate and quantification over variable assignments. It is stronger that the well-known *de dicto* version stating that whatever is necessary is also true.

Of course, for a deeper discussion, we would have to specify a semantics or a deductive system for the *de re* modalities. In chapter 7 we develop possible-worlds semantics for languages with modal predicates, but only for unary modal predicates. This semantics can be adapted to binary modal predicates, that is, *de dicto* modalities. There are some tricky and metaphysically interesting problems, some of which are discussed in (Halbach 2021). We may consider a semantics where different worlds can have different domains. Presumably then also different variable assignments exist in different worlds, because a variable assignment cannot contain an only possibly existing object. A variable assignment assigning Pluto to the first variable exists in the actual world, but it may fail to exist in a world where Pluto has never been formed. Here we break off the discussion and refer the reader to work that has been done in this direction, for instance, by Bealer (1993), Halbach and Sturm (2004), and Halbach, Leitgeb, and Welch (2003); but many questions in this area are still open and modal metaphysics could benefit from considering languages with great expressive power and predicates for *de re* modalities.

3.6 The Paradoxes in Context

Large parts of this monograph are dedicated to the analysis of paradoxes that arise from diagonalization, such as the liar paradox and Montague's paradox. Opponents of the predicate view may regard our struggle with these paradoxes as evidence that the predicate approach is ultimately not promising. If we have to go through elaborate theories of paradox first before we can even start to tackle the philosophically interesting questions, then we should draw the conclusion that the predicate approach is hopeless and that Montague (1963) showed irrefutably that the predicate approach forces us to sacrifice too much. The operator conception of modalities seems to offer an elegant way of separating interesting philosophical problems from the fruitless and frustrating debates about the paradoxes.

However, we do not expect that there are solutions to the paradoxes that allow us to separate the discussion of the paradoxes from other issues in metaphysics, philosophy of language, philosophical logic, and epistemology. The paradoxes are a sign of the expressive power of the predicate approach. They permit the expression of claims that cannot be expressed otherwise, but they also impose restrictions on our theorizing. They have already had an enormous impact in philosophy. Tarski's distinction between object language and metalanguage is one way to block the paradoxes. This distinction is nowadays deeply entrenched in philosophy and other disciplines. Here, taking the paradoxes seriously and exploring Tarski's solution has led to great progress.

Other parts of philosophy have resisted. For instance, in epistemology the paradoxes involving modal predicates such as the liar paradox have not had an influence on mainstream epistemology. We think that they should have been given more attention. Even if these paradoxes are not genuinely epistemological, but more general, they cannot be ignored. Ignoring these paradoxes is no better than ignoring the Gettier problem or Fitch's paradox.[10]

The paradoxes in the main body of this book are thus to be understood not just as follies in the philosophical landscape that can be admired or laughed at before one moves along on a philosophical itinerary. Rather we think of the paradoxes as serious philosophical crossroads that force us to give up or modify naive beliefs that we have gotten used to but that lead to inconsistency, triviality, or otherwise unacceptable consequences.

We understand the reluctance of many philosophers outside logic to engage with the paradoxes from diagonalization. Very often logicians working on the paradoxes are quick to suggest that the best solution is to modify logic, to abandon, restrict, or modify some rules or axioms of our logical calculus. In fact some of the proposed modifications do not look that dramatic at first glance and seem to do an excellent job in dodging the paradoxes. But when the philosophers then return to the traditional problems in their field, all of that field would have to be rewritten using the new modified logic. That does not sound too tempting.

We do not believe that we should modify our logic in the light of the paradoxes. We are wary of the quietist attitude shared by many philosophers. They seem to be happy to leave the paradoxes to the specialist logicians, hoping that they will come up with a viable solution some day that does not bring too much disruption to other fields of philosophy. We do not expect that such a pain-free solution is available. The nature of these paradoxes, the fact that they need only extremely weak assumptions, makes it improbable that they have a straightforward solution that has no knock-on effects in other parts of philosophy. Rather on the contrary, the fact that logicians have been bold enough to suggest that we should adopt a paraconsistent or paracomplete logic or tinker with structural rules such as contraction makes it unlikely that they will find a solution that does not interfere with other parts of philosophy.

[10] Moreover, traditionally 'epistemological' paradoxes such as the Fitch paradox interact with the paradoxes considered here. See, for instance, (Halbach 2008) and Paseau (2008, 2009) .

4 Paradoxes over Logic

In order to construct the liar sentence and many other paradoxes, we need to be able to prove certain assumptions about the objects that can be true. More specifically, we need to build a sentence that is equivalent to the claim that that sentence is not true. For this logicians usually employ certain operations on sentences, such as substitution of variables with terms. These operations and suitable assumptions about them will enable us to prove many further paradoxes in later chapters. Many of these paradoxes, that is, inconsistency results, hold only in the presence of certain basic assumptions on these operations. Additional assumptions about the modal predicate – assumptions that are plausible if the predicate is read as truth, necessity, knowledge, or the like – will then yield inconsistencies. The assumptions on the operations on sentences can be shown to be essential for the inconsistency proofs.

There are also some closely related paradoxes for which these assumptions on syntactic operations are not required. The most famous paradox of this kind is Russell's paradox. All that is required for it is a binary predicate symbol Sat and suitable assumptions on it. No syntactic assumption or other assumptions on the objects to which the predicate is to be ascribed are needed. Using the binary predicate we can 'diagonalize' formulæ. In the general case, in particular, for unary predicates such as the truth predicate, we need the syntactic assumptions to prove the diagonal lemma, that is, lemma 5.12.

4.1 Russell's Paradox

In mathematics, philosophy, and other disciplines expressions of the form $\{ x: \ldots x \ldots \}$ are frequently used to denote the set of all objects x such that . . . x . . . For instance, the set $\{ x: x \text{ is a person} \}$ contains exactly all the persons; $\{ x: x \in \mathbb{R} \text{ and } 2 < x < 4 \}$ contains exactly all the real numbers between 2 and 4, if $\mathbb{R}$ is the set of real numbers. In many cases (certainly in the first author's school), it is taken for granted that the sets $\{ x: \ldots x \ldots \}$ exist. Let us make this assumption explicit and assume that for any formula $\varphi(x)$ the set $\{\, x\colon \varphi(x) \,\}$ exists. This assumption is known as *unrestricted comprehension*. That is, for each formula $\varphi(x)$ we assume the existence of a set containing exactly those objects x for which $\varphi(x)$ holds. Russell's paradox shows that this assumption is inconsistent.

4.1 THEOREM · RUSSELL'S PARADOX *The schema* $\exists y \forall x (\mathrm{Sat}\, y\, x \leftrightarrow \varphi(x))$ *is logically inconsistent, where the formula* $\varphi(x)$ *can be any formula with* x *but not* y *free.*

We state the theorem with the binary predicate symbol Sat for later use. Of course it does not matter which specific symbol we use for the binary predicate symbol. For the application to sets we would write $x \in y$ instead of $\mathrm{Sat}\, y\, x$. With this notation the schema becomes $\exists y \forall x (x \in y \leftrightarrow \varphi(x))$. The schema then tells us that for any formula $\varphi(x)$ there is a corresponding set $\{x : \varphi(x)\}$.

Of course, the schema is also inconsistent if we admit all formulæ, even those with y free; but such instances are not required to justify the existence of the sets $\{\, x\colon \ldots x \ldots \}$, and this particular inconsistency should not bother us too much because $\exists y \forall x (\mathrm{Sat}\, y\, x \leftrightarrow \neg \mathrm{Sat}\, y\, x)$ is an obviously inconsistent instance. The theorem tells us that even with the restriction to $\varphi(x)$ without free occurrences of y the schema is inconsistent.

To show the inconsistency of the schema of unrestricted comprehension we need only one instance, namely $\exists y \forall x (\mathrm{Sat}\, y\, x \leftrightarrow \neg \mathrm{Sat}\, x\, x)$.

PROOF The proof can easily be given in a formal calculus such as Natural Deduction. Here we outline the proof; its full formalization should be obvious. Assume that there is an a such that $\forall x (\mathrm{Sat}\, a\, x \leftrightarrow \neg \mathrm{Sat}\, x\, x)$. Now we eliminate the universal quantifier, instantiating it with a, and obtain $\mathrm{Sat}\, a\, a \leftrightarrow \neg \mathrm{Sat}\, a\, a$. This equivalence is propositionally inconsistent. ⊣

The schema of unrestricted comprehension cannot be used in set theory without rendering set theory trivial. Hence, we *cannot* assume that for any formula $\varphi(x)$ there is a set $\{\, x\colon \varphi(x) \,\}$. In particular, there is no set $\{\, x\colon \neg x \in x \,\}$. The axioms for set theory have to be formulated more carefully. Modern axiomatizations of set theory have weakened forms of comprehension.

Notoriously, Frege (1893) used axioms similar to the schema in the theorem. However, the inconsistency spotted by Bertrand Russell in Frege's text was not as obvious as the inconsistency of simple unrestricted comprehension. The version here is a streamlined version that soon emerged to be at the root of the inconsistency.

Russell's paradox is not only relevant to Sat read as set-theoretic membership. It also shows that we have to be cautious with our assumptions about the existence of properties. Perhaps we may want to assume that for any formula $\varphi(x)$ there is a property of being $\varphi(x)$. For instance, many philosophers assume that there is a property of being red and that exactly all the red objects have this property. They may also assume that there is a property of not seeing oneself; exactly those objects that do not see themselves have this property; those who happen to look into a mirror or the like don't have it. Thus, one may also expect that there is a property of not having oneself as a property. For instance, the property of being red itself is presumably not red; it is an abstract object without any colour. Thus, the property of being red should *have* the property of not having itself as a property. The property of being abstract, in contrast, should *not* have the property of not having itself as a property, because the property of being abstract is itself abstract. But Russell's paradox shows that there cannot be a generally applicable property of not having oneself as a property. This is more or less Grelling's 'heterological' paradox. The paradox coincides with Russell's paradox if Sat y x is read as 'x has y (as a property)'.

4.2 Satisfaction

As the choice of the notation Sat in theorem 4.1 indicates, we are interested in still another application of Russell's paradox. Sat y x can be read as 'x satisfies y' or 'y is true of x'. In this case we can still think of y as a property, but also as a formula with one free variable. Assume that we have a unary predicate symbol P expressing 'is red'. Then $\exists y \forall x (\mathrm{Sat}\, y\, x \leftrightarrow Px)$ would say that there is something, viz, a formula, that is satisfied by exactly all red objects. Usually the lesson drawn from Russell's paradox when Sat y x is read in the set-theoretic way as $x \in y$ is that there cannot be a set $\{x\colon \varphi(x)\}$ for every formula $\varphi(x)$. If we draw the analogous conclusion for the reading of Sat as satisfaction, Russell's paradox would show that there cannot be a formula that is true of exactly those objects that are not true of themselves. We cannot deny the existence of the formula $\neg \mathrm{Sat}\, x\, x$; we can only deny that it is not true of itself. So while the paradoxes of satisfaction and set-membership are basically the same, the two different readings point at different conclusions we should draw from the inconsistency.

Russell's paradox with satisfaction can be brought into a form that makes it better comparable to the truth-theoretic paradoxes in later chapters and prepares for later definitions. To this end we introduce individual constants for all formulæ of the language; we call them 'quotation constants'.

4.2 DEFINITION The symbols of $\mathcal{L}_q$ are:

(i) infinitely many variable symbols $\mathsf{v}_0, \mathsf{v}_1, \mathsf{v}_2, \mathsf{v}_3, \ldots$,

(ii) a binary predicate symbol Sat,

(iii) the connectives $\neg$, $\rightarrow$ and the quantifier symbol $\forall$,

(iv) auxiliary symbols (and),

(v) possibly finitely many further function and predicate symbols, and

(vi) for each string e of symbols there is exactly one constant in the language $\mathcal{L}_q$. The constant for e is called the *quotation constant* of e. We write $\overline{e}$ for the quotation constant of e.

All the mentioned symbols are pairwise different. As before, we write x for v_0, y for v_1, and z for v_2.

The quotation constants in (vi) may require some explanation. For instance, we have a quotation constant $\overline{\wedge}$ for the conjunction symbol. Therefore, $\overline{\wedge}\mathsf{v}_2\neg$ is a string of symbols of $\mathcal{L}_q$ and therefore the language contains also a quotation constant $\overline{\overline{\wedge}\mathsf{v}_2\neg}$. Of course, we could generate the quotation constants recursively, but this is not required. The quotation constants could simply be symbols of the form $c_1, c_2, c_3, \ldots$ Clause (vi) requires that there be a one–one mapping between the set of expressions e of $\mathcal{L}_q$ and the set of quotation constants. Any such mapping will suffice. We will return to quotation constants and how to understand them in the next chapter.

In what follows, the notation $\varphi(\mathsf{x})$ indicates that φ is a formula containing at most x free.

4.3 PROPOSITION · SATISFACTION PARADOX
The set of all sentences $\forall \mathsf{x}\big(\mathrm{Sat}\,\overline{\varphi(\mathsf{x})}\,\mathsf{x} \leftrightarrow \varphi(\mathsf{x})\big)$ *is inconsistent.*

The use of the first variable x could be replaced with the use of another variable, of course. We could equally have stated the sentences as $\forall y\big(\mathrm{Sat}\,\overline{\varphi(\mathsf{x})}\,y \leftrightarrow \varphi(y)\big)$, where y is any variable such that there is no occurrence of x in $\varphi(\mathsf{x})$ that is in the scope of a quantifier $\forall y$.

Obviously, the sentences $\forall \mathsf{x}\left(\mathrm{Sat}\,\overline{\varphi(\mathsf{x})}\,\mathsf{x} \leftrightarrow \varphi(\mathsf{x})\right)$ can be understood as formalizations of the following semiformal schema:

For all x: a formula '$\varphi(\mathsf{x})$' is true of x iff $\varphi(\mathsf{x})$.

But there are other readings, inspired by the application mentioned above:

An object x has the property expressed by '$\varphi(\mathsf{x})$' iff $\varphi(\mathsf{x})$.

The following is even closer to Russell's paradox:

An object x is in $\left\{\mathsf{x}\colon \varphi(\mathsf{x})\right\}$ iff $\varphi(\mathsf{x})$.

PROOF The proof is a variant of Russell's paradox. Choose $\varphi(\mathsf{x})$ as $\neg\mathrm{Sat}\,\mathsf{x}\,\mathsf{x}$. This single instance of the schema $\forall \mathsf{x}\left(\mathrm{Sat}\,\overline{\varphi(\mathsf{x})}\,\mathsf{x} \leftrightarrow \varphi(\mathsf{x})\right)$ is already inconsistent:

$$\forall \mathsf{x}\left(\mathrm{Sat}\,\overline{\neg\mathrm{Sat}\,\mathsf{x}\,\mathsf{x}}\,\mathsf{x} \leftrightarrow \neg\mathrm{Sat}\,\mathsf{x}\,\mathsf{x}\right)$$

implies, by choosing x as $\overline{\neg\mathrm{Sat}\,\mathsf{x}\,\mathsf{x}}$, the blatantly inconsistent

$$\mathrm{Sat}\,\overline{\neg\mathrm{Sat}\,\mathsf{x}\,\mathsf{x}}\;\overline{\neg\mathrm{Sat}\,\mathsf{x}\,\mathsf{x}} \leftrightarrow \neg\mathrm{Sat}\,\overline{\neg\mathrm{Sat}\,\mathsf{x}\,\mathsf{x}}\;\overline{\neg\mathrm{Sat}\,\mathsf{x}\,\mathsf{x}}. \qquad \dashv$$

The satisfaction paradox is very close to the liar paradox, but it requires a binary satisfaction predicate rather than a unary truth predicate.

The only difference between the satisfaction paradox and Russell's paradox, as stated above, is that in Russell's paradox there is no constant $\overline{\varphi(\mathsf{x})}$. This argument place is existentially quantified. Thus, the satisfaction paradox is just a particular reading of Russell's paradox. This is very well known. What is less known is that the technique can be used to obtain more sophisticated paradoxes that are commonly proved by invoking the diagonal lemma, that is, lemma 5.12 below or a similar trick. Even Yablo's and Visser's paradoxes, which we will consider later, can be obtained over logic without using the diagonal lemma, as Halbach and Zhang (2016) have shown.

If we prove the paradoxes without using a theory of the objects to which modalities can be ascribed, we gain information about what exactly is needed to obtain the paradoxes. The satisfaction paradox tells us that we are not safe from semantic and liar-like paradoxes even in the absence of a theory that allows us to construct sentences that are usually considered to be self-referential. Hence, we cannot hope to block the paradoxes completely by drastically weakening or modifying the background theory of the objects to which modalities such as truth are ascribed.

Should we be focusing more on paradoxes that do not require a theory of expressions, propositions, and the like? Should we rewrite the paradoxes usually proved with the diagonal lemma by using predicate symbols with higher arities as in (Halbach and Zhang 2016)? We do not think so. At least for our purposes we are interested in theories that incorporate such a theory. First, the paradoxes in the present chapter require fewer resources than those in future chapters, because a theory of expressions or the like is not required. In another respect, however, they require more resources because they need binary predicates rather than just unary predicates as in the usual liar paradox. More importantly, it is not clear to what extent such a rewriting of paradoxes with an underlying ontology of propositions or expressions as paradoxes without such an ontology is always possible. Ontological assumptions will be needed for other results. If there are no syntactic assumptions at all we will be unable to define many important predicates. In particular, we will not be able to define provability predicates.

We are interested in philosophically useful theories of modalities, or at least formal frameworks for developing such theories. For such theories it is important that they can be combined with theories of expressions. In fact, the more advanced axioms for modalities such as truth or necessity do not make much sense if separated from a theory of expressions or some theory of the objects that can be true or necessary.

5 A Theory of Expressions

In this chapter we develop a theory of syntax, in which the diagonal lemma, lemma 5.12, is provable. The paradoxes, including the liar paradox but also more sophisticated paradoxes such as Visser's and Yablo's paradoxes, can be studied in this theory. It is relatively weak, but it allows us to go straight to the paradoxes and investigate them without the detour via arithmetic or a sophisticated and more complicated theory of syntax. It helps to keep control over the resources used to generate the paradoxes. A relatively strong theory, such as Peano arithmetic or the syntax theory described in chapter 8, are not needed for proving those paradoxes. Of course, if we pass on to a stronger theory of expressions, the paradoxes remain and inconsistency results will still obtain. Thus, by using a weak theory we prove stronger results. A more powerful theory of syntax that is strong enough to prove the Gödel incompleteness theorems is introduced in chapter 8.

5.1 The Symbols

We specify conditions on languages of first-order logic. In what follows we assume that the language $\mathcal{L}$ satisfies these conditions. Of course, the results that we are going to prove about $\mathcal{L}$ apply to all languages satisfying these conditions. Talking as if we were dealing only with a single language seems easier to us than preceding all results with a conditional sentence of the kind 'If $\mathcal{L}$ is a language satisfying all conditions in the definition above, then ...'

Expressions of a language are finite strings of symbols of that language. The strings are obtained by concatenating symbols. Hence, an expression of $\mathcal{L}$ is an arbitrary finite string of the following symbols. A single symbol is an expression of length 1. We admit also the string or expression of length 0.

5.1 DEFINITION The symbols of $\mathcal{L}$ are:

(i) infinitely many variable symbols $\mathsf{v}_0, \mathsf{v}_1, \mathsf{v}_2, \mathsf{v}_3, \ldots,$

(ii) predicate symbols = and □,

(iii) function symbols q, ⌢, and sub,

(iv) the connectives ¬, → and the quantifier symbol ∀,

(v) auxiliary symbols (and),

(vi) possibly finitely many further function and predicate symbols of arbitrary arities and finitely many further auxiliary symbols, and

(vii) for each string e of symbols exactly one constant.

All symbols are pairwise distinct. For instance, v_0 is distinct from $\mathsf{v}_1, \mathsf{v}_2, \ldots, =$, and so on; v_1 is distinct from $\mathsf{v}_2, \ldots, =$, and so on. In particular, if e is any string of symbols, the constant for e is distinct from e itself and from all symbols in (i)–(vi); and if f is a string of symbols distinct from e, then the constants for e and f are also distinct. Consequently, the constant for e is distinct from the constant for the *constant* of e, and so on. For (vii) we assume that each constant is also associated with an expression, although this will be needed only later.

There are no further symbols in $\mathcal{L}$ beyond those in (i)–(vii).

The constant for e is called the quotation constant of e. We write $\overline{e}$ for the quotation constant of e. We write x for v_0, y for v_1, z for v_2, and w for v_3 to make the notation less cluttered.

For the definition of a formula of the language it does not matter what the intended meanings of these symbols are. But it may help to add some explanations here. We have three special function symbols. The binary function symbol ⌢ stands for concatenation, that is, $x \frown y$ is the result of concatenating x and y, that is, x followed by y. Here x and y are any variables of the language. The unary function symbol q expresses the function that takes an expression to its quotation, that is, $\mathsf{q}x$ is the quotation constant of x. Finally, sub is a ternary function symbol and $\mathsf{sub}\,xyz$ is the result of substituting the symbol y with the expression z in x. The unary predicate symbol □ can be read in different ways, for instance, as a truth or necessity predicate. We will consider different readings and axiomatizations of □.

In (vi) we require the additional function and predicate symbols to have 'arbitrary arity'. As explained in section 2.1, this merely means that with each function and predicate symbol some natural number is associated.

Except for the last condition (vii) on quotation constants, the list of symbols is fairly standard. But even in the other clauses there are some tricky details that are usually brushed over.

In more carefully written logic books, it is explicitly stated that all the symbols are pairwise distinct, that is, y is distinct from ¬, q is distinct from the left bracket (, and so on. This means that no symbol is 'used twice'. We make this assumption in our definition. But the assumption alone does not suffice. We said that the internal structure of the symbols does not matter. Hence, so far nothing keeps us from using ¬¬ as the eleventh variable or even ∀y□y as the connective →; ¬¬ and ∀y□y can still be different from any symbol, though not from any string of symbols. Hence, we will want to rule out that any symbol is part of another symbol. We will also not admit that combining two symbols gives us another symbol. Symbols should be irreducible units. Whenever we go through a string of symbols we should be able to identify the sequence of symbols. There should be only one way to parse a given string of symbols of $\mathcal{L}$ into its constituent symbols. Often, this assumption is left implicit. We impose the following constraint explicitly. It states that no string of symbols of $\mathcal{L}$ can be obtained by composing symbols of $\mathcal{L}$ in a different way. By 'composing' we mean concatenating the symbols.

5.2 UNIQUE READABILITY ASSUMPTION *Assume that $a_1, \ldots, a_n, b_1, \ldots, b_k$ are symbols of $\mathcal{L}$. If the string $a_1 \ldots a_n$ is identical to the string $b_1 \ldots b_k$, then $n = k$, $a_1 = b_1, \ldots,$ and $a_n = b_k$.*

This obviously rules out the possibility that a string of symbols could be obtained in two different ways. For instance, we cannot use ¬¬ as the eleventh variable or ∀y□y as the connective →, as this would violate our assumption.

The assumption of the unique readability of strings of symbols is by no means a trivial assumption, although it is widely relied upon in logic, often without being made explicit.

We distinguish between the language $\mathcal{L}$ itself and our particular notation for $\mathcal{L}$. We do not actually assume that the first variable of $\mathcal{L}$ is the sans serif letter v followed by the Arabic numeral for zero in a somewhat lowered position and reduced in size. Similarly, we do not assume that the constant for the expression $\overline{\neg=}$ is composed from the glyphs ¬ and = with a line on top. Overlining glyphs is only our way of *naming* the corresponding quotation constant. The only operation on symbols is concatenation. Again, we do not assume that concatenation follows the left-to-right direction. However, a few assumptions about concatenation are implicit. In particular, concatenation is associative: concatenating e with f and the result with g yields the same string as concatenating e with the concatenation of f and g. This is important when we write $a_1 \ldots a_n$ for the concatenation of the symbols $a_1, \ldots, a_n$ (in this order). Without associativity of concatenation, we would have to indicate by means of brackets or similar devices in which order the symbols have been concatenated. Other properties that are usually assumed about strings of symbols follow from assumption 5.2: If concatenation were commutative, the assumption would fail. Moreover, the assumption rules out that a concatenation of symbols yields another symbol.

We should ascertain that our notation could serve as a particular instantiation of $\mathcal{L}$. That is, we should show that assumption 5.2 is satisfied if the symbols are of the particular shape we have chosen and concatenation is expressed in the way we use. This is not completely trivial, and the reader may find such worries outlandish. For instance, we follow the convention of leaving a little space between notations of expressions when we write the concatenation of the notations. Our notation for the concatenation of the quotation constant for the negation symbol with itself is $\overline{\neg}\ \overline{\neg}$, not $\overline{\neg\neg}$. If we did not leave some space, the notation for the concatenation of the quotation constant with itself would be the same as the notation for the single quotation constant for the negation symbol concatenated with itself.

These or similar problems arise for most formal languages. In the definition above, there is an additional issue, namely the generation of the quotation constants. If we had chosen, for instance, to generate quotation constants in our notation by enclosing an expression in asterisks, then the expression $*\neg*\neg*\neg*$ could be of length 1 and be the quotation constant for the following: the negation symbol, followed by the *constant* for the negation symbol, followed by the negation symbol again; or it could have length 3 and be the quotation constant for negation, followed by the negation symbol, followed by the quotation constant for $\neg$ again. Overlining avoids pitfalls of this kind.

Our particular notation satisfies unique readability, and all notations for distinct symbols are distinct. A full argument for the pairwise distinctness of all symbols and unique readability could proceed via a main induction on the maximal number of overlinings in a notation for an expression and a side induction on the length of the expression. Our notation has the nice feature that symbols are always separated by horizontal spaces but there are no horizontal spaces *within* symbols, and that symbols are thus contiguous. The last claim has two exceptions: (1) We do not count the horizontal spaces in sub. This could have been easily avoided by using only one letter instead of three; it only would have made it harder to remember. (2) We also disregard all spaces before and within Arabic numerals. The last condition means that we consider the notations for variables as contiguous. Obviously there would have been ways to make them genuinely contiguous, but we can stipulate that we ignore gaps involving glyphs in index position.

Overlining thus achieves a special feat: applied to a notation, it eliminates or 'fills' all horizontal spaces: $\neg\!\rightarrow\!\neg$ contains two horizontal spaces, while $\overline{\neg\!\rightarrow\!\neg}$ does not contain any. Overlining thus converts a noncontiguous expression into a contiguous symbol. The price for this is that we have a nonlinear notation. There are linear notations for $\mathcal{L}$, but overlining for generating quotation constants is a highly readable notation, and that is why we prefer it over all linear options that came to our minds.

It may be asked why we have chosen to treat quotations as constants rather than complex expressions composed from symbols; even variables might be seen as composed. There are reasons for these choices that depend on our axioms for the theory of syntax in section 5.3. In a nutshell, our choice helps us to keep the theory simple. The choice of symbols will be different in our more expressive theory in chapter 8.

5.2 Formulæ and Sentences

We now define the notions of a term and a formula of $\mathcal{L}$. They are certain expressions of $\mathcal{L}$, that is, certain strings of symbols.

5.3 DEFINITION The $\mathcal{L}$-terms are defined as follows:

(i) All variables are terms.

(ii) All quotation constants are terms.

(iii) If t, r, and s are terms, then $\mathsf{q}t$, $\frown st$, and $\mathsf{sub}\, rst$ are terms.

(iv) If $t_1, \dots, t_n$ are terms and f is one of the additional function symbols of arity n, then $ft_1 \dots t_n$ is a term.

(v) Nothing else is an $\mathcal{L}$-term.

The term $\frown st$ will be written as $(s \frown t)$. $(s \frown t \frown u)$ is short for $\big((s \frown t) \frown u\big)$. We will also often add brackets and commas for readability and write, for instance, $\mathsf{sub}(r, s, t)$ instead of $\mathsf{sub}\, rst$. In the following definitions we drop the analogous clauses stating that nothing else is a formula, sentence, and so on.

It follows from the unique readability of strings of symbols that there is exactly one string of length 0, the empty string. Since the empty string is a string of symbols, $\overline{}$ is a term (this is the empty expression overlined). Since $\overline{}$ looks so odd, we write $\underline{0}$ for $\overline{}$. The empty string is a weird thing. One might be inclined to say that it is not anything and that concatenating an expression with the empty string is really concatenating the expression with nothing. A major discussion could be added here that is reminiscent of that about holes in the style of (D. K. Lewis and S. Lewis 1970). However, nothing depends on our assumption that the empty string exists. Assuming the existence of the empty string simplifies some things, but it is not indispensable. What the empty string is for the expressions is the number zero for the natural numbers.

Formulæ, sentences, and free and bound occurrences of variables are defined in the usual way.

5.4 DEFINITION The atomic $\mathcal{L}$-formulæ are defined as follows:

(i) If s and t are terms, then $=st$ and $\Box s$ are atomic formulæ.

(ii) If $t_1, \ldots, t_n$ are terms and P is one of the additional predicate symbols of arity n, then $Pt_1 \ldots t_n$ is an atomic formula.

The atomic formula $=st$ is also written as $s = t$.

5.5 DEFINITION If φ and ψ are formulæ and x is a variable, then $\neg\varphi$, $(\varphi \rightarrow \psi)$, and $\forall x\, \varphi$ are formulæ.

Finally we define free and bound occurrences of variables.

5.6 DEFINITION

(i) Every occurrence of a variable in an atomic formula is free in that formula.

(ii) All occurrences of free variables y in φ are also free in $\forall x\, \varphi$ iff y is distinct from x. All other occurrences of variables are not free.

An occurrence of a variable in a formula is bound iff it is not free.

For instance, in the formula $\forall \underline{\mathsf{x}}(\Box \underline{\mathsf{x}} \to \Box \underline{\mathsf{x}}) \to \mathsf{x} = \mathsf{x}$, all underlined occurrences of x are bound; the remaining two are free.

5.7 DEFINITION A formula is a sentence iff it does not contain a free occurrence of a variable.

The following two formulæ are examples of sentences:

$$\neg\Big(\forall \mathsf{v}_3\big(\mathsf{v}_3 = \overline{\to\forall} \to \neg \mathsf{v}_3 = \overline{\overline{\to\forall}}\big) \to \Box\overline{\mathsf{v}_3}\Big),$$

$$\overline{\mathsf{v}_{12}} = \overline{\neg\Box\overline{\neg}}.$$

We will often have to replace variables in formulæ with other terms. If, for instance, a formula $\varphi(\mathsf{x})$ and some term t are given, we write $\varphi(t)$ for the result of substituting all free occurrences of x in $\varphi(\mathsf{x})$ with the term t. We will always make clear which variable is replaced by mentioning the formula first and the variable whose free occurrences are going to be replaced by writing the variable in brackets. This looks less cluttered than $\varphi(t/\mathsf{x})$ or the like.

The reason for the restriction to free occurrences becomes obvious by considering a formula such as $\Box\mathsf{x} \to \forall\mathsf{x}\,\Box\mathsf{x}$. If this formula is our formula $\varphi(\mathsf{x})$, then $\varphi(\overline{\neg})$ should be $\Box\overline{\neg} \to \forall\mathsf{x}\,\Box\mathsf{x}$ and not $\Box\overline{\neg} \to \forall\overline{\neg}\Box\overline{\neg}$. The latter is not even a formula. In most cases the term t will not contain free variables, but if it does, the occurrences of variables in t should not be bound by quantifiers in $\varphi(t)$. To avoid this problem, we can use different variables in $\varphi(\mathsf{x})$.

In what follows we omit or include brackets to make the notation less cluttered. The bracketing conventions for formulæ from page 14 are used.

5.3 The Basic Axioms

We are now going to specify axioms and rules for the syntax theory E. Actually, we state only minimal conditions for E, and then E can be any theory containing these axioms.

5.8 DEFINITION All instances of the following schemas are axioms of E:

A1 $\overline{a}{}^\frown\overline{b} = \overline{ab}$, where a and b are arbitrary strings of symbols

A2 $\mathsf{q}(\overline{a}) = \overline{\overline{a}}$

A3 $\mathsf{sub}(\overline{a}, \overline{b}, \overline{c}) = \overline{d}$, where a and c are arbitrary strings of symbols, b is a symbol (or, equivalently, a length-1 string of symbols), and d is the string of symbols obtained from a by replacing all occurrences of the symbol b with c

A4 $\forall x \forall y \forall z \big((x^\frown y)^\frown z\big) = \big(x^\frown (y^\frown z)\big)$

A5 $\forall x \forall y \big(x^\frown y = \underline{0} \rightarrow x = \underline{0} \wedge y = \underline{0}\big)$

A6 $\forall x \forall y (x^\frown y = x \leftrightarrow y = \underline{0}) \wedge \forall x \forall y (y^\frown x = x \leftrightarrow y = \underline{0})$

A7 $\forall x \forall y\, \mathsf{sub}(x^\frown \overline{a}, \overline{a}, y) = \mathsf{sub}(x, \overline{a}, y)^\frown y$, where a is a symbol

A8 $\forall x \forall y \forall z \forall w$
$\big(x^\frown y = z^\frown w \leftrightarrow \exists v_4\big((x = z^\frown v_4 \wedge v_4{}^\frown y = w) \vee (x^\frown v_4 = z \wedge y = v_4{}^\frown w)\big)\big)$

In A2, A3, and A7 we have added brackets for readability. The official version of A4 is $\forall x \forall y \forall z = {}^\frown{}^\frown xyz^\frown x^\frown yz$.

We do not stipulate that E must not contain further axioms or rules of deduction. In fact, we often assume that E contains further theorems in the formulation of our results in the next chapter.

We write $\mathsf{E} \vdash \varphi$ if and only if the formula φ can be proved using the rules and axioms of E.

REMARK ON A1 The concatenation of two expressions e_1 and e_2 is the expression e_1 followed by e_2. For instance, $\neg\neg x$ is the concatenation of $\neg$ and $\neg x$. Therefore both $\overline{\neg}^\frown \overline{\neg x} = \overline{\neg\neg x}$ and $\overline{\neg\neg}^\frown \overline{x} = \overline{\neg\neg x}$ are instances of A1. Concatenating the empty string with any expression e gives again the same expression e. Therefore, we have, for example, $\overline{\forall}^\frown \underline{0} = \overline{\forall}$ as an instance of A1.

The axioms A1–A3 describe the functions of concatenation, quotation, and substitution by providing function values for specific entries. In definition 5.1 we required that our language $\mathcal{L}$ contain exactly one quotation constant for each expression of the language. This does not only mean that we have as many quotation constants as strings of symbols, but also that each expression e has a quotation constant $\overline{e}$ that is associated with it. So far this has not mattered, and we have not made any use of the connection between expressions and their quotation constants. However, in stating axioms A1–A3 we do make use of this connection. Whether a specific $\mathcal{L}$-sentence is an instance of A1–A3 depends on this connection. If c_1 is the quotation constant for the expression a, c_2 the one for the expression b, and c_3 the quotation constant for the concatenation of a with b, then $c_1{}^\frown c_2 = c_3$ is an axiom according to A1. But we could have associated different constants with a, b, and c, and then $c_1{}^\frown c_2 = c_3$ would not be an A1-axiom.

REMARK ON A2 The symbol q describes the function that takes an expression and returns its quotation constant. Thus, axiom A2 makes the association of constants with expressions explicit in the language $\mathcal{L}$. For each expression a, the axiom tells us that $\overline{a}$ is its quotation constant. The sentences $\mathsf{q}(\overline{\rightarrow\rightarrow}) = \overline{\overline{\rightarrow\rightarrow}}$ and $\mathsf{q}(\overline{\mathsf{x}\neg}) = \overline{\overline{\mathsf{x}\neg}}$, for example, are A2-axioms. In the former axiom, $\overline{\overline{\rightarrow\rightarrow}}$ is the quotation constant for the quotation constant of the expression $\rightarrow\rightarrow$.

The use of quotation constants of quotation constants may look somewhat puzzling. But something similar is required in informal English. If we want to say that a certain expression is the quotation of the name 'Plato', we could do so using the following sentence:

> " 'Plato' " is the quotation of the name 'Plato'.

Here we have used double quotation marks for quoting expressions containing single quotation marks.[1] If we dropped one layer of quotation marks and wrote instead

> 'Plato' is the quotation of the name Plato,

we would be saying nonsense. Also, if we didn't use the name 'Plato' in the example but rather a sentence such as 'Snow is white', we would have an expression that is not an English sentence. Equally, in $\mathcal{L}$ the expression $\mathsf{q}(\rightarrow\rightarrow) = \overline{\rightarrow\rightarrow}$ is not a well-formed sentence, because $\rightarrow\rightarrow$ is not a term and so it cannot be used as an argument for the function q.[2]

[1] The standard (British English) convention to use double quotation marks within single quotes is problematic because the quoted expression is changed. Thus, on this convention, the quotation of an expression is not always obtained by enclosing the expression in quotation marks. When the expression contains quotation marks, it has to be modified. The quotation of Plato's name is ' "Plato" ' and obtained by enclosing the name in single quotation marks. Strangely, the expression within the single quotes contains double instead of the original single quotes.

[2] In spoken English we do not pronounce quotation marks. Perhaps we may use gestures in logic classes to indicate how spoken sentences would be written down. The modern quotation marks have a complicated history, and different devices for marking quotations were used before the modern conventions came into use. Without any quotation marks an expression such as 'Plato' is ambiguous. The expression 'Plato' can then stand either for the person or for the name of Plato (or for the *name* of the name, and so on). In the terminology of medieval philosophers, the former would be called 'formal' and the latter 'material supposition'.

REMARK ON A3 Examples of A3-axioms are the following sentences:

$$\mathsf{sub}(\overline{)\rightarrow\Box \mathsf{v}_{12}}, \overline{\Box}, \overline{\rightarrow}) = \overline{)\rightarrow\rightarrow \mathsf{v}_{12}},$$
$$\mathsf{sub}(\overline{\forall \mathsf{x}\Box \mathsf{x}}, \overline{\mathsf{x}}, \overline{\overline{\neg}}) = \overline{\forall\overline{\neg}\Box\overline{\neg}},$$
$$\mathsf{sub}(\overline{\neg\neg}, \overline{\neg}, \overline{\neg\neg\neg}) = \overline{\neg\neg\neg\neg\neg\neg}.$$

In an A3-axiom $\mathsf{sub}(\overline{a}, \overline{b}, \overline{c}) = \overline{d}$ the expression b must be a (single) symbol, not a string of symbols with more than one symbol or the empty string. This does not imply that the substitution function cannot be applied to complex expressions; it just means that, while $\mathsf{sub}(\overline{a}, \overline{b}, \overline{c}) = \overline{d}$ is a well-formed sentence, it is not an A3-axiom if b is not a single symbol. Axiom A3 does not say anything about the result of substituting a complex expression. The reason for this restriction is that the result of the substitution of a complex string may be not unique. For instance, the result of substituting $\neg$ for $\rightarrow\rightarrow$ in $\rightarrow\rightarrow\rightarrow$ might be either $\rightarrow\neg$ or $\neg\rightarrow$. This problem does not arise if only single symbols are replaced. The problem could also be fixed in other ways, for instance, by always replacing the first occurrence of an expression; but we do not need to substitute complex expressions in what follows, and we avoid the problem by the restriction of b to single symbols.

The symbols of $\mathcal{L}$ are listed in definition 5.1. In particular, all variables and quotation constants are single symbols. Thus, the following sentence is an A3-axiom:

$$\mathsf{sub}(\overline{\forall \mathsf{x}(\mathsf{x}=\overline{\neg} \rightarrow \neg \mathsf{x}=\overline{\overline{\neg}})}, \overline{\overline{\neg}}, \overline{\mathsf{q}(\mathsf{z})}) = \overline{\forall \mathsf{x}(\mathsf{x}=\mathsf{q}(\mathsf{z}) \rightarrow \neg \mathsf{x}=\overline{\overline{\neg}})}.$$

Single symbols can be replaced with other expressions, but nothing can be replaced 'within' single symbols. Thus, the following, for instance, is an A3-axiom:

$$\mathsf{sub}(\overline{\mathsf{x}=\mathsf{x} \rightarrow \overline{\mathsf{x}}=\overline{\mathsf{x}}}, \overline{\mathsf{x}}, \overline{\mathsf{z}}) = \overline{\mathsf{z}=\mathsf{z} \rightarrow \overline{\mathsf{x}}=\overline{\mathsf{x}}}.$$

The axioms A1–A3 are already sufficient for proving the crucial diagonal lemma (lemma 5.12) and therefore for proving the paradoxes in section 6.1. The other axioms are needed only later. But since we prefer to have the axioms of E in one place, we introduce the remaining axioms already here.

REMARK ON A4 In contrast to A1–A3, the following axioms A4–A7 are only single axioms, that is, whereas each of A1–A3 specifies infinitely many axioms, axioms A4–A7 each specify a single axiom. The axiom $\forall \mathsf{x}\forall \mathsf{y}\forall \mathsf{z}\,((\mathsf{x} \frown \mathsf{y}) \frown \mathsf{z}) = (\mathsf{x} \frown (\mathsf{y} \frown \mathsf{z}))$ simplifies reasoning with strings a great deal. It says that concatenation is associative, that is, it does not matter whether we concatenate first *a* and *b* and then the result with *c* or whether we concatenate first *b* with *c* and then precede this with *a*.

The axiom A4 does not follow from the axioms in A1–A3. For any expressions *a*, *b*, and *c*, logic and A1 allow us to prove the following:

$$\begin{aligned}(\overline{a}^\frown\overline{b})^\frown\overline{c} &= \overline{ab}^\frown\overline{c}\\ &= \overline{abc}\\ &= \overline{a}^\frown\overline{bc}\\ &= \overline{a}^\frown(\overline{b}^\frown\overline{c}).\end{aligned}$$

But this can be proved only for individual expressions. There is no way to conclude the universally quantified sentence $\forall x \forall y \forall z \left((x^\frown y)^\frown z\right) = \left(x^\frown(y^\frown z)\right)$ from all these sentences with arbitrary expressions *a*, *b*, and *c*. Similar remarks apply to other universally quantified claims, including the following axioms.

REMARK ON A5–A6 These axioms will be invoked only in section 6.5. The axiom A5 tells us that if either *a* or *b* is not the empty expression, then the concatenation of *a* and *b* is non-empty as well. Axiom A6 postulates that only the empty string does not change an object if it is concatenated with this object.

REMARK ON A7 This axiom says that the result of substituting a symbol *a* in an expression whose last symbol is *a* with an expression *c* is the same as substituting first *a* in the part before the last occurrence of *a* with *c* and then appending *c*. The reason for substituting only a single symbol – rather than also complex expressions – is the same as in axiom A3.

REMARK ON A8 If the concatenation of x and y is identical to the concatenation of z with w, then x and z (and y and w) need not be identical. The expression z could also be a proper initial segment of x. Here is an illustration of this case:

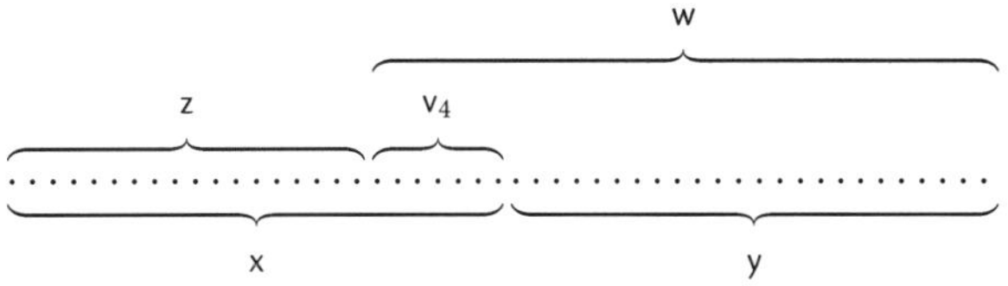

In this case there must be an expression v_4 such that x is z followed by v_4 and w is v_4 followed by y. Formally this means that the following obtains:

$$\exists v_4(x = z^\frown v_4 \wedge v_4{}^\frown y = w).$$

Of course, there is another possibility. The expression x could conversely be an initial segment of z. In that case we have

$$\exists v_4(x^\frown v_4 = z \wedge y = v_4{}^\frown w).$$

It is also possible that x and z are the same expression. This case is already covered because v_4 is then the empty string.[3] Therefore, the two cases are exhaustive and there are no other possibilities if $x^\frown y = z^\frown w$. This justifies the left-to-right direction of axiom A8:

$$\forall x \forall y \forall z \forall w \Big(x^\frown y = z^\frown w \leftrightarrow \exists v_4\big((x = z^\frown v_4 \wedge v_4{}^\frown y = w) \vee (x^\frown v_4 = z \wedge y = v_4{}^\frown w)\big)\Big).$$

Axiom A8 expresses the linearity of expressions in the following sense. If appending the same expression to an expression *a* and to an expression *b* yields the same result, then *a* and *b* must be identical. This can be seen by choosing from the following instance of the axiom:

$$\forall x \forall y \forall z \Big(x^\frown y = z^\frown y \leftrightarrow \exists v_4\big((x = z^\frown v_4 \wedge v_4{}^\frown y = y) \vee (x^\frown v_4 = z \wedge y = v_4{}^\frown y)\big)\Big).$$

From axiom A6 it follows that $\forall v_4(v_4{}^\frown y = y \to v_4 = \underline{0})$. Therefore, the following obtains:

$$\forall x \forall y \forall z (x^\frown y = z^\frown y \to x = z).$$

The same applies to prefixing expressions. All this requires only the left-to-right direction of A8.

The right-to-left direction is equivalent to the associativity of concatenation, as will be shown in proposition 8.50. Therefore, we could omit axiom A4 without loss.

The axioms A1–A8 are very weak. They can be satisfied in a model that has just one element, say 0, in its domain, as will be shown in section 5.5. Of course,

[3] Tarski's (1935, p. 173) original formulation Axiom 4 lists three possibilities, exactly because Tarski does not admit the empty expression.

the theory E may contain additional axioms, such as $\neg(\overline{\neg} = \underline{0})$, that preclude this trivial model. Proving the results in chapter 6 in such a weak theory makes those results stronger. Most of our observations on E are negative, in the sense that they show that certain axioms that look plausible and might be included in E have unacceptable consequences; in particular we will show that many axioms lead to inconsistency. If these negative results are proved for a weak theory such as E, it makes them stronger: if already E is inconsistent with certain assumptions, then any stronger theory properly containing E is inconsistent as well.

When motivating the axioms, we already sketched the intended models of our theory. These models are the instantiations of $\mathcal{L}$ or, for short, $\mathcal{L}$ is its own intended model. That is, the domain of the intended model of E is the set of expressions, conceived as strings of symbols. The function symbols are interpreted as the corresponding syntactic functions. No assumptions are made how $\Box$ and possible further symbols are interpreted, because this obviously depends on how we want to read E and these further symbols. The intended model will be described in more detail in section 5.5.

5.4 The Diagonal Lemma

As has been mentioned above, axioms A1–A3 suffice for proving the diagonal lemma.[4] The diagonal function dia is defined in the following way:

5.9 DEFINITION $\mathsf{dia}(x) := \mathsf{sub}\big(x, \bar{\mathsf{x}}, \mathsf{q}(x)\big)$.

There are different ways to understand definitions of this kind. Here we understand them as metalinguistic abbreviations of $\mathcal{L}$-expressions. That is, dia is not an additional function symbol of $\mathcal{L}$. The definition of dia is intended to express the following: if t is a term, $\mathsf{dia}(t)$ is shorthand for $\mathsf{sub}\big(t, \bar{\mathsf{x}}, \mathsf{q}(t)\big)$. Thus, dia has a status similar to $\wedge$, $\vee$, $\leftrightarrow$, and $\exists$. They, too, are not symbols of our language $\mathcal{L}$, as we explain on page 14; they merely allow us to abbreviate formulæ. Similarly,

[4]There is no such cheap way to Gödel's theorems, though. Gödel showed that functions corresponding to those expressed by sub and q (and further operations) can be defined in an arithmetical theory for numerical codes of expressions. To this end he proved that all recursive functions can be represented in a fixed arithmetical system. And then he proved that certain operations, like substitution, *are* recursive. Gödel did neither state nor prove the diagonal lemma in his celebrated (1931), although the main idea is found in that paper. For an overview of the history of the diagonal lemma, see (Smoryński 1981).

dia is not a function symbol of $\mathcal{L}$. It merely allows us to communicate certain terms more efficiently.

In most situations it does not make a big difference whether we think of such definitions as definitions in the object language such that dia, for instance, is introduced as a new function symbol in $\mathcal{L}$ or whether we understand them as parts of metalinguistic abbreviations. In the present context, however, the situation is more complicated. If dia were a function symbol of $\mathcal{L}$, the quotation constants $\overline{\mathsf{dia}(\mathsf{y})}$ and $\overline{\mathsf{sub}(\mathsf{y}, \overline{\mathsf{x}}, \mathsf{q}(\mathsf{y}))}$ would be distinct constants. On our understanding, they are the same constant because $\mathsf{dia}(\mathsf{y})$ is the same expression as $\mathsf{sub}(\mathsf{y}, \overline{\mathsf{x}}, \mathsf{q}(\mathsf{y}))$. The metalinguistic expressions $\overline{\mathsf{dia}(\mathsf{y})}$ and $\overline{\mathsf{sub}(\mathsf{y}, \overline{\mathsf{x}}, \mathsf{q}(\mathsf{y}))}$ are different ways to refer to one and the same constant of $\mathcal{L}$.

In the definition of dia we have fixed the quotation constant $\overline{\mathsf{x}}$, which is the quotation constant for the first variable x, that is, v_0. In what follows we always diagonalize formulæ in the variable x. There is nothing specific about the choice of x. We could have used any other variable instead.

5.10 LEMMA *Assume $\varphi(\mathsf{x})$ is a formula not containing bound occurrences of* x. *Then the following holds:*

$$\mathsf{E} \vdash \mathsf{dia}\big(\overline{\varphi(\mathsf{dia}(\mathsf{x}))}\big) = \overline{\varphi\Big(\mathsf{dia}\big(\overline{\varphi(\mathsf{dia}(\mathsf{x}))}\big)\Big)}.$$

PROOF In E the following equations can be proved. The first line is the definition of dia and therefore there is the same term on the left and the right side of the identity symbol. In the second line axiom A2 is used, and axiom A3 yields the last line.

$$\begin{aligned}
\mathsf{dia}\big(\overline{\varphi(\mathsf{dia}(\mathsf{x}))}\big) &= \mathsf{sub}\Big(\overline{\varphi(\mathsf{dia}(\mathsf{x}))}, \overline{\mathsf{x}}, \mathsf{q}\big(\overline{\varphi(\mathsf{dia}(\mathsf{x}))}\big)\Big) \\
&= \mathsf{sub}\Big(\overline{\varphi(\mathsf{dia}(\mathsf{x}))}, \overline{\mathsf{x}}, \overline{\overline{\varphi(\mathsf{dia}(\mathsf{x}))}}\Big) \\
&= \overline{\varphi\Big(\mathsf{dia}\big(\overline{\varphi(\mathsf{dia}(\mathsf{x}))}\big)\Big)}.
\end{aligned}$$ ⊣

Had we allowed that $\varphi(\mathsf{x})$ contain bound occurrences of the specific variable x, the proof would fail in the last step. On page 61 we defined, for a given formula $\varphi(\mathsf{x})$ and term t, the formula $\varphi(t)$ as the result of substituting all free occurrences of x with the term t. Thus, in the proof above, $\varphi\big(\mathsf{dia}\big(\overline{\varphi(\mathsf{dia}(\mathsf{x}))}\big)\big)$ is the result of substituting all *free* occurrences of x in $\varphi(\mathsf{x})$ with the term $\mathsf{dia}\big(\overline{\varphi(\mathsf{dia}(\mathsf{x}))}\big)$.

The A3-axiom used in the last step is the following:

$$\mathsf{sub}\Big(\overline{\varphi(\mathsf{dia}(\mathsf{x}))}, \overline{\mathsf{x}}, \overline{\overline{\varphi(\mathsf{dia}(\mathsf{x}))}}\Big) = \overline{d},$$

where d is the result of replacing *all* occurrences of x in $\varphi(\mathsf{dia}(\mathsf{x}))$ with $\overline{\varphi(\mathsf{dia}(\mathsf{x}))}$. If $\varphi(\mathsf{dia}(\mathsf{x}))$ contains no bound occurrences of x then d is the same string of symbols as $\varphi(\mathsf{dia}(\overline{\varphi(\mathsf{dia}(\mathsf{x}))}))$. If, however, $\varphi(\mathsf{dia}(\mathsf{x}))$ does contain bound occurrences then in the last step these bound occurrences would be replaced, too, not giving $\varphi(\mathsf{dia}(\overline{\varphi(\mathsf{dia}(\mathsf{x}))}))$ but an expression that is not even a formula, because all occurrences of x would have been replaced, even those in quantifiers.

For future reference we state this lemma in a slightly less specific way:

5.11 STRONG DIAGONAL LEMMA *If $\varphi(\mathsf{x})$ is a formula of $\mathcal{L}$ with no bound occurrences of* x*, then one can find a term t such that the following holds:*

$$\mathsf{E} \vdash t = \overline{\varphi(t)},$$

and therefore

$$\mathsf{E} \vdash \varphi(t) \leftrightarrow \varphi(\overline{\varphi(t)}).$$

PROOF The term $\mathsf{dia}(\overline{\varphi(\mathsf{dia}(\mathsf{x}))})$ can serve as the term t. ⊣

The strong diagonal lemma shows that $\varphi(\mathsf{dia}(\overline{\varphi(\mathsf{dia}(\mathsf{x}))}))$ resembles self-referential sentences of natural languages in some important aspects. For instance, the English sentence

(5.1) Sentence (5.1) is a sentence

arguably says about itself that it is a sentence; and the sentence

The first sentence on page 69 containing the word 'first' is an example

says about itself that it is an example. Both sentences contain an expression designating the respective sentence itself. In the first sentence this is the phrase *the sentence* (5.1) and in the second it is the phrase *the first sentence on page 69 containing the word 'first'*. Similarly, the sentence $\varphi(\mathsf{dia}(\overline{\varphi(\mathsf{dia}(\mathsf{x}))}))$ of the language $\mathcal{L}$ contains a term that designates the sentence itself, namely, $\mathsf{dia}(\overline{\varphi(\mathsf{dia}(\mathsf{x}))})$. This property will be important in our discussion of self-reference in later chapters.

We also state the diagonal lemma in its more common weak version. The weak version becomes more relevant when we try to generalize the diagonal lemma to other languages and theories. In many theories there are no function symbols corresponding to our q and sub. This is the case for the standard formulation of set theory, whose language contains only the predicate symbol $\in$ as its single non-logical symbol and no function symbols at all. Also many arithmetical languages have only a very limited stock of symbols. For such languages and theories only the following weak version of the diagonal lemma is provable.

5.12 DIAGONAL LEMMA, GÖDEL'S FIXED-POINT LEMMA *If $\varphi(\mathsf{x})$ is a formula of $\mathcal{L}$ with no bound occurrences of* x, *then one can find a sentence γ such that the following holds:*

$$\mathsf{E} \vdash \gamma \leftrightarrow \varphi(\overline{\gamma}).$$

PROOF For a given formula $\varphi(\mathsf{x})$ we can, by the previous lemma, find a term t with $\mathsf{E} \vdash t = \overline{\varphi(t)}$. So the claim

$$\mathsf{E} \vdash \varphi(t) \leftrightarrow \varphi(\overline{\varphi(t)})$$

follows by the laws of identity. Thus, $\varphi(t)$ has the properties required of γ. ⊣

Concatenation alone is sufficient for this weak form of the diagonal lemma (see Grzegorczyk 2005 also for some historical observations). In the strong diagonal lemma, we started from a formula $\varphi(\mathsf{x})$ with only x as free variable. If the formula contains additional free variables, the proof goes through in the same way:

5.13 DIAGONAL LEMMA WITH FREE VARIABLES *If $\varphi(\mathsf{x},\mathsf{y})$ is a formula of $\mathcal{L}$ with no bound occurrences of* x, *then one can find a formula $\theta(\mathsf{y})$ such that the following holds:*[5]

$$\mathsf{E} \vdash \forall \mathsf{y}\Big(\theta(\mathsf{y}) \leftrightarrow \varphi\big(\overline{\theta(\mathsf{y})},\mathsf{y}\big)\Big).$$

Here $\overline{\theta(\mathsf{y})}$ is the quotation constant for the formula $\theta(\mathsf{y})$. Thus, the variable y does not occur in $\overline{\theta(\mathsf{y})}$ and therefore cannot be bound in $\overline{\theta(\mathsf{y})}$. There is also a version of this lemma where occurrences of y 'inside' $\overline{\theta(\mathsf{y})}$ can be bound, using a trick. This will be shown in lemma 6.17.

The proof is the same as for the diagonal lemma. Of course, we could allow more free variables, but we will need only the version with y.

[5]The reader may have noticed that we are using θ instead of γ for the diagonal formula. This has typographical reasons: the variables y and γ look almost the same in our typeface, and using another Greek letter is intended to improve readability.

5.5 Standard Models

In this section we describe the standard or 'intended' models for E. They will be used heavily in chapter 7. The reader only interested in the paradoxes and the applications of the diagonal lemma can jump ahead to chapter 6, because the models of E will play only a marginal role in that chapter.

If a theory has a model, it is consistent. If we only try to show that the obligatory axioms of E, that is, A1–A8, are consistent, a trivial model suffices. There is no axiom that tells us that there are any distinct expressions, that is, that there is more than one expression. We can use a domain that contains exactly one object, for instance, the number 0. In such a model all quotation constants denote the same object and all function symbols are interpreted by functions that have constant value 0. It is not hard to check that the axioms A1–A8 are satisfied in such a model. We could exclude such trivial models by adding all sentences $\neg\overline{a}=\overline{b}$ as axioms, whenever $\overline{a}$ and $\overline{b}$ are distinct quotation constants. This would rule out models with a finite domain. But, for reasons discussed above, we prefer to work with very weak assumptions on E.

Of course, our theory should not only be consistent but also sound under the intended interpretation. When motivating our axioms A1–A8, we already mentioned how we intend to interpret the quotation constants and the function symbols q, $\frown$, and sub, but not $\Box$ or any additional function or predicate symbols. Let $\mathcal{L}_{qc}$ be language consisting of these symbols alone. That is, the symbols of $\mathcal{L}_{qc}$ are the logical symbols, the function symbols q, $\frown$, and sub, and all quotation constants from $\mathcal{L}$.

The standard model $\mathbb{E}$ of $\mathcal{L}_{qc}$ has as its domain the set of all expressions of the full language $\mathcal{L}$, that is, the set of all finite strings of symbols of $\mathcal{L}$. $\mathcal{L}$ and $\mathcal{L}_{qc}$ cannot coincide, because at least $\Box$ is a symbol of $\mathcal{L}$ but not of $\mathcal{L}_{qc}$.

The quotation constants and the function symbols q, $\frown$, and sub are interpreted in $\mathbb{E}$ as follows:

(i) For every expression e, the interpretation in $\mathbb{E}$ of its quotation constant $\overline{e}$ is the expression e itself.

(ii) The function symbol q is interpreted in $\mathbb{E}$ by the function that assigns to every expression its quotation constant.

(iii) The function symbol $\frown$ is interpreted in $\mathbb{E}$ by the function that assigns to every two expressions (in a specific order) their concatenation.

(iv) The function symbol sub is interpreted in $\mathbb{E}$ by a function that, applied to some expression a, some symbol b, and some expression c, yields the result of substituting c for b in a; if b is not a symbol the function returns a.

If φ is a sentence of $\mathcal{L}_{\mathrm{qc}}$, we write $\mathbb{E} \vDash \varphi$ to express that the sentence φ is true in $\mathbb{E}$.

The full language $\mathcal{L}$ contains at least $\Box$ and possibly further function and predicate symbols beyond those of $\mathcal{L}_{\mathrm{qc}}$. The model $\mathbb{E}$ does not provide an interpretation of $\Box$ and the further predicate and function symbols.

We call any model of $\mathcal{L}$ that interprets the vocabulary of $\mathcal{L}_{\mathrm{qc}}$ in the same way as $\mathbb{E}$ a *standard model*. The predicate symbol $\Box$ and the further symbols can be interpreted in any way. This is expressed in standard terminology by saying that the model is an expansion of $\mathbb{E}$ to the language $\mathcal{L}$, which means that the model adds interpretations of the additional function and predicate symbols, while keeping the domain and the interpretations of q, $\frown$, and sub fixed.

5.14 DEFINITION Every model of $\mathcal{L}$ that is an expansion of $\mathbb{E}$ to $\mathcal{L}$ is a standard model. We write models of $\mathcal{L}$ as $\langle \mathbb{E}, V, S \rangle$, where S is a set of expressions of $\mathcal{L}$ (as an interpretation of $\Box$), and V is a function providing interpretations for all remaining function and predicate symbols. If $\Box$ is the only additional symbol of $\mathcal{L}$ beyond those of $\mathcal{L}_{\mathrm{qc}}$, V is not needed and we write $\langle \mathbb{E}, S \rangle$.

We collect a few easy observations on standard models. The first remark says that a universally quantified sentence is true in a standard model iff the formula without the quantifier is satisfied by all expressions:

5.15 LEMMA *Let $\langle \mathbb{E}, V, S \rangle$ be a standard model of $\mathcal{L}$ and $\varphi(x)$ be a formula of $\mathcal{L}$. Then $\langle \mathbb{E}, V, S \rangle \vDash \forall x\, \varphi(x)$ obtains if and only if $\langle \mathbb{E}, V, S \rangle \vDash \varphi(\overline{e})$ holds for all quotation constants $\overline{e}$.*

Of course, standard models validate all of A1–A8. Therefore, we have the following:

5.16 LEMMA · SOUNDNESS OF STANDARD MODELS *Every standard model satisfies all axioms A1–A8.*

One can inductively prove that all theorems proved from A1–A8 are true in the standard model. The theory E may contain further axioms and rules that restrict the permissible interpretations of $\Box$ or of the additional vocabulary and thereby rule out certain standard models. In particular, we will consider certain axioms for $\Box$ that characterize $\Box$ as a truth or necessity predicate. As expected, these axioms will be compatible only with certain extensions of $\Box$.

If the theory E is consistent, it has a model. The model need not be standard. In fact we will encounter theories with additional axioms for $\Box$ which rule out standard models. An easy, but artificial, way to produce such a theory is to assume that $\mathcal{L}$ contains an additional constant c and that E contains all sentences $\neg c = \overline{e}$ as axioms for all expressions e. Adding these axioms to the obligatory axioms A1–A8 and even all axioms $\neg \overline{a} = \overline{b}$ for distinct expressions a and b, mentioned above, is still consistent, because in any given proof, c could be replaced with a quotation constant $\overline{e}$ that does not occur in the proof. Therefore, the theory with all these axioms is consistent and thus has a model by the completeness theorem. But in a standard model there is no possible interpretation of the constant c, and therefore the theory does not have a standard model.

Nonstandard models cannot be ruled out by adding stronger axioms for syntax. In fact, even if we add all sentences that are true in all standard models, the trick with the additional constant c still works and there is a nonstandard model that satisfies all of these sentences.

Later we will encounter consistent theories that are less artificial, but still do not have standard models. Very often the absence of a standard model for a theory is thought to show that the theory is unacceptable. Therefore, a theory of truth or necessity need not be inconsistent in order to be paradoxical; it may also be paradoxical because it lacks a standard model. Hence, a mere consistency proof is insufficient for showing that such a theory is 'safe'. We may expect an acceptable theory of truth or necessity not only to be consistent, but also to have a standard model. The theory CT introduced in chapter 11 is an example of a theory of truth with a standard model.

Nonstandard models have been studied in detail in the case of arithmetic. Kaye (1991) provides an introduction to their study. Via coding, results on nonstandard models of arithmetic can be applied to syntax theories. Substantial work has been done on the theory of so-called satisfaction classes, which provides deeper insights into nonstandard syntax theories (see again Kaye 1991).

6 The Paradoxes

In this chapter we use the diagonal lemma to prove the inconsistency of certain assumptions with E; other assumptions merely lead to ω-inconsistency or otherwise unpalatable consequences such as in theorem 6.4 below; still others impose limits on the expressive power of the language with these axioms. Many of these results are known in the literature as paradoxes, others as theorems. Our use of the term 'paradox' in the chapter title is very loose. Here a paradox is not much more than a surprising result proved from plausible-looking assumptions.

When we write 'inconsistent' in what follows, we mean inconsistent with E without any assumptions on E beyond those explicitly stated. Since we did not fix the axioms of E and admitted further axioms in E, inconsistency results could also be formulated by saying, 'E is inconsistent if it contains the sentence ψ', instead of 'ψ is inconsistent (with E)'.

6.1 Some Simple Applications of Diagonalization

The first inconsistency result is the famous liar paradox. If $\Box$ is understood as a truth predicate, the T-schema assumes the following form in $\mathcal{L}$:

$$\Box\overline{\psi} \leftrightarrow \psi, \tag{6.1}$$

for all sentences ψ of $\mathcal{L}$. This schema corresponds to the schema

'*A*' is true if and only if *A*,

where *A* is any English declarative sentence.

The schema is often thought to be fundamental to truth, and many truth theories are based on refinements of it.

6.1 THEOREM · LIAR PARADOX *The T-schema $\Box\overline{\psi} \leftrightarrow \psi$ for all sentences ψ of $\mathcal{L}$ is inconsistent.*

PROOF Apply the diagonal lemma 5.12 to the formula $\neg\Box x$. Then lemma 5.12 implies the existence of a sentence γ such that the following holds: $\mathsf{E} \vdash \gamma \leftrightarrow \neg\Box\overline{\gamma}$. Together with the instance $\Box\overline{\gamma} \leftrightarrow \gamma$ of the T-schema, this yields $\gamma \leftrightarrow \neg\gamma$ and thus an inconsistency. ⊣

We refer to the sentence γ in the proof as the 'liar sentence'. Of course, γ is not the only sentence φ satisfying $\mathsf{E} \vdash \varphi \leftrightarrow \neg\Box\overline{\varphi}$. Any such sentence would suffice for the proof, and often all of these sentences are also called 'liar sentences'. When we use the singular, we refer specifically to the γ in the proof above.

Since the T-schema is inconsistent, a truth predicate satisfying the schema cannot be defined in E, unless E itself is inconsistent. This result is known as *Tarski's theorem on the undefinability of truth*, which was proved in a different form in (Tarski 1935).

6.2 TARSKI'S THEOREM ON THE UNDEFINABILITY OF TRUTH *If* E *is consistent, there is no formula* $\tau(x)$ *such that* $\tau(\overline{\psi}) \leftrightarrow \psi$ *can be derived in* E *for all sentences* ψ *of* $\mathcal{L}$.

PROOF Apply the diagonalization lemma to $\neg\tau(x)$ as above. If $\tau(x)$ contains bound occurrences of x, they can be renamed such that there are none. The proof is then exactly as for the liar paradox, only with τ instead of $\Box$. ⊣

It is not so surprising that the axioms listed explicitly as axioms for E do not allow for a definition of a truth predicate $\tau(x)$. After all, the axioms explicitly listed for E are not very strong. According to definition 5.8, however, E may contain arbitrary additional axioms. Thus, Tarski's theorem in the form above says that assuming E to contain further axioms for $\Box$ which *allow* for a truth definition renders E inconsistent. Hence, whatever axioms we might add, they will never suffice for a definition of truth.

Nevertheless, one can usually consistently add a new predicate symbol Tr *not in* $\mathcal{L}$, and include $\mathrm{Tr}\overline{\psi} \leftrightarrow \psi$ as an axiom schema for all sentences of $\mathcal{L}$, as Tarski (1935) observed. In this case ψ cannot contain the symbol Tr because Tr is not a symbol of $\mathcal{L}$.

6.3 THEOREM *Assume that* $\mathsf{E} \vdash \neg\overline{a} = \overline{b}$, *if* a *and* b *are distinct expressions. Assume further that the language* $\mathcal{L}$ *is expanded by a new predicate symbol* Tr *and that all sentences* $\mathrm{Tr}\overline{\psi} \leftrightarrow \psi$ *are added to* E, *where* ψ *is a sentence of* $\mathcal{L}$ *without the new predicate symbol* Tr. *Then the resulting theory is consistent iff* E *is consistent.*

PROOF We show that a given proof of a contradiction $\bot$, for instance, $\neg\overline{\forall}=\overline{\forall}$, in the theory

$$\mathsf{E} \cup \{\, \mathsf{Tr}\overline{\psi} \leftrightarrow \psi\colon\ \psi \text{ is a sentence of } \mathcal{L}\,\}$$

can be transformed into a proof of $\bot$ in E itself.

Suppose that there is a proof of $\bot$ with the additional axioms $\mathsf{Tr}\overline{\psi} \leftrightarrow \psi$. In the given proof only finitely many axioms with Tr can occur because E itself does not contain any axioms with Tr. Let

$$\mathsf{Tr}\,\overline{\psi_0} \leftrightarrow \psi_0,\ \mathsf{Tr}\,\overline{\psi_1} \leftrightarrow \psi_1,\ \ldots,\ \mathsf{Tr}\,\overline{\psi_n} \leftrightarrow \psi_n$$

be these axioms. $\tau(x)$ is the following formula of the language $\mathcal{L}$:

$$(x=\overline{\psi_0} \wedge \psi_0) \vee (x=\overline{\psi_1} \wedge \psi_1) \vee \cdots \vee (x=\overline{\psi_n} \wedge \psi_n).$$

If ψ_k is a sentence distinct from ψ_i for $k \leq n$, then $\mathsf{E} \vdash \neg\overline{\psi_k} = \overline{\psi_i}$ by assumption, and thus we have the following:

$$\mathsf{E} \vdash \Big((\overline{\psi_k}=\overline{\psi_0} \wedge \psi_0) \vee (\overline{\psi_k}=\overline{\psi_1} \wedge \psi_1) \vee \cdots \vee (\overline{\psi_k}=\overline{\psi_n} \wedge \psi_n)\Big) \leftrightarrow \psi_k.$$

That is, we have for all sentences ψ_k with $k \leq n$ the following:

$$\mathsf{E} \vdash \tau(\overline{\psi_k}) \leftrightarrow \psi_k.$$

To finish the proof, replace everywhere in the given proof any formula $\mathsf{Tr}\,t$, where t is an arbitrary term, with $\tau(t)$ and add above any former axiom $\mathsf{Tr}\overline{\psi_k} \leftrightarrow \psi_k$ a proof of $\tau(\overline{\psi_k}) \leftrightarrow \psi_k$, respectively. The resulting structure is a proof in E of the contradiction $\bot$. ⊣

The claim fails if we remove the assumption that $\mathsf{E} \vdash \neg\overline{a}=\overline{b}$ for distinct expressions a, b. Using the schema $\mathsf{Tr}\overline{\psi} \leftrightarrow \psi$, we can prove that a given E-provable sentence is distinct from any given E-refutable sentence. For instance, $\forall x\, x=x$ is provable, and from

$$\mathsf{Tr}\,\overline{\forall x\ x=x} \leftrightarrow \forall x\ x=x$$

we can prove $\mathsf{Tr}\,\overline{\forall x\ x=x}$. Analogously we can show $\neg\mathsf{Tr}\,\overline{\forall x\,\neg x=x}$, and hence also $\neg\,\overline{\forall x\ x=x} = \overline{\forall x\,\neg x=x}$. Thus, the schema $\mathsf{Tr}\overline{\psi} \leftrightarrow \psi$ is not ontologically neutral: it forces the existence of at least two objects. The lack of ontological neutrality may be a problem for certain kinds of deflationism about truth (see Halbach 2001). It can be demonstrated that with the schema alone, that is, without any E-axioms, we cannot show that any further objects are distinct. The schema is compatible with the assumption that all true sentences are identical with each other and, analogously, that all false sentences are identical with each other.

The next theorem belongs to a family of results of which *Curry's paradox* is the first (Curry 1942). As the liar paradox theorem 6.1 shows, one cannot use all instances of the T-schema (6.1) as axioms for truth. A theory of truth relying exclusively on certain select instances of the T-schema, however, has been thought to have certain philosophical merits. A simple idea for amending the T-schema is to drop the instances that lead to an inconsistency.[1] As McGee (1992) has shown, however, there are more troublesome instances of the T-schema than just those which lead to inconsistency. By employing a suitable *consistent* instance of the T-schema one can decide *any* contingent sentence in either way. In what follows, $\mathsf{E}+\varphi$ for a sentence φ in our language is the theory obtained by adding φ as an axiom to E.

6.4 MCGEE'S THEOREM ON T-SENTENCES *Assume* $\mathsf{E} \nvdash \neg\varphi$. *Then there is a sentence* γ *such that* $\mathsf{E}+(\Box\overline{\gamma}\leftrightarrow\gamma)$ *is consistent and* $\mathsf{E}+(\Box\overline{\gamma}\leftrightarrow\gamma)\vdash\varphi$.

We prove in E that every sentence φ is equivalent to a T-sentence $\Box\overline{\gamma}\leftrightarrow\gamma$. This is line (6.2) in the following proof.

PROOF The diagonalization lemma, applied to $\Box x\leftrightarrow\varphi$, yields a sentence γ with the following property:

$$\mathsf{E}\vdash\gamma\leftrightarrow(\Box\overline{\gamma}\leftrightarrow\varphi),$$

$$\mathsf{E}\vdash(\gamma\leftrightarrow\Box\overline{\gamma})\leftrightarrow\varphi, \qquad \text{propositional logic} \tag{6.2}$$

$$\mathsf{E}+(\Box\overline{\gamma}\leftrightarrow\gamma)\vdash\varphi.$$

Because $\gamma\leftrightarrow\Box\overline{\gamma}$ is provably equivalent to φ, which is consistent with E by assumption, $\mathsf{E}+(\Box\overline{\gamma}\leftrightarrow\gamma)$ must be consistent by (6.2). ⊣

This result spells doom for the suggestion that we should endorse a maximal consistent set of T-sentences. At the moment of writing, at least as far as I know, it is logically consistent with what we believe that Graham Leigh will be the Prime

[1] Horwich (1998), for instance, has pursued such a strategy. Horwich conceived truth as a predicate of propositions rather than sentences. This difference does not matter for the present discussion. Horwich imposes also the restriction that the 'good' instances of the schema must be effectively recognizable.

Minister of England in 2028. I could use a T-sentence consistent with what I believe to prove that Graham Leigh will be the Prime Minister of England in 2028. It is also consistent that he will *not* be Prime Minister, and I could prove this, too, by using *another* consistent set of T-sentences.

The theorems show that outright inconsistency is not the only way a theory can be paradoxical. It is important to keep this in mind when searching for solutions to the paradoxes: it is not sufficient to show that the chosen assumptions do not lead to an inconsistency; there are more kinds of paradoxes than those that lead to plain inconsistency.

In what follows we introduce some further axioms, axiom schemas, and rules of inference that have analogues in modal logic. The schema $\Box\overline{\psi} \rightarrow \psi$ is analogous to the characteristic schema of the modal system T. This is the reason for designating the schema with the predicate also with T:

$$\text{(T)} \qquad \Box\overline{\psi} \rightarrow \psi.$$

We say that a theory, usually E, 'contains' an axiom schema such as T iff the theory contains all instances of the schema. This means, for instance, that E contains T iff E contains the sentences $\Box\overline{\psi} \rightarrow \psi$ for all sentences ψ of $\mathcal{L}$.

The next theorem is a strengthening of the liar paradox, that is, theorem 6.1. For notions like necessity or knowledge the schema $\Box\overline{\psi} \rightarrow \psi$ can be retained, but one would not postulate the converse direction, that is, all sentences $\psi \rightarrow \Box\overline{\psi}$, as axioms. The following rule of inference is more plausible: Once ψ has been derived, one may conclude $\Box\overline{\psi}$. We call this inference rule the rule of *necessitation*. We say that a theory is *closed under necessitation* if and only if, whenever the theory proves (i.e., contains) a sentence ψ, it also proves $\Box\overline{\psi}$. With these weakened assumptions on $\Box$, the argument for the liar paradox still goes through.

Before we state the theorem, we introduce more terminology. The rule of necessitation is designated by NEC in what follows. Thus, NEC is the rule that allows us to pass from a proof of ψ (without any undischarged assumptions) to a proof of $\Box\overline{\psi}$ by appending $\Box\overline{\psi}$ as the last line in the proof. If we work in Natural Deduction it is important that the proof of ψ does not rely on undischarged assumptions. If undischarged assumptions were permitted, NEC would trivially collapse into the axiom schema $\psi \rightarrow \Box\overline{\psi}$, because we could assume ψ, conclude $\Box\overline{\psi}$ (with ψ as undischarged premiss), and then arrive at $\psi \rightarrow \Box\overline{\psi}$ by discharging the assumption ψ.

6.5 THEOREM · MONTAGUE'S PARADOX, MONTAGUE 1963 *If* E *contains* T *and is closed under necessitation, then* E *is inconsistent.*

PROOF Assume that E contains T and is closed under necessitation. We apply the diagonalization lemma to the formula $\neg\Box x$, as in the proof of the liar paradox, to obtain a sentence γ. This yields the first line below:

$\mathsf{E} \vdash \gamma \leftrightarrow \neg\Box\overline{\gamma}$	
$\mathsf{E} \vdash \neg\Box\overline{\gamma} \rightarrow \gamma$	weakening
$\mathsf{E} \vdash \Box\overline{\gamma} \rightarrow \gamma$	T
$\mathsf{E} \vdash \gamma$	two preceding lines
$\mathsf{E} \vdash \Box\overline{\gamma}$	NEC
$\mathsf{E} \vdash \neg\gamma$	first line $\dashv$

It does not follow from the theorem that, if E is closed under necessitation, $\Box\overline{\psi} \rightarrow \psi$ is inconsistent (with E). In fact, in this case E may still be consistent. The difference is that, if E is closed under necessitation, then adding all sentences $\Box\overline{\psi} \rightarrow \psi$ may yield a theory that is *not* closed under necessitation. Once we have proved a sentence χ using an instance of $\Box\overline{\psi} \rightarrow \psi$, we may be unable to apply NEC, if we have only assumed that E is closed under NEC, but not E with the additional axioms of T.

Montague's paradox is a problem for various readings of $\Box$. In particular, if we understand $\Box$ as necessity, then NEC and the schema T look highly plausible. But also when we think of $\Box$ as knowledge of some kind, we get into a problem. If $\Box$ stands for 'can be known', then NEC seems sound. Even if $\Box$ is a predicate expressing 'subject X knows', Montague's paradox causes trouble. For a specific subject, NEC may not be plausible, but we need to apply NEC only once. We can show the subject a proof and thus the subject should accept the sentence that has been proved. Therefore, the person knows it. But that is sufficient for the argument.

The reasoning behind Montague's paradox is closely related to a part of the proof of the first incompleteness theorem.

6.6 GÖDEL'S FIRST INCOMPLETENESS THEOREM *Suppose for all sentences* φ *of* $\mathcal{L}$ *that* $\mathsf{E} \vdash \varphi$ *iff* $\mathsf{E} \vdash \Box\overline{\varphi}$. *Then there is a sentence* γ *such that neither* γ *itself nor its negation is derivable in* E, *or* E *is inconsistent.*

PROOF Choose γ as the liar sentence, that is, as in the proof of theorem 6.1. If, on the one hand, $\mathsf{E} \vdash \gamma$, then by assumption $\mathsf{E} \vdash \Box\overline{\gamma}$ and by the choice of γ also $\mathsf{E} \vdash \neg\Box\overline{\gamma}$; so E would be inconsistent. If, on the other hand, $\mathsf{E} \vdash \neg\gamma$, then $\mathsf{E} \vdash \Box\overline{\gamma}$ and by assumption $\mathsf{E} \vdash \gamma$ and E is inconsistent in this case as well. ⊣

The reason for labelling this result as Gödel's first incompleteness theorem is the following. Gödel showed that a provability predicate $\mathsf{Bew}(\mathsf{x})$ can be defined in a certain system of arithmetic. Very roughly speaking and transposed to our setting, he defined a formula $\mathsf{Bew}(\mathsf{x})$ that satisfies the following condition for all formulæ ψ of $\mathcal{L}$ (with a suitably strong E instead of his system of arithmetic):

$$\mathsf{E} \vdash \psi \quad \text{if and only if} \quad \mathsf{E} \vdash \mathsf{Bew}(\overline{\psi}).$$

In section 10.4 we define a provability predicate with this property for a more expressive theory E^* of syntax and then use the reasoning above to prove Gödel's first incompleteness theorem for E^*.

We turn to a slightly more sophisticated application of the diagonal lemma. The diagonal lemma allows us to diagonalize formulae such as $\neg\Box\mathsf{x}$ or $\Box\mathsf{x} \leftrightarrow \varphi$ (for some fixed sentence φ). It is not obvious how to diagonalize a formula such as $\neg\Box\overline{\Box\mathsf{x}}$ with respect to the variable x. After all, the variable x does not occur in $\neg\Box\overline{\Box\mathsf{x}}$, which is a sentence that merely contains *a quotation constant for a formula* in which x occurs. In the proof of the following theorem we show how to obtain a sentence γ with $\mathsf{E} \vdash \gamma \leftrightarrow \neg\Box\overline{\Box\overline{\gamma}}$ by applying the diagonal lemma, not directly to $\neg\Box\overline{\Box\mathsf{x}}$, but to a different formula with an actual occurrence of x. This sentence γ allows us to prove a result that is stronger than the liar paradox, that is, theorem 6.1. The liar paradox shows that the schema $\Box\overline{\varphi} \leftrightarrow \varphi$ is inconsistent. The schema $\Box\overline{\Box\overline{\varphi}} \leftrightarrow \varphi$ is weaker than the T-schema in the sense that it logically follows from it, but does not logically imply it. However, $\Box\overline{\Box\overline{\varphi}} \leftrightarrow \varphi$ is still inconsistent with the axioms of E. The inconsistency can easily be proved with the sentence γ above.

6.7 THEOREM E *is inconsistent if it contains the schema* $\Box\overline{\Box\overline{\varphi}} \leftrightarrow \varphi$.

PROOF For any for all sentences φ of $\mathcal{L}$ and indeed any expression φ we have the following:

$$\mathsf{E} \vdash \overline{\Box}^\frown \mathsf{q}(\overline{\varphi}) = \overline{\Box}^\frown \overline{\overline{\varphi}} \qquad \text{axiom A2}$$

$$\mathsf{E} \vdash \overline{\Box}^\frown \mathsf{q}(\overline{\varphi}) = \overline{\Box\overline{\varphi}} \qquad \text{axiom A1}$$

The diagonal lemma is applied to the formula $\neg\Box\big(\overline{\Box}{}^\frown\mathsf{q}(\mathsf{x})\big)$:

$$\begin{aligned} &\mathsf{E} \vdash \gamma \leftrightarrow \neg\Box\big(\overline{\Box}{}^\frown\mathsf{q}(\overline{\gamma})\big) && \\ &\mathsf{E} \vdash \gamma \leftrightarrow \neg\Box\overline{\Box\overline{\gamma}} && \text{remark above} \\ &\mathsf{E} \vdash \gamma \leftrightarrow \neg\gamma && \text{assumption} \end{aligned}$$

⊣

There is an informal analogue to this sentence γ with $\Box$ as truth, the so-called postcard paradox: on the one side of a postcard is the sentence 'The sentence on the other side is not true'; on the other side is the sentence 'The sentence on the other side is true.'

We introduce another axiom schema. The analogue of the following schema in modal logic is common to all so-called normal modal logics. The minimal normal modal logic is called K, and we use the letter here to designate the following schema for $\Box$ as a predicate (without assuming that a system with K is closed under NEC as in modal logic):

(K) $$\Box\overline{\varphi\rightarrow\psi} \rightarrow (\Box\overline{\varphi} \rightarrow \Box\overline{\psi}).$$

For later use we prove the following lemma:

6.8 LEMMA $\mathsf{E} \vdash \Box\overline{\varphi\wedge\psi} \leftrightarrow \Box\overline{\varphi}\wedge\Box\overline{\psi}$, *if* E *contains* K *and is closed under* NEC.

On page 14 we introduced the connective $\wedge$ as an abbreviation: $\varphi\wedge\psi$ is short for $\neg(\varphi\rightarrow\neg\psi)$.

PROOF For the left-to-right direction we reason as follows:

$$\begin{aligned} &\mathsf{E} \vdash \varphi\wedge\psi \rightarrow \varphi && \text{logic} \\ &\mathsf{E} \vdash \Box\overline{\varphi\wedge\psi \rightarrow \varphi} && \text{NEC} \\ &\mathsf{E} \vdash \Box\overline{\varphi\wedge\psi} \rightarrow \Box\overline{\varphi} && \text{K and modus ponens} \end{aligned}$$

From a similar argument we obtain also $\mathsf{E} \vdash \Box\overline{\varphi\wedge\psi} \rightarrow \Box\overline{\psi}$. This yields the left-to-right direction. For the converse direction we proceed as follows:

$$\begin{aligned} &\mathsf{E} \vdash \varphi \rightarrow \big(\psi \rightarrow (\varphi\wedge\psi)\big) && \text{logic} \\ &\mathsf{E} \vdash \Box\overline{\varphi} \rightarrow (\Box\overline{\psi} \rightarrow \Box\overline{\varphi\wedge\psi}) && \text{NEC and K} \end{aligned}$$

⊣

As we mentioned above in the context of McGee's theorem 6.4, plain inconsistency is not the only way a system can fail to be acceptable: there are axioms for $\Box$ that decide previously undecided $\Box$-free sentences that should not be decided by axioms for truth or necessity. Hence, McGee's theorem shows that $\Box$-free consequences of a consistent theory can be paradoxical. Consistent theories, however, can also be unacceptable because of theorems with $\Box$. Internal-inconsistency is an example. A theory $\mathcal{T}$ is internally inconsistent (with respect to $\Box$) if and only if $\mathcal{T} \vdash \Box\overline{\varphi}$ and $\mathcal{T} \vdash \Box\overline{\neg\varphi}$ for some sentence φ. An internally inconsistent theory need not prove $\Box\overline{\varphi}$ for all sentences, but under certain natural assumptions it does.

6.9 LEMMA *Assume* E *is closed under* NEC. *Then every internally inconsistent theory containing* E *and* K *proves* $\Box\overline{\psi}$ *for all sentences* ψ.

The result is stronger than the claim that, if E is internally inconsistent, contains K, and is closed under NEC, then it proves $\Box\overline{\psi}$ for all sentences ψ. This is because a theory containing E may fail to be closed under NEC, even if E is. For the proof of the lemma it is therefore important that we apply NEC only to sentences proved in E without using K or any sentences that are in the internally inconsistent theory but not in E. In fact, we apply NEC only to sentences that are propositional tautologies. Therefore, we do not even have to assume that E is closed under NEC, only that it contains $\Box\overline{\varphi}$ whenever φ is a propositional tautology.

PROOF Assume that E is as described in the lemma. For all sentences φ and ψ we then have the following:

$\mathsf{E} \vdash \varphi \to (\neg\varphi \to \psi)$	logic
$\mathsf{E} \vdash \Box\overline{\varphi \to (\neg\varphi \to \psi)}$	NEC
$\mathsf{E} \vdash \Box\overline{\varphi} \to \Box\overline{\neg\varphi \to \psi}$	K and modus ponens
$\mathsf{E} \vdash \Box\overline{\varphi} \to (\Box\overline{\neg\varphi} \to \Box\overline{\psi})$	K and modus ponens

Assume now that $\mathcal{T} \supseteq \mathsf{E}$ is internally inconsistent. Then there is a sentence φ with $\mathcal{T} \vdash \Box\overline{\varphi}$ and $\mathcal{T} \vdash \Box\overline{\neg\varphi}$. Together with the last line this implies $\mathcal{T} \vdash \Box\overline{\psi}$. ⊣

As an example of internal inconsistency we consider a result, which is related to theorem 2 in Thomason 1980. We introduce the following schema whose analogue in modal logic is well known:

(4) $$\Box\overline{\varphi} \to \Box\overline{\Box\overline{\varphi}}.$$

For the theorem, we may read $\Box$ as idealized belief or as 'can be believed by an ideally rational person'. For belief, as opposed to knowledge, we reject factivity, that is, schema T. A person may rationally believe something that is not true. The schema K is sound: if a rational person believes $\varphi \to \psi$ and φ, then they are also entitled to believe ψ. The schema 4 expresses a faculty of introspection: whenever the ideally rational person believes something, they realize this and *believe* that they believe it. Moreover, we assume the rule NEC for E. This is only justified if E is sufficiently weak and does not contain further axioms not believed by the ideal subject. In fact, much weaker versions of NEC will suffice. The theorem then shows that the subject cannot consistently believe in the factivity of their own belief. If they believed that $\Box\overline{\varphi} \to \varphi$, that is, if they believed in the reliability of their beliefs, they can rationally believe anything. One might take this as an argument for the claim that an ideally rational subject cannot rationally endorse factivity for their own beliefs.

6.10 THEOREM · THOMASON 1980 *Assume* E *is closed under* NEC. *Then any theory* $\mathcal{T}$ *containing* E *and the schemas* K, 4, *and* $\Box\overline{\Box\overline{\varphi} \to \varphi}$ *is internally inconsistent and proves* $\Box\overline{\psi}$ *for all* $\mathcal{L}$*-sentences* ψ.

We are in the situation decribed above after lemma 6.9: the theory $\mathcal{T}$ need not be closed under NEC. This means for the proof that we can apply NEC only to theorems proved in E, but not to sentences proved using the further schemas K, 4, or $\Box\overline{\Box\overline{\varphi} \to \varphi}$. Therefore, the result is not a trivial consequence of Löb's theorem 6.11, below, because there we apply NEC to a sentence whose proof relies on 4.

PROOF Roughly speaking, we run the proof of Montague's paradox in the scope of $\Box$. Assume that E and $\mathcal{T}$ have the properties mentioned in the theorem.

$\mathsf{E} \vdash \gamma \leftrightarrow \neg\Box\overline{\gamma}$	liar sentence
$\mathsf{E} \vdash \Box\overline{\Box\overline{\gamma} \to \neg\gamma}$	logic and NEC
$\mathsf{E} \vdash (\Box\overline{\gamma} \to \gamma) \to ((\Box\overline{\gamma} \to \neg\gamma) \to \neg\Box\overline{\gamma})$	logic
$\mathsf{E} \vdash (\Box\overline{\gamma} \to \gamma) \to ((\Box\overline{\gamma} \to \neg\gamma) \to \gamma)$	first line
$\mathsf{E} \vdash \Box\overline{\Box\overline{\gamma} \to \gamma} \to (\Box\overline{\Box\overline{\gamma} \to \neg\gamma} \to \Box\overline{\gamma})$	NEC and K
$\mathcal{T} \vdash (\Box\overline{\Box\overline{\gamma} \to \neg\gamma} \to \Box\overline{\gamma})$	$\Box\overline{\Box\overline{\varphi} \to \varphi}$
$\mathcal{T} \vdash \Box\overline{\gamma}$	second line

Now we invoke 4 to conclude $\mathcal{T} \vdash \Box\overline{\Box\overline{\gamma}}$ from $\mathcal{T} \vdash \Box\overline{\gamma}$. From the first line above we also get $\mathsf{E} \vdash \Box\overline{\gamma} \to \Box\overline{\neg\Box\overline{\gamma}}$ by NEC and K. Combining this with the last line, we obtain the following internal inconsistency:

$$\mathcal{T} \vdash \Box\overline{\neg\Box\overline{\gamma}} \wedge \Box\overline{\Box\overline{\gamma}}.$$

Since E and $\mathcal{T}$ satisfy the conditions of lemma 6.9, we have $\mathcal{T} \vdash \Box\overline{\psi}$ for all sentences ψ. ⊣

The following theorem is a formalized version of Löb's theorem. In the real theorem, □ is the provability predicate. Later we define a provability predicate in a more expressive theory and prove Löb's theorem for this theory as theorem 10.77. Löb (1955) actually proved a rule version, which we obtain as a corollary.

The assumptions of Löb's theorem, that is, the rule NEC and the two schemas K and 4 are satisfied for a suitable formula expressing provability. With a provability predicate instead of □, NEC, K and 4 are known as the Löb derivability conditions. We will also call NEC, K and 4 themselves the Löb derivability conditions.[2]

In a sense Löb's theorem is a strengthening of Montague's paradox, at least in the presence of K and 4 as axiom schemas. We can ask for which sentences we can have $\Box\overline{\varphi} \to \varphi$. We know that we cannot have $\Box\overline{\gamma} \to \gamma$ for the liar sentence γ; but we may still hope to have it for all well-behaved (in a sense to be specified) sentences. Löb's theorem dooms these hopes. By corollary 6.12 below, we have $\Box\overline{\varphi} \to \varphi$ only in the trivial case when φ is already provable.

6.11 LÖB'S THEOREM *If* E *is closed under* NEC *and contains* K *and* 4, *then we have* $\mathsf{E} \vdash \Box\overline{\Box\overline{\varphi} \to \varphi} \to \Box\overline{\varphi}$ *for all sentences* φ *of* $\mathcal{L}$.

PROOF φ is the sentence for which we prove the theorem. Apply the diagonal lemma 5.12 to the formula $\Box x \to \varphi$. This yields a diagonal sentence γ and we continue as follows:

$\mathsf{E} \vdash \gamma \leftrightarrow (\Box\overline{\gamma} \to \varphi)$	diagonal lemma
$\mathsf{E} \vdash \gamma \to (\Box\overline{\gamma} \to \varphi)$	weakening
$\mathsf{E} \vdash \Box\overline{\gamma \to (\Box\overline{\gamma} \to \varphi)}$	NEC

[2] The Löb derivability conditions are also called 'Bernays–Löb conditions' or 'Hilbert–Bernays–Löb conditions', because Löb's conditions are a slight modification of those employed by Hilbert and Bernays (1939).

$\mathsf{E} \vdash \Box\overline{\gamma} \to (\Box\overline{\Box\overline{\gamma}} \to \Box\overline{\varphi})$	K used twice
$\mathsf{E} \vdash \Box\overline{\gamma} \to \Box\overline{\Box\overline{\gamma}}$	4
$\mathsf{E} \vdash \Box\overline{\gamma} \to \Box\overline{\varphi}$	two preceding lines
$\mathsf{E} \vdash (\Box\overline{\varphi} \to \varphi) \to (\Box\overline{\gamma} \to \varphi)$	previous line
$\mathsf{E} \vdash (\Box\overline{\varphi} \to \varphi) \to \gamma$	first line
$\mathsf{E} \vdash \Box\overline{\Box\overline{\varphi} \to \varphi} \to \Box\overline{\gamma}$	NEC and then K
$\mathsf{E} \vdash \Box\overline{\Box\overline{\varphi} \to \varphi} \to \Box\overline{\varphi}$	sixth line ⊣

6.12 COROLLARY *Assume that* E *is closed under* NEC *and contains* K *and* 4. *Then for any* φ *of* $\mathcal{L}$ *the following rule of inference holds: If* $\mathsf{E} \vdash \Box\overline{\varphi} \to \varphi$, *then* $\mathsf{E} \vdash \varphi$.

PROOF Assume $\mathsf{E} \vdash \Box\overline{\varphi} \to \varphi$ and reason as follows:

$\mathsf{E} \vdash \Box\overline{\varphi} \to \varphi$	assumption
$\mathsf{E} \vdash \Box\overline{\Box\overline{\varphi} \to \varphi}$	NEC
$\mathsf{E} \vdash \Box\overline{\varphi}$	theorem above
$\mathsf{E} \vdash \varphi$	assumption in first line ⊣

We discuss Löb's theorem for provability in later chapters. In provability logic the kind of reasoning above is carried out in operator modal logic. The reader is referred to the monographs (Smoryński 1985) and (Boolos 1993) on provability logic. But the importance of Löb's theorem transcends the analysis of the provability predicate. In chapter 7 we show that in a sense many other paradoxes can be reduced to Löb's theorem. It imposes restrictions on the accessibility relation in our possible-worlds semantics. If possible-worlds semantics has any significance in metaphysics, then Löb's theorem is a deeper metaphysical insight than so many other trivial observations about possible-worlds semantics for operator modal logic.

An analogue of Gödel's second incompleteness theorem follows easily from Löb's theorem. As above, $\bot$ is an abbreviation for the fixed contradiction $\neg\overline{\forall}=\overline{\forall}$. Of course, any other sentence that is refutable in E could be used just as well.

6.13 GÖDEL'S SECOND INCOMPLETENESS THEOREM *Assume that* E *is closed under* NEC *and contains* K *and* 4. *Then* $\mathsf{E} \vdash \neg\Box\overline{\bot}$ *implies that* E *is inconsistent.*

The contraposition of this formulation may be more familiar: $\mathsf{E} \nvdash \neg\Box\overline{\bot}$, if E is consistent.

PROOF Assume $\mathsf{E} \vdash \neg\Box\overline{\bot}$. Then also $\mathsf{E} \vdash \Box\overline{\bot} \rightarrow \bot$ and by corollary 6.12 $\mathsf{E} \vdash \bot$, that is, E is inconsistent. ⊣

This result is not only surprising when $\Box$ is a formal provability predicate, as in Gödel's second incompleteness theorem for arithmetic. If $\Box$ is read as informal provability or the like, one would expect that one can assert that a contradiction cannot be informally proved. But that is not feasible. If we simply add $\neg\Box\overline{\bot}$ as a new axiom to a theory containing the schemas K and 4 and closed under NEC, the theory becomes inconsistent.

6.2 Paradoxes from Interaction of Modalities

So far we have focused on a single modal predicate $\Box$ and assumptions about it that lead to paradoxes. But paradoxes can also arise from the interaction of two or more modal predicates. As a first, simple example we consider an inconsistency result in (Halbach 2006).

We said that the language $\mathcal{L}$ may contain further predicate symbols beyond $=$ and $\Box$. For the interaction paradoxes we obviously require at least two predicates. Besides $\Box$, we use Tr and assume that both predicates belong to $\mathcal{L}$. The axioms we use allow us to read $\Box$ as 'is necessary', 'can be known', perhaps also as 'is analytic' or 'holds a priori'. The predicate Tr is the truth predicate. Of course, truth is prone to paradox, and we know already that the unrestricted T-schema leads to the liar paradox. Similarly, we know that very weak assumptions on the necessity predicate suffice for Montague's paradox.

To dodge the inconsistencies, we resort to the relatively crude method of typing. In theorem 6.3 we showed that we can consistently add a new predicate Tr and axioms $\mathrm{Tr}\overline{\psi} \leftrightarrow \psi$ for all sentences ψ of $\mathcal{L}$. The reason why we used a predicate Tr that is not in $\mathcal{L}$ was that if we had used $\Box$, then there could have been axioms in E already that involve Tr. In that case our consistency proof would not have succeeded. This time both predicates Tr and $\Box$ are predicates in $\mathcal{L}$.

6.14 THEOREM *Assume* E *satisfies the following three conditions:*

(i) *If ψ is a sentence of $\mathcal{L}$ not containing* Tr, *then* E *contains* $\mathrm{Tr}\overline{\psi} \leftrightarrow \psi$.

(ii) *If ψ is a sentence of $\mathcal{L}$ not containing $\Box$, then* E *contains* $\Box\overline{\psi} \to \psi$.

(iii) *If ψ is a sentence of $\mathcal{L}$ not containing $\Box$ with* $\mathsf{E} \vdash \psi$, *then also* $\mathsf{E} \vdash \Box\overline{\psi}$ *holds.*

Then E *is inconsistent.*

Since $\Box$ is a symbol of $\mathcal{L}$, $\Box$ may occur in ψ in (i); similarly, Tr may occur in the ψ in (ii) and (iii). Because $\Box$ and Tr are symbols of $\mathcal{L}$ we have quotation constants for all sentences with $\Box$ and Tr in $\mathcal{L}$. As before, $\Box$ does not occur in a formula $\mathsf{Tr}\overline{\Box\overline{\varphi}}$, which merely contains a *quotation constant* for a sentence with $\Box$.

By theorem 6.3 the axiom schema (i) alone is consistent with E, if E is consistent and does not contain any further axioms on Tr. The schema (ii) and the restricted rule of necessitation (iii) are even weaker. Therefore, taken separately, the axioms and rules for truth and necessity do not engender a paradox, but taken together they do.

PROOF We apply the diagonal lemma to the formula $\neg\mathsf{Tr}\big(\overline{\Box}\,\hat{}\,\mathsf{q}(x)\big)$ and reason as follows:

$\mathsf{E} \vdash \gamma \leftrightarrow \neg\mathsf{Tr}\big(\overline{\Box}\,\hat{}\,\mathsf{q}(\overline{\gamma})\big)$	diagonal lemma
$\mathsf{E} \vdash \gamma \leftrightarrow \neg\mathsf{Tr}\overline{\Box\overline{\gamma}}$	axioms A1 and A2; cf. proof of theorem 6.7
$\mathsf{E} \vdash \mathsf{Tr}\overline{\Box\overline{\gamma}} \to \neg\gamma$	logic
$\mathsf{E} \vdash \Box\overline{\gamma} \to \neg\gamma$	(i)
$\mathsf{E} \vdash \Box\overline{\gamma} \to \gamma$	(ii)
$\mathsf{E} \vdash \neg\Box\overline{\gamma}$	two preceding lines
$\mathsf{E} \vdash \neg\mathsf{Tr}\overline{\Box\overline{\gamma}}$	(i)
$\mathsf{E} \vdash \gamma$	second line
$\mathsf{E} \vdash \Box\overline{\gamma}$	(iii)

The last line and the fourth line from the bottom establish the claim. ⊣

Another, more refined interaction paradox is Horsten's and Leitgeb's (2001) *no future paradox*. Assume $\mathcal{L}$ contains four predicates G, H, F, and P. The intended reading of Gx is 'x will always be the case', while Hx is read as 'x has always been the case'. Similarly, Fx is to be read as 'x will be the case at some point (in the future)', and Px, finally, stands for 'x has been the case at some point (in the past)'. G and H can easily be defined from F and P, respectively (or also vice versa). The four predicates correspond to the well-known operators from temporal logic, the difference being that here G and H are predicates rather than operators.

We list some axioms and rules that are plausible for the given readings of the four temporal predicates. The sentences φ and ψ are in the language $\mathcal{L}$. This means that φ and ψ may contain the predicates G, H, F, and P.

(G1) $\mathsf{G}\overline{\varphi \to \psi} \to (\mathsf{G}\overline{\varphi} \to \mathsf{G}\overline{\psi})$,

(H1) $\mathsf{H}\overline{\varphi \to \psi} \to (\mathsf{H}\overline{\varphi} \to \mathsf{H}\overline{\psi})$,[3]

(G2) $\varphi \to \mathsf{HF}\overline{\overline{\varphi}}$,

(H2) $\varphi \to \mathsf{GP}\overline{\overline{\varphi}}$,

(G3) $\mathsf{G}\overline{\varphi} \leftrightarrow \neg\mathsf{F}\overline{\neg\varphi}$,

(H3) $\mathsf{H}\overline{\varphi} \leftrightarrow \neg\mathsf{P}\overline{\neg\varphi}$,

(N) $\dfrac{\varphi}{\mathsf{G}\overline{\varphi}}$ and $\dfrac{\varphi}{\mathsf{H}\overline{\varphi}}$ for all sentences φ.

In N the notation $\frac{\varphi}{\mathsf{G}\overline{\varphi}}$ means that we can conclude $\mathsf{G}\overline{\varphi}$ from a proof of φ. This is the rule of necessitation, only with G in the place of $\Box$. Analogously for H.

If E contains all these axioms and is closed under the rules in N, then E may be consistent, but it is internally inconsistent. As before, $\bot$ is a fixed contradiction.

6.15 THEOREM · NO FUTURE PARADOX, HORSTEN AND LEITGEB 2001
If E *contains* G1, H1, G2, H2, G3, *and* H3 *and is closed under* N, *we have* $\mathsf{E} \vdash \mathsf{H}\overline{\bot} \wedge \mathsf{G}\overline{\bot}$.

Thus, we can prove that at all moments in the future $\bot$ will hold. Since $\bot$ is a contradiction, there cannot *be* any moment in the future. Therefore, there is no future. Analogously, but less dramatically, there has also never been a moment in the past.

PROOF I shall only prove that there is no future, that is, $\mathsf{E} \vdash \mathsf{G}\overline{\bot}$. The first line is obtained as in the proof of theorem 6.14:

$$
\begin{aligned}
(6.3) \qquad & \mathsf{E} \vdash \gamma \leftrightarrow \mathsf{GP}\overline{\overline{\neg\gamma}} & \\
& \mathsf{E} \vdash \neg\gamma \leftrightarrow \neg\mathsf{GP}\overline{\overline{\neg\gamma}} & \\
& \mathsf{E} \vdash \neg\gamma \to \mathsf{GP}\overline{\overline{\neg\gamma}} & \text{H2}
\end{aligned}
$$

[3] In the original paper (Horsten and Leitgeb 2001, p. 260), there is a typo in the formulation of this axiom: the occurrence of G there should be an H, too.

(6.4)	$\mathsf{E} \vdash \gamma$	preceding two lines
(6.5)	$\mathsf{E} \vdash \mathsf{G}\overline{\mathsf{P}\overline{\neg\gamma}}$	from (6.3) and previous line
	$\mathsf{E} \vdash \mathsf{H}\overline{\gamma}$	N and (6.4)
	$\mathsf{E} \vdash \neg\mathsf{P}\overline{\neg\gamma}$	H3
(6.6)	$\mathsf{E} \vdash \mathsf{G}\overline{\neg\mathsf{P}\overline{\neg\gamma}}$	N
(6.7)	$\mathsf{E} \vdash \mathsf{G}\overline{\bot}$	(6.5), (6.6), and G1

The last line follows because, by N, we have $\mathsf{G}\varphi \to \overline{(\neg\varphi \to \bot)}$ for all φ and in particular for $\mathsf{P}\overline{\neg\gamma}$. ⊣

With these temporal predicates one can assert that there is a future by saying that if φ will always be the case, then φ will be the case at some point:

$$\text{(FUT)} \qquad \mathsf{G}\overline{\varphi} \to \mathsf{F}\overline{\varphi}.$$

Adding the assumption that there is a future leads to an outright inconsistency.

6.16 COROLLARY · HORSTEN AND LEITGEB 2001 *If* E *contains* H2, G3, H3, *and* FUT *and is closed under* N, *then* E *is inconsistent.*[4]

PROOF One proves (6.5) and (6.6) as in the preceding theorem and applies FUT to the latter in order to obtain $\mathsf{F}\overline{\neg\mathsf{P}\overline{\neg\gamma}}$, which in turn implies $\neg\mathsf{G}\overline{\mathsf{P}\overline{\neg\gamma}}$ by G3 and is therefore inconsistent with (6.5). ⊣

We present only two examples of paradoxes that arise from the interaction of modal predicates. More are known. Generally, however, these paradoxes remain not very well explored. Stern and Fischer (2015) have provided some deeper analysis and explored to what extent the paradoxes are really new and not in some sense variants of old paradoxes with a single modality. Theorem 6.14 looks very much like a variant of Montague's paradox and is somehow derivative. The no future paradox, in contrast, can be shown not to be reducible to a paradox with a single modal predicate in a sense made precise by Stern and Fischer (2015).

[4]Horsten and Leitgeb (2001) proved the dual of this corollary.

6.3 Quantifying-In

We now look at a somewhat more complicated family of paradoxes. It includes, among others, Yablo's, Visser's, and McGee's ω-inconsistency paradoxes. An ω-inconsistent theory cannot be interpreted in the intended way, with the set of all $\mathcal{L}$-expressions as domain and the function symbols q, $\frown$, and sub as the intended functions on this set, although it may still be consistent. As a preparation we develop our syntax theory a little further.

In the sentence $\Box\overline{\mathsf{x}=\mathsf{z}}$ there is no occurrence of a variable. The expression $\overline{\mathsf{x}=\mathsf{z}}$ is a quotation constant and a single symbol, which does not contain any further symbols. Our method for communicating formulæ requires us to mention x and z, but that holds only for our chosen instantiation of $\mathcal{L}$. Since there are no occurrences of variables in $\Box\overline{\mathsf{x}=\mathsf{z}}$, no occurrence of a variable can be bound by adding quantifiers. The quantifiers in $\exists\mathsf{x}\exists\mathsf{z}\Box\overline{\mathsf{x}=\mathsf{z}}$ are idling; they do not bind any occurrence of a variable. However, loosely speaking, there are ways to bind variables 'within' quotation constants. The trick is well known.

Assume $\Box$ is read as 'necessary' and we want to say that every expression is necessarily identical with itself, that is, we want to say that for all expressions e the sentence $\overline{e} = \overline{e}$ is necessary. We cannot do this by writing $\forall\mathsf{x}\Box\overline{\mathsf{x}=\mathsf{x}}$, but we can formulate our claim in the following way:

> For all expressions e: if we replace in the formula $\mathsf{x} = \mathsf{x}$ every occurrence of x by the quotation constant for e, then the resulting sentence is necessary.

This can be expressed in $\mathcal{L}$ using the following formula:

$$\forall\mathsf{x}\,\Box\mathsf{sub}\big(\overline{\mathsf{x}=\mathsf{x}}, \overline{\mathsf{x}}, \mathsf{q}(\mathsf{x})\big).$$

From this we can derive, for instance, $\Box\overline{\overline{\neg}=\overline{\neg}}$ in E in the following way:

$$\begin{array}{ll}
\forall\mathsf{x}\,\Box\mathsf{sub}\big(\overline{\mathsf{x}=\mathsf{x}}, \overline{\mathsf{x}}, \mathsf{q}(\mathsf{x})\big) & \text{assumption} \\
\Box\mathsf{sub}\big(\overline{\mathsf{x}=\mathsf{x}}, \overline{\mathsf{x}}, \mathsf{q}(\overline{\neg})\big) & \text{logic} \\
\Box\mathsf{sub}\big(\overline{\mathsf{x}=\mathsf{x}}, \overline{\mathsf{x}}, \overline{\overline{\neg}}\big) & \text{A2} \\
\Box\overline{\overline{\neg}=\overline{\neg}} & \text{A3}
\end{array}$$

Thus, $\forall \mathsf{x} \Box \mathsf{sub}(\overline{\mathsf{x}=\mathsf{x}}, \bar{\mathsf{x}}, \mathsf{q}(\mathsf{x}))$ implies $\Box \overline{\bar{e}=\bar{e}}$ for each expression e of $\mathcal{L}$. The trick can be generalized. Assume $\varphi(y)$ is a formula with no bound occurrences of the variable y, then

$$\overline{\varphi(\underset{\cdot}{x})} \text{ abbreviates } \mathsf{sub}(\overline{\varphi(y)}, \bar{y}, \mathsf{q}(x)).$$

The reason for demanding that $\varphi(y)$ does not contain any bound occurrences of the variable y is that we intend to replace only free occurrences of the variable y with the quotation constant. But sub replaces *all* occurrences, whether they are bound or not. So we better make sure that only *free* occurrences of y are replaced with x, by banning bound occurrences of y altogether. It is not possible to tell from the abbreviation $\overline{\varphi(\underset{\cdot}{x})}$ which variable is substituted with the quotation constant of x. But we will always mention the formula first and mark the variable. For instance, after we have introduced a formula $\varphi(\mathsf{x},\mathsf{y})$, $\overline{\varphi(\mathsf{x},\underset{\cdot}{\mathsf{v}_4})}$ abbreviates $\mathsf{sub}(\overline{\varphi(\mathsf{x},\mathsf{y})}, \bar{\mathsf{y}}, \mathsf{q}(\mathsf{v}_4))$. By not indicating which variable is replaced, we have prioritized aesthetics and simplicity over precision. When we use this notation, we assume that $\varphi(y)$ does not have any bound occurrences of y, without always making this assumption explicit. In many cases we start with a formula $\varphi(x)$ and pass on to $\overline{\varphi(\underset{\cdot}{x})}$, that is, $\mathsf{sub}(\overline{\varphi(x)}, \bar{x}, \mathsf{q}(x))$, that is, we use the very same variable that is replaced to quantify over the quotations. This, however, is not always the case, because occasionally we need to use another variable for quantification, as in section 6.4 below.

If $\Box$ stands for necessity, the sentence $\forall \mathsf{x} \Box \overline{\underset{\cdot}{\mathsf{x}}=\underset{\cdot}{\mathsf{x}}}$ expresses that the sentences $\bar{e}=\bar{e}$ for all quotation constants $\bar{e}$ are necessary. It does not express that all objects are necessarily self-identical. It also does not imply that all sentences $t=t$, where t is some closed term (not necessarily a quotation constant), are necessary. The method is a way of quantifying-in in some sense, but we do not claim that it gives us full *de re* modality in the sense of section 3.5. Quantifying over quotation constants may come close to *de re* modality, but only if certain extra assumptions are made. The limitations become obvious if we consider a situation where the domain does not only contain expressions. In this case the function expressed by q would have to map an object to its constant or some kind of canonical name, and we may lack such a constant or name. But even in a setting where we have only expressions in the domain, quantifying over quotation constants is often not enough, as in intensional contexts coextensive terms may fail to be substitutable *salva veritate*. For proper *de re* modality we should better use a binary predicate, as discussed in section 3.5.

If $\Box$ stands for truth, then coextensional terms should be substitutable. The trick with underdotting becomes a way to express a notion of truth with substitutional quantification. The function described by q yields a standard name for each object. Hence, $\forall x \Box \overline{\varphi(\underset{.}{x})}$ expresses the following:

> The result of replacing x in φ with the standard name of an arbitrary object is true.

This is at least close to the claim that all objects satisfy the formula $\varphi(x)$.[5] It is plausible to assume that truth is closed under substitution of coreferential terms. Hence, if $\varphi(\overline{e})$ is true for all quotation constants $\overline{e}$, then $\varphi(t)$ should be true for all closed terms. But this behaviour is specific to truth. For necessity, we cannot assume that, if a sentence $\varphi(\overline{e})$ is necessary and t some term, also $\varphi(t)$ is necessary, if $t = \overline{e}$. This does not mean that anything is wrong with the underdotting method. It just means we should not expect too much from it.

Using the underdotting notation, we establish a generalization of the diagonal lemma, lemma 5.12, which was proved by Ehrenfeucht and Feferman (1960) for arithmetic.[6]

6.17 UNIFORM DIAGONAL LEMMA, PARAMETRIZED DIAGONAL LEMMA *Let* $\varphi(x, y)$ *be a formula with the two free variables* x *and* y *that does not contain a bound occurrence of* y. *Then there is a formula* $\theta(y)$ *such that*

$$E \vdash \forall y\Big(\theta(y) \leftrightarrow \varphi\big(\overline{\theta(\underset{.}{y})}, y\big)\Big).$$

The only difference to the diagonal lemma 5.13 with free variables is that now y is underdotted and bound 'from outside' in θ on the right-hand side.

We have formulated the uniform diagonal lemma with the first two variables, x and y. Of course, we can prove the uniform diagonal lemma also for other variables; and thus we could state it with metavariables x and y instead, with appropriate conditions on the variables.

---

[5]There are many subtleties, and substitutional quantification and satisfaction can come apart in many ways. The literature is notoriously full of mistakes on this. Enayat and Visser (2015) demonstrate some of the problems.

[6]In arithmetic, overdotting is used instead of our underdotting, which latter is more readable in conjunction with the overlining for quotation constants.

PROOF By applying the diagonal lemma 5.13 with free variables to the formula

$$\varphi\Big(\mathsf{sub}\big(\mathsf{x}, \bar{\mathsf{y}}, \mathsf{q}(\mathsf{y})\big), \mathsf{y}\Big),$$

we obtain a formula $\theta(\mathsf{y})$ such that the following holds:

$$\mathsf{E} \vdash \forall \mathsf{y}\Big(\theta(\mathsf{y}) \leftrightarrow \varphi\Big(\mathsf{sub}\big(\overline{\theta(\mathsf{y})}, \bar{\mathsf{y}}, \mathsf{q}(\mathsf{y})\big), \mathsf{y}\Big)\Big).$$

This is exactly the claim, since $\overline{\theta(\dot{\mathsf{y}})}$ is defined as $\mathsf{sub}\big(\overline{\theta(\mathsf{y})}, \bar{\mathsf{y}}, \mathsf{q}(\mathsf{y})\big)$. ⊣

6.4 Yablo's and Visser's Paradoxes

Yablo (1993) presented his paradox as an infinitely descending list of sentences:

(S_1)	For all $k > 1$, S_k is untrue.
(S_2)	For all $k > 2$, S_k is untrue.
(S_3)	For all $k > 3$, S_k is untrue.
	$\vdots$

Assume that one of the sentences in the list, S_n, is true. Then all sentences below that sentence are untrue. Take any sentence below S_n. It must be untrue, but it says correctly that all sentences below it are untrue. That is a contradiction, so, contrary to our assumption, S_n is not true. Hence, *none* of the sentences in the list is true. But each of them says correctly that all sentences below it are untrue. Hence, they are all true. This is an outright contradiction.

The significance of Yablo's paradox does not lie in the result it proves. A careful analysis of the argument above shows that we invoke instances of the T-schema. But we do not need Yablo's paradox to show the inconsistency of the unrestricted T-schema, because of the liar paradox. The fascination lies in the proof: the derivation of the inconsistency does not obviously rely on a circular or self-referential sentence; each of the sentences makes only claims about the sentences below, but not about itself or sentences above. None of the sentences in the list seem to make any direct or indirect claims about themselves. This first impression has been argued to be misleading, but at any rate there is something puzzling here.

By formalizing the paradox, we pursue multiple aims: First, we demonstrate that the paradox can be reconstructed in a rigorous setting, because some logicians have voiced objections to the use of an infinite list of sentences. In particular, Priest (1997) asked for a justification of the assumption that such a list or some analogue exists (and showed how to answer the question in an arithmetical setting). Secondly, by analyzing the argument for the inconsistency in a formal setting, we can keep track of what exactly is needed for the argument and whether some kind of circularity is involved. Thirdly, we may try to use the reasoning employed in the paradox to prove new inconsistencies that are not immediate consequences of known inconsistencies.

Yablo (1993) presented the sequence of sentences using natural numbers as indices. Ketland (2005) showed that only very weak assumptions on the ordering of the sentences are needed, and our version of Yablo's paradox follows Ketland in using only weak assumptions on the order of the sentences. By using a primitive axiomatized predicate $<$ it becomes easier to see exactly which conditions on the ordering are required for Yablo's and other paradoxes, even though orderings with the relevant properties can be defined in E without extra vocabulary. Ketland (2005) used only two assumptions on the ordering in the proof of Yablo's paradox, seriality and transitivity:

(SER) $$\forall x \exists y\, x<y,$$

(TRANS) $$\forall x \forall y \forall z \big(x<y \rightarrow (y<z \rightarrow x<z)\big).$$

The conditions SER and TRANS can be satisfied by a relation in which objects do not have unique successors. This is the case, for instance, for the 'smaller than' ordering on the rational numbers. For a given rational number, there is no single 'next' number or successor, because the relation is dense, that is, between any two numbers there is another one. It is also not excluded that we have $\exists x\, x<x$. Hence, we are not ruling out loops in the relation.

We could define a formula in $\mathcal{L}$ that satisfies SER and TRANS. However, that would make it harder to control what exactly is used in the proof. Therefore, we assume that $<$ is a primitive symbol of $\mathcal{L}$ and that SER and TRANS are axioms of E.

There are several formalizations of Yablo's paradox. Some yield only ω-inconsistencies; ω-inconsistent theories lack a standard model. The phenomenon of ω-inconsistency will be explained in definition 6.28 below. Here we prove an outright inconsistency. For this we use not the simple T-schema, but a 'uniform' version:

(UTS) $$\forall y \big(\Box\overline{\varphi(\dot{y})} \leftrightarrow \varphi(y)\big).$$

Here $\varphi(y)$ can be any formula (as long as it satisfies the variable condition); in particular, it can contain $\Box$. This schema is intended as an analogue to English sentences such as the following (reversing the order of the formulæ in the biconditional):

> For every object, the object is white if and only if it is true that it is white.

It is perhaps not so clear that instances of UTS are actually formalizations of this sentence. As pointed out above, it might be better to use a binary satisfaction predicate. Moreover, UTS tells us only something about the truth of sentences with quotation constants in place of y, because that is how the notation has been defined. But the 'weakness' of the schema – compared to versions with a satisfaction predicate – does not matter, as we are going to show that it suffices for the inconsistency. Of course, we could get the inconsistency in the same way as in the liar paradox; but, as has been explained above, the proof itself is interesting.

6.18 THEOREM · YABLO'S PARADOX *Assume that* E *contains all the following sentences:*

(SER) $\forall x \exists y\, x{<}y,$

(TRANS) $\forall x \forall y \forall z \big(x{<}y \rightarrow (y{<}z \rightarrow x{<}z)\big),$

(UTS) $\forall y \big(\Box \overline{\varphi(\underset{\cdot}{y})} \leftrightarrow \varphi(y)\big).$

Then E *is inconsistent.*

PROOF The proof follows our informal argument for the infinite list. We write $y{>}x$ for $x{<}y$ and abbreviate $\forall z\,(z{>}y \rightarrow \psi)$ as $\forall z{>}y\, \psi$ and $\exists z\,(z{>}y \wedge \psi)$ as $\exists z{>}y\, \psi$. We apply the diagonal lemma 5.13 with a free variable to the formula

$$\forall z{>}y\, \neg\Box \mathrm{sub}\big(x, \bar{y}, q(z)\big),$$

which has exactly x and y as free variables. This yields a formula $\theta(y)$ with the following property:

$$E \vdash \forall y \Big(\theta(y) \leftrightarrow \forall z{>}y\, \neg\Box \mathrm{sub}\big(\overline{\theta(y)}, \bar{y}, q(z)\big)\Big).$$

Using our underdotting convention, this can be abbreviated as follows:

$$E \vdash \forall y \big(\theta(y) \leftrightarrow \forall z{>}y\, \neg\Box \overline{\theta(\underset{\cdot}{z})}\big). \tag{6.8}$$

The sentences $\theta(\overline{e})$ for arbitrary expressions e correspond to the Yablo sentences. Priest (1997) defined the Yablo sentences in this way in arithmetic, after Visser (1989) had used a similar method to obtain his paradox (see theorem 6.19 below). The contradiction can now be derived in the following way in E:

$$
\begin{array}{lll}
\mathsf{E} \vdash \forall \mathsf{y}\big(\Box\overline{\theta(\dot{\mathsf{y}})} \leftrightarrow \theta(\mathsf{y})\big) & & \text{UTS} \\
& \leftrightarrow \forall \mathsf{z}{>}\mathsf{y}\, \neg\Box\overline{\theta(\dot{\mathsf{z}})} & (6.8) \\
& \rightarrow \exists \mathsf{z}{>}\mathsf{y}\, \neg\Box\overline{\theta(\dot{\mathsf{z}})} & \text{SER} \\
& \rightarrow \exists \mathsf{z}{>}\mathsf{y}\, \forall \mathsf{w}{>}\mathsf{z}\, \neg\Box\overline{\theta(\dot{\mathsf{w}})} & \text{second line and TRANS} \\
& \rightarrow \exists \mathsf{z}{>}\mathsf{y}\, \theta(\mathsf{z}) & (6.8) \\
& \rightarrow \exists \mathsf{z}{>}\mathsf{y}\, \Box\overline{\theta(\dot{\mathsf{z}})} & \text{UTS}
\end{array}
$$

The right-hand side formulæ in the second and last lines are contradictory. Therefore we have established $\forall \mathsf{y}\, \neg\Box\overline{\theta(\dot{\mathsf{y}})}$ and we can proceed as follows:

$$
\begin{array}{ll}
\mathsf{E} \vdash \forall \mathsf{y}\, \neg\theta(\mathsf{y}) & \text{UTS} \\
\mathsf{E} \vdash \forall \mathsf{y}\, \exists \mathsf{z}{>}\mathsf{y}\, \Box\overline{\theta(\dot{\mathsf{z}})} & (6.8)
\end{array}
$$

The last line contradicts the previously derived $\forall \mathsf{y}\, \neg\Box\overline{\theta(\dot{\mathsf{y}})}$. ⊣

There are some variations of our version of Yablo's paradox. The relation $<$ is defined on all objects; and SER implies that every object is related to some object by $<$. Now one might prefer not to use all objects in the ordering, because it means that all objects are indices for sentences in the sequence of Yablo sentences, and that looks somewhat odd. It is possible to restrict SER and TRANS to a non-empty domain; that is, the two assumptions on $<$ are replaced with the following three assumptions for some formula $\rho(\mathsf{x})$:

$$
\begin{array}{ll}
(\text{SER}_\rho) & \forall \mathsf{x}\big(\rho(\mathsf{x}) \rightarrow \exists \mathsf{y}\big(\rho(\mathsf{y}) \wedge \mathsf{x}{<}\mathsf{y}\big)\big), \\
(\text{TRANS}_\rho) & \forall \mathsf{x} \forall \mathsf{y} \forall \mathsf{z}\big(\rho(\mathsf{x}) \wedge \rho(\mathsf{y}) \wedge \rho(\mathsf{z}) \rightarrow \big(\mathsf{x}{<}\mathsf{y} \rightarrow (\mathsf{y}{<}\mathsf{z} \rightarrow \mathsf{x}{<}\mathsf{z})\big)\big), \\
(\text{INHABIT}_\rho) & \exists \mathsf{x}\, \rho(\mathsf{x}).
\end{array}
$$

The proof of Yablo's paradox still goes through if all quantifiers over objects in the ordering are thus restricted to ρ.

The conditions SER and TRANS are easy to satisfy. In fact, in E we can define many relations that satisfy SER and TRANS, without adding any assumptions. For instance, we can define $x<y$ as the identity relation $x=y$ or as the total relation; these relations are serial and transitive.

With ρ it is even easier. We can choose a single loop of length 1. For instance, we can use $x = \overline{\neg}$ as the formula ρ and then stipulate $\overline{\neg} < \overline{\neg}$. The conditions SER$_\rho$, TRANS$_\rho$, and INHABIT$_\rho$ are satisfied with this assumption. Ketland's (2005) analysis of Yablo's paradox and the proof above show that transitivity and seriality suffice. Loops and the ordering $<$ on the natural numbers (as in the original version of Yablo's paradox) are just different ways to satisfy the conditions and obtain a transitive and serial ordering.

Our formalized version of Yablo's paradox is nevertheless somewhat disappointing because it yields an inconsistency that is the most familiar in the theory of paradoxes: We know already from the liar paradox that the T-schema is inconsistent. For the usual proof of this inconsistency, we neither need the uniform version UTS of the schema nor any assumptions on an ordering $<$. There is only a vague feeling that the proof of Yablo's paradox is 'less circular' than the usual simple proof of the liar paradox. Hence, as announced above, what is surprising about the formalized version of Yablo's paradox is not the result as stated in theorem 6.18, but rather its proof.

The absence of circularity in Yablo's paradox can be made explicit by introducing a hierarchy of truth predicates. This will allow us to use the reasoning behind Yablo's paradox to prove a new result, Visser's paradox, that cannot be proved with a simple, liar-style sentence. In a hierarchy a given truth predicate applies only to sentences that are 'lower' in the hierarchy. A hierarchy of truth predicates can be obtained by iterating theorem 6.3: First, a truth predicate Tr_1 is added to $\mathcal{L}$ and all axioms $\mathsf{Tr}_1\overline{\psi} \leftrightarrow \psi$ with ψ a sentence in $\mathcal{L}$ are added to E. Then a further truth predicate Tr_2 is added to the language and all axioms $\mathsf{Tr}_2\overline{\psi} \leftrightarrow \psi$, where ψ is a sentence in $\mathcal{L}$ expanded with Tr_1. This procedure can be iterated, and theorem 6.3 ensures the consistency of these theories, as long as E is consistent.[7] A truth hierarchy in which truth predicates apply only to sentences with truth predicates lower in the hierarchy blocks the liar paradox: in the proof of the liar paradox, that is, theorem 6.1, an instance of $\Box\overline{\psi} \leftrightarrow \psi$ is used in which ψ contains $\Box$. Therefore, it is perhaps surprising that level indices can be attached to

[7] Tarski (1935) discussed already the hierarchy of languages. The hierarchy can be iterated along the transfinite ordinals (see Halbach 1995), although some additional difficulties arise. The hierarchy can be introduced either by defining suitable models or with axioms as above and in (Halbach 2014, section 9.1).

the 'untrue' predicate in Yablo's paradox and the paradox still ensues:

(S_1) For all $k > 1$, S_k is untrue$_1$.

(S_2) For all $k > 2$, S_k is untrue$_2$.

(S_3) For all $k > 3$, S_k is untrue$_3$.

$\vdots$

Compared to the Tarskian hierarchy sketched above, the level indices are 'upside down': the lower the numerical index of a truth predicate is, the higher it sits in the hierarchy of truth predicates. The topmost truth predicate 'is untrue$_1$' can be applied to all sentences containing truth predicates with indices greater than 1, that is, to all sentences except those with 'is untrue$_1$' itself. There is no lowest level in this hierarchy: one can always go further down. In the Tarskian hierarchy, in contrast, there is a lowest level.

We can now repeat the argument for Yablo's paradox for the list above by attaching level indices: Assume that one of the sentences in the list, S_{n+1}, is true$_n$. Then all sentences below that sentence are untrue$_{n+1}$. Take any sentence S_k below S_{n+1}. It says correctly that all sentences below it are untrue$_k$, and therefore S_k is true$_n$. That is a contradiction. Hence, there is no n such that the sentence S_{n+1} is true$_n$. But each of these sentences says that all sentences below it are untrue$_{n+1}$. Hence, for every n, the sentence S_{n+1} is true$_n$. This is an outright contradiction.[8]

The argument can be formalized by adding hierarchy levels to the formal proof of Yablo's paradox, theorem 6.18. We follow the informal argument above and permit quantification of the level indices.[9] That is, we use a binary predicate $\Box_y x$. We write y in index position, although it is just a normal argument, hoping that this is suggestive and makes it clear that y is intended to be understood as indicating the level in the hierarchy. We can assume that this binary predicate symbol is one of the additional symbols of $\mathcal{L}$. As for Yablo's paradox, we assume that our language $\mathcal{L}$ contains a primitive binary symbol $<$ as above.

The assumptions SER and TRANS on $<$, seriality and transitivity, will stay the same, but the disquotation schema UTS needs to be modified so that the binary

[8] For an informal comparison of Yablo's and Visser's paradox, see (Halbach 2016).

[9] In order to obtain an ω-inconsistency the level indices need not be quantifiable. For a proof of Visser's paradox in an arithmetical setting with infinitely many truth predicates Tr_n whose index cannot be quantified over, see (Halbach 2014, section 9.2). Truth hierarchies with quantifiable indices have been analyzed by Feferman (mentioned in conversation) and Fujimoto (2012).

predicate $\Box$ obeys the restriction on language levels. To this end we need to define the language levels, which is not as straightforward as with fixed level indices, and with quantifiable indices there are various possibilities. We define language levels by bounding the quantifiers that range over indices in the truth predicate. As long as the variable x in $\Box_x s$ ranges only over indices $x > \overline{e}$, the predicate $\Box_{\overline{e}}$ with the fixed index e can safely be applied to a sentence containing $\Box_x s$. We spell out this restriction formally.

A term t *occurs in index position in* a formula φ iff $\Box_t s$ is a subformula of φ for some term s. For instance, $\mathrm{v}_3{}^\frown\mathrm{v}_4$ occurs in index position in $\Box_{\mathrm{v}_3{}^\frown\mathrm{v}_4}\overline{\neg\neg}$, while v_3 and v_4 do not. We focus on sentences in which all terms in index position are variables, not complex terms or constants.

An occurrence of a quantifier $\forall x$ is restricted by $\zeta(x)$ in a formula φ iff (the occurrence of) the subformula of φ beginning with $\forall x$ is of the form $\forall x\big(\zeta(x) \rightarrow \ldots\big)$. Of course the notion should be defined properly by induction.

We employ the following typed version of the uniform T-schema UTS:

$$\text{(VUTS)} \qquad \forall \mathrm{y}\big(\Box_{\mathrm{y}}\overline{\varphi(\underset{\cdot}{\mathrm{y}})} \leftrightarrow \varphi(\mathrm{y})\big),$$

where all terms occurring in index position in $\varphi(\mathrm{y})$ are variables $x_1, x_2, \ldots, x_k$ distinct from y (but not complex terms or constants) and all quantifiers $\forall x_1$, $\forall x_2$, …, $\forall x_k$ in $\varphi(\mathrm{y})$ are restricted by $x_i > \mathrm{y}$, respectively.

The following sentences are instances of the axiom schema VUTS:

$$\forall \mathrm{y}\Big(\Box_{\mathrm{y}}\overline{\forall \mathrm{v}_3 {>} \underset{\cdot}{\mathrm{y}}\, \exists \mathrm{v}_7\big(\Box_{\mathrm{v}_3}(\overline{\neg}{}^\frown \mathrm{v}_7) \wedge \neg\Box_{\mathrm{v}_3}\mathrm{v}_7\big)} \leftrightarrow \forall \mathrm{v}_3 {>} \mathrm{y}\, \exists \mathrm{v}_7\big(\Box_{\mathrm{v}_3}(\overline{\neg}{}^\frown \mathrm{v}_7) \wedge \neg\Box_{\mathrm{v}_3}\mathrm{v}_7\big)\Big),$$

$$\forall \mathrm{y}\Big(\Box_{\mathrm{y}}\overline{\exists \mathrm{v}_4 {>} \underset{\cdot}{\mathrm{y}}\, \Box_{\mathrm{v}_4}\overline{\underset{\cdot}{\mathrm{v}_4} = \overline{\neg}}} \leftrightarrow \exists \mathrm{v}_4 {>} \mathrm{y}\, \Box_{\mathrm{v}_4}\overline{\underset{\cdot}{\mathrm{v}_4} = \overline{\neg}}\Big).$$

In the rest of this section we prove two claims: First, the proof of Yablo's paradox is unaffected by this restriction on truth predicates. Secondly, the paradox disappears if we drop seriality SER from our assumptions. The second point demonstrates why the version with indices is more interesting: the schema UTS is already by itself inconsistent, without any assumptions on $<$. The inconsistency of VUTS arises only when we assume that the list does not bottom out. This can be due to cycles in $<$ such as if $a < a$ or because there is an infinite chain $a_1 > a_2 > \cdots$ of distinct elements. Therefore, the converse ill-foundedness of $<$ (that is, the existence of a cycle or an infinite chain) is the source of the paradox. We will elaborate on this in chapter 7. We can still assume that the hierarchy is infinite.

In Tarski's hierarchy there is for every language level a higher level, but there is not for every level a lower level.[10]

6.19 THEOREM · VISSER'S PARADOX *If* E *contains* SER, TRANS, *and* VUTS, *then* E *is inconsistent.*

PROOF As we said above, the proof follows exactly the reasoning for Yablo's paradox with language levels added. We obtain a sentence $\theta(y)$ by diagonalization:

$$\mathsf{E} \vdash \forall y\big(\theta(y) \leftrightarrow \forall z{>}y\ \neg\Box_z\overline{\theta(\dot{z})}\big). \tag{6.9}$$

The formula $\theta(y)$ obtained by lemma 5.13 is of the form $\forall z > y\ \neg\Box_z t$ for some complex term t. Therefore, the only term occurring in index position in $\theta(y)$ is z, which is bound by the restricted quantifier $\forall z{>}y$, and thus the following is an instance of VUTS:

$$\begin{aligned} \mathsf{E} \vdash \forall y\big(\Box_y\overline{\theta(\dot{y})} \leftrightarrow{} & \theta(y)\big) & \\ \leftrightarrow{} & \forall z{>}y\ \neg\Box_z\overline{\theta(\dot{z})} & \text{(6.9)} \\ \rightarrow{} & \exists z{>}y\ \neg\Box_z\overline{\theta(\dot{z})} & \text{SER} \\ \rightarrow{} & \exists z{>}y\ \forall w{>}z\ \neg\Box_w\overline{\theta(\dot{w})} & \text{second line and TRANS} \\ \rightarrow{} & \exists z{>}y\ \theta(z) & \text{(6.9)} \\ \rightarrow{} & \exists z{>}y\ \Box_z\overline{\theta(\dot{z})} & \text{VUTS} \end{aligned}$$

The right-hand-side formulæ in the second and last lines are contradictory. Thus, we have established $\forall y\ \neg\Box_y\overline{\theta(\dot{y})}$. This is the place where quantification over language levels is essentially required. If we used infinitely many predicates $\Box_n$, we could prove this only for each truth predicate separately. The proof concludes as above:

$$\begin{aligned} \mathsf{E} \vdash \forall y\big(\neg\Box_y\overline{\theta(\dot{y})} \leftrightarrow{} & \neg\theta(y)\big) & \text{VUTS} \\ \leftrightarrow{} & \exists z{>}y\ \Box_z\overline{\theta(\dot{z})} & \text{(6.9)} \end{aligned}$$

[10] Kripke (1975, page 697) mentioned ill-founded hierarchies. It seems that his remarks prompted work on ill-founded hierarchies by McCarthy (1988), Visser (1989), and others, although Kripke had had different hierarchies in mind, as he explained in his (2019). The history of the work on ill-founded hierarchies is somewhat complicated. Yablo and Visser had found their paradoxes long before their papers quoted here appeared. These paradoxes are closely related to various ω-inconsistency phenomena in axiomatic theories of truth and rule-of-revision semantics by Herzberger (1982) and Belnap and Gupta (1993). See (Leitgeb 2001) for an analysis of the relations between them. Cook's monograph (2014) provides a detailed analysis of Yablo's paradox.

The last line contradicts $\forall y\, \neg\Box_y \overline{\theta(\dot{y})}$. ⊣

Visser's (1989) version of the paradox differs from ours in various aspects. His theory is formulated in arithmetic and does not use a quantified version of the T-schema and is therefore only ω-inconsistent, while our result is an outright inconsistency.

As we mentioned above, VUTS by itself is consistent – unlike the unrestricted T-schema UTS of Yablo's paradox. To narrow down the source of the paradox, we prove a stronger result than the mere consistency of VUTS. Having an infinite list, for instance, does not generate a paradox. Seriality in the other direction, that is, converse seriality,

(CONV-SER) $$\forall x \exists y\; y < x,$$

does not cause a paradox. We can also add asymmetry

(ASYM) $$\forall x \forall y (x < y \rightarrow \neg y < x)$$

as well as totality

(TOT) $$\forall x \forall y (x < y \vee y < x)$$

and keep transitivity. These axioms can be satisfied only in an infinite domain.

For the consistency proof we restrict the underlying syntax theory E to the obligatory axioms. Let the theory V be given by CONV-SER, ASYM, TOT, TRANS, VUTS, and the obligatory axioms A1–A8 from definition 5.8. The language $\mathcal{L}$ of V contains at least $<$ and the binary predicate symbol $\Box$, but may contain further symbols.

The consistency result we are going to prove shows that we can have reasonable truth hierarchies with quantified level indices. In quantified hierarchies a truth predicate can be defined by $\exists z\, \Box_z x$. The formula cannot be used to generate a paradox because it is located nowhere in the hierarchy. The relevant quantifier $\exists z$ is not restricted, and therefore $\exists z\, \Box_z x$ cannot be meaningfully applied to itself. Under suitable assumptions, one will always have sentences in a hierarchy with quantified indices that are outside the hierarchy, because they feature an unrestricted quantifier over level indices.

We define a standard model in the sense of section 5.5 for V. A suitable interpretation of $<$ is obtained by ordering all expressions of the language in the way the natural numbers are ordered by $>$:

$$\cdots \sqsubset e_3 \sqsubset e_2 \sqsubset e_1.$$

Here the direction of the order may feel odd, because $\sqsubset$ corresponds to $>$, not $<$. It does not matter which order we choose. We could pick some lexical order. This relation satisfies CONV-SER, ASYM, TOT, and TRANS.

Our notation is the same as in section 5.5, with the difference that we now focus on a *binary* predicate symbol $\Box$ instead of the unary $\Box$. In the rest of the section we write $\langle \mathbb{E}, V, S \rangle$ for standard models, as before, but S is now the extension of the binary $\Box$, that is, a set of ordered pairs. A unary $\Box$ can be covered by V, just like the other surplus vocabulary. An interpretation V of this vocabulary is now fixed; call this interpretation $V_{\sqsubset}$. It needs to interpret $<$ as $\sqsubset$; no further assumptions on $V_{\sqsubset}$ are needed. For the next lemma we do not impose any restriction on the interpretation of the binary $\Box$.

6.20 LEMMA $\langle \mathbb{E}, V_{\sqsubset}, S \rangle \vDash \forall z > \overline{e_n}\ \varphi(z)$ *iff* $\langle \mathbb{E}, V_{\sqsubset}, S \rangle \vDash \varphi(\overline{e_1}) \wedge \cdots \wedge \varphi(\overline{e_{n-1}})$ *for all sets S of expressions.*

We skip the proof, which should be obvious from the definition of $\sqsubset$, because for every expression e there are only finitely many expressions g with $e \sqsubset g$. For a sentence φ, the sentence φ' is obtained by replacing every subformula of the form $\forall z > \overline{e_n}\ \varphi(z)$ with $\varphi(\overline{e_1}) \wedge \cdots \wedge \varphi(\overline{e_{n-1}})$. It follows by induction from the lemma that φ and φ' are equivalent in any standard model $\langle \mathbb{E}, V_{\sqsubset}, S \rangle$.

A sequence S_n of extensions of $\Box$ is defined inductively as follows (the sets S_n are the levels of the Tarskian hierarchy):

$$S_0 := \varnothing.$$

We start with the empty extension for $\Box$ and define the first level as the set of sentences true in the model with $S_0 = \varnothing$ as the extension of the binary symbol $\Box$, and then continue in this way.

$$S_{n+1} := S_n \cup \{ \langle e_{n+1}, \varphi \rangle : \langle \mathbb{E}, V_{\sqsubset}, S_n \rangle \vDash \varphi \}.$$

Finally, we take the union of all these sets as our interpretation of the binary truth predicate:

$$S_\omega := \bigcup_{n \in \omega} S_n.$$

At any level n only pairs $\langle e_n, \varphi\rangle$ are added, not pairs with an index different from e_n. In particular, after this level only pairs $\langle e_k, \varphi\rangle$ with $k > n$ are added. This yields the following lemma:

6.21 LEMMA *For all* $i \leq n$, $\langle e_i, \varphi\rangle \in S_n$ *iff* $\langle e_i, \varphi\rangle \in S_\omega$.

From this lemma the following can be proved by induction on the length of φ:

6.22 LEMMA *If all occurrences of the binary predicate symbol* $\Box$ *in* φ *are of the form* $\Box_{\overline{e_k}} t$, *where* $\overline{e_k}$ *is some quotation constant with* $k \leq n$ *and* t *some term, then* $\langle \mathbb{E}, V_\sqsubset, S_n\rangle \vDash \varphi$ *is equivalent to* $\langle \mathbb{E}, V_\sqsubset, S_\omega\rangle \vDash \varphi$.

The next theorem shows that V has a standard model and is therefore consistent.

6.23 THEOREM $\langle \mathbb{E}, V_\sqsubset, S_\omega\rangle \vDash \mathsf{V}$.

PROOF It only remains to check that $\langle \mathbb{E}, V_\sqsubset, S_\omega\rangle \vDash$ VUTS, that is, we have to show

$$\langle \mathbb{E}, V_\sqsubset, S_\omega\rangle \vDash \forall \mathsf{y}\big(\Box_{\mathsf{y}}\overline{\varphi(\dot{\mathsf{y}})} \leftrightarrow \varphi(\mathsf{y})\big),$$

where all terms occurring in index position in $\varphi(\mathsf{y})$ are variables $x_1, x_2, \ldots, x_k$ distinct from y and all quantifiers $\forall x_1, \forall x_2, \ldots, \forall x_k$ in $\varphi(\mathsf{y})$ are restricted by $>\mathsf{y}$. If $\varphi(\mathsf{y})$ is such a formula, then $\varphi(\overline{e_n})'$ contains only occurrences of $\Box$ of the form $\Box_{\overline{e_k}} t$ with $k < n$.

Since $\langle \mathbb{E}, V_\sqsubset, S_\omega\rangle$ is a standard model, it is sufficient to prove

$$\langle \mathbb{E}, V_\sqsubset, S_\omega\rangle \vDash \Box_{\overline{e_n}}\overline{\varphi(\overline{e_n})} \leftrightarrow \varphi(\overline{e_n})$$

for all $n \geq 1$ by lemma 5.15 and the axioms for substitution and quotation (for the elimination the underdotting).

$$
\begin{array}{llll}
\langle \mathbb{E}, V_\sqsubset, S_\omega\rangle \vDash \Box_{\overline{e_n}}\overline{\varphi(\overline{e_n})} & \text{iff} & \langle e_n, \varphi(\overline{e_n})\rangle \in S_\omega & \\
& \text{iff} & \langle e_n, \varphi(\overline{e_n})\rangle \in S_n & \text{def. } S_\omega \\
& \text{iff} & \langle \mathbb{E}, V_\sqsubset, S_{n-1}\rangle \vDash \varphi(\overline{e_n}) & \text{def. } S_n \\
& \text{iff} & \langle \mathbb{E}, V_\sqsubset, S_{n-1}\rangle \vDash \varphi(\overline{e_n})' & \text{lem. 6.20} \\
& \text{iff} & \langle \mathbb{E}, V_\sqsubset, S_\omega\rangle \vDash \varphi(\overline{e_n})' & \text{lem. 6.22} \\
& \text{iff} & \langle \mathbb{E}, V_\sqsubset, S_\omega\rangle \vDash \varphi(\overline{e_n}) & \text{lem. 6.20} \quad \dashv
\end{array}
$$

This brings us closer to an assessment of what is at the root of Visser's and Yablo's paradox: Seriality and transitivity are sufficient to generate the paradox, even when we have language levels. If there is an infinitely descending chain of language levels, the disquotation axioms VUTS generate an inconsistency.

If a serial relation is finite, that is, contains only finitely many ordered pairs, then there have to be loops; in a finite domain, circularity is the only way to obtain seriality. In an infinite domain, however, we can have seriality without circularity. Thus, Yablo's and Visser's paradoxes provide some evidence for the claim that at the root of paradox is the ill-foundedness of $>$, not circularity. In terms of $<$, the paradox arises iff $<$ fails to be converse well-founded (or 'upwards well-founded', or 'Noetherian'). Circularity is just a special form of ill-foundedness. This observation matches the semantic diagnosis in chapter 7.

If we do have loops, the proof of inconsistency becomes easier. For instance, we can obtain the paradox by adding the axiom $\exists x \left(x{<}x \wedge \forall y(x{<}y \rightarrow y{=}x)\right)$, which expresses that there is at least one simple loop in $<$, and collapse the paradox into a version of the liar paradox. We can still use the proof of theorem 6.19 to obtain the inconsistency. We only need to use a version with a relativizing $\rho(x)$ as we did in the case of Yablo's paradox.

For the simpler proof we diagonalize as above:

$$\mathsf{E} \vdash \forall y\left(\theta(y) \leftrightarrow \forall z{>}y\ \neg\Box_z\overline{\theta(\dot{z})}\right).$$

We instantiate the universal quantifier with an a such that $a < a \wedge \forall y(a < y \rightarrow y = a)$, whose existence is stated by the condition on $<$:

$$\theta(a) \leftrightarrow \forall z{>}a\ \neg\Box_z\overline{\theta(\dot{z})}.$$

The right-hand side $\forall z{>}a\ \neg\Box_z\overline{\theta(\dot{z})}$ is then equivalent to $\neg\Box_a\overline{\theta(\dot{a})}$, because a is the one and only object $>$-greater than a.

A simple loop expressed by is only the simplest case. Assuming $\exists x\ x{<}x$ also yields an inconsistency, via a slightly more complicated proof, because now there can be other objects $>$-greater than a. There are more variations, and we will look into them from a semantic perspective in chapter 7.

6.5 Arithmetic in E

As mentioned above, syntax can be reduced to arithmetic by coding expressions in the numbers. Conversely, arithmetic can also be reduced to syntax. In this book, syntax deals with strings of different symbols. In $\mathcal{L}$ there are infinitely many symbols. Arithmetic can be viewed as the theory of syntax of a very limited alphabet, namely the alphabet with exactly one symbol, by identifying each number *n* with the string of *n* occurrences of that symbol.

The theory of strings of a single symbol is already contained in our theory E. In this section we develop arithmetic in E. Using a modicum of arithmetic will allow us to prove McGee's ω-inconsistency theorem in the next section.

We use strings xxx... as natural numbers and call expressions $\overline{\mathsf{xxx}\ldots}$ *numerals*; they act as constants for numbers. Moreover, $\underline{n}$, the *numeral of n*, stands for

$$\overline{\underbrace{\mathsf{x}\ldots\mathsf{x}}_{n}}.$$

For instance, $\underline{4}$, that is, $\overline{\mathsf{xxxx}}$, is the numeral for 4.

6.24 DEFINITION $\mathsf{Nat}(x)$ is defined as $\mathsf{sub}(x, \overline{\mathsf{x}}, \underline{0}) = \underline{0}$.

The idea is that substituting the empty string for x in a string of xs gives the empty string. If the original string had contained some symbol different from x, the symbol would not have been replaced and thus remained. The empty string is the empty string of occurrences of x, and therefore it is a natural number, provably in E.

6.25 LEMMA $\mathsf{E} \vdash \mathsf{Nat}(\underline{n})$ *for all natural numbers n.*

PROOF For each $\underline{n}$, the sentence $\mathsf{sub}(\underline{n}, \overline{\mathsf{x}}, \underline{0}) = \underline{0}$ is an instance of A3. ⊣

We write $\forall n\, \varphi(n)$ for $\forall x\big(\mathsf{Nat}(x) \to \varphi(x)\big)$, for any variable x, and similarly $\exists n\, \varphi(n)$ for $\exists x\big(\mathsf{Nat}(x) \wedge \varphi(x)\big)$. This abbreviation is used in conjunction with the underdotting convention as in $\forall k\, \overline{\varphi(\underset{\cdot}{k})}$, which is short for

$$\forall x\Big(\mathsf{Nat}(x) \to \mathsf{sub}\big(\mathsf{q}x, \overline{x}, \overline{\varphi(x)}\big)\Big),$$

where x is a variable with no bound occurrences in φ.

Addition and multiplication can be mimicked in $\mathcal{L}$ by concatenation and substitution, respectively. We skip the proof of the following observation:

6.26 LEMMA *Assume* $\underline{n}$, $\underline{k}$, $\underline{n{+}k}$, *and* $\underline{n{\cdot}k}$ *are numerals for* n, k, $n{+}k$, *and* $n{\cdot}k$, *respectively. Then the following holds:*

(i) $\mathsf{E} \vdash \underline{n}^\frown\underline{k} = \underline{n+k}$,

(ii) $\mathsf{E} \vdash \mathsf{sub}(\underline{k}, \overline{\mathsf{x}}, \underline{n}) = \underline{n \cdot k}$.

In particular we have $\mathsf{E} \vdash \underline{n}^\frown\underline{1} = \underline{n+1}$.

We expect that every number except $\underline{0}$ has a unique predecessor. However, this relies on the linearity of expressions, which is expressed by axiom A8.

6.27 LEMMA $\mathsf{E} \vdash \forall n \forall k\, (n^\frown\underline{1} = k^\frown\underline{1} \rightarrow n = k)$.

PROOF The following is an instantiation of axiom A8:

$$\forall n \forall k \Big(n^\frown\underline{1} = k^\frown\underline{1} \leftrightarrow \exists \mathsf{v}_4\big((n = k^\frown\mathsf{v}_4 \wedge \mathsf{v}_4{}^\frown\underline{1} = \underline{1}) \vee (n^\frown\mathsf{v}_4 = k \wedge \underline{1} = \mathsf{v}_4{}^\frown\underline{1})\big)\Big).$$

Axiom A6 implies $\forall \mathsf{v}_4(\mathsf{v}_4{}^\frown\underline{1} = \underline{1} \rightarrow \mathsf{v}_4 = \underline{0})$. Thus, if the first disjunct obtains, n and k must be identical by axiom A6. The other case is analogous. ⊣

In the theory of paradoxes, inconsistency may look like the only evil that can arise, as long as the axioms themselves are plausible. As we will see, inconsistency is far from being the only evil. Many logicians see ω-inconsistency as a mortal sin in theories of numbers.

6.28 DEFINITION E is *ω-inconsistent* if and only if there is a formula $\varphi(\mathsf{x})$ with the following properties:

(i) $\mathsf{E} \vdash \varphi(\underline{k})$ for all natural numbers k,

(ii) $\mathsf{E} \vdash \neg\forall n\, \varphi(n)$.

Thus, if E is ω-inconsistent, E proves $\varphi(\underline{k})$ for each particular natural number k, but at the same time also claims that there is some number for which $\varphi(\mathsf{x})$ does not hold. This does not imply that E is plainly inconsistent because one cannot derive $\forall n\, \varphi(n)$ from all the sentences $\varphi(\underline{0}), \varphi(\underline{1}), \varphi(\underline{2}), \ldots$ That is, E is not closed under the so-called ω-rule:

$$\frac{\varphi(\underline{0}) \quad \varphi(\underline{1}) \quad \varphi(\underline{2}) \quad \varphi(\underline{3}) \quad \ldots}{\forall \mathsf{x}\big(\mathsf{Nat}(\mathsf{x}) \rightarrow \varphi(\mathsf{x})\big)}$$

In the proof of the next lemma we invoke axioms A6 and A7.

6.29 LEMMA $\mathsf{E} \vdash \forall x\big(\mathsf{Nat}(x) \rightarrow \mathsf{Nat}(x^\frown\underline{1})\big)$.

PROOF In E one can reason as follows:

$$\begin{aligned} \mathsf{sub}(x^\frown\overline{\mathsf{x}}, \overline{\mathsf{x}}, \underline{0}) &= \mathsf{sub}(x, \overline{\mathsf{x}}, \underline{0})^\frown\underline{0} && \text{A7} \\ &= \mathsf{sub}(x, \overline{\mathsf{x}}, \underline{0}) && \text{A6} \end{aligned}$$

Thus, $\mathsf{sub}(x, \overline{\mathsf{x}}, \underline{0}) = \underline{0} \rightarrow \mathsf{sub}(x^\frown\overline{\mathsf{x}}, \overline{\mathsf{x}}, \underline{0}) = \underline{0}$ is provable in E. ⊣

From this the next lemma follows:

6.30 LEMMA *The theory* E *proves* $\forall n\, \varphi(n) \rightarrow \forall n\, \varphi(n^\frown\underline{1})$ *for all formulæ* $\varphi(x)$ *of* $\mathcal{L}$.

6.6 McGee's Theorem on ω-Inconsistency

McGee's (1985) paradox is closely related to Yablo's and Visser's paradoxes. Leitgeb (2001) described the connections between these paradoxes in some detail. To provide an informal idea of how the paradoxes are related, we look at the following well-known variant of Yablo's paradox with existential instead of universal quantifiers:

(S_1) For some $k > 1$, S_k is not true.
(S_2) For some $k > 2$, S_k is not true.
(S_3) For some $k > 3$, S_k is not true.
⋮

The contradiction is derived in a way similar to the one for Yablo's paradox. The sentences in the list differ only in their labels. We now make them differ in another feature:

(S_1) For some $k > 1$, S_k is not true.
(S_2) For some $k > 2$, 'S_k is true' is not true.
(S_3) For some $k > 3$, ' "S_k is true" is true' is not true.
⋮

That is, we add to each S_{n+1} a further n-many iterated truth predicates. The labels are no longer needed, because the sentences are all distinct anyway, as they differ in the number of truth predicates. This allows us to collapse the list into a single sentence:

(S) For some k: sentence (S) with k many truth predicates is not true.

The phrase 'with k many truth predicates' expresses k many applications of the truth predicate to S. Thus, 'Snow is white' with 3 truth predicates is

' " 'Snow is white' is true" is true' is true.

The sentence (S) says that at least one of the following sentences is not true:

(S)
(S) is true.
'(S) is true' is true.
' "(S) is true" is true' is true.
$\vdots$

McGee's ω-inconsistency theorem can be obtained by formalizing (S).

On page 71 we showed that the obligatory axioms of E can be satisfied by a model with a domain that contains only one element, because there is no axiom that tells us that some objects are distinct. All results in section 6.5 are equalities and thus satisfiable in models with one element. To distinguish between the different lines in the construction above, we make an additional assumption: we assume that every number is either the empty string $\underline{0}$ or a successor number, but not both. This is axiom (v) in the following result. Axiom A6 shows that this forces infinite models and that $\underline{k}$ and $\underline{n}$ must denote distinct objects if $k \neq n$. Also, in this respect, too, McGee's theorem is very similar to Yablo's and Visser's paradoxes, where the infinity of the list is forced by axioms for $<$. Leitgeb (2001) provided details of how Yablo's, Visser's, and McGee's paradoxes are related.

6.31 MCGEE'S ω-INCONSISTENCY THEOREM *Assume that* E *is closed under the rule in* (i) *and contains the formula* (v) *and the schemas* (ii)–(iv) *for all sentences* φ *and* ψ *and all formulæ* $\chi(\mathsf{x})$ *having at most* x *free.*

(i) NEC,
(ii) $\Box\overline{\varphi \to \psi} \to (\Box\overline{\varphi} \to \Box\overline{\psi})$,

(iii) $\Box\overline{\neg\varphi} \to \neg\Box\overline{\varphi}$,

(iv) $\forall x\, \Box\overline{\chi(\dot{x})} \to \Box\overline{\forall x\, \chi(x)}$,

(v) $\forall n\, (n=\underline{0} \vee \exists k\; n=k^\frown\underline{1}) \wedge \neg\exists k\; \underline{0}=k^\frown\underline{1}$.

Then E *is* ω*-inconsistent.*

Much stronger axioms have been thought to be plausible for $\Box$ as truth. The theorem contains only the part that is responsible for the ω-inconsistency. In particular, it has been thought that a theory of truth might claim that the truth predicate commutes with all connectives and quantifiers and that conecessitation and its inverse rule should hold for truth. For instance, one would use the axiom $\forall x\big(\Box(\overline{\neg}^\frown x) \to \neg\Box x\big)$ (where perhaps x is restricted to range over sentences only) instead of the weaker schema (iii).

It has been shown by Friedman and Sheard (1987) that such a system is consistent over an arithmetical base theory. When it was realized that the system is ω-inconsistent, hardly anybody thought such a system could be a sensible theory of truth. Nevertheless, the theory has been further investigated by some people.

For the proof of the theorem we follow McGee in using the diagonal lemma twice. The first application yields a method that is useful also for other purposes. Let σ be a sentence. Then there is a formula $\theta(w, z, y)$ such that the following holds:

$$\text{(6.10)}\quad \mathsf{E} \vdash \forall n \forall z \forall y\Big(\theta(n, z, y) \leftrightarrow \exists k\big(n = k^\frown\underline{1} \wedge z = \overline{\forall z(\theta(\dot{k}, z, \dot{y}) \to \Box z)}\big) \vee \big(n=\underline{0} \wedge z=y\big)\Big).$$

The version of the diagonal lemma we need is a generalization of the uniform diagonal lemma 6.17. Generalizing it to formulæ with three free variables, such as $\theta(w, z, y)$, is straightforward. For this formula $\theta(w, z, y)$ we prove a lemma:

6.32 LEMMA *Assume that* E *satisfies the conditions mentioned in the theorem above and* σ *is some sentence of* $\mathcal{L}$*. Then the following hold:*

(i) $\mathsf{E} \vdash \forall z\big(\theta(\underline{0}, z, \overline{\sigma}) \leftrightarrow z = \overline{\sigma}\big)$,

(ii) $\mathsf{E} \vdash \forall n \forall z\Big(\theta(n^\frown\underline{1}, z, \overline{\sigma}) \leftrightarrow z = \overline{\forall z\big(\theta(\dot{n}, z, \overline{\sigma}) \to \Box z\big)}\Big)$.

We would like $\theta(n, \mathrm{z}, \overline{\sigma})$ to express that z is the sentence

$$\underbrace{\Box\Box\cdots\Box}_{n}\overline{\overline{\vdots\,\overline{\sigma}}}.$$

It would be easier to present the idea with a binary function symbol f with arguments n and σ. The function expressed by f would yield as output the expression above. However, in the absence of such a function symbol, we use the formula $\theta(n, \mathrm{z}, \overline{\sigma})$. If we did have a suitable function symbol f, then we could restate the two sentences in the lemma by the following two 'recursive' clauses:

(i) $f(\underline{0}, \overline{\sigma}) = \overline{\sigma}$,

(ii) $f(n^\frown\underline{1}, \overline{\sigma}) = \overline{\Box}^\frown\mathrm{q}\big(f(n, \overline{\sigma})\big)$.

The lemma is now proved in the following way:

PROOF From (v) we derive $n = \underline{0} \rightarrow \neg\exists k\ n = k^\frown\underline{1}$, which in turn implies the formula $\forall n\forall \mathrm{z}\forall \mathrm{y}\big(n = \underline{0} \rightarrow \big(\theta(n, \mathrm{z}, \mathrm{y}) \leftrightarrow (n = \underline{0} \wedge \mathrm{z} = \mathrm{y})\big)\big)$. This yields (i).

For (ii), observe that lemma 6.29 shows that $n^\frown\underline{1}$ is a number if n is. Therefore, we obtain the following from (6.10):

$$\begin{aligned}\mathsf{E} \vdash \forall n\forall \mathrm{z}\forall \mathrm{y}\Big(&\theta(n^\frown\underline{1}, \mathrm{z}, \mathrm{y}) \leftrightarrow \\ &\exists k\big(n^\frown\underline{1} = k^\frown\underline{1} \wedge \mathrm{z} = \overline{\forall \mathrm{z}(\theta(\underset{.}{k}, \mathrm{z}, \underset{.}{\mathrm{y}}) \rightarrow \Box \mathrm{z})}\big) \vee (n^\frown\underline{1} = \underline{0} \wedge \mathrm{z} = \mathrm{y})\Big).\end{aligned}$$

The second disjunct can be dropped because of our assumption (v). Using the uniqueness of predecessors, lemma 6.27, the result can be further simplified as follows:

$$\mathsf{E} \vdash \forall n\forall \mathrm{z}\forall \mathrm{y}\Big(\theta(n^\frown\underline{1}, \mathrm{z}, \mathrm{y}) \leftrightarrow \mathrm{z} = \overline{\forall \mathrm{z}\big(\theta(\underset{.}{n}, \mathrm{z}, \underset{.}{\mathrm{y}}) \rightarrow \Box \mathrm{z}\big)}\Big).$$

To obtain (ii), it remains to instantiate $\forall \mathrm{y}$ with $\overline{\sigma}$. ⊣

The second application of the diagonal lemma is to $\neg\forall n\forall \mathrm{z}\big(\theta(n, \mathrm{z}, \mathrm{x}) \rightarrow \Box \mathrm{z}\big)$. This use of the diagonal lemma is straightforward and requires only the plain version, that is, lemma 5.12.

(6.11) $$\mathsf{E} \vdash \sigma \leftrightarrow \neg\forall n\forall \mathrm{z}\big(\theta(n, \mathrm{z}, \overline{\sigma}) \rightarrow \Box \mathrm{z}\big).$$

Of course, σ is the formal counterpart of the sentence (S) above.

PROOF OF MCGEE'S THEOREM We start with (6.11):

$$
\begin{aligned}
&\mathsf{E} \vdash \neg\sigma \leftrightarrow \forall n \forall \mathrm{z}\big(\theta(n, \mathrm{z}, \overline{\sigma}) \to \Box \mathrm{z}\big) \\
&\qquad \to \forall \mathrm{z}\big(\theta(\underline{0}, \mathrm{z}, \overline{\sigma}) \to \Box \mathrm{z}\big) \\
(6.12) \quad &\qquad \to \Box\overline{\sigma}. && \text{lemma 6.32(i)}
\end{aligned}
$$

An application of NEC to (6.11) and assumption (ii) in the statement of McGee's theorem yield the following implications:

$$
\begin{aligned}
&\mathsf{E} \vdash \Box\overline{\sigma} \to \Box\overline{\neg\forall n \forall \mathrm{z}\big(\theta(n, \mathrm{z}, \overline{\sigma}) \to \Box \mathrm{z}\big)} \\
&\qquad \to \neg\Box\overline{\forall n \forall \mathrm{z}\big(\theta(n, \mathrm{z}, \overline{\sigma}) \to \Box \mathrm{z}\big)} && \text{assumption (iii)} \\
&\qquad \to \neg\forall n\, \Box\overline{\forall \mathrm{z}\big(\theta(\underset{\cdot}{n}, \mathrm{z}, \overline{\sigma}) \to \Box \mathrm{z}\big)} && \text{assumption (iv)} \\
&\qquad \to \neg\forall n \forall \mathrm{z}\Big(\mathrm{z} = \overline{\forall \mathrm{z}\big(\theta(\underset{\cdot}{n}, \mathrm{z}, \overline{\sigma}) \to \Box \mathrm{z}\big)} \to \Box \mathrm{z}\Big) \\
&\qquad \to \neg\forall n \forall \mathrm{z}\big(\theta(n \frown \underline{1}, \mathrm{z}, \overline{\sigma}) \to \Box \mathrm{z}\big) && \text{lemma 6.32(ii)} \\
&\qquad \to \neg\forall n \forall \mathrm{z}\big(\theta(n, \mathrm{z}, \overline{\sigma}) \to \Box \mathrm{z}\big) && \text{lemma 6.30} \\
(6.13) \quad &\qquad \to \sigma && \text{(6.11)}
\end{aligned}
$$

Combining (6.12) and (6.13) yields $\mathsf{E} \vdash \neg\sigma \to \sigma$ and therefore $\mathsf{E} \vdash \sigma$, which in turn implies by (6.11):

$$
(6.14) \qquad \mathsf{E} \vdash \neg\forall n \forall \mathrm{z}\big(\theta(n, \mathrm{z}, \overline{\sigma}) \to \Box \mathrm{z}\big).
$$

From $\mathsf{E} \vdash \sigma$, however, we have also by NEC:

$$
\begin{aligned}
&\mathsf{E} \vdash \Box\overline{\sigma} \\
(6.15) \quad &\mathsf{E} \vdash \forall \mathrm{z}\big(\theta(\underline{0}, \mathrm{z}, \overline{\sigma}) \to \Box \mathrm{z}\big) && \text{lemma 6.32(i)} \\
&\mathsf{E} \vdash \Box\overline{\forall \mathrm{z}\big(\theta(\underline{0}, \mathrm{z}, \overline{\sigma}) \to \Box \mathrm{z}\big)} && \text{NEC} \\
&\mathsf{E} \vdash \forall \mathrm{z}\Big(\mathrm{z} = \overline{\forall \mathrm{z}\big(\theta(\underline{0}, \mathrm{z}, \overline{\sigma}) \to \Box \mathrm{z}\big)} \to \Box \mathrm{z}\Big) \\
&\mathsf{E} \vdash \forall \mathrm{z}\big(\theta(\underline{0} \frown \underline{1}, \mathrm{z}, \overline{\sigma}) \to \Box \mathrm{z}\big) && \text{lemma 6.32(ii)} \\
(6.16) \quad &\mathsf{E} \vdash \forall \mathrm{z}\big(\theta(\underline{1}, \mathrm{z}, \overline{\sigma}) \to \Box \mathrm{z}\big) && \text{axiom A1} \\
&\mathsf{E} \vdash \Box\overline{\forall \mathrm{z}\big(\theta(\underline{1}, \mathrm{z}, \overline{\sigma}) \to \Box \mathrm{z}\big)} && \text{NEC} \\
&\mathsf{E} \vdash \forall \mathrm{z}\Big(\mathrm{z} = \overline{\forall \mathrm{z}\big(\theta(\underline{1}, \mathrm{z}, \overline{\sigma}) \to \Box \mathrm{z}\big)} \to \Box \mathrm{z}\Big) \\
&\mathsf{E} \vdash \forall \mathrm{z}\big(\theta(\underline{1} \frown \underline{1}, \mathrm{z}, \overline{\sigma}) \to \Box \mathrm{z}\big) && \text{lemma 6.32(ii)} \\
(6.17) \quad &\mathsf{E} \vdash \forall \mathrm{z}\big(\theta(\underline{2}, \mathrm{z}, \overline{\sigma}) \to \Box \mathrm{z}\big) && \text{axiom A1} \\
&\qquad \vdots
\end{aligned}
$$

(6.14) and the sequence of lines continuing (6.15), (6.16), and (6.17) establish the ω-inconsistency of E in the sense of definition 6.28. ⊣

6.7 The Road Ahead

The emphasis of this book is on the paradoxes themselves, not their potential solutions – whatever may count as a potential solution. Here we merely mention some points that help to motivate later chapters, especially chapter 11 on axiomatic theories of truth. Beall, Glanzberg, and Ripley (2020) provided a starting point for exploring the literature on 'solutions' of the paradoxes. By a 'solution' we simply mean a move that avoids the triviality of our theories, ω-inconsistency, or other unwanted consequences.

There are various classes of solutions. Among them are the following: the weakening or rejection of fundamental principles of the modal predicates, the restriction of the applicability of modal predicates, and the mutilation of (classical) logic. We cannot browse through all the options, but list some general requirements that guide our choice.

Classical logic should be retained.

What may look like a tiny change of the truth tables of the connectives or a minuscule modification of the rules of Natural Deduction in a toy system is most likely to have repercussions in many areas. Sometimes it is claimed that classical logic only needs to be changed for some pathological sentences; otherwise it can be retained. It is suggested that the resulting systems are still classical, or 'almost' classical. But what makes a law logical is its universality. Therefore, a law that allows for exceptions is not a logical one. It may help to compare the revisions of logic for the sake of the paradoxes, with intuitionistic logic. Intuitionistic logicians usually advocate changes to classical logic by rejecting the law of excluded middle not completely, but only for certain instances. It is widely agreed that intuitionistic logic is a departure from classical. We view the restrictions of the usual classical laws of logic in the same way. It would be misleading to label them as *classical* laws, even if many classical theorems and rules are retained.

When allegedly smaller changes to classical logic are advocated, the consequences of these changes are often underestimated. In claims such as those that everything that is necessary is also true, that some a priori truths are necessary, or that there may be truths that cannot be known, we quantify also over pathological cases. The allegedly small changes to classical logic affect also those claims and therefore vast parts of philosophy. Abandoning classical logic can have far-reaching effects on our philosophical reasoning.

The rejection of classical logic does also affect other areas such as mathematical reasoning or reasoning about syntax. There are patterns of reasoning we would not easily give up. In fact, we would rather dispense with the modal predicates than lose those patterns. Halbach and Horsten (2006) and Halbach and Nicolai (2018) investigated how particular patterns of mathematical reasoning are affected by adopting certain paracomplete and paraconsistent logics for sentences with the truth predicate and showed that proofs of transfinite induction are no longer logically correct, with repercussions for the provability of sentences that do *not* contain the truth predicate. Of course, this is only a case study, but we suspect that all solutions involving nonclassical logic block some common patterns of classical mathematical reasoning.

Some hardcore proponents of nonclassical logics will be prepared to pay this price and accept that changes have to be made to classical mathematical reasoning patterns. We do not have strong arguments which show that such a move is unfeasible. We would get into a territory that makes a discussion with nonclassical logicians very hard because the participants do no longer agree on what valid logical arguments are. We do not intend to follow the nonclassical logicians on their road, because we are not prepared to make the required incisions to our reasoning.

A solution should not make it impossible to formulate relevant philosophical claims in the object language.

This is the point we already made in chapter 3. Modal notions should be treated in such a way that we can formalize philosophical discourse in our object language. This was the reason for rejecting modal operator logic as a solution to the paradoxes. Nowadays philosophers do not think of modal logic as a solution to the paradoxes. But in the early years of modal logic and its applications in philosophy, this was one of the factors that brought about the victory of operator modal logic over predicate treatments of the modalities, with the exception of truth and formal provability where the predicate view prevailed.

The reason why we do not think that operator modal logic is a viable solution of the paradoxes is the restriction of expressive power. In standard first-order quantified modal logic we cannot express the claims that there are synthetic a priori truths, that what is true is knowable, and so on, at least not without adding further fancy devices to the language. We called this the 'quantification problem'.

All modal predicates should be accommodated.

One main shortcoming of many proposals is that they are confined to a single predicate. There is a risk that we devise an ingenious theory of truth that avoids the paradoxes, and then another theory for knowledge or metaphysical necessity. Both theories can be successful in avoiding inconsistencies when reasoning *only* about truth or *only* about necessity; but when we merge them together, they clash. In theorem 6.14 we presented an observation that shows how two simple and straightforward solutions can be incompatible. In a nutshell, we chose a 'typing' approach for the two predicates: we postulate the T-sentences for the truth predicates, but only for instances that do not contain the truth predicate; and then we impose a similar restriction on the necessity predicate – and get a contradiction. The problem is that the ψ in the T-sentences $\mathsf{Tr}\overline{\psi} \leftrightarrow \psi$ is not allowed to contain the truth predicate Tr, but may contain the necessity predicate. Thus our truth theory is given by axioms with occurrences of the necessity predicate (that is also why the interpolation theorem does not apply). To fix the problem we may also rule out occurrences of the necessity predicate in ψ, and impose a similar restriction on the axioms for necessity. Clearly, we would have to do the same for knowledge, analyticity, and so on. All these notions cannot be applied to any sentence containing the notion itself or any of the other notions. This makes the strict solution nearly useless. We would have to say that *no* modal, epistemic, or alethic belief can constitute knowledge, simply because knowledge cannot be applied to sentences (or propositions or the like) that contain these other notions. We would declare large parts of philosophical discourse illegitimate.

When we require that a solution should accommodate all modal predicates, we do not intend to demand that all modal notions should be treated uniformly. We hinted at a non-uniform or 'mixed' approach in section 3.2, where we considered the strategy by Halbach and Welch (2009) of treating modal notions like necessity as modal operators while truth is conceived as a predicate. The modal predicate 'is necessary' is replaced with 'is necessarily true'. The adverb 'necessarily' can then readily be formalized by a modal operator. One worry is that such non-uniform treatments make further adjustments necessary. The strategy may work for necessity, but it hardly works for knowledge, for instance. 'Victor knows that x' is hardly equivalent to 'Victor knows that x is true', where now 'Victor knows that' is treated as a modal operator. We refer the reader to (Halbach and Welch 2009) and (Stern 2016) for further discussion.

The paradoxes should be taken seriously.

This may sound obvious in the context of this book, but in many areas of philosophy that are less formal, paradoxes of the kind we have discussed in this chapter are not taken seriously. Very often the attitude in epistemology, for instance, is that these paradoxes should be left to the logicians and not interfere with the usual debates in epistemology. But ignoring them is as bad as ignoring the Gettier problem and other 'genuinely epistemological' paradoxes and puzzles. The results in the present chapter may force us to reject certain definitions of knowledge as inadequate. Because they are independent of particular epistemological stances, results such as Montague's theorem 6.5 and Thomason's theorem 6.10 are more fundamental than more specifically epistemological paradoxes.

The epistemologist can block the paradoxes by rejecting some of our fundamental assumptions, for instance, by denying that the objects of belief are structures like our sentences or that the diagonal lemma can be applied to beliefs. Instead beliefs may be conceived as sets of possible worlds. We do not argue against this approach here, which has its own problems and cannot escape the set-theoretic paradoxes easily. We only insist that pushing aside as irrelevant paradoxes arising from diagonalization will make it harder to develop precise theories of knowledge, because these paradoxes will re-emerge once we try to develop precise theories.

This concludes our list of requirements that a solution of the paradoxes should satisfy. The situation can be compared with that in set theory. Georg Cantor and others developed set theory without a formal theory. Early set theorists were aware of the problems posed by proper classes and perhaps of paradoxes such as the Burali–Forti paradox of the set of all ordinals, but they lacked a clear systematic way of blocking the paradoxes. They proved important results that still stand. However, Zermelo's axiomatization of set theory and his later account of the cumulative hierarchy opened the way to the development of modern set theory.

Of course, there are also fundamental differences. In particular, the notion of set-theoretic membership has always been fairly technical without a strong grounding in pre-theoretical intuitions. This is very different from knowledge, necessity, and truth. Our pre-theoretical intuitions and the extensive use of these notions in our philosophical theorizing make revisions of our basic assumptions about them more difficult. Therefore, the temptations to consider radical solutions such as the rejection of classical logic are stronger.

7 Possible-Worlds Semantics

In chapter 3 we identified two main reasons for the rise of the operator over the predicate conception of modalities: first, Montague's (1963) theorem showed that the predicate approach runs into problems with the paradoxes, and secondly, and perhaps more importantly, the development of possible-worlds semantics for the operator conception of modalities offered so much room for further work, while nothing comparable was forthcoming for modal predicates. In this chapter we show how to set up possible-worlds semantics for modal predicates. As far as we know, Asher and Kamp (1989) first adapted possible-worlds semantics to a language with modal predicates, and we follow their account in many respects. Because we slightly change the language, our semantics is greatly simplified compared to that by Halbach, Leitgeb, and Welch (2003).

There are several motivations for investigating possible-worlds semantics for modal predicates. First, as we have argued in chapter 3, we need the expressive power of modal predicates to express quantified claims such as 'There are synthetic a priori truths.' We would like to have a possible-worlds semantics for a language in which such claims can be expressed. This would allow us to transfer many insights gained from possible-worlds semantics for modal operators to modal predicates.

The second motive for considering possible-worlds semantics for predicates comes from metaphysics. There lies a certain irony in the fact that possible-worlds semantics restricted to modal operators is at the centre of modern analytic metaphysics, given that the operator conception of modalities avoids metaphysics to a large extent. As we argued in section 3.4, the operator account does not require any objects of which modalities can be predicated. Therefore, we can avoid any ontological commitments to such objects and escape the category problem. It looks like an advantage of the operator approach that it allows us to discuss modalities without having to address such ontological questions. It is surprising, however, that metaphysicians cling to a framework that excels at avoiding ontological commitment, at least in the object language. The entire resurgence of analytic metaphysics was prompted by metaphysical questions about modality, and from the beginning the entire discussion has been couched by Kripke (1972) and many others in the framework of possible-worlds semantics for modal operators. If we want to discuss traditional metaphysical questions such as the question whether universals exist *ante rem* or *in rebus*, the operator account and its possible-worlds semantics are less useful. On the usual operator accounts we cannot talk about properties or propositions in the object language. Universals are relegated to the metatheory and live in a completely different sphere than ordinary objects. Of course metaphysicians have explored alternatives. For instance, one can give up modal logic altogether and talk directly about possible worlds. In this case, discourse about possible worlds is no longer used as a semantics but becomes an object theory (which is fully extensional). One can then try to translate modal logic into the theory of possible worlds as D. K. Lewis (1968) did.[1] We, however, prefer to treat modal notions as primitive notions with possible-worlds semantics. This strikes us as a more promising framework for modal metaphysics than operator modal logic.

Finally, the paradoxes also provide a reason to care about possible-worlds semantics for modal predicates. We will use possible-worlds semantics to explore the origins of the paradoxes and to devise a general theory of paradoxes. In particular, possible-worlds semantics can shed some light on the question whether self-reference is at the root of paradox.

The chapter does not presuppose any prior knowledge of modal logic and possible-worlds semantics. However, a grasp of the basics of possible-worlds semantics for operators would be useful, because our possible-worlds semantics resembles possible-worlds semantics for operators in many details and in terminology. Sider (2010), Boolos (1993), Chellas (1980), Hughes and Cresswell (1996), and Chagrov and Zakharyaschev (1997) give much more detail than is needed here for our purposes.

In this chapter we keep the account of possible-worlds semantics very simple. We cover only *de dicto* modality (see section 3.5) and consider only a unary

[1]We assume that, perhaps inspired by his teacher Quine, one of Lewis's main motives for adopting a realist view of possible worlds as in his 1986 was the attempt to escape intensionality by talking directly about possible worlds. He puts it as follows in 1968, p. 116: 'Counterpart theory is a theory, not a special-purpose intensional logic', and talks about the 'obscurity of quantified modal logic'. By adopting the predicate view of modalities, as Quine preferred, we avoid the 'obscurity of quantified modal logic' and work in classical first-order predicate logic without having to talk explicitly about possible worlds in the object language.

modal predicate. The vocabulary of the syntax theory will be interpreted in the intended way at all possible worlds. The 'contingent' vocabulary, whose interpretation may vary between worlds, will be restricted to a single sentence symbol (a propositional variable). We do not include further contingent predicate symbols; at least the results below are not affected by the addition of further sentence or predicate symbols of higher arity. The domain is kept constant through all possible worlds and contains exactly all expressions of the language.

These choices are by no means intended to deliver the best, most general, or most interesting account of possible-worlds semantics. However, by keeping our possible-worlds semantics simple we are able to concentrate on the interplay between the paradoxes and possible-worlds semantics and concentrate on the points that are specific to the predicate approach. If we were more interested in an account of possible-worlds semantics that sheds some light on metaphysical issues, we would choose a far more general account, include more contingent vocabulary, and use a domain that contains besides all expressions also further objects of different kinds. New questions arise from the addition of further contingent vocabulary beyond the single sentence symbol and the admission of more inclusive domains. Many of them have been discussed by modal logicians and metaphysicians; others arise from the additional expressive power of the predicate approach. Here we do not address them.

The use of the sentence symbol will greatly simplify some problems. Halbach, Leitgeb, and Welch (2003) consider possible-worlds semantics for a language that features only syntactic vocabulary and the modal predicate. The resulting problems required some non-trivial applications of descriptive set theory by Welch.

7.1 Fundamentals of Possible-Worlds Semantics

For the sake of simplicity, the additional vocabulary of $\mathcal{L}$ is now fixed: there is only a sentence parameter p beyond the obligatory symbols of definition 5.1. To mark this assumption we call our language $\mathcal{L}_p$. Consequently, the only non-logical symbols of $\mathcal{L}_p$ are p, the quotation constants, the function symbols q, $\frown$, and sub, and the predicate symbol $\Box$.

In what follows, the notation of section 5.5 is used. In particular, a standard model for $\mathcal{L}_p$ is of the form $\langle \mathbb{E}, V, S \rangle$, where V assigns a truth value *true* or *false* to p and S is the extension of $\Box$, that is, we have the following:

$$\langle \mathbb{E}, V, S \rangle \models \Box \overline{e} \quad \text{iff} \quad e \in S.$$

The notion of a frame is exactly the same as in operator modal logic:

7.1 DEFINITION A *frame* is an ordered pair $\langle W, R\rangle$ where W is non-empty and R is a binary relation on W.

The elements of W are called *worlds*, R is the *accessibility* relation. If w and v are elements of W, we write wRv iff the ordered pair $\langle W, v\rangle$ is in R. We follow the usual terminology in saying that *w sees v* or that *w can access v* iff wRv.

We can now define what a possible-worlds model for the language $\mathcal{L}_p$ is. Let a frame $\langle W, R\rangle$ be given. In a nutshell, a possible-worlds model assigns a standard model to each world in W in such a way that $\Box\overline{\varphi}$ is true at a world w iff φ is true at all worlds accessible from w. We first explain the definition in some detail and then state the full definition 7.2 below.

We distinguish three kinds of nonlogical vocabulary. First, there is the syntactic vocabulary. These are all symbols except for p and $\Box$, that is, all quotation constants, q, $\frown$, and sub. The interpretation of the syntactic vocabulary is kept fixed throughout all worlds. This means that, for instance, the concatenation symbol $\frown$ is interpreted as concatenation at every world. Similarly, a quotation constant $\overline{e}$ denotes the expression e at all worlds. Expressions and relations on them are considered as abstract objects whose interpretation does not vary between worlds. This assumption is related to the discussion in section 3.4.

The second class of vocabulary is what we called 'contingent' vocabulary. In the case of $\mathcal{L}_p$ there is only one such symbol, the sentence symbol p. As in operator modal logic, the interpretation of the contingent vocabulary can be varied in arbitrary ways between worlds. The interpretation of p in a possible-worlds model is given by what we call a 'valuation'. A valuation V for a frame $\langle W, R\rangle$ is a function that assigns to every $w \in W$ a truth value *true* or *false*. Therefore, whereas in a standard model $\langle \mathbb{E}, V, S\rangle$ the function V needs to specify only a truth value for p, in a possible-worlds model it needs to specify a truth value for p for each world.

The last kind of vocabulary is the modal predicate $\Box$. For a frame $\langle W, R\rangle$ an interpretation B of $\Box$, a '$\Box$-interpretation' for short, is a function that assigns a set S of expressions to every $w \in W$. Therefore, $\big\langle \mathbb{E}, V(w), B(w)\big\rangle$ is a standard model for each $w \in W$. A *possible-worlds model*, or 'PW-model' for short, will be defined as a quadruple $\langle W, R, V, B\rangle$ with V a valuation for $\langle W, R\rangle$ and B a $\Box$-interpretation for $\langle W, R\rangle$; the quadruple $\langle W, R, V, B\rangle$ also has to satisfy an extra condition to be a PW-model.

The definition of a PW-model somewhat resembles that of a possible-worlds model in operator modal logic. However, there are important differences. In operator modal logic there is no need for a $\Box$-interpretation B. Whether a sentence of the form $\underline{\Box}\varphi$ (where $\underline{\Box}$ is the modal *operator*) is true at a world is *defined* inductively in such a way that $\underline{\Box}\varphi$ is true at a world w iff φ is true at all worlds that can be seen by w, that is, at all u such that wRu. In particular, if all worlds can see each other, a sentence is necessarily true at a world iff the sentence is true at *all* worlds.

Our possible-worlds semantics for modal predicates preserves the fundamental feature of possible-worlds semantics: necessity is truth in all accessible worlds. However, given a valuation V for a frame $\langle W, R\rangle$, we cannot *define* by induction on the complexity of φ what it means for φ to be true at a world of the frame. In particular, we may not be able to define a suitable $\Box$-interpretation. In operator modal logic, in contrast, such a definition is possible, because $\underline{\Box}\varphi$ has a higher complexity than φ. With a modal predicate this is not generally possible. Consider a sentence $\Box t$ where t is some closed term. The term t may denote a very complex sentence. In fact, t can even denote $\Box t$ itself again, as we know from the diagonal lemma. Thus, we cannot easily transfer the inductive definition of truth at a world from operator modal logic to our possible-worlds semantics for modal predicates. Depending on the frame, it may not be possible to define a suitable $\Box$-interpretation at all.

Of course, the conception of necessity as truth at all accessible worlds will be retained. Since we cannot use it in a definition, we impose it as a condition on our PW-models:[2]

7.2 DEFINITION A *PW-model* is a quadruple $\langle W, R, V, B\rangle$ such that $\langle W, R\rangle$ is a frame, V is a valuation for $\langle W, R\rangle$, and B is a $\Box$-interpretation for $\langle W, R\rangle$ satisfying the following condition, where $\mathcal{L}_p$ is the set of all $\mathcal{L}_p$-sentences:

$$B(w) = \Big\{ \varphi \in \mathcal{L}_p\text{: for all } u \in W\text{: if } wRu \text{ then } \big\langle \mathbb{E}, V(u), B(u)\big\rangle \vDash \varphi \Big\}. \tag{7.1}$$

Of course, $\langle \mathbb{E}, V(u), B(u)\rangle \vDash \varphi$ means that the sentence φ is true in the standard model $\langle \mathbb{E}, V(u), B(u)\rangle$ in the usual sense of first-order predicate logic; and the expression $\langle \mathbb{E}, V(u), B(u)\rangle \vDash \varphi$ can be read as 'φ is true at world u in the PW-model $\langle W, R, V, B\rangle$'.

[2] This is Asher and Kamp's (1989, p. 103) *Convention B*.

Condition (7.1) on PW-models requires that a sentence is in the extension of $\Box$ at a world w if and only if it is true in all worlds seen by w. Thus, if $\langle W, R, V, B\rangle$ is a PW-model, the following holds for all sentences $\varphi \in \mathcal{L}_P$ and all $w \in W$:

$$\langle \mathbb{E}, V(w), B(w)\rangle \vDash \Box\overline{\varphi} \quad \text{iff} \qquad (7.2)$$
$$\text{for all } u \in W\text{: if } wRu \text{ then } \langle \mathbb{E}, V(u), B(u)\rangle \vDash \varphi.$$

The definition does not imply the existence of any PW-models at all. As we will see, we cannot obtain PW-models for all frames; but we will single out those frames for which we *can* define PW-models. This leads to the following definition:

7.3 DEFINITION A frame $\langle W, R\rangle$ *admits a PW-model on every valuation* iff for every valuation V on $\langle W, R\rangle$ there is a B such that $\langle W, R, V, B\rangle$ is a PW-model. A frame *admits a PW-model* iff the frame admits a PW-model on some valuation, that is, iff there is a valuation V and a $\Box$-interpretation B such that $\langle W, R, V, B\rangle$ is a PW-model.

Here we are more interested in the question whether a frame admits a PW-model for *all* valuations than in the question whether it does so on *some* valuation. We would like to be able to interpret the contingent vocabulary arbitrarily and still be able to interpret $\Box$ in such a way that condition (7.1) is satisfied. Halbach, Leitgeb, and Welch (2003), in contrast, asked the other question, that is, they asked which frames admit PW-models at all.

The focus on the former question can be motivated by a look at operator modal logic. There we are usually not interested in whether there is some valuation that makes, for instance, $\underline{\Box}\varphi \rightarrow \varphi$ true. This schema can be made true on all frames – including frames that are not reflexive – by not varying the interpretation of the contingent vocabulary between worlds. Under this specific interpretation, $\underline{\Box}\varphi \rightarrow \varphi$ is true at all worlds, even if the frame is not reflexive. What we are interested in are the frames that make $\underline{\Box}\varphi \rightarrow \varphi$ true at all worlds under *arbitrary* interpretations of the contingent vocabulary. The set of frames that will make $\underline{\Box}\varphi \rightarrow \varphi$ true at all worlds on all valuations (in the sense of operator modal logic) is exactly the set of all reflexive frames. Similar claims hold for $\underline{\Box}\varphi \rightarrow \underline{\Box\Box}\varphi$ and transitive frames. Many more adequacy results of this kind are known. Hence, in operator modal logic we are interested in sets of frames that allow us to vary the interpretation of the contingent vocabulary arbitrarily without losing the validity of a certain sentence or sentence schema.

Also, in possible-worlds semantics for modal predicates we are interested not in frames where we can finesse a suitable $\Box$-interpretation by cleverly choosing a valuation first; rather we want to know for which frames we can *always* get a PW-model while being completely free in the choice of the valuation. Thus, we pose what we call the Strong Characterization Problem (in order to distinguish it from the Characterization Problem in Halbach, Leitgeb, and Welch 2003):

STRONG CHARACTERIZATION PROBLEM *Which frames admit a PW-model on every valuation?*

Before tackling this problem, we show that possible-worlds semantics for predicates resembles its counterpart for modal operators in many aspects. Analogous definitions of frames and models for modal operators lead to the so-called *normal* systems of modal logic with the minimal system K (see any of the books on modal logic cited above). These systems are closed under necessitation for $\Box$, and the necessity operator distributes over material implication. For the predicate account, something similar can be shown:

7.4 LEMMA · NORMALITY *Suppose $\langle W, R, V, B\rangle$ is a PW-model, $w \in W$, and φ, ψ sentences of $\mathcal{L}_P$. Then the following hold:*

(i) *If $\langle \mathbb{E}, V(u), B(u)\rangle \vDash \varphi$ for all $u \in W$, then $\langle \mathbb{E}, V(w), B(w)\rangle \vDash \Box\overline{\varphi}$.*

(ii) $\langle \mathbb{E}, V(w), B(w)\rangle \vDash \Box\overline{\varphi \to \psi} \to (\Box\overline{\varphi} \to \Box\overline{\psi})$.

PROOF For the proof of the first claim assume $\langle \mathbb{E}, V(w), B(w)\rangle \vDash \Box\overline{\varphi \to \psi}$ and $\langle \mathbb{E}, V(w), B(w)\rangle \vDash \Box\overline{\varphi}$. By (7.2) we also obtain the following for all v with wRv:

$$\langle \mathbb{E}, V(v), B(v)\rangle \vDash \varphi \to \psi,$$
$$\langle \mathbb{E}, V(v), B(v)\rangle \vDash \varphi.$$

This implies that $\langle \mathbb{E}, V(v), B(v)\rangle \vDash \psi$ for all v with wRv. Consequently, using the other direction of (7.2), we conclude $\langle \mathbb{E}, V(w), B(w)\rangle \vDash \Box\overline{\psi}$. ⊣

Clause (ii) of the lemma says that the axiom schema K on page 82 is satisfied at all worlds in all PW-models. The result can be generalized: not only do we obtain the schema $\Box\overline{\varphi \to \psi} \to (\Box\overline{\varphi} \to \Box\overline{\psi})$ for all sentences φ and ψ, but also the universally quantified principle $\forall x \forall y\big(\Box(x \,\dot{\to}\, y) \to (\Box x \to \Box y)\big)$. Analogous remarks apply to several results below, for instance, to lemma 7.5(i).

Many results on modal principles can be transferred from operator modal logic. We give only two examples. A frame $\langle W, R\rangle$ is said to be *transitive* iff for all v, w, and u in W the following holds:

$$\text{if } vRw \text{ and } wRu, \text{ then } vRu.$$

A frame is *reflexive* iff wRw for all $w \in W$.

7.5 LEMMA

(i) *If a frame $\langle W, R\rangle$ is transitive and $\langle W, R, V, B\rangle$ a* PW*-model on that frame, we have for all sentences φ in $\mathcal{L}_P$ and worlds $w \in W$:*

$$\langle \mathbb{E}, V(w), B(w)\rangle \models \Box\overline{\varphi} \to \Box\overline{\Box\overline{\varphi}}.$$

(ii) *If a frame $\langle W, R\rangle$ is reflexive and $\langle W, R, V, B\rangle$ a* PW*-model on that frame, we have for all sentences φ in $\mathcal{L}_P$ and worlds $w \in W$:*

$$\langle \mathbb{E}, V(w), B(w)\rangle \models \Box\overline{\varphi} \to \varphi.$$

We skip the proofs. The second claim is somewhat frivolous, because no reflexive frame admits a PW-model, as is shown in the next section.

7.2 The Paradoxes Revisited

The paradoxes show that certain frames do not admit a PW-model on any valuation. We do not begin with the most general result, but rather show how certain paradoxes from the previous chapter translate into proofs establishing that certain frames do not admit a PW-model. When we say that a frame does not admit a PW-model, we mean that it does not admit a PW-model on *any* valuation.

For our first example, which corresponds to the liar paradox, we consider a frame $\langle W_1, R_1\rangle$ with exactly one element w in W_1; this world sees itself, that is, wR_1w. This frame can be pictured in the following way:

7.6 THEOREM · LIAR PARADOX *The frame $\langle W_1, R_1\rangle$ does not admit a* PW-*model.*

Strictly speaking, talking about *the* frame $\langle W_1, R_1\rangle$ is not correct. Here w is not a specific object and the result is proved for any singleton W_1. But obviously it does not matter what w and worlds in general are. 'Up to isomorphism', as mathematicians say, there is only one frame that has the graph above. Thus, we will continue to talk as if there were only one such frame.

PROOF We give this proof is great detail as an example Suppose that $\langle W_1, R_1\rangle$ admits a PW-model $\langle W_1, R_1, V_1, B_1\rangle$. There is a liar sentence γ with $\mathsf{E} \vdash \gamma \leftrightarrow \neg\Box\overline{\gamma}$. The existence of such a sentence γ is guaranteed by the diagonalization lemma 5.12, and the sentence from the proof of theorem 6.1 can be used as γ. By the soundness lemma 5.16, we have

$$\langle \mathbb{E}, V_1(w), B_1(w)\rangle \vDash \gamma \leftrightarrow \neg\Box\overline{\gamma}. \tag{7.3}$$

We show that both $\langle \mathbb{E}, V_1(w), B_1(w)\rangle \vDash \gamma$ and $\langle \mathbb{E}, V_1(w), B_1(w)\rangle \nvDash \gamma$ lead to a contradiction.

Case 1. If $\langle \mathbb{E}, V_1(w), B_1(w)\rangle \vDash \gamma$, then by the normality lemma 7.4(i) we have also $\langle \mathbb{E}, V_1(w), B_1(w)\rangle \vDash \Box\overline{\gamma}$ because w is the only world in W_1. The assumption, however, implies also $\langle \mathbb{E}, V_1(w), B_1(w)\rangle \vDash \neg\Box\overline{\gamma}$. This is a contradiction.

Case 2. $\langle \mathbb{E}, V_1(w), B_1(w)\rangle \vDash \neg\gamma$ implies $\langle \mathbb{E}, V_1(w), B_1(w)\rangle \vDash \Box\overline{\gamma}$, which in turn yields $\langle \mathbb{E}, V_1(w), B_1(w)\rangle \vDash \gamma$ by (7.2) because wR_1w. ⊣

In order to visualize this proof in a diagram, consider the diagram for the first case:

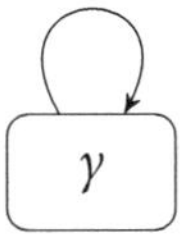

By writing γ in the box for the world we indicate that γ holds at that world. Then (7.3) yields also $\neg\Box\overline{\gamma}$ at w.

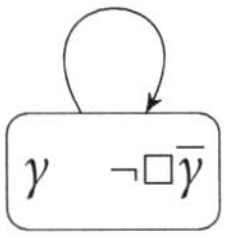

The sentence γ holds at all worlds that can be seen from w – which is only w itself. This allows us to add $\Box\overline{\gamma}$:

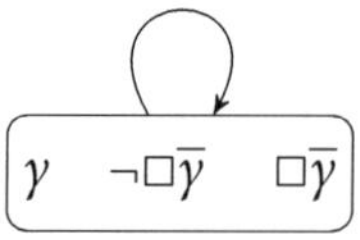

Thus, we have a contradiction at the world w. The other case can be visualized in a similar fashion.

In general, there are the following rules for refuting the existence of a PW-model on a frame by a diagram. Assume that a diagram is drawn as above. The worlds are the nodes in this diagram. If a sentence is true at a world, you may write this sentence in the box corresponding to this world.

(i) At every world every theorem of E is true.

(ii) A sentence φ is true at w, if φ follows in E from some sentences true at w.

(iii) A sentence $\forall x\, \varphi(x)$ is true at w, if $\varphi(\overline{e})$ is true at w for all expressions e. The soundness of this rule follows from lemma 5.15.

(iv) A sentence $\Box\overline{\varphi}$ is true at w, if φ is true at all worlds seen from w, that is, if φ holds at all nodes for which there are arrows from w.

We shall now turn to further examples. Montague's theorem is a generalization of the liar paradox.

7.7 EXAMPLE · MONTAGUE'S PARADOX *If $\langle W, R\rangle$ admits a PW-model (on some valuation), then $\langle W, R\rangle$ is not reflexive.*

The trivial proof resembles Montague's proof showing that the predicate version of the modal system T is inconsistent. The (operator) modal system T is a normal modal system with the characteristic axiom schema $\Box\varphi \to \varphi$. It is very well known that T is valid on all reflexive frames (see any of the books on modal logic mentioned above).

PROOF Assume that there is a PW-model $\langle W_2, R_2, V_2, B_2\rangle$ with a reflexive frame $\langle W_2, R_2\rangle$, that is, with wR_2w for all $w \in W_2$. Pick an arbitrary world $w \in W_2$ and let γ be the liar sentence as in (7.3) of the previous proof.

If $\langle \mathbb{E}, V_2(w), B_2(w)\rangle \vDash \neg\gamma$, then $\langle \mathbb{E}, V_2(w), B_2(w)\rangle \vDash \Box\overline{\gamma}$ by the choice of γ. From $\langle \mathbb{E}, V_2(w), B_2(w)\rangle \vDash \Box\overline{\gamma}$ and wRw it follows that $\langle \mathbb{E}, V_2(w), B_2(w)\rangle \vDash$

γ. Thus, the assumption $\langle\mathbb{E}, V_2(w), B_2(w)\rangle \vDash \neg\gamma$ yields a contradiction and we must have $\langle\mathbb{E}, V_2(w), B_2(w)\rangle \vDash \gamma$ for *all* worlds $w \in W_2$, because w was arbitrary.

Since W_2 is not empty, there must be $w \in W_2$ with $\langle\mathbb{E}, V_2(w), B_2(w)\rangle \vDash \gamma$. Because γ is a liar sentence, we also have $\langle\mathbb{E}, V_2(w), B_2(w)\rangle \vDash \neg\Box\overline{\gamma}$. Hence, there must be a world $v \in W_2$ such that $V_2(v) \vDash \neg\gamma$. But it has already been shown that there is no such world. ⊣

The arguments showing that a given frame does not admit a PW-model proceed by diagonal arguments. In the above examples we employed the liar sentence. The next examples require slightly more complex diagonal sentences, as in the possible-worlds version of the postcard paradox:

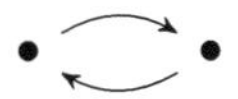

7.8 EXAMPLE *The frame where 'two worlds see each other' displayed above does not admit a PW-model.*

The existence of a suitable $\Box$-interpretation can be ruled out by considering a sentence satisfying $\mathsf{E} \vdash \gamma \leftrightarrow \neg\Box\overline{\Box\overline{\gamma}}$. The existence of such a sentence follows from the diagonal lemma as in theorem 6.7.

This example can be generalized in the obvious way. For instance, the frame with the diagram

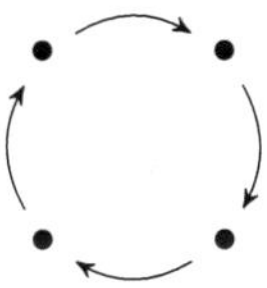

can be shown to admit no PW-model by considering a sentence satisfying

$$\mathsf{E} \vdash \gamma \leftrightarrow \neg\Box\overline{\Box\overline{\Box\overline{\Box\overline{\gamma}}}}.$$

For each n, we can employ a different instance of the diagonal lemma to refute the existence of a PW-model for a loop of length n.

As in the examples above, various inconsistency results for rules and axioms for $\Box$ can be turned into proofs showing that certain frames do not admit PW-models. The results can be used to visualize paradoxes: the liar paradox shows that a frame which is just a simple loop does not admit a PW-model; Montague's paradox shows that no reflexive frame admits a PW-model; and so on. All negative results so far rule out that circular frames admit PW-models. In none of the frames considered so far was there a 'dead end', that is, a world that does not see any world. In all the frames above, every world is in a loop. Therefore, one might suspect that somehow circularity is at the root of paradox. In the next example we consider a simple frame with one dead end. Thus, not all worlds in the frame are in a loop.

7.9 EXAMPLE *The frame 'one world sees itself and one other world' does not admit a PW-model.*

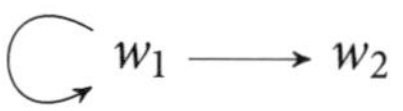

We call the frame $\langle W_3, R_3 \rangle$.

PROOF For the proof, we employ again the diagonal lemma applied to the formula $\Box \mathsf{x} \rightarrow \Box(\overline{\neg}\,\hat{}\,\mathsf{x})$, which gives us a sentence γ with the following property:

$$\mathsf{E} \vdash \gamma \leftrightarrow (\Box\overline{\gamma} \rightarrow \Box\overline{\neg\gamma}).$$

Assume that this frame admits a PW-model $\langle W_3, R_3, V_3, B_3 \rangle$ and thus the following holds:

$$\big\langle \mathbb{E}, V_3(w), B_3(w) \big\rangle \vDash \gamma \leftrightarrow (\Box\overline{\gamma} \rightarrow \Box\overline{\neg\gamma}) \quad \text{for all worlds } w \in W_3.$$

The world w_2 does not see any world. Therefore, we have $\big\langle \mathbb{E}, V_3(w_2), B_3(w_2) \big\rangle \vDash \Box\overline{\varphi}$ for all sentences φ. In particular, we have $\big\langle \mathbb{E}, V_3(w_2), B_3(w_2) \big\rangle \vDash \Box\overline{\neg\gamma}$ and therefore also $\big\langle \mathbb{E}, V_3(w_2), B_3(w_2) \big\rangle \vDash \Box\overline{\gamma} \rightarrow \Box\overline{\neg\gamma}$ and consequently, by the choice of γ, $\big\langle \mathbb{E}, V_3(w_2), B_3(w_2) \big\rangle \vDash \gamma$. This yields the following diagram:

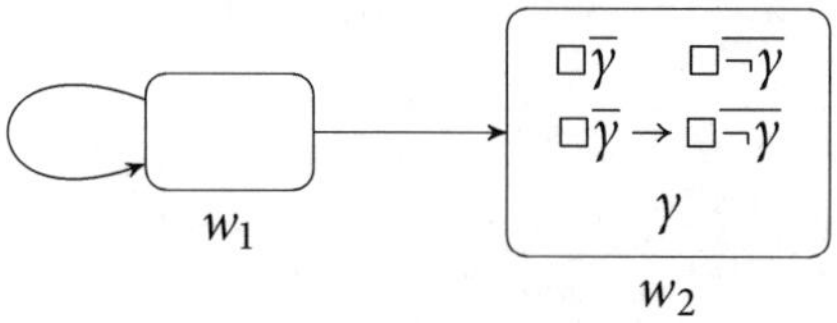

Now we distinguish two cases:

Case 1. $\big\langle \mathbb{E}, V_3(w_1), B_3(w_1) \big\rangle \vDash \gamma$. Then $\big\langle \mathbb{E}, V_3(w_1), B_3(w_1) \big\rangle \vDash \Box\overline{\gamma} \rightarrow \Box\overline{\neg\gamma}$ obtains. Since γ holds at both worlds, we also have $\big\langle \mathbb{E}, V_3(w_1), B_3(w_1) \big\rangle \vDash \Box\overline{\gamma}$. This yields the following diagram:

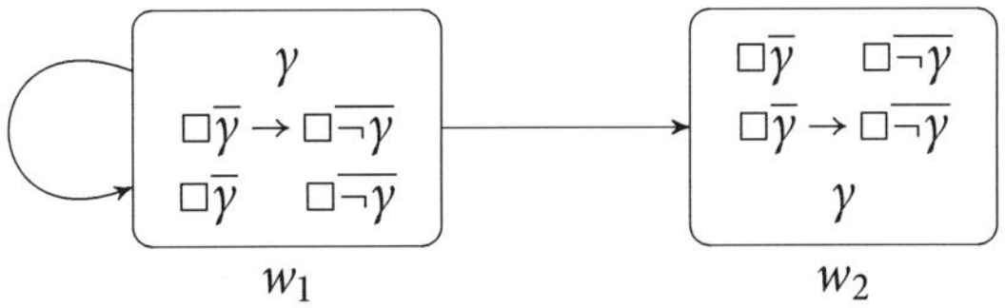

The last formula in the left box, that is, in w_1, is an application of modus ponens. But $\langle \mathbb{E}, V_3(w_1), B_3(w_1) \rangle \models \Box\overline{\neg\gamma}$ contradicts $\langle \mathbb{E}, V_3(w_1), B_3(w_1) \rangle \models \gamma$ (and also $\langle \mathbb{E}, V_3(w_2), B_3(w_2) \rangle \models \gamma$).

Case 2. $\langle \mathbb{E}, V_3(w_1), B_3(w_1) \rangle \models \neg\gamma$. This case is easy, because w_2 does not have to be considered. From the choice of γ we conclude $\langle \mathbb{E}, V_3(w_1), B_3(w_1) \rangle \models \neg(\Box\overline{\gamma} \rightarrow \Box\overline{\neg\gamma})$ and thus $\langle \mathbb{E}, V_3(w_1), B_3(w_1) \rangle \models \Box\overline{\gamma}$.

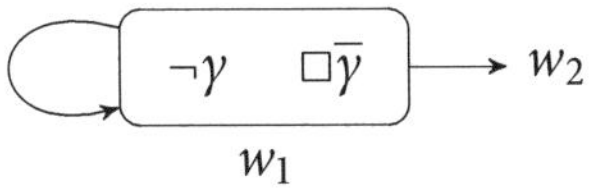

This is impossible, as $\langle \mathbb{E}, V_3(w_1), B_3(w_1) \rangle \models \Box\overline{\gamma}$ implies $\langle \mathbb{E}, V_3(w_1), B_3(w_1) \rangle \models \gamma$, because $w_1 R_3 w_1$. ⊣

The frame $\langle W_3, R_3 \rangle$ still involves some circularity, namely the loop attached to the first world w_1. Hence, the question arises whether all frames that do not admit a PW-model contain some loop. Here is an example of a frame that does not involve any loop, but still does not admit a PW-model. The result is a possible-worlds counterpart of McGee's ω-inconsistency theorem 6.31.

7.10 EXAMPLE *The frame* $\langle \omega, \mathrm{Pre} \rangle$ *does not admit a* PW*-model. Here* ω *is the set of all natural numbers and* Pre *is the relation that obtains between* n *and* k *iff* n *is the predecessor of* k*. Hence every world* n *sees* $n+1$*, but no other world.*

The frame $\langle \omega, \mathrm{Pre} \rangle$ can be displayed by the following diagram:

$$0 \longrightarrow 1 \longrightarrow 2 \longrightarrow \cdots$$

PROOF Assume there is a PW-model $\langle \omega, \mathrm{Pre}, V_{\mathrm{M}}, B_{\mathrm{M}} \rangle$ for $\langle \omega, \mathrm{Pre} \rangle$. In the proof of theorem 6.31, we established the existence of a sentence σ with the following property:

$$\text{(6.11)} \qquad \mathsf{E} \vdash \sigma \leftrightarrow \neg\forall n \forall z \big(\gamma(n, z, \overline{\sigma}) \rightarrow \Box z\big).$$

Every sentence provable in E is true at all worlds. Now let $k \in \omega$ and assume $\langle \mathbb{E}, V_M(k), B_M(k) \rangle \models \neg\sigma$. As in the proof of McGee's ω-inconsistency theorem, we use (6.11) and instantiate the universally quantified n with 0 (as in step 6.12):

$$\langle \mathbb{E}, V_M(k), B_M(k) \rangle \models \Box\overline{\sigma}.$$

Since (6.11) holds at all worlds, we also have the following for all $k \in \omega$:

$$\langle \mathbb{E}, V_M(k), B_M(k) \rangle \models \Box\overline{\sigma \leftrightarrow \neg\forall n \forall z \big(\gamma(n, z, \overline{\sigma}) \to \Box z\big)}.$$

As in the proof of McGee's theorem, we can use this observation to derive

$$\langle \mathbb{E}, V_M(k), B_M(k) \rangle \models \Box\overline{\sigma} \to \sigma,$$

that is, line (6.13) in the proof of theorem 6.31. Consequently, σ holds at all worlds k:

$$\langle \mathbb{E}, V_M(k), B_M(k) \rangle \models \sigma. \tag{7.4}$$

Each world k sees only its successor world. Therefore, we have the following for all worlds k and sentences φ:

$$\langle \mathbb{E}, V_M(k), B_M(k) \rangle \models \Box\overline{\varphi} \quad \text{iff} \quad \langle \mathbb{E}, V_M(k+1), B_M(k+1) \rangle \models \varphi. \tag{7.5}$$

Thus, at world k the predicate $\Box$ applies exactly to the sentences that are true at world $k+1$.

Since $\langle \mathbb{E}, V_M(k), B_M(k) \rangle \models \sigma$ for all $k \in \omega$, we also have for all $i \in \omega$ the following with i times iterated $\Box$ symbols:

$$\langle \mathbb{E}, V_M(k), B_M(k) \rangle \models \Box \overline{\cdots \Box\overline{\sigma}}.$$

This allows us to conclude for all k and n:

$$\langle \mathbb{E}, V_M(k), B_M(k) \rangle \models \forall z \big(\gamma(\underline{n}, z, \overline{\sigma}) \to \Box z\big).$$

Since we are dealing with standard models, this yields the following claim by lemma 5.15:

$$\langle \mathbb{E}, V_M(k), B_M(k) \rangle \models \forall n \forall z \big(\gamma(n, z, \overline{\sigma}) \to \Box z\big).$$

From (7.4) and (6.11) above, we also get the following for all k:

$$\langle \mathbb{E}, V_M(k), B_M(k) \rangle \models \neg\forall n \forall z \big(\gamma(n, z, \overline{\sigma}) \to \Box z\big).$$

In this way we obtain a contradiction and have thus refuted the existence of a valuation V_M. ⊣

The same argument works also without a starting point 0, that is, for $\langle \mathbb{Z}, \mathrm{Pre} \rangle$, where $\mathbb{Z}$ is the set of the integers. The transitive versions $\langle \omega, < \rangle$ of $\langle \mathbb{Z}, < \rangle$ can be shown not to admit a PW-model by an argument resembling the proof of Yablo's paradox. However, Hsiung (2021) observed that the liar sentence suffices in this case:

7.11 THEOREM *The frames $\langle \omega, < \rangle$ and $\langle \mathbb{Z}, < \rangle$ do not admit* PW*-models. Here $<$ is the usual 'smaller than' relation on the integers.*

The frame $\langle \omega, < \rangle$ can be displayed by the following diagram:

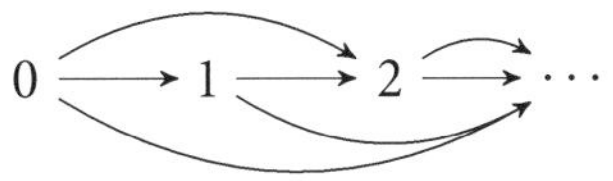

PROOF Assume there is a PW-model $\langle \omega, <, V_Y, B_Y \rangle$ for $\langle \omega, < \rangle$. For the liar sentence γ the following obtains at all worlds n:

$$\langle \mathbb{E}, V_Y(n), B_Y(n) \rangle \vDash \gamma \leftrightarrow \neg \Box \overline{\gamma}.$$

We claim that there is a k with $\langle \mathbb{E}, V_Y(k), B_Y(k) \rangle \vDash \neg\gamma$. If, to the contrary, we had

$$\langle \mathbb{E}, V_Y(n), B_Y(n) \rangle \vDash \gamma$$

and thus $\langle \mathbb{E}, V_Y(n), B_Y(n) \rangle \vDash \neg\Box\overline{\gamma}$ for all $n \in \omega$, there would still have to be a $k > n$ with

$$\langle \mathbb{E}, V_Y(k), B_Y(k) \rangle \vDash \neg\gamma.$$

Fix such a world $k \in \omega$. Because γ is a diagonal sentence of $\neg\Box\overline{x}$, this implies $\langle \mathbb{E}, V_Y(k), B_Y(k) \rangle \vDash \Box\overline{\gamma}$. Consequently, all $i > k$ will have to satisfy

$$\langle \mathbb{E}, V_Y(i), B_Y(i) \rangle \vDash \gamma$$

and thus also $\langle \mathbb{E}, V_Y(i), B_Y(i) \rangle \vDash \neg\Box\overline{\gamma}$. Hence, contrary to what we just derived, there would have to be $i > k$ with $\langle \mathbb{E}, V_Y(i), B_Y(i) \rangle \vDash \neg\gamma$. ⊣

In none of the proofs so far did the valuation play any role. We showed that for frames with certain properties no suitable □-interpretation can be found. For the proofs, we started from the assumption that a frame has a PW-model with some valuation and some □-interpretation and then derived a contradiction from this assumption. In section 7.4 we will make use of specific valuations, which will enable us to prove a very general negative result.

7.3 Frames with Possible-Worlds Models

In section 7.2 we showed for many frames that they do not admit a PW-model; and so far we have not seen a single frame that *does* admit a PW-model. First, we show that the frame with exactly one world that is a dead end admits a PW-model on any valuation. (As before, a dead end is a world that cannot see any world.)

7.12 EXAMPLE *The frame $\langle \{w\}, \varnothing \rangle$ admits a PW-model on every valuation.*

In what follows, $\mathcal{L}_p^S$ is the set of all *sentences* of $\mathcal{L}_p$. We set $B(w) = \mathcal{L}_p^S$. Then it is not hard to see that $\langle W, R, V, B \rangle$ is a PW-model for any V. There are only two such PW-models, of course. They differ in the truth value of p. Generally, also in other frames, if $\langle W, R, V, B \rangle$ is any PW-model and $w \in W$ a dead end, then $B(w)$ must be the set of all $\mathcal{L}_p$-sentences.

7.13 EXAMPLE *The frame 'one world sees another world' admits a PW-model on every valuation.*

The frame has the following diagram:

$$1 \longrightarrow 0$$

PROOF Let any valuation V be given. For the dead end 0 we set $B(0) = \mathcal{L}_p^S$ and for 1 we define

$$B(1) := \left\{ \varphi \in \mathcal{L}_p^S \colon \langle \mathbb{E}, V(0), B(0) \rangle \vDash \varphi \right\}.$$

Then $\langle W, R, V, B \rangle$ is easily seen to be a PW-model. ⊣

In any PW-model on this frame, $\Box$ is interpreted at 1 as a truth predicate for 0. That is, we obtain the following for all sentences φ, as we observed in the proof of example 7.10, step (7.5) already:

$$\langle \mathbb{E}, V(1), B(1) \rangle \vDash \Box\overline{\varphi} \quad \text{iff} \quad \langle \mathbb{E}, V(0), B(0) \rangle \vDash \varphi.$$

If this is iterated, we obtain a PW-model that captures the revision theory of truth for finite stages, in the sense of Belnap and Gupta (1993). The frame has the following diagram:

$$\cdots \longrightarrow 2 \longrightarrow 1 \longrightarrow 0$$

By Suc we denote the relation $\{\langle k, n\rangle : k = n+1\}$ on the set ω of the natural numbers.

7.14 EXAMPLE *The frame $\langle \omega, \mathrm{Suc}\rangle$ admits a PW-model on every valuation.*

For the proof, we just iterate the construction above. At every level k above 0 the predicate $\Box$ is interpreted as the truth predicate for the previous world $k-1$. Again we can assign any truth value to p at every world k. Of course, the choice of this truth value $V(k)$ will then influence $B(n)$ for $n < k$.

Many observations from revision semantics apply to this PW-model. For instance, if γ is a liar sentence with $\mathsf{E} \vdash \gamma \leftrightarrow \neg\Box\overline{\gamma}$ and $\langle \omega, \mathrm{Suc}, V, B\rangle$ is a PW-model, then the truth value of γ will flip at every stage. Since 0 is a dead end, $\Box\overline{\gamma}$ holds at 0, and therefore we have the following:

$$\begin{aligned} \langle \mathbb{E}, V(0), B(0)\rangle &\vDash \neg\gamma, \\ \langle \mathbb{E}, V(1), B(1)\rangle &\vDash \gamma, \\ \langle \mathbb{E}, V(2), B(2)\rangle &\vDash \neg\gamma, \\ \langle \mathbb{E}, V(3), B(3)\rangle &\vDash \gamma, \\ &\vdots \end{aligned}$$

We can also define a PW-model if we use the transitive closure of Suc, that is, the ordering $>$. The frame $\langle \omega, >\rangle$ admits a PW-model, where $>$ is the 'bigger than' relation on the nonnegative integers. As long as there is no infinite chain $w_1, w_2, w_2 \ldots$ of worlds such that $w_1 R w_2$, $w_2 R w_3$, and so on, the frame admits a PW-model. The absence of such a chain is captured by the following definition:

7.15 DEFINITION A frame $\langle W, R\rangle$ is *converse well-founded* (or 'Noetherian') iff for every non-empty $M \subseteq W$ there is a $w \in M$ that is R-maximal in M.

More formally, a frame $\langle W, R\rangle$ is converse well-founded iff the following condition obtains:

$$\forall M \subseteq W \big(M \neq \varnothing \rightarrow \exists w \in M\ \forall v \in M\ \neg wRv\big).$$

The frames $\langle \omega, >\rangle$ and $\langle \omega, \mathrm{Suc}\rangle$ are converse well-founded; the frames $\langle \omega, <\rangle$ and $\langle \omega, \mathrm{Pre}\rangle$, and all frames with loops, are not.

7.16 LEMMA *Every converse well-founded frame $\langle W, R\rangle$ admits a PW-model on every valuation.*

PROOF Let a valuation V be given. Then a $\Box$-interpretation B can be defined by transfinite recursion on the well-founded relation R^{-1} (the inverse of R). For each $w \in W$ the extension of $\Box$ at w is defined as the set of all sentences that hold at all worlds u that can be seen from w:

$$B(w) := \{ \varphi \in \mathcal{L}_p^S : \forall u(wRu \to \langle \mathbb{E}, V(u), B(u) \rangle \models \varphi) \}.$$

The extension $B(w)$depends on the extensions $B(u)$ with wRu, and thus $B(w)$ is defined is defined by transfinite recursion. The principle of transfinite induction guarantees that there is exactly one function B that satisfies the equation above. This principle applies to all well-founded relations, and to R^{-1} in particular. Here it is applied in the following way: Assume B were not uniquely determined for some elements $w \in W$, and let M be the set of all such w. Then there is an R^{-1}-minimal (that is, an R-maximal) element $w_{\max}$ in M, because R is converse well-founded. However, all u with $w_{\max}Ru$ are not in M and thus the sets $B(u)$ are uniquely determined. $B(w_{\max})$ then has to be the unique intersection of all $B(u)$ with $w_{\max}Ru$. Therefore, $B(w_{\max})$ is uniquely determined too, contrary to the assumption. ⊣

7.4 The Strong Characterization Problem

The semantic version of Montague's paradox, example 7.7, implies the semantic version of the liar paradox, theorem 7.6: that reflexive frames do not admit PW-models implies, in particular, that a single world that exactly sees itself does not admit a PW-model. This implication among semantic results mirrors the strength of the original paradoxes in their original syntactic versions (theorems 6.1 and 6.5): Montague's paradox implies the liar paradox, but the converse direction does not hold (in a sense we do not make precise here). There are more such implications.

In the present section we search for the most general limitative result, the most general paradox of this kind. It is difficult to give a precise formulation of the question in purely proof-theoretic terms. Here we give the question a semantic shape and return to what we called the Strong Characterization Problem: Which frames do for all valuations not admit PW-models?

We have already ruled out circularity (the presence of loops) as this condition for the non-existence of a PW-model. It is a sufficient condition, because no frame with a loop admits a PW-model; but it is not necessary, because there are frames such as $\langle \omega, \mathrm{Pre} \rangle$ from example 7.10 that do not contain any circularity but still do not admit a PW-model on any valuation. In what follows we give a complete answer to the Strong Characterization Problem by proving the converse of lemma 7.16. Thus, a frame admits a PW-model on every valuation iff it is converse well-founded. We take this to be further support for the claim that the source of a large set of paradoxes is converse ill-foundedness and not circularity. Circularity is merely a special case of converse ill-foundedness.

7.17 THEOREM · STRONG CHARACTERIZATION THEOREM *A frame admits a* PW*-model on every valuation iff it is converse well-founded.*

The right-to-left direction is lemma 7.16. For the left-to-right direction the presence of 'contingent' vocabulary – in our case the sentence letter p – is crucial. Halbach, Leitgeb, and Welch (2003) showed that the left-to-right direction fails in the absence of contingent vocabulary that can be interpreted arbitrarily at each world.

We first give the proof idea. If the frame is transitive, Löb's theorem

$$\Box\overline{\Box\overline{\varphi} \to \varphi} \to \Box\overline{\varphi}$$

will hold at any world. This follows from lemma 7.5(i), which gives us $\Box\overline{\varphi} \to \Box\overline{\Box\overline{\varphi}}$, and Löb's theorem, that is, theorem 6.11.

From operator modal logic we know that Löb's theorem and converse well-foundedness are closely related. The propositional modal system GL (for 'Gödel–Löb') is an extension of the minimal normal modal logic K with what is called the 'Löb axiom', which is just the formula above with an operator instead of a predicate.[3] The system GL rose to great prominence because it captures the 'modal' (in the operator sense) properties of the canonical provability predicate in any sufficiently strong system, in particular, in Peano arithmetic. It is known that GL is valid in all transitive converse well-founded frames. We can use almost the same argument as used in the proof of that result to show that, if we can prove the predicate counterpart of the GL axioms, a frame that admits a PW-model on each valuation must be converse well-founded. The problem now is that we have used the assumption that the frame is transitive. To dispense with this assumption we

[3]The monographs (Boolos 1993) and (Smoryński 1985) deal with GL and its properties in depth. For a concise overview, see (Verbrugge 2017).

prove Löb's theorem not for $\Box$ – which may be impossible – but for a new predicate $\Box^*$, which is related to the transitive closure of R in the same way $\Box$ relates to R. As usual, the transitive closure of R is the relation obtained by taking the intersection of all transitive relations containing R, which itself can be shown to be transitive. The transitive closure of R is denoted R^*.

After having sketched the plan, we fill in the details. We will start by defining $\Box^*$. In (6.10) on page 110, we defined a formula $\gamma(\mathrm{w}, \mathrm{z}, \mathrm{y})$ with the following property:

$$\text{(6.10)}\quad \mathsf{E} \vdash \forall n \forall \mathrm{z} \forall \mathrm{y} \Big(\gamma(n, \mathrm{z}, \mathrm{y}) \leftrightarrow \exists k \big(n = k^\frown \underline{1} \wedge \mathrm{z} = \overline{\forall \mathrm{z} (\gamma(\dot{k}, \mathrm{z}, \dot{\mathrm{y}}) \to \Box \mathrm{z})} \big) \vee (n = \underline{0} \wedge \mathrm{z} = \mathrm{y}) \Big).$$

The next lemma is a semantic counterpart to lemma 6.32 in the proof of McGee's ω-inconsistency theorem. For a given sentence φ, we define $\Box^n \overline{\varphi}$ inductively in the metalanguage:

$$\Box^0 \overline{\varphi} := \Box \overline{\varphi},$$
$$\Box^{n+1} \overline{\varphi} := \Box \overline{\Box^n \overline{\varphi}}.$$

The sentences $\Box^n \overline{\varphi}$ are all of the form $\Box \overline{e}$ where $\overline{e}$ is the quotation constant for some sentence e. In particular, the definition is not in the object language and thus the variable n is also metalinguistic and cannot be quantified over in the object language.

7.18 LEMMA *For every* PW*-model* $\langle W, R, V, B \rangle$*, every* $w \in W$*, and all* $n \in \mathbb{N}$*,*

$$\langle \mathbb{E}, V(w), B(w) \rangle \vDash \forall \mathrm{z} \big(\gamma(\underline{n}, \mathrm{z}, \overline{\varphi}) \to \Box \mathrm{z} \big) \leftrightarrow \Box^n \overline{\varphi}.$$

The proof is by induction on n, similar to that of lemma 6.32. We define $\Box^*$ as follows:

$$\text{(7.6)}\qquad \Box^* \mathrm{y} := \forall n \forall \mathrm{z} \big(\gamma(n, \mathrm{z}, \mathrm{y}) \to \Box \mathrm{z} \big).$$

Thus, $\Box^* \overline{\sigma}$ expresses at a world w that σ holds at all worlds that are R^*-accessible from w. This is the content of the following lemma:

7.19 LEMMA *For all* φ *in* $\mathcal{L}_p^{\mathrm{S}}$*, all* PW*-models* $\langle W, R, V, B \rangle$*, and all* $w \in W$*,*

$$\langle \mathbb{E}, V(w), B(w) \rangle \vDash \Box^* \overline{\varphi} \quad \textit{iff} \quad \textit{for all } v \textit{ with } wR^*v\text{: } \langle \mathbb{E}, V(v), B(v) \rangle \vDash \varphi.$$

PROOF For $n \in \mathbb{N}$, we write $w_1 R^n w_2$ to abbreviate that there are $v_0, v_1, \ldots, v_n$ such that $v_0 = w_1$, $v_n = w_2$, and $v_k R v_{k+1}$ for all $k < n$. In particular, $w_1 R^1 w_2$ iff $w_1 R w_2$. By induction on n and using (7.2) on page 124, it can be shown that the following holds for all $n \geq 1$:

$$\text{(7.7)}\quad \langle \mathbb{E}, V(w), B(w) \rangle \vDash \Box^n \overline{\varphi} \quad \text{iff} \quad \text{for all } v \text{ with } wR^n v\text{: } \langle \mathbb{E}, V(v), B(v) \rangle \vDash \varphi.$$

It is not hard to see that w_1 and w_2 are related via the transitive closure of R iff w_2 can be reached from w_1 in finitely many R-steps. More formally, $w_1 R^* w_2$ iff, for some n, $w_1 R^n w_2$. This observation is used in the last step below:

$$\begin{array}{lll}
\langle \mathbb{E}, V(w), B(w) \rangle \vDash \Box^* \overline{\varphi} & & \\
\text{iff} \ \ \langle \mathbb{E}, V(w), B(w) \rangle \vDash \forall n \forall z \big(\gamma(n, z, \overline{\varphi}) \to \Box z\big) & & (7.6) \\
\text{iff} \ \ \text{for all } n \in \omega\text{: } \langle \mathbb{E}, V(w), B(w) \rangle \vDash \forall z \big(\gamma(\underline{n}, z, \overline{\varphi}) \to \Box z\big) & & (5.15) \\
\text{iff} \ \ \text{for all } n \in \omega\text{: } \langle \mathbb{E}, V(w), B(w) \rangle \vDash \Box^n \overline{\varphi} & & \text{lemma 7.18} \\
\text{iff} \ \ \text{for all } n \in \omega \text{ and } v \text{ with } wR^n v\text{: } \langle \mathbb{E}, V(v), B(v) \rangle \vDash \varphi & & (7.7) \\
\text{iff} \ \ \text{for all } v \text{ with } wR^* v\text{: } \langle \mathbb{E}, V(v), B(v) \rangle \vDash \varphi & & \dashv
\end{array}$$

7.20 LEMMA *For all $\mathcal{L}_P$-sentences φ and ψ and PW-models $\langle W, R, V, B \rangle$ the following hold:*

(i) *If $\langle \mathbb{E}, V(w), B(w) \rangle \vDash \varphi$ for all $w \in W$, then $\langle \mathbb{E}, V(w), B(w) \rangle \vDash \Box^* \overline{\varphi}$.*

(ii) $\langle \mathbb{E}, V(w), B(w) \rangle \vDash \Box^* \overline{\varphi \to \psi} \to (\Box^* \overline{\varphi} \to \Box^* \overline{\psi})$.

(iii) $\langle \mathbb{E}, V(w), B(w) \rangle \vDash \Box^* \overline{\varphi} \to \Box^* \overline{\Box^* \overline{\varphi}}$.

(iv) $\langle \mathbb{E}, V(w), B(w) \rangle \vDash \Box^* \overline{\Box^* \overline{\varphi} \to \varphi} \to \Box^* \overline{\varphi}$.

Lemma 7.19 yields (i) and (ii), and (iii) follows from the above by lemma 7.5. Clauses (i)–(iii) show that $\Box^*$ satisfies the conditions for $\Box$ in theorem 6.11, which gives Löb's theorem, that is, (iv).

7.21 LEMMA *The transitive closure R^* of the accessibility relation R of any frame that admits a PW-model on every valuation is converse well-founded.*

In what follows we say that a relation R is converse ill-founded iff it is not converse well-founded.

PROOF The proof idea is well known from the operator modal system GL (see, e.g., Boolos 1993, pp. 75f.). Assume that there is a frame $\langle W, R\rangle$ such that $\langle W, R^*\rangle$ is converse ill-founded. We define a valuation V and show that the assumption that there is a PW-model $\langle W, R, V, B\rangle$ leads to a contradiction, because we would have $\langle \mathbb{E}, V(u), B(u)\rangle \nvDash \Box^*\overline{\Box^*\overline{p} \to p} \to \Box^*\overline{p}$ for the sentence letter p of $\mathcal{L}_p$ for some $u \in W$, which contradicts the previous lemma.

Since $\langle W, R^*\rangle$ is converse ill-founded, there is a non-empty set $M \subseteq W$ without an R^*-maximal element. Define a valuation V as follows:

$$V(w)(p) := \begin{cases} \text{true}, & \text{if } w \notin M, \\ \text{false}, & \text{if } w \in M. \end{cases}$$

Assume now that for this V there is a $\Box$-interpretation B such that $\langle W, R, V, B\rangle$ is a PW-model. Since M is non-empty, there is a $u \in M$. We show

(i) $\langle \mathbb{E}, V(u), B(u)\rangle \vDash \Box^*\overline{\Box^*\overline{p} \to p}$,

(ii) $\langle \mathbb{E}, V(u), B(u)\rangle \nvDash \Box^*\overline{p}$.

For the proof of (i) assume uR^*v. Then clause (i) is established by proving that $\langle \mathbb{E}, V(v), B(v)\rangle \vDash \Box^*\overline{p} \to p$. We distinguish two cases:

Case 1. $v \in M$. Since v is not R^*-maximal in M, there must be still another $w \in M$ with vR^*w. Thus, $\langle \mathbb{E}, V(w), B(w)\rangle \nvDash p$ and $\langle \mathbb{E}, V(v), B(v)\rangle \nvDash \Box^*\overline{p}$ and therefore $\langle \mathbb{E}, V(v), B(v)\rangle \vDash \Box^*\overline{p} \to p$.

Case 2. $v \notin M$. Then $\langle \mathbb{E}, V(v), B(v)\rangle \vDash p$ and thus $\langle \mathbb{E}, V(v), B(v)\rangle \vDash \Box^*\overline{p} \to p$, too.

For (ii), we observe that there is a $v \in M$ with uR^*v, because u is not R^*-maximal in M. Since $v \in M$, we have $\langle \mathbb{E}, V(v), B(v)\rangle \nvDash p$, which yields (ii).

From (i) and (ii) one can conclude $\langle \mathbb{E}, V(u), B(u)\rangle \nvDash \Box^*\overline{\Box^*\overline{p} \to p} \to \Box^*\overline{p}$. ⊣

This lemma is the only place where we make use of the contingent vocabulary in $\mathcal{L}_p$. Obviously it is crucial to the proof that we can define a valuation that makes p true at all converse well-founded worlds and false at all converse *ill-founded* worlds. Here, a world w is called *converse ill-founded* (in a frame $\langle W, R\rangle$) iff there exists an infinite chain w, w_1, w_2, … of worlds in W such that wRw_1, w_1Rw_2, and so on; otherwise it is converse well-founded. For more information, see (Halbach, Leitgeb, and Welch 2003).

7.22 LEMMA *A frame $\langle W, R\rangle$ is converse well-founded iff its transitive closure $\langle W, R^*\rangle$ is converse well-founded.*

PROOF For the left-to-right direction, assume that the frame $\langle W, R\rangle$ is converse well-founded. Let M be some subset of W. If there is a finite R-path $v_1 R w_1 R w_2 R \ldots R w_n R v_2$ connecting two elements v_1 and v_2 of M, add all elements $w_1, \ldots, w_n$ in the path to M. This gives a set M'. By assumption, $M' \subseteq W$ contains an R-maximal element w. The world w must be an element of the original set M, because it is not between two worlds v_1 and v_2. It is also R^*-maximal in M, because it is R-maximal in M', and M' contains all paths that could be cut short by R^*.

For the converse direction assume that $\langle W, R^*\rangle$ is converse well-founded. That is, every $M \subseteq W$ contains an R^*-maximal element. But any element of M that is R^*-maximal is also R-maximal. Therefore, $\langle W, R\rangle$ is converse well-founded. ⊣

This concludes the proof of the left-to-right direction of the Strong Characterization Theorem: Lemma 7.21 shows that the transitive closure of the accessibility relation of any frame that admits a PW-model on every valuation is converse well-founded. The last lemma then shows that the accessibility relation itself is converse well-founded.

The Strong Characterization Theorem puts the blame for paradox on converse ill-foundedness. This can be compared with Yablo's and Visser's paradoxes, that is, theorem 6.18 and related results. In each case converse ill-foundedness plays a crucial role in generating paradoxes. Of course, Yablo's paradox and the Strong Characterization Theorem seem highly disparate: The former is an inconsistency in a formal deductive system, the latter a limitation on models of a certain kind. Our possible-worlds semantics brings out the connection between these results. It shows how in the end all the paradoxes in section 7.2 can be converted into limitative results on the existence of PW-models and that the Strong Characterization Theorem implies all these limitative results. All evidence points at converse ill-foundedness as the culprit and the root of paradox.

8 An Expressive Theory of Expressions

The language $\mathcal{L}$ of our weak theory of syntax includes a constant for each string of symbols from the language. In the presence of the axioms of E many of these quotation constants are superfluous. The constant $\overline{\forall\overline{\neg}}$ is provably equal to the term $\overline{\forall}{}^\frown\overline{\overline{\neg}}$ by axiom A1 and so to $\overline{\forall}{}^\frown(\mathsf{q}\overline{\neg})$ using A2. In any model of E – whether standard or not – these three terms denote the same expression because equality is interpreted as identity in every model. Thus, in a theorem of E, any occurrence of the term $\overline{\forall\overline{\neg}}$ can be replaced by $\overline{\forall}{}^\frown(\mathsf{q}\overline{\neg})$, and the result remains a theorem of E. A similar replacement can be carried out for occurrences of $\overline{\forall\overline{\neg}}$ within quotation constants. If e is the expression $f\overline{\forall\overline{\neg}}g$, then the quotation constant for e, viz, $\overline{e}$, is provably equal to a term that does not rely on the expression $\overline{\forall\overline{\neg}}$, for instance $\overline{f}{}^\frown\mathsf{q}\big(\overline{\forall}{}^\frown(\mathsf{q}\overline{\neg})\big){}^\frown\overline{g}$. In short, if we designate the term $\overline{\forall}{}^\frown(\mathsf{q}\overline{\neg})$ as expressing the quotation of $\forall\overline{\neg}$ rather than the constant $\overline{\forall\overline{\neg}}$, we have reduced neither the expressive capacity of the language nor the deductive capability of the theory. It should come as no surprise that this method of decomposing quotation constants into terms applies more broadly and permits every quotation constant to be expressed as a term constructed from just the function symbols for concatenation and quotation, and quotation constants for the basic symbols of $\mathcal{L}$, that is, quotation constants for symbols of $\mathcal{L}$ that are not themselves quotation constants.[1] Quotation constants of these basic symbols, and the constant $\underline{0}$ denoting the empty expression, will be referred to as *syntactic constants*.

The argument above should be compared with formal theories of arithmetic where we do not usually introduce a constant for each natural number, because every natural number can be expressed by a closed term built from a single constant denoting 0 and a unary function symbol for successor.[2] For our theory of

[1] We will, in fact, present two translations of $\mathcal{L}$-expressions into the language with just the first level of quotation constants. The translations will agree on the interpretation of quotation constants for expressions in this minimal language but diverge on deeper nesting of quotation. Both translations will preserve provable equality meaning that a quotation constant and its two interpretations are all provably equal in the theory E.

[2] Or constants for 0 and 1 and a binary function for addition.

expressions, concatenation and quotation are the primitive constructors which generate from the syntactic constants of $\mathcal{L}$ terms for all $\mathcal{L}$-expressions. These terms are not uniquely determined. The term $\underline{0}^\frown t$ denotes the same expression as t; likewise, the terms $(r^\frown s)^\frown t$ and $r^\frown(s^\frown t)$. There is also a subtlety with quotation as to whether the quotation of $\bar{\bar{\neg}}$ should be expressed as $\mathsf{q}(\mathsf{q}\bar{\neg})$ or $\bar{\mathsf{q}}^\frown\mathsf{q}\bar{\neg}$. Both terms are provably equal over the axioms of E. These considerations aside, there are naturally arising reductions of the language $\mathcal{L}$ to the language comprising only the basic symbols and syntactic constants. We can then ask whether there is a natural theory of syntax that can be formulated within this simple language that is as expressive as E, in the sense that the translation of each theorem of E to the new language is provable.

The present chapter is devoted to developing such a theory. We present a language $\mathcal{L}^*$ comprising a finite number of basic symbols and their associated quotations. The language contains no further quotation constants. Instead, the infinitely many quotation constants in $\mathcal{L}$ are expressed in $\mathcal{L}^*$ as terms via a reduction of $\mathcal{L}$ to $\mathcal{L}^*$ in the manner described. Within this language, an axiomatic theory of $\mathcal{L}^*$-expressions is defined. The theory, denoted E*, replaces the axiom schemas of E by a finite collection of axioms that define the three basic operations on expressions: concatenation, quotation, and substitution. In the case of concatenation, the universal axioms A4–A6 and A8 of E provide a suitable starting point, but are not sufficient in themselves. To them, we must add axioms corresponding to the unique readability of expressions, namely a means by which assumption 5.2 can be derived as a theorem of E*. The operations of substitution and quotation are expressed entirely by schemas in E. These axiom schemas are replaced by six quantified axioms in E*, from which all instances of the axiom schemas of E are derivable.

These considerations alone do not warrant referring to E* as being more expressive than E. However, the shift to a finite language and the quantified nature of the axioms overcome other limitations of E which become apparent only when we look beyond the paradoxes to the expression of concepts such as provability, denotation, and truth. These particular issues will be touched upon only briefly in this chapter, being the main focus of chapters 9 to 11. The present chapter lays the necessary groundwork for these investigations.

The new language, $\mathcal{L}^*$, is introduced in two stages. First, we explore the sublanguage of $\mathcal{L}$ obtained by dropping all quotation constants except those for basic symbols. This language, which we name $\mathcal{L}^-$, is not finite because it contains the infinitely many variable symbols and a quotation constant for each. Nevertheless, $\mathcal{L}^-$ provides an appropriate starting point to examine the reductions of $\mathcal{L}$ described earlier. We will compare two natural formulations of the theory E in this language and discuss the limitations of both $\mathcal{L}$ and $\mathcal{L}^-$ as languages for formalizing syntax. The reader who wishes to proceed directly to the definition of $\mathcal{L}^*$ can begin in section 8.2, where the language and a refined notion of quotation is presented. The axioms of our 'expressive' theory E^* of expressions, and their immediate consequences, are the subject of sections 8.3 and 8.4. To ease presentation, the axioms are separated into groups according to the main syntactic property they concern: symbols, concatenation, quotation, substitution, and, finally, the axiom schema of induction. The formal reduction of E to E^* is covered in section 8.5.

8.1 Generating Quotations

Consider the following sublanguage of $\mathcal{L}$, which we name $\mathcal{L}^-$, formed from a limited collection of quotation constants:

8.1 DEFINITION The symbols of $\mathcal{L}^-$ are:

(i) all variable symbols of $\mathcal{L}$,

(ii) all connectives, quantifiers, and auxiliary symbols of $\mathcal{L}$,

(iii) all function and predicate symbols of $\mathcal{L}$ and all constants that are not quotation constants,

(iv) the quotation constant $\overline{u}$ for each symbol u in clause (i), (ii), and (iii),

(v) the quotation constant $\underline{0}$.

The symbols in the first three clauses are called the basic symbols of $\mathcal{L}^-$. The remaining symbols, from clauses (iv) and (v), are called syntactic constants. An $\mathcal{L}^-$-expression is a finite string of $\mathcal{L}^-$-symbols.

Clause (iv) provides a quotation constant for each basic symbol of $\mathcal{L}$. But the language lacks quotation constants for more complex expressions, such as strings of length 2 or greater, or quotation constants. The quotation constant $\overline{\neg\neg}$ from $\mathcal{L}$ is not a symbol of $\mathcal{L}^-$ because $\neg\neg$ is not a symbol. The $\mathcal{L}$-symbol $\overline{\neg}$ *is* a symbol of $\mathcal{L}^-$, but since it is not a *basic* symbol of $\mathcal{L}^-$, the $\mathcal{L}$-symbol $\overline{\overline{\neg}}$ is not in $\mathcal{L}^-$. There are still infinitely many syntactic constants because there is one associated to each variable symbol. But the definition of $\mathcal{L}^-$ avoids the extra level of recursion needed in enumerating all symbols of $\mathcal{L}$.

The descriptive simplicity of $\mathcal{L}^-$ would be of little significance if the language were too weak to provide an interesting framework for a theory of expressions. The language is clearly sufficient for formulating simple statements such as 'If the expression "¬" is written as a concatenation of two expressions then one of these expressions is the empty expression':

(8.1) $$\forall \mathsf{x} \forall \mathsf{y} \left(\mathsf{x}^\frown \mathsf{y} = \overline{\neg} \rightarrow \mathsf{x} = \underline{0} \vee \mathsf{y} = \underline{0} \right).$$

The property of being a basic symbol of $\mathcal{L}^-$ can also be expressed: the basic symbols are precisely the expressions of length 1 that are not quotations of any expression. Formalized in $\mathcal{L}^-$ with the free variable x this becomes

(8.2) $$\forall \mathsf{y} \forall \mathsf{z} \left(\mathsf{x} = \mathsf{y}^\frown \mathsf{z} \rightarrow \mathsf{y} = \mathsf{x} \vee \mathsf{z} = \mathsf{x} \right) \wedge \forall \mathsf{z} \neg \mathsf{x} = \mathsf{q}\mathsf{z}.$$

Less clear is whether we can express the statement 'The formula in (8.2) has four occurrences of the symbol x' in $\mathcal{L}^-$, because $\mathcal{L}^-$ lacks a quotation constant for the string of symbols in (8.2).

Nevertheless, there is a sense in which the sublanguage $\mathcal{L}^-$ is as expressive as $\mathcal{L}$. We can show that every term t of $\mathcal{L}$ can be associated with a term t^- of $\mathcal{L}^-$ such that $\mathsf{E} \vdash t = t^-$. In particular, each expression e of $\mathcal{L}^-$ can be assigned a term of $\mathcal{L}^-$, denoted $\ulcorner e \urcorner$, such that $\mathsf{E} \vdash \overline{e} = \ulcorner e \urcorner$. We call $\ulcorner e \urcorner$ the quotation of e. The definition mirrors the decomposition of quotation constants into terms described at the beginning of the chapter. To facilitate the broader reduction of $\mathcal{L}$-expressions to $\mathcal{L}^-$ it is helpful to define $\ulcorner e \urcorner$ even in the case that e is not an $\mathcal{L}^-$-expression, but maintaining the property $\mathsf{E} \vdash \overline{e} = \ulcorner e \urcorner$, and that $\ulcorner e \urcorner$ is an expression of $\mathcal{L}^-$ if e is.

To aid the definition of quotation, as well as other later definitions, it will prove helpful to introduce an abbreviation for when two expressions of $\mathcal{L}$ are identical, i.e., are the same strings of $\mathcal{L}$-symbols. For this we introduce the symbol $\equiv$, and use $e \equiv f$ as shorthand for the statement that e and f are identical as strings of $\mathcal{L}$-symbols. Moreover, we will use 0 for the empty expression, so $e \equiv 0$ is notational shorthand for the statement 'e is the (unique) expression of length 0'. By definition, we have $e0 \equiv 0e \equiv e$ for every e. Note that $\equiv$ and 0 are not symbols of the formal language $\mathcal{L}$ but merely metalinguistic abbreviations for concepts that, until now, we have expressed only in text. These abbreviations will prove particularly helpful in defining operations on expressions, such as quotation, which we now present.

A subexpression of e is a sequence of consecutive symbols within e, that is, any expression f such that $e \equiv gfh$ for some g and h, which may be empty. If $e \equiv fg$, then we call f a prefix, and g a suffix, of e.

8.2 DEFINITION Let e be an expression of $\mathcal{L}$. The quotation of e is the $\mathcal{L}$-expression $\ulcorner e \urcorner$ defined recursively by conditions (i)–(iv):

(i) The quotation of the empty expression 0 is the quotation constant $\underline{0}$.

(ii) If e is a basic symbol of $\mathcal{L}^-$, then $\ulcorner e \urcorner$ is the quotation constant $\overline{e}$.

(iii) If $e \equiv \overline{f}$ is a quotation constant, then $\ulcorner e \urcorner$ is the term $\mathsf{q}\overline{f}$.

(iv) If $e \equiv fu$ is an expression of length at least 2 and u is a symbol, then $\ulcorner e \urcorner$ is the expression ${}^\frown \ulcorner f \urcorner \ulcorner u \urcorner$.

We occasionally refer to expressions $\ulcorner e \urcorner$ as quotation *terms* to distinguish them from quotation *constants*.

Quotation, in the sense of definition 8.2, behaves quite differently to the quotation constants of $\mathcal{L}$. The quotation $\ulcorner e \urcorner$ of an $\mathcal{L}$-expression e will only be a symbol if e happens to be a basic symbol or the empty expression. Otherwise, $\ulcorner e \urcorner$ is an expression of length at least 2. The symbols $\ulcorner$ and $\urcorner$ are not part of the language. Expressions $\ulcorner e \urcorner \ulcorner f \urcorner$ have a unique reading, namely as appending the quotation of f to the right of the quotation of e. In the next section we will return to the more familiar notation of writing $\overline{e}$ for quotation, once we have dispensed with quotation constants entirely. For now we keep the notational distinction introduced above, whereby $\overline{e}$ denotes the quotation constant in $\mathcal{L}$ associated with the expression e (which happens to be a symbol of $\mathcal{L}^-$ if e is a basic symbol) and $\ulcorner e \urcorner$ denotes the quotation of e as specified in definition 8.2.

8.3 EXAMPLE *The quotation of the expression* $\neg\mathsf{x}$ *is* $\ulcorner \neg\mathsf{x} \urcorner \equiv {}^\frown \overline{\neg}\,\overline{\mathsf{x}}$, *which we also write as* $(\overline{\neg} {}^\frown \overline{\mathsf{x}})$. *The quotation of* this *expression is the term*

$$\ulcorner\ulcorner \neg\mathsf{x} \urcorner\urcorner \equiv \ulcorner {}^\frown \overline{\neg}\,\overline{\mathsf{x}} \urcorner \equiv {}^\frown {}^\frown \overline{{}^\frown}\, \mathsf{q}\overline{\neg}\, \mathsf{q}\overline{\mathsf{x}},$$

which may also be written as $\big((\overline{{}^\frown} {}^\frown (\mathsf{q}\overline{\neg})) {}^\frown (\mathsf{q}\overline{\mathsf{x}})\big)$.

Definition 8.2 presents quotation as an operation on expressions in $\mathcal{L}$, not merely for the sublanguage $\mathcal{L}^-$ we have been discussing. It remains to be shown that the quotation of an expression in $\mathcal{L}^-$ is indeed an expression in $\mathcal{L}^-$ and, in particular, a term in $\mathcal{L}^-$, as we have claimed. The two quotations in example 8.3 support our claim, and a proof of the general statement is not difficult to find. In fact, we can easily show that quotation terms satisfy many of the properties we have already observed for quotation constants. For instance, quotations of distinct expressions are distinct and the theory E proves that quotation terms satisfy the same equations as the axioms state for quotation constants. The next three propositions lay out these results.

8.4 PROPOSITION *The quotation of an expression of $\mathcal{L}^-$ (or $\mathcal{L}$) is a term of $\mathcal{L}^-$ (resp. $\mathcal{L}$). Moreover, every $\mathcal{L}$-expression is the quotation of at most one $\mathcal{L}$-expression. In other words, $\ulcorner a \urcorner \equiv \ulcorner b \urcorner$ if and only if $a \equiv b$.*

PROOF The first claim is a straightforward induction on the length of $\mathcal{L}$-expressions. The second claim is proved similarly, arguing by induction on the length of a that for every b, if $\ulcorner a \urcorner \equiv \ulcorner b \urcorner$ then $a \equiv b$. ⊣

8.5 PROPOSITION *For any two expressions a and b of $\mathcal{L}$, $\mathsf{E} \vdash \ulcorner ab \urcorner = \ulcorner a \urcorner \frown \ulcorner b \urcorner$. The derivation in E of these equations requires only predicate logic and the axioms A4 and A6.*

PROOF By induction on the length of b. If b is the empty string, then $\ulcorner b \urcorner \equiv \underline{0}$ and A6 $\vdash \ulcorner a \urcorner \frown \ulcorner b \urcorner = \ulcorner ab \urcorner$. Otherwise, $b \equiv cu$ for some $\mathcal{L}$-symbol u and $\mathcal{L}$-expression c, whence

$$
\begin{aligned}
\text{A4+A6} \vdash \ulcorner ab \urcorner &= \ulcorner ac \urcorner \frown \ulcorner u \urcorner, && \\
&= (\ulcorner a \urcorner \frown \ulcorner c \urcorner) \frown \ulcorner u \urcorner, && \text{induction hypothesis} \\
&= \ulcorner a \urcorner \frown (\ulcorner c \urcorner \frown \ulcorner u \urcorner), && \text{A4} \\
&= \ulcorner a \urcorner \frown \ulcorner b \urcorner. && \text{definition of } \ulcorner b \urcorner
\end{aligned}
$$

The first equality above is the definition of $\ulcorner ab \urcorner$ if ac is not the empty expression, and follows from A6 otherwise. ⊣

8.6 PROPOSITION *For every $\mathcal{L}$-expression a, $\mathsf{E} \vdash \overline{a} = \ulcorner a \urcorner$.*

PROOF By induction on a. If $a \equiv 0$ then $\overline{a}$ and $\ulcorner a \urcorner$ are both the quotation constant $\underline{0}$. Otherwise, $a \equiv bu$ where u is a symbol of $\mathcal{L}$ and b is a (possibly empty) expression. By the induction hypothesis, $\mathsf{E} \vdash \overline{b} = \ulcorner b \urcorner$, and by proposition 8.5 it suffices to show that $\mathsf{E} \vdash \overline{u} = \ulcorner u \urcorner$. If u is not a quotation constant the two terms are identical by definition. Otherwise, we may assume that $u \equiv \overline{e}$, whereby $\ulcorner u \urcorner \equiv \mathsf{q}\overline{e}$ and $\mathsf{E} \vdash \overline{u} = \ulcorner u \urcorner$ is an instance of A2. ⊣

The simplest $\mathcal{L}$-expressions that are not expressions of $\mathcal{L}^-$ are those built from the basic symbols and quotation constants for arbitrary $\mathcal{L}^-$-expressions. Proposition 8.4 offers a way to translate each expression of this kind into $\mathcal{L}^-$ by replacing every quotation constant by the corresponding quotation term. That is, given an expression a, we obtain a new expression $a^\natural$ defined by recursion: if $a \equiv 0$, set $a^\natural \equiv 0$; if $a \equiv b\overline{e}$, set $a^\natural \equiv b^\natural \ulcorner e \urcorner$; and if $a \equiv bu$ for a basic symbol u, set $a^\natural \equiv b^\natural u$.

The translation can be applied to any $\mathcal{L}$-expression, though $a^\natural$ will only be an expression of $\mathcal{L}^-$ if all quotation constants in a are for $\mathcal{L}^-$-expressions. If, for example, a contains a quotation constant $\overline{e}$ and e contains a quotation constant $\overline{f}$, then in forming $a^\natural$, the symbol $\overline{e}$ will have been replaced by the expression $\ulcorner e \urcorner$, which still contains the symbol $\overline{f}$. Nevertheless, the step from a to $a^\natural$ has brought us closer to the language $\mathcal{L}^-$: by replacing $\overline{e}$ with $\ulcorner e \urcorner$, one level of quotation has been stripped away.

We thus have a procedure to translate arbitrary $\mathcal{L}$-expressions into $\mathcal{L}^-$. If a is not already an expression of $\mathcal{L}^-$, we consider the expression $a^\natural$. If this is in $\mathcal{L}^-$ we are done. Otherwise, we proceed to $a^{\natural\natural}$, $a^{\natural\natural\natural}$, and so on, each time removing one more level of quotation constants from the starting expressions a, until eventually an $\mathcal{L}^-$-expression is reached.

It remains to be proven that every expression of $\mathcal{L}$ is reduced to $\mathcal{L}^-$ by some number of applications of the translation $^\natural$. We will turn to this task shortly. First, we present the translation more precisely and establish a generalization of proposition 8.6 connecting expressions and their translations in the theory E.

8.7 DEFINITION For each a we obtain an $\mathcal{L}$-expression $a^\natural$ defined via the following conditions:

(i) $0^\natural \equiv 0$;

(ii) if $a \equiv bu$ and u is a basic symbol then $a^\natural \equiv b^\natural u$;

(iii) if $a \equiv bu$ and $u \equiv \overline{c}$ is a quotation constant, then $a^\natural \equiv b^\natural \ulcorner c \urcorner$.

Applying the translation to a quotation constant, the definition yields $\overline{e}^\natural \equiv \ulcorner e \urcorner$ for every $\mathcal{L}$-expression e. Proposition 8.6 therefore implies $\mathsf{E} \vdash \overline{e} = \overline{e}^\natural$. If e is a basic symbol (so $\overline{e}$ is a symbol of $\mathcal{L}^-$) then, in fact, $\overline{e}^\natural \equiv \overline{e}$. So the translation has no effect on the symbols and expressions of $\mathcal{L}^-$. To examine a more complex expression not in $\mathcal{L}^-$, consider the following translations involving the quotation constant $\overline{\overline{\neg}=\overline{\mathsf{x}}}$, which we denote by s:

$$s^\natural \equiv \ulcorner \overline{\neg}=\overline{\mathsf{x}} \urcorner \equiv \mathsf{q}\overline{\neg}{}^\frown\overline{=}{}^\frown\mathsf{q}\overline{\mathsf{x}} \qquad \text{and} \qquad \overline{s}^\natural \equiv \ulcorner s \urcorner \equiv \mathsf{q}s.$$

The translation of s is a term of $\mathcal{L}^-$, whereas the translation of $\overline{s}$ is a term, but not of $\mathcal{L}^-$. Applying the translation a second time to $\overline{s}$ does return a term in $\mathcal{L}^-$:

$$\overline{s}^{\natural\natural} \equiv \ulcorner s \urcorner^\natural \equiv \mathsf{q}\ulcorner \overline{\neg}=\overline{\mathsf{x}} \urcorner \equiv \mathsf{q}s^\natural.$$

The next lemma establishes some basic properties of the translation.

8.8 LEMMA *Let a and b be arbitrary expressions of $\mathcal{L}$.*

(i) $(ab)^\natural \equiv a^\natural b^\natural$;

(ii) *if a is in $\mathcal{L}^-$ then $a^\natural \equiv a$;*

(iii) *if a is a term, then $a^\natural$ is a term containing the same variables as a;*

(iv) *if a is a formula, then $a^\natural$ is a formula with the same free and bound variables.*

PROOF All four claims are proved by induction on the length of a. Clause (i) is a direct consequence of the definition. To show (ii), it suffices to examine the case that a is a symbol: if a is a basic symbol, then $a^\natural \equiv a$ by definition, otherwise, $a \equiv \overline{u}$ where u is a basic symbol and $a^\natural \equiv \ulcorner u \urcorner \equiv \overline{u}$. For (iii), proposition 8.4 and (ii) imply that the translation of every constant (whether it be a basic symbol or a quotation constant) is a term. Proceeding by induction, if $a \equiv \mathsf{f}s_1 \cdots s_n$ is a term where f is an n-ary function symbol and $s_1, \ldots, s_n$ are terms, then $a^\natural$ is, by clauses (i) and (ii), the expression $\mathsf{f}s_1^\natural \cdots s_n^\natural$. By induction hypothesis, each $s_i^\natural$ is a term, so $a^\natural$ is a term. The proof of (iv) follows a similar argument and is left as an exercise. ⊣

A consequence of proposition 8.6 and lemma 8.8 is that $\mathsf{E} \vdash \mathsf{c} = \mathsf{c}^\natural$ obtains for every constant c in the language $\mathcal{L}$. Generalizing, the translation preserves provable equality between terms and provable equivalence between formulæ.

8.9 PROPOSITION *Let s be a term of $\mathcal{L}$ and φ a formula of $\mathcal{L}$. Then $\mathsf{E} \vdash s = s^\natural$ and $\mathsf{E} \vdash \varphi \leftrightarrow \varphi^\natural$.*

PROOF The claims are proved by induction on the length of the term/formula involved. In both cases the translation only replaces constants in the term/formula by provably equal terms. Hence, every complex term is translated to a provably equal term and every formula to a provably equivalent formula. ⊣

All that remains is to prove that starting from an arbitrary $\mathcal{L}$-expression and iteratively applying the translation $^\natural$, an expression of $\mathcal{L}^-$ is obtained. This is the goal of the next proposition.

8.10 PROPOSITION *Let a be any expression and suppose* $a \equiv a_0, a_1, a_2, \ldots$ *is the sequence of expressions where* $a_{k+1} \equiv a_k^\natural$ *for every* $k \geq 0$*. There exists* $n \geq 0$ *such that* a_n *is in* $\mathcal{L}^-$ *and* $a_n \equiv a_{n+j}$ *for every* $j > 0$.

The proof proceeds by induction on the nesting depth of quotation. All expressions of $\mathcal{L}^-$ are considered have quotation depth 0. An expression has quotation depth $n + 1$ if and only if it is a string of basic symbols and quotation constants for expressions with quotation depth $\leq n$, and contains at least one quotation constant for an expression with quotation depth n.

PROOF Let $\mathcal{E}_n$ be the set of $\mathcal{L}$-expressions of quotation depth $\leq n$. Any expression formed from the basic symbols of $\mathcal{L}^-$ and quotation constants for expressions in $\mathcal{E}_n$ is an element of $\mathcal{E}_{n+1}$. In addition, each set $\mathcal{E}_n$ is closed under quotation: if $a \in \mathcal{E}_n$, then $\ulcorner a \urcorner \in \mathcal{E}_n$.

We show that $a \in \mathcal{E}_{n+1}$ implies $a^\natural \in \mathcal{E}_n$ by induction on a. If $a \equiv 0$, the claim is obvious, as the empty expression is contained in every level. For the induction step, assume that $a \equiv bu \in \mathcal{E}_{n+1}$ and $b^\natural \in \mathcal{E}_n$. If u is a basic symbol, then $a^\natural \equiv b^\natural u \in \mathcal{E}_n$. If u is a quotation constant, say $u \equiv \overline{c}$, then $u^\natural \in \mathcal{E}_n$ because $\mathcal{E}_n$ is closed under quotation, whence $a^\natural \equiv b^\natural \ulcorner c \urcorner \in \mathcal{E}_n$.

To prove the proposition, let a_0 be any expression of $\mathcal{L}$ and suppose $a_0, a_1, \ldots$ is the sequence of $\mathcal{L}$-expressions given by $a_{k+1} = a_k^\natural$ for every $k \geq 0$. Let n be such that $a \in \mathcal{E}_n$. By the above it follows that $a_n \in \mathcal{E}_0$. ⊣

Proposition 8.10 confirms that the translation of $\mathcal{L}$ into $\mathcal{L}^-$ given by iterating the operation $a \mapsto a^\natural$ is well defined: given a, define $a^\#$ to be the first $\mathcal{L}^-$-expression encountered in the sequence $a, a^\natural, a^{\natural\natural}, a^{\natural\natural\natural}, \ldots$ The next lemma and theorem are consequences of the results we established for $^\natural$.

8.11 LEMMA *The following hold for any two* $\mathcal{L}$*-expressions a and b:*

(i) $a^\#$ *is an* $\mathcal{L}^-$*-expression and* $a^{\natural\#} = a^\#$,

(ii) $(ab)^\# \equiv a^\# b^\#$,

(iii) $\overline{a}^\# \equiv \ulcorner a \urcorner^\#$.

PROOF Application of the definition and the properties of the translation $^\natural$. For clause (iii), we observe that $\overline{a}^\# \equiv \overline{a}^{\natural\#} \equiv \ulcorner a \urcorner^\#$. ⊣

8.12 THEOREM *Let* s *be a term and* φ *a formula. Then* $s^\#$ *is a term in the language* $\mathcal{L}^-$ *such that* $\mathsf{E} \vdash s = s^\#$, *and* $\varphi^\#$ *is a formula in the language* $\mathcal{L}^-$ *such that* $\mathsf{E} \vdash \varphi \leftrightarrow \varphi^\#$.

PROOF Repeatedly applying proposition 8.9 yields $\mathsf{E} \vdash s = s^\natural \wedge s^\natural = s^{\natural\natural} \wedge s^{\natural\natural} = s^{\natural\natural\natural} \wedge \cdots$. So $\mathsf{E} \vdash s = s^\#$. Similarly for formulæ related by equivalence. ⊣

A corollary of the theorem is that every statement about $\mathcal{L}$-expressions that can be expressed as a formula of $\mathcal{L}$ is expressed by a formula of the sublanguage $\mathcal{L}^-$ where the only quotation constants are the syntactic constants, namely, quotation constants for basic symbols. There are two immediate corollaries of theorem 8.12 which we will appeal to later:

8.13 COROLLARY *Let* φ *be any formula. Then* $\mathsf{E} \vdash \varphi$ *if and only if* $\mathsf{E} \vdash \varphi^\#$.

8.14 COROLLARY *Any two models of* E_{min} *(not necessarily standard) that make true the same sentences of* $\mathcal{L}^-$, *make true the same sentences of* $\mathcal{L}$.

The translation $^\#$ motivates two versions of the theory E which are formulated solely within the sublanguage $\mathcal{L}^-$. The first is the theory axiomatized by the translations of the axioms of E. The second theory uses the axiom schemas of E but with $\mathcal{L}^-$-quotations instead of quotation constants. We will examine both these theories, starting with the former.

8.15 DEFINITION The axioms of $\mathsf{E}^\#$ are the translations of the axioms of E. In particular, $\mathsf{E}^\#_{\text{min}}$ is given by the following axioms:

A1$^\#$ $\ulcorner a \urcorner^\# {}^\frown \ulcorner b \urcorner^\# = \ulcorner ab \urcorner^\#$, where a and b are arbitrary $\mathcal{L}$-expressions.

A2$^\#$ These axioms are trivial, as the translation of a quotation constant $\overline{\overline{a}}$ is precisely the term $\mathsf{q}\overline{a}^\#$.

- A3$^{\#}$ Axiom A3 becomes the axiom $\mathsf{sub}(\ulcorner a \urcorner^{\#}, \ulcorner b \urcorner^{\#}, \ulcorner c \urcorner^{\#}) = \ulcorner d \urcorner^{\#}$, where a and c are arbitrary $\mathcal{L}$-expressions, b is any symbol of $\mathcal{L}$, and d is the result of substituting c for b in a.
- A7$^{\#}$ The sentence $\forall \mathsf{x} \forall \mathsf{y}\ \mathsf{sub}(\mathsf{x} ^\frown \ulcorner b \urcorner^{\#}, \ulcorner b \urcorner^{\#}, \mathsf{y}) = \mathsf{sub}(\mathsf{x}, \ulcorner b \urcorner^{\#}, \mathsf{y}) ^\frown \mathsf{y}$, where b is a symbol of $\mathcal{L}$.
- – Axioms A4, A5, A6, and A8 are formulæ of $\mathcal{L}^-$ and remain unchanged by the translation.

In A3$^{\#}$ and A7$^{\#}$, b is restricted to symbols of $\mathcal{L}$. This can be either a basic symbol or a quotation constant. In the former case, $\ulcorner b \urcorner^{\#}$ is the syntactic constant $\overline{b}$ (of $\mathcal{L}^-$), and in the latter, $b \equiv \overline{e}$ for some $\mathcal{L}$-expression e and $\ulcorner b \urcorner^{\#} \equiv \mathsf{q} \ulcorner e \urcorner^{\#}$. Therefore A7$^{\#}$ may be reformulated as the following pair of schemas:

(i) $\forall \mathsf{x} \forall \mathsf{y}\ \mathsf{sub}(\mathsf{x} ^\frown \overline{b}, \overline{b}, \mathsf{y}) = \mathsf{sub}(\mathsf{x}, \overline{b}, \mathsf{y}) ^\frown \mathsf{y}$, where b is a basic symbol of $\mathcal{L}^-$;

(ii) $\forall \mathsf{x} \forall \mathsf{y}\ \mathsf{sub}(\mathsf{x} ^\frown \mathsf{q} \ulcorner b \urcorner^{\#}, \mathsf{q} \ulcorner b \urcorner^{\#}, \mathsf{y}) = \mathsf{sub}(\mathsf{x}, \mathsf{q} \ulcorner b \urcorner^{\#}, \mathsf{y}) ^\frown \mathsf{y}$, where b is an expression of $\mathcal{L}$.

Similarly for A3$^{\#}$. Note, the term $\ulcorner b \urcorner^{\#}$ in schema (ii) cannot be simplified further, as every instance of (ii) is the translation of some instance of A7.

We will prove that $\mathsf{E}^{\#}$ is equivalent to E in a strong sense: the two theories have the same $\mathcal{L}^-$-theorems and the translation under $^{\#}$ of every theorem of E is a theorem of $\mathsf{E}^{\#}$. We begin with the observation that $\mathsf{E}^{\#}$ is a subtheory of E.

8.16 PROPOSITION *If* $\mathsf{E}^{\#} \vdash \varphi$, *then* $\mathsf{E} \vdash \varphi$.

PROOF If φ is an axiom of $\mathsf{E}^{\#}$, then $\varphi \equiv \psi^{\#}$ for an axiom ψ of E and corollary 8.13 implies $\mathsf{E} \vdash \varphi$. The rest of the argument is by induction on the length of the derivation of φ in $\mathsf{E}^{\#}$. ⊣

8.17 THEOREM *For every sentence* φ *of* $\mathcal{L}$, $\mathsf{E} \vdash \varphi$ *if and only if* $\mathsf{E}^{\#} \vdash \varphi^{\#}$.

PROOF That $\mathsf{E}^{\#} \vdash \varphi^{\#}$ implies $\mathsf{E} \vdash \varphi$ is a consequence of proposition 8.16 and corollary 8.13. For the other direction, we note that the translation preserves derivability: if φ is logically derivable from Γ, then $\varphi^{\#}$ is logically derivable from the set $\{ \gamma^{\#} : \gamma \in \Gamma \}$. Since every axiom of E is, by definition, translated to an axiom of $\mathsf{E}^{\#}$, we deduce that $\mathsf{E} \vdash \varphi$ implies $\mathsf{E}^{\#} \vdash \varphi^{\#}$. ⊣

Combining theorem 8.17 and corollary 8.13, we conclude that E and $\mathsf{E}^{\#}$ have the same $\mathcal{L}^{-}$-theorems.

8.18 COROLLARY *Let φ be any sentence in $\mathcal{L}^{-}$. Then $\mathsf{E} \vdash \varphi$ iff $\mathsf{E}^{\#} \vdash \varphi$.*

The definition of $\mathsf{E}^{\#}$ is far from satisfactory. Although each axiom is a formula of $\mathcal{L}^{-}$, in specifying which sentences are axioms of $\mathsf{E}^{\#}$ we refer to expressions outside the language. This is not easily avoided. For example, consider the following sentence of $\mathcal{L}^{-}$:

$$(8.3) \qquad \mathsf{sub}\Big(\big(\mathsf{q}\bar{\neg}{}^\frown\mathsf{q}(\bar{\forall}{}^\frown\mathsf{q}\bar{\to})\big){}^\frown\bar{\mathsf{x}},\ \mathsf{q}(\bar{\forall}{}^\frown\mathsf{q}\bar{\to}),\ \mathsf{q}\bar{\mathsf{x}}{}^\frown\bar{\neg}\Big) = \big((\mathsf{q}\bar{\neg}{}^\frown\mathsf{q}\bar{\mathsf{x}}){}^\frown\bar{\neg}\big){}^\frown\bar{\mathsf{x}}.$$

It is not difficult to convince oneself that this formula is true under the intended interpretation of the symbols and, moreover, a theorem of E. But is (8.3) an axiom of $\mathsf{E}^{\#}$? We suspect the answer is not immediate. In comparison, it is trivial whether a given formula of $\mathcal{L}$ is an instance of an axiom of $\mathsf{E}_{\mathrm{min}}$. In fact, (8.3) is the instance of A3$^{\#}$ where $a \equiv \bar{\neg}\overline{\forall\bar{\to}}\mathsf{x}$, $b \equiv \overline{\forall\bar{\to}}$, and $c \equiv \bar{\mathsf{x}}\neg$. The complexity lies in the translation. If the translation mapped every quotation constant to a quotation term of an $\mathcal{L}^{-}$-expression, we could hope to formulate the substitution axiom as

$$(8.4) \qquad \mathsf{sub}(\ulcorner a\urcorner, \ulcorner b\urcorner, \ulcorner c\urcorner) = \ulcorner d\urcorner$$

with the expected conditions on a, b, c, and d. But the terms occurring in (8.3) are not quotations, and the axioms of $\mathsf{E}^{\#}$ do not have the simple form of (8.4).

The second reformulation of E as a theory in the language $\mathcal{L}^{-}$ is motivated by an axiomatization in the style of (8.4) instead of (8.3). Where an axiom of E refers to quotation *constants*, we will consider the corresponding axiom schema about quotation *terms*. We call this theory E^{-}.

8.19 DEFINITION All instances of the following schemas are axioms of E^{-}:

- A2^{-} $\mathsf{q}\ulcorner a\urcorner = \ulcorner\ulcorner a\urcorner\urcorner$;
- A3^{-} $\mathsf{sub}(\ulcorner a\urcorner, \ulcorner b\urcorner, \ulcorner c\urcorner) = \ulcorner d\urcorner$, if b is a symbol or quotation of an $\mathcal{L}^{-}$-expression and d is the string of symbols obtained from a by replacing all occurrences of the string b with c;
- A7^{-} $\forall\mathsf{x}\forall\mathsf{z}\ \mathsf{sub}(\mathsf{x}{}^\frown\ulcorner b\urcorner, \ulcorner b\urcorner, \mathsf{z}) = \mathsf{sub}(\mathsf{x}, \ulcorner b\urcorner, \mathsf{z}){}^\frown\mathsf{z}$, provided b is either a symbol of $\mathcal{L}^{-}$ or a quotation;
- – A4, A5, A6, and A8 from E.

The axioms of E^- are just the axioms of E, but with quotation (of $\mathcal{L}^-$-expressions) replacing all references to quotation constants (of $\mathcal{L}$). Axiom A2$^-$, for instance, is obtained by reading the nested quotation constant $\overline{\overline{a}}$ as an iterated quotation. This is already different from the interpretation under $^\#$, where $\overline{\overline{a}}^\# \equiv \ulcorner\overline{a}\urcorner^\# \equiv \mathsf{q}\ulcorner a\urcorner^\#$, and which trivializes the translation of A2. A similar interpretation is involved in the formulation of A7$^-$, for which we recall that a symbol of $\mathcal{L}$ is either a symbol of $\mathcal{L}^-$ or a quotation constant. An axiom corresponding to A1 is not required, as proposition 8.5 shows that the version with quotations is provable directly from the axioms A4 and A6.

Concerning the formulation of A3$^-$, recall the original statement of A3:

A3 $\mathsf{sub}(\overline{a}, \overline{b}, \overline{c}) = \overline{d}$, where a and c are arbitrary strings of symbols, b is a symbol [of $\mathcal{L}$], and d is the string of symbols obtained from a by replacing all occurrences of the symbol b with c.

In $\mathcal{L}$ every quotation constant is a symbol, so one instance of this axiom is given by choosing $a \equiv \neg\overline{\wedge\vee}$, $b \equiv \overline{\wedge\vee}$, $c \equiv \neg$, and $d \equiv \neg\neg$. According to the reading of quotation constants as quotations of expressions, the following sentence ought to be an instance, or derivable from instances, of A3$^-$.

$$\mathsf{sub}(\ulcorner\neg\ulcorner\mathsf{x}\neg\urcorner\urcorner, \ulcorner\ulcorner\mathsf{x}\neg\urcorner\urcorner, \ulcorner\neg\urcorner) = \ulcorner\neg\neg\urcorner.$$

But the expression $\ulcorner\mathsf{x}\neg\urcorner$ is not a symbol of $\mathcal{L}^-$, so to cover all instances of A3 it is necessary to permit in A3$^-$ cases where b is not a symbol but a term.

The restriction of the expression b to symbols in A3 is to ensure that the result of the substitution, namely the expression d, is uniquely determined. Uniqueness is lost if b can range over arbitrary expressions (cf. the remark on A3 in section 5.3). For instance, if $a \equiv {\to}{\to}{\to}$ and $b \equiv {\to}{\to}$, then d could be taken as $c{\to}$ or ${\to}c$, which are distinct provided $c \not\equiv {\to}$. This particular example is avoided in A3$^-$ because here b is neither a symbol of $\mathcal{L}^-$ nor a quotation. In fact, the restriction on b given in A3$^-$ is sufficient for the expression d to be uniquely determined. In order to prove this claim, it is necessary to be precise in saying what is meant by the phrase 'd is obtained from a by replacing all occurrences of the string b with c'. It will be helpful to shorten this long statement by the concept of a substitution instance.

8.20 DEFINITION A substitution instance is any quadruple (a, b, c, d) of expressions generated by the following two conditions, where b is non-empty.

(i) If b is not a subexpression of a, then (a, b, c, a) is a substitution instance for every expression c.

(ii) If (a, b, c, d) and (a', b, c, d') are substitution instances, then the quadruple (aba', b, c, dcd') is a substitution instance.

As a trivial instance of case (i), the tuple $(0, b, c, 0)$ is a substitution instance for every non-empty expression b and every expression c. By an application of (ii) with a, a', d, and d' all empty, this implies that (b, b, c, c) is the substitution instance whenever b is non-empty.

As another example, fix $b \equiv {\to}{\to}$ and consider the expressions d for which $({\to}{\to}{\to}, b, \neg, d)$ is a substitution instance. The first clause of the definition produces the substitution instances

$$(0, b, \neg, 0), \qquad (\to, b, \neg, \to).$$

Writing the expression ${\to}{\to}{\to}$ first as $0b{\to}$ and then as ${\to}b0$, the following substitution instances derive from (ii):

$$({\to}{\to}{\to}, b, \neg, \neg{\to}), \qquad ({\to}{\to}{\to}, b, \neg, {\to}\neg).$$

These correspond respectively to performing the substitution by parsing the expression ${\to}{\to}{\to}$ left-to-right and right-to-left.

That they are the only substitution instances follows from reversing the argument. Suppose d is such that $({\to}{\to}{\to}, b, \neg, d)$ is a substitution instance. Because b is a subexpression of ${\to}{\to}{\to}$, this substitution instance must have been generated by clause (ii) of the definition. There are only two ways of writing ${\to}{\to}{\to}$ in the form aba': either a is empty and $a' \equiv \to$, or vice versa. The two scenarios give rise to precisely the two substitution instances computed above.

There are also exactly two expressions d that make $({\to}{\to}{\to}{\to}, b, \neg, d)$ a substitution instance:

$$({\to}{\to}{\to}{\to}, b, \neg, \neg\neg), \qquad ({\to}{\to}{\to}{\to}, b, \neg, {\to}\neg{\to}).$$

They arise from decomposing ${\to}{\to}{\to}{\to}$ as, respectively, $0bb$ (or $bb0$) and ${\to}b{\to}$.

Naturally, there are conditions that can be placed on the first three components of substitution instances which ensure that the final component – the 'result' of the substitution – is uniquely determined. For example, for every choice of a and b, provided b is non-empty, there is exactly one expression d such that (a, b, b, d) is a substitution instance, namely $d \equiv a$. In order to prove a claim such as this, it is helpful to observe an equivalent definition of substitution instances.

8.21 LEMMA *Let a, b, c, d be arbitrary strings of $\mathcal{L}$-symbols with b non-empty. Then (a, b, c, d) is a substitution instance if and only if a can be written as a concatenation $a \equiv a_0 b a_1 b \cdots b a_n$ for some n, where b is not a subexpression of any a_i, and $d \equiv a_0 c a_1 c \cdots c a_n$.*

The lemma is proved by induction on a; we omit the details.

As the examples on the previous page demonstrate, the subexpressions $a_0, \ldots, a_n$ in the statement of lemma 8.21 may not be uniquely determined. But if, for a particular choice of a and b, there is a unique decomposition $a \equiv a_0 b a_1 \cdots b a_n$ satisfying the conditions in the lemma, then it immediately follows that the 'result' of the substitution – the expression d above – is unique. This is always the case if b is a symbol. It also holds if b is a term, as the next lemmas demonstrate.

8.22 LEMMA *Suppose a and b are non-empty expressions such that ab is a term or formula of $\mathcal{L}$. Then for no expression c is bc a term or formula.*

We leave the proof of the lemma as an exercise and proceed directly to its consequence for substitution instances.

8.23 LEMMA *Suppose (a, b, c, d) and (a, b, c, d') are two substitution instances. If b is a symbol, term, or formula, then $d \equiv d'$.*

PROOF If b does not occur as a subexpression of a, then $d \equiv a \equiv d'$ by lemma 8.21. Otherwise, let a' be the shortest expression such that $a'b$ is a prefix of a. In particular, b is not a subexpression of a'. Furthermore, let $a''b$ be any other prefix of a. (If there is no other, then b occurs exactly once in a and $d \equiv d'$.) We claim that $a'b$ is a prefix of a''. Suppose not. As a' is strictly shorter than a'', we can write b as a concatenation of two non-empty expressions b_0 and b_1 such that $a'' \equiv a'b_0$. So $a'b \equiv a''b_1$ is a prefix of $a''b$, and we find a non-empty expression b_2 such that $b \equiv b_1 b_2$. Therefore, $b \equiv b_0 b_1 \equiv b_1 b_2$, which contradicts lemma 8.22. Therefore, $a'b$ is a prefix of a'', from which we conclude that there is exactly one decomposition $a \equiv a_0 b a_1 b \cdots b a_n$ where each a_i does not contain b as a subexpression. ⊣

As a result of lemma 8.23, the formulation of A3$^-$ in E$^-$ is unproblematic.

We now turn to the task of providing a translation from $\mathcal{L}$ into $\mathcal{L}^-$ which maps theorems of E into theorems of E$^-$. The translation $^\#$ introduced earlier actually suffices. But this is far from obvious, as the $^\#$-translation of an axiom of E is not in general an instance of any axiom in E$^-$. Rather, we will present an alternative translation which more closely follows the structure of the axioms of E^-. In particular, this translation will map every quotation constant of $\mathcal{L}$ to the quotation of some $\mathcal{L}^-$-expression.

8.24 DEFINITION We define a translation $^-$ mapping expressions in $\mathcal{L}$ into expressions in the sublanguage $\mathcal{L}^-$. Let a be an $\mathcal{L}$-expression. The $\mathcal{L}^-$-expression a^- is given by the following clauses:

(i) $0^- \equiv 0$;

(ii) if $a \equiv bu$ and u is a basic symbol, $a^- \equiv b^- u$;

(iii) if $a \equiv bu$ and $u \equiv \overline{e}$ is a quotation constant, $a^- \equiv b^- \ulcorner e^- \urcorner$.

This translation differs from the previous one in the treatment of quotation constants. Suppose $a \equiv \overline{e}$ is a quotation constant. To form a^- we first apply the translation to the $\mathcal{L}$-expression e and then form the quotation of the result. For instance, if $e \equiv \overline{\mathsf{x}\neg}\forall$, we compute $e^- \equiv \ulcorner \mathsf{x}\neg \urcorner \forall \equiv {}^\frown\overline{\mathsf{x}}\,\overline{\neg}\,\forall$, whereby $a^- \equiv \ulcorner {}^\frown\overline{\mathsf{x}}\,\overline{\neg}\,\forall \urcorner$. The translation $^\#$ works in the opposite order: $a^\#$ is the translation of the quotation of e, namely, $a^\# \equiv \ulcorner \overline{\mathsf{x}\neg}\forall \urcorner^\#$. An argument by induction on the construction of a (using the $\mathcal{E}_n$-hierarchy we saw in proposition 8.10) implies that a^- is an expression of $\mathcal{L}^-$: if e^- is an $\mathcal{L}^-$-expression, then so is $\overline{e}^- \equiv \ulcorner e^- \urcorner$, because quotation does not leave the sublanguage $\mathcal{L}^-$.

This new translation satisfies many of the same properties. It preserves concatenation, leaves expressions of $\mathcal{L}^-$ unaltered, and maps terms to terms and formulæ to formulæ:

8.25 LEMMA *For a and b expressions of $\mathcal{L}$,*

(i) $(ab)^- \equiv a^- b^-$;

(ii) *if a is an expression in $\mathcal{L}^-$, then $a^- \equiv a$;*

(iii) *if a is a term (formula) in $\mathcal{L}$, a^- is a term (formula) in $\mathcal{L}^-$ and has the same free and bound variables as a.*

Examining its effect on the axioms of E, we see that every instance of A2 is translated into an equation

$$\mathsf{q}\ulcorner a^- \urcorner = \ulcorner \ulcorner a^- \urcorner \urcorner.$$

This equation is an instance of A2$^-$ because a^- is an $\mathcal{L}^-$-expression. Likewise, the translation of an instance of A3 is an instance of A3$^-$. Translations of A1 have the form

$$\ulcorner a \urcorner {}^\frown \ulcorner b \urcorner = \ulcorner ab \urcorner,$$

where a and b are $\mathcal{L}^-$-expressions, which, as we have seen, are derivable from A4 and A6. As a consequence, the following result is not surprising.

8.26 THEOREM *Let φ be a theorem of* E. *Then* $\mathsf{E}^- \vdash \varphi^-$. *Hence, every $\mathcal{L}^-$-theorem of* E *is provable in* E^-.

E may contain axioms than the minimal collection listed in definition 5.8, and we have not yet clarified how these should be formulated in the corresponding $\mathcal{L}^-$-theory. Our motivation for the minimal set of $\mathcal{L}^-$-axioms in definition 8.19 has been made precise by the translation $\varphi \mapsto \varphi^-$, which we can now use to define E^-. Given a theory E that extends E_{min}, we define E^- to be the theory comprising the axioms listed in definition 8.19 plus an axiom φ^- for each additional axiom φ in E.

PROOF Same argument as for theorem 8.17. ⊣

8.27 COROLLARY *Let t be any term in the language $\mathcal{L}$ and φ any formula in $\mathcal{L}$. Then* $\mathsf{E}^- \vdash s^- = s^\#$ *and* $\mathsf{E}^- \vdash \varphi^- \leftrightarrow \varphi^\#$.

PROOF Fix a term s and a formula φ, both from the language $\mathcal{L}$. By theorem 8.12 we have $\mathsf{E} \vdash s = s^\#$ and $\mathsf{E} \vdash \varphi \leftrightarrow \varphi^\#$. Theorem 8.26 therefore yields $\mathsf{E}^- \vdash s^- = s^{\#-}$ and $\mathsf{E}^- \vdash \varphi^- \leftrightarrow \varphi^{\#-}$. But $s^{\#-} \equiv s^\#$ and $\varphi^{\#-} \equiv \varphi^\#$ because $s^\#$ and $\varphi^\#$ are both expressions in $\mathcal{L}^-$. ⊣

8.28 COROLLARY $\mathsf{E}^\#$ *is a subtheory of* E^-.

PROOF Suppose $\mathsf{E}^\# \vdash \varphi$. Then $\mathsf{E} \vdash \varphi$ and $\mathsf{E}^- \vdash \varphi^-$. But φ is $\mathcal{L}^-$, so $\varphi \equiv \varphi^-$. ⊣

In theorem 8.17 we showed that $\mathsf{E}^\# \vdash \varphi^\#$ implies $\mathsf{E} \vdash \varphi$. The analogous statement for E^- does not hold, as the next result demonstrates.

8.29 COROLLARY *There exists a formula φ of $\mathcal{L}$ such that* $\mathsf{E}^- \vdash \varphi^-$ *but* $\mathsf{E}_{\text{min}} \nvdash \varphi$.

The strategy of the proof is to present a theorem of E^- which is not true in any standard model of $\mathcal{L}$.

PROOF Let a be any expression involving a quotation constant from $\mathcal{L}$ not in $\mathcal{L}^-$. Let $b \equiv a^-$ and consider the formula $\varphi \equiv \overline{a} = \overline{b}$. The translation of φ is $\ulcorner b \urcorner = \ulcorner b \urcorner$, which is clearly a theorem of E^-. However, since b is an expression in $\mathcal{L}^-$ we have $a \not\equiv b$. As such, if $\mathbb{E}$ is a standard model of E then $\mathbb{E} \models \neg\, \overline{a} = \overline{b}$. Hence, the formula $\overline{a} = \overline{b}$ is not derivable from the axioms of E. ⊣

Corollary 8.29 questions the adequacy of E^- as a theory of expressions. Given corollary 8.27, it implies that $\mathsf{E}^-_{\text{min}}$ is not a subtheory of E_{min} and, moreover, no standard model of $\mathcal{L}$ is a model of E^-. As a theory of $\mathcal{L}^-$-expressions, however, we should evaluate E^- against standard models of $\mathcal{L}^-$. A standard model of $\mathcal{L}^-$ is a structure $\langle \mathbb{E}^-, V \rangle$ for the language $\mathcal{L}^-$. As before, $\mathbb{E}^-$ provides the domain as well as the interpretation of the quotation constants and the function symbols $\frown$, sub, and q; the valuation V provides the interpretation of the remaining nonlogical symbols in $\mathcal{L}^-$.[3] The domain of $\mathbb{E}^-$ is the set of $\mathcal{L}^-$-expressions. The only quotation constants present in $\mathcal{L}^-$ are syntactic constants. These are interpreted as the empty expression in the case of $\underline{0}$ and the associated basic symbol in other cases. The function symbols for substitution and concatenation are interpreted as before. The quotation function symbol q is interpreted as quotation on $\mathcal{L}^-$-expressions as per definition 8.2. That is, q is interpreted as the unary function $\mathsf{q}^{\mathbb{E}^-}$ mapping an expression a to its quotation $\ulcorner a \urcorner$. As the quotation of any $\mathcal{L}^-$-expression is in $\mathcal{L}^-$, the function $\mathsf{q}^{\mathbb{E}^-}$ is well defined.

We leave the proof of the following result to the reader.

8.30 THEOREM *Every standard model of $\mathcal{L}^-$ is a model of $\mathsf{E}^-_{\text{min}}$.*

In many respects E^- is a simplification of E. It is formulated in the sublanguage $\mathcal{L}^-$ which, although infinite, dispenses with the extra level of recursion needed to express all symbols of $\mathcal{L}$. The axioms of E^- are specified by a finite list of axiom schemas ranging over expressions of $\mathcal{L}^-$, in analogy to the axioms of E (and in contrast to $\mathsf{E}^\#$, whose axioms are defined as translations of $\mathcal{L}$-expressions). Moreover, every theorem of E is provably equivalent (over E) to a theorem of E^-. Finally, E^- unites the two natural translations of $\mathcal{L}$ into $\mathcal{L}^-$ in a strong sense (corollary 8.27) which, by corollary 8.29, is not provable in either $\mathsf{E}^\#$ or E.

[3] In chapter 5 a standard model for $\mathcal{L}$ was defined as a triple $\langle \mathbb{E}, V, S \rangle$ with S representing the interpretation of the unary relation symbol $\Box$. For the present definition, we consider the interpretation of $\Box$ to be given by V.

Nevertheless, there are respects in which E^- is weak as a theory of syntax. For a start, $\mathsf{E}^-_{\mathrm{min}}$ admits a trivial model, although this can be easily avoided by expanding the theory with axioms expressing that all basic symbols and syntactic constants are pairwise distinct. More importantly, there are simple properties of $\mathcal{L}^-$-expressions which lack natural definitions in E^-. An example is the set of all variable symbols, whose only definition in $\mathcal{L}^-$ (in a sense made precise below) is as the set of basic symbols minus the finitely many non-variables. This has ramifications on the expression of the terms and sentences of $\mathcal{L}^-$, as well as of numerous syntactic operations on them. For example, one approach to the treatment of many-sorted languages relies on partitioning the variables into two infinite collections, which cannot be achieved by any formula of $\mathcal{L}^-$ or $\mathcal{L}$.

Beginning with the next section, we present a more general theory of expressions which can talk and reason about variables, terms, and formulæ directly, and in a way that is closer to our informal descriptions of these objects as expressions. Ending our study of $\mathcal{L}$, we prove the two claims made above about expressing properties had by infinitely many symbols of $\mathcal{L}^-$.

8.31 LEMMA *Suppose $\varphi(\mathsf{x})$ is an $\mathcal{L}^-$-formula such that, for every string a of $\mathcal{L}^-$-symbols, $\mathsf{E}^- \vdash \varphi(\ulcorner a \urcorner)$ if and only if a is a variable. Then $\varphi(\mathsf{x})$ contains the syntactic constant of every non-variable basic symbol of $\mathcal{L}^-$.*

PROOF Suppose $\varphi(\mathsf{x})$ is such that $\mathsf{E}^- \vdash \varphi(\ulcorner a \urcorner)$ if and only if a is a variable, and u is a non-variable basic symbol whose associated syntactic constant $\overline{u}$ does not occur in φ. Let k be such that neither the variable v_k nor its quotation occurs in φ. Define a mapping f on the symbols of $\mathcal{L}^-$ which exchanges u and v_k:

$$f(v) \equiv \begin{cases} u, & \text{if } v \equiv \mathsf{v}_k, \\ \mathsf{v}_k, & \text{if } v \equiv u, \\ v, & \text{otherwise.} \end{cases}$$

By definition, $f(f(v)) \equiv v$ for every $\mathcal{L}^-$-symbol. Let a^f be the expression defined as follows. If $a \equiv 0$, then $a^f \equiv 0$. If $a \equiv b\overline{v}$ for some b and v, then $a^f \equiv b^f\overline{f(v)}$. Otherwise, a has the form bv where v is a basic symbol, and $a^f \equiv b^f v$.

Note, for every term t and formula ψ, the expression t^f is a term and ψ^f is a formula, as f only affects syntactic constants and does not alter any of the basic symbols through which t and ψ are constructed. In particular, ψ^f is an axiom of E^- whenever ψ is, and $\mathsf{E}^- \vdash \psi$ if and only if $\mathsf{E}^- \vdash \psi^f$. Since, by assumption, $\mathsf{E}^- \vdash \varphi(\overline{\mathsf{v}_k})$ and $\varphi^f \equiv \varphi$, we deduce $\mathsf{E}^- \vdash \varphi(\overline{u})$, yielding a contradiction. ⊣

The second claim concerning the inexpressibility of certain partitionings of the $\mathcal{L}^-$-symbols is captured by the next lemma. We leave the proof to the reader.

8.32 LEMMA *Let B be the set of basic symbols of $\mathcal{L}^-$ and let V be any set of $\mathcal{L}^-$-expressions. If there is formula $\varphi(\mathsf{x})$ of $\mathcal{L}^-$ such that for every $\mathcal{L}^-$-expression a, $\mathsf{E}^- \vdash \varphi(\ulcorner a \urcorner)$ if and only if $a \in V$, then one of the sets $B \cap V$ and $B \setminus V$ is finite,*

8.2 The Symbols

The language for our more general theory shares many similarities with $\mathcal{L}^-$. It comprises a collection of basic symbols (predicate and function symbols, connectives, and auxiliary symbols) and a quotation constant for each basic symbol and for the empty expression. As before, we refer to these quotation constants as syntactic constants. In contrast to $\mathcal{L}^-$ and $\mathcal{L}$, the language is derived from a finite set of symbols. In particular, there is not a distinct symbol for each variable. Instead, variables will be expressions formed from a particular auxiliary symbol.

The next definition fixes the requirements we impose on this language, which we henceforth denote as $\mathcal{L}^*$. As with previous languages, we assume that $\mathcal{L}^*$ comprises a certain minimal collection of symbols which are required for a theory of syntax. Beyond this, the language may contain finitely many other basic symbols. This includes, for instance, the unary predicate symbol $\Box$, which we no longer assume is present in the minimal $\mathcal{L}^*$-language. Hence, except where stated otherwise, the results and constructions we present in this chapter apply to any set $\mathcal{L}^*$ of symbols which satisfies the requirements of the definition.

8.33 DEFINITION The symbols of $\mathcal{L}^*$ are the following:

- Basic symbols:
  - (i) predicate symbols: sym (unary) and $=$ (binary),
  - (ii) function symbols: q (unary), $\frown$ (binary), sub (ternary),
  - (iii) connectives $\neg$, $\rightarrow$, and the quantifier symbol $\forall$,
  - (iv) auxiliary symbols: parentheses (and) and symbols v and e,
  - (v) possibly finitely many other function, relation, and auxiliary symbols.
- Syntactic symbols: a constant $\underline{0}$ and for each basic symbol u, a constant $\underline{u}$.

We let $\mathcal{L}^*_{\text{min}}$ denote the minimal language given by removing condition (v) from the definition. As usual, the symbols listed in the definition are assumed to be pairwise distinct, so expressions of $\mathcal{L}^*$ satisfy the unique readability criterion of assumption 5.2. Unless otherwise stated, *symbol* and *expression* refer to the symbols and expressions of $\mathcal{L}^*$, though in cases of ambiguity we reserve the terms $\ast$-*symbol* and $\ast$-*expression* to refer exclusively to, respectively, symbols and finite strings of symbols of $\mathcal{L}^*$.

The syntactic symbols replace the quotation constants of $\mathcal{L}$ and form the building blocks for quotations of $\mathcal{L}^*$-expressions in the same way as in $\mathcal{L}^-$. We name and draw them differently – writing $\underline{u}$ instead of $\overline{u}$ – to emphasize the shift to a language with only finitely many quotation constants as symbols. In addition to this change of notation, there are three distinguished symbols in $\mathcal{L}^*$ that were not assumed in previous languages: the predicate symbol sym and the auxiliary symbols v and e. The first of these symbols defines the basic symbols of $\mathcal{L}^*$, in the sense that the intended interpretation of this unary predicate is the (finite) set of basic $\ast$-symbols. The symbol v will be used to generate the variables of $\mathcal{L}^*$, which are not symbols. It is convenient for some later considerations to assume that $\mathcal{L}^*$ contains a symbol which does not occur in our most frequently utilized $\ast$-expressions, namely terms and formulæ of $\mathcal{L}^*$. This is the purpose of the final auxiliary symbol e. Each of the new symbols has an associated syntactic constant, $\underline{\mathsf{sym}}$, $\underline{\mathsf{v}}$ and $\underline{\mathsf{e}}$, respectively.

Strictly speaking, none of these additional symbols are necessary for an adequate definition of the theory E^*. For every particular language $\mathcal{L}^*$ satisfying definition 8.33, a formula equivalent to $\mathsf{sym}\,x$ can be given. That formula depends on the particular choice of $\mathcal{L}^*$, however, whereas the predicate sym provides a uniform means to refer to the basic symbols of any such language. The symbols v and e have a similar role. The former is used to generate variables, but any basic $\ast$-symbol can replace its use with an appropriate adjustment of definitions. The symbol e ensures that the language contains a symbol that does not occur in any term, formula, or quotation. Any $\ast$-expression that is not a subexpression of any variable, term, formula, or quotation, can replace the use of e in the following.

Despite these additional symbols not being among the obligatory symbols of our weak language $\mathcal{L}$, we can assume that these symbols are among the 'possibly finitely many further [...] symbols' of $\mathcal{L}$. Therefore, we may treat $\mathcal{L}^*$ as a sublanguage of both $\mathcal{L}$ and $\mathcal{L}^-$. As the languages $\mathcal{L}^-$ and $\mathcal{L}$ contain infinitely many symbols, neither can be a sublanguage of $\mathcal{L}^*$ in the strict sense.

8.34 DEFINITION A variable is an expression $(\mathsf{v}\cdots\mathsf{v})$ where $\mathsf{v}\cdots\mathsf{v}$ is a string consisting of the symbol v only. The variable containing exactly k-many occurrences of v is written as v_k:

$$\mathsf{v}_k := (\underbrace{\mathsf{v}\cdots\mathsf{v}}_{k}).$$

Notice that a variable encloses the string $\mathsf{v}\cdots\mathsf{v}$ in matching braces, so the symbol v is not a variable by itself. In particular, variables are not basic symbols of the language and are expressions formed by juxtaposing two or more symbols. The expressions $()$ and (v) are the variables v_0 and v_1 respectively. As before, we introduce abbreviations for commonly used variables: x, y, z, and w for v_0, v_1, v_2, and v_3, respectively, and we use x, y, z (possibly with indices) as metavariables for variables.

The terms and formulæ of $\mathcal{L}^*$ are now defined in the expected way.

8.35 DEFINITION The $\mathcal{L}^*$-terms are defined as follows.

(i) All variables are terms.

(ii) If $t_1, \ldots, t_n$ are terms and f is a function symbol of arity n, then $ft_1\cdots t_n$ is a term.

A term is closed if and only if it contains no variables. A subterm of a term t is any term which is a subexpression of t.

8.36 DEFINITION The $\mathcal{L}^*$-formulæ are defined as follows.

(i) If $t_1, \ldots, t_n$ are terms and P is a predicate symbol of arity n, then $Pt_1\cdots t_n$ is an atomic formula.

(ii) If φ is a formula and x is a variable, then $\forall x\, \varphi$ is a formula.

(iii) If φ and ψ are formulæ, so are $\neg\varphi$ and $(\varphi \to \psi)$.

A subformula of a formula φ is any formula which is a subexpression of φ. Free and bound occurrences of variables are defined as usual (see definition 5.6). A sentence is a formula with no free occurrences of any variable.

We inherit the same conventions of notation as the preceding chapters. These include introducing parentheses and commas for readability, such as writing $\mathsf{sub}(r, s, t)$ instead of $\mathsf{sub}\, rst$, and placing binary function and predicate symbols between their arguments, as in $s^\frown t$ and $s = t$, which stand for ${}^\frown st$ and $=st$ respectively. As before, $r^\frown s^\frown t$ is shorthand for $((r^\frown s)^\frown t)$.

REMARK ON NOTATION The notational abbreviations introduced have the potential to introduce ambiguity in parsing expressions. The expression $\underline{\forall}\,{}^\frown\,\underline{\mathsf{v}}$, for instance, may be interpreted either as the concatenation of the three symbols $\underline{\forall}$, ${}^\frown$, and $\underline{\mathsf{v}}$ in that order or as the term ${}^\frown\underline{\forall}\,\underline{\mathsf{v}}$. Context dictates which reading is appropriate. Since the expression $\underline{\forall}\,{}^\frown\,\underline{\mathsf{v}}$ is not officially a term, in any situation where a term is expected, such as writing $\mathsf{x} = \underline{\forall}{}^\frown\underline{\mathsf{v}}$ or $\varphi(\underline{\forall}{}^\frown\underline{\mathsf{v}})$ for a formula φ, the term ${}^\frown\underline{\forall}\,\underline{\mathsf{v}}$ is intended. But where we refer only to an expression, such as in 'the concatenation of b with the expression $\underline{\forall}{}^\frown\underline{\mathsf{v}}$', the literal reading takes precedence. Generally, our convention of using letters r, s, and t as metavariables for terms will disambiguate most cases. The same rules apply to our notational abbreviations for formulæ.

8.37 EXAMPLE *The following expressions are formulæ using the abbreviations of notation.*

(i) $\mathsf{x} = \underline{\forall}\,{}^\frown\,\underline{\mathsf{v}}$. *As a formula, this expression abbreviates the expression* $=()^\frown\underline{\forall}\,\underline{\mathsf{v}}$.

(ii) $\exists\mathsf{y}\,(\mathsf{y} = \mathsf{q}\underline{\mathsf{v}})$. *This is a sentence. Formally, it is the expression* $\exists(\mathsf{v}){=}(\mathsf{v})\mathsf{q}\underline{\mathsf{v}}$ *and is distinct from the formula* $\exists\mathsf{y}\,(\mathsf{y} = \mathsf{qx})$.

(iii) $\Box\,\mathsf{sub}\big(\mathsf{w}^\frown\mathsf{y},\ \underline{\mathsf{v}},\ \mathsf{y}^\frown(\mathsf{qw})\big)$, *if* $\Box$ *is a unary predicate symbol of* $\mathcal{L}^*$.

8.38 LEMMA *If t is a term and e is any expression except the empty string, then neither of the expressions te and et is a term. Similarly, if φ is a formula then neither φe nor $e\varphi$ is a formula, provided e is not empty.*

Lemma 8.38 implies unique readability for terms and formulæ. In the case of terms, if $s_1, \ldots, s_k$ and $t_1, \ldots, t_l$ are two sequences of terms such that $s_1 \cdots s_k \equiv t_1 \cdots t_l$, then $k = l$ and $s_i \equiv t_i$ for every i with $1 \le i \le k$. As a consequence, if t is a term of the form $\mathsf{f}e$ where f is a function symbol, then lemma 8.38 ensures there is exactly one sequence of terms $t_1, \ldots, t_n$ such that $t \equiv \mathsf{f}t_1 \cdots t_n$. In particular, n will be the arity of f.

PROOF We prove the claim for terms by induction on the length of t. By the induction hypothesis we may assume that for every term s shorter than t, there is no non-empty expression f such that sf or fs is a term. With t fixed, assume that e is an expression of non-zero length such that te is a term. By the definition of $\mathcal{L}^*$-terms, te is either a variable or function symbol suffixed by terms. Since t is a term (and e is non-empty), te is not a variable. So, there is a function symbol f

and terms $s_1, \ldots, s_n$, where n is the arity of f, such that $te \equiv \mathsf{f}s_1 \cdots s_n$. As t is a term and the leftmost symbol of t is f, it follows that there are terms $t_1, \ldots, t_n$ such that $t \equiv \mathsf{f}t_1 \cdots t_n$. So $s_1 \cdots s_n \equiv t_1 \cdots t_n e$. But as e has non-zero length, there is some $1 \leq i \leq n$ and a non-empty expression f such that $s_i \equiv t_i f$ or $t_i \equiv s_i f$. As s_i and t_i are both expressions shorter than t, this contradicts the induction hypothesis. A similar argument establishes that et is not a term. ⊣

In the previous section we introduced quotation as an operation that associates to each expression e a term $\ulcorner e \urcorner$ which acts as a surrogate for the quotation constant $\overline{e}$ in the language $\mathcal{L}$. We make use of precisely the same construction for the language $\mathcal{L}^*$. As we are no longer directly concerned with the weak theory E and its language $\mathcal{L}$ we can safely, without introducing ambiguity, return to the familiar notation of overlining an expression to represent its quotation.

8.39 DEFINITION The quotation of a $*$-expression e is the $\mathcal{L}^*$-term $\overline{e}$ defined as follows.

(i) If e is the empty string, $\overline{e}$ is the expression $\underline{0}$.

(ii) If e is a basic symbol, $\overline{e}$ is the syntactic constant $\underline{e}$.

(iii) If e is a syntactic constant, $\overline{e}$ is the term $\mathsf{q}e$.

(iv) If $e \equiv fu$ is an expression of length at least 2 and u is a $*$-symbol, $\overline{e}$ is the term $\frown \overline{f}\,\overline{u}$.

The following are immediate consequences of the definition.

8.40 PROPOSITION *For all expressions a and b, and all symbols u,*

(i) *$\overline{a}$ is a closed term;*

(ii) *$\overline{a}$ is a constant if and only if a is a basic symbol or the empty expression;*

(iii) *$\overline{a} \equiv \mathsf{q}u$ if and only if $a \equiv u$ and u is a syntactic constant;*

(iv) *$\overline{a} \equiv \overline{b}$ if and only if $a \equiv b$.*

The quotation of every $*$-expression is a term of $\mathcal{L}^*$. As the next definition and lemma demonstrate, the collection of terms that are quotations can be characterized quite naturally. We call these the pure terms:

8.41 DEFINITION The pure terms are the terms of $\mathcal{L}^*$ generated by the following clauses.

(i) $\mathsf{q}\underline{0}$ is a pure term.

(ii) $\underline{u}$ and $\mathsf{q}\underline{u}$ are pure terms if u is a basic symbol.

(iii) if r is any pure term and s is a pure term of type (i) or (ii), then ${}^\frown rs$ is a pure term.

8.42 LEMMA *The pure terms are exactly the quotations of non-empty $\star$-expressions.*

PROOF By induction on the length of $\star$-expressions. The quotation of any symbol is a pure term of type (i) or (ii). If $a \equiv bu$ where u is a symbol and $b \not\equiv 0$, then $\overline{a}$ is, by definition, the term ${}^\frown \overline{b}\overline{u}$. By the induction hypothesis, $\overline{b}$ is a pure term and $\overline{u}$ is a pure term of type (i) or (ii). Hence, $\overline{a}$ is a pure term. The converse direction is an equally straightforward induction on the generation of the pure terms. ⊣

8.43 LEMMA *For every syntactic constant u, $\overline{\overline{u}}$ is the pure term $\underline{\mathsf{q}}{}^\frown(\mathsf{q}u)$.*

PROOF Suppose u is a syntactic constant. By the definition of quotation, $\overline{u}$ is the expression $\mathsf{q}u$, so $\overline{\overline{u}} \equiv \overline{\mathsf{q}u} \equiv {}^\frown \underline{\mathsf{q}}\overline{u} \equiv {}^\frown \underline{\mathsf{q}}\mathsf{q}u$, which we write as the term $\underline{\mathsf{q}}{}^\frown(\mathsf{q}u)$. ⊣

Because variables are not symbols, neither are their quotations. The quotation of the variable v_0 is the expression $\overline{(\,)}$, namely the term ${}^\frown\underline{(}\,\underline{)}$. The quotation of v_k is the term

$$\underline{(}{}^\frown\underbrace{\underline{\mathsf{v}}{}^\frown\cdots{}^\frown\underline{\mathsf{v}}}_{k}{}^\frown\underline{)}.$$

The property of being a variable is expressed by the following $\star$-formula:

$$\mathsf{Var}(\mathsf{x}) := \exists \mathsf{z}\left(\mathsf{x} = \left(\underline{(}{}^\frown\mathsf{z}{}^\frown\underline{)}\right) \wedge \mathsf{sub}(\mathsf{z}, \underline{\mathsf{v}}, \underline{0}) = \underline{0}\right).$$

Under the same intended semantics as in previous sections, $\mathsf{Var}(\overline{a})$ is true just in case that a is a $\star$-expression of the kind $(\mathsf{v}\cdots\mathsf{v})$, that is, a variable of $\mathcal{L}^\star$.

8.3 The Basic Axioms

We now present the axioms of the expressive theory $\mathsf{E}^\star$. The axioms naturally split into six groups, based on which part of our syntax theory they formalize:

predicate logic, the basic symbols and syntactic constants, the operations of concatenation, quotation, and substitution, and the principle of induction. The final category deserves special consideration and is treated separately in section 8.4. We will present each group of axioms in turn, accompanied by a brief study of their immediate consequences. The complete list of obligatory axioms of E^* is summarized at the end of the chapter in section 8.5.

Our approach of presenting the axioms of E^* one group at a time will introduce some redundancy among the axioms, whereby some axioms in the initial groups will be derivable from later presented ones. In most cases, it is the axiom schema of induction that creates the redundancy. We favour this mode of presentation, however, as it allows us to focus on one aspect of syntax at a time and to observe a certain modularity among the axiom groups.

As with the previous theories of syntax, further axioms and rules may be added, such as axioms expressing that the unary predicate symbol $\Box$ satisfies conditions akin to truth. The axioms presented in the present chapter determine the *minimal* expressive theory, the axioms of syntax that form the core of the theories that are examined in subsequent chapters. That is, E^* is assumed to contain the following axioms but may contain other axioms in addition to those listed. Some extensions of the minimal theory will be examined in detail in later chapters. The present chapter, however, concerns the minimal set of axioms only and their immediate consequences.

To assist readability, we adopt the convention of capitalizing names for defined $\mathcal{L}^*$-formulæ (such as Var above, and Sing and Term introduced shortly) and marking primitive symbols, namely sym, sub, q, and other $\ast$-symbols, in lowercase.

8.3.1 Axioms for Symbols

The first group of basic axioms formalize some elementary properties of $\ast$-symbols, namely that they are pairwise distinct, indecomposable, and formed of basic symbols and quotations of basic symbols only. Many of these properties are not expressed by the axioms of the weak theory E yet are central to our understanding of expressions and implicit in the assumption of unique readability of $\ast$-expressions (assumption 5.2).

What we recognize as $\ast$-symbols are, by virtue of unique readability, precisely the non-empty expressions which admit only trivial decompositions. These are the expressions that hold of the formula Sing defined as follows.

8.44 DEFINITION $\mathsf{Sing}(\mathsf{x}) \;\equiv\; \mathsf{x}\neq\underline{0} \wedge \forall \mathsf{w}\forall \mathsf{z}(\mathsf{x}=\mathsf{w}^\frown \mathsf{z} \rightarrow \mathsf{w}=\mathsf{x} \vee \mathsf{z}=\mathsf{x})$.

An expression e for which $\mathsf{Sing}(\overline{e})$ holds is called a *singleton*. From the basic axioms of E^* we can deduce that every $\star$-symbol is a singleton and that every singleton is either a basic symbol or a syntactic constant. The unary predicate symbol sym serves to demarcate the basic symbols from the syntactic symbols. As there are only finitely many $\star$-symbols, the formula $\mathsf{sym}\,\mathsf{x}$ could be defined as a disjunction of equations $\mathsf{x} = \underline{u}$ where u ranges over the basic symbols of $\mathcal{L}^*$. Utilizing such a definition, however, would cause formulæ using this predicate to have their intended interpretations only for the specific choice of $\mathcal{L}^*$ for which the formula was defined. Furthermore, there will be no formula of $\mathcal{L}^*$ which uniformly expresses the property of being a syntactic constant over all languages satisfying the requirements laid out in definition 8.33. For these reasons we favour an axiomatization sym of the $\star$-symbols.

The following sentences are basic axioms of E^*.

B1 $\mathsf{sym}\,\underline{u}$ for each basic $\star$-symbol u,

B2 $\forall \mathsf{x}\big(\mathsf{sym}\,\mathsf{x} \rightarrow \mathsf{Sing}(\mathsf{x})\big)$,

B3 $\forall \mathsf{x}\big(\mathsf{x}=\underline{0} \vee \mathsf{sym}\,\mathsf{x} \rightarrow \mathsf{Sing}(\mathsf{qx})\big)$,

B4 $\forall \mathsf{x}\big(\mathsf{Sing}(\mathsf{x}) \rightarrow \mathsf{sym}\,\mathsf{x} \vee \mathsf{x}=\mathsf{q}\underline{0} \vee \exists \mathsf{y}(\mathsf{sym}\,\mathsf{y} \wedge \mathsf{x}=\mathsf{qy})\big)$,

B5 $\forall \mathsf{x}\,\neg\mathsf{sym}(\mathsf{qx})$,

B6 for each pair of distinct basic symbols u and v, the sentence $\underline{u}\neq\underline{v}$.

Recalling the standard models of $\mathcal{L}$, the axiom schema B1 expresses that the interpretation of the unary predicate sym comprises (at least) the basic $\star$-symbols. The remaining axioms explicate our basic assumptions underlying the symbols of $\mathcal{L}^*$: basic symbols are singletons (B2); likewise the syntactic constants (B3); these are the only kind of singleton expressions (B4); no quotation is a basic symbol (B5); and basic symbols are pairwise distinct (B6). The combination of B4 and B5 expresses that the syntactic constants are the only quotations which are singletons. In other words, the quotation of a quotation is never a singleton. Recall that quotation in $\mathcal{L}^*$ refers to the operation $a \mapsto \overline{a}$ and that $\overline{a}$ is an expression of unit length – a symbol – if and only if a is a basic symbol or a is empty. As there are only finitely many $\star$-symbols, instantiations of B1 and B6 are finite in number.

8.45 PROPOSITION *If a is a symbol, then* $\mathsf{E}^* \vdash \mathsf{Sing}(\overline{a})$.

PROOF By B1 and B2 if a is a basic $\ast$-symbol, or B1 and B3 if a is a syntactic constant. ⊣

The basic symbols are characterized by the predicate symbol sym. Syntactic constants can be recognized in two ways, either as the quotations of basic symbols and the empty expression, or as the symbols of $\mathcal{L}^*$ which are not basic symbols. We start by introducing, in the first definition, a formula expressing the property of being a syntactic constant.

8.46 DEFINITION $\mathsf{Syn}(\mathsf{x}) := \mathsf{x} = \mathsf{q}\underline{0} \vee \exists \mathsf{y}(\mathsf{sym}\,\mathsf{y} \wedge \mathsf{x} = \mathsf{q}\mathsf{y})$.

Axioms B3 and B4 appeal to this characterization of syntactic constants. The conjunction of these two axioms is equivalent to

$$\forall x\big(\mathsf{Sing}(x) \leftrightarrow \mathsf{sym}\,x \vee \mathsf{Syn}(x)\big). \tag{8.5}$$

As a consequence, we see that the two classifications of syntactic constants are equivalent over E^*.

8.47 PROPOSITION $\mathsf{E}^* \vdash \forall x\big(\mathsf{Syn}(x) \leftrightarrow \mathsf{Sing}(x) \wedge \neg\mathsf{sym}\,x\big)$.

PROOF One direction of the equivalence is a consequence of (8.5):

$$\mathsf{E}^* \vdash \forall x\big(\mathsf{Sing}(x) \wedge \neg\mathsf{sym}\,x \rightarrow \mathsf{Syn}(x)\big),$$

The other implication, is equivalent to

$$\mathsf{E}^* \vdash \forall x\big(\mathsf{Syn}(x) \rightarrow \mathsf{Sing}(x) \wedge \neg\mathsf{sym}\,x\big).$$

By (8.5), $\mathsf{E}^* \vdash \forall x\big(\mathsf{Syn}(x) \rightarrow \mathsf{Sing}(x)\big)$. As B5 implies $\mathsf{E}^* \vdash \forall x\big(\mathsf{Syn}(x) \rightarrow \neg\mathsf{sym}\,x\big)$, we are done. ⊣

8.48 PROPOSITION *Suppose u is a basic symbol and v is any symbol distinct from u. Then* $\mathsf{E}^* \vdash \overline{u} \neq \overline{v}$.

The reason that proposition 8.48 is restricted to the case that u is a basic symbol is that we currently lack axioms which rule out $\mathsf{q}\underline{u} = \mathsf{q}\underline{v}$ for distinct u and v. From our axioms for the quotation function, given shortly, the more general statement will follow. Proposition 8.48 (indeed, axiom B6) rules out as a model of E^* the trivial model with domain the singleton set consisting of the empty string only. The axioms of concatenation will imply that the domain of any model of E^* is infinite.

PROOF If v is a basic symbol, then proposition 8.48 is an instance of B6. So the interesting case is if v is a syntactic constant, for which are required to show that $\underline{v} \equiv \underline{0}$ or $\mathsf{E}^* \vdash \underline{u} \neq \mathsf{q}\underline{v}$ for every pair of basic symbols u and v (not necessarily distinct). This is a consequence of B5, because $\mathsf{E}^* \vdash \mathsf{sym}\,\underline{u}$. ⊣

8.3.2 *Axioms for Concatenation*

The theory E^* has the following axioms for concatenation:

C1 $\forall x \forall y (x ^\frown y = \underline{0} \rightarrow x = \underline{0} \wedge y = \underline{0})$,

C2 $\forall x \forall y (x ^\frown y = x \leftrightarrow y = \underline{0}) \wedge \forall x \forall y (x ^\frown y = y \leftrightarrow x = \underline{0})$,

C3 $\forall x \forall y \forall z \forall w$
$$\big(x ^\frown y = z ^\frown w \leftrightarrow \exists v_4 \big((x = z ^\frown v_4 \wedge v_4 ^\frown y = w) \vee (x ^\frown v_4 = z \wedge y = v_4 ^\frown w)\big)\big).$$

These axioms are all axioms of E. We refer the reader to the remarks in section 5.3 for their explanation. Axiom C3 is called the axiom of linearity.

Tarski (1935) was the first to present axioms for a theory of expressions, and our three axioms for concatenation form a version of Tarski's theory (Tarski did not admit the empty string as an expression, but that is not an essential difference). Corcoran, Frank, and Maloney (1974) add second-order logic to Tarski's axioms and show that the resulting theory is equivalent to the second-order theory of (Peano) arithmetic. Even in the setting of first-order logic, the simple theory of expressions given by the axioms for concatenation and symbols is surprisingly expressive.

We begin with the observation that, equipped with these axioms, the non-empty expressions are provably such.

8.49 PROPOSITION *If a is non-empty,* $\mathsf{E}^* \vdash \overline{a} \neq \underline{0}$.

PROOF Suppose $a \equiv bu$ and u is a symbol. By the definition of quotation, $\mathsf{E}^* \vdash \overline{a} = \overline{b} ^\frown \overline{u}$. But then $\mathsf{E}^* \vdash \overline{a} = \underline{0} \rightarrow \overline{u} = \underline{0}$ by C1, and proposition 8.45 implies $\mathsf{E}^* \vdash \overline{a} \neq \underline{0}$. ⊣

We have remarked that the associativity of concatenation is a consequence of the axiom of linearity C3. Given the importance of associativity, we prove this fact before proceeding to other consequences of the axioms.

8.50 PROPOSITION $\mathsf{E}^* \vdash \forall x \forall y \forall z\; x ^\frown (y ^\frown z) = (x ^\frown y) ^\frown z$.

PROOF The following formula can be derived from the axioms of predicate logic:

$$\forall x \forall y \forall z \exists \mathsf{v}_4 \big(x^\frown \mathsf{v}_4 = x^\frown y \wedge y^\frown z = \mathsf{v}_4{}^\frown z\big). \tag{8.6}$$

Now instantiate C3 with $\mathsf{x} = x$, $\mathsf{y} = y^\frown z$, $\mathsf{z} = x^\frown y$, and $\mathsf{w} = z$. From (8.6) and predicate logic, we conclude $\mathsf{E}^* \vdash \forall x \forall y \forall z\ x^\frown(y^\frown z) = (x^\frown y)^\frown z$. ⊣

We make frequent use of proposition 8.50 without explicit reference.

An important concept is that of subexpression. Given a and b, we say that a is a subexpression of b, and write $a \subseteq b$, if and only if there exist (possibly empty) expressions c and d such that $b \equiv cad$. This relation is expressed by the formula

$$x \subseteq y := \exists w \exists z (w^\frown x^\frown z = y).$$

The negated formula, namely $\neg x \subseteq y$, will often be abbreviated to $x \nsubseteq y$. An expression a is a proper subexpression of b if and only if a is a subexpression of b and $a \not\equiv b$. This relation is expressed by the formula $x \subseteq y \wedge \neg x = y$, which we shorten to $x \subset y$.

In addition to the preceding abbreviations, it is convenient to introduce shorthands for quantification over the subexpressions of a fixed expression. We thus introduce two derived quantifiers, called bounded quantifiers, expressing the statements 'For all subexpressions of x, …' and 'There exists a subexpression of x such that …':

$$\begin{aligned} \forall x \subseteq t\ \varphi &\quad \text{abbreviates} \quad \forall x (x \subseteq t \rightarrow \varphi), \\ \exists x \subseteq t\ \varphi &\quad \text{abbreviates} \quad \neg \forall x \subseteq t\ \neg \varphi. \end{aligned}$$

Observe that $\exists x \subseteq t\ \varphi$ is logically equivalent to the formula $\neg \forall x \neg (x \subseteq t \wedge \varphi)$. When we write $\forall x \subseteq t\ \varphi$ and $\exists x \subseteq t\ \varphi$, there is an implicit assumption that the quantified variable x does not occur in the term t. Strict versions of the bounded quantifiers, $\forall x \subset t\ \varphi$ and $\exists x \subset t\ \varphi$, are also available and defined analogously.

8.51 LEMMA *The following two sentences are theorems of* E^*.

(i) $\forall x \big(\mathsf{Sing}(x) \leftrightarrow x \neq \underline{0} \wedge \forall y \subseteq x\, \forall z \subseteq x (x = y^\frown z \rightarrow x = \underline{0} \vee y = \underline{0})\big)$,

(ii) $\forall x \forall y \big(\mathsf{Sing}(xy) \leftrightarrow (\mathsf{Sing}(x) \wedge y = \underline{0}) \vee (\mathsf{Sing}(y) \wedge x = \underline{0})\big)$.

PROOF We use C2 and the definition of Sing. ⊣

8.52 PROPOSITION *If a has length at least 2, then* $\mathsf{E}^* \vdash \neg\mathsf{Sing}(\overline{a})$.

PROOF Let $a \equiv buv$ be any expression of length at least 2, where u and v are $\star$-symbols. If $b \equiv 0$, then $\overline{a} \equiv \overline{u}\,{}^\frown\,\overline{v}$; otherwise, $\overline{a} \equiv (\overline{b}\,{}^\frown\,\overline{u})\,{}^\frown\,\overline{v}$. In either case, $\mathsf{E}^* \vdash \overline{a} = \overline{b}{}^\frown\overline{u}{}^\frown\overline{v}$. So

$$\begin{aligned} \mathsf{E}^* \vdash \mathsf{Sing}(\overline{a}) &\rightarrow \overline{bu} = \underline{0} \vee \overline{v} = \underline{0} \\ &\rightarrow \overline{u} = \underline{0} \vee \overline{v} = \underline{0}. \end{aligned}$$

Hence $\mathsf{E}^* \vdash \neg\mathsf{Sing}(\overline{a})$. ⊣

The next two lemmas present a number of properties of concatenation derivable from the axioms we have laid down so far. The first lemma only requires the axioms of concatenation C1–C3 and does not depend on the axioms for $\star$-symbols. The second lemma lists joint consequences of the two sets of axioms.

8.53 LEMMA *The following are derivable in* E^*:

(i) $\forall x\; x \subseteq x$,

(ii) $\forall x \forall y \forall z (x^\frown y = x^\frown z \rightarrow y = z) \wedge \forall x \forall y \forall z (y^\frown x = z^\frown x \rightarrow y = z)$,

(iii) $\forall x \forall y \forall z (x \subseteq y \wedge y \subseteq z \rightarrow x \subseteq z)$,

(iv) $\forall x (x \subseteq \underline{0} \rightarrow x = \underline{0})$,

(v) $\forall w \forall x \forall y \forall z (wx = yz \rightarrow x \subseteq z \vee z \subseteq x)$.

PROOF With the exception of (ii), the claims are immediate consequences of the axioms: (i) follows directly from C2; associativity of concatenation implies (iii); (iv) is a consequence of C1; and (v) is an application of the linearity axiom.

This leaves (ii). Assume that $ab = ac$. By the axiom of linearity, there exists an expression d such that $ad = a$ and either $b = dc$ or $c = db$. By C2 we deduce $d = \underline{0}$, and so $b = c$. This establishes the first conjunct; the second follows by a symmetric argument. ⊣

8.54 LEMMA *The following are derivable in* E^*:

(i) $\forall x \big(\mathsf{Sing}(x) \rightarrow \forall y \subseteq x\, (y = \underline{0} \vee y = x)\big)$,

(ii) $\forall x \forall y \forall z \big(\mathsf{Sing}(x) \wedge x \subseteq y^\frown z \rightarrow (x \subseteq y \vee x \subseteq z)\big)$,

(iii) $\forall w \forall x \forall y \forall z \big(w^\frown z = x^\frown y \wedge \mathsf{Sing}(y) \wedge \mathsf{Sing}(z) \rightarrow w = x \wedge z = y\big)$,

(iv) $\forall w \forall x \forall y \forall z \big(w^\frown z \subseteq x^\frown y \wedge z \neq \underline{0} \wedge \mathsf{Sing}(y) \rightarrow w \subseteq x \big)$,

(v) $\forall w \forall x \forall y \forall z \big(w \subseteq x^\frown y^\frown z \wedge \mathsf{Sing}(y) \rightarrow y \subseteq w \vee w \subseteq x \vee w \subseteq z \big)$.

PROOF For all parts, we argue in the theory consisting of the axioms for symbols and concatenation.

(i). Assume that a is a singleton and let $b \subseteq a$. We may assume that $b \neq \underline{0}$, whereby we are required to show that $a = b$. Let $a = cbd$. Since a is a symbol, lemma 8.51 implies that $cb = \underline{0}$ or $d = \underline{0}$. Given $b \neq \underline{0}$, the first option is impossible because of C1, so $d = \underline{0}$. However, lemma 8.51 also implies that either $c = \underline{0}$ or $bd = \underline{0}$, from which we deduce $c = \underline{0}$. Hence $a = cbd = b$.

(ii). Let a be a symbol and assume that $a \subseteq bc$. We are required to show $a \subseteq b \vee a \subseteq c$. By way of contradiction assume $a \not\subseteq b$ and $a \not\subseteq c$. Since $a \subseteq bc$ there exist d and d' such that $dad' = bc$. Applying the axiom of linearity, there exists an e such that

- $de = b$ and $ec = ad'$, or
- $d = be$ and $c = ead'$.

The second option contradicts the assumption $a \not\subseteq c$, so in particular $b = de$ and $ec = ad'$ for some e. For the same reason it follows that e is non-empty. By a symmetric argument, there exists a non-empty e' such that $c = e'd'$. So, $dad' = dee'd'$ and, by part (ii), we deduce $a = ee'$. But both e and e' are non-empty, contradicting the assumption that a is a singleton.

(iii). Suppose $ab = cd$ and each of b and d is a singleton. By (v) either $b \subseteq d$ or $d \subseteq b$. In either case, (i) implies $b = d$, whence also $a = c$ by (ii).

We leave (iv) and (v) to the reader. ⊣

As we observed at the start of the chapter, C2 and associativity of concatenation suffice to prove that concatenation of $*$-expressions is expressed by the function symbol $^\frown$.

8.55 PROPOSITION *For any a and b,* $\mathsf{E}^* \vdash \overline{a}^\frown \overline{b} = \overline{ab}$.

PROOF The proof is identical to the proof of proposition 8.5, in which we established the analogous claim for E. That proof only relied on the axioms A4 and A6 of E, both of which are provable in E^*. ⊣

8.56 PROPOSITION *If a is a subexpression of b then* $\mathsf{E}^* \vdash \overline{a} \subseteq \overline{b}$.

PROOF This is a consequence of proposition 8.55. If a is a subexpression of b it means there exist (possibly empty) expressions e and f such that $eaf \equiv b$. So we deduce $\mathsf{E}^* \vdash \overline{e}\frown\overline{a}\frown\overline{c} = \overline{b}$, from which $\mathsf{E}^* \vdash \overline{a} \subseteq \overline{b}$ follows. ⊣

There are two approaches to formulating a converse to proposition 8.55. The literal version is the statement that for any a, b, and c, if $\mathsf{E}^* \vdash \overline{a}\frown\overline{b} = \overline{c}$ then $ab \equiv c$. By proposition 8.55 shows this to be a special case of the property

$$\text{(8.7)} \qquad \mathsf{E}^* \vdash \overline{a} = \overline{b} \quad \text{implies} \quad a \equiv b,$$

which states that only true equalities between expressions are derivable. The second form of a converse is the implication

$$\text{(8.8)} \qquad a \not\equiv b \quad \text{implies} \quad \mathsf{E}^* \vdash \neg\, \overline{a} = \overline{b}.$$

Under the assumption that E^* is consistent, (8.7) is a consequence of (8.8) and proposition 8.55: if $\mathsf{E}^* \vdash \overline{a} = \overline{b}$, then $\mathsf{E}^* \nvdash \neg\, \overline{a} = \overline{b}$ by the consistency of E^*, and (8.8) implies $a \equiv b$. If one of a and b is a basic symbol, (8.8) is implied by axiom B6. However, we do not yet have sufficient axioms to establish (8.8) in the case that a and b are syntactic constants, that is, if $\overline{a} \equiv \mathsf{q}\underline{u}$ and $\overline{b} \equiv \mathsf{q}\underline{v}$ for u and v distinct basic symbols. These statements will become provable from the axioms of quotation we present shortly. For now we can show that this is the only obstacle in establishing (8.8):

8.57 PROPOSITION *Suppose* $\mathsf{E}^* \vdash \mathsf{q}\underline{u} \neq \mathsf{q}\underline{v}$ *for each pair of distinct syntactic constants* $\underline{u}$ *and* $\underline{v}$. *Then for any two distinct* $\star$*-expressions* a *and* b,

$$\mathsf{E}^* \vdash \neg\, \overline{a} = \overline{b}.$$

PROOF Fix distinct $\star$-expressions a and b and let c be their longest common suffix, namely c is the longest $\star$-expression such that $a \equiv dc$ and $b \equiv ec$ for some (possibly empty) d and e. Axiom C1 covers the case that one of a and b has length 0. By extending either a or b if necessary, we may assume that there are distinct symbols u and v such that uc is a suffix of a and vc is a suffix of b. Lemma 8.53(ii) and lemma 8.54(iii) together imply $\mathsf{E}^* \vdash \overline{a} = \overline{b} \rightarrow \overline{u} = \overline{v}$, so it suffices to show that

$$\text{(8.9)} \qquad \mathsf{E}^* \vdash \neg\, \overline{u} = \overline{v}.$$

The hypothesis of the lemma covers the case that u and v are both syntactic constants. If u and v are both basic symbols, (8.9) is an axiom, and if just one of u and v is a basic symbol, then (8.9) follows from B5. Hence $\mathsf{E}^* \vdash \neg\, \overline{a} = \overline{b}$. ⊣

Before presenting the next set of axioms, we will introduce some more advanced machinery available in the theory of concatenation, namely representing finite sequences of expressions as single expressions. Sequencing on a domain of objects is an operation $n, a_1, \ldots, a_n \mapsto \langle a_1, \ldots, a_n \rangle$ mapping a natural number n and n many objects to a new object $\langle a_1, \ldots, a_n \rangle$ satisfying the property that if $\langle a_1, \ldots, a_n \rangle \equiv \langle b_1, \ldots, b_m \rangle$, then $m = n$ and $a_i = b_i$ for each $1 \leq i \leq m$.

Many mathematical domains permit sequencing. In arithmetic, sequencing can be defined in multiple ways. One approach is to define, given natural numbers $a_1, \ldots, a_n$, the 'sequence' $\langle a_1, \ldots, a_n \rangle$ to be $2^{a_1+1} \times 3^{a_2+1} \times \cdots \times p_n^{a_n+1}$, where p_n denotes the n-th prime number. The number 1 denotes the empty sequence $\langle\rangle$ with no elements, 4 the singleton sequence $\langle 1 \rangle$, 18 the two-element sequence $\langle 0, 1 \rangle$, and so on. The fundamental theorem of arithmetic implies that every non-zero natural number encodes a unique sequence $\langle a_1, \ldots, a_n \rangle$. In set theory the Kuratowski definition of ordered pairs, which maps two sets x and y to the two-element (or one-element if $x = y$) set $\{\{x\}, \{x, y\}\}$, can be readily expanded to encode finite sequences of sets as sets.

For $\star$-expressions the challenge is to find a way of combining finitely many expressions into a single expression in a way that the original sequence of expressions can be uniquely recovered. A natural first approach is to represent the sequence $a_1, \ldots, a_n$ as an expression $ua_1ua_2u \cdots ua_n$ where u is some symbol that does not occur in any a_i. Let us abbreviate this expression as $[a_1, \ldots, a_n]_u$. The expression representing the empty sequence (where $n = 0$) is $[\,]_u$, which is the empty expression. The single-element sequence a_1 is expressed as $[a_1]_u \equiv ua_1$, and the two-element sequence a_1, a_2 as $[a_1, a_2]_u$, namely ua_1ua_2. The assumption that u does not occur in any a_i means that u occurs exactly n times in $[a_1, \ldots, a_n]_u$. Now suppose $b_1, \ldots, b_m$ are expressions and v is any symbol not occurring in any b_i. If $[a_1, \ldots, a_n]_u \equiv [b_1, \ldots, b_m]_v$, then $u \equiv v$, $m = n$, and $a_i \equiv b_i$ for each $1 \leq i \leq n$. Therefore, for every expression a, there is a unique $\star$-symbol u, natural number n, and expressions $a_1, \ldots, a_n$ such that u does not occur in any a_i, and $a = [a_1, \ldots, a_n]_u$.

This approach to building sequences has much in common with the separation of written text into words and sentences in many languages, for instance in the language of this book. Words are finite strings of symbols from a fixed alphabet; sentences are sequences of words demarcated by a non-alphabetic symbol, the space; paragraphs are sequences of sentences delineated by full-stops; and so on. Each level in the 'hierarchy' requires a mark which can serve as a separator between constituents and protects against ambiguity when decomposing a given sequence back into its parts. The method is typed – a sentence cannot normally be used in place of a word and a paragraph cannot (normally) be used as a sentence. This is in contrast to sequencing in arithmetic and set theory where $\langle i, j\rangle$ is defined for any i and j, even those that represent sequences. What is more, the method assumes that given expressions $a_1, \ldots, a_n$ we can select some symbol (or expression) u which can be used as a separator so that the 'elements' $a_1, \ldots, a_n$ are uniquely determined from the 'sequence' $[a_1, \ldots, a_n]_u$. Once we have introduced axioms for the quotation function, we will be able to introduce an untyped sequencing operation for expressions based on the above approach. But for now we will be content with a typed account sequences which, to disambiguate, we call *lists*.

Our primary application of sequences is to express finite lists of terms and formulæ.[4] These expressions are therefore our 'words'. As the symbol e does not occur in any term or formula,[5] we use that symbol as the 'space' inserted between words to form sentences. There different ways to lift the analogy to the level of paragraphs. We could require that $\mathcal{L}^*$ contains another auxiliary symbol, in addition to e, to be used as separator between lists. Alternatively, if the words are terms and formulæ, then the two-symbol expression ee never occurs as a subexpression of a list and can be utilized for the same purpose.

To formalize our analogy, a *word* is any expression that does not contain the symbol e. A *list* is a string of words, each immediately preceded by the symbol e. That is, an expression is a list if and only if it is the empty expression or its leftmost symbol is e. Given words $a_1, \ldots, a_n$, we write $[a_1, \ldots, a_n]$ for the list $[a_1, \ldots, a_n]_\mathrm{e}$, namely, $[a_1, \ldots, a_n] \equiv \mathrm{e}a_1\mathrm{e}a_2\mathrm{e}\cdots\mathrm{e}a_n$. The empty list $[\,]$ is the empty expression, whereas $[0]$ is the list of one (empty) word and given by the expression e. Lists are closed under concatenation: if $a_1, \ldots, a_n, b_1, \ldots, b_m$ are words, then $[a_1, \ldots, a_n][b_1, \ldots, b_m] \equiv [a_1, \ldots, a_n, b_1, \ldots, b_m]$.

An element of a list l is any word a such that either $\mathrm{e}a$ is a suffix of l or $\mathrm{e}a\mathrm{e} \subseteq l$. Equivalently, a is an element of l if and only if there exist lists $l_0, l_1 \subset l$ such that $l \equiv l_0\mathrm{e}al_1$. We write $a \in l$ to express that a is an element of (the list) l. An initial segment of l is any list l_0 such that the unique l_1 satisfying $l \equiv l_0 l_1$ is also a list. In other words, l_0 is an initial segment of l if and only if $l_0\mathrm{e}$ is a prefix of $l\mathrm{e}$. Every element of an initial segment of a list is an element of the list. An initial

[4]We will consider lists of quotations, but quotations are terms.

[5]A term can contain the syntactic constant $\underset{\sim}{\mathrm{e}}$, but this is distinct from e.

segment of l is proper if it is distinct from l. These definitions are expressed by the following formulæ.

$$\begin{aligned}\mathsf{Word}(\mathsf{x}) &:= \neg\,\underline{\mathsf{e}} \subseteq \mathsf{x},\\ \mathsf{List}(\mathsf{x}) &:= \mathsf{x} = \underline{0} \vee \exists \mathsf{w}(\mathsf{x} = \underline{\mathsf{e}}^\frown \mathsf{w}),\\ \mathsf{x} \in \mathsf{y} &:= \mathsf{Word}(\mathsf{x}) \wedge \big(\underline{\mathsf{e}}^\frown \mathsf{x}^\frown \underline{\mathsf{e}} \subseteq \mathsf{y} \vee \exists \mathsf{w}(\mathsf{w}^\frown \underline{\mathsf{e}}^\frown \mathsf{x} = \mathsf{y})\big),\\ \mathsf{Init}(\mathsf{x},\mathsf{y}) &:= \mathsf{List}(\mathsf{x}) \wedge \exists \mathsf{w}\big(\mathsf{List}(\mathsf{w}) \wedge \mathsf{x}^\frown \mathsf{w} = \mathsf{y}\big).\end{aligned}$$

We introduce two bounded quantifiers referring to the element-relation for lists: $\forall x \in t\ \varphi$ and $\exists x \in t\ \varphi$ for $\forall x(x \in t \to \varphi)$ and $\exists x(x \in t \wedge \varphi)$ respectively. Since elements of lists are subexpressions of them, these quantifiers are special cases of the bounded quantifiers already introduced.

Concerning the formal notion of a word, we observe the following property of E^*:

8.58 LEMMA *For every $*$-expression a, $\mathsf{E}^* \vdash \mathsf{Word}(\overline{a})$ if a is a word, and $\mathsf{E}^* \vdash \neg\mathsf{Word}(\overline{a})$ otherwise.*

PROOF The second statement follows directly from proposition 8.56. The first part is straightforward to prove by induction on a. The empty expression is a word and, indeed, $\mathsf{E}^* \vdash \mathsf{Word}(\underline{0})$ by lemma 8.54(iv). Moreover, if $a \equiv bu$ is a word and u is a symbol, then $\mathsf{E}^* \vdash \mathsf{Word}(\overline{b})$ by the induction hypothesis and $\mathsf{E}^* \vdash \overline{u} \neq \underline{\mathsf{v}}$ by proposition 8.48. As $\mathsf{E}^* \vdash \mathsf{Sing}(\overline{u})$, we apply proposition 8.55 and lemma 8.54(ii) to deduce $\mathsf{E}^* \vdash \mathsf{Word}(\overline{a})$. ⊣

In relation to the other formulæ introduced, we observe the following:

8.59 PROPOSITION *The following are derivable in E^*:*

(i) $\forall x \forall y \forall z\big(\mathsf{List}(x) \wedge \mathsf{Init}(y,x) \wedge \mathsf{Init}(z,x) \to \mathsf{Init}(y,z) \vee \mathsf{Init}(z,y)\big)$.

(ii) $\forall x \forall y\big(\mathsf{Init}(x,y) \to \forall z \in x\ z \in y\big)$.

(iii) $\forall x \forall y\big(\mathsf{List}(x) \wedge \mathsf{List}(y) \to \big(\mathsf{List}(x^\frown y) \wedge \forall z(z \in x^\frown y \leftrightarrow z \in x \vee z \in y)\big)\big)$.

PROOF Exercise; lemma 8.54(v) is needed. ⊣

8.60 PROPOSITION *Suppose $a_1, \ldots, a_k$ are words and l is the list $[a_1, \ldots, a_k]$. For each $i \leq k$ let $l_i = [a_1, \ldots, a_i]$. Then*

(i) $\mathsf{E}^* \vdash \mathsf{List}(\overline{l})$,

(ii) $\mathsf{E}^* \vdash \forall y\big(y \in \overline{l} \rightarrow y = \overline{a_1} \vee \cdots \vee y = \overline{a_k}\big)$,

(iii) $\mathsf{E}^* \vdash \forall y\big(\mathsf{Init}(y, \overline{l}) \rightarrow y = \overline{l_0} \vee \cdots \vee y = \overline{l_k}\big)$.

Our first application of lists will be to show that the property of being a well-bracketed word is expressible in E^*. An expression w is well-bracketed if every opening bracket (in w can be associated with a unique closing bracket) in w occurring to the right. The expression $(\neg()((\mathsf{v})\mathsf{x}))$ is well-bracketed whereas $((()()))$ is not. Every term and formula is a well-bracketed word. More precisely, an expression is well-bracketed if and only if it can be generated via three recursive rules:

(i) Every expression containing neither the symbol (nor the symbol) is well-bracketed.

(ii) If a is well-bracketed, so is (a).

(iii) If a and b are well-bracketed, so is ab.

A proof that a given expression is well-bracketed consists in specifying how the expression can be generated via the three rules.

8.61 LEMMA *An expression a is well-bracketed if and only if there exists a sequence of expressions a_0, a_1, …, a_n such that $a_n \equiv a$ and for each $i \leq n$ either a_i contains neither the symbol (nor the symbol), or $a_i \equiv (a_j)$ for some $j < i$, or $a_i \equiv a_j a_k$ for some j, $k < i$.*

If a is a well-bracketed word then the shortest sequence $a_0, \ldots, a_n$ satisfying the lemma will be a sequence of words and can be represented as a list. Moreover, there is a formula of $\mathcal{L}^*$ which expresses that each element of a list fulfils one of the three criteria of the lemma. The property of not containing either bracket is given by the formula $\neg(\underline{(} \subseteq \mathsf{x} \vee \underline{)} \subseteq \mathsf{x})$. Since this is rather difficult to read let l and r denote the left and right bracket respectively. Being a well-bracketed word is expressed by the formula $\mathsf{Wbw}(\mathsf{x})$, defined as

$$\exists \mathsf{y}\Big(\mathsf{List}(\mathsf{y}) \wedge \mathsf{x} \in \mathsf{y} \wedge \\ \forall \mathsf{x} \in \mathsf{y}\big(\neg(\underline{r} \subseteq \mathsf{x} \vee \underline{l} \subseteq \mathsf{x}) \vee \exists \mathsf{w} \in \mathsf{y}\ \mathsf{x} = \underline{l}^\frown \mathsf{w}^\frown \underline{r} \vee \exists \mathsf{w} \in \mathsf{y}\ \exists \mathsf{z} \in \mathsf{y}\ \mathsf{x} = \mathsf{w}^\frown \mathsf{z}\big)\Big).$$

The variable y in $\mathsf{Wbw}(\mathsf{x})$ represents in the form of a list the sequence $a_0, \ldots, a_n$ in lemma 8.61, but without any restriction on the order of the elements. Under this reading, the quantifier $\forall \mathsf{x} \in \mathsf{y}$ ranges over the constituent words $a_0, \ldots, a_n$ and the rest of the formula expresses that each individual word satisfies one of the requirements (i)–(iii) with respect to the other elements of the list.

8.62 LEMMA *If a is a well-bracketed word, then* $\mathsf{E}^* \vdash \mathsf{Wbw}(\overline{a})$.

At present, we cannot capture the larger class of well-bracketed expressions, as these include expressions such as (e) which interfere with the decomposition of lists as sequences of words. That will become possible with untyped sequences at our disposal.

Through a similar use of lists we can capture the notion of a term. Let $\mathcal{F}$ be the (finite) set of basic function symbols of $\mathcal{L}^*$. The arity of a function symbol $\mathsf{f} \in \mathcal{F}$ is denoted a_f. In addition to basic function symbols, terms can be constructed from syntactic constants. These, recall, are expressed by the formula $\mathsf{Syn}(x)$ specified in definition 8.46.

8.63 DEFINITION For each function symbol f of $\mathcal{L}^*$, we introduce a term $\dot{\mathsf{f}}$ of the same arity, defined by $\dot{\mathsf{f}}(x_1, \ldots, x_{a_\mathsf{f}}) := \underline{\mathsf{f}}{}^\frown x_1{}^\frown \cdots {}^\frown x_{a_\mathsf{f}}$ and abbreviated as $\dot{\mathsf{f}} x_1 \cdots x_{a_\mathsf{f}}$. $\mathsf{Term}(\mathsf{x})$ is the formula

$$\exists \mathsf{y}\Big(\mathsf{List}(\mathsf{y}) \wedge \mathsf{x} \in \mathsf{y} \wedge \forall \mathsf{x} \in \mathsf{y}\,\big(\mathsf{Var}(\mathsf{x}) \vee \mathsf{Syn}(\mathsf{x}) \vee \bigvee_{\mathsf{f} \in \mathcal{F}} \exists \mathsf{v}_2 \in \mathsf{y} \cdots \exists \mathsf{v}_{a_\mathsf{f}+1} \in \mathsf{y}\ \mathsf{x} = \dot{\mathsf{f}} \mathsf{v}_2 \cdots \mathsf{v}_{a_\mathsf{f}+1}\big)\Big).$$

The variables $\mathsf{v}_2, \ldots, \mathsf{v}_{a_\mathsf{f}+1}$ in the final conjunct of Term represent a_f-many elements from the list y. Since both x and y occur free in the third conjunct, it is necessary to start the indexing at the third variable, v_2.

REMARK ON NOTATION The notation $\bigvee_{\mathsf{f} \in \mathcal{F}}$ abbreviates a disjunction of formulæ indexed by the elements of $\mathcal{F}$. In general, given a finite set $I = \{i_1, \ldots, i_k\}$ and a formula φ_i for each $i \in I$, we write

$$\bigvee_{i \in I} \varphi_i \quad \text{to abbreviate} \quad \varphi_{i_1} \vee \varphi_{i_2} \vee \cdots \vee \varphi_{i_k},$$

$$\bigwedge_{i \in I} \varphi_i \quad \text{to abbreviate} \quad \varphi_{i_1} \wedge \varphi_{i_2} \wedge \cdots \wedge \varphi_{i_k}.$$

If I is the empty set, then $\bigvee_{i\in I}\varphi_i$ is $\bot$ and $\bigwedge_{i\in I}\varphi_i$ is $\neg\bot$. The order in which the elements of I are enumerated is unimportant as the different choices lead to logically equivalent formulæ. In the indexed disjunction of definition 8.63, $I = \mathcal{F}$ and φ_{f} is the formula $\exists \mathsf{v}_2 \in \mathsf{y} \cdots \exists \mathsf{v}_{a_{\mathsf{f}}+1} \in \mathsf{y}\ \mathsf{x} = \underset{\cdot}{\mathsf{f}}\mathsf{v}_2 \cdots \mathsf{v}_{a_{\mathsf{f}}+1}$ for each $\mathsf{f} \in \mathcal{F}$.

If I is a set of consecutive natural numbers, say $I = \{m, m+1, \ldots, n\}$, we write $\bigvee_{j=m}^{n}\varphi_j$ for $\bigvee_{j\in I}\varphi_j$, and likewise for conjunction.

Term is a well-formed formula as $\mathcal{F}$ is a finite set and for each $\mathsf{f} \in \mathcal{F}$ the sequence of existential quantifiers $\exists \mathsf{v}_1 \in \mathsf{y} \cdots \exists \mathsf{v}_{a_{\mathsf{f}}} \in \mathsf{y}$ is finite in length. Closed terms can be expressed as terms without any variables:

$$\mathsf{CTerm}(\mathsf{x}) := \mathsf{Term}(\mathsf{x}) \wedge \forall \mathsf{y} \subseteq \mathsf{x}\ \neg \mathsf{Var}(\mathsf{y}).$$

The two formulæ Term and CTerm will be used extensively in subsequent chapters, where also the next lemma will be proved. For now, we leave the following as an exercise for the reader.

8.64 PROPOSITION *For every term t,* $\mathsf{E}^* \vdash \mathsf{Term}(\overline{t})$. *If t is closed,* $\mathsf{E}^* \vdash \mathsf{CTerm}(\overline{t})$.

8.3.3 *Axioms for Quotation*

In the theories E and E^-, axioms for the quotation function q were given pointwise, that is, term by term. Separately, we also introduced an operation on the languages of these theories which associated to each expression a a term $\ulcorner a \urcorner$, the quotation of a, and proved in each theory that the function symbol q provides an internal representation of this operation. The quotation axioms of E^* will be motivated from the other direction: they comprise axioms stating that the function q satisfies the defining properties of the quotation operation $a \mapsto \overline{a}$. From these axioms we will be able to derive analogues of the axiom schemas of E and E^-, namely the equation $\mathsf{q}\overline{a} = \overline{\overline{a}}$ for every $*$-expression a.

The following three formulæ are axioms of E^*. The first axiom expresses that the quotation of au, where u is a $*$-symbol and a is not empty, is the concatenation of the quotations of a and u, namely the expression $\frown\overline{a}\overline{u}$. The second axiom defines the quotation of the syntactic constants, recalling that $\overline{u} \equiv \mathsf{q}\underline{u}$ if u is a basic symbol. The final axiom states that quotation is an injective operation, a fact we proved in proposition 8.40.

D1 $\forall \mathsf{x} \forall \mathsf{y}(\mathsf{x} \neq \underline{0} \wedge \mathsf{Sing}(\mathsf{y}) \rightarrow \mathsf{q}(\mathsf{x}\frown\mathsf{y}) = \underline{\frown}\frown\mathsf{qx}\frown\mathsf{qy}),$

D2 $\forall x(\mathsf{sym}\, x \rightarrow \mathsf{q}(\mathsf{q}x) = \underline{\mathsf{q}}{}^\frown \mathsf{q}x)$,

D3 $\forall x \forall y(\mathsf{q}x = \mathsf{q}y \rightarrow x = y)$.

Our first observation is a new characterization of the basic symbols that results from D3:

8.65 PROPOSITION $\mathsf{E}^* \vdash \forall x\,(\mathsf{sym}\, x \leftrightarrow x \neq \underline{0} \wedge \mathsf{Sing}(\mathsf{q}x))$.

PROOF The left-to-right direction is a consequence of the axioms for symbols. For the converse, assume that $x \neq \underline{0}$ and $\mathsf{Sing}(\mathsf{q}x)$. By the axioms for symbols there exists y such that $\mathsf{sym}\, y$ and $\mathsf{q}x = \mathsf{q}y$, from which D3 implies $\mathsf{sym}\, x$. ⊣

The next result recalls the notion of a pure term from definition 8.41:

8.66 PROPOSITION *For every pure term t,* $\mathsf{E}^* \vdash \overline{t} = \mathsf{q}t$. *In particular, for every expression a,* $\mathsf{E}^* \vdash \overline{\overline{a}} = \mathsf{q}\overline{a}$.

PROOF We argue by induction on the formation of t. If t is a syntactic constant then $\overline{t} \equiv \mathsf{q}t$ by definition. Otherwise t is either $\mathsf{q}s$ or ${}^\frown rs$ for pure terms r and s. In the former case, s is a syntactic constant and $\overline{t} \equiv \underline{\mathsf{q}}{}^\frown \overline{t}$. We instantiate the universal quantifier in D2 with s to conclude

$$\mathsf{E}^* \vdash \mathsf{q}t = \overline{t}.$$

In the second scenario, $t \equiv {}^\frown rs$ and $s \equiv \mathsf{q}\underline{u}$ or $s \equiv \underline{u}$ for some syntactic constant $\underline{u}$. The induction hypothesis implies $\mathsf{E}^* \vdash \overline{r} = \mathsf{q}r \wedge \overline{s} = \mathsf{q}s$. Moreover, $\mathsf{E}^* \vdash \mathsf{Sing}(s)$ is derivable from either B2 or B3 depending on the form of s. Thus from D1 we deduce

$$\mathsf{E}^* \vdash \mathsf{q}t = \mathsf{q}(r^\frown s) = \underline{\frown}{}^\frown \mathsf{q}r^\frown \mathsf{q}s = \underline{\frown}{}^\frown \overline{r}^\frown \overline{s} = \overline{{}^\frown rs} = \overline{t}.$$

The penultimate equation is an application of proposition 8.55. The second part of the proposition is a consequence of the first, choosing the pure term $t \equiv \overline{a}$. ⊣

It is straightforward to find non-pure terms that fail the property in the statement of proposition 8.66. For example, choosing $t \equiv {}^\frown \underline{0}\mathsf{q}\underline{\neg}$, namely the term $\underline{0}{}^\frown \mathsf{q}\underline{\neg}$, we have

$$\mathsf{E}^* \vdash \overline{t} = \underline{\frown}{}^\frown \mathsf{q}\underline{0}{}^\frown \underline{\mathsf{q}}{}^\frown \mathsf{q}\underline{\neg},$$

yet

$$\mathsf{E}^* \vdash \mathsf{q}t = \underline{\mathsf{q}}{}^\frown \mathsf{q}\underline{\neg}$$

by D1 and D2. Thus, according to E^*, $\mathsf{q}t$ is an expression of length 2 whereas the length of $\overline{t}$ is 4. The two terms are therefore provably distinct by repeated applications of lemma 8.54(iii). The function symbol sub for substitution also provides counterexamples to proposition 8.66. For now, let us assume

$$\mathsf{E}^* \vdash \mathsf{sub}\underline{\forall}\,\underline{\forall}\,\underline{\neg} = \underline{\neg}.$$

This theorem follows from the axioms of substitution we will present shortly. Let t be the term $\mathsf{sub}\underline{\forall}\,\underline{\forall}\,\underline{\neg}$. Clearly, $\mathsf{E}^* \vdash \mathsf{q}t = \mathsf{q}\underline{\neg}$, whereas $\overline{t}$ is a non-singleton expression with leftmost symbol $\underline{\mathsf{sub}}$.

Axiom D3 is particularly relevant in the derivation of negative facts about quotations, the main one being that quotations of distinct expressions are provably distinct:

8.67 PROPOSITION *For any two distinct $*$-expressions a and b,* $\mathsf{E}^* \vdash \neg\,\overline{a} = \overline{b}$.

PROOF Proposition 8.57 yields the desired result provided we establish $\mathsf{E}^* \vdash \overline{u} \neq \overline{v}$, where u and v are any two distinct syntactic constants. That requirement is provided by D3. ⊣

Generalizing the proposition, we obtain the following lemma:

8.68 LEMMA *If a is not a subexpression of b, then* $\mathsf{E}^* \vdash \neg\,\overline{a} \subseteq \overline{b}$.

PROOF Given an expression a, let S_a be the set of all subexpressions of a, which is finite. By induction over the length of b we show $\mathsf{E}^* \vdash \forall x\,(x \subseteq \overline{b} \rightarrow \bigvee_{c\in S_b} x = \overline{c})$. By the previous lemma, however, $\mathsf{E}^* \vdash \bigwedge_{c\in S_b} \neg\,\overline{a} = \overline{c}$. ⊣

The next lemma establishes some further usual properties of quotation:

8.69 LEMMA *The following are theorems of* E^*.

(i) $\forall x \forall y\,(\mathsf{sym}\,x \wedge \mathsf{sym}\,y \rightarrow x \not\subseteq \mathsf{q}y)$;

(ii) $\mathsf{q}\overline{a} \not\subseteq \overline{a}$ *for every a;*

(iii) $\mathsf{Word}(\mathsf{q}\overline{a})$ *for every a.*

PROOF For (i), apply lemma 8.54(i) and the axioms for symbols. Clause (ii) follows by induction on the length of a. The case that a is a symbol or the empty expression is a consequence of the axioms for symbols. In the other cases, a is an expression of length ≥ 2, and the length of $\overline{a}$ is always strictly greater than that of a. So lemma 8.68 implies $\mathsf{E}^* \vdash \underline{\overline{\overline{a}}} \not\subset \underline{\overline{a}}$. As $\mathsf{E}^* \vdash \underline{\overline{\overline{a}}} = \mathsf{q}\underline{\overline{a}}$, we are done. For (iii) it is required to prove $\mathsf{E}^* \vdash \underline{\mathsf{e}} \not\subset \mathsf{q}\underline{\overline{a}}$ for every a. Again, we proceed by induction on a. If a is a symbol or the empty expression, this follows from lemma 8.69. In the other cases, we apply the induction hypothesis and D1. ⊣

Clause (iii) of the previous lemma provides the missing ingredient for turning the typed sequences into a method of representing arbitrary sequences of $\star$-expressions as single $\star$-expressions. In section 8.3.2 we introduced the abbreviation $[a_1, \ldots, a_m] \equiv \mathsf{e}a_1\mathsf{e}\cdots\mathsf{e}a_m$ for forming lists of words. This construction is typed, as it assumes that $a_1, \ldots, a_m$ do not contain the delimiting symbol e and so cannot be lists (of non-zero length) themselves. Without such an assumption it is not possible to uniquely determine $a_1, \ldots, a_m$ given $[a_1, \ldots, a_m]$.

Because the quotation of each $\star$-expression is a word (and this fact is derivable from the axioms of E^*), lists of quotations do not suffer from ambiguity. For each natural number n and expressions $a_1, \ldots, a_n$ we introduce the abbreviation

$$\langle a_1, \ldots, a_n \rangle := [\overline{a_1}, \ldots, \overline{a_n}] \equiv \mathsf{e}\overline{a_1}\mathsf{e}\cdots\mathsf{e}\overline{a_n}.$$

An expression of the form $\langle a_1, \ldots, a_n \rangle$ is called a sequence. We refer to $a_1, \ldots, a_n$ as the components of the sequence $\langle a_1, \ldots, a_n \rangle$. Being a list of quotations, the elements of $\langle a_1, \ldots, a_n \rangle$ are the expressions $\overline{a_1}, \ldots, \overline{a_n}$. The empty sequence $\langle\,\rangle$ is the empty list, namely the empty expression, and a sequence of length 1 is an expression $\langle a \rangle \equiv \mathsf{e}\overline{a}$ obtained by prefixing the symbol e to a quotation.

Sequences are expressed in $\mathcal{L}^*$ by the function symbol for quotation. For each $n \geq 0$, we introduce a term $\langle \mathsf{v}_1, \ldots, \mathsf{v}_n \rangle$ in the variables $\mathsf{v}_1, \ldots, \mathsf{v}_n$ defined as

$$\langle \mathsf{v}_1, \ldots, \mathsf{v}_n \rangle := \underline{\mathsf{e}}{}^\frown \mathsf{q}\mathsf{v}_1{}^\frown \underline{\mathsf{e}}{}^\frown \cdots {}^\frown \underline{\mathsf{e}}{}^\frown \mathsf{q}\mathsf{v}_n.$$

These terms are such that if $a \equiv \langle a_1, \ldots, a_n \rangle$ is a sequence, then

$$\mathsf{E}^* \vdash \underline{\overline{a}} = \langle \underline{\overline{a_1}}, \ldots, \underline{\overline{a_n}} \rangle.$$

Moreover, if $a_1, \ldots, a_m$ and $b_1, \ldots, b_n$ are such that either $m \neq n$ or $a_i \not\equiv b_i$ for some i, then, applying proposition 8.67, lemma 8.69, and D3, we deduce

$$\mathsf{E}^* \vdash \langle \underline{\overline{a_1}}, \ldots, \underline{\overline{a_m}} \rangle \neq \langle \underline{\overline{b_1}}, \ldots, \underline{\overline{b_n}} \rangle.$$

The next formulæ specify the properties of being a sequence and being a component, respectively:

$$\mathsf{Seq}(y) := \mathsf{List}(y) \wedge \forall x \in y \, \exists z \; x = \mathsf{q}z,$$
$$x \in_{\mathrm{seq}} y := \mathsf{q}x \in y.$$

The next lemma demonstrates that these definitions operate as intended.

8.70 LEMMA *Let $a_1, \ldots, a_n$, and b be expressions. The following are derivable in* E^*.

(i) $\mathsf{Seq}\big(\langle \overline{a_1}, \ldots, \overline{a_n} \rangle\big)$,

(ii) $\overline{b} \in_{\mathrm{seq}} \langle \overline{a_1}, \ldots, \overline{a_n} \rangle \leftrightarrow \bigvee_{i=1}^{n} \overline{b} = \overline{a_i}$.

We conclude our examination of the axioms of quotation by considering a variation of axiom D2 that may intuitively seem plausible. The curious reader may have wondered whether it is necessary for the variable x in D2 to be restricted to basic symbols ('$\mathsf{sym}\,\mathsf{x} \to \ldots$') and if restricting to singletons, replacing D2 by the formula

(8.10) $$\forall \mathsf{x}\big(\mathsf{Sing}(\mathsf{x}) \to \mathsf{qqx} = \underline{\mathsf{q}}\,\widehat{}\,\mathsf{qx}\big),$$

or placing no restriction whatsoever, would be sufficient.

We show that (8.10) is inconsistent with the axioms of E^*. In particular, it is important that the properties expressed by D1 and D2 are mutually exclusive: D1 evaluates quotations of expressions of length at least 2, and D2 applies only to quotations of symbols. When evaluating a term $\mathsf{qq}s$, it is therefore necessary to evaluate the subterm s first. If s is a basic symbol, then D2 applies. Otherwise, s is either a syntactic constant or an expression of length at least 2, and $\mathsf{q}s$ will be a non-singleton expression. In this case, $\mathsf{qq}s$ is evaluated via D1.

8.71 LEMMA $\mathsf{E}^* + (8.10)$ *is inconsistent.*

PROOF We have $\mathsf{E}^* \vdash \mathsf{sym}\,\underline{\mathsf{v}}$, so $\mathsf{E}^* \vdash \mathsf{Sing}(\underline{\mathsf{v}})$. Hence, by D2,

(8.11) $$\mathsf{E}^* \vdash \mathsf{qq}\underline{\mathsf{v}} = \underline{\mathsf{q}}\,\widehat{}\,\mathsf{q}\underline{\mathsf{v}}.$$

Therefore,

	$\mathsf{E}^* \vdash \mathsf{qqq}\underline{\mathsf{v}} = \mathsf{q}(\underline{\mathsf{q}}\,\widehat{}\,\mathsf{q}\underline{\mathsf{v}})$	(8.11)
	$= \overline{\widehat{}\,\mathsf{qq}\underline{\mathsf{v}}}$	proposition 8.66
(8.12)	$= \underline{\widehat{}}\,\underline{\widehat{}}\,\mathsf{q}\underline{\mathsf{q}}\,\widehat{}\,\underline{\mathsf{q}}\,\widehat{}\,\mathsf{q}\underline{\mathsf{v}}.$	definition 8.39

Since $\mathsf{E}^* \vdash \mathsf{Sing}(\mathsf{q}\underline{\mathsf{v}})$, we also obtain

$$\mathsf{E}^* + (8.10) \vdash \mathsf{qq}\underline{\mathsf{q}}\underline{\mathsf{v}} = \underline{\mathsf{q}}{}^\frown\mathsf{qq}\underline{\mathsf{v}} \qquad (8.10)$$

$$(8.13) \qquad = \underline{\mathsf{q}}{}^\frown\underline{\mathsf{q}}{}^\frown\mathsf{q}\underline{\mathsf{v}}. \qquad (8.11)$$

Combining (8.12) and (8.13), and applying lemma 8.53(ii), we deduce $\mathsf{E}^*+(8.10) \vdash \underline{\mathsf{q}} = \underline{\ }^\frown{}^\frown\mathsf{q}\underline{\mathsf{q}}$, that is, $\mathsf{E}^*+(8.10) \vdash \mathsf{Sing}(\underline{\mathsf{q}}) \wedge \neg\mathsf{Sing}(\underline{\mathsf{q}})$. ⊣

8.3.4 Axioms for Substitution

In the weak theory E, the substitution function is given by two forms of axiom: the finitely many instances of axiom A7 and the infinite collection of axioms $\mathsf{sub}(\overline{a}, \overline{b}, \overline{c}) = \overline{d}$ where (a, b, c, d) is a substitution instance in which b is an $\mathcal{L}$-symbol (cf. definition 8.20). The axioms of E^- generalized this equation to include substitution instances in which b may be a complex expression, but still the output expression d is uniquely determined.

Following in the vein of the axioms for concatenation and quotation, we want to present a system of finitely many axioms from which for every choice of a, b, and c, with b non-empty, there exists an expression d that makes (a, b, c, d) a substitution instance and the equation $\mathsf{sub}(\overline{a}, \overline{b}, \overline{c}) = \overline{d}$ derivable in E^*. A natural way to achieve this is to axiomatize a particular strategy for computing substitution instances. For instance, we can always determine a suitable d by parsing the expression a symbol by symbol starting, say, from the rightmost symbol in a. If a is recognized as being of the form $a_0 b$, we set d to be $d_0 c$ where d_0 is the expression which makes (a_0, b, c, d_0) the substitution instance computed via this method. If a is non-empty but not of the above form, it suffices to set $d \equiv d_0 u$ where u is the symbol such that $a \equiv a_0 u$ for some a_0 and (a_0, b, c, d_0) is the substitution instance computed recursively. This is the approach we adopt in our axiomatization of substitution. Other strategies are also possible. As before, our main use of substitution is in computing $\mathsf{sub}(\overline{a}, \overline{b}, \overline{c})$ where b is a term or symbol. Lemma 8.23 established, for the language $\mathcal{L}^-$, that in this case there is a unique expression d making (a, b, c, d) a substitution instance. We leave to the reader the task of proving the analogous claim for $\star$-expressions.

The following sentences are axioms of E^*.

E1 $\forall y \forall z(\mathsf{sub}(\underline{0}, y, z) = \underline{0} \wedge \mathsf{sub}(y, \underline{0}, z) = y)$,

E2 $\forall x \forall y \forall z(y \neq \underline{0} \to \mathsf{sub}(x^\frown y, y, z) = \mathsf{sub}(x, y, z)^\frown z)$,

E3 $\forall w \forall x \forall y \big(\mathsf{Sing}(w) \wedge \forall z\ x^\frown w \neq z^\frown y \rightarrow \forall z\ \mathsf{sub}(x^\frown w, y, z) \equiv \mathsf{sub}(x, y, z)^\frown w\big)$.

Note that E1 also includes the definition $\mathsf{sub}(y, \underline{0}, z) = y$, which ensures that substitution can be evaluated on all choices of its three arguments.

8.72 PROPOSITION *Let* (a, b, c, d) *be a substitution instance in which d was obtained from a by successively replacing the rightmost occurrence of b in a by c. Then* $\mathsf{E}^* \vdash \mathsf{sub}(\overline{a}, \overline{b}, \overline{c}) = \overline{d}$.

PROOF Induction on the length of a. ⊣

A negative version of the proposition is also available:

8.73 PROPOSITION *Suppose* (a, b, c, d) *is not a substitution instance and b is non-empty. Then* $\mathsf{E}^* \vdash \neg\, \mathsf{sub}(\overline{a}, \overline{b}, \overline{c}) = \overline{d}$.

PROOF Suppose that b is non-empty and let (a, b, c, d) be the substitution instance described in the previous proposition. So $\mathsf{E}^* \vdash \mathsf{sub}(\overline{a}, \overline{b}, \overline{c}) = \overline{d}$. If e is any expression for which (a, b, c, e) is not a substitution instance, then $d \not\equiv e$. Proposition 8.67 implies $\mathsf{E}^* \vdash \neg\, \overline{d} = \overline{e}$, and we are done. ⊣

So far we have seen two kinds of expressions defined in terms of substitution. The first is natural numbers, introduced in chapter 6 as the formula

$$\mathsf{Nat}(x) \;\equiv\; \mathsf{sub}(x, \bar{\mathsf{x}}, \underline{0}) = \underline{0}.$$

The second is the definition of the variables in $\mathcal{L}^*$ from the previous section:

$$\mathsf{Var}(x) \;\equiv\; \exists y\big(x = (\underline{^\frown} y \underline{^\frown}) \wedge \mathsf{sub}(y, \underline{\mathsf{v}}, \underline{0}) = \underline{0}\big).$$

We may now use propositions 8.72 and 8.73 to show that both formulæ capture the respective sets of expressions. The proof of the next result is now straightforward.

8.74 PROPOSITION *For each* $\star$*-expression a,*

(i) $\mathsf{E}^* \vdash \mathsf{Var}(\overline{a})$ *if a is a variable, and* $\mathsf{E}^* \vdash \mathsf{Nat}(\overline{a})$ *if a is a numeral;*

(ii) $\mathsf{E}^* \vdash \neg \mathsf{Var}(\overline{a})$ *if a is not a variable, and* $\mathsf{E}^* \vdash \neg \mathsf{Nat}(\overline{a})$ *if a is not a numeral.*

With axioms for concatenation, substitution, and quotation in place, and having derived from them versions of the most important axioms of E, we can start to reprove in E^* theorems of E. In section 8.5 we describe how to import any theorem of E as a theorem of E^*. Such a general result is largely unnecessary because most of the theorems of E that we presented are logical consequences of the strong diagonal lemma 5.11, and proving this single result in E^* suffices to transport the most interesting results from one theory into the other.

8.75 STRONG DIAGONAL LEMMA *If $s(\mathsf{x})$ is a term of $\mathcal{L}^*$, then there exists a term t such that $\mathsf{E}^* \vdash t = s(\overline{t})$.*

We have taken the opportunity to state a slight generalization of the strong diagonal lemma from chapter 6, with an application in mind to a paradox on function symbols we will present in section 9.2. A direct reformulation of the lemma would state that if $\varphi(\mathsf{x})$ is a formula with no bound occurrences of x, then there is a closed term t such that the equation $t = \overline{\varphi(t)}$ is a theorem of E^*. We obtain this version by selecting $\mathsf{sub}(\overline{\varphi(\mathsf{x})}, \overline{\mathsf{x}}, \mathsf{x})$ for the term $s(\mathsf{x})$ in lemma 8.75.

The reader can verify that this strengthening also holds for E.

PROOF We use the same diagonal function $\mathsf{dia}(\mathsf{x}) := \mathsf{sub}(\mathsf{x}, \overline{\mathsf{x}}, \mathsf{qx})$ as in chapter 5. Given a term $s(\mathsf{x})$, let r be the term $s(\mathsf{dia}(\mathsf{x}))$. As in E, the following equations are derivable in E^*:

$$\begin{aligned} \mathsf{E}^* \vdash \mathsf{dia}(\overline{r}) &= \mathsf{sub}(\overline{s(\mathsf{dia}(\mathsf{x}))}, \overline{\mathsf{x}}, \overline{\overline{r}}) && \text{proposition 8.66} \\ &= \overline{s(\mathsf{dia}(\overline{r}))}. && \text{proposition 8.72} \end{aligned}$$

Let $t \equiv s(\mathsf{dia}(\overline{r}))$. We have $\mathsf{E}^* \vdash t = s(\overline{t})$. ⊣

Before we demonstrate how to derive the traditional diagonal lemma as a consequence of lemma 8.75, we consider a version of Tarski's theorem on the undefinability of truth for terms:

8.76 THEOREM *Let $\mathcal{L}^*$ contains a unary function symbol t and suppose that $\mathsf{E}^* \vdash \mathsf{t}\overline{\varphi} = \underline{\mathsf{v}} \leftrightarrow \varphi$ for every sentence φ in the language $\mathcal{L}^*$. Then E^* is inconsistent.*

The condition in theorem 8.76 is equivalent to the assumption that a predicate satisfying the unrestricted T-schema for $\mathcal{L}^*$ is definable. Let $\tau(\mathsf{x}) := \mathsf{tx} = \underline{\mathsf{v}}$. If $\mathsf{E}^* \vdash \mathsf{t}\overline{\varphi} = \underline{\mathsf{v}} \leftrightarrow \varphi$ for a sentence φ, then $\mathsf{E}^* \vdash \tau(\overline{\varphi}) \leftrightarrow \varphi$. Conversely, if τ is a formula which satisfies the T-schema, a function symbol t introduced with the axiom $\forall x\big(\tau(x) \to \mathsf{t}x = \underline{\mathsf{v}}\big) \wedge \forall x\big(\neg\tau(x) \to \mathsf{t}x = \underline{\mathsf{v}}\underline{\mathsf{v}}\big)$ can be added to the theory. Theorem 8.76 implies that the extension of E^* by this axiom is inconsistent. As, in this case, t is a definable function, it follows that the theory E^* itself is inconsistent by the argument on eliminating function symbols given in chapter 2.

PROOF OF THEOREM 8.76 We give a direct proof of the theorem using the strong diagonal lemma for terms. Suppose $\mathsf{E}^* \vdash \mathsf{t}\overline{\varphi} = \underline{\mathsf{v}} \leftrightarrow \varphi$ for every sentence φ. Let $u(\mathsf{x})$ be the term $\mathsf{t}\big(\mathsf{sub}(\overline{\neg\mathsf{x} = \underline{\mathsf{v}}}, \overline{\mathsf{x}}, \mathsf{qx})\big)$. By lemma 8.75 we find a term s such that

$$\mathsf{E}^* \vdash s = \mathsf{t}(\overline{\neg s = \underline{\mathsf{v}}}).$$

Thus, $\mathsf{E}^* \vdash s = \underline{\mathsf{v}} \leftrightarrow \neg s = \underline{\mathsf{v}}$, and E^* is inconsistent. ⊣

8.77 COROLLARY *If $\varphi(\mathsf{x})$ is a formula of $\mathcal{L}^*$ with no bound occurrences of x, then there exists a formula γ such that*

$$\mathsf{E}^* \vdash \gamma \leftrightarrow \varphi(\overline{\gamma}).$$

PROOF Given φ, consider the term $s(\mathsf{x}) \equiv \mathsf{sub}(\overline{\varphi}, \overline{\mathsf{x}}, \mathsf{qx})$. Lemma 8.75 provides a closed term t such that

$$\mathsf{E}^* \vdash t = s(\overline{t}) = \overline{\varphi(\overline{t})}.$$

The second equality claim is an application of proposition 8.72. Now let $\gamma \equiv \varphi(t)$. Therefore, $\mathsf{E}^* \vdash \gamma \leftrightarrow \varphi(\overline{\gamma})$. ⊣

8.4 The Axiom Schema of Induction

The final group of axioms concerns a method of proof which we have used repeatedly but which is not captured by the other axioms or the rules of predicate logic. This is the principle of mathematical induction for $\star$-expressions. We have seen many applications of induction so far. For example, that the quotation of every expression is a term was proved by induction on the length of expressions. A second example is lemma 8.69, where we proved that $\mathsf{E}^* \vdash \mathsf{Word}(\mathsf{q}\overline{a})$ for every $\star$-expression a. This proof also proceeds by induction on a and appeals to the axioms of quotation and concatenation. The generalization,

$$\forall x\ \mathsf{Word}(\mathsf{q}x), \tag{8.14}$$

is not a consequence of lemma 8.69: the basic axioms provide no general way of deriving $\forall x\, \varphi(x)$ from the collection of assumptions $\varphi(\overline{a})$ for every a. Even the fairly innocuous claim that every non-empty expression is the concatenation of an expression and a symbol, expressed by the formula

$$\forall x \Big(x \neq \underline{0} \to \exists y \exists u \big(\mathsf{Sing}(u) \wedge x = yu \big) \Big), \tag{8.15}$$

is not derivable from the axioms presented in the previous section.[6] Each instance of (8.15) with x replaced by a quotation constant is easily proven in E^*, and we can derive both examples by incorporating the principle of proof by induction into E^*.

Before proceeding with the formal details, it is perhaps appropriate to clarify what we mean precisely by the principle of induction for $\star$-expressions. Induction as a method of proof is usually associated with the natural numbers. This principle of induction can be expressed as the following claim about properties of natural numbers (here we use the term 'property' in a neutral sense without commitment to any particular interpretation).

PRINCIPLE OF INDUCTION FOR NATURAL NUMBERS *Suppose P is a property of natural numbers which holds of* 0 *and holds of* $n+1$ *whenever it holds of* n. *Then P holds of* all *natural numbers.*

We may use induction to prove, for example, that addition on numbers is commutative: $m+n = n+m$ for all m and n. A closely related property can be stated for expressions:

WEAK PRINCIPLE OF INDUCTION *Suppose P is a property of $\star$-expressions which holds of the empty expression and holds of the $\star$-expression au whenever u is a symbol and P holds of a. Then P holds of all $\star$-expressions.*

The hypothesis consists of two parts: that P holds of the empty expression, called the *base* case, and that for every expression a and symbol u, if P holds of a, then P holds of au, the inductive case. In the inductive case, the assumption that P holds of a is called the induction hypothesis. If P is such that it satisfies both

[6] That (8.14) and (8.15) are not derivable from the axioms we have so far presented can be deduced by providing a model of this fragment of E^* in which the formulæ are false. This result, however, is beyond the scope of the present work.

the base case and inductive case then, from the principle of weak induction, we may deduce that P holds of all expressions.

We can prove that the formula in (8.15) is correct as a statement about $*$-expressions by appealing to the weak induction principle. Let P be the property expressed of the variable x by (8.15), namely that if x is not empty, then x is the concatenation of some expression and a singleton. The proof is straightforward. The base case holds because the empty expression does not satisfy the antecedent of the implication. The inductive case holds because if a is an expression and u is a symbol, then P holds of the expression au, because every such expression satisfies the consequent. So, by the principle of induction for expressions, we conclude that P holds of all expressions and that thus the statement expressed by (8.15) is true.

If the property which we are attempting to prove by induction is presented as a formula $\varphi(\mathsf{x})$, then the principle of weak induction for this property can also be written as a formula. This is the formula

$$\varphi(\underline{0}) \land \forall \mathsf{x}\Big(\varphi(\mathsf{x}) \to \forall \mathsf{y}\big(\mathsf{Sing}(\mathsf{y}) \to \varphi(\mathsf{xy})\big)\Big) \to \forall \mathsf{x}\, \varphi.$$

Weak induction is useful for deriving a number of generalized statements about expressions. It is not difficult, however, to find examples of proof by induction which do not readily fit into the template of weak induction. One such example is the statement that all terms are well-bracketed words. As a statement about $\mathcal{L}^*$-expressions, the claim is easily proved by induction on the recursive definition of terms: every constant and variable is a well-bracketed word, and as complex terms do not introduce parentheses these are well-bracketed words provided the constituent subterms are. Hence, all terms are well-bracketed. In section 8.3.2 we introduced the formulæ $\mathsf{Wbw}(x)$ and $\mathsf{Term}(x)$, expressing the properties of being a well-bracketed word and a term, respectively. The claim we wish to establish is given by the formula $\forall x\, \varphi(x)$ where

$$\varphi(x) := \mathsf{Term}(x) \to \mathsf{Wbw}(x).$$

Replicating the informal argument behind this claim, we want to assume as the induction hypothesis the statement that $\mathsf{Wbw}(y)$ for every expression y that is a subterm of x, and from this deduce $\varphi(x)$. That is, our informal argument establishes $\forall y \sqsubset x\ \varphi(y) \to \varphi(x)$. But the induction hypothesis for the weak induction principle is the assumption $\varphi(y)$ for the unique y such that $x = yu$ for some symbol u. As y will not be a term in this case, the weak induction hypothesis is of no use. Although a proof of the claim can be given using weak induction, the argument will no longer closely mirror the informal proof on the inductive definition of terms.

These examples motivate an apparently stronger principle of induction for expressions:

STRONG PRINCIPLE OF INDUCTION *Suppose P is a property of expressions such that for every expression a, if P is true of every proper subexpression of a then P is true of a. Then P is true of all expressions.*

In order to deduce, using this principle, that P holds of all expressions, it suffices to show that P holds of an arbitrary expression e under the assumption that P holds of all proper subexpressions of e. This single requirement replaces both the base case and the induction case of weak induction. In the special case that e is the empty expression, the condition becomes to show that P is true of e, as the empty expression has no proper subexpressions. And in the case that e is a composite expression, say fu, the principle of strong induction allows us to assume that P holds of all proper subexpressions of fu, including, among other assumptions, that P holds of f.

In the case of arithmetic, strong induction can be likened to course-of-values induction on natural numbers:

COURSE-OF-VALUES INDUCTION FOR NATURAL NUMBERS *Suppose P is a property of natural numbers such that for every natural number n, if P is true of every $m < n$ then P is true of n. Then P is true of all natural numbers.*

Despite the name, weak induction is not weaker than strong induction. In fact, the two principles, taken as axiom schemas, are equivalent over a weak theory of arithmetic. The name is because the induction hypothesis of the weak principle is a consequence of the induction hypothesis of the strong principle, but the converse is not always the case. We sketch the easier direction of the equivalence, namely that weak induction follows from strong induction. A formal derivation of this result is given in proposition 8.79, and the more difficult direction is presented in proposition 9.44 in the next chapter. We begin with the observation that the property expressed by (8.15) can be proved by strong induction, but this is straightforward. Now let P be some property for which we want to establish the weak induction principle. We can assume that P satisfies the hypothesis of the weak induction principle, namely that P holds of the empty expression and that P holds of an expression au whenever P holds of a and u is a symbol. The aim is to prove that P also satisfies the hypothesis of the strong induction principle. Therefore, let e be an arbitrary $\ast$-expression and assume that P holds of all proper subexpressions of e. We are required to show that P holds of e. We have assumed that P holds of the empty expression, so it suffices to consider the case that e is not empty. Now, (8.15) implies that $e \equiv au$ for some expression a and symbol u. As a is a proper subexpression of e, P holds of a by assumption. So P holds of e by the weak induction hypothesis. Invoking the principle of strong induction, we deduce that P holds of all $\ast$-expressions.

The final kind of axiom we will add to form E^* is the formal counterpart to the principle of strong induction for $\ast$-expressions. If the property P is expressed by $\varphi(\mathsf{x})$, then the strong principle of induction for P is expressed by the formula

$$\forall \mathsf{x}\big(\forall \mathsf{y}{\subset}\mathsf{x}\ \varphi(\mathsf{y}) \to \varphi(\mathsf{x})\big) \to \forall \mathsf{x}\, \varphi(\mathsf{x}). \tag{8.16}$$

The axiom says that if $\varphi(\mathsf{x})$ is such that

$$\forall \mathsf{x}\big(\forall \mathsf{y}{\subset}\mathsf{x}\ \varphi(\mathsf{y}) \to \varphi(\mathsf{x})\big), \tag{8.17}$$

then $\varphi(x)$ holds for every x. Sentence (8.17) expresses the antecedent of the strong induction principle: for any expression x, if $\varphi(y)$ for every y that is a proper subexpression of x, then $\varphi(x)$. A formula $\varphi(x)$ which satisfies (8.17) is said to be progressive (in x). The axiom of induction for φ states that if φ is progressive, then φ holds of all expressions.

Our formulations of induction in natural language quantify over properties. The language $\mathcal{L}^*$ does not have a way to talk about properties or sets of $\ast$-expressions in any general sense. Therefore, we stipulate (8.16) as an axiom schema, with a separate axiom for each formula of the language. Also, we require that the axioms of a theory are sentences. Rather than restricting the axiom to formulæ with just one free variable, we take the universal closure of all instances of (8.16). Thus, E^* contains the following axiom schema:

F1 the universal closure of $\forall \mathsf{x}\big(\forall \mathsf{y}{\subset}\mathsf{x}\ \varphi(\mathsf{y}) \to \varphi(\mathsf{x})\big) \to \forall \mathsf{x}\, \varphi(\mathsf{x})$ for each formula $\varphi(\mathsf{x})$ of $\mathcal{L}^*$.

We refer to the collection of instances of F1 as the axiom schema of induction. As remarked, φ may contain free variables in addition to x. These act as parameters in induction arguments. We can, for instance, prove a formula $\forall x \forall y\, \varphi(x,y)$ by appealing to the induction axiom for $\varphi(\mathsf{x},y)$, where y remains a free variable of the induction. If we prove that $\varphi(\mathsf{x},y)$ is progressive in x we may deduce $\forall x\, \varphi(x,y)$ and conclude $\forall x \forall y\, \varphi(x,y)$ by logic.

Sometimes it is helpful to consider the contrapositive of the induction axiom. If φ is a negated formula, say $\varphi \equiv \neg\psi$, then F1 is logically equivalent to

$$\exists x\, \psi(x) \to \exists x\big(\psi(x) \wedge \forall y \subset x\; \neg\psi(y)\big).$$

This statement expresses a natural minimality principle for $*$-expressions: if P holds of some expression, then there exists an expression e such that P holds of e but not of any proper subexpression of e.

We begin with some simple applications of the strong induction axiom.

8.78 LEMMA *The following are derivable in* E^*.

(i) $\forall x\big(x = \underline{0} \vee \exists y \exists z\big(\mathsf{Sing}(z) \wedge x = y^\frown z\big)\big)$,

(ii) $\forall x\, \mathsf{Word}(\mathsf{q}x)$,

(iii) $\forall x\, \mathsf{q}x \not\subseteq x$,

(iv) $\forall x \forall y\big(x \subseteq y \wedge y \subseteq x \to x = y\big)$.

PROOF (i). Let $\varphi(x) \equiv x = 0 \vee \exists y \exists z\big(\mathsf{Sing}(z) \wedge x = y^\frown z\big)$. We argue informally within E^*. To deduce $\forall x\, \varphi(x)$ by induction it suffices to show that $\varphi(x)$ is progressive in x. Fix an arbitrary expression a and assume $\forall y \subset a\; \varphi(y)$. From this, we want to deduce $\varphi(a)$. If $a = 0$ or $\mathsf{Sing}(a)$, then $\varphi(a)$ holds by definition. Thus we may assume

a. $a \neq 0$;

b. $\neg\mathsf{Sing}(a)$;

c. for every non-empty $b \subset a$ there exists an expression c and a singleton u such that $b = c^\frown u$.

Combining a and b, it follows that $a = a_0{}^\frown a_1$ for non-empty expressions a_0 and a_1. In particular, a_1 is a non-empty proper subexpression of a. By c, $a_1 = a_2{}^\frown u$ for some expression a_2 and singleton u. Letting $y = a_0{}^\frown a_2$ and $z = u$, we have shown $\varphi(a)$. Applying F1, we conclude that $\forall x\, \varphi(x)$.

(ii). We prove that $\varphi(x)$ is progressive in x, where now $\varphi(x) = \mathsf{Word}(\mathsf{q}x)$. Fix an arbitrary a and assume $\varphi(b)$ for every $b \subset a$. By (i) it suffices to assume three cases: $a = 0$, a is a singleton, or $a = c^\frown u$ for some singleton u and non-empty c. We already know that $\overline{0}$ is a word by the axioms for symbols, as is $\overline{a}$ if a is a singleton. In the third alternative, D1 implies $\mathsf{Word}(\mathsf{q}a) \leftrightarrow \mathsf{Word}(\mathsf{q}c) \wedge \mathsf{Word}(\mathsf{q}u)$, and we are done. So $\varphi(x)$ is progressive, and (ii) is established.

(iii). The statement clearly holds if $x = \underline{0}$. Furthermore, if $x = y^\frown u$ with u a singleton, then $\mathsf{q}y^\frown \mathsf{q}u$ is a subexpression of $\mathsf{q}x$. Thus, from $\mathsf{q}x \subseteq x$ we deduce $\mathsf{q}y \subseteq y$. Hence, the formula $\mathsf{qx} \nsubseteq \mathsf{x}$ is progressive in x.

(iv). We prove the claim that no expression is a proper subexpression of itself, expressed in $\mathcal{L}^*$ as $\forall x \forall z_1 \forall z_2 \big(x = z_1{}^\frown x^\frown z_2 \rightarrow z_1 = \underline{0} \wedge z_2 = \underline{0}\big)$. That this implies the desired result follows from the fact that if two distinct expressions are subexpressions of one another, then each expression is a proper subexpression of itself. The preceding formula is proved by induction on the variable x using (i). Suppose $z_1 = \underline{0} \wedge z_2 = \underline{0}$. If x is empty then both z_1 and z_2 are empty by C1. Moreover, if z_2 is empty, then C2 implies that z_1 is empty. This leaves the case that neither x nor z_2 is the empty expression. We show that this case is in contradiction with the induction hypothesis. Let $x = y^\frown u$ and $z_2 = z_3{}^\frown v$, where u and v are singletons. Then $y^\frown u = z_1{}^\frown x^\frown z_3{}^\frown v$, so $u = v$ and $y = z_1{}^\frown x^\frown z_3$ by lemma 8.53(ii). Therefore, $y = z_1{}^\frown y^\frown (u^\frown z_3)$. As y is a proper subexpression of x, the induction hypothesis implies $u^\frown z_3 = \underline{0}$, contradicting the assumption that u is a singleton. ⊣

The axiom schema of induction can be used to formalize proofs which employ induction on the recursive construction of certain collections of expressions. The argument that all terms are well-bracketed words has this form, for instance, and the reader can confirm that the informal proof given on page 191 can be presented as an instance of the induction axiom for the formula $\mathsf{Term}(\mathsf{x}) \rightarrow \mathsf{Wbw}(\mathsf{x})$. Lemma 8.80 provides more examples of formal proofs appealing to the strong induction principle.

The next proposition confirms that weak induction is a theorem of E^*:

8.79 PROPOSITION E^* *derives the following two statements for every formula* φ.

$$\varphi(\underline{0}) \wedge \forall \mathsf{x}\Big(\varphi(\mathsf{x}) \rightarrow \forall \mathsf{y}\big(\mathsf{Sing}(\mathsf{y}) \rightarrow \varphi(\mathsf{x}^\frown \mathsf{y})\big)\Big) \rightarrow \forall \mathsf{x}\, \varphi,$$

$$\varphi(\underline{0}) \wedge \forall \mathsf{x}\Big(\varphi(\mathsf{x}) \rightarrow \forall \mathsf{y}\big(\mathsf{Sing}(\mathsf{y}) \rightarrow \varphi(\mathsf{y}^\frown \mathsf{x})\big)\Big) \rightarrow \forall \mathsf{x}\, \varphi.$$

PROOF We show that the first is a theorem of E*. Fix a formula $\varphi(\mathsf{x})$ and, arguing within E*, assume

$$\varphi(\underline{0}) \wedge \forall \mathsf{x}\Big(\varphi(\mathsf{x}) \rightarrow \forall \mathsf{y}\big(\mathsf{Sing}(\mathsf{y}) \rightarrow \varphi(\mathsf{x}^\frown \mathsf{y})\big)\Big). \tag{8.18}$$

We claim that $\varphi(\mathsf{x})$ is progressive in x. To that aim, fix an arbitrary a and assume

$$\forall \mathsf{y} \subset a\ \varphi(\mathsf{y}). \tag{8.19}$$

We use (i) from the previous lemma. If $a = \underline{0}$, (8.18) implies $\varphi(a)$ directly. Otherwise, $a = bu$ for some b and some singleton u. By (8.19) we have $\varphi(b)$, whence (8.18) implies $\varphi(a)$, as required. ⊣

The three induction schemas – F1 and the two presentations of weak induction in proposition 8.79 – are equivalent in the sense that over the basic axioms of E* every instance of one of the schemas is provable from some instance of either of the other two. That strong induction is derivable from either form of weak induction is proved in the next chapter, namely in proposition 9.44.

As the definition of the function symbols sub and q was given recursively on the generation of expressions, induction permits deriving many generalizations of earlier lemmas.

8.80 LEMMA *The following are derivable in* E*.

(i) $\forall x \forall y\ \mathsf{sub}(x,y,y) = x$,

(ii) $\forall w \forall x \forall y \forall z\Big(\mathsf{Sing}(y) \rightarrow \mathsf{sub}(w^\frown x, y, z) = \mathsf{sub}(w,y,z)^\frown \mathsf{sub}(x,y,z)\Big)$,

(iii) $\forall x \forall y\Big(\mathsf{Sing}(y) \rightarrow \big(\mathsf{sub}(x,y,\underline{0}) = \underline{0} \leftrightarrow \forall z \subseteq x\ (\mathsf{Sing}(z) \rightarrow z = y)\big)\Big)$,

(iv) $\forall x \forall y \forall z\Big(\mathsf{List}(x) \wedge \mathsf{Word}(y^\frown z) \rightarrow \mathsf{List}\big(\mathsf{sub}(x,y,z)\big)\Big)$,

(v) $\forall x \forall y \forall z\Big(\mathsf{List}(x) \wedge \mathsf{Word}(y^\frown z) \rightarrow$
$\qquad \forall w\big(w \in \mathsf{sub}(x,y,z) \leftrightarrow \exists w'(w' \in x \wedge w = \mathsf{sub}(w',x,y))\big)\Big)$,

(vi) $\forall x\big(\mathsf{Term}(x) \rightarrow \mathsf{Wbw}(x)\big)$,

(vii) $\forall x\Big(\mathsf{Term}(x) \rightarrow \forall y\big(\mathsf{Term}(x^\frown y) \vee \mathsf{Term}(y^\frown x) \rightarrow y = \underline{0}\big)\Big)$.

PROOF We leave the proof as an exercise. ⊣

The next application of induction is to the theory of sequences in E^*. In section 8.3.3 we introduced the term

$$\langle \mathsf{v}_1, \ldots, \mathsf{v}_n \rangle \equiv \underline{\mathsf{e}}^\frown \mathsf{q}\mathsf{v}_1{}^\frown \underline{\mathsf{e}}^\frown \cdots {}^\frown \underline{\mathsf{e}}^\frown \mathsf{q}\mathsf{v}_n$$

and saw that E^* proves that these terms behave as sequences of expressions with unique decompositions. As lemma 8.78 shows, E^* does not only prove that each quotation is a word, but also the general claim that all quotations (of $\ast$-expressions) are words. This observation immediately provides quantified versions of the unique decomposition of sequences from lemma 8.70:

8.81 LEMMA *The following are theorems of* E^*.

(i) $\forall x_1 \cdots \forall x_k\, \mathsf{Seq}(\langle x_1, \ldots, x_k \rangle)$,

(ii) $\forall x_1 \cdots \forall x_k \forall y \big(y \in_{\mathsf{seq}} \langle x_1, \ldots, x_k \rangle \leftrightarrow \bigvee_{i=1}^{k} y = x_i \big)$,

(iii) $\forall x_1 \cdots \forall x_k \forall y_1 \cdots \forall y_k \big(\langle x_1, \ldots, x_k \rangle = \langle y_1, \ldots, y_k \rangle \to \bigwedge_{i=1}^{k} x_i = y_i \big)$.

The weak and strong induction principles are not as structurally different as may first appear. To see this, we consider the relation of immediate prefix, defined by e being the immediate prefix of f if and only if $f \equiv eu$ for some symbol u. According to this definition, the empty expression has no immediate prefix and every non-empty expression has exactly one immediate prefix. The weak induction principle can be rephrased using the template of strong induction but for the relation of immediate prefix rather than subexpression:

REVISED WEAK PRINCIPLE OF INDUCTION *Suppose P is a property of expressions such that for every expression e, if P holds of the immediate prefix of e then P holds of e. Then P holds of all expressions.*

Other versions of induction for expressions can be formulated by inserting other relations. For instance, we may consider the relation of proper prefix, where e is a proper prefix of f if and only if there exists a non-empty g such that $eg \equiv f$.

PRINCIPLE OF PREFIX INDUCTION *Suppose P is a property of expressions such that for every expression e, if P holds of all proper prefixes of e then P holds of e. Then P holds of all $\ast$-expressions.*

Since the immediate prefix of an expression is a proper prefix, and every proper prefix is a subexpression, strong induction implies prefix induction, which in turn implies weak induction.

Not all binary relations give rise to sound induction principles. A statement of induction which uses the relation of identity in place of (proper) subexpression is simply false. If P is the empty property, which holds of no expressions at all, then the implication 'If P holds of all expressions identical to e, then P holds of e' is trivially the case. Yet the conclusion of such an induction, that P holds of all expressions, is clearly false. In general, an induction principle based on a binary relation $\prec$ on expressions is sound if and only if there are no infinite descending $\prec$-sequences of expressions, that is, no infinite sequence of expressions $e_0, e_1, \dots$ such that $e_{i+1} \prec e_i$ for every $i \geq 0$. A relation which has this property is called well-founded. The relations of immediate prefix, proper prefix, and proper subexpression are examples of well-founded relations.

PRINCPLE OF WELL-FOUNDED INDUCTION *Let $\prec$ be a well-founded relation on expressions. Suppose P is a property of expressions such that for every expression e, if P is true of all expressions $f \prec e$ then P is true of e. Then P is true of all expressions.*

Expressed as a schema, this induction principle is the collection of formulæ

$$\forall \mathsf{x}\big(\forall \mathsf{y}(\psi(\mathsf{y},\mathsf{x}) \rightarrow \varphi(\mathsf{y})) \rightarrow \varphi(\mathsf{x})\big) \rightarrow \forall \mathsf{x}\, \varphi(\mathsf{x}) \tag{8.20}$$

where φ ranges over all $\mathcal{L}^*$-formula and $\psi(x, y)$ over formulæ that express well-founded relations. The axiom schema FI of induction is the set of universal closures of instances of (8.20) where $\psi(x, y) \equiv x \subset y$.

The schema of well-founded induction is much stronger than the axiom of induction. It is possible to present an $\mathcal{L}^*$-formula $\psi(x, y)$ expressing a well-founded relation on expressions and a formula $\varphi(x)$ for which the instance of (8.20) is not provable in $\mathsf{E}^*_{\text{min}}$.[7] However, the specific examples of well-founded induction that we have in mind are derivable from the axioms of E^*. These are the weak induction schema and an induction principle based on the measure of the quotation complexity of expressions, which we introduce below.

[7]The reader will find examples of unprovable instances of well-founded induction in most textbooks on proof theory, for example Troelstra and Schwichtenberg (2000).

Recall that the expressions of the language $\mathcal{L}$ are generated from a set of basic symbols by the operation of concatenation and the introduction of a fresh constant for each expression (the quotation constants). In proposition 8.10 we used this perspective on the expressions of $\mathcal{L}$ to define a hierarchy $\mathcal{E}_0 \subseteq \mathcal{E}_1 \subseteq \cdots$ of sets of expressions and proved, by induction on the level in the hierarchy, that a particular translation of expressions in $\mathcal{L}$ into the initial set $\mathcal{E}_0$ is well defined. For $n > 0$, $\mathcal{E}_n$ was defined to be the set of expressions which can be formed by concatenating, in any order, expressions from $\mathcal{E}_0$ and quotation constants $\overline{e}$ for $e \in \mathcal{E}_{n-1}$.

A hierarchy of $\ast$-expressions analogous to the one above can be defined. Let $\lhd$ be the binary relation on $\ast$-expressions given by $e \lhd f$ if and only if $\overline{e} \subseteq f$. We can think of this relation as stating that e is *mentioned* in f. For example, $\neg$ is mentioned in $\underline{\neg}{}^\frown\underline{\rightarrow}$, as $\underline{\neg}$ is a subexpression of $\underline{\neg}{}^\frown\underline{\rightarrow}$. Let $\mathcal{E}_0^*$ be the set of expressions in the basic symbols of $\mathcal{L}^*$ only. For $n \geq 0$, let $\mathcal{E}_{n+1}^*$ be the set of expressions e such that $f \in \mathcal{E}_n^*$ for every $f \lhd e$. In particular, $\mathcal{E}_1^*$ is the set of expressions for which the only quotations that occur as subexpressions are quotations of strings of basic symbols. This set includes the quotation of every expression in $\mathcal{E}_0^*$. The set also includes all expressions formed exclusively from the syntactic constants, because $\overline{e}$ is a subexpression of such an expression if and only if e is a basic symbol or the empty expression.

The hierarchy of $\ast$-expressions provides a measure on the 'quotation complexity' of expressions in a way which is closely related to the hierarchy of $\mathcal{L}$-expressions based on quotation constants. We define the rank of an expression e to be the least number n such that $e \in \mathcal{E}_n^*$. All expressions in $\mathcal{E}_0^*$ have rank 0 by definition. The syntactic constants all have rank 1, as does the quotation of any expression from $\mathcal{E}_0^*$. The expression $\mathsf{q}\underline{\neg}$ is an example of a rank-2 expression: it has precisely two subexpressions that are quotations, namely $\overline{\neg}$ and $\overline{\underline{\neg}}$. That is to say, $e \lhd \mathsf{q}\underline{\neg}$ if and only if $e \equiv \neg$ or $e \equiv \underline{\neg}$. The rank of $\neg$ is 0 and the rank of $\underline{\neg}$ is 1. An example of an expression of rank 3 is ${}^\frown\underline{\mathsf{q}}\,\mathsf{q}\underline{\neg}$. This expression features four quotations as subexpressions, specifically the quotations of q, $\neg$, $\underline{\neg}$, and $\mathsf{q}\underline{\neg}$. The rank of the final expression is, as we have seen, 2. The other three expressions have smaller rank.

Our definition of rank assumes that every $\ast$-expression is present in at least one set in the sequence $\mathcal{E}_0^*, \mathcal{E}_1^*, \ldots$ But we have not yet shown this, and there could be expressions which are not enumerated into any set. Nor have we proved that the sets actually form a hierarchy, that is, that $\mathcal{E}_n^*$ is contained in $\mathcal{E}_m^*$ for every $n < m$. We now prove these claims.

8.82 PROPOSITION

(i) *For every* $m \leq n$, *we have* $\mathcal{E}^*_m \subseteq \mathcal{E}^*_n$.

(ii) *For every* $*$*-expression* e *there exists* $n \geq 0$ *such that* $e \in \mathcal{E}^*_n$.

PROOF We show by induction on $n \geq 0$ that $\mathcal{E}^*_n \subseteq \mathcal{E}^*_{n+1}$. The base case, $n = 0$, is a consequence of the definition: If $e \in \mathcal{E}^*_0$ then, since e is a string of basic symbols only, there is no expression f such that $f \lhd e$. Therefore $e \in \mathcal{E}^*_1$. For the induction step, suppose $n = m+1$ and $e \in \mathcal{E}^*_n$. If $f \lhd e$, then $f \in \mathcal{E}^*_m$ by definition, and the induction hypothesis yields $f \in \mathcal{E}^*_n$. So $e \in \mathcal{E}^*_{n+1}$.

The second claim is proved by induction on the length of the expression e. Indeed, we prove that $e \in \mathcal{E}^*_n$, where n is the length of e. We start, however, with the observation that the length of a quotation $\overline{e}$ is never less than the length of e and that $\overline{e}$ and e have the *same* length if and only if e is a basic symbol. In other words, if $e \lhd f$ and f is not a syntactic constant, then the length of e is strictly less than the length of f. Now let e be an expression and n its length. If $n = 0$, then e is empty and $e \in \mathcal{E}^*_0$, as required. If $n = 1$, then $e \in \mathcal{E}^*_1$ because $\mathcal{E}^*_1$ contains all $*$-symbols. Now suppose $n > 1$ and consider an arbitrary $f \lhd e$. Let the length of f be m. As observed, $m < n$, so the induction hypothesis implies $f \in \mathcal{E}^*_m$. As this is the case for every $f \lhd e$, we have that $e \in \mathcal{E}^*_{m+1}$ and, by (i), $e \in \mathcal{E}^*_n$. ⊣

The next claim follows almost immediately from proposition 8.82.

8.83 PROPOSITION *The relation* $\lhd$ *is well-founded.*

PROOF Let e_0 be any $*$-expression and suppose $e_1, e_2, \ldots$ is an infinite sequence of expressions such that $e_{i+1} \lhd e_i$ for each $i \geq 0$. By the previous proposition, each e_i has finite rank, say $e_i \in \mathcal{E}^*_{n_i}$. But then $n_0 > n_1 > \cdots$ is an infinite descending sequence of natural numbers, which is impossible. ⊣

Unlike the well-founded relations considered earlier, $\lhd$ is not transitive. That is, there exist expressions $e_0 \lhd e_1 \lhd e_2$ with $e_0 \ntriangleleft e_2$. Nevertheless, as the relation is well-founded, the induction principle for $\lhd$ is sound:

PRINCIPLE OF RANK INDUCTION *Suppose* P *is a property of expressions such that for every expression* e, *if* P *holds of every expression* $f \lhd e$, *then* P *holds of* e. *Then* P *holds of all expressions.*

In the language $\mathcal{L}^*$, the relation $\lhd$ is expressed by the formula $\mathsf{q}x \subseteq y$, which we abbreviate as $x \lhd y$. This formula was considered in lemma 8.78, where we proved that $\lhd$ is irreflexive, specifically, $\mathsf{E}^* \vdash \forall x \neg x \lhd x$. The principle of rank induction for a formula $\varphi(\mathsf{x})$ is expressed by the formula

$$\forall \mathsf{x}\big(\forall \mathsf{y} \lhd \mathsf{x}\ \varphi(\mathsf{y}) \rightarrow \varphi(\mathsf{x})\big) \rightarrow \forall \mathsf{x}\, \varphi(\mathsf{x}), \tag{8.21}$$

where $\forall \mathsf{y} \lhd \mathsf{x}\ \varphi(\mathsf{y})$ follows the convention of bounded quantification and abbreviates $\forall \mathsf{y}(\mathsf{y} \lhd \mathsf{x} \rightarrow \varphi(\mathsf{y}))$. The contrapositive of (8.21) presents the following version of the minimality principle:

$$\exists x\, \varphi(x) \rightarrow \exists x\Big(\varphi(x) \wedge \forall y\big(y \lhd x \rightarrow \neg\varphi(y)\big)\Big).$$

Rank induction is another example of an induction principle which is provable in the theory E^*. The proof of this claim will be postponed to the next chapter (proposition 9.47) as we currently lack the resources to formalize the argument of propositions 8.82 and 8.83 within E^* itself.

8.84 PROPOSITION *The principle of rank induction* (8.21) *for arbitrary formulæ of* $\mathcal{L}^*$ *is provable in* E^*.

8.5 Expressions Revisited

Having laid out the axioms of the strong theory of expressions, it remains to compare this theory to E. First, we summarize the definition of E^*:

8.85 DEFINITION The following are all axioms of E^*. The minimal theory $\mathsf{E}^*_{\min}$ of $\mathcal{L}^*$ comprises these axioms only.

- Axioms for symbols:
  - B1 $\mathsf{sym}\,\underline{u}$ for each basic symbol u of $\mathcal{L}^*$;
  - B2 $\forall \mathsf{x}\big(\mathsf{sym}\,\mathsf{x} \rightarrow \mathsf{Sing}(\mathsf{x})\big)$,
  - B3 $\forall \mathsf{x}\big(\mathsf{x} = \underline{0} \vee \mathsf{sym}\,\mathsf{x} \rightarrow \mathsf{Sing}(\mathsf{qx})\big)$,
  - B4 $\forall \mathsf{x}\big(\mathsf{Sing}(\mathsf{x}) \rightarrow \mathsf{sym}\,\mathsf{x} \vee \mathsf{x} = \mathsf{q}\underline{0} \vee \exists \mathsf{y}(\mathsf{sym}\,\mathsf{y} \wedge \mathsf{x} = \mathsf{qy})\big)$,
  - B5 $\forall \mathsf{x} \neg \mathsf{sym}(\mathsf{qx})$,

B6 for each pair of distinct basic symbols u and v, the axiom $\underline{u} \neq \underline{v}$.

- Axioms for concatenation:

C1 $\forall x \forall y (x^\frown y = \underline{0} \rightarrow x = \underline{0} \wedge y = \underline{0})$,

C2 $\forall x \forall y (x^\frown y = x \leftrightarrow y = \underline{0}) \wedge \forall x \forall y (x^\frown y = y \leftrightarrow x = \underline{0})$,

C3 $\forall x \forall y \forall z \forall w$
$\big(x^\frown y \equiv z^\frown w \leftrightarrow \exists v_4 \big((x = z^\frown v_4 \wedge v_4{}^\frown y = w) \vee (x^\frown v_4 = z \wedge y = v_4{}^\frown w)\big)\big)$.

- Axioms for quotation:

D1 $\forall x \forall y \big(x \neq \underline{0} \wedge \mathsf{Sing}(y) \rightarrow q(x^\frown y) = \underline{\frown}^\frown qx^\frown qy\big)$,

D2 $\forall x \big(\mathsf{sym}\, x \rightarrow q(qx) = \underline{q}^\frown qx\big)$,

D3 $\forall x \forall y (qx = qy \rightarrow x = y)$.

- Axioms for substitution:

E1 $\forall y \forall z \big(\mathsf{sub}(\underline{0}, y, z) = \underline{0} \wedge \mathsf{sub}(y, \underline{0}, z) = y\big)$,

E2 $\forall x \forall y \forall z \big(y \neq \underline{0} \rightarrow \mathsf{sub}(x^\frown y, y, z) = \mathsf{sub}(x, y, z)^\frown z\big)$,

E3 $\forall w \forall x \forall y$
$\big(\mathsf{Sing}(w) \wedge \forall z (x^\frown w \neq z^\frown y) \rightarrow \forall z\ \mathsf{sub}(x^\frown w, y, z) = \mathsf{sub}(x, y, z)^\frown w\big)$.

- Axiom schema of induction:

F1 the universal closure of $\forall x \big(\forall y \subset x\ \varphi(y) \rightarrow \varphi(x)\big) \rightarrow \forall x\ \varphi(x)$ for each formula $\varphi(x)$ of $\mathcal{L}^*$.

The language $\mathcal{L}^-$ from section 8.1 can be viewed as the expansion of $\mathcal{L}^*$ by an infinite set of symbols for variables, $v_0, v_1, \ldots$, and syntactic constants for each. The auxiliary symbol v has no essential role in this instantiation of $\mathcal{L}^-$ and does not occur in the expressions that are terms or formulæ of $\mathcal{L}^-$. We can also treat $\mathcal{L}^-$ and $\mathcal{L}^*$ as sublanguages of $\mathcal{L}$, with $\mathcal{L}$ being obtained from $\mathcal{L}^-$ by recursively adding a fresh constant $\overline{e}$ for each finite string of symbols e. To reduce ambiguity between the quotation constants of $\mathcal{L}$ and quotation as defined for $\mathcal{L}^*$, we temporarily follow the notation of section 8.3.3 and write $\ulcorner e \urcorner$ for the quotation (term) of e defined in accordance with definition 8.39, reserving $\overline{e}$ for the corresponding quotation constant in $\mathcal{L}$.

There is a natural translation of $\mathcal{L}^-$-expressions into $\mathcal{L}^*$, given by leaving the symbols common to both languages unaltered, translating the variables of $\mathcal{L}^-$ as the corresponding expression in $\mathcal{L}^*$ and their syntactic constants as the quotations of the variables in $\mathcal{L}^*$. We will denote the result of applying this translation to an $\mathcal{L}^-$-expression a as a^*. If a is a term of $\mathcal{L}^-$, then the translation a^* is a term of $\mathcal{L}^*$. Likewise, formulæ of $\mathcal{L}^-$ are mapped to formulæ of $\mathcal{L}^*$.

8.86 LEMMA *If* $\mathsf{E}^- \vdash \varphi$, *where* E^- *is the theory axiomatized in definition 8.19, then* $\mathsf{E}^* \vdash \varphi^*$.

We leave the details to the reader, but remark that the axiom schema of induction is not necessary to witness the provability of φ^* in E^*, and that E^* in the lemma can be replaced by the finite set of basic axioms.

In section 8.1, we introduced two translations of $\mathcal{L}$ into $\mathcal{L}^-$. These translations also leave the symbols common to both languages unaltered but contrast in their explication of the 'internal structure' of quotation. One translation maps a quotation constant $\overline{a}$ to the expression $\overline{a}^- \equiv \ulcorner a^- \urcorner$; the other maps it to the expression $\overline{a}^\# \equiv \ulcorner a \urcorner^\#$. Under the first translation quotation constants are always expressed as concatenations of symbols. The second translation utilizes quotation as a primitive generator of expressions. As a simple example we consider the translation of the two-symbol $\mathcal{L}$-expression $a \equiv \forall\overline{\neg\to}$:

$$\overline{a}^- \equiv \ulcorner\forall\ulcorner\neg\to\urcorner\urcorner \equiv {}^\frown{}^\frown{}^\frown\underline{\forall}\,\underline{{}^\frown}\mathsf{q}\underline{\neg}\mathsf{q}\underline{\to} \quad \text{and} \quad \overline{a}^\# \equiv {}^\frown\underline{\forall}\mathsf{q}\ulcorner\neg\to\urcorner \equiv {}^\frown\underline{\forall}\mathsf{q}{}^\frown\underline{\neg}\underline{\to}.$$

The first translation maps $\overline{a}$ to the $\mathcal{L}^-$-term expressing the concatenation of the symbol $\forall$, the function symbol ${}^\frown$, and quotations of the two symbols $\neg$ and $\to$. The second translation interprets $\overline{a}$ as the concatenation of $\forall$ with the quotation of the two-symbol expression $\neg\to$.

We believe both translations describe modes of quotation. Our strong theory of expressions appears to presuppose the former view of quotations as concatenations of symbols. The definition of quotation in the language $\mathcal{L}^*$ is precisely of this kind. Moreover, we have proved, combining our work in section 8.1 and lemma 8.86, that if $\mathsf{E}_{\mathrm{min}} \vdash \varphi$, then $\mathsf{E}^* \vdash \varphi^{-*}$. But we also saw that over E^-, and hence over E^*, the two interpretations give rise to equal terms and equivalent formulæ. Restating that result for the strong theory E^* of expressions:

8.87 PROPOSITION *For every term s and every formula φ of $\mathcal{L}$,*

$$\mathsf{E}^* \vdash s^{-*} = s^{\#*} \quad \textit{and} \quad \mathsf{E}^* \vdash \varphi^{-*} \leftrightarrow \varphi^{\#*}.$$

PROOF Corollary 8.27 and lemma 8.86. ⊣

8.88 THEOREM *Let $\mathcal{L}$ and $\mathcal{L}^*$ be languages satisfying definitions 5.1 and 8.33, respectively, and suppose every symbol of $\mathcal{L}^*$ is a symbol of $\mathcal{L}$. For all $\mathcal{L}$-formulæ φ, if $\mathsf{E}_{\mathrm{min}} \vdash \varphi$ then $\mathsf{E}^*_{\mathrm{min}} \vdash \varphi^{-*} \wedge \varphi^{\#*}$. In fact, there is a finite set of axioms of $\mathsf{E}^*_{\mathrm{min}}$ witnessing the above claim for all φ.*

PROOF Apply theorem 8.26, proposition 8.87, , and lemma 8.86. As lemma 8.86 does not require the axiom schema of induction, and there are finitely many basic axioms of $\mathsf{E}^*_{\mathrm{min}}$, the stronger claim of the theorem holds. ⊣

This final theorem, and proposition 8.87 in particular, shows that, like the weak theory E, the strong theory does not force one particular perspective of quotation. The definition of quotation in $\mathcal{L}^*$ expresses the operation as a transformation of expressions one symbol at a time, and the translation $a \mapsto a^{-*}$ of expressions in $\mathcal{L}$ into $\mathcal{L}^*$ applies this construction to quotations in $\mathcal{L}$. The alternative view of generating expressions through a combination of the operations of concatenation and quotation, used explicitly in the construction of the weak language $\mathcal{L}$, is also present in $\mathcal{L}^*$ as the set of expressions $a^{\#*}$ where a ranges over expressions in $\mathcal{L}$. The two approaches are syntactically distinct: it is straightforward to construct examples of $\mathcal{L}$-expressions a such that $a^{-*} \not\equiv a^{\#*}$. Nevertheless, proposition 8.87 proves that these two translations of $\mathcal{L}$ into $\mathcal{L}^*$ are equally expressive and interchangeable in all formal contexts.

9 Consistency, Denotation, and Arithmetic

In this chapter we begin our examination of the metatheory of the strong theory of expressions introduced in the previous chapter. The first task is to prove the consistency of the theory. Although the axioms of E^* were all motivated by properties of the set of $*$-expressions, these explanations have been based on informal interpretations of the various predicates, function symbols, and defined formulæ. Just as in chapter 5, these informal interpretations will be made precise, with the result that the set of $*$-expressions determines a standard model for the axioms of the minimal expressive theory $\mathsf{E}^*_{\mathrm{min}}$.

The second task undertaken is an axiomatization of denotation. The denotation of a closed term of $\mathcal{L}^*$ is the expression the term denotes in a fixed standard model of $\mathcal{L}^*$. As a function from closed terms to expressions, denotation is the inverse to quotation, as the denotation of a quotation $\overline{a}$ is precisely the expression a itself across all standard models. But the domain of the denotation function contains not only quotations but all closed terms, including, in the case that $\mathcal{L}^*$ contains a basic function symbol or constant not in $\mathcal{L}^*_{\mathrm{min}}$, terms whose interpretation differs across the standard models. In section 9.2 we examine extensions of E^* by a function or predicate symbol expressing denotation and deduce a variant of the liar paradox for theories with a primitive denotation function. We also prove that for any choice of $\mathcal{L}^*$ there is a formula of $\mathcal{L}^*$ which provably in $\mathsf{E}^*_{\mathrm{min}}$ expresses the denotation function for closed terms of $\mathcal{L}^*$.

Finally, we revisit the reduction of arithmetic to syntax in the context of the strong theory of expressions. Theories of syntax are usually conceived as subtheories of arithmetic via a coding of expressions as natural numbers. In the case of the language $\mathcal{L}^*$, each $*$-expression is assigned a unique natural number via a coding scheme, and the syntactic operations on $*$-expressions – concatenation, substitution and quotation – are interpreted as arithmetic functions operating on codes of $*$-expressions. The standard choice of theory for the arithmetization of syntax is Peano arithmetic, and this theory is well known to be sufficient to simulate our expressive theory $\mathsf{E}^*_{\mathrm{min}}$ via any of the usual methods of coding expressions in arithmetic. Peano arithmetic is axiomatized by the defining equations for the successor, addition, and multiplication functions on natural numbers, plus the axiom schema of induction for arithmetic (see definition 9.33).

In this chapter we reverse the usual reduction and develop arithmetic as a subtheory of the theory of expressions. As in chapter 6, arithmetic is identified with the theory of expressions built from a single symbol. In this way, we demonstrate that Peano arithmetic is a subtheory of the strong theory of expressions $\mathsf{E}^*_{\text{min}}$.

9.1 Standard Models

The axioms of E^* were chosen with a particular reading of the logical symbols in mind: syntactic constants denote specific symbols of $\mathcal{L}^*$, and the three designated function symbols express the operations of concatenation, substitution, and quotation. In section 5.5 we established that this interpretation of the symbols of $\mathcal{L}_{\text{min}}$ validates all the axioms (and, thereby, also the theorems) of the theory E_{min}. We did this via the notion of a standard model of $\mathcal{L}$, namely the set of all $\mathcal{L}$-expressions equipped with the primitive operations of concatenation, substitution, and quotation as well as possibly other operations interpreting any additional constants and function or predicate symbols.

In this section we establish an analogous result for the strong theory E^* of expressions. A standard model of $\mathcal{L}^*$ has as its domain the set of $\ast$-expressions. The syntactic constants of $\mathcal{L}^*$ and the obligatory basic function and predicate symbols are given their intended interpretations. The interpretations of other $\ast$-symbols, namely the basic function or predicate symbols of $\mathcal{L}^*$ that are not symbols of $\mathcal{L}^*_{\text{min}}$, are not fixed. If $\mathcal{L}^*$ extends $\mathcal{L}^*_{\text{min}}$ by at least one function or predicate symbol, there will not be a unique standard model of $\mathcal{L}^*$ and each interpretation of the additional symbols will induce a different standard model. We show that the axioms of the minimal theory $\mathsf{E}^*_{\text{min}}$ are true in all standard models of $\mathcal{L}^*$, that is, they are true statements about $\ast$-expressions.

Standard models of $\mathcal{L}^*$ can be seen as refinements of models of $\mathcal{L}$. Every standard model of $\mathcal{L}^*$ can be expanded to a model of E by interpreting the missing quotation constants of $\mathcal{L}$ as $\ast$-expressions in the way described in section 8.1. This model will not be a standard model of $\mathcal{L}$ because its domain of the model is the set of $\ast$-expressions rather than the (strictly larger) set of $\mathcal{L}$-expressions. In the other direction, every standard model of $\mathcal{L}$ can be transformed into a standard model of $\mathcal{L}^*$ using the translations of $\mathcal{L}$ into $\mathcal{L}^*$ seen in the previous chapter (namely the composite translation ${}^{-*}$ of section 8.5).

We fix a language $\mathcal{L}^*$ satisfying definition 8.33 for use throughout this section and let $\mathcal{E}^*$ be the set of $*$-expressions. The $*$-symbols fall in two categories: the basic symbols, comprising finitely many predicate, function, connective, and auxiliary symbols, and the syntactic constants, namely the symbol $\underline{0}$ and a symbol $\underline{u}$ for each basic symbol u. We have discussed at length how we intend to interpret the basic function and predicate symbols of $\mathcal{L}^*_{\text{min}}$ and the syntactic constants of $\mathcal{L}^*$. Let $\mathcal{L}^*_{\text{syn}}$ be the language consisting of these symbols alone.

9.1 DEFINITION The symbols of $\mathcal{L}^*_{\text{syn}}$ are the basic symbols of $\mathcal{L}^*_{\text{min}}$ and the (finitely many) syntactic constants of $\mathcal{L}^*$.

The language $\mathcal{L}^*_{\text{syn}}$ is sufficient to express many syntactic properties of $*$-expressions. The quotation of every $*$-expression is a term in $\mathcal{L}^*_{\text{syn}}$. The basic axioms of E^* are all formulæ of $\mathcal{L}^*_{\text{syn}}$, as are the formula Term expressing the property of being a term of $\mathcal{L}^*$ and the corresponding formulæ for lists and sequences.

The standard model $\mathbb{E}^*$ of $\mathcal{L}^*_{\text{syn}}$ has as its domain the set $\mathcal{E}^*$ of all $*$-expressions. The function and predicate symbols of $\mathcal{L}^*_{\text{syn}}$ are interpreted in $\mathbb{E}^*$ as follows:

(i) The interpretation of a syntactic constant $\underline{a}$ is the $*$-expression $a \in \mathcal{E}^*$.

(ii) The function symbol $\frown$ is interpreted by the function of concatenation function on $\mathcal{E}^*$.

(iii) The function symbol q is interpreted by the function that assigns to every expression its quotation.

(iv) The function symbol sub is interpreted by the ternary function $\mathsf{sub}^{\mathbb{E}^*}$ on $\mathcal{E}^*$ defined by the following:

- $\mathsf{sub}^{\mathbb{E}^*}(e, 0, g) := e$ for all $e, g \in \mathcal{E}^*$;
- for $f \not\equiv 0$, $\mathsf{sub}^{\mathbb{E}^*}(e, f, g)$ is determined by recursion on e:
  (a) $\mathsf{sub}^{\mathbb{E}^*}(0, f, g) := 0$,
  (b) $\mathsf{sub}^{\mathbb{E}^*}(ef, f, g) := \mathsf{sub}^{\mathbb{E}^*}(e, f, g)g$,
  (c) $\mathsf{sub}^{\mathbb{E}^*}(eu, f, g) := \mathsf{sub}^{\mathbb{E}^*}(e, f, g)u$ if u is a symbol and there is no $e' \in \mathcal{E}^*$ such that $eu \equiv e'f$.

(v) The predicate symbol sym is interpreted by the set of basic symbols of $\mathcal{L}^*$.

In clause (i), a is either a basic symbol of $\mathcal{L}^*$ or the empty expression. In either case, the intended interpretation of $\underline{a}$ is the expression a.

9.2 DEFINITION A standard model of $\mathcal{L}^*$ is any model of $\mathcal{L}^*$ with domain $\mathcal{E}^*$ that agrees with $\mathbb{E}^*$ on the interpretation of the symbols of $\mathcal{L}^*_{\text{syn}}$ We write standard models of $\mathcal{L}^*$ as $\langle \mathbb{E}^*, V \rangle$, where V is a function providing interpretations for all remaining function and predicate symbols.

We will prove that the axioms of $\mathsf{E}^*_{\text{min}}$ are true in every standard model of $\mathcal{L}^*$. First, however, it is helpful to take a closer look at the denotations of terms in standard models. Let $\langle \mathbb{E}^*, V \rangle$ of $\mathcal{L}^*$ be any standard model.

9.3 DEFINITION A variable assignment is a function $\mathfrak{b}\colon \mathbb{N} \to \mathcal{E}^*$ from the natural numbers into the expressions. Given a variable assignment $\mathfrak{b}$ and a term t of $\mathcal{L}^*$, the denotation of t under $\mathfrak{b}$, written $t^{\mathfrak{b}}$, is the $\star$-expression obtained by replacing each variable symbol v_i in t by the expression $\mathfrak{b}(i)$ and each function symbol in t by the interpretation supplied by $\langle \mathbb{E}^*, V \rangle$:

- If $t \equiv \underline{0}$, then $t^{\mathfrak{b}} \equiv 0$.
- If $t \equiv \underline{u}$ where u is a basic symbol, then $t^{\mathfrak{b}} \equiv u$.
- If $t \equiv \mathsf{v}_i$ is a variable then $t^{\mathfrak{b}} \equiv \mathfrak{b}(i)$. That is, the denotation of v_i under $\mathfrak{b}$ is the expression which $\mathfrak{b}$ assigns to i.
- If $t \equiv {\frown} rs$ then $t^{\mathfrak{b}} \equiv r^{\mathfrak{b}} s^{\mathfrak{b}}$, i.e., the concatenation of the expressions $r^{\mathfrak{b}}$ and $s^{\mathfrak{b}}$.
- If $t \equiv \mathsf{sub}\, rsu$ then $t^{\mathfrak{b}} \equiv \mathsf{sub}^{\mathbb{E}^*}(r^{\mathfrak{b}}, s^{\mathfrak{b}}, u^{\mathfrak{b}})$.
- If $t \equiv \mathsf{q} r$ then $t^{\mathfrak{b}} \equiv \overline{r^{\mathfrak{b}}}$.
- If $t \equiv \mathsf{f} s_1 \cdots s_k$ and f is a function symbol not in $\mathcal{L}^*_{\text{syn}}$ then $t^{\mathfrak{b}} \equiv \mathsf{f}^V(s_1^{\mathfrak{b}}, \ldots, s_k^{\mathfrak{b}})$ where f^V is the k-ary function on $\star$-expressions which V assigns to f.

9.4 LEMMA *Let t be a term and let $\mathfrak{b}$ and $\mathfrak{c}$ be variable assignments. If $x^{\mathfrak{b}} \equiv x^{\mathfrak{c}}$ for every variable x occurring in t, then $t^{\mathfrak{b}} \equiv t^{\mathfrak{c}}$. If t is closed, then $t^{\mathfrak{b}} \equiv t^{\mathfrak{c}}$ for all $\mathfrak{b}$ and $\mathfrak{c}$.*

PROOF By induction on the construction of t. ⊣

A consequence of the above lemma is that the denotation of a closed term is independent of the chosen variable assignment. We emphasize this by writing $t^{\mathbb{E}^*}$ in place of $t^{\mathfrak{b}}$ for closed terms t and variable assignments $\mathfrak{b}$.

The next lemmas examine the denotations of quotations.

9.5 LEMMA *For every term t and variable assignment $\mathfrak{b}$, the expression $(\mathsf{q}t)^{\mathfrak{b}}$ is a closed term.*

9.6 LEMMA *For every $\star$-expression e, $\overline{e}^{\mathbb{E}^*} \equiv e$. In particular, $(\mathsf{q}\overline{e})^{\mathfrak{b}} \equiv \overline{e}$.*

PROOF The first part is proved by induction on the length of e. To see the second part, note for every assignment $\mathfrak{b}$:

$$
\begin{aligned}
(\mathsf{q}\overline{e})^{\mathfrak{b}} &\equiv \overline{\overline{e}^{\mathfrak{b}}} && \text{definition}\\
&\equiv \overline{e} && \text{first part}
\end{aligned}
$$

⊣

Lemma 9.5 tells us that the denotation of $\mathsf{q}t$ is always a term of $\mathcal{L}^*$, regardless of the particular standard model and variable assignment. If t is closed, then $\mathsf{q}t$ denotes just one possible term, namely the term $\overline{e}$ where $e \equiv t^{\mathbb{E}^*}$. If, however, t contains a free variable, then $\mathsf{q}t$ can denote different terms under different variable assignments. For example, the denotation of the term $t \equiv \mathsf{q}(x^\frown y)$ under an assignment $\mathfrak{b}$ is the quotation of the expression $x^{\mathfrak{b}}y^{\mathfrak{b}}$, that is, $t^{\mathfrak{b}} \equiv \overline{x^{\mathfrak{b}}y^{\mathfrak{b}}}$. No matter which variable assignment is chosen, $\mathsf{q}(x^\frown y)$ denotes a closed term. Lemma 9.6 goes one step further, by computing the denotation of terms $\mathsf{q}\overline{e}$. Since quotations are closed terms, we know from lemma 9.5 that the denotation of $\mathsf{q}\overline{e}$ does not depend on the standard model or the variable assignment. The result should not be surprising as it aligns with the interpretation of quotation in standard models of the weak theory E. In $\mathcal{L}$, the quotation of an expression is a constant whose interpretation is specified as a certain element of the domain, and this interpretation is fixed across all standard models. In contrast, quotations in $\mathcal{L}^*$ are closed terms, and lemma 9.6 proves that the denotation of a quotation is indeed the expression which is quoted.

As a consequence of lemma 9.6, we obtain the following result strengthening the connection between quotation and denotation:

9.7 LEMMA *For every term t and assignment $\mathfrak{b}$, $\left((\mathsf{q}t)^{\mathfrak{b}}\right)^{\mathbb{E}^*} \equiv t^{\mathfrak{b}}$.*

PROOF By definition, $(\mathsf{q}t)^{\mathfrak{b}} \equiv \overline{t^{\mathfrak{b}}}$ for all t and $\mathfrak{b}$. Applying lemma 9.6, we deduce $\left((\mathsf{q}t)^{\mathfrak{b}}\right)^{\mathbb{E}^*} \equiv t^{\mathfrak{b}}$. ⊣

Another consequence of lemma 9.6 is the next lemma.

9.8 LEMMA *Let $t(x)$ be a term and $\mathfrak{b}$ a variable assignment such that $x^{\mathfrak{b}} \equiv e$. Then $t^{\mathfrak{b}} \equiv t(\overline{e})^{\mathfrak{b}}$.*

The proof of lemma 9.8 proceeds by induction on the term t. We leave the argument as an exercise. Repeated applications of lemma 9.8 yield the following:

9.9 PROPOSITION *Let $t(x_0, \ldots, x_k)$ be a term in which every variable occurring in t is among $x_0, \ldots, x_k$. If $x_i^{\mathfrak{b}} \equiv e_i$ for each $i \leq k$, then $t^{\mathfrak{b}} \equiv t(\overline{e_0}, \ldots, \overline{e_k})^{\mathbb{E}^*}$.*

Next we show how formulæ of $\mathcal{L}^*$ are evaluated in standard models. This is the usual relation of satisfaction for a formula of $\mathcal{L}^*$ relative to a model and a variable assignment described in chapter 2 and utilized in section 5.5 for the weak theory E. We present the formal definition below, though we restrict attention to standard models of $\mathcal{L}^*$.

We define the relation $\langle \mathbb{E}^*, V \rangle \vDash_{\mathfrak{b}} \varphi$, expressing that φ is satisfied in $\langle \mathbb{E}^*, V \rangle$ under the assignment $\mathfrak{b}$, by recursion on φ:

(i) $\langle \mathbb{E}^*, V \rangle \vDash_{\mathfrak{b}} s = t$ if and only if $s^{\mathfrak{b}} \equiv t^{\mathfrak{b}}$.

(ii) $\langle \mathbb{E}^*, V \rangle \vDash_{\mathfrak{b}} \mathsf{sym}\, s$ if and only if $s^{\mathfrak{b}}$ is a basic symbol of $\mathcal{L}^*$.

(iii) $\langle \mathbb{E}^*, V \rangle \vDash_{\mathfrak{b}} \mathsf{R} s_1 \cdots s_k$ if and only if $\mathsf{R}^V s_1^{\mathfrak{b}} \cdots s_k^{\mathfrak{b}}$, for all k-ary predicate symbols R of $\mathcal{L}^*$ that are not symbols of $\mathcal{L}^*_{\text{syn}}$.

(iv) $\langle \mathbb{E}^*, V \rangle \vDash_{\mathfrak{b}} \neg\varphi$ if and only if $\langle \mathbb{E}^*, V \rangle \nvDash_{\mathfrak{b}} \varphi$.

(v) $\langle \mathbb{E}^*, V \rangle \vDash_{\mathfrak{b}} (\varphi \to \psi)$ if and only if $\langle \mathbb{E}^*, V \rangle \nvDash_{\mathfrak{b}} \varphi$ or $\langle \mathbb{E}^*, V \rangle \vDash_{\mathfrak{b}} \psi$.

(vi) $\langle \mathbb{E}^*, V \rangle \vDash_{\mathfrak{b}} \forall \mathsf{v}_i\, \varphi$ if and only if $\langle \mathbb{E}^*, V \rangle \vDash_{\mathfrak{c}} \varphi$ for every assignment $\mathfrak{c}$ such that $\mathfrak{c}(j) \equiv \mathfrak{b}(j)$ for all $j \neq i$.

9.10 DEFINITION Let $\langle \mathbb{E}^*, V \rangle$ be a standard model of $\mathcal{L}^*$ and φ a formula of $\mathcal{L}^*$. We say that φ is true in $\langle \mathbb{E}^*, V \rangle$, written $\langle \mathbb{E}^*, V \rangle \vDash \varphi$, if and only if $\langle \mathbb{E}^*, V \rangle \vDash_{\mathfrak{b}} \varphi$ for every variable assignment $\mathfrak{b}$. A formula is said to be true if and only if it is true in all standard models of $\mathcal{L}^*$.

Applying the definition of satisfaction to the derived connectives yields the following equivalences.

9.11 LEMMA *The following hold for all φ, ψ, and $\mathfrak{b}$:*

(i) *$\langle \mathbb{E}^*, V \rangle \vDash_{\mathfrak{b}} \varphi \wedge \psi$ if and only if $\langle \mathbb{E}^*, V \rangle \vDash_{\mathfrak{b}} \varphi$ and $\langle \mathbb{E}^*, V \rangle \vDash_{\mathfrak{b}} \psi$.*

(ii) *$\langle \mathbb{E}^*, V \rangle \vDash_{\mathfrak{b}} \varphi \vee \psi$ if and only if $\langle \mathbb{E}^*, V \rangle \vDash_{\mathfrak{b}} \varphi$ or $\langle \mathbb{E}^*, V \rangle \vDash_{\mathfrak{b}} \psi$.*

(iii) *$\langle \mathbb{E}^*, V \rangle \vDash_{\mathfrak{b}} \exists \mathsf{v}_i\, \varphi$ if and only if $\langle \mathbb{E}^*, V \rangle \vDash_{\mathfrak{c}} \varphi$ for some assignment $\mathfrak{c}$ such that $\mathfrak{c}(j) \equiv \mathfrak{b}(j)$ for all $j \neq i$.*

The next three lemmas are easily proved by induction on the formula φ:

9.12 LEMMA *Let φ be a sentence of $\mathcal{L}^*_{\text{syn}}$. Then φ is true in some standard model of $\mathcal{L}^*$ if and only if φ is true (in all standard models).*

9.13 LEMMA *If $x^{\mathfrak{b}} \equiv x^{\mathfrak{c}}$ for each variable x which occurs free in φ, then $\langle \mathbb{E}^*, V \rangle \vDash_{\mathfrak{b}} \varphi$ if and only if $\langle \mathbb{E}^*, V \rangle \vDash_{\mathfrak{c}} \varphi$.*

9.14 LEMMA *Let $\varphi(x)$ be a formula and t a term such that no variable in t is bound in φ. If $t^{\mathfrak{b}} \equiv x^{\mathfrak{b}}$ then $\langle \mathbb{E}^*, V \rangle \vDash_{\mathfrak{b}} \varphi$ if and only if $\langle \mathbb{E}^*, V \rangle \vDash_{\mathfrak{b}} \varphi(t)$.*

Applying the previous lemma to the quantifier clauses leads to the following characterization of truth in standard models:

9.15 LEMMA *Let $\varphi(x)$ be a formula of $\mathcal{L}^*$.*

(i) $\langle \mathbb{E}^*, V \rangle \vDash \forall x\, \varphi$ *if and only if* $\langle \mathbb{E}^*, V \rangle \vDash \varphi(\overline{e})$ *for every* $e \in \mathcal{E}^*$.

(ii) $\langle \mathbb{E}^*, V \rangle \vDash \exists x\, \varphi$ *if and only if* $\langle \mathbb{E}^*, V \rangle \vDash \varphi(\overline{e})$ *for some* $e \in \mathcal{E}^*$.

Lemma 9.15 greatly simplifies the process of assessing whether a given sentence is true in some/all standard models by removing the need to reason about variable assignments or formulæ with free variables. The proof of the next result is an example of the value of lemma 9.15.

9.16 THEOREM *Let $\langle \mathbb{E}^*, V \rangle$ be a standard model of $\mathcal{L}^*$. The following obtain for every $*$-expression e:*

(i) $\langle \mathbb{E}^*, V \rangle \vDash \mathsf{Sing}(\overline{e})$ *if and only if e is a symbol of $\mathcal{L}^*$.*

(ii) $\langle \mathbb{E}^*, V \rangle \vDash \mathsf{Syn}(\overline{e})$ *if and only if e is a syntactic constant of $\mathcal{L}^*$.*

(iii) $\langle \mathbb{E}^*, V \rangle \vDash \mathsf{Word}(\overline{e})$ *if and only if e is a word.*

(iv) $\langle \mathbb{E}^*, V \rangle \vDash \mathsf{List}(\overline{e})$ *if and only if e is a list.*

(v) $\langle \mathbb{E}^*, V \rangle \vDash \mathsf{Seq}(\overline{e})$ *if and only if e is a sequence.*

(vi) $\langle \mathbb{E}^*, V \rangle \vDash \mathsf{Term}(\overline{e})$ *if and only if e is a term.*

(vii) $\langle \mathbb{E}^*, V \rangle \vDash \mathsf{CTerm}(\overline{e})$ *if and only if e is a closed term.*

PROOF We provide the argument behind (i); the remainder is left to the reader. Fix any $*$-expression e. Recall that $\mathsf{Sing}(\overline{e})$ is the formula $\overline{e} \neq \underline{0} \wedge \forall \mathsf{w} \forall \mathsf{z}(\overline{e} = \mathsf{w}^\frown \mathsf{z} \to \mathsf{w} = \overline{e} \vee \mathsf{z} = \overline{e})$. Lemma 9.15 and the definition of satisfaction entail that $\langle \mathbb{E}^*, V \rangle \vDash \mathsf{Sing}(\overline{e})$ if and only if e is non-empty and for all $f, g \in \mathcal{E}^*$, if $e \equiv fg$ then either $e \equiv f$ or $e \equiv g$. In other words, $\langle \mathbb{E}^*, V \rangle \vDash \mathsf{Sing}(\overline{e})$ if and only if e is a $*$-symbol. ⊣

Finally, we can prove the main claim of this section, namely that the obligatory axioms of the strong theory of expressions are true statements about $*$-expressions.

9.17 THEOREM · SOUNDNESS OF STANDARD MODELS *The axioms of* $\mathsf{E}^*_{\min}$ *are true in all standard models.*

PROOF Fix a standard model $\langle \mathbb{E}^*, V \rangle$. That the axioms of symbols, B1–B6, are all true in $\langle \mathbb{E}^*, V \rangle$ is an immediate consequence of theorem 9.16(i). The axioms of concatenation, C1–C3, and of substitution, E1–E3, are similarly straightforward. We show that the axiom schema F1 of induction is true in $\langle \mathbb{E}^*, V \rangle$ by appealing to the strong principle of induction for $*$-expressions. Notice that $\langle \mathbb{E}^*, V \rangle \vDash \overline{a} \subset \overline{b}$ if and only if a is a proper subexpression of b. Given a formula $\varphi(\mathsf{x})$ where x is the only variable occurring free, the statement that the axiom schema of induction for $\varphi(\mathsf{x})$ is true in $\langle \mathbb{E}^*, V \rangle$ is precisely the instance of strong induction for the property $\{ e \in \mathcal{E}^* : \langle \mathbb{E}^*, V \rangle \vDash \varphi(\overline{e}) \}$. Of the axioms of $\mathsf{E}^*_{\min}$, only the axioms of quotation remain. To see that D1 is true in $\langle \mathbb{E}^*, V \rangle$, let $a \in \mathcal{E}^*$ be any non-empty expression and u any $*$-symbol. Lemma 9.6 and the definition of quotation imply

$$\mathsf{q}(\overline{a}^\frown \overline{u})^{\mathbb{E}^*} \equiv \overline{au} \equiv \left(\underline{\frown}^\frown(\mathsf{q}\overline{a})^\frown(\mathsf{q}\overline{u})\right)^{\mathbb{E}^*}.$$

Applying lemma 9.15 and theorem 9.16(i), we deduce that $\langle \mathbb{E}^*, V \rangle \vDash$ D1. Similar reasoning shows that D2 expresses that the terms $\overline{\overline{u}}$ and $\mathsf{q}\overline{u}$ denote the same expression if u is a basic symbol and, therefore, is a consequence of lemma 8.43. Finally, proposition 8.40 implies that $\langle \mathbb{E}^*, V \rangle \vDash$ D3. ⊣

9.18 COROLLARY *Suppose* $\mathsf{E}^*_{\min} \vdash \varphi$. *Then* φ *is true in every standard model of* $\mathcal{L}^*$. *In particular,* $\mathsf{E}^*_{\min}$ *is consistent.*

9.2 Denotation

In chapter 6 we observed that $\mathsf{E}_{\min}$ can be consistently extended by the T-schema

$$\Box\overline{\varphi} \leftrightarrow \varphi \tag{9.1}$$

if $\square$ is a fresh predicate symbol and φ ranges only over sentences of $\mathcal{L}_{\text{min}}$ that do not contain $\square$. The same result holds for $\mathsf{E}^*_{\text{min}}$. This will be shown in chapter 11. Focusing on the case that φ is an equation, (9.1) describes the schema

(9.2) $$\square\overline{s=t} \leftrightarrow s=t,$$

where s and t range over closed terms. Let $\square_=(x,y)$ abbreviate the formula $\square(\underline{=}{}^\frown x{}^\frown y)$, which, reading $\square$ as a truth predicate and assuming x and y range over closed terms, expresses that the equation between the terms x and y is true. Over E^*, (9.2) is equivalent to

(9.3) $$\square_=(\overline{s},\overline{t}) \leftrightarrow s=t.$$

The collection of axioms of the form (9.3) attempts to express the claim

(9.4) An equality statement between two closed terms is true if and only if the terms denote the same expression.

Statement (9.4) explicitly quantifies over terms whereas the quantification in (9.3) is simulated by an infinite lot of equivalences. Quantification over expressions which are closed terms is possible via the formula CTerm. But to fully represent (9.4) would require a way to express within $\mathcal{L}^*$ that two terms denote the same expression.

As an approximation to (9.4), we may consider the sentence

(9.5) $$\forall x\forall y\big(\square_=(\mathsf{q}x,\mathsf{q}y) \leftrightarrow x=y\big).$$

Split into its two constituent implications, (9.5) is equivalent to the conjunction of

(9.6) $$\forall x\,\square_=(\mathsf{q}x,\mathsf{q}x),$$

(9.7) $$\forall x\forall y\big(\square_=(\mathsf{q}x,\mathsf{q}y) \rightarrow x=y\big).$$

Still reading $\square\overline{\varphi}$ as 'φ is true in all standard models', (9.6) and (9.7) express that every equation of the form $\overline{e}=\overline{e}$ is true, and that these are the *only* true equations between quotations. A standard model validating (9.5) is easily obtained: consider any standard model of $\mathcal{L}^*$ in which the predicate symbol $\square$ is interpreted as the set of expressions $=\overline{e}\,\overline{e}$ for $e\in\mathcal{E}^*$. This particular model confirms that (9.5) does not imply (9.3). As an example, let $s\equiv\underline{\forall}$ and $t\equiv\mathsf{sub}\,\underline{\neg}\,\underline{\neg}\,s$. Clearly $\mathsf{E}^*_{\text{min}}\vdash s=t$, so any model of $\mathsf{E}^*_{\min}+(9.3)$ must satisfy $\Box_=(\bar{s},\bar{t})$. But as t is not a pure term, that is, t is not $\bar{a}$ for some non-empty expression a, the standard model described above does not satisfy $\Box_=(\bar{s},\bar{t})$.

The problems of formalizing (9.4) disappear if one can refer to the denotation of a term. Suppose $\mathcal{L}^*$ contains a unary function symbol d, and E^* derives, for each closed term s, the sentence

$$\mathsf{d}\bar{s} = s. \tag{9.8}$$

The intention is that d is a function which, provided with a closed term as input, returns the denotation of this term in the standard model. More precisely, the intended semantics for d in a standard model $\langle \mathbb{E}^*, V\rangle$ of $\mathcal{L}^*$ is that d maps any expression which is a closed term to its denotation. That is, we require, for all closed terms e,

$$\mathsf{d}^V(e) \equiv e^{\mathbb{E}^*}.$$

There is no restriction on the value of $\mathsf{d}^V(e)$ if e is not a closed term. Applying the definition, if s is any term, $\mathfrak{b}$ is a variable assignment, and $s^{\mathfrak{b}}$ is a closed term, then $(\mathsf{d}s)^{\mathfrak{b}} \equiv (s^{\mathfrak{b}})^{\mathbb{E}^*}$.

An axiom schema of the form (9.8) can be shown to follow from a finite number of statements governing the behaviour of the denotation function d. We take the axioms of a primitive denotation function to be

DF1 $\forall \mathsf{x}\ \mathsf{d}(\mathsf{qx}) = \mathsf{x}$,

DF2 for each $k \geq 0$ and each function symbol f of $\mathcal{L}^*$ of arity k, the sentence

$$\forall \mathsf{v}_1 \cdots \forall \mathsf{v}_k \Big(\mathsf{CTerm}(\mathsf{v}_1) \wedge \cdots \wedge \mathsf{CTerm}(\mathsf{v}_k) \rightarrow \mathsf{d}(\underset{\cdot}{\mathsf{f}}\mathsf{v}_1 \cdots \mathsf{v}_k) = \mathsf{f}(\mathsf{d}\mathsf{v}_1) \cdots (\mathsf{d}\mathsf{v}_k)\Big).$$

The first axiom expresses that the denotation of a quotation is the quoted expression. The second axiom expresses, using the abbreviation introduced in definition 8.63, that the denotation of an expression of the form $\mathsf{f}s_1 \cdots s_k$, where each s_i is a closed term, is the result of applying the interpretation of f to the denotations of the arguments. A special case of DF2 is the equation $\mathsf{d}\underline{\mathsf{c}} = \mathsf{c}$ for every basic constant c of $\mathcal{L}^*$. Recall that every term of the form $\mathsf{f}e$ admits a unique decomposition of the form $\mathsf{f}s_1 \cdots s_k$ (see lemma 8.38); lemma 8.80(vii) shows that this unique readability property is derivable in E^*.

9.19 PROPOSITION *Suppose that* E^* *derives* DF1 *and all instances of* DF2. *Then* $\mathsf{E}^* \vdash \mathsf{d}\bar{s} = s$ *for every closed term* s.

PROOF By structural induction on the closed term *s*. ⊣

A primitive denotation function allows us to express statements that refer to the denotation of quantified terms, such as the equational T-schema (9.2) which becomes the statement

$$\forall x \forall y \Big(\mathsf{CTerm}(x) \wedge \mathsf{CTerm}(y) \rightarrow \big(\Box_{=}(x,y) \leftrightarrow \mathsf{d}x = \mathsf{d}y\big)\Big). \tag{9.9}$$

In fact, (9.9) shows that in the theory with a primitive denotation function, the property of being a true equation between closed terms is definable. Combining (9.9) with the conclusion of proposition 9.19 yields the equivalence $\Box\overline{s=t} \leftrightarrow s=t$ for every pair s, t of closed terms.

However, any set of axioms which implies (9.8) for all closed terms turns out to be inconsistent:

9.20 THEOREM · DENOTATION PARADOX *Suppose* $\mathsf{d}(x)$ *is a term of* $\mathcal{L}^*$ *and* E^* *derives the equation* $\mathsf{d}(\overline{s}) = s$ *for every closed term* s *of* $\mathcal{L}^*$*. Then* E^* *is inconsistent.*

PROOF We apply the strong diagonal lemma 8.75 to the term $\underline{\forall}{}^\frown\mathsf{d}(\mathsf{x})$. This yields a closed term s such that

$$\mathsf{E}^*_{\min} \vdash s = \underline{\forall}{}^\frown\mathsf{d}(\overline{s}).$$

Assuming that $\mathsf{E}^* \vdash \mathsf{d}(\overline{s}) = s$, we deduce $\mathsf{E}^* \vdash s = \underline{\forall}{}^\frown s$, from which it follows that $\mathsf{E}^* \vdash \underline{\forall} = \underline{0}$. ⊣

Just as Tarski's theorem shows that a consistent E^* cannot contain a truth predicate for all sentences in the language $\mathcal{L}^*$, the 'paradox' of theorem 9.20 shows that a consistent E^* cannot admit a primitive denotation function operating on all closed terms of $\mathcal{L}^*$. There are parallels in the two proofs: under the assumption that truth is definable, a sentence equivalent to its own negation can be constructed. From a definable denotation function, an expression can be defined which is a proper subexpression of itself, a state of affairs ruled out by the axioms of $\mathsf{E}^*_{\min}$.

Consistency can be recovered if the primitive denotation function is treated as a partial function which is defined only for closed terms that do not themselves refer to denotation. That is, we drop from the instances of DF2 the case that f is the function symbol d. Formally, there are no 'partial' functions in predicate logic. For any k-place function symbol f, the sentence $\forall x_1 \cdots \forall x_k \exists y\ \mathsf{f}x_1 \cdots x_k = y$, expressing that f returns a value on all inputs, is a logical validity. We can, however, simulate partial functions simply by not specifying (and never referring to) the value of the function on arguments outside the intended domain. Our axiomatization of a denotation function via DF1 and DF2 is already of this style. Neither axiom determines the value of the interpreting function d^V on arguments that are not closed terms. This observation is somewhat moot because, taken together, DF1 and DF2 are inconsistent. But it is not the totality of the denotation function which is the source of the contradiction. Rather, it is the assumption of a denotation function operating on terms which can reference this very function. Indeed, as the proof of theorem 9.20 shows, even for an interpretation of the denotation function symbol d as a *partial* function, there will be closed terms of $\mathcal{L}^*$ (such as the term s used in the proof) on which this function is undefined.[1]

In addition to removing the instance of DF2 for the symbol d, it may be necessary to exclude other function symbols of $\mathcal{L}^*$ from this axiom, depending on how these are axiomatized in E^*. For instance, if e is a unary function symbol distinct from d and $\mathsf{E}^* \vdash \forall x(\mathsf{d}x = \mathsf{e}x)$, then the instance of DF2 referring to e likewise leads to inconsistency. In general, as with combining distinct modalities, it is non-trivial which interactions between denotation and other primitive functions avoid, or lead to, inconsistency.

But beyond consistency it is hard to justify why a primitive denotation function should be defined only for terms which do not themselves refer to denotation. In such a case it is more natural to express denotation as a binary relation satisfying the uniqueness condition. With this in mind, we suppose that $\mathcal{L}^*$ contains a binary predicate symbol den and that E^* has the following sentences as axioms:

DP1 $\forall x \forall y \forall z(\mathsf{den}\,xy \wedge \mathsf{den}\,xz \rightarrow y = z)$,

DP2 $\forall x\ \mathsf{den}(\mathsf{q}x)x$,

DP3 for each $k \geq 0$ and each function symbol f in $\mathcal{L}^*$ with arity k, the formula

$$\forall v_1 \cdots \forall v_{2k}\Big(\bigwedge_{1 \leq i \leq k} \mathsf{den}\, v_i v_{k+i} \rightarrow \mathsf{den}(\underset{\cdot}{\mathsf{f}} v_1 \cdots v_k)(\mathsf{f} v_{k+1} \cdots v_{2k})\Big).$$

[1] As noted, to validate classical logic function symbols must be interpreted as total functions on the domain. There are logics which admit interpretations of function symbols as *partial* functions, for instance the logic of partial terms (see, e.g., Troelstra and Dalen 1988, §2.2). The proof of theorem 9.20 generalizes to formulations of the theory E^* over this logic.

Reading $\mathsf{den}\,xy$ as 'x denotes y', the first axiom expresses that the interpretation of den is a (partial) function, that is, every expression denotes at most one expression. The other axioms serve two purposes: they stipulate the domain of this function, and then 'denotation' of each expression in the domain. Axiom schema DP3 states that the denotation of an expression $\mathsf{f}e$, where f is a function symbol of arity k, is determined by decomposing e into k many denoting expressions – captured by the variables $\mathsf{v}_1, \ldots, \mathsf{v}_k$ in the axiom – and applying to their denotation the function that f is interpreted as. Compared to the axiom for a primitive denotation function, the variables $\mathsf{v}_1, \ldots, \mathsf{v}_k$ in DP3 range over all denoting expressions, not only terms. To learn from the axiom that an expression $\mathsf{f}e$ denotes, where f is a binary function symbol and e is any expression, it suffices to find a decomposition of e into two denoting expressions, say $e \equiv gh$. Then $\mathsf{f}e$ 'denotes' the result of applying the function interpreting f to the denotations of g and h. If, however, there were a second decomposition of e into two denoting expressions, this could produce a second 'denotation' of $\mathsf{f}e$, contradicting DP1. But provided that the domain of the function expressed by den consists solely of terms or some other collection of expressions that satisfies the unique readability property in lemma 8.38, the problematic scenario can never arise.

Before turning our attention to consistency, we observe that the axioms indeed express that den is a denotation function:

9.21 PROPOSITION *Suppose the axioms* DP1–DP3 *are provable in* E^*. *Then* $\mathsf{E}^* \vdash \forall x\big(\mathsf{CTerm}(x) \rightarrow \exists y\, \mathsf{den}\, xy\big)$. *In particular,* $\mathsf{E}^* \vdash \mathsf{den}\,\bar{s}s$ *for every closed term* s *of* $\mathcal{L}^*$.

The proof of the proposition proceeds by formal induction on terms and relies on the final three axioms of denotation.

A standard model of $\mathcal{L}^*$ with a denotation predicate is not difficult to construct. In fact, there is a canonical choice for the interpretation of den which applies to all standard models of $\mathcal{L}^*$: the set of pairs $\langle s, e\rangle$ where s is a closed term of $\mathcal{L}^*$ and e is the denotation of s in the given standard model. We call $\langle \mathbb{E}^*, V\rangle$ a *standard model with denotation* if it is a standard model of $\mathcal{L}^*$ and the binary predicate symbol den is interpreted as the relation

$$\mathsf{den}^V = \left\{ \langle s, e\rangle \in \mathcal{E}^* \times \mathcal{E}^* \colon s \text{ is a closed term of } \mathcal{L}^* \text{ and } s^{\mathbb{E}^*} \equiv e \right\}. \tag{9.10}$$

The next proposition establishes that the axioms for denotation predicates are true in every standard model with denotation:

9.22 PROPOSITION *Let $\langle \mathbb{E}^*, V\rangle$ be a standard model with denotation. Then for all e, f, $g \in \mathcal{E}^*$ the following two conditions hold:*

(i) *If* $\langle e, f\rangle \in \mathsf{den}^V$ *and* $\langle e, g\rangle \in \mathsf{den}^V$ *then* $f \equiv g$;

(ii) $\langle \overline{e}, e\rangle \in \mathsf{den}^V$.

PROOF (i) is trivial, and (ii) is a consequence of lemma 9.6. ⊣

Item (i) of proposition 9.22 confirms that the interpretation of den in a standard model with denotation is a function on expressions in the form of a functional relation on $\mathcal{E}^*$.

9.23 THEOREM *The axioms of a primitive denotation predicate are true in every standard model with denotation. In particular, the theory* $\mathsf{E}^*_{\mathrm{min}}$ *plus the axioms for a primitive denotation predicate* den *is consistent and has a standard model (with denotation).*

PROOF Let $\langle \mathbb{E}^*, V\rangle$ be a standard model with denotation. We show that the axioms DP1–DP3 are true in $\langle \mathbb{E}^*, V\rangle$. The first axiom is a consequence of proposition 9.22(i). The case of DP2 reduces to showing that $\langle \mathbb{E}^*, V\rangle \models \mathsf{den}(\mathsf{q}\overline{a})\overline{a}$ for every $*$-expression a. Lemma 9.6 yields $(\mathsf{q}\overline{a})^{\mathbb{E}^*} \equiv \overline{a}$ for every a, and proposition 9.22(ii) completes this case. To verify that $\langle \mathbb{E}^*, V\rangle \models$ DP3, suppose that f is a function symbol of $\mathcal{L}^*$, that the arity of f is k, and that $a_1, \ldots, a_k, b_1, \ldots, b_k$ are expressions such that $\langle a_i, b_i\rangle \in \mathsf{den}^V$ for each $1 \le i \le k$. Let $\mathsf{f}^{\langle \mathbb{E}^*, V\rangle}$ be the k-place function interpreting f. That is, $\mathsf{f}^{\langle \mathbb{E}^*, V\rangle}$ is $\mathsf{f}^{\mathbb{E}^*}$ or f^V, according to whether f is a basic symbol. The definition of den^V, (9.10), requires that each a_i is a closed term and that b_i is the denotation of a_i in $\langle \mathbb{E}^*, V\rangle$. Therefore $\mathsf{f}a_1 \cdots a_k$ is a closed term and, by definition, its denotation in $\langle \mathbb{E}^*, V\rangle$ is the expression $\mathsf{f}^{\langle \mathbb{E}^*, V\rangle}(b_1, \ldots, b_k)$, as desired. ⊣

Utilizing a denotation predicate, we can express equality for closed terms. This is the binary relation that holds between two expressions if and only if they are closed terms with the same value.

9.24 PROPOSITION *Suppose the axioms* DP1–DP3 *are provable in* E^*. *Then there is a formula* $\varphi(x, y)$ *of* $\mathcal{L}^*$ *such that* $\mathsf{E}^* \vdash \varphi(\overline{s}, \overline{t}) \leftrightarrow s = t$.

PROOF Let $\varphi(x, y) := \mathsf{CTerm}(x) \wedge \mathsf{CTerm}(y) \wedge \forall z(\mathsf{den}\, xz \leftrightarrow \mathsf{den}\, yz)$. Proposition 9.21 implies that the desired equivalence is provable in E^*. ⊣

In chapter 11 we will prove a strengthening of proposition 9.24 showing that, given a denotation predicate, truth predicates for large classes of formulæ, not only atomic formulæ, can be obtained.

The reason we did not include the axioms for denotation in E^* is that they are expressible. That is, there is a formula $\mathsf{Den}(x,y)$ in the language $\mathcal{L}^*$ which provably in $\mathsf{E}^*_{\min}$ fulfils the requirements of axioms DP1–DP3 when den is replaced by Den. This formula is constructed in a similar way to the formula Term in that $\mathsf{Den}(x,y)$ asserts the existence of a list whose elements satisfy a recursive definition of the relation of denotation: The denotations of constants – the simplest closed terms – are determined by a case distinction between the basic and syntactic constants. Denotations of complex terms are determined recursively, based on the denotations of the immediate subterms. In order to record subterms with their denotations, the elements of the list over which the formula Den existentially quantifies will be pairs $\langle s, a\rangle$ such that s is a closed term and a is the denotation of s.

In the following definition, $\mathcal{F}$ is the finite set of basic function symbols of $\mathcal{L}^*$. For each $\mathsf{f} \in \mathcal{F}$ let $a_\mathsf{f} \geq 0$ be the arity of f. Basic constants are treated as basic function symbols with arity 0.

9.25 DEFINITION The formula $\mathsf{Den}(x,y)$ is defined as

$$\exists z\Big(\mathsf{Seq}(z) \wedge \langle x,y\rangle \in_{\mathrm{seq}} z \wedge \forall w_0 \forall w_1\big(\langle w_0, w_1\rangle \in_{\mathrm{seq}} z \rightarrow \psi_{\mathsf{Den}}(w_0, w_1, z)\big)\Big),$$

where ψ_{Den} abbreviates

$$\begin{aligned}\psi_{\mathsf{Den}}(w_0, w_1, z) \;:=\; & \big(\mathsf{Sing}(w_0) \wedge w_0 = \mathsf{q}w_1\big) \vee \\ & \bigvee_{\mathsf{f}\in\mathcal{F}} \exists x_1 \cdots \exists x_{a_\mathsf{f}} \exists y_1 \cdots \exists y_{a_\mathsf{f}} \Big(w_0 = \underset{\cdot}{\mathsf{f}} x_1 \cdots x_k \wedge w_1 = \mathsf{f} y_1 \cdots y_{a_\mathsf{f}} \wedge \bigwedge_{i=1}^{a_\mathsf{f}} \langle x_i, y_i\rangle \in_{\mathrm{seq}} z\Big).\end{aligned}$$

The formula Den expresses the partial denotation function in the following sense:

9.26 PROPOSITION *The following are derivable in* E^*.

(i) $\mathsf{Den}(\overline{s}, s)$ *for each closed term* s,

(ii) $\forall x\big(\mathsf{CTerm}(x) \rightarrow \exists y\, \mathsf{Den}(x,y)\big)$,

(iii) $\forall x\, \mathsf{Den}(\mathsf{q}x, x)$,

(iv) $\forall x \forall y\big(\mathsf{Den}(x,y) \rightarrow \mathsf{CTerm}(x)\big)$,

(v) $\forall x \forall y \forall z \big(\mathsf{Den}(x,y) \wedge \mathsf{Den}(x,z) \rightarrow y = z\big)$.

PROOF (i). Let l be a sequence of pairs $\langle \bar{t}, t\rangle$ where each t is a subterm of s. The order of the components of l is unimportant. It is straightforward to show

$$\mathsf{E}^* \vdash \forall w_0 \forall w_1 \big(\langle w_0, w_1\rangle \in_{\mathsf{seq}} \bar{l} \rightarrow \psi_{\mathsf{Den}}(w_0, w_1, \bar{l})\big).$$

Moreover, $\mathsf{E}^* \vdash \mathsf{Seq}(\bar{l}) \wedge \langle \bar{s}, s\rangle \in_{\mathsf{seq}} \bar{l}$, so $\mathsf{E}^* \vdash \mathsf{Den}(\bar{s}, s)$, as desired.

(ii) is similar to (i), but the proof proceeds by formal induction on x, using the definition of $\mathsf{CTerm}(x)$. If x is a syntactic constant, that is, if $\mathsf{Syn}\, x$, then $x = \mathsf{q}y$ for some y and $\mathsf{Den}(x,y)$. Otherwise, $x \equiv \mathsf{f}x_1 \cdots x_{a_\mathsf{f}}$ for a function symbol f and closed subterms $x_1, \ldots, x_{a_\mathsf{f}}$ of x. The induction hypothesis yields expressions $y_1, \ldots, y_{a_\mathsf{f}}$ and sequences $l_1, \ldots, l_{a_\mathsf{f}}$ satisfying

(a) $\langle x_i, y_i\rangle$ is a component of l_i;

(b) $\psi_{\mathsf{Den}}(w_0, w_1, l_i)$ for all pairs $\langle w_0, w_1\rangle$ in l_i.

Let l be the concatenation of the l_i extended by the pair $\langle x, \mathsf{f}y_1 \cdots y_{a_\mathsf{f}}\rangle$. This sequence serves as the witness to verify $\mathsf{Den}(x,y)$.

(iii) is a special case of the proof of (ii) and is shown by induction on x.

(iv) is established by induction on the sequences satisfying the closure condition in Den. Namely, we argue, by formal induction on l, that if l satisfies

$$\forall w_0 \forall w_1 \big(\langle w_0, w_1\rangle \in_{\mathsf{seq}} l \rightarrow \psi_{\mathsf{Den}}(w_0, w_1, l)\big), \tag{9.11}$$

then for every pair $\langle x, y\rangle \in_{\mathsf{seq}} l$, x is a closed term. We leave the details of this argument to the reader.

(v) is also proved by formal induction. It suffices to show, within E^*, that if l is a sequence fulfilling condition (9.11) then for any two pairs $\langle w, x\rangle, \langle w, y\rangle \in_{\mathsf{seq}} l$, we have $x = y$. If w is a singleton expression then, since $\langle w, x\rangle \in_{\mathsf{seq}} l$, either $w = \mathsf{q}x$ is a syntactic constant or $w = \underline{\mathsf{c}}$ is a basic constant and $x = \mathsf{c}$ is the denoted expression. In either case x is uniquely determined. If w is not a singleton expression then, under the assumption that $\langle w, x\rangle \in_{\mathsf{seq}} l$, there is a function symbol f with non-zero arity a, a decomposition $w = \underline{\mathsf{f}}w_1 \cdots w_a$ of w, and expressions $x_1, \ldots, x_a$ such that $\langle w_i, x_i\rangle \in_{\mathsf{seq}} l$ for each i and $x = \mathsf{f}x_1 \cdots x_a$. By (ii), $w, w_1, \ldots, w_a$ are all closed terms. Lemma 8.78(vii) implies that the choice of w_1, w_2, and so on until w_a, is unique. The induction hypothesis implies that x_i is uniquely determined given w_i. So x is uniquely determined. ⊣

The previous results lead to the definability of denotation:

9.27 THEOREM *The axioms for denotation predicates,* DP1–DP3, *with* Den *replacing* den, *are derivable in* $\mathsf{E}^*_{\min}$. *In particular, if* $\mathsf{E}^*_{\min}$+DP1–DP3 $\vdash \varphi$ *and* φ *does not contain the symbol* den, *then* $\mathsf{E}^*_{\min} \vdash \varphi$.

PROOF The first part of the theorem is a consequence of proposition 9.26 in the case of the translation of the axioms DP1 and DP2, and the definition of Den for the remaining two axioms. The second part follows from the first. ⊣

A consequence of the definability of denotation is that the true equations between closed terms are directly expressible in $\mathsf{E}^*_{\min}$. Define formulæ Eq and $\mathsf{Tr}_{\mathsf{eq}}$ as follows:

$$\begin{aligned}\mathsf{Eq}(x,y) &:= \mathsf{CTerm}(x) \wedge \mathsf{CTerm}(y) \wedge \exists z\big(\mathsf{Den}(x,z) \wedge \mathsf{Den}(y,z)\big),\\ \mathsf{Tr}_{\mathsf{eq}}(x) &:= \exists y \exists z\big(x = \underline{=}^\frown y^\frown z \wedge \mathsf{Eq}(y,z)\big).\end{aligned}$$

The first formula is similar to the formula given in the proof of proposition 9.24 expressing that x and y are closed terms with the same denotation. $\mathsf{Tr}_{\mathsf{eq}}(x)$ therefore expresses that x is a true equation between closed terms, that is, x is an expression of the type $=st$ and s and t are closed terms denoting the same expression. Proposition 9.26 shows that $\mathsf{Eq}(x, y)$ is equivalent to the formula

$$\mathsf{CTerm}(x) \wedge \mathsf{CTerm}(y) \wedge \forall z\big(\mathsf{Den}(x,z) \leftrightarrow \mathsf{Den}(y,z)\big).$$

Equations are not the only atomic formulæ. Building on $\mathsf{Tr}_{\mathsf{eq}}$, it is not difficult to express the property of being a true atomic sentence. By definition, $\mathcal{L}^*$ contains only finitely many predicate symbols. Suppose these are $\mathsf{R}_0, \ldots, \mathsf{R}_k$ and that this list includes the equality predicate. For each i, let a_i be the arity of the predicate symbol R_i. Writing $\underset{\cdot}{\mathsf{R}}_i x_1 \cdots x_{a_i}$ as a shorthand for the term $\underline{\mathsf{R}}_i{}^\frown x_1{}^\frown \cdots {}^\frown x_{a_i}$, we define

$$\mathsf{Tr}_{\mathsf{at}}(x) := \bigvee_{i=0}^{k} \exists x_1 \cdots \exists x_{a_i} \exists y_1 \cdots \exists y_{a_i} \Big(x = \underset{\cdot}{\mathsf{R}}_i x_1 \cdots x_{a_i} \wedge \mathsf{R}_i y_1 \cdots y_{a_i} \wedge \bigwedge_{j=1}^{a_i} \mathsf{Den}(x_i, y_i)\Big).$$

The variables x_i are intended to range over closed terms, which is enforced by the conjunction of the $\mathsf{Den}(x_i, y_i)$ and proposition 9.26(iv). So $\mathsf{Tr}_{\mathsf{at}}(x)$ expresses that x is an atomic sentence, namely a $*$-expression of the form $\mathsf{R}s_1 \cdots s_n$, and that the relation expressed by R holds of the $*$-expressions denoted by these closed terms. In short, $\mathsf{Tr}_{\mathsf{at}}(x)$ states that x is a true atomic sentence.

It readily follows that the formula $\mathsf{Tr}_{\mathrm{at}}$ satisfies the T-schema for atomic sentences:

$$\mathsf{E}^*_{\min} \vdash \mathsf{Tr}_{\mathrm{at}}(\overline{\varphi}) \leftrightarrow \varphi \quad \text{for atomic sentences } \varphi.$$

$\mathsf{Tr}_{\mathrm{at}}$ is an example of a definable truth predicate, albeit one that works only for atomic sentences. Truth predicates for larger classes of formulæ will be defined in chapter 11.

9.3 Arithmetic in E*

Arithmetic can be interpreted in E^* in precisely the same way as in E, by identifying natural numbers with finite strings of some fixed symbol. In chapter 6 we used strings composed of the variable symbol x. But x is not a symbol of $\mathcal{L}^*$. Rather, it abbreviates the two-symbol expression $()$. This does not pose any particular problem and we could continue to identify natural numbers with expressions of the form $\mathsf{xx}\cdots\mathsf{x}$. But it will prove convenient for each natural number to be expressed as a string of corresponding length. Therefore, we will employ the symbol v in place of the expression x. Nevertheless, with only minor changes the present section could be carried out using natural numbers as defined in chapter 6.

Henceforth, the natural number n is identified with the expression $\mathsf{v}\cdots\mathsf{v}$ consisting of n many occurrences of v. The *numeral of* n, written as $\underline{n}$, is the quotation of this expression:

$$\underline{n} := \overline{\underbrace{\mathsf{v}\cdots\mathsf{v}}_{n}}.$$

Notice that the natural number 0 is the empty expression, and that the numeral of 0 is just the quotation of the empty string, the syntactic constant $\underline{0}$. The numeral of 1 is the constant $\underline{\mathsf{v}}$ and the numeral of $n+1$ is the term $\underline{n}\frown\underline{\mathsf{v}}$ if $n > 0$. Although $\underline{n}$ was a symbol of $\mathcal{L}$, in $\mathcal{L}^*$ it is a term which denotes the natural number n in every standard model of $\mathcal{L}^*$. The property of being a natural number is expressed by the following formula.

9.28 DEFINITION $\mathsf{Nat}^*(\mathsf{x}) := \mathsf{sub}(\mathsf{x}, \underline{\mathsf{v}}, \underline{0}) = \underline{0}$.

9.29 PROPOSITION *For each $*$-expression a,*

(i) $\mathsf{E}^* \vdash \mathsf{Nat}^*(\overline{a})$ *if a is a natural number,*

(ii) $\mathsf{E}^* \vdash \neg\mathsf{Nat}^*(\overline{a})$ *if a is not a natural number.*

PROOF This is a consequence of propositions 8.72 and 8.73. ⊣

As previously, successor, addition, and multiplication are expressed via concatenation and substitution:

9.30 DEFINITION We introduce defined terms $\mathsf{S}(\mathsf{x})$, $\mathsf{x}+\mathsf{y}$, and $\mathsf{x}\cdot\mathsf{y}$ given by

$$\mathsf{S}(\mathsf{x}) := \mathsf{x}\frown\underline{\mathsf{v}}, \qquad \mathsf{x}+\mathsf{y} := \mathsf{x}\frown\mathsf{y}, \qquad \mathsf{x}\cdot\mathsf{y} := \mathsf{sub}(\mathsf{y}, \underline{\mathsf{v}}, \mathsf{x}).$$

With these definitions, we can consider the language of arithmetic as a sublanguage of $\mathcal{L}^*$. Terms of $\mathcal{L}^*$ that can be constructed from variables and the constant $\underline{0}$ by use of the three defined terms S, +, and · will be called arithmetic terms. A formula φ is in the language of arithmetic if all terms in φ are arithmetic and all quantifiers in φ are relativized to the predicate Nat^*. By the latter condition we mean that if $\forall \mathsf{v}_i\, \psi$ is any subformula of φ, then ψ is of the form $\psi \equiv (\mathsf{Nat}^*(\mathsf{v}_i) \to \chi)$ for some χ.

The next results develop the theory of arithmetic within the theory E^*, starting with the provable properties of numerals.

9.31 LEMMA *For all natural numbers m and n,*

(i) $\mathsf{E}^* \vdash \mathsf{S}(\underline{m}) = \underline{m+1}$,

(ii) $\mathsf{E}^* \vdash \underline{m}+\underline{n} = \underline{m+n}$,

(iii) $\mathsf{E}^* \vdash \underline{m}\cdot\underline{n} = \underline{m\cdot n}$.

The theory E can already prove an analogous lemma. Within E^*, however, it is possible to derive quantified versions of the claims. In theorem 9.34 we show that the axioms of the first-order theory known as Peano arithmetic are derivable in E^*. Before proceeding to that result, it is necessary to observe that our definitions of successor, addition, and multiplication preserve the property of being a natural number. Lemma 9.31 establishes this fact for each particular instantiation of the terms by numerals. The next result presents the generalized statement.

9.32 PROPOSITION *The following are derivable in* E^*:

(i) $\forall x\big(\mathsf{Nat}^*(x) \to x=\underline{0} \vee \exists y(x=\mathsf{S}(y) \wedge \mathsf{Nat}^*(y))\big)$,

(ii) $\forall x\big(\mathsf{Nat}^*(x) \leftrightarrow \mathsf{Nat}^*(\mathsf{S}(x))\big)$,

(iii) $\forall x \forall y\big(\mathsf{Nat}^*(x) \wedge \mathsf{Nat}^*(y) \rightarrow \mathsf{Nat}^*(x+y)\big)$,

(iv) $\forall x \forall y\big(\mathsf{Nat}^*(x) \wedge \mathsf{Nat}^*(y) \rightarrow \mathsf{Nat}^*(x \cdot y)\big)$.

PROOF The first clause is a consequence of lemma 8.78(i). This lemma establishes that every non-empty expression is the result of appending a singleton to some expression. Therefore, if $\mathsf{Nat}^*(x)$ and $x \neq \underline{0}$, then $x = y^\frown \underline{\mathsf{v}}$ for some expression y and $\mathsf{Nat}^*(y)$ holds because $\mathsf{sub}(y, \underline{\mathsf{v}}, \underline{0}) = \mathsf{sub}(y^\frown \underline{\mathsf{v}}, \underline{\mathsf{v}}, \underline{0})$. (ii) follows from the same observation.

Concerning (iii) and (iv), we use the basic axioms of concatenation and substitution in E^* combined with weak induction (proposition 8.79). Let $\varphi(y)$ be the formula $\mathsf{Nat}^*(y) \rightarrow \forall x\big(\mathsf{Nat}^*(x) \rightarrow \mathsf{Nat}^*(x+y)\big)$. We argue informally within E^* and prove $\forall y\, \varphi(y)$ by weak induction, from which the first of the two remaining claims follows. The base case of the induction, $\varphi(\underline{0})$, is trivial. For the induction case, we assume that $y = z^\frown u$ for a singleton u and the induction hypothesis $\varphi(z)$, and are required to show $\varphi(y)$. To that aim, suppose $\mathsf{Nat}^*(y)$. As $y \neq \underline{0}$, (i) implies $y = \mathsf{S}(z)$ and therefore $\mathsf{Nat}^*(z)$. Now let x be any natural number. The induction hypothesis implies $\mathsf{Nat}^*(x^\frown z)$, so $\mathsf{Nat}^*(\mathsf{S}(x^\frown z))$ by (ii) and, hence, $\mathsf{Nat}^*(x^\frown y)$ by the associativity of concatenation.

Clause (iv) uses a similar argument. Let $\varphi(y)$ now be the formula $\mathsf{Nat}^*(y) \rightarrow \forall x\big(\mathsf{Nat}^*(x) \rightarrow \mathsf{Nat}^*(x \cdot y)\big)$. The base case of the induction, namely $\varphi(\underline{0})$, is trivial. For the induction case we may assume, as before, that $y = \mathsf{S}(z)$, that z is a natural number, and $\varphi(z)$. If x is a natural number, then $x \cdot y = (x \cdot z) + x$. From the induction hypothesis, we know $\mathsf{Nat}^*(x \cdot z)$, whereby $\mathsf{Nat}^*(x \cdot y)$ follows by (iii). $\dashv$

The two applications of induction in the proof were somewhat awkward because of the need to specialize the induction schema – a statement about arbitrary expressions – to the domain of natural numbers by appealing to previously established general results about expressions. Both proofs would be greatly streamlined if we had access to an induction principle specifically for the natural numbers. The next theorem proves such a numerical induction principle.

As in chapter 6, we introduce abbreviations for quantifiers which are restricted to natural numbers. We use letters m and n (possibly ornamented) in this role as formal metavariables for natural numbers. So $\forall n\, \varphi(n)$ abbreviates the formula $\forall x\big(\mathsf{Nat}^*(x) \rightarrow \varphi(x)\big)$ for an appropriate choice of variable x, and similarly for $\exists n$.

For example, statement (i) from the previous proposition is abbreviated as

$$\mathsf{E}^* \vdash \forall m\big(m = \underline{0} \vee \exists n\ m = \mathsf{S}(m)\big),$$

and (iii) simply becomes $\mathsf{E}^* \vdash \forall m \forall n\ \mathsf{Nat}^*(m+n)$.

The most important formal theory of arithmetic is Peano arithmetic. Conceived as a theory in the language $\mathcal{L}^*$, it is axiomatized as follows:

9.33 DEFINITION Peano arithmetic is the theory axiomatized by the following sentences.

PA1 $\forall m\ \mathsf{S}(m) \neq \underline{0}$,

PA2 $\forall m \forall n \big(\mathsf{S}(m) = \mathsf{S}(n) \rightarrow m = n\big)$,

PA3 $\forall m\ m + \underline{0} = m$,

PA4 $\forall m \forall n\ m + \mathsf{S}(n) = \mathsf{S}(m+n)$,

PA5 $\forall m\ m \cdot \underline{0} = \underline{0}$,

PA6 $\forall m \forall n\ m \cdot \mathsf{S}(n) = (m \cdot n) + m$,

PA7 the universal closure of $\varphi(\underline{0}) \wedge \forall n\big(\varphi(n) \rightarrow \varphi(\mathsf{S}(n))\big) \rightarrow \forall n\ \varphi(n)$ for every formula $\varphi(\mathsf{x})$.

The final axiom, called the axiom schema of numerical induction, is stipulated for formulæ in the language $\mathcal{L}^*$. A reasonable restriction would be that φ must be a formula in the language of arithmetic. The principle of numerical induction, however, applies to all properties of natural numbers regardless of the linguistic resources used in their definition. In particular, to properties expressed by arbitrary formulæ of $\mathcal{L}^*$. This general formulation of numerical induction scheme is provable in E*.

9.34 THEOREM *The axioms of Peano arithmetic are provable in* E*.

We actually prove a stronger claim than stated, as we will show that the axioms of Peano arithmetic are consequences of the *weak* principle of induction (over the basic axioms of E*). Weak induction, recall, is the collection of all formulæ of the form

$$\varphi(\underline{0}) \wedge \forall \mathsf{x}\Big(\varphi(\mathsf{x}) \rightarrow \forall \mathsf{y}\big(\mathsf{Sing}(\mathsf{y}) \rightarrow \varphi(\mathsf{x}^\frown \mathsf{y})\big)\Big) \rightarrow \forall \mathsf{x}\, \varphi(\mathsf{x}).$$

Although it was remarked in that chapter that the two induction schemas are equivalent over the basic axioms of E^*, we have not yet proved this result. In fact, our argument that weak induction implies strong induction will proceed via numerical induction: we show that the strong induction principle can be reduced to numerical induction which, in turn, can be proven from weak induction and the basic axioms of E^*.

PROOF Expanding the abbreviations, PA1 and PA2 are the formulæ

- $\forall x\big(\mathsf{Nat}^*(x) \to x^\frown \underline{\mathsf{v}} \neq \underline{0}\big)$,
- $\forall x \forall y\big(\mathsf{Nat}^*(x) \wedge \mathsf{Nat}^*(y) \wedge x^\frown \underline{\mathsf{v}} = y^\frown \underline{\mathsf{v}} \to x = y\big)$.

Both axioms are consequences of the axioms of concatenation. Axiom PA3 is an instance of axiom C2; axiom PA4 states the associativity of concatenation and is a consequence of proposition 8.50. Axioms PA5 and PA6 are the formulæ

- $\forall x\big(\mathsf{Nat}^*(x) \to \mathsf{sub}(\underline{0}, \underline{\mathsf{v}}, x) = \underline{0}\big)$,
- $\forall x \forall y\big(\mathsf{Nat}^*(x) \wedge \mathsf{Nat}^*(y) \to \mathsf{sub}(y^\frown \underline{\mathsf{v}}, \underline{\mathsf{v}}, x) = \mathsf{sub}(y, \underline{\mathsf{v}}, x)^\frown x\big)$.

These are consequences of the axioms of substitution.

Finally, we derive the axiom schema of numerical induction in E^*. The argument is similar to the proof by induction in proposition 9.32. Fix an arbitrary formula $\varphi(\mathsf{x})$ and assume, arguing in E^*, that

$$\varphi(\underline{0}) \wedge \forall n\big(\varphi(n) \to \varphi(\mathsf{S}(n))\big). \tag{9.12}$$

We are required to show $\forall x\big(\mathsf{Nat}^*(x) \to \varphi(x)\big)$, for which we appeal to weak induction (proposition 8.79). Define $\psi(\mathsf{x}) \equiv \mathsf{Nat}^*(\mathsf{x}) \to \varphi(\mathsf{x})$. From (9.12) and proposition 9.32(i), we easily deduce the formula

$$\psi(\underline{0}) \wedge \forall x \forall y\big(\psi(x) \wedge \mathsf{Sing}(y) \to \psi(x^\frown y)\big).$$

Applying weak induction, we conclude $\forall x\, \psi(x)$, as required. ⊣

The following is an immediate consequence of theorem 9.34:

9.35 COROLLARY *If* $\mathsf{PA} \vdash \varphi$ *then* $\mathsf{E}^* \vdash \varphi$.

The common approach to a theory of syntax is to view it as a subtheory of Peano arithmetic via a coding of $\ast$-expressions as natural numbers. We will not present the details of this reduction – the reader can consult almost any textbook covering Gödel's theorems, for instance Shoenfield (1967) or Boolos, Burgess, and Jeffrey (2007) – but any reasonable coding of the language $\mathcal{L}^*$ in arithmetic will induce a mapping of each $\ast$-formula φ to a formula φ^* in the language of arithmetic satisfying a converse to corollary 9.35: $\mathsf{E}^*_{\min} \vdash \varphi$ implies $\mathsf{PA} \vdash \varphi^*$. As the translation can be chosen so that $\mathsf{PA} \vdash \varphi^* \leftrightarrow \varphi$ whenever φ is in the language of arithmetic, theorem 9.34 admits a strengthening directly connecting arithmetic in E^* with Peano arithmetic:

9.36 THEOREM $\mathsf{E}^*_{\min}$ *and* PA *derive the same theorems in the language of arithmetic.*

The main value of theorem 9.34 for our purposes is the axiom schema PA7 of numerical induction that the theorem shows to be derivable in E^*. Naturally, this formulation of induction is useful for proving quantified statements about the natural numbers. We present some examples of later use:

9.37 LEMMA

(i) $\mathsf{E}^* \vdash \forall m \forall n \forall n' \;\; m+(n+n') = (m+n)+n'$,

(ii) $\mathsf{E}^* \vdash \forall m \forall n \forall n' \;\; m\cdot(n\cdot n') = (m\cdot n)\cdot n'$,

(iii) $\mathsf{E}^* \vdash \forall m \forall n \;\; m+n = n+m$,

(iv) $\mathsf{E}^* \vdash \forall m \forall n \;\; m\cdot n = n\cdot m$.

PROOF We leave the proof of this lemma to the reader. ⊣

The standard ordering of the natural numbers, $0 < 1 < 2 < \cdots$, can be defined in terms of addition:

9.38 DEFINITION $x \leq y$ is defined as $\mathsf{Nat}^*(y) \wedge \exists n\; x+n = y$. We define $x < y$ to be $x \leq y \wedge x \neq y$.

The formula $x \leq y$ states that y is a natural number which can be obtained by appending some, possibly empty, expression to x. The same relation can be defined as 'subexpression' restricted to natural numbers. We can prove, by numerical induction, that the two definitions are equivalent:

9.39 PROPOSITION $\mathsf{E}^* \vdash \forall n \forall x (x \leq n \leftrightarrow x \subseteq n)$.

PROOF The implication $\forall n \forall x (x \leq n \rightarrow x \subseteq n)$ is straightforward since addition is concatenation. For the converse direction, we prove $\forall m \forall x (x \subseteq m \rightarrow \exists n\, x^\frown n = m)$ by induction on the variable m. The base case of the induction is trivial. For the induction step, we assume that x is a subexpression of m and that $m = \mathsf{S}(m_0)$ for a natural number m_0. If x is a subexpression of m_0, then the induction hypothesis implies $x^\frown n = m$ for some n. Otherwise, $x = \mathsf{S}(x_0)$ for some $x_0 \subseteq m_0$. The induction hypothesis implies $x_0{}^\frown n = m_0$ for some n, and $x^\frown n = m$ results from lemma 9.37(iii). ⊣

An important application of arithmetic in a theory of expressions is the ability to compare expressions by length or by some other numerical measure of complexity. Length is a relation which associates to each expression a natural number such that 0 is assigned to the empty expression and the natural number $n+1$ is assigned to a non-empty expression au under the condition that u is a singleton and n is assigned to a. This property is readily expressed as a formula of $\mathcal{L}^*$:

9.40 DEFINITION $\mathsf{Len}(x, n)$ is defined as the formula

$$\mathsf{Len}(x, n) := \exists z \Big(\mathsf{Seq}(z) \wedge \langle x, n \rangle \in_{\mathsf{seq}} z \wedge \forall y \forall m \big(\langle y, m \rangle \in_{\mathsf{seq}} z \rightarrow \psi_{\mathsf{Len}}(y, m, z) \big) \Big)$$

where

$$\begin{aligned} \psi_{\mathsf{Len}}(y, m, z) := \ & (y = \underline{0} \wedge m = \underline{0}) \vee \\ & \exists x \forall u \forall n \big(\mathsf{Sing}(u) \wedge y = x^\frown u \wedge m = \mathsf{S}(n) \wedge \langle x, n \rangle \in_{\mathsf{seq}} z \big). \end{aligned}$$

Our formula for length is similar in structure to the formula Den defined on page 219. For arbitrary expressions x and w, $\mathsf{Len}(x, w)$ expresses the existence of a sequence of pairs of expressions which contains the pair $\langle x, w \rangle$, contains a pair $\langle a, n \rangle$ if the pair $\langle au, n+1 \rangle$ is present for some symbol u, and contains $\langle 0, n \rangle$ only if $n \equiv 0$.

9.41 PROPOSITION *The following are provable in* E^*.

(i) $\forall x \exists m\ \mathsf{Len}(x, m)$,

(ii) $\forall x \forall y \forall z \big(\mathsf{Len}(x, y) \wedge \mathsf{Len}(x, z) \rightarrow y = z \big)$.

Given proposition 9.41, we can simplify uses of the formula Len via an introduced function symbol. In the following we write $|s| = t$ instead of $\mathsf{Len}(s, t)$. As detailed in chapter 2, there are two ways to manage this abuse of notation formally. One approach is to introduce $|\cdot|$ as a unary function symbol in $\mathcal{L}^*$ and add the axiom $\forall x\, \mathsf{Len}(x, |x|)$ to E^*. The second method is to replace every formula using the function symbol by a logically equivalent formula in which the only use of the length function is of the form $|s| = t$, and then to replace these equations by the corresponding formulæ $\mathsf{Len}(s, t)$. For present considerations, either method is suitable.

Making use the introduced notation, the next proposition builds on the definition of Len:

9.42 PROPOSITION *The following are provable in* E^**:*

(i) $\forall x\big(|x| = \underline{0} \leftrightarrow x = \underline{0}\big)$,

(ii) $\forall x \forall y\ |x^\frown y| = |x| + |y|$,

(iii) $\forall x \forall y\big(x \sqsubset y \rightarrow |x| < |y|\big)$.

We will not prove propositions 9.41 and 9.42, as the arguments are of the same flavour as those for the properties we established for the formula Den in proposition 9.26. More arguments of this kind are presented in detail in chapter 11, for example propositions 11.6 and 11.12.

The next proposition is a simple application of arithmetic induction using (ii) from proposition 9.42:

9.43 PROPOSITION $\mathsf{E}^* \vdash \forall n\ |n| = n.$

It was mentioned in the preceding chapter that the axiom of induction in E^* is equivalent to the weak induction schema introduced in proposition 8.79. The proof of the equivalence appeals to arithmetic induction, which, as the proof of theorem 9.34 demonstrates, is derivable from weak induction alone. We can now show that the axiom schema of induction is derivable from arithmetic induction. In the following let E^*_0 name the theory axiomatized by the basic axioms for expressions. That is, E^*_0 is the subtheory of $\mathsf{E}^*_{\mathrm{min}}$ with the axiom schema of induction omitted.

9.44 PROPOSITION *Over* E^*_0*, the axiom schema* F1 *of (strong) induction is derivable from the schema of weak induction.*

PROOF Let $\varphi(x)$ be any formula. We claim to be able to prove

$$\forall x\big(\forall y{\sqsubset}x\ \varphi(y) \to \varphi(x)\big) \to \forall x\, \varphi(x) \tag{9.13}$$

in the theory $\mathsf{E}_0^* + \text{PA7}$, which extends E_0^* by the schema of arithmetic induction. We choose the instance of weak induction for the formula

$$\psi(y) := \forall x\big(|x| \leq y \to \varphi(x)\big). \tag{9.14}$$

This formula expresses that φ holds of all expressions whose length is no greater than (the natural number) y. By proposition 9.41(i) we know that

$$\mathsf{E}_0^* \vdash \forall m\, \psi(m) \to \forall x\, \varphi(x).$$

We now argue within $\mathsf{E}_0^* + \text{PA7}$. With the aim being to establish (9.13), we assume the antecedent, the claim that $\varphi(x)$ is progressive in x:

$$\forall x\big(\forall y{\sqsubset}x\ \varphi(y) \to \varphi(x)\big). \tag{9.15}$$

Instantiating x with $\underline{0}$ and applying proposition 9.42(i), we deduce $\psi(\underline{0})$. We claim that (9.15) also implies

$$\forall m\big(\psi(m) \to \psi(\mathsf{S}(m))\big). \tag{9.16}$$

Fix an arbitrary natural number m, suppose $\psi(m)$, and, with the aim to conclude $\psi\big(\mathsf{S}(m)\big)$, assume that x is any expression such that $|x| \leq m + \underline{1}$. By proposition 9.42(iii) and the transitivity of $\leq$ we know that if y is a proper subexpression of x, then $|y| \leq m$. So, from $\psi(m)$ we deduce $\forall y{\sqsubset}x\ \varphi(x)$ and, invoking (9.15), also $\varphi(x)$. Thus (9.16) is implied by (9.15). From (9.16) and $\psi(\underline{0})$ follows $\forall m\ \psi(m)$, which entails $\forall x\ \varphi(x)$. Hence we have shown that the induction axiom for φ, namely (9.13), is provable in $\mathsf{E}_0^* + \text{PA7}$. $\dashv$

In the previous chapter we also claimed that the principle of rank induction is derivable in E^*. We conclude this section with a proof of this claim. Recall, rank induction is the schema

$$\forall x\big(\forall y{\lhd}x\ \varphi(y) \to \varphi(x)\big) \to \forall x\, \varphi(x), \tag{9.17}$$

where $\lhd$ is defined as

$$x \lhd y \equiv \mathsf{q}x \subseteq y.$$

Rank induction, too, can be shown to be a consequence of numerical induction. More specifically, we use the induction schema implicit in the proof of proposition 9.44, namely induction on the length of expressions. To begin, we require an observation on the length of quotations:

9.45 LEMMA *The following are provable in* E*.

(i) $\forall x\ |x| \leq |\mathsf{q}x|$,

(ii) $\forall x\big(|x| = |\mathsf{q}x| \rightarrow \mathsf{sym}\, x\big)$.

The first condition expresses that the length of $\overline{a}$ is never smaller than the length of a. The second claim adds that the only case in which an expression and its quotation have the same length are the basic symbols. These statements directly correspond to the two observations we relied on in the proof that $\lhd$ is a well-founded relation (proposition 8.83).

PROOF Both claims are proved by weak induction. In the case of (i), we observe that the length of the empty expression is 0 whereas $\mathsf{q}\underline{0}$ has unit length. The induction step of the argument splits into two cases. It is easily proved that the length of a singleton is 1 and that the length of the quotation of a singleton is non-zero. This leaves the case that the length of x is greater than 1, i.e., $x = yuv$ for symbols u and v, and some, possibly empty, expression y. By axiom D1, $\mathsf{q}x = \underline{\frown}{}^\frown \mathsf{q}(y^\frown u)^\frown \mathsf{q}v$. Applying proposition 9.42(v), the length of $\mathsf{q}x$ is the sum of the lengths of the three expressions $\underline{\frown}$, $\mathsf{q}(y^\frown u)$, and $\mathsf{q}v$. The induction hypothesis implies $|y^\frown u| \leq |\mathsf{q}(y^\frown u)|$, meaning that the length of $\mathsf{q}x$ is not less than the length of x.

Claim (ii) is derived by a similar argument: if x is not a basic symbol, then either x is a syntactic constant or $x = yu$, where u is a symbol and y has non-zero length. In the former case, $\mathsf{q}x = \underline{\mathsf{q}}^\frown x$ is an expression one symbol longer than x. In the latter case, the length of $\mathsf{q}x$ is strictly greater than the sum of the lengths of $\mathsf{q}y$ and $\mathsf{q}u$, which we know from (i) is not less than the length of x. Hence, if x and $\mathsf{q}x$ are of the same length, then x is a basic symbol, as claimed in (ii). ⊣

Connecting the previous lemma to the rank relation $\lhd$, we deduce:

9.46 PROPOSITION $\mathsf{E}^* \vdash \forall y \forall x \lhd y\big(|x| < |y| \vee \mathsf{sym}\, x\big)$.

PROOF As $x \lhd y$ abbreviates $\mathsf{q}x \subseteq y$, the combination of proposition 9.42(iii) and lemma 9.45 implies the proposition. ⊣

We can now derive rank induction within E^*:

9.47 PROPOSITION *The schema of rank induction, that is, (9.17) for every formula φ, is derivable in E^*.*

PROOF Fix a formula φ and assume, with the aim of deducing $\forall x\, \varphi(x)$, the formula

$$\forall x\big(\forall y \lhd x\ \varphi(y) \to \varphi(x)\big). \tag{9.18}$$

As in the proof of proposition 9.44, we show $\forall x\, \varphi(x)$ by induction on the length of expressions. Let $\psi(m)$ be the formula from (9.14) stating that $\varphi(x)$ holds for every expression x with length $\leq m$. (9.18) implies $\varphi(\underline{0})$, so $\psi(\underline{0})$ holds also. Now assume $\psi(m)$ for a natural number m, and fix an arbitrary expression x of length at most $m+1$. If $|x| \leq m$, then $\varphi(x)$ is a consequence of $\psi(m)$. So it suffices to suppose $|x| = m+1$. If $m = 0$, then x is a basic symbol or syntactic constant, and $\varphi(x)$ results from one or two applications of (9.18). This leaves the case that $m \neq 0$, i.e., x has length at least 2. By proposition 9.46 it follows that the length of any $y \lhd x$ is no greater than m. The induction hypothesis, $\psi(m)$, therefore implies $\forall y \lhd x\ \varphi(y)$, whence $\varphi(x)$ obtains from (9.18).

Thus, we have shown $\psi(\underline{0}) \wedge \forall m\big(\psi(m) \to \psi(\mathsf{S}(m))\big)$. Hence, we conclude $\forall m\, \psi(m)$ by arithmetic induction and, therefore, $\forall x\, \varphi(x)$. ⊣

10 Formal Language

We now turn to the task of developing the theory of syntax within the strong theory of expressions. This endeavour will culminate in proofs of Gödel's incompleteness theorems for theories that extend the minimal theory $\mathsf{E}^*_{\min}$. We encountered the incompleteness phenomenon in chapter 6, where it was shown that a theory of expressions which can express its own notion of theoremhood is either incomplete or inconsistent. At that time we were unable to present examples of such theories except by way of an explicit predicate symbol satisfying the criteria desired of a provability predicate. What we lacked were a language and a theory in which formulæ expressing provability could be constructed.

The first step towards formalizing syntax was already taken in chapter 8, where we presented a formula of $\mathcal{L}^*$ expressing the property of being a term of that language. This will be complemented by formulæ expressing the properties of being a formula of $\mathcal{L}^*$ and being provable in the theory $\mathsf{E}^*_{\min}$. Indeed, for a broad range of theories E^*, including all examples from previous chapters, a formula $\mathsf{Bew}(\mathsf{x})$ can be defined such that for every expression φ,

$$\text{(10.1)} \qquad \mathsf{E}^* \vdash \varphi \text{ if and only if } \mathsf{E}^*_{\min} \vdash \mathsf{Bew}(\overline{\varphi}).$$

We begin our study not with incompleteness but completeness. Our main result in this direction is the completeness of $\mathsf{E}^*_{\min}$ with respect to existential sentences of $\mathcal{L}^*_{\mathrm{syn}}$ where this is the language introduced in chapter 9 that sits intermediate between $\mathcal{L}^*$ and the minimal language $\mathcal{L}^*_{\min}$. We prove that for every sentence of $\mathcal{L}^*_{\mathrm{syn}}$ of the form $\exists x\,\varphi$ where all quantifiers of φ are bounded, if $\exists x\,\varphi$ is true in some standard model, then $\mathsf{E}^*_{\min} \vdash \exists x\,\varphi$. We call any sentence which is provably equivalent to such an existentially quantified formula a Σ-sentence. The completeness of $\mathsf{E}^*_{\min}$ with respect to Σ-sentences subsumes many observations on provability in E^* from previous chapters. These range from the provability of all true equations between closed terms to the provable instances of the formulæ expressing the length and denotation functions. The result also facilitates proofs of the incompleteness theorems. By ensuring that Bew is a Σ-formula, the equivalence in (10.1) becomes immediate: the 'if' direction is due to soundness and the 'only if' direction a corollary of completeness for Σ-sentences.

10.1 Expressing Relations

We have claimed of many formulæ that they express particular properties of or relations between $\ast$-expressions. To name a few, we stated that the formula $\mathsf{x} \subseteq \mathsf{y}$ expresses the relation of subexpression, $\mathsf{Sing}(\mathsf{x})$ of being a singleton, $\mathsf{Syn}(\mathsf{x})$ of being a syntactic constant, and $\mathsf{Term}(\mathsf{x})$ of being a term of $\mathcal{L}^*$. In chapter 8 assertions of this kind were supported by the informal semantics of formulæ as statements about the domain of $\ast$-expressions, and used to motivate the axioms of $\mathsf{E}^*_{\min}$ and the definitions of various formulæ. The notion of a standard model introduced in chapter 9 brought formal clarity to our semantic claims and culminated in theorem 9.16 confirming that the four formulæ above, among other examples, indeed define the anticipated relations between expressions in the sense that each formula is true of precisely the expressions – or tuples of expressions – in the corresponding set or relation.

Definability is not the same as expressibility though. Later in this chapter we will have the resources to construct a formula $\varphi(\mathsf{x}, \mathsf{y})$ such that $\varphi(\overline{a}, \overline{b})$ is true in any standard model if and only if b is a theorem of $\mathsf{E}^*_{\min}$ and a is a subexpression of some line in a proof of b. Using this formula, we can express the property that x does not occur in any $\mathsf{E}^*_{\min}$-proof of inconsistency by the formula $\varphi'(\mathsf{x}) := \neg\varphi(\mathsf{x}, \overline{\bot})$, where $\bot$ is a fixed contradiction such as $\neg\overline{\forall} = \overline{\forall}$. As $\mathsf{E}^*_{\min}$ is consistent, φ' defines the set of *all* expressions. Yet we would not claim that φ' *expresses* the property of being an arbitrary string of $\ast$-symbols. For a start, the assertion that φ' holds of the empty string is equivalent to stating that $\mathsf{E}^*_{\min}$ is consistent, because the empty string is a subexpression of every expression. So the axioms of $\mathsf{E}^*_{\min}$ do not suffice to prove that the property expressed by φ' is non-empty. The theory of arithmetic provides other examples. Letting $\psi(\mathsf{x})$ state that x is a natural number n for which there exist positive integers a, b, and c such that $a^n + b^n = c^n$, we know from Fermat's 'last theorem' – proved only in 1995 by Andrew Wiles – that $\psi(\mathsf{x})$ defines the two-element set $\{1, 2\}$ of expressions. But it would be a stretch to say that ψ *expresses* the property of being an element of this set.[1]

[1] At the time of writing, it is an open question whether Fermat's last theorem is provable in Peano

The conditions under which a formula can be said to express a property will be examined in detail in the final chapter. For the formalization of syntax, it suffices to isolate a proof-theoretic approximation to the notion of expressing a property which, like definability, is determined pointwise. A formula $\varphi(\mathsf{x})$ *pointwise expresses* a set $X \subseteq \mathcal{E}^*$ in E^* if and only if for all $e \in \mathcal{E}^*$ we have $\mathsf{E}^* \vdash \varphi(\overline{e})$ if and only if $e \in X$. For example, the set of all expressions is pointwise expressed in $\mathsf{E}^*_{\mathrm{min}}$ by the formula $\mathsf{x} = \mathsf{x}$ (or any other logically valid formula) but not by the formula φ' from the previous paragraph, for the reasons described. In contrast, the formula $\psi(\mathsf{x})$ pointwise expresses the set $\{1, 2\}$ in $\mathsf{E}^*_{\mathrm{min}}$: that $\mathsf{E}^*_{\mathrm{min}} \vdash \psi(\underline{1}) \wedge \psi(\underline{2})$ is easily verified, and $\mathsf{E}^*_{\mathrm{min}} \nvdash \psi(\underline{n})$ for $n > 2$ by soundness.

The relation of pointwise expression is ternary, as it is a relation between a set of expressions, a formula, *and* a theory. It is entirely possible for a formula to pointwise express different sets of expressions relative to different theories. An example is the formula φ', which pointwise expresses the empty set in $\mathsf{E}^*_{\mathrm{min}}$ but the set of all expressions in the stronger (and consistent) theory $\mathsf{E}^*_{\mathrm{min}} + \neg\varphi(\underline{0}, \underline{\perp})$. Using the same formula for expressing provability – to be introduced in section 10.4 – it is possible to construct a single formula of $\mathcal{L}^*$ which, by varying the choice of the theory, pointwise expresses infinitely many distinct sets of expressions.

One immediate conclusion that we can draw from these examples is that pointwise expression is not expression. From a formula pointwise expressing a property we cannot infer that it expresses said property. Nor does expressibility necessarily imply pointwise expressibility. Pointwise expressibility is, like definability, merely approximate to expressibility. Nevertheless, it is a notion with a rich theory that provides a valuable test bed for the study of expressibility, a matter we return to in detail in chapter 12.

Looking back at chapter 8 we see that the properties of being a syntactic constant, a singleton, a list, and a term – as well as many others – are pointwise expressed in the minimal theory $\mathsf{E}^*_{\mathrm{min}}$ by formulæ of $\mathcal{L}^*$. In this section we establish a direct connection between pointwise expressibility and definability which subsumes all these examples into a single result known as the Σ-completeness theorem. As remarked, the Σ-completeness theorem shows that every true merely

arithmetic, which is to say that it is unknown whether $\mathsf{E}^*_{\mathrm{min}} \vdash \forall n(n > \underline{2} \to \neg\psi(n))$. McLarty (2010) discusses the assumptions underlying Wiles' proof and whether the argument can be formalized in Zermelo–Fraenkel set theory or, even, Peano arithmetic. Although exponentiation x^n is not included in Peano arithmetic, it is not difficult to show that this function can be expressed in $\mathcal{L}^*$ and that its relevant properties are provable in $\mathsf{E}^*_{\mathrm{min}}$.

existential sentence is provable in $\mathsf{E}^*_{\min}$. A corollary of this result is that every relation on expressions that can be defined by an existential formula is pointwise expressed by that formula in $\mathsf{E}^*_{\min}$.

Our notion of pointwise expressing a property is analogous to a set of natural numbers being weakly represented in a theory of arithmetic ('numerated' in the terminology of Feferman 1960). A set $X \subseteq \mathbb{N}$ of natural numbers is weakly represented in a theory A of arithmetic if there is a formula $\varphi(\mathsf{x})$ in the language of A such that $\mathsf{A} \vdash \varphi(\underline{n})$ if and only if $n \in X$, where $\underline{n}$ is the numeral for n. Indeed, theorem 9.36 ensures that a set of natural numbers is weakly represented in Peano arithmetic if and only if it is pointwise expressed in $\mathsf{E}^*_{\min}$.

Much of this section and the next will be familiar to readers who have studied representability of relations and functions in theories of arithmetic, such as covered by, for example, Boolos, Burgess, and Jeffrey (2007). There are some notable differences, however. Many of our results require new or modified proofs to address the increase in expressivity of $\mathcal{L}^*$ over the language of arithmetic. Theorem 10.13, showing that every Σ_1-formula of $\mathcal{L}^*$ is provably equivalent to a formula containing just one unbounded existential quantifier, is a prime example.

But the main distinction in our approach stems from the flexibility afforded the object language. A direct translation of results about weak representability to our setting will apply only to theories formulated in the minimal language $\mathcal{L}^*_{\min}$. To accommodate languages with additional symbols – as will be needed in the next chapter – it is necessary to examine pointwise expressibility for languages beyond $\mathcal{L}^*_{\min}$ and generalize many of the standard results on representability in arithmetic. The Σ-completeness theorem described earlier, for instance, establishes a sufficient condition for a true sentence of $\mathcal{L}^*$ to be provable in E^* that includes formulæ beyond the minimal language.

Before we give the formal definition of pointwise expressibility, we should clarify what we mean by a formula of $\mathcal{L}^*$ defining a set or relation. Let R be a set or relation on $*$-expressions. We say of an $\mathcal{L}^*$-formula φ that it *defines* R if the extension of φ is R in every standard model of $\mathcal{L}^*$; R is *definable* if and only if it is defined by some $\mathcal{L}^*$-formula. Recall, the extension of a formula is the set of expressions for which that formula is true (in the specified model). Formally, the extension of a formula $\varphi(\mathsf{v}_0, \dots, \mathsf{v}_k)$, with at most $\mathsf{v}_0, \dots, \mathsf{v}_k$ free, in a standard model $\mathbb{E}^*$ is the set E_φ of $(k+1)$-tuples $\langle a_0, \dots, a_k \rangle$ for which $\varphi(\overline{a_0}, \dots, \overline{a_k})$ is true in $\mathbb{E}^*$, that is,

$$E_\varphi = \left\{ \langle a_0, \dots, a_k \rangle \in \mathcal{E}^* \times \cdots \times \mathcal{E}^* \colon\ \mathbb{E}^* \vDash \varphi(\overline{a_0}, \dots, \overline{a_k}) \right\}.$$

Writing $Ra_0 \cdots a_k$ for $\langle a_0, \ldots, a_k \rangle \in R$, the extension of φ in $\mathbb{E}^*$ is the $(k+1)$-ary relation E_φ satisfying $E_\varphi a_0 \cdots a_k$ if and only if $\mathbb{E}^* \vDash \varphi(\overline{a_0}, \ldots, \overline{a_k})$.[2] If the extensions of φ are the same across all standard models of $\mathcal{L}^*$, we speak of *the* extension of φ. For example, the extension of $\mathsf{Term}(\mathsf{x})$ is the same in all standard models, namely the set of terms of $\mathcal{L}^*$. Likewise, the extension of $\mathsf{v}_0 \subseteq \mathsf{v}_1$ is the relation of subexpression in all standard models: $E_\subseteq = \{ \langle a, b \rangle \in \mathcal{E}^* \times \mathcal{E}^* \colon a \text{ is a subexpression of } b \}$. Thus, we say that $\mathsf{Term}(\mathsf{x})$ *defines* the property of being a term of $\mathcal{L}^*$, and that $\mathsf{v}_0 \subseteq \mathsf{v}_1$ defines the relation of subexpression. Lemma 9.12 implies that all formulæ of the language $\mathcal{L}^*_{\text{syn}}$ have the same extension in all standard models. In contrast, the extension of $\Box\mathsf{x} \wedge \mathsf{Term}(\mathsf{x})$ varies with the model: for every set T of terms there is a standard model of $\mathcal{L}^*$ in which the extension of the formula is T. Some of these sets will be definable, but none are *defined* by the formula $\Box\mathsf{x} \wedge \mathsf{Term}(\mathsf{x})$.

10.1 DEFINITION Let R be a k-ary relation on $*$-expressions and $\varphi(\mathsf{v}_1, \ldots, \mathsf{v}_k)$ a formula in k variables. We say that φ *pointwise expresses* R in E^*, or that R is *pointwise expressed by* φ in E^*, if and only if for all $a_1, \ldots, a_k \in \mathcal{E}^*$,

$$\mathsf{E}^* \vdash \varphi(\overline{a_1}, \ldots, \overline{a_k}) \text{ if and only if } Ra_1 \cdots a_k.$$

If, in addition, the complement of R is pointwise expressed by $\neg\varphi(\mathsf{v}_1, \ldots, \mathsf{v}_k)$, then φ *strongly pointwise expresses* R. A relation on $*$-expressions is (*strongly*) *pointwise expressed* in E^* if it is (strongly) pointwise expressed by some formula.

We occasionally write 'weakly pointwise express' in place of 'pointwise express' in order to contrast with the 'strong' notion of expressibility. We also drop explicit mention of E^* if it can be inferred from context.

10.2 PROPOSITION *Let R be a k-ary relation. Then the following are equivalent:*

(i) $\varphi(\mathsf{v}_1, \ldots, \mathsf{v}_k)$ *strongly pointwise expresses R in* E^*.

(ii) E^* *is consistent and for all* $a_1, \ldots, a_k \in \mathcal{E}^*$,

   (a) *if* $Ra_1 \cdots a_k$, *then* $\mathsf{E}^* \vdash \varphi(\overline{a_1}, \ldots, \overline{a_k})$;

   (b) *if not* $Ra_1 \cdots a_k$, *then* $\mathsf{E}^* \vdash \neg\varphi(\overline{a_1}, \ldots, \overline{a_k})$.

[2] We are restricting attention to standard models, though the notion of extension applies to arbitrary $\mathcal{L}^*$-structures, in which case the set $\mathcal{E}^*$ is replaced by the domain of the structure and satisfaction is defined in terms of a variable assignment.

PROOF To establish that (i) implies (ii) we need only show that if any relation is strongly pointwise expressed in E^* then the theory is consistent. This is an immediate application of the definition, for if R is strongly pointwise expressed by $\varphi(\mathsf{v}_1, \ldots, \mathsf{v}_k)$, then

$$\mathsf{E}^* \vdash \varphi(\underline{0}, \ldots, \underline{0}) \quad \text{implies} \quad \langle 0, \ldots, 0\rangle \in R$$

and

$$\mathsf{E}^* \vdash \neg\varphi(\underline{0}, \ldots, \underline{0}) \quad \text{implies} \quad \langle 0, \ldots, 0\rangle \notin R.$$

In particular, either $\mathsf{E}^* \nvdash \varphi(\underline{0}, \ldots, \underline{0})$ or $\mathsf{E}^* \nvdash \neg\varphi(\underline{0}, \ldots, \underline{0})$, so E^* is consistent.

For the converse, if $\mathsf{E}^* \vdash \varphi(\overline{a_1}, \ldots, \overline{a_k})$ and E^* is consistent, then $Ra_1 \cdots a_k$ by property (b). So φ pointwise expresses R. By an analogous argument, $\neg\varphi$ pointwise expresses the complement of R. ⊣

As already noted, we have encountered many properties of $*$-expressions that are pointwise expressed in $\mathsf{E}^*_{\min}$, including identity, singletons, variables, lists, terms, and well-bracketed words. In the case of the first three notions we also established conditions (a) and (b) of proposition 10.2, from which it follows that these concepts are strongly pointwise expressed in $\mathsf{E}^*_{\min}$. The soundness of standard models (theorem 9.17) implies that pointwise expressibility in $\mathsf{E}^*_{\min}$ implies definability.

In this section we show that for some kinds of formula the implication can be inverted. That is, if a relation is definable and the defining formula has a certain syntactic form, then that relation is pointwise expressed in E^*. In some special cases, we will be able to deduce strong pointwise expressibility via proposition 10.2. General results such as these allow us to focus on semantic arguments – definability and reasoning about expressions – rather than provability from a chosen set of axioms in each case. For example, it is relatively easy to show that the formula $\mathsf{Term}(x)$ defines the set of terms of $\mathcal{L}^*$. Yet, to show that this set is pointwise expressed by the formula is considerably harder. That the terms are pointwise expressible in $\mathsf{E}^*_{\min}$ is just one of many corollaries of this section. Later we will apply the same reasoning to deduce pointwise expressibility of other relations on expressions including denotation, formulæ, and provability.

Our first result concerns formulæ involving restricted quantification only.

10.3 DEFINITION A formula is bounded if all quantifiers in the formula are bounded. That is, the bounded formulæ of $\mathcal{L}^*$ are the formulæ which can be built from atomic formulæ using the connectives of $\mathcal{L}^*$ and the bounded quantifiers $\forall x \subseteq t$ where x is a variable and t is a term which does not contain x.

Since the bounded existential quantifier is defined as a negated bounded universal quantifier – recall, $\exists x \subseteq t\ \varphi$ abbreviates $\neg\forall x \subseteq t\ \neg\varphi$ – the former can also be utilized subject to the same restrictions on the term t. The defined connectives $\wedge$ and $\vee$ are also available for constructing bounded formulæ.

10.4 PROPOSITION *The formulæ* $\subseteq$, $\in$, Var, Sing, *and* Syn *introduced in chapter 8 are provably equivalent to bounded formulæ. In particular, the following equivalences are derivable in* $\mathsf{E}^*_{\text{min}}$*:*

(i) $\forall x \forall y \big(x \subseteq y \leftrightarrow \exists w \subseteq y\ \exists z \subseteq y\ \ y = w{}^\frown x{}^\frown z\big)$,

(ii) $\forall x \forall y \big(x \in y \leftrightarrow \neg \underline{\mathsf{e}} \subseteq x \wedge \big(\underline{\mathsf{e}}{}^\frown x{}^\frown \underline{\mathsf{e}} \subseteq y \vee \exists w \subseteq y\ (w{}^\frown \underline{\mathsf{e}}{}^\frown x = y)\big)\big)$,

(iii) $\forall x \big(\mathsf{Var}(x) \leftrightarrow \exists y \subseteq x \,(x = (\underline{{}^\frown} y \underline{{}^\frown}) \wedge \mathsf{sub}(y, \underline{\mathsf{v}}, \underline{0}) = \underline{0})\big)$,

(iv) $\forall x \big(\mathsf{Sing}(x) \leftrightarrow x \neq \underline{0} \wedge \forall y \subseteq x\ \forall z \subseteq x\ (x = y{}^\frown z \rightarrow y = x \vee z = x)\big)$,

(v) $\forall x \big(\mathsf{Syn}(x) \leftrightarrow \mathsf{Sing}(x) \wedge \neg\, \mathsf{sym}\, x\big)$.

The minimal language, $\mathcal{L}^*_{\text{min}}$, has sym and = as the only predicate symbols, and q, $^\frown$, and sub as the only basic function symbols. The constants of $\mathcal{L}^*_{\text{min}}$ comprise the symbol $\underline{0}$ and the syntactic constants for the above symbols, the connectives, quantifier, and four auxiliary symbols. The language $\mathcal{L}^*$, in contrast, is either $\mathcal{L}^*_{\text{min}}$ or some fixed extension of it by finitely many further symbols and a syntactic constant for each new symbol. For the present section, we also make use of the language intermediate between $\mathcal{L}^*_{\text{min}}$ and $\mathcal{L}^*$, which extends the minimal language by these new syntactic constants. This language was used in the previous chapter in the definition of a standard model of $\mathcal{L}^*$, where it was named $\mathcal{L}^*_{\text{syn}}$.

10.5 DEFINITION The language $\mathcal{L}^*_{\text{syn}}$ consists of the basic symbols of $\mathcal{L}^*_{\text{min}}$ and the (finitely many) syntactic constants of $\mathcal{L}^*$.

The minimal theory of expressions, $\mathsf{E}^*_{\text{min}}$, is a theory formulated in the language $\mathcal{L}^*$ (as opposed to $\mathcal{L}^*_{\text{min}}$). So this theory derives statements beyond the logical validities, such as that each syntactic constant of $\mathcal{L}^*$ is a singleton, which are expressible in the language $\mathcal{L}^*_{\text{syn}}$ but not the language $\mathcal{L}^*_{\text{min}}$. Our main result concerning bounded formulæ is that the minimal theory suffices to prove all true bounded sentences in this language:

10.6 BOUNDED COMPLETENESS THEOREM *Let φ be a bounded sentence in the language $\mathcal{L}^*_{\mathrm{syn}}$. If φ is true, then $\mathsf{E}^* \vdash \varphi$.*

This theorem implies that the minimal theory of expressions is complete with respect to bounded sentences: for every bounded sentence φ of $\mathcal{L}^*_{\mathrm{syn}}$, one of φ and $\neg\varphi$ is derivable in $\mathsf{E}^*_{\mathrm{min}}$. Before we proceed to the proof of theorem 10.6 we remark three important consequences.

10.7 COROLLARY *Let φ be a bounded sentence of $\mathcal{L}^*_{\mathrm{syn}}$. Then either $\mathsf{E}^*_{\mathrm{min}} \vdash \varphi$ or $\mathsf{E}^*_{\mathrm{min}} \vdash \neg\varphi$.*

PROOF Since φ is a sentence, one of φ and $\neg\varphi$ is true. Applying theorem 10.6 completes the proof. ⊣

10.8 COROLLARY *Suppose E^* is consistent. Then E^* and $\mathsf{E}^*_{\mathrm{min}}$ derive the same bounded sentences of $\mathcal{L}^*_{\mathrm{syn}}$.*

PROOF Let φ be a bounded sentence of $\mathcal{L}^*_{\mathrm{syn}}$ derivable in E^*. If φ is not derivable in $\mathsf{E}^*_{\mathrm{min}}$, then $\mathsf{E}^*_{\mathrm{min}} \vdash \neg\varphi$ by corollary 10.7, and $\mathsf{E}^* \vdash \neg\varphi$. But this contradicts the consistency of E^*. ⊣

10.9 COROLLARY *Every relation on $\star$-expressions defined by a bounded formula of $\mathcal{L}^*_{\mathrm{syn}}$ is strongly pointwise expressed in $\mathsf{E}^*_{\mathrm{min}}$ by that formula.*

PROOF Let $\varphi(\mathsf{v}_1, \ldots, \mathsf{v}_k)$ be a bounded formula and R the relation defined by φ. By theorem 10.6 and the soundness of $\mathsf{E}^*_{\mathrm{min}}$, $\mathsf{E}^*_{\mathrm{min}} \vdash \varphi(\overline{a_1}, \ldots, \overline{a_k})$ if and only if $\varphi(\overline{a_1}, \ldots, \overline{a_k})$ is true, if and only if $Ra_1 \cdots a_k$. Similarly, $\mathsf{E}^*_{\mathrm{min}} \vdash \neg\varphi(\overline{a_1}, \ldots, \overline{a_k})$ if and only if not $Ra_1 \cdots a_k$. So φ strongly pointwise expresses R in $\mathsf{E}^*_{\mathrm{min}}$. ⊣

We now turn to the proof of theorem 10.6, which proceeds by induction on φ. In the base case we require to show that if $s = t$ is a true equality between closed terms then it is derivable in E^*. We rely on the following result:

10.10 PROPOSITION *If s is a closed term of $\mathcal{L}^*_{\mathrm{syn}}$ and $a = s^{\mathbb{E}^*}$, then $\mathsf{E}^* \vdash s = \overline{a}$.*

PROOF Induction on the construction of s. The result is immediate if s is a syntactic constant. The remaining cases follow from results in chapter 8: proposition 8.55 covers the case where s is a concatenation of two closed terms, proposition 8.72 the case that $s \equiv \mathsf{sub}\, r_1 r_2 r_3$ for terms r_1, r_2, and r_3, and proposition 8.66 the case that $s \equiv \mathsf{q} r$ for some r. ⊣

PROOF OF THEOREM 10.6 Suppose φ is an atomic formula of $\mathcal{L}^*_{\text{syn}}$, so either $\varphi \equiv \mathsf{sym}\, s$ for a closed term s or $\varphi \equiv s = t$ for closed terms s and t. In the latter case, proposition 10.10 yields expressions a and b such that $\mathsf{E}^* \vdash s = \overline{a} \wedge t = \overline{b}$, whence propositions 8.55 and 8.67 imply $\mathsf{E}^* \vdash \varphi$ if $a \equiv b$, and $\mathsf{E}^* \vdash \neg\varphi$ otherwise. In the case where $\varphi \equiv \mathsf{sym}\, s$, let a be given by applying proposition 10.10 to the term s. If φ is true, then a is a basic symbol and $\mathsf{E}^* \vdash \varphi$. Otherwise, either a is the empty expression or $\overline{a}$ is an expression of length at least 2, and axioms B2 and B3 imply $\mathsf{E}^* \vdash \neg\varphi$. For φ a complex formula, the only non-trivial case is that of bounded quantification: Suppose $\varphi \equiv \forall x \subseteq t\ \psi(x)$, where t is a closed term of $\mathcal{L}^*_{\text{syn}}$. Let a be an expression and let $a_0, \ldots, a_k$ be an enumeration of all subexpressions of a. By induction on the length of a we prove

$$\mathsf{E}^* \vdash \forall x\Big(x \subseteq \overline{a} \leftrightarrow \bigvee_{i=0}^{k} x = \overline{a_i}\Big).$$

Choosing a to be the denotation of t and applying proposition 10.10 we deduce that

$$\mathsf{E}^* \vdash \varphi \leftrightarrow \bigwedge_{i=0}^{k} \psi(\overline{a_i}).$$

If φ is true, then so is $\psi(\overline{a_i})$ for each $i \leq k$, and $\mathsf{E}^* \vdash \varphi$ follows from the induction hypothesis. Conversely, if φ is false, $\mathsf{E}^* \vdash \neg\psi(\overline{a_i})$ for some i and $\mathsf{E}^* \vdash \neg\varphi$, as desired. ⊣

The restriction on quantification in bounded formulæ severely limits the applicability of theorem 10.6. In contrast to an unbounded quantifier, which ranges over the set of all expressions, bounded quantifiers are restricted to finite domains, namely the subexpressions of the 'bounding' expression. We have seen that some important classes of expressions – variables, singletons, and syntactic constants – can be defined in this way. But other concepts relevant to a theory of syntax, such as terms, formulæ, and denotation, are not expressed by bounded formulæ over $\mathsf{E}^*_{\text{min}}$.

The remainder of this section examines pointwise expressibility for properties whose definition naturally utilizes unbounded quantification. Looking back at the formulæ introduced for various syntactic notions – lists, sequences, terms, denotation (more will be presented in section 10.3) – the majority of them are properties which are weakly pointwise expressed using the existential quantifier as the only unbounded quantifier. This observation needs careful formulation to be useful, because the logical equivalence $\forall x\, \varphi \leftrightarrow \neg\exists x\, \neg\varphi$ permits every formula to be conceived as having been built using the unbounded existential quantifier as the only quantifier. What we mean is that each of the preceding examples can be expressed by a formula built from bounded formulæ via the connectives $\wedge$ and $\vee$, bounded quantifiers $\forall \mathsf{v}_i \subseteq s$ and $\exists \mathsf{v}_i \subseteq s$, and unbounded existential quantifiers $\exists \mathsf{v}_i$. Formulæ of this kind are called Σ_1 and suffice for defining many important concepts of a theory of syntax. The dual kind of formulæ, permitting the universal quantifier as the only unbounded quantifier, are called Π_1.

10.11 DEFINITION The Σ_1-formulæ is the set of $\mathcal{L}^*$-formulæ generated by the following clauses:

(i) All bounded formulæ are Σ_1.

(ii) If φ, ψ are both Σ_1, then $\varphi \vee \psi$ and $\varphi \wedge \psi$ are Σ_1.

(iii) If φ is Σ_1, v a variable, and t a term not containing v, then $\forall v \subseteq t\ \varphi$ and $\exists v \subseteq t\ \varphi$ are Σ_1.

(iv) If φ is Σ_1 and v a variable, then $\exists v\, \varphi$ is Σ_1.

The Π_1-formulæ are defined by the same clauses but with the following in place of (iv):

(iv) If φ is Π_1 and v a variable, then $\forall v\, \varphi$ is Π_1.

In addition to bounded formulæ, the Σ_1-formulæ permit arbitrary (unbounded) existential quantifiers provided they occur under the scope of the defined connectives $\wedge$ and $\vee$, and bounded quantifiers only. Negation and implication occur in a Σ_1-formula only within bounded (sub)formulæ and in uses of the defined connectives and bounded quantifiers.

10.12 LEMMA *Every Σ_1-formula is logically equivalent to the negation of a Π_1-formula, and vice versa.*

PROOF Induction on formulæ using the equivalences $\neg(\alpha \wedge \beta) \leftrightarrow \neg\alpha \vee \neg\beta$, $\neg(\alpha \vee \beta) \leftrightarrow \neg\alpha \wedge \neg\beta$, $\neg\forall x\, \alpha \leftrightarrow \exists x \neg\alpha$, and $\neg\exists x \subseteq t\ \alpha \leftrightarrow \forall x \subseteq t\ \neg\alpha$, which are theorems of predicate logic. ⊣

The proof of lemma 10.12 provides a method to transform any negated Π_1-formula into an equivalent Σ_1-formula by 'pushing' the leading negation through the connectives and quantifiers until all unbounded universal quantifiers have been removed. With this procedure in mind it is possible to treat negated Π_1-formulæ as Σ_1-formulæ and assume that the collection of Σ_1-formulæ includes formulæ constructed from negated Π_1-formulæ via the rules (ii)–(iv) of the definition. Similarly, we consider a formula built from negated Σ_1-formulæ using the rules for Π_1 as still being in the class Π_1.

Many useful properties of Σ_1-formulæ apply also to formulæ that are provably equivalent to formulæ in this class. But there are different degrees of equivalence, depending on the theory over which the equivalence is derivable. Lemma 10.12 concerned equivalences provable over pure logic. Less discerning than logical equivalence is provable equivalence over the theory E^* of expressions. The next theorem establishes a normal form theorem for the minimal theory $\mathsf{E}^*_{\mathrm{min}}$. It shows that every Σ_1-formula can be proved equivalent to a bounded formula prefixed by exactly one unbounded existential quantifier.

10.13 THEOREM *Let φ be a Σ_1-formula. Then there is a bounded formula ψ and a variable x such that $\mathsf{E}^*_{\mathrm{min}} \vdash \varphi \leftrightarrow \exists x\, \psi$. Dually, let φ be a Π_1-formula. Then there is a bounded formula ψ and a variable x such that $\mathsf{E}^*_{\mathrm{min}} \vdash \varphi \leftrightarrow \forall x\, \psi$.*

Every formula is logically equivalent to a formula in so-called prenex normal form, that is, to a formula of the kind $Q_1x_1 \cdots Q_kx_k\psi$ where each Q_i is a quantifier, either $\forall$ or $\exists$, and ψ is bounded. Theorem 10.13 adds to this result in two ways, if we focus on derivability in $\mathsf{E}^*_{\mathrm{min}}$ instead of predicate logic. First, starting from an arbitrary Σ_1-formula, the 'prenex' unbounded quantifiers $Q_1, \ldots, Q_k$ can be assumed to be without exception existential quantifiers. This result does not hold over predicate logic because the initial Σ_1-formula may contain bounded universal quantifiers and there is no logical equivalence that permits, except in very special circumstances, permuting a bounded universal and an unbounded existential quantifier. Indeed, the main challenge in the proof of theorem 10.13 is establishing the equivalences needed for this particular transformation. The second contribution of the theorem is that multiple unbounded existential quantifiers can be merged into a single quantifier. This, again, requires the axioms of $\mathsf{E}^*_{\mathrm{min}}$.

The proof of theorem 10.13 proceeds by induction on the Σ_1-formula φ. The desired bounded formula ψ is straightforward to define: it can be obtained from φ by converting all unrestricted existential quantifiers to bounded quantifiers using a fresh variable x as the bound. As already remarked, proving the desired equivalence is non-trivial, with bounded universal quantifiers in φ presenting the most difficult case. The second claim of the theorem is implied by lemma 10.12.

PROOF Given φ and a term s whose variables are distinct from those occurring in φ, we obtain a bounded formula φ_s by inserting s as a bound to every unbounded quantifier in φ. Since existential quantifiers are defined as negations of universal quantifiers, φ_s arises by replacing in φ each unbounded quantifier $\forall y$ by the bounded quantifier $\forall y \subseteq s$. Bounded quantifiers in φ are not modified. We claim that if φ is Σ_1 and x is a variable not occurring in φ, then

$$\mathsf{E}^*_{\min} \vdash \varphi \leftrightarrow \exists x\, \varphi_x. \tag{10.2}$$

As φ_x is a bounded formula by design, (10.2) establishes the theorem. In the proof of (10.2) we make use of the following observation, which is easily proved by induction on φ:

$$\mathsf{E}^*_{\min} \vdash \forall x (\varphi_x \leftrightarrow \forall y \forall z\, \varphi_{y^\frown x^\frown z}). \tag{10.3}$$

We now proceed with the proof of (10.2). If φ is a bounded formula, then (10.2) is derivable by predicate logic since $\varphi_x \equiv \varphi$ and it is assumed that x does not occur in φ. If $\varphi \equiv \alpha \wedge \beta$ is a conjunction, then $\varphi_x \equiv \alpha_x \wedge \beta_x$ and the following equivalences are derivable, where x and y are distinct variables not occurring in φ.

$$\begin{aligned}
\mathsf{E}^*_{\min} \vdash \varphi &\leftrightarrow \exists x\, \alpha_x \wedge \exists y\, \beta_y && \text{induction hypothesis}\\
&\leftrightarrow \exists x \exists y (\alpha_x \wedge \beta_y) && \text{predicate logic}\\
&\leftrightarrow \exists x \exists y (\alpha_{x^\frown y} \wedge \beta_{x^\frown y}) && \text{(10.3)}\\
&\leftrightarrow \exists x (\alpha_x \wedge \beta_x) && \text{predicate logic}
\end{aligned}$$

The case where φ is a disjunction is similar. Now suppose φ is a quantified formula. We begin with the bounded existential quantifier: If $\varphi \equiv \exists y \subseteq s\, \alpha$ and x does not occur in φ, then

$$\begin{aligned}
\mathsf{E}^*_{\min} \vdash \varphi &\leftrightarrow \exists y \subseteq s\, \exists x\, \alpha_x && \text{induction hypothesis}\\
&\leftrightarrow \exists x \exists y \subseteq s\, \alpha_x && \text{predicate logic}
\end{aligned}$$

The second equivalence holds because x does not occur in s. In the case of an unbounded quantifier, $\varphi \equiv \exists y\, \alpha$ and therefore

$$\begin{aligned} \mathsf{E}^*_{\min} \vdash \varphi &\leftrightarrow \exists y \exists x\, \alpha_x && \text{induction hypothesis} \\ &\leftrightarrow \exists x \exists y\, \alpha_x \\ &\leftrightarrow \exists x \exists y\, \alpha_{x^\frown y} && (10.3) \\ &\leftrightarrow \exists x \exists y (y \subseteq x^\frown y \wedge \alpha_{x^\frown y}) \\ &\leftrightarrow \exists x\, \varphi_x && \text{as } \varphi_x \equiv \exists y \subseteq x\ \alpha_x. \end{aligned}$$

The final case is the bounded universal quantifier. Assume that $\varphi \equiv \forall y \subseteq s\ \alpha(y)$. Following the other cases, we show that $\exists x\, \varphi_x$ is equivalent to $\forall y \subseteq s\, \exists x\, \alpha_x(y)$ over $\mathsf{E}^*_{\min}$ and appeal to the induction hypothesis to deduce (10.2). One direction of the equivalence follows by logic. For the other direction, we show:

$$\mathsf{E}^*_{\min} \vdash \forall z \big(\forall y \subseteq z\, \exists x\, \alpha_x(y) \rightarrow \exists x\, \forall y \subseteq z\ \alpha_x(y) \big).$$

The claim is proved by numerical induction on the length of z. We argue within $\mathsf{E}^*_{\min}$. Fix an expression z. The goal is to establish

$$\forall y \subseteq z\, \exists x\ \alpha_x(y) \rightarrow \exists x\, \forall y \subseteq z\ \alpha_x(y).$$

This is trivial if z is the empty expression. Otherwise, there are symbols u_0 and u_1, and (possibly empty) expressions w_0 and w_1 such that $z = u_0 w_0$ and $z = w_1 u_1$. From the definition of subexpression, we observe

$$\forall y \big(y \subseteq z \leftrightarrow (y = z \vee y \subseteq w_0 \vee y \subseteq w_1) \big).$$

Moreover, the induction hypothesis applies to the expressions w_0 and w_1 as each is strictly shorter than z. So we obtain

$$\begin{aligned} \forall y \subseteq z\, \exists x\, \alpha_x(y) &\leftrightarrow \exists x\, \alpha_x(z) \wedge \forall y \subseteq w_0\, \exists x\, \alpha_x(y) \wedge \forall y \subseteq w_1\, \exists x\, \alpha_x(y) \\ &\rightarrow \exists x\, \alpha_x(z) \wedge \exists x\, \forall y \subseteq w_0\ \alpha_x(y) \wedge \exists x\, \forall y \subseteq w_1\ \alpha_x(y) && \text{ind. hyp.} \\ &\rightarrow \exists x \big(\alpha_x(z) \wedge \forall y \subseteq w_0\ \alpha_x(y) \wedge \forall y \subseteq w_1\ \alpha_x(y) \big) && (10.3) \\ &\leftrightarrow \exists x\, \forall y \subseteq z\, \alpha_x(y). \end{aligned}$$

With the claim shown, the proof is complete. $\dashv$

Given theorem 10.13 it is easy to lift our completeness theorem for bounded formulæ to Σ_1-formulæ:

10.14 Σ_1-COMPLETENESS THEOREM *Let φ be a true Σ_1-sentence in the language $\mathcal{L}^*_{\text{syn}}$. Then $\mathsf{E}^* \vdash \varphi$.*

PROOF Fix a Σ_1-sentence φ in $\mathcal{L}^*_{\text{syn}}$ and let φ_x be the bounded formula constructed in the proof of theorem 10.13. We have that φ_x is in the language $\mathcal{L}^*_{\text{syn}}$ and $\mathsf{E}^*_{\text{min}} \vdash \varphi \leftrightarrow \exists x\, \varphi_x$. If φ is true then, by the soundness of $\mathsf{E}^*_{\text{min}}$, there is an expression a such that $\varphi_{\overline{a}}$ is true. Theorem 10.6 implies $\mathsf{E}^*_{\text{min}} \vdash \varphi_{\overline{a}}$, so $\mathsf{E}^* \vdash \varphi$. ⊣

As a corollary of completeness for bounded formulæ, theorem 10.6, we observed that for every bounded sentence φ of $\mathcal{L}^*_{\text{syn}}$, either $\mathsf{E}^*_{\text{min}} \vdash \varphi$ or $\mathsf{E}^*_{\text{min}} \vdash \neg\varphi$. Theorem 10.14 does not yield the analogous claim for Σ_1-sentences because this class is not closed under negation. In chapter 11 (theorem 11.15) we present a Σ_1-formula whose negation is not equivalent to a Σ_1-formula over any consistent extension of $\mathsf{E}^*_{\text{min}}$. As a statement about pointwise expressibility, theorem 10.14 can be restated as the following:

10.15 COROLLARY *Every relation on expressions which is definable by a Σ_1-formula of $\mathcal{L}^*_{\text{syn}}$ is pointwise expressed in $\mathsf{E}^*_{\text{min}}$ by that formula. That is, given an n-ary relation R on expressions defined by a Σ_1-formula $\varphi(x_1, \ldots, x_n)$ of $\mathcal{L}^*_{\text{syn}}$, for all $a_1, \ldots, a_n \in \mathcal{E}^*$, we have $Ra_1 \cdots a_n$ if and only if $\mathsf{E}^*_{\text{min}} \vdash \varphi(\overline{a_1}, \ldots, \overline{a_n})$.*

The formulæ Term and Wbw introduced in chapter 8 are two examples of formulæ that, although not Σ_1 as defined, are equivalent to Σ_1-formulæ of $\mathcal{L}^*_{\text{syn}}$. In each case, the equivalence can be established in the minimal theory $\mathsf{E}^*_{\text{min}}$ using proposition 10.4. Applying corollary 10.15 to their Σ_1-form, we deduce that each formula pointwise expresses in $\mathsf{E}^*_{\text{min}}$ the property or relation they were designed to express. Rather than always converting a formula to an explicitly Σ_1-form and applying completeness for Σ_1-formulæ, it is convenient to introduce a broader class of formulæ to which theorem 10.14 and corollary 10.15 apply.

10.16 DEFINITION A formula is Σ if and only if it is provably equivalent over E^* to a Σ_1-formula of $\mathcal{L}^*_{\text{syn}}$. A formula is Π if and only if its negation is Σ.

Expanding the definition, φ is a Σ-formula if and only if there exists a Σ_1-formula ψ of $\mathcal{L}^*_{\text{syn}}$ such that $\mathsf{E}^* \vdash \varphi \leftrightarrow \psi$. Dually, φ is Π if and only if there exists a Π_1-formula ψ of $\mathcal{L}^*_{\text{syn}}$ such that $\mathsf{E}^* \vdash \varphi \leftrightarrow \psi$. There is no restriction on the language of the formula φ in definition 10.16. For example, $\Box x \to \Box x$ is not a formula of $\mathcal{L}^*_{\mathrm{syn}}$ but is a Σ-formula as it is provably equivalent (over predicate logic) to the $\mathcal{L}^*_{\mathrm{syn}}$-formula $x = x$. Note, a formula is Π if and only if its negation is Σ.

10.17 DEFINITION A formula is Δ if and only if it is Σ and Π.

We will write that φ is $\Sigma/\Pi/\Delta$ *over* E^* to draw attention to a particular choice of theory over which the equivalences hold.

For a formula $\varphi(x)$ to be Δ we do not require that it be both Σ_1 and Π_1, a condition equivalent to φ being bounded. Definition 10.17 merely expresses that there exist a Σ_1-formula ψ and a Π_1-formula χ, each in the language $\mathcal{L}^*_{\mathrm{syn}}$, such that $\mathsf{E}^* \vdash \forall x(\varphi(x) \leftrightarrow \psi(x))$ and $\mathsf{E}^* \vdash \forall x(\varphi(x) \leftrightarrow \chi(x))$.

Examples of Σ-formulæ include Term and Wbw mentioned above, the formula Seq expressing sequences (introduced on page 185), and the formulæ $\subseteq$, $\in$, Var, Sing, Syn that are provably equivalent to bounded formulæ. These latter formulæ are examples of Δ-formulæ. If $\mathcal{L}^*$ and $\mathcal{L}^*_{\mathrm{min}}$ coincide, then every Σ_1-formula is Σ, and every bounded formula is Δ. But assuming that $\mathcal{L}^*$ properly extends the minimal language it is straightforward to find bounded formulæ that are not Σ and, therefore, not Δ.

10.18 PROPOSITION *Suppose $\mathcal{L}^*$ extends $\mathcal{L}^*_{\mathrm{min}}$ by a function or predicate symbol. Then there exists a bounded formula in $\mathcal{L}^*$ which is not equivalent to any formula of $\mathcal{L}^*_{\mathrm{syn}}$ over $\mathsf{E}^*_{\mathrm{min}}$.*

PROOF There are two cases, depending on whether $\mathcal{L}^*$ contains a predicate symbol not in $\mathcal{L}^*_{\mathrm{min}}$ or a function symbol. The argument for the latter is more general, so we assume that case. Let f be a function symbol not in $\mathcal{L}^*_{\mathrm{min}}$. Without loss of generality, we assume that f is a unary function. Consider the bounded sentence $\mathsf{f}\underline{0} = \underline{0}$. Clearly, there is a standard model of $\mathcal{L}^*$ in which this sentence is true and another in which it is false. By lemma 9.12, the formula is not provably equivalent to any formula of $\mathcal{L}^*_{\mathrm{syn}}$ over $\mathsf{E}^*_{\mathrm{min}}$. ⊣

The next propositions are useful for showing that formulæ are Σ, Π, or Δ without explicitly presenting the equivalent formula of $\mathcal{L}^*_{\mathrm{syn}}$. There proofs follow from the definitions of the respective formula classes.

10.19 PROPOSITION *The set of Σ-formulæ contains all Δ-formulæ and is closed under the (defined) connectives conjunction and disjunction, bounded universal quantification, and unbounded existential quantification.*

10.20 PROPOSITION *The set of Π-formulæ contains all Δ-formulæ and is closed under the (defined) connectives conjunction and disjunction, bounded existential quantification, and unbounded universal quantification.*

10.21 PROPOSITION *The set of Δ-formulæ is closed under all logical connectives and under bounded universal and existential quantification.*

We now give the generalization of the Σ_1-completeness theorem 10.14 we mentioned above.

10.22 Σ-COMPLETENESS THEOREM *Suppose* E^* *admits a standard model and* φ *is a* Σ*-sentence which is true in this model. Then* $\mathsf{E}^* \vdash \varphi$.

PROOF Let $\mathbb{E}^* \models \mathsf{E}^*$ be a standard model and suppose φ is a Σ-sentence true in this model. By definition, there is a Σ_1-sentence ψ of $\mathcal{L}^*_{\text{syn}}$ such that $\mathbb{E}^* \models \psi$. Lemma 9.12 entails that ψ is true in all standard models of $\mathcal{L}^*$. So $\mathsf{E}^*_{\text{min}} \vdash \psi$ by theorem 10.14 and thus $\mathsf{E}^* \vdash \varphi$. ⊣

The Σ-completeness theorem extends a result for theories of arithmetic known by the same name which states that every true Σ_1-sentence in the language of arithmetic is provable in Peano arithmetic. As Peano arithmetic can be conceived as a subtheory of E^* (theorem 9.34) and under this identification every Σ_1-formula in the language of arithmetic is automatically a Σ-formula, the mentioned result is a consequence of theorem 10.22 and the fact that PA and $\mathsf{E}^*_{\text{min}}$ derive the same theorems in the language of arithmetic (theorem 9.36).[3]

There is no restriction on the language or complexity of the formula φ in the theorem except that it be provably equivalent to a Σ_1-formula in the language $\mathcal{L}^*_{\text{syn}}$ over some extension of $\mathsf{E}^*_{\text{min}}$ and that this theory admits a standard model. In particular, both φ and the theory E^* may utilize vocabulary – predicate, function, and auxiliary symbols – outside the language $\mathcal{L}^*_{\text{syn}}$ and the formula need not be equivalent to any Σ_1-formula or $\mathcal{L}^*_{\text{syn}}$-formula over the minimal theory $\mathsf{E}^*_{\text{min}}$. In

[3] It is known that the full strength of Peano arithmetic is not required for the Σ-completeness theorem and that every true Σ_1-sentence of arithmetic can be derived in the subtheory in which the numerical induction schema is asserted for Σ_1-formulæ only. The analogous claim is true for theories of expressions: theorem 10.22 holds if E^* is any theory in the language $\mathcal{L}^*$ which contains at least the basic axioms of $\mathsf{E}^*_{\text{min}}$ and the schema of induction for Σ_1-formulæ. The main ingredient for establishing this result is showing that the proof of theorem 10.13 requires no more than the induction schema for Σ_1-formulæ.

addition, there is no assumption that φ is true in *all* standard models of $\mathcal{L}^*$. There may be standard (and nonstandard) models in which φ is false. But provided E^* proves that φ is equivalent to a sentence of $\mathcal{L}^*_{\text{syn}}$, lemma 9.12 implies that the truth value of φ will be the same across all standard models of E^*.

As before, from completeness we infer expressibility:

10.23 COROLLARY · POINTWISE EXPRESSIBILITY FOR Σ AND Δ *Let R be a relation on $*$-expressions defined by a formula φ. Then the following hold:*

(i) *If φ is Σ in $\mathsf{E}^*_{\text{min}}$, then φ pointwise expresses R in $\mathsf{E}^*_{\text{min}}$.*

(ii) *If φ is Δ in $\mathsf{E}^*_{\text{min}}$, then φ strongly pointwise expresses R in $\mathsf{E}^*_{\text{min}}$.*

PROOF Let $\varphi(\mathsf{v}_1, \ldots, \mathsf{v}_n)$ define an n-ary relation R. Then $\varphi(\overline{a_1}, \ldots, \overline{a_n})$ is true iff $Ra_1 \cdots a_n$. By theorem 10.22, if φ is Σ in $\mathsf{E}^*_{\text{min}}$, then $\mathsf{E}^*_{\text{min}} \vdash \varphi(\overline{a_1}, \ldots, \overline{a_n})$ whenever $Ra_1 \cdots a_n$. The soundness of $\mathsf{E}^*_{\text{min}}$ with respect to standard models yields the converse. So φ pointwise expresses R in $\mathsf{E}^*_{\text{min}}$. If also $\neg\varphi$ is Σ, then $\neg\varphi$ pointwise expresses the complement of R, whence φ strongly pointwise expresses R. ⊣

Theorem 10.22 will prove extremely helpful in the next section, where many of the predicates we define for the formalization of syntax in E^* will be Σ-formulæ. The importance of the class Δ lies in the fact that these formulæ can be used to express more complex syntactic relations and functions while maintaining applicability of the Σ-completeness theorem. For instance, the Δ-formula Len can be utilized in both positive and negative contexts within an (otherwise) Σ-formula and the resulting formula will remain Σ. Moreover, once we have established a formula as being Δ, we can directly appeal to corollary 10.23 to deduce that the relation defined by the formula is strongly pointwise expressed by it.

10.2 Expressing Functions

So far we have considered expressing relations in E^*. As discussed in chapter 2, functions can be treated as special kinds of relations. Recall that an $n+1$-ary relation R is an n-ary function on the set $\mathcal{E}^*$ of $*$-expressions if two conditions are satisfied:

- For all $a_1, \ldots, a_n \in \mathcal{E}^*$ there is a $b \in \mathcal{E}^*$ such that $Ra_1 \cdots a_n b$.
- For all $a_1, \ldots, a_n \in \mathcal{E}^*$, if $Ra_1 \cdots a_n b$ and $Ra_1 \cdots a_n c$, then $b \equiv c$.

We call the relation R above the graph of f. Analogously, we will say that a formula $\varphi(\mathsf{v}_0, \ldots, \mathsf{v}_n)$ expresses a function in E^* if the $\mathcal{L}^*$-formulæ corresponding to the statements above are provable in E^*:

- $\forall x_0 \cdots \forall x_{n-1} \exists y\ \varphi(x_0, \ldots, x_{n-1}, y)$,
- $\forall x_0 \cdots \forall x_{n-1} \forall y \forall z \big(\varphi(x_0, \ldots, x_{n-1}, y) \wedge \varphi(x_0, \ldots, x_{n-1}, z) \rightarrow y = z\big)$.

Thus, to say that a function is pointwise expressible in E^* we require not only that the graph of the function be pointwise expressed by a formula but also that this formula expresses a function in E^*.

10.24 DEFINITION Let f be a k-ary function on $*$-expressions. A formula $\varphi(\mathsf{v}_0, \ldots, \mathsf{v}_k)$ pointwise expresses f in E^* if the following three conditions are satisfied:

(i) $\mathsf{E}^* \vdash \varphi\big(\overline{a_1}, \ldots, \overline{a_k}, \overline{f a_1 \cdots a_k}\big)$ for all $a_1, \ldots, a_k \in \mathcal{E}^*$.

(ii) $\mathsf{E}^* \vdash \forall \mathsf{v}_0 \cdots \forall \mathsf{v}_{k-1} \exists \mathsf{v}_k\ \varphi(\mathsf{v}_0, \ldots, \mathsf{v}_k)$.

(iii) $\mathsf{E}^* \vdash \forall \mathsf{v}_0 \cdots \forall \mathsf{v}_{k+1} \big(\varphi(\mathsf{v}_0, \ldots, \mathsf{v}_{k-1}, \mathsf{v}_k) \wedge \varphi(\mathsf{v}_0, \ldots, \mathsf{v}_{k-1}, \mathsf{v}_{k+1}) \rightarrow \mathsf{v}_k = \mathsf{v}_{k+1}\big)$.

It might seem odd that we have seemingly competing requirements on functions being expressed in a theory compared to their graphs. The first requirement of definition 10.24 asserts just one half of the equivalence needed for φ to weakly pointwise express the relation corresponding to f. The second and third property assert that the existence and uniqueness conditions – necessary for a relation to define a function – are provable in E^*.

As will be shown shortly, the first and third condition of definition 10.24 suffice to demonstrate that if E^* is consistent then the graph of every pointwise expressed function is *strongly* pointwise expressed in E^*. In fact, by reversing our perspective and viewing relations as derived from functions, the two notions of pointwise expressing a property turn out to coincide: With every relation R there is associated a unique function c_R, called the *characteristic function* of R, defined as follows. If R is a k-ary relation on expressions, c_R is the k-ary function such that $c_R a_1 \cdots a_k \equiv 0$ if $R a_1 \cdots a_k$ holds, and $c_R a_1 \cdots a_k \equiv \mathsf{v}$ otherwise. That is, c_R returns the empty string if the tuple of its arguments is in the relation R, and otherwise returns the auxiliary symbol v. The relation R can be retrieved from c_R as the set of k-tuples to which c_R assigns the empty string. The choice of 0 and v is unimportant; any other pair of distinct expressions would do just as well.

Strongly pointwise expressing a relation and pointwise expressing its characteristic function are equivalent conditions on consistent theories:

10.25 PROPOSITION *Let* E^* *be consistent. A relation R is strongly pointwise expressed in* E^* *if and only if the characteristic function of R is pointwise expressed in* E^*.

PROOF We begin with the 'only if' direction. Suppose the k-ary relation R is strongly pointwise expressed in E^* by $\psi(\mathsf{v}_0,\ldots,\mathsf{v}_{k-1})$. We claim that the formula

$$\varphi(\mathsf{v}_0,\ldots,\mathsf{v}_k) \;\equiv\; \big(\mathsf{v}_k=\underline{0} \wedge \psi(\mathsf{v}_0,\ldots,\mathsf{v}_{k-1})\big) \vee \big(\mathsf{v}_k=\underline{\mathsf{v}} \wedge \neg\psi(\mathsf{v}_0,\ldots,\mathsf{v}_{k-1})\big)$$

pointwise expresses the characteristic function of R, the k-ary function c_R. Let $a_1, \ldots, a_k \in \mathcal{E}^*$. If $Ra_1\cdots a_k$ holds, then $\mathsf{E}^* \vdash \psi(\overline{a_1},\ldots,\overline{a_k})$ by assumption and, therefore, $\mathsf{E}^* \vdash \varphi(\overline{a_1},\ldots,\overline{a_k},\overline{c_R a_1\cdots a_k})$. Otherwise, $\mathsf{E}^* \vdash \neg\psi(\overline{a_1},\ldots,\overline{a_k})$, whence $\mathsf{E}^* \vdash \varphi(\overline{a_1},\ldots,\overline{a_k},\overline{c_R a_1\cdots a_k})$ also obtains. Hence, condition (i) of definition 10.24 holds. Requirements (ii) and (iii) follow directly from the construction of φ.

For the 'if' direction, let $\varphi(\mathsf{v}_0,\ldots,\mathsf{v}_k)$ pointwise express the characteristic function of R in E^*. Observe that if $Ra_1\cdots a_k$ then $\mathsf{E}^* \vdash \varphi(\overline{a_1},\ldots,\overline{a_k},\underline{0})$ by condition (i) of definition 10.24. Similarly, $\mathsf{E}^* \vdash \neg\varphi(\overline{a_1},\ldots,\overline{a_k},\underline{0})$ if not $Ra_1\cdots a_k$, because of (i), (iii), and $\mathsf{E}^* \vdash \neg\, \underline{0} = \underline{\mathsf{v}}$. So by proposition 10.2, $\varphi(\mathsf{v}_0,\ldots,\mathsf{v}_{k-1},\underline{0})$ strongly pointwise expresses R. ⊣

The next two propositions employ a similar argument to relate the pointwise expressibility of functions and of their graphs.

10.26 PROPOSITION *Let f be a k-ary function pointwise expressed in* E^* *by a formula* $\varphi(x_1,\ldots,x_{k+1})$. *Then* φ *strongly pointwise expresses the graph of f if and only if* E^* *is consistent.*

PROOF By proposition 10.2 it suffices to show that $\mathsf{E}^* \vdash \neg\varphi(\overline{a_1},\ldots,\overline{a_k},\overline{b})$ for all expressions $a_1, \ldots, a_k, b$ such that $b \not\equiv fa_1\cdots a_k$. Letting $c \equiv fa_1\cdots a_k$, condition (i) of definition 10.24 implies $\mathsf{E}^* \vdash \varphi(\overline{a_1},\ldots,\overline{a_n},\overline{c})$. Since $\mathsf{E}^* \vdash \overline{b} \neq \overline{c}$, clause (iii) of the definition yields $\mathsf{E}^* \vdash \neg\varphi(\overline{a_1},\ldots,\overline{a_n},\overline{b})$, as required. ⊣

10.27 PROPOSITION *Let* $\varphi(\mathsf{v}_0,\ldots,\mathsf{v}_k)$ *pointwise express a k-ary function. If* φ *is* Σ_1, *then* φ *is* Δ_1. *If* φ *is* Σ, *then* φ *is* Δ.

PROOF By (ii) and (iii) of definition 10.24, $\neg\varphi(\mathsf{v}_0,\ldots,\mathsf{v}_k)$ is provably equivalent to the Σ-formula $\exists y\big(\varphi(\mathsf{v}_0,\ldots,\mathsf{v}_{k-1},y) \wedge \mathsf{v}_k \neq y\big)$. ⊣

Any function that can be expressed as a term in $\mathcal{L}^*_{\text{syn}}$ is pointwise expressed in $\mathsf{E}^*_{\text{min}}$ in the sense of definition 10.24. This observation is a consequence of theorem 10.6. If there exists a term $t(x_1, \ldots, x_k)$ with at most $x_1, \ldots, x_k$ free such that for all $a_1, \ldots, a_k \in \mathcal{E}^*$

$$\mathsf{E}^* \vdash \overline{fa_1 \cdots a_k} = t(\overline{a_1}, \ldots, \overline{a_k}), \tag{10.4}$$

then the formula $\mathsf{v}_k = t(\mathsf{v}_0, \ldots, \mathsf{v}_{k-1})$ expresses f in the sense of definition 10.24. In particular, the basic functions of concatenation, substitution, and quotation are pointwise expressed in every consistent extension of $\mathsf{E}^*_{\text{min}}$ by the atomic formulæ $\mathsf{z} = \mathsf{x}^\frown\mathsf{y}$, $\mathsf{w} = \mathsf{sub}(\mathsf{x}, \mathsf{y}, \mathsf{z})$, and $\mathsf{y} = \mathsf{qx}$, respectively.

We have already seen two other functions on expressions whose underlying relations are strongly pointwise expressed in $\mathsf{E}^*_{\text{min}}$. These are the length function, assigning to each expression its length, and the denotation function for closed terms. Propositions 9.41 and 9.43 show that the formula Len pointwise expresses the length function.

10.28 PROPOSITION *The function ascribing to each expression its length is pointwise expressed in* $\mathsf{E}^*_{\text{min}}$ *by the binary formula* Len(x,y).

The denotation function does not fit the schema of definition 10.24. As a function on expressions it is partial, being defined on closed terms only, meaning that clause (i) of definition 10.24 is not well defined. In section 9.2 we argued against extending the denotation function to a total function on expressions. However, we still claimed that the results of that section, namely proposition 9.26, show that denotation is expressed by the formula Den(x, y). We now demonstrate how to generalize definition 10.24 to obtain a notion of pointwise expressibility suitable for partial functions.

The first change to the definition is the restriction of clause (i) to the domain of the partial function.[4] Condition (ii) is adjusted similarly, by restricting the range of the universal quantifiers to a formula pointwise expressing the domain of the function. The requirement that the domain is pointwise expressed is important for deducing an analogue of proposition 10.26. (Note, the domain of a total

[4] For convenience, we will assume that all argument places of a partial function have the same domain. That is, we restrict attention to partial functions of type $S \times \cdots \times S \to \mathcal{E}^*$ for some $S \subseteq \mathcal{E}^*$. Functions where different argument places may be associated with distinct domains can be accommodated by minor changes to definition 10.29.

function is strongly pointwise expressed by the formula $x = x$.) Condition (iii) is unchanged. Finally, we add a fourth clause to the definition, expressing that the function is defined on arguments from its domain only.

10.29 DEFINITION Let f be an n-ary partial function on a set S of $\star$-expressions and let $\sigma(x)$ be a formula. A formula $\varphi(\mathsf{v}_0, \dots, \mathsf{v}_n)$ pointwise expresses f in E^* relative to σ if and only if S is strongly pointwise expressed in E^* by $\sigma(\mathsf{x})$ and the following four conditions are satisfied.

(i) $\mathsf{E}^* \vdash \varphi(\overline{a_1}, \dots, \overline{a_n}, \overline{fa_1 \cdots a_n})$ for all $a_1, \dots, a_n \in S$.

(ii) $\mathsf{E}^* \vdash \forall x_1 \cdots \forall x_n \big(\bigwedge_{i=1}^{n} \sigma(x_i) \to \exists y\, \varphi(x_1, \dots, x_n, y) \big)$.

(iii) $\mathsf{E}^* \vdash \forall x_1 \cdots \forall x_n \forall y \forall z \big(\varphi(x_1, \dots, x_n, y) \wedge \varphi(x_1, \dots, x_n, z) \to y = z \big)$.

(iv) $\mathsf{E}^* \vdash \forall x_1 \cdots \forall x_n \forall y \big(\varphi(x_1, \dots, x_n, y) \to \bigwedge_{i=1}^{n} \sigma(x_i) \big)$.

When the formula expressing the domain of f is clear from context we omit explicit mention of it. Applying the definition to the denotation function yields:

10.30 PROPOSITION *The formula* Den *pointwise expresses the denotation function on closed $\mathcal{L}^*$-terms in* E^* *relative to* CTerm.

PROOF Proposition 9.26. ⊣

The next two propositions provide analogues of propositions 10.26 and 10.27 for partial functions:

10.31 PROPOSITION *Let f be a k-ary partial function pointwise expressed by $\varphi(\mathsf{v}_0, \dots, \mathsf{v}_k)$. Then φ strongly pointwise expresses the graph of f in* E^* *if and only if* E^* *is consistent.*

PROOF By a similar argument as in proposition 10.26, the formula $\sigma(\mathsf{v}_0) \wedge \cdots \wedge \sigma(\mathsf{v}_{k-1}) \wedge \varphi(\mathsf{v}_0, \dots, \mathsf{v}_k)$ strongly pointwise expresses the graph of f. ⊣

10.32 PROPOSITION *Let f be a k-ary function on a set S which is defined by a Δ-formula $\sigma(x)$. Suppose $\varphi(\mathsf{v}_0, \dots, \mathsf{v}_k)$ pointwise expresses f relative to σ. If φ is Σ_1, then φ is Δ_1. If φ is Σ, then φ is Δ.*

PROOF The following formula is equivalent to $\varphi(x_0, \dots, x_k)$:

$$\bigwedge_{i=0}^{k-1} \sigma(x_i) \wedge \forall z \big(\varphi(x_0, \dots, x_{k-1}, z) \to x_k \neq z \big).$$ ⊣

The denotation function is an example of a function which is pointwise expressed by a formula but cannot be consistently expressed by any term. In theorem 9.20 we showed that if there is a term $d(x)$ such that $\mathsf{E}^* \vdash d(\overline{s}) = s$ for every closed term s of $\mathcal{L}^*_{\mathrm{syn}}$, then E^* is inconsistent. This observation does not preclude our adding fresh function symbols for expressed functions. Suppose φ satisfies the second and third condition of definition 10.24:

(ii) $\mathsf{E}^* \vdash \forall x_1 \cdots \forall x_n \exists y\ \varphi(x_1, \ldots, x_n, y)$.

(iii) $\mathsf{E}^* \vdash \forall x_1 \cdots \forall x_n \forall y \forall z \big(\varphi(x_1, \ldots, x_n, y) \wedge \varphi(x_1, \ldots, x_n, z) \rightarrow y = z\big)$.

Over E^*, the formula φ expresses an n-ary function. We can 'complete' definition 10.24 by extending the vocabulary of E^* by a symbol for the expressed function. Let $\mathcal{L}^*_{\mathsf{f}}$ expand $\mathcal{L}^*$ by a new function symbol f of arity n. The following sentence states that the formula and function symbol express the same function.

$\text{FUN}_{\mathsf{f},\varphi}$ $\forall x_1 \cdots \forall x_n\ \varphi(x_1, \ldots, x_n, \mathsf{f} x_1 \cdots x_n)$.

The theory $\mathsf{E}^* + \text{FUN}_{\mathsf{f},\varphi}$ is consistent if E^* is. Any model of E^* for the language $\mathcal{L}^*$ can be expanded to a model for the language $\mathcal{L}^*_{\mathsf{f}}$ by interpreting the function symbol f as the function whose graph is the denotation of $\varphi(\mathsf{v}_0, \ldots, \mathsf{v}_n)$ in this model. The resulting model satisfies the theory $\mathsf{E}^* + \text{FUN}_{\mathsf{f},\varphi}$.

In chapter 2 we detailed how function symbols can be eliminated from a theory by the use of predicate symbols. Following that argument, but now using the formula φ in place of a fresh predicate symbol, the introduction of f into E^* can be reversed by converting every derivation in the theory $\mathsf{E}^* + \text{FUN}_{\mathsf{f},\varphi}$ into a derivation from the axioms of E^* alone. The described reduction establishes a strong connection between the two theories, a consequence of which is an alternative proof that the consistency of E^* implies the consistency of $\mathsf{E}^* + \text{FUN}_{\mathsf{f},\varphi}$:

10.33 PROPOSITION *Let* E^*, $\mathcal{L}^*_{\mathsf{f}}$, *and* φ *be as above. For every formula* ψ *in the language* $\mathcal{L}^*$, *if* $\mathsf{E}^* + \text{FUN}_{\mathsf{f},\varphi} \vdash \psi$, *then* $\mathsf{E}^* \vdash \psi$.

The primary motivation behind expanding the language in the way described above is to increase the legibility of formulæ. Function symbols allow us to express in formulæ operations on strings whose intension, or denotation, is more easily read as a function than via defining formulæ. As the proof behind proposition 10.33 clearly shows, new symbols can mask complexity. The formula $\mathsf{f}x = y$ is atomic, but the formula it replaces, say $\varphi(x, y)$, can be arbitrarily complex. In particular, a Σ_1-formula containing an introduced function symbol need not be equivalent to a Σ_1-formula in the language without that function symbol. While this observation has little bearing on our study of E^* thus far – for example, an instance of the induction axiom containing the function symbol f remains an instance once occurrences of f have been replaced – we now have a collection of results which depend on the syntactic complexity of the formulæ to which they apply. Notably: does the Σ-completeness theorem hold for a Σ_1-formula in the language expanded with a function symbol for an expressible function?

The answer to this particular question is negative. The argument relies on a result we have remarked on several times which will be proved in section 10.4: that $\mathsf{E}^*_{\min}$ is an incomplete theory, meaning that there exist sentences γ in the language $\mathcal{L}^*_{\min}$ such that neither $\mathsf{E}^*_{\min} \vdash \gamma$ nor $\mathsf{E}^*_{\min} \vdash \neg\gamma$. The result is a consequence of theorem 10.63.

As the independent formula γ is in the language $\mathcal{L}^*_{\min}$, it follows that one of γ and $\neg\gamma$ must be true in all standard models of $\mathcal{L}^*_{\min}$. Without loss of generality, we assume the former. Define $\varphi(\mathsf{x}) \equiv (\gamma \wedge \mathsf{x} = \underline{\forall}) \vee (\neg\gamma \wedge \mathsf{x} = \underline{\neg})$. Because γ is true, φ defines the symbol $\underline{\forall}$ in all standard models. That is, for every standard model $\mathbb{E}^*$ of $\mathcal{L}^*_{\min}$, we have $\mathbb{E}^* \vDash \varphi(\overline{a})$ if and only if $a \equiv \forall$. By logic, $\mathsf{E}^*_{\min} \vdash \gamma \vee \neg\gamma$, so $\mathsf{E}^*_{\min} \vdash \varphi(\underline{\forall}) \vee \varphi(\underline{\neg})$, from which the existence condition for φ is derivable:

$$\mathsf{E}^*_{\min} \vdash \exists y\, \varphi(y).$$

Moreover, $\mathsf{E}^*_{\min} \vdash \big(\varphi(\underline{\forall}) \leftrightarrow \gamma\big) \wedge \big(\varphi(\underline{\neg}) \leftrightarrow \neg\gamma\big)$, hence the uniqueness condition is derivable:

$$\mathsf{E}^*_{\min} \vdash \forall x \forall y \big(\varphi(x) \wedge \varphi(y) \rightarrow x = y\big).$$

Suppose $\mathcal{L}^*$ contains a constant c that is not a symbol of $\mathcal{L}^*_{\min}$, and let E^* be the theory $\mathsf{E}^*_{\min}$ with one additional axiom: $\varphi(\mathsf{c})$. As we know from proposition 10.33, every theorem of E^* that does not feature the additional constant c is a theorem of $\mathsf{E}^*_{\min}$. Moreover, we have a canonical notion of a standard model for the theory E^*, namely the standard models of $\mathcal{L}^*$ which interpret c as $\forall$.

If the completeness theorem for Σ_1-sentences (theorem 10.14) held for arbitrary Σ_1-formulæ and not only those in the language $\mathcal{L}^*_{\text{syn}}$, then we could deduce that $\mathsf{E}^* \vdash \mathsf{c} = \underline{\forall}$, so $\mathsf{E}^* \vdash \varphi(\underline{\forall})$, and $\mathsf{E}^* \vdash \gamma$. Proposition 10.33 would then imply $\mathsf{E}^*_{\min} \vdash \gamma$, in contradiction with the choice of γ. This argument uses an introduced symbol to present the independent formula γ as a Σ_1-formula. The Σ-completeness theorem tells us that the defining formula $\varphi(x)$ is not Σ, for if it were, $\varphi(\underline{\forall})$ would be a true Σ-formula and so provable in $\mathsf{E}^*_{\min}$.

The following theorem establishes a result in the other direction: if $\mathcal{L}^*$ extends $\mathcal{L}^*_{\text{min}}$ by function symbols only, each of which is Σ-definable in E^*, then every Σ_1-formulæ of $\mathcal{L}^*$ is Σ.

10.34 THEOREM *Let* $\mathsf{f}_0, \ldots, \mathsf{f}_n$ *be function symbols of* $\mathcal{L}^*$ *and suppose that for each* $i \leq n$ *there is a* Σ*-formula* φ_i *which expresses a function in* E^* *and is such that* $\mathsf{E}^* \vdash \text{FUN}_{\mathsf{f}_i,\varphi_i}$. *Then every* Σ_1*-formula in the expansion of* $\mathcal{L}^*_{\text{syn}}$ *by the function symbols* $\mathsf{f}_0, \ldots, \mathsf{f}_n$ *is* Σ.

PROOF Given $\varphi_i(\mathsf{v}_0, \ldots, \mathsf{v}_{k_i})$ as above, where k_i is the arity of f_i, the proof of proposition 10.27 shows that conditions (ii) and (iii) of definition 10.24 suffice to deduce that φ_i is Δ. Using the method described in chapter 2 to eliminate occurrences of function symbols, it is clear that a Σ_1-formula in the expansion of $\mathcal{L}^*_{\text{syn}}$ by $\mathsf{f}_0, \ldots, \mathsf{f}_n$ will be transformed into a Σ-formula in $\mathcal{L}^*_{\text{syn}}$. ⊣

Theorem 10.34 shows that we can introduce function symbols for functions that are pointwise expressed in E^* by Σ-formulæ and that E^* is complete for Σ_1-sentences involving the new symbols. This is particularly useful for the development of syntax in $\mathsf{E}^*_{\text{min}}$ where syntactic operations such as instantiating variables in formulæ and forming the universal closure of a formula play a central role, and can be safely replaced by function symbols once we have established that the operations are pointwise expressed by Σ-formulæ.

10.3 Formal Syntax

Recall the formulæ Sing, Syn, and Var expressing respectively the singletons, syntactic constants, and variables of $\mathcal{L}^*$:

$$\begin{aligned} \mathsf{Sing}(\mathsf{x}) &\equiv \mathsf{x} \neq \underline{0} \wedge \forall \mathsf{w} \forall \mathsf{z}(\mathsf{x} = \mathsf{w}^\frown \mathsf{z} \rightarrow \mathsf{w} = \mathsf{x} \vee \mathsf{z} = \mathsf{x}), \\ \mathsf{Syn}(\mathsf{x}) &\equiv \mathsf{x} = \mathsf{q}\underline{0} \vee \exists \mathsf{y}(\mathsf{sym}\,\mathsf{y} \wedge \mathsf{x} = \mathsf{q}\mathsf{y}), \\ \mathsf{Var}(\mathsf{x}) &\equiv \exists \mathsf{z}\big(\mathsf{x} = (\underline{\frown}\mathsf{z}\underline{\frown}) \wedge \mathsf{sub}(\mathsf{z}, \underline{\mathsf{v}}, \underline{0}) = \underline{0}\big). \end{aligned}$$

Proposition 10.4 established that each of these formulæ is provably equivalent to a bounded formula. As a consequence of completeness for bounded formulæ, they strongly pointwise express the corresponding set of $*$-expressions. In the case of variables, we have that, for every expression a,

- $\mathsf{E}^* \vdash \mathsf{Var}(\overline{a})$ if a is a variable;

- $\mathsf{E}^* \vdash \neg\mathsf{Var}(\overline{a})$ if a is not a variable.

We have already observed that the formula Term introduced in chapter 8 pointwise expresses the terms of $\mathcal{L}^*$. This result also follows from theorem 10.14 as the formula is Σ_1. By showing that Term is Δ we can deduce that terms are strongly pointwise expressed in $\mathsf{E}^*_{\text{min}}$.

In what follows, it will prove convenient to introduce abbreviations for quantifiers which range over terms, that is, quantifiers of the sort $\forall x(\mathsf{Term}(x) \to \cdots)$. We will follow our practice in the metalanguage and use symbols r, s, and t (possibly embellished by subscripts etc.) as formal metavariables for terms. Henceforth, $\forall t\, \varphi(t)$ is shorthand for $\forall \mathsf{v}_i(\mathsf{Term}(\mathsf{v}_i) \to \varphi(\mathsf{v}_i))$ for an appropriate choice of i, and $\exists t\, \varphi(t)$ abbreviates $\exists \mathsf{v}_i(\mathsf{Term}(\mathsf{v}_i) \wedge \varphi(\mathsf{v}_i))$.

When we employ induction in the metalanguage to prove that some property P holds of all terms we typically argue by induction on the recursive definition of terms: 'If P holds of all variables and all constants, and holds of a complex term whenever it holds of all its proper subterms, then P holds of all terms.' Given that variables and constants have, by definition, no proper subterms, induction can be simply stated as: 'If P holds of an arbitrary term t whenever it holds of all proper subterms of t, then P holds of all terms.' The formal version of this statement, where $\varphi(x)$ expresses the property P, is the formula

$$\forall t\big(\forall s \sqsubset t\; \varphi(s) \to \varphi(t)\big) \to \forall t\, \varphi(t). \tag{10.5}$$

As remarked in section 8.4, (10.5) is provably equivalent to the strong induction principle for the formula $\mathsf{Term}(x) \to \varphi(x)$, and so is derivable in $\mathsf{E}^*_{\text{min}}$. Therefore, the induction principle (10.5) can be utilized in formal derivations. We present an example of a formal proof by induction on terms before moving to our main result on the expression of terms in E^*:

10.35 PROPOSITION *The following are provable in* E^*:

(i) $\forall x\big(\mathsf{Term}(x) \leftrightarrow \mathsf{Var}(x) \vee \mathsf{Syn}(x) \vee \bigvee_{\mathsf{f}\in\mathcal{F}} \exists t_1 \cdots \exists t_{a_\mathsf{f}}\; x = \underline{\mathsf{f}}{}^\frown t_1{}^\frown \cdots {}^\frown t_{a_\mathsf{f}}\big)$,

(ii) $\forall t \forall y\big(\mathsf{Term}(t^\frown y) \vee \mathsf{Term}(y^\frown t) \to y = \underline{0}\big)$,

(iii) $\forall t \forall r \forall s\; \mathsf{Term}\big(\mathsf{sub}(t, r, s)\big)$.

The preceding formulæ are all true in any standard model of $\mathcal{L}^*$ and express basic syntactic properties of terms. The first claim matches the formula Term to the inductive definition of terms, and is easy to verify. Claim (ii) is a restatement of the unique readability property for terms proved in lemma 8.80. Finally, (iii) expresses that terms are invariant under replacing a subterm by another term. A special case of (iii) is that $t(s)$ is a term whenever $t(x)$ and s are terms.

PROOF The first claim is not proved by term induction, but is a direct consequence of the definition of the formula Term. The second claim was proved in lemma 8.80. To see the third claim, let y and y_0 be the lists witnessing that t and s, respectively, are terms. We claim $z = y_0 {}^\frown \mathsf{sub}(y, r, s)$ is a list which witnesses that $\mathsf{sub}(t, r, s)$ is a term. Lemma 8.80 ensures that z is a list and that its elements are simply the elements of y_0 and the elements of y under the substitution of s for r. As y contains t as its final element, so z contains $\mathsf{sub}(t, r, s)$. Thus, fix an initial segment z_0 of z and let w_0 be its final element. If $w_0 \in y_0$, there is nothing to check. Otherwise, $w_0 = \mathsf{sub}(w, r, s)$ for some $w \in y$ and we proceed by a case distinction on w: if w is a variable or a syntactic constant then either w_0 is as well or $w_0 = s$, which is an element of y_0, whereas if $w = \underline{\mathsf{f}} {}^\frown w_1 {}^\frown \cdots {}^\frown w_{a_\mathsf{f}}$ is a complex term and each w_j is an element of y, then $w_0 = \underline{\mathsf{f}} {}^\frown w'_1 {}^\frown \cdots {}^\frown w'_{a_\mathsf{f}}$ where $w'_j = \mathsf{sub}(w_j, r, s)$. ⊣

10.36 THEOREM *The formula* Term *is* Δ.

We have already remarked that Term is Σ, so it remains to show that the formula is Π, that is, that $\mathsf{Term}(x)$ is provably equivalent to a Π_1-formula of $\mathcal{L}^*_{\mathrm{syn}}$ over $\mathsf{E}^*_{\mathrm{min}}$. Here we employ a standard trick for Σ-formulæ of this kind. The set of terms of $\mathcal{L}^*$ is, by definition, a set $\mathcal{T}$ of $*$-expressions containing

(i) all variables,

(ii) all syntactic constants, and

(iii) the expression $\mathsf{f}e_1 \cdots e_{a_\mathsf{f}}$ for every $\mathsf{f} \in \mathcal{F}$ and $e_1, \ldots, e_{a_\mathsf{f}} \in \mathcal{T}$.

It is not, however, an arbitrary such set. The set $\mathcal{E}^*$ of all $*$-expressions has this property. Rather, the set of $\mathcal{L}^*$-terms is the *smallest* such $\mathcal{T}$ in the sense that the set of terms is a subset of every set $\mathcal{T}$ containing (i)–(iii). We have thus arrived at an alternative definition of terms: an expression e is a term of $\mathcal{L}^*$ if and only if for every set $\mathcal{T}$ of $*$-expressions which contains (i)–(iii), we have $e \in \mathcal{T}$.

It is this reformulation of the definition which leads us to the realization that Term is Π: the set of terms of $\mathcal{L}^*$ can be defined as the intersection of all sets of expressions satisfying (i)–(iii). Our formal language $\mathcal{L}^*$ lacks the vocabulary to quantify over sets. But it is not necessary to resort to set theory to express the $*$-terms. The characterization of terms can be refined so as to refer only to properties of $*$-expressions: a $*$-expression e is a term of $\mathcal{L}^*$ if and only if e is contained in every list L of words which includes

(i′) all variable symbols occurring in e,

(ii′) all syntactic constants occurring in e, and

(iii′) the $*$-expression $\mathsf{f}e_1\cdots e_{a_\mathsf{f}}$ whenever this is a subexpression of e, f is a function symbol in $\mathcal{F}$, and $e_1, \ldots, e_{a_\mathsf{f}}$ are elements of L.

Expressing these properties is the formula Term*:

$$\psi_{\mathsf{Term}}(w, y) := \mathsf{Var}(w) \lor \mathsf{Syn}(w) \lor \bigvee_{\mathsf{f}\in\mathcal{F}} \exists w_1 \in y \cdots \exists w_{a_\mathsf{f}} \in y \; w = \underset{\cdot}{\mathsf{f}} w_1 \cdots w_{a_\mathsf{f}},$$

$$\mathsf{Term}^*(x) := \forall y \Big(\mathsf{List}(y) \land \forall w \subseteq x \big(\psi_{\mathsf{Term}}(w, y) \to w \in y\big) \to x \in y\Big).$$

The notation $\underset{\cdot}{\mathsf{f}} w_1 \cdots w_{a_\mathsf{f}}$, recall, is shorthand for the term $\underline{\mathsf{f}}^\frown w_1{}^\frown \cdots {}^\frown w_{a_\mathsf{f}}$. Up to renaming of variables, ψ_{Term} is a subformula of our original characterization of terms:

$$\mathsf{Term}(x) \equiv \exists y \big(\mathsf{List}(y) \land x \in y \land \forall w \in y \; \psi_{\mathsf{Term}}(w, y)\big).$$

As the only unbounded quantifier in Term* is the leading universal quantifier $\forall y$, this formula is Π_1. The subformula

$$\forall w \subseteq x \big(\psi_{\mathsf{Term}}(w, y) \to w \in y\big)$$

expresses that y satisfies (i′)–(iii′) relative to expression x, and $\mathsf{Term}^*(x)$ simply states that x is a $*$-expression contained in every such y.

PROOF OF THEOREM 10.36 We show $\mathsf{E}^* \vdash \mathsf{Term}(x) \leftrightarrow \mathsf{Term}^*(x)$. Here we will not be formal with the argument but provide an informal proof using only the language and assumptions available in E^*.

$\mathsf{E}^* \vdash \mathsf{Term}(x) \to \mathsf{Term}^*(x)$: Based on our abbreviations, this claim is rendered as $\forall s\, \mathsf{Term}^*(s)$, which we can establish via term induction, (10.5), with $\varphi(x) \equiv \mathsf{Term}^*(x)$. To that aim, it is sufficient to suppose that t is an arbitrary term of $\mathcal{L}^*$ and that for every proper subterm $s \subset t$ we have $\mathsf{Term}^*(s)$. If t is a variable or syntactic constant of $\mathcal{L}^*$, then there are no proper subterms, but $\mathsf{Term}^*(t)$ holds by definition. Otherwise, $t \equiv \mathsf{f}s_1 \cdots s_k$ for a function symbol f with arity k and terms

$s_1, \ldots, s_k$. By assumption, $\mathsf{Term}^*(s_i)$ for each $1 \leq i \leq k$. With the aim to show that $\mathsf{Term}^*(t)$, let l be any list satisfying

$$\forall w \subseteq t\big(\psi_{\mathsf{Term}}(w, l) \to w \in l\big). \tag{10.6}$$

As s_i is a proper subexpression of t, (10.6) and $\mathsf{Term}^*(s_i)$ yield $s_i \in l$ for each $1 \leq i \leq k$. Hence $\psi_{\mathsf{Term}}(t, l)$, from which (10.6) implies $t \in l$, as desired.

$\mathsf{E}^* \vdash \mathsf{Term}^*(x) \to \mathsf{Term}(x)$: Given an arbitrary word a, let l_a be a list comprising all proper subexpressions of a satisfying the formula Term^*. That is, l_a is such that $\forall w\big(w \in l_a \leftrightarrow w \not\subseteq a \wedge \mathsf{Term}^*(w)\big)$. Such a list can be proven to exist by strong induction. Now suppose $\mathsf{Term}^*(a)$. We may assume that $\mathsf{Term}(w)$ for every $w \in l_a$, from which l_a, concatenated with a, witnesses $\mathsf{Term}(a)$. ⊣

A corollary of the theorem is that terms are strongly pointwise expressed in E^*:

10.37 PROPOSITION *Let a be any $*$-expression.*

- *If a is a term, then* $\mathsf{E}^* \vdash \mathsf{Term}(\overline{a})$.
- *If a is not a term, then* $\mathsf{E}^* \vdash \neg\mathsf{Term}(\overline{a})$.

PROOF Theorem 10.36 and corollary 10.23. ⊣

Variants of the formula Term can be readily given which strongly pointwise express terms of particular sublanguages of $\mathcal{L}^*$, such as $\mathcal{L}^*_{\mathrm{syn}}$:

$$\begin{aligned}
\mathsf{Term}_{\mathrm{syn}}(x) &:= \exists y\big(\mathsf{List}(y) \wedge x \in y \wedge \forall w \in y\ \psi_{\mathsf{T_S}}(w, y)\big), \\
\psi_{\mathsf{T_S}}(w, y) &:= \mathsf{Var}(w) \vee \mathsf{Syn}(w) \vee \\
&\quad \vee \exists w_1 \in y\, \exists w_2 \in y\, \exists w_3 \in y\big(w = w_1 \underset{.}{\frown} w_2 \vee w = \underset{.}{\mathsf{sub}}\, w_1 w_2 w_3 \vee w = \underset{.}{\mathsf{q}}\, w_1\big).
\end{aligned}$$

The task of verifying that $\mathsf{Term}_{\mathrm{syn}}$ is Δ and behaves as intended is left to the reader.

The general template of the formulæ Term and Term* can be used to prove that other collections of expressions are strongly pointwise expressed. For example, the Σ-formula Wbw, expressing well-bracketed words, shares the construction with Term but with ψ_{Term} replaced by

$$\begin{aligned}
\psi_{\mathsf{Wbw}}(w, y) &:= \neg\big(\underline{)} \subseteq w \wedge \underline{(} \subseteq w\big) \vee \exists x \in y\, \exists z \in y\big(w = \underline{(}\frown x \frown \underline{)} \vee w = x \frown z\big), \\
\mathsf{Wbw}(x) &:= \exists y\big(\mathsf{List}(y) \wedge x \in y \wedge \forall w \in y\ \psi_{\mathsf{Wbw}}(w, y)\big).
\end{aligned}$$

A similar argument shows that Wbw has an equivalent Π_1-form:

$$\mathsf{Wbw}^*(x) \;:=\; \forall y\Big(\mathsf{List}(y) \wedge \forall w\subseteq x\big(\psi_{\mathsf{Wbw}}(w,y) \to w\in y\big) \;\to\; x\in y\Big).$$

Concerning terms, the same template provides Σ- and Π-formulæ describing closed terms and pure terms. For these two examples, however, simpler Σ-definitions are available:

$$\begin{aligned}\mathsf{CTerm}(x) &:= \mathsf{Term}(x) \wedge \forall v\subseteq x\; \neg\mathsf{Var}(v),\\ \mathsf{PTerm}(x) &:= \exists w(w\neq \underline{0} \wedge x = \mathsf{q}w).\end{aligned}$$

The first formula expresses the closed terms as the terms which do not contain variables. An equivalent Π-definition is obtained by replacing the subformula $\mathsf{Term}(x)$ with $\mathsf{Term}^*(x)$. The second definition appeals to the characterization of pure terms in lemma 8.42 as the quotations of non-empty expressions.

As remarked, both properties can also be expressed by their inductive definition: closed terms follow the same construction as terms lacking the clause for variables; pure terms follow the inductive definition in definition 8.41. The formulæ CTerm′, CTerm*, PTerm′, and PTerm* below provide Σ- and Π-definitions for the two kinds of $\ast$-expressions.

$$\begin{aligned}\psi_{\mathsf{CTerm}}(w,z) &:= \mathsf{Syn}(w) \vee \bigvee_{\mathsf{f}\in\mathcal{F}} \exists w_1\in z \cdots \exists w_{a_\mathsf{f}}\in z\;\, w = \underset{\cdot}{\mathsf{f}} w_1\cdots w_{a_\mathsf{f}},\\ \mathsf{CTerm}'(x) &:= \exists y\big(\mathsf{List}(y) \wedge x\in y \wedge \forall w\in y\;\psi_{\mathsf{CTerm}}(w,y)\big),\\ \mathsf{CTerm}^*(x) &:= \forall y\Big(\mathsf{List}(y) \to \big(\forall w\subseteq x\big(\psi_{\mathsf{CTerm}}(w,y) \to w\in y\big) \to x\in y\big)\Big),\end{aligned}$$

$$\begin{aligned}\psi_0(x) &:= \big(\mathsf{Syn}(x) \wedge x\neq \mathsf{q}\underline{0}\big) \vee \exists w\big(\mathsf{Syn}(w) \wedge x = \mathsf{q}w\big),\\ \psi_{\mathsf{PTerm}}(w,y) &:= \psi_0(w) \vee \exists w_1\subseteq w\;\exists w_2\subseteq w\big(w_1\in y \wedge \psi_0(w_2) \wedge w = w_1 \,\underset{\cdot}{\frown}\, w_2\big),\end{aligned}$$

$$\begin{aligned}\mathsf{PTerm}'(x) &:= \exists y\big(\mathsf{List}(y) \wedge x\in y \wedge \forall w\in y\;\psi_{\mathsf{PTerm}}(w,y)\big),\\ \mathsf{PTerm}^*(x) &:= \forall y\Big(\mathsf{List}(y) \to \big(\forall w\subseteq x\big(\psi_{\mathsf{PTerm}}(w,y) \to w\in y\big) \to x\in y\big)\Big).\end{aligned}$$

The formulæ CTerm′ and CTerm* are Σ_1 and Π_1 respectively, and their equivalence is easily proved in E^* by reducing to the formula CTerm. Although PTerm′ is Σ_1, PTerm* is not Π_1 because of the unbounded existential quantifier in ψ_0. We have seen, however, that Syn is equivalent to a bounded formula. As the quotation of a syntactic constant is the result of prepending that constant by the symbol q, we have

$$\mathsf{E}^* \vdash \forall w\big(\mathsf{Syn}(w) \to \mathsf{q}w = \underset{\cdot}{\mathsf{q}}w\big).$$

Hence, the existential quantifier in ψ_0 can be replaced by a bounded quantifier $\exists w \subseteq x$. So, PTerm^* is Π. We leave the proof of equivalence between PTerm' and PTerm^* to the reader, and focus on the equivalence between the two Σ-definitions of pure terms, the one given by the inductive construction of definition 8.41, the other by the characterization of pure terms as quotations in lemma 8.42.

10.38 LEMMA $\mathsf{E}^* \vdash \forall x\big(\mathsf{PTerm}(x) \leftrightarrow \mathsf{PTerm}'(x)\big)$.

PROOF The left-to-right direction is the claim that $\forall w\big(w \neq \underline{0} \to \mathsf{PTerm}'(\mathsf{q}w)\big)$ is provable in E^*, which we show by induction on w. If w is non-empty, then $w = x \frown u$ for a singleton u and an expression x. By proposition 8.47 we know $\mathsf{Syn}(u) \vee \mathsf{sym}\, u$, that is, u is either a basic symbol or a syntactic constant. In either case we deduce that $\psi_0(\mathsf{q}u)$. Now, if x is trivial then $\mathsf{PTerm}'(\mathsf{q}w)$ for this reason. Otherwise, $\mathsf{q}w = \underline{\frown}{}^\frown \mathsf{q}x{}^\frown \mathsf{q}u$ and, applying the induction hypothesis, we may assume that $\mathsf{PTerm}'(\mathsf{q}x)$. But then $\mathsf{PTerm}'(\mathsf{q}w)$ follows by definition.

The right-to-left direction is the formal counterpart of lemma 8.42 and follows the same proof as that result. ⊣

As a consequence, we have Δ-definitions for the closed and pure terms:

10.39 THEOREM *The formulæ* CTerm *and* PTerm *are* Δ. *Thus, the closed and pure terms are strongly pointwise expressed in* $\mathsf{E}^*_{\min}$ *by these formulæ.*

It is an easy argument to show in $\mathsf{E}^*_{\min}$ that every pure term is closed. We proceed by induction on pure terms, using the formula PTerm. First it is necessary to show $\mathsf{E}^*_{\min} \vdash \forall x\big(\psi_0(x) \to \mathsf{CTerm}(x)\big)$, from which follows

$$\mathsf{E}^*_{\min} \vdash \forall y \forall w\Big(\mathsf{List}(y) \wedge \psi_{\mathsf{PTerm}}(w, y) \to \exists z\big(\mathsf{List}(z^\frown y) \wedge \psi_{\mathsf{CTerm}}(w, z^\frown y)\big)\Big).$$

The 'witness' to the existential quantifier $\exists y$ is simply the list of syntactic constants present in the pure term w.

10.40 LEMMA $\mathsf{E}^*_{\min} \vdash \forall x\big(\mathsf{PTerm}(x) \to \mathsf{CTerm}(x)\big)$.

Our simple definition of pure terms also serves as a definition of quotations since an expression is a quotation if and only if it is a pure term or $\underline{0}$. So, quotations are also Δ-definable. As a consequence, sequences are expressed by a Δ-formula in $\mathsf{E}^*_{\min}$:

$$\mathsf{E}^*_{\min} \vdash \forall x\Big(\mathsf{Seq}(x) \leftrightarrow \mathsf{List}(x) \wedge \forall w \in x\big(w = \mathsf{q}\underline{0} \vee \mathsf{PTerm}(w)\big)\Big).$$

Moreover, the function which returns the nth component of a sequence has a straightforward Σ-representation:

$$\mathsf{Proj}_n(x, y) := \exists z_1 \cdots \exists z_n \exists z \;\; x = \langle z_1, \ldots, z_n, y\rangle^\frown z,$$

where, recall, $\langle x_1, \ldots, x_k\rangle \equiv \underline{\mathsf{e}}^\frown \mathsf{q}x_1{}^\frown \underline{\mathsf{e}}^\frown \cdots {}^\frown \underline{\mathsf{e}}^\frown \mathsf{q}x_k$. Given that the set of sequences is pointwise expressed by a Δ-formula, theorem 10.34 allows us to assume that $\mathcal{L}^*_{\mathrm{syn}}$ contains unary function symbols p_0, …, p_n expressing (finitely many of) these operations, and that E^* contains the following axiom for each $i \leq n$:

(PROJ$_i$) $$\forall x\big(\mathsf{Seq}(x) \to \mathsf{Proj}_i(x, \mathsf{p}_i x)\big).$$

In particular, in the presence of function symbols for projections quantification over components of a sequence reduces to a bounded quantifier relativized to a Δ-formulæ, allowing these quantifiers to be freely used in the construction of other Δ-formulæ.

10.41 PROPOSITION $\mathsf{E}^*_{\min} \vdash \forall x \forall y\big(y \in_{\mathrm{seq}} x \leftrightarrow \exists z \subseteq x\big(\mathsf{Seq}(z) \wedge y = \mathsf{p}_0 z\big)\big)$.

Employing the theory of arithmetic developed in the previous chapter, it is possible to combine the infinite lot of projection function symbols as a single, two-place, function which takes as its first argument a natural number for the index. That is, we can readily define a single Σ-formula $\mathsf{Proj}(x_0, x_1, y)$ satisfying the following conditions:

$$\mathsf{E}^* \vdash \forall x\Big(\mathsf{Seq}(x) \to \forall y\big(\mathsf{Proj}(\underline{n}, x, y) \leftrightarrow \mathsf{Proj}_n(x, y)\big)\Big) \quad \text{for every } n,$$
$$\mathsf{E}^* \vdash \forall m \forall x\big(\mathsf{Seq}(x) \to \exists y\, \mathsf{Proj}(m, x, y)\big),$$
$$\mathsf{E}^* \vdash \forall m \forall x \forall y \forall y'\big(\mathsf{Seq}(x) \wedge \mathsf{Proj}(m, x, y) \wedge \mathsf{Proj}(m, x, y') \to y = y'\big).$$

As we will have no need for the projection functions beyond p_0 and p_1, we omit the definition of Proj and verification of the above.

To summarize the section so far, we have established the following theorem, which serves to add several important examples to our growing stock of Δ-formulæ:

10.42 THEOREM *The formulæ* Term, PTerm, CTerm, Wbw, Seq, *and* $\mathsf{p}_n x = y$ *for each* n *are all* Δ.

Theorem 10.42 has an immediate consequence for the expression of the denotation function on closed terms, which we can now show has an equivalent Σ_1-presentation, and is Δ for some specific sublanguages of $\mathcal{L}^*$. It is straightforward to provide variants of this formula tailored to terms of sublanguages of $\mathcal{L}^*$, such as $\mathcal{L}^*_{\min}$ and $\mathcal{L}^*_{\text{syn}}$. Fix any set $\mathcal{F}$ of function symbols of $\mathcal{L}^*$, and let the arity of $\mathsf{f} \in \mathcal{F}$ be a_f. Following the template of the formula Den (definition 9.25), we define

$$\psi_{\mathsf{Den}_\mathcal{F}}(w_0, w_1, z) \ := \ \big(\mathsf{Sing}(w_0) \wedge w_0 = \mathsf{q}w_1\big) \ \vee$$
$$\bigvee_{\mathsf{f}\in\mathcal{F}} \exists x_1 \cdots \exists x_{a_\mathsf{f}} \exists y_1 \cdots \exists y_{a_\mathsf{f}} \Big(w_0 = \underset{\cdot}{\mathsf{f}} x_1 \cdots x_{a_\mathsf{f}} \ \wedge \ w_1 = \mathsf{f} y_1 \cdots y_{a_\mathsf{f}} \ \wedge \ \bigwedge_{i=1}^{a_\mathsf{f}} \langle x_i, y_i \rangle \in_{\text{seq}} z \Big).$$

The formula $\mathsf{Den}_\mathcal{F}(x, y)$ is

$$\mathsf{Den}_\mathcal{F}(x, y) \ := \ \exists y \big(\mathsf{Seq}(z) \ \wedge \ \langle x, y \rangle \in_{\text{seq}} y \ \wedge \ \forall w \in_{\text{seq}} y \ \psi_{\mathsf{Den}_\mathcal{F}}(\mathsf{p}_0 w, \mathsf{p}_1 w, y)\big).$$

This formula uses the projection functions on sequences introduced above instead of explicitly quantifying over components. By the same observations, $\mathsf{Den}_\mathcal{F}$ is provably equivalent to a Σ_1-formula in the language $\mathcal{L}^*_{\text{syn}}$ expanded by the symbols in $\mathcal{F}$. Function symbols in $\mathcal{F}$ are necessary to state the subformula $\psi_{\mathsf{Den}_\mathcal{F}}$, so this formula need not be Σ.

10.43 PROPOSITION *Let* $\mathcal{F}$ *be a set of function symbols of* $\mathcal{L}^*$. *The denotation function on closed terms of* $\mathcal{F}$ *is pointwise expressed in* $\mathsf{E}^*_{\min}$ *by the formula* $\mathsf{Den}_\mathcal{F}$. *If every function symbol of* $\mathcal{F}$ *is pointwise expressed in* E^* *by a* Σ*-formula, then* $\mathsf{Den}_\mathcal{F}$ *is* Δ.

PROOF The first claim is a consequence of theorem 10.42 and the natural reformulation of proposition 9.26 for a given sublanguage $\mathcal{F}$. The second claim is an application of theorem 10.34. ⊣

Having dealt with terms we proceed to formulæ. Formulæ are generated from atoms by the connectives $\neg$ and $\rightarrow$ and the quantifier $\forall v$. We can describe them in E^* in much the same way as terms, using their recursive definition. At this point it will prove helpful to introduce shorthands for the common connectives, quantifiers, and some basic formulæ. We have already seen the abbreviation $\underset{\cdot}{\mathsf{f}}$ for the term constructing the expression $\mathsf{f}e_1 \cdots e_k$ from expressions $e_1, \ldots, e_k$, where k

is the arity of f. We now introduce similar terms for the connectives, quantifiers, and basic formulæ. The convention of writing a dot under the symbol for the induced term goes back to Feferman (1960).

$$
\begin{aligned}
x \underset{\cdot}{\to} y &:= (\underline{(}^\frown x^\frown \underline{\to}^\frown y^\frown \underline{)}), & \underset{\cdot}{\neg} x &:= \underline{\neg}^\frown x,\\
x \underset{\cdot}{\vee} y &:= (\underset{\cdot}{\neg} x) \underset{\cdot}{\to} y, & \underset{\cdot}{\forall} v x &:= \underline{\forall}^\frown v^\frown x,\\
x \underset{\cdot}{\wedge} y &:= \underset{\cdot}{\neg}(x \underset{\cdot}{\to} (\underset{\cdot}{\neg} y)), & \underset{\cdot}{\exists} v x &:= \underset{\cdot}{\neg}(\underset{\cdot}{\forall} v (\underset{\cdot}{\neg} x)),\\
x \underset{\cdot}{\leftrightarrow} y &:= (x \underset{\cdot}{\to} y) \underset{\cdot}{\wedge} (y \underset{\cdot}{\to} x), & x \underset{\cdot}{=} y &:= \underline{=}^\frown x^\frown y,\\
\underset{\cdot}{\mathsf{R}} x_1 \cdots x_k &:= \underline{\mathsf{R}}^\frown x_1{}^\frown \cdots {}^\frown x_k, & x \underset{\cdot}{\subseteq} y &:= \underset{\cdot}{\exists} \bar{\mathsf{x}}(\underset{\cdot}{\exists} \bar{\mathsf{y}}(\bar{\mathsf{x}} \underset{\cdot}{\frown} (x \underset{\cdot}{\frown} \bar{\mathsf{y}}) \underset{\cdot}{=} y)).
\end{aligned}
$$

The penultimate definition introduces a term for each predicate symbol R with k being its arity. The final abbreviation, $x \underset{\cdot}{\subseteq} y$, expresses the subexpression relation between the denotations of x and y. In this term, $\bar{\mathsf{x}}$ and $\bar{\mathsf{y}}$ name the specific variables v_0 and v_1. So, for terms r and s not containing x or y, $\bar{r} \underset{\cdot}{\subseteq} \bar{s}$ denotes the formula $r \subseteq s$. We appeal to the same conventions regarding omitting brackets and binding. The expression $x \underset{\cdot}{\wedge} y \underset{\cdot}{\wedge} z$ is shorthand for $(x \underset{\cdot}{\wedge} y) \underset{\cdot}{\wedge} z$ and $x \underset{\cdot}{\wedge} y \underset{\cdot}{\to} z$ abbreviates $(x \underset{\cdot}{\wedge} y) \underset{\cdot}{\to} z$. For later considerations, it is convenient to incorporate the same notational abbreviations for bounded quantifiers:

$$
\begin{aligned}
\underset{\cdot}{\forall} v \underset{\cdot}{\subseteq} x\ y \quad &\text{abbreviates} \quad \underset{\cdot}{\forall} v((v \underset{\cdot}{\subseteq} x) \underset{\cdot}{\to} y);\\
\underset{\cdot}{\exists} v \underset{\cdot}{\subseteq} x\ y \quad &\text{abbreviates} \quad \underset{\cdot}{\neg}(\underset{\cdot}{\forall} v \underset{\cdot}{\subseteq} x\ \underset{\cdot}{\neg} y).
\end{aligned}
$$

As with terms, we introduce abbreviations to express quantification over formulæ. In keeping with the use of lowercase Greek figures for formulæ, these symbols are used as bound variables that are relativized to the formula Form. However, to reduce potentially problematic naming clashes (such as in $\forall\varphi\ \varphi(\varphi)$), we favour use of the symbols α, β, and γ for 'formula' variables and reserve our usual labels φ, ψ, and so on, for actual formulæ. Thus, in analogy with term quantification, $\forall\alpha\ \varphi(\alpha)$ abbreviates $\forall \mathsf{v}_i(\mathsf{Form}(\mathsf{v}_i) \to \varphi(\mathsf{v}_i))$ for some appropriate v_i.

10.44 DEFINITION Let $\mathcal{R}$ be the finite set of relation symbols of $\mathcal{L}^*_\square$, including equality. The arity of $\mathsf{R} \in \mathcal{R}$ is denoted a_{R}. Define

$$
\begin{aligned}
\mathsf{Atom}(x) &:= \bigvee_{\mathsf{R} \in \mathcal{R}} \exists t_1 \subseteq x \cdots \exists t_{a_{\mathsf{R}}} \subseteq x\ \ x = \underset{\cdot}{\mathsf{R}} t_1 \cdots t_{a_{\mathsf{R}}},\\
\psi_{\mathsf{Form}}(x,y) &:= \mathsf{Atom}(x) \vee \\
&\qquad \exists w_1 \in y\, \exists w_2 \in y \big(x = \underset{\cdot}{\neg} w_1 \vee x = w_1 \underset{\cdot}{\to} w_2 \vee \exists v \subseteq x (\mathsf{Var}(v) \wedge x = \underset{\cdot}{\forall} v\, w_1)\big),\\
\mathsf{Form}(x) &:= \exists y (\mathsf{List}(y) \wedge x \in y \wedge \forall w \in y\ \psi_{\mathsf{Form}}(w,y)).
\end{aligned}
$$

The formula Atom expresses the atomic formulæ of $\mathcal{L}^*$. Formulæ of $\mathcal{L}^*$ are expressed using the same template as for terms, via the existence of a list of all subformulæ. As with terms, we can restrict attention to specific classes of formulæ. For instance, replacing Atom in definition 10.44 by

$$\mathsf{Atom}_{\mathrm{syn}}(x) := \exists t \subseteq x\ \exists s \subseteq x \big(\mathsf{Term}_{\mathrm{syn}}(t \,\dot{\frown}\, s) \wedge (x = \mathsf{sym}\,\dot{t} \vee x = t \dot{=} s)\big),$$

we arrive at a formula $\mathsf{Form}_{\mathrm{syn}}$ expressing that x is a formula of $\mathcal{L}^*_{\mathrm{syn}}$. Altering instead the final disjunct of ψ_{Form}, we obtain a formula $\mathsf{Form}_{\Delta_0}(\mathsf{x})$ expressing the property of being a bounded formula of $\mathcal{L}^*$.

10.45 PROPOSITION *The following are derivable in* E^*.

(i) $\mathsf{Form}(x) \leftrightarrow \mathsf{Atom}(x) \vee \exists\alpha\exists\beta\Big(x = \dot{\neg}\alpha \vee x = \alpha \dot{\rightarrow} \beta \vee \exists z\big(\mathsf{Var}(z) \wedge x = \dot{\forall} z\,\alpha\big)\Big)$,

(ii) $\forall\alpha\forall\beta\Big(\mathsf{Form}(\alpha \dot{\wedge} \beta) \wedge \mathsf{Form}(\alpha \dot{\vee} \beta) \wedge \forall v\big(\mathsf{Var}(v) \rightarrow \mathsf{Form}(\dot{\exists} v\,\alpha)\big)\Big)$,

(iii) $\forall\alpha\,\neg\mathsf{Term}(\alpha) \wedge \forall t\,\neg\mathsf{Form}(t)$,

(iv) $\forall\alpha\forall y\big(\mathsf{Form}(\alpha \frown y) \vee \mathsf{Form}(y \frown \alpha) \rightarrow y = \underline{0}\big)$,

(v) $\forall\alpha\forall\beta\forall\gamma\big(\alpha \subseteq \beta \frown \gamma \rightarrow \alpha \subseteq \beta \vee \alpha \subseteq \gamma\big)$.

10.46 PROPOSITION Form *is* Δ.

PROOF As Term is Δ, so are Atom and ψ_{Form}. Therefore, Form is Σ. Let Form^* be the Π-formula analogous to Term^* from theorem 10.36:

$$\mathsf{Form}^*(\mathsf{x}) := \forall z\Big(\mathsf{List}(z) \wedge \forall w \subseteq \mathsf{x}\big(\psi_{\mathsf{Form}}(w, z) \rightarrow w \in z\big) \rightarrow \mathsf{x} \in z\Big).$$

A similar argument shows the equivalence of Form and Form^* over $\mathsf{E}^*_{\mathrm{min}}$. ⊣

10.47 PROPOSITION Form *strongly pointwise expresses the set of* $\mathcal{L}^*$*-formulas.*

An important concept concerning formulæ is the notion of free and bound occurrences of variables. The bound variables of a formula are simply the variables that occur adjacent to quantifiers. The following formula expresses that v is a bound variable in α:

$$\mathsf{BV}(\alpha, v) := \mathsf{Var}(v) \wedge \underline{\forall} \frown v \subseteq \alpha.$$

To talk about free variables we need the notion of a variable occurrence. The formula $\varphi := \mathsf{sym}\,\mathsf{q}\mathsf{v}_0 \rightarrow \forall \mathsf{v}_0\ \mathsf{v}_0 \frown \mathsf{v}_1 = \mathsf{q}\mathsf{v}_0$ has four occurrences of v_0. Of interest are the leftmost and two rightmost instances of v_0, where the variable occurs as a term in an atomic subformula of φ. We can identify the occurrences of v_0 in φ by considering the formulæ in which a single instance of v_0 is emphasized by renaming it. In our example, the three occurrences of v_0 can be identified with the single occurrence of v_2 in each of three formulæ:

$$\begin{aligned}\varphi_0 &\equiv \mathsf{sym}\,\mathsf{q}\mathsf{v}_2 \to \forall \mathsf{v}_0\ \mathsf{v}_0{}^\frown\mathsf{v}_1 = \mathsf{q}\mathsf{v}_0,\\ \varphi_1 &\equiv \mathsf{sym}\,\mathsf{q}\mathsf{v}_0 \to \forall \mathsf{v}_0\ \mathsf{v}_2{}^\frown\mathsf{v}_1 = \mathsf{q}\mathsf{v}_0,\\ \varphi_2 &\equiv \mathsf{sym}\,\mathsf{q}\mathsf{v}_0 \to \forall \mathsf{v}_0\ \mathsf{v}_0{}^\frown\mathsf{v}_1 = \mathsf{q}\mathsf{v}_2.\end{aligned}$$

In φ_1 and φ_2 the unique occurrence of v_2 is under the scope of the quantifier $\forall\mathsf{v}_0$. These two formulæ therefore identify bound occurrences of v_0 in φ. As the v_2 in φ_0 is *not* in the scope of such a quantifier, it corresponds to a free occurrence of v_0 and witnesses that v_0 is a free variable of φ. The same technique can be used to mark occurrences of terms. The following formulæ use the variable v_2 to isolate the two occurrences of the term $\mathsf{q}\mathsf{v}_0$ in φ:

$$\begin{aligned}\varphi'_0 &\equiv \mathsf{sym}\,\mathsf{v}_2 \to \forall \mathsf{v}_0\ \mathsf{v}_0{}^\frown\mathsf{v}_1 = \mathsf{q}\mathsf{v}_0,\\ \varphi'_1 &\equiv \mathsf{sym}\,\mathsf{q}\mathsf{v}_0 \to \forall \mathsf{v}_0\ \mathsf{v}_0{}^\frown\mathsf{v}_1 = \mathsf{v}_2.\end{aligned}$$

10.48 DEFINITION Let φ be a formula and t a term. An occurrence of t in φ is a pair (ψ, v_i) of a formula and a variable such that

(i) v_i is not a subexpression of φ,

(ii) v_i occurs exactly once in ψ and is not a bound variable of ψ,

(iii) φ is the result of replacing v_i with t in ψ, that is, $\varphi \equiv \mathsf{sub}^{\mathbb{E}^*}(\psi, \mathsf{v}_i, t)$.

A triple (ψ, v_i, t) such that (ψ, v_i) is an occurrence of t in φ is called a term occurrence or, simply, an occurrence in φ.

The next formula pointwise expresses the quaternary relation that (α, v, r) is an occurrence (of r) in β:

$$\begin{aligned}\mathsf{Occ}(\alpha, v, r, \beta) := \ &\mathsf{Form}(\alpha) \wedge \mathsf{Var}(v) \wedge \mathsf{Term}(r) \wedge \mathsf{Form}(\beta) \wedge\\ &\wedge v \not\subset \beta \wedge \neg\mathsf{BV}(\alpha, v) \wedge\\ &\wedge \exists x \exists y(\alpha = x^\frown v^\frown y \wedge v \not\subset x \wedge v \not\subset y) \wedge\\ &\wedge \beta = \mathsf{sub}(\alpha, v, r).\end{aligned}$$

An occurrence (ψ, v_j) of a variable v_i in φ is bound if the single occurrence of v_j in ψ is in the scope of a quantifier $\forall \mathsf{v}_i$. More generally, we say of a term occurrence (ψ, v_j, t) that it is *bound* if the variable v_j occurs under the scope of a quantifier $\forall \mathsf{v}_i$ for some variable $\mathsf{v}_i \subseteq t$. An occurrence which is not bound is called *free*. The formula $\mathsf{FOcc}(\alpha, v, r)$ expresses that the occurrence (α, v, r) is free:

$$\mathsf{FOcc}(\alpha, v, r) \ := \ \forall w \forall y \big(\mathsf{Var}(w) \wedge \underset{.}{\forall} w y \subseteq \alpha \wedge v \subseteq y \rightarrow w \not\subseteq r\big).$$

With the notion of a free occurrence, we can express the free variables of a formula as the variables which have at least one free occurrence:

$$\mathsf{FV}(v, \alpha) \ := \ \exists \beta \exists w \big(\mathsf{Occ}(\beta, w, v, \alpha) \wedge \mathsf{FOcc}(\beta, w, v)\big).$$

Finally, a sentence is a formula without free variables:

$$\mathsf{Sent}(x) \ := \ \mathsf{Form}(x) \wedge \forall v \subseteq x \big(\mathsf{Var}(v) \rightarrow \neg \mathsf{FV}(v, x)\big).$$

From these definitions we may deduce that

10.49 PROPOSITION E^* *proves the following.*

(i) $\forall \alpha \Big(\mathsf{Atom}(\alpha) \rightarrow \forall v \big(\mathsf{FV}(v, \alpha) \leftrightarrow v \subseteq \alpha\big)\Big)$,

(ii) $\forall v \forall \alpha \forall \beta \big(\mathsf{FV}(v, \alpha \underset{.}{\rightarrow} \beta) \leftrightarrow \mathsf{FV}(v, \alpha) \vee \mathsf{FV}(v, \beta)\big)$,

(iii) $\forall v \forall \alpha \big(\mathsf{FV}(v, \underset{.}{\neg} \alpha) \leftrightarrow \mathsf{FV}(v, \alpha)\big)$,

(iv) $\forall v \forall w \forall \alpha \big(\mathsf{FV}(v, \underset{.}{\forall} w \alpha) \leftrightarrow v \neq w \wedge \mathsf{FV}(v, \alpha)\big)$,

(v) $\forall \alpha \big(\mathsf{Sent}(\alpha) \leftrightarrow \mathsf{Sent}(\underset{.}{\neg} \alpha)\big)$,

(vi) $\forall \alpha \forall \beta \big(\mathsf{Sent}(\alpha) \wedge \mathsf{Sent}(\beta) \leftrightarrow \mathsf{Sent}(\alpha \underset{.}{\rightarrow} \beta)\big)$,

(vii) $\forall \alpha \forall v \Big(\mathsf{Sent}(\underset{.}{\forall} w \alpha) \leftrightarrow \mathsf{Form}(\alpha) \wedge \forall w \big(\mathsf{FV}(w, \alpha) \rightarrow w = v\big)\Big)$,

(viii) $\forall \alpha \forall v \big(\neg \mathsf{BV}(v, \alpha) \rightarrow \forall s\, \mathsf{Form}(\mathsf{sub}(\alpha, v, s))\big)$.

The first four claims of the proposition express the inductive definition of free variables. Items (v), (vi), and (vii) specialize to the case of sentences. The final claim states that formulæ are closed under replacing variables which are not bound by terms. The restriction to unbound variables ensures that the substitution does not alter quantifiers: for instance, $\mathsf{sub}(\forall \mathsf{v}_0 = \mathsf{v}_0 \mathsf{v}_0, \mathsf{v}_0, \sqsupseteq) \equiv \forall \sqsupseteq = \sqsupseteq \sqsupseteq$, which is not a formula.

PROOF We sketch the proof of (ii) as an example. Suppose v is a free variable of $\varphi \to \psi$, and let (χ, w, v) be a free occurrence of v in this formula. The formula χ necessarily has the form of an implication, say $\varphi_0 \to \psi_0$, and because w occurs precisely once in χ either (φ_0, w, v) is a free occurrence of v in φ (and $\psi_0 \equiv \psi$) or (ψ_0, w, v) is a free occurrence of v in ψ (and $\varphi_0 \equiv \varphi$). So v is free in either φ or ψ. The converse direction uses a similar argument, as do (i), (iii), and (iv). Items (v), (vi) and (vii) are direct applications of the earlier parts; (viii) is proved by induction on α. ⊣

It is clear that FV is a Σ-formula. As a result, Sent is Π. It is reasonable to expect that Sent is Δ. We leave this simple task to the reader.

10.50 THEOREM *The sentences of $\mathcal{L}^*$ are strongly pointwise expressed by the Δ-formula* Sent(x).

Before we move, on it is perhaps worth remarking that there are other, equivalent, ways to express the free variables of a formula. For example, one can define the free and bound variables of a formula in parallel with the inductive construction of formulæ (cf. the formula φ_{FV} on page 305). While this method is sufficient for specifying the free variables of a formula, it does not immediately assist in defining the ternary relation 'v is free for t in φ'. A more involved construction can be imagined that encodes also the 'free for' relation, but this takes us even further from the simple definition we are trying to emulate, namely that a sentence is merely a formula with no free variable occurrences. A second approach is to formalize the statement 'All occurrences of v in φ are within the scope of quantifiers $\forall v$', which is equivalent to v not being free in φ. This can be expressed as finding a sequence $(\varphi_i)_{i \le n}$ of formulæ such that $\varphi_0 \equiv \varphi$, φ_n does not contain $\forall v$, and $\varphi_{i+1} \equiv \mathsf{sub}^{\mathbb{E}^*}(\varphi_i, \forall v\, \psi, p)$ for all $i \le n$, where $\forall v\, \psi$ is a subformula of φ_i and p is some fixed atomic formula not containing any variables. Then v is free in φ if and only if v occurs in φ_n. A definition of this kind will be Δ because the final formula in the sequence, φ_n, is uniquely determined up to the choice of p.

The reason for taking such care over free and bound variables is that substitution of terms for variables in formulæ is a complex operation. Given a formula $\varphi(v)$ and a term t, the result of the 'substitution' $\varphi(t)$ presupposes that v is *free for t in φ*, which is to say that for every free occurrence (ψ, v_i, v) of v in φ it is the case that (ψ, v_i, t) is also free. If v is not free for t in φ, then by writing $\varphi(t)$ we actually mean $\psi(t)$ for a formula $\psi(v)$ obtained from $\varphi(v)$ by renaming certain bound variables in such a way that v is free for t in $\psi(v)$. In our formalization of substitution, these two steps are separated. The statement that v is free for t in φ is expressed by the formula $\mathsf{FreeFor}(v,t,\varphi)$:

$$\mathsf{FreeFor}(v,t,\varphi) \;:=\; \forall\psi\forall w\big(\mathsf{Occ}(\psi,w,v,\varphi) \wedge \mathsf{FOcc}(\psi,w,v) \rightarrow \mathsf{FOcc}(\psi,w,t)\big).$$

The operational part of substitution, describing the result $\varphi(t)$, is expressed as $\mathsf{sub}(\chi,w,t)$ for a variable w and a formula χ which is identical to φ except that all free occurrences of v have been replaced by w. We express this 'construction' by a four-place formula $\mathsf{Sub}(\alpha,r,v,\beta)$ which holds if – assuming α is a formula, r is a term, and v is a variable – β is the result of replacing all free occurrences of v in α by r:

$$\begin{aligned}\mathsf{Sub}(\alpha,r,v,\beta) \;:=\; \exists w\exists y\big(&\mathsf{Var}(w) \wedge w\notin\alpha \wedge \neg\mathsf{FV}(v,y) \wedge \neg\mathsf{BV}(w,y) \wedge \\ &\wedge \forall y_0\subseteq y(\dot{\forall} v\, y_0\subseteq y \rightarrow w\not\subset y_0) \wedge \\ &\wedge \alpha=\mathsf{sub}(y,w,v) \wedge \beta=\mathsf{sub}(y,w,r)\big).\end{aligned}$$

The first and third line of the formula above enforce that the existential quantifiers $\exists w\exists y$ correspond, respectively, to a fresh variable and a copy of α in which (at least) all free occurrences of v have been replaced by w. The second line expresses that no bound occurrence of v has been replaced. Witnesses to the existential quantifier $\exists y$ are uniquely determined up to the choice of variable symbol expressed by w. If v does not occur free in α, then $\alpha=y=\beta$. Otherwise, y expresses the result of replacing every free occurrence of v in α by w. In particular, the final argument of the formula, namely β, is independent of the choices for w and y and uniquely determined by the other arguments.

10.51 PROPOSITION *The formula* Sub *pointwise expresses the function which, given a formula* φ*, variable* v*, and term* t*, returns the result of replacing every free occurrence of* v *by* t *in* φ*. In particular, the following two formulæ are provable in* E^**:*

$$\forall\alpha\forall v\forall t\big(\mathsf{Var}(v) \rightarrow \exists\beta\,\mathsf{Sub}(\alpha,t,v,\beta)\big),$$
$$\forall y\forall z\big(\mathsf{Sub}(\alpha,t,v,y) \wedge \mathsf{Sub}(\alpha,t,v,z) \rightarrow y=z\big).$$

The proposition only claims that $\mathsf{Sub}(\mathsf{x},\mathsf{y},\mathsf{z},\mathsf{w})$ represents the operation of term instantiation for terms that are known to be free for the variable being replaced. That is, we have $\mathsf{E}^* \vdash \mathsf{Sub}(\overline{\varphi(v)},\overline{v},\overline{s},\overline{\varphi(s)})$ if s is free for v in $\varphi(v)$. It is possible to capture the more general use of term substitution by incorporating into the formula renaming bound variables to ensure that the freeness condition is met. Unless we assume some canonical method for renaming bound variables, however, this notion of substitution is not uniquely determined.

A corollary of the previous proposition is that we can assume that our formal language contains a ternary function symbol s such that

$$\mathsf{E}^* \vdash \forall\alpha\forall v\forall t\big(\mathsf{Var}(v) \to \mathsf{Sub}(\alpha, t, v, \mathsf{s}(\alpha, v, t))\big).$$

To improve readability we introduce the shorthand $\alpha[t/v]$ for $\mathsf{s}(\alpha, v, t)$. We emphasize that although defined for all α, v, and t, the 'function' $\cdot[\cdot/\cdot]$ only expresses the operation of substitution in the case where t is free for v in α.

It is occasionally useful to consider simultaneous substitutions, corresponding to obtaining $\varphi(s,t)$ from $\varphi(x,y)$, s, and t. Such operations are readily expressed by generalizing the formula Sub. We therefore assume, for each $k \geq 0$, a $(2k+3)$-ary function symbol, written $\alpha[t_0/v_0, \ldots, t_k/v_k]$, expressing in $\mathsf{E}^*_{\mathrm{min}}$ the result of simultaneously substituting in α the terms $t_0, \ldots, t_k$ for variables $v_0, \ldots, v_k$, respectively, subject to the restriction that each t_i is free for v_i in α and $v_i \neq v_j$ if $i \neq j$. In the case where t_i is a closed term for each $i \leq k$, the simultaneous substitution $\alpha[t_0/v_0, \ldots, t_k/v_k]$ can be identified with iterated substitution $\alpha[t_0/v_0]\cdots[t_k/v_k]$. However, in the general case, t_i may denote a term containing a variable v_j where $i < j$, whereby the two terms express different results. We introduce $\alpha[t_0, \ldots, t_k]$ as shorthand for $\alpha[t_0/\overline{\mathsf{v}_0}, \ldots, t_k/\overline{\mathsf{v}_k}]$.

Before concluding the section on formal syntax, we present formal counterparts to two further operations on formulæ. Both operations are about constructing sentences from formulæ with free variables. The first is the universal closure of a formula. Recall, a universal closure of φ is any result of prefixing universal quantifiers for all free variables of φ. This definition does not uniquely determine a sentence as the universal quantifiers can be introduced in different orders. Lack of uniqueness has not caused any difficulties thus far because the universal closures of formulæ are logically equivalent. However, it will be convenient to fix some canonical choice for the universal closure of a formula so that in formal statements we can talk about 'the' universal closure as though it were uniquely determined. With this in mind, we define 'the' universal closure of a formula φ to be the sentence $\forall \mathsf{v}_{i_1}\forall \mathsf{v}_{i_2}\cdots\forall \mathsf{v}_{i_k}\varphi$ such that $\mathsf{v}_{i_1}, \ldots, \mathsf{v}_{i_k}$ are precisely the free variables of φ and $i_1 < i_2 < \cdots < i_k$. Given the considerations of this section, it should be clear that the property of being the universal closure of a formula is strongly pointwise expressed in $\mathsf{E}^*_{\min}$ by a Δ-formula. In the following, we assume a function symbol ucl for expressing the universal closure. For convenience, we assume that the function is defined on all inputs, though how it is defined on expressions that are not formulæ is unimportant.

The second method of obtaining a sentence from a formula is through substituting closed terms for all free variables. We let $\mathsf{Ins}(x,y)$ be a Δ-formula of $\mathcal{L}^*$ expressing that y is a formula, x is a sentence, and x can be obtained from y by instantiating the free variables of y with arbitrary closed terms. An instantiation of a formula φ requires that all free occurrences of a given variable v_i in φ are replaced by the same closed term. For instance, $\exists z\ \underline{0}^\frown z = \underline{\forall}$ is an instantiation of $\exists z\ x^\frown z = y$ but not an instantiation of $\exists z\ x^\frown z = x$.

10.4 Formal Provability

We now have the ingredients to express provability within E^*. Recall that $\Gamma \vdash \varphi$ means that φ is logically derivable from Γ, where $\Gamma \cup \{\varphi\}$ is assumed to be a set of sentences. At a minimum, we desire pointwise expressibility of provability, which means a formula $\mathsf{Bew}_\Gamma(\mathsf{x})$ associated to the theory or set of axioms Γ such that

$$\mathsf{E}^*_{\min} \vdash \mathsf{Bew}_\Gamma(\overline{\varphi}) \text{ if and only if } \Gamma \vdash \varphi.$$

Of particular interest is when Γ is the minimal theory $\mathsf{E}^*_{\min}$ or some extension of it. Mirroring the proof of Gödel's first incompleteness theorem in chapter 6, pointwise expressibility of provability for $\mathsf{E}^*_{\min}$ is sufficient to establish that $\mathsf{E}^*_{\min}$ is incomplete. The second incompleteness theorem – which entails the stronger conclusion that $\neg\mathsf{Bew}_{\mathsf{E}^*_{\min}}(\overline{\bot})$ is not derivable in $\mathsf{E}^*_{\min}$ – depends on the provability predicate satisfying different properties than pointwise expressibility: we require analogues of the axioms K and 4, and rule NEC, from section 6.1.

So far, we have not specified any particular calculus for logical derivability. The reader may have had in mind a system of natural deduction, an axiomatic calculus, a sequent calculus, or some other sound and complete system for first-order predicate logic. The choice was not important because each calculus induces the same notion of logical derivability for sentences.[5] But if we want to present a formula that expresses logical derivability, then it is necessary to specify a calculus

[5] Different calculi may define different notions of derivability for formulæ. Axiomatic calculi on formulæ often admit the inference $\{\varphi\} \vdash \forall x \varphi$ which is not present in most presentations of natural deduction.

and the accompanying notion of a derivation. It should be noted that the choice is primarily one of convenience. Our construction of provability predicates can be applied to other calculi for predicate logic and the equivalence of the resulting provability predicates will be provable in $\mathsf{E}^*_{\min}$. That is not to suggest that all provability predicates for a given theory are provably equivalent. An example to the contrary is given in theorem 10.65, and others are discussed in chapter 12. We merely mean that the 'canonical' provability predicate for the theory E^* obtained by following the construction laid out below is largely independent of the choice of logical calculus.

We will assume an axiomatic calculus for classical predicate logic. Known also as *Hilbert* (or *Frege*) *systems*, axiomatic calculi comprise a collection of *logical axioms* and *rules of inference*. Typically, in an axiomatic calculus the number of rules is low compared with the number of axioms.[6] These calculi are desirable for expressing provability because they are easy to state, and thus easy to express in a formal syntax theory.

The *logical axioms* of predicate logic, PL, are given by the following six axiom schemas and one axiom.[7] As usual, φ, ψ, and χ range over formulæ of $\mathcal{L}^*$, t over terms of $\mathcal{L}^*$, and i over natural numbers.

PL1 $\varphi \to (\psi \to \varphi)$,

PL2 $(\varphi \to (\psi \to \chi)) \to ((\varphi \to \psi) \to (\varphi \to \chi))$,

PL3 $(\neg\varphi \to \neg\psi) \to (\psi \to \varphi)$,

PL4 $\forall \mathsf{v}_i\, \varphi(\mathsf{v}_i) \to \varphi(t)$, if v_i is free for t in φ,

PL5 $\forall \mathsf{v}_i (\psi \to \varphi) \to (\psi \to \forall \mathsf{v}_i\, \varphi)$, if v_i is not free in ψ,

PL6 $\forall \mathsf{x}\; \mathsf{x}{=}\mathsf{x}$,

PL7 $\forall \mathsf{x} \forall \mathsf{y} (\mathsf{x}{=}\mathsf{y} \to (\varphi(\mathsf{x}) \to \varphi(\mathsf{y})))$, if x is free for y in φ.

In addition to the logical axioms there are two rules of inference. Combined with the logical axioms, these determine our relation of logical derivability. The rules will be presented shortly. First, we examine how the logical axioms, as well as other sets of axioms, can be expressed in the language $\mathcal{L}^*$.

[6] In contrast to, say, calculi of natural deduction, which usually favour few (if any) axioms and introduction and elimination rules for each connective and quantifier.

[7] We follow the presentation of Hamilton (1988); Troelstra and Schwichtenberg (2000) present a similar Hilbert system for predicate logic and prove the equivalence of various Hilbert systems and natural deduction and sequent calculi for classical and other logics.

With the exception of PL6, all the logical axioms are axiom schemas: PL1–PL3 describe an axiom for every choice of formulæ φ, ψ, and χ; PL4 is an axiom for every formula φ, term t, and i for which v_i is free for t in φ; PL5 for every φ and ψ in which v_i does not occur free; and PL7 for every choice of φ in which x is free for y. Setting aside the restrictions in PL4, PL5, and PL7, the logical axioms are expressed by instantiations of the following seven terms, where variables α, β, and γ are intended to range over formulæ, v over variables, and s over terms:

$$\begin{aligned}
\mathsf{la}_1(\alpha,\beta) &:= \alpha \underset{\cdot}{\to} (\beta \underset{\cdot}{\to} \alpha),\\
\mathsf{la}_2(\alpha,\beta,\gamma) &:= \big(\alpha \underset{\cdot}{\to} (\beta \underset{\cdot}{\to} \gamma)\big) \underset{\cdot}{\to} \big((\alpha \underset{\cdot}{\to} \beta) \underset{\cdot}{\to} (\alpha \underset{\cdot}{\to} \gamma)\big),\\
\mathsf{la}_3(\alpha,\beta) &:= (\underset{\cdot}{\neg}\alpha \underset{\cdot}{\to} \underset{\cdot}{\neg}\beta) \underset{\cdot}{\to} (\beta \underset{\cdot}{\to} \alpha),\\
\mathsf{la}_4(\alpha,v,s) &:= \underset{\cdot}{\forall} v\,\alpha \underset{\cdot}{\to} x[s/v],\\
\mathsf{la}_5(\alpha,\beta,v) &:= \underset{\cdot}{\forall} v(\beta \underset{\cdot}{\to} \alpha) \underset{\cdot}{\to} (\beta \underset{\cdot}{\to} \underset{\cdot}{\forall} v\,\alpha),\\
\mathsf{la}_6 &:= \overline{\forall \mathsf{x}\;\mathsf{x}=\mathsf{x}},\\
\mathsf{la}_7(\alpha) &:= \underset{\cdot}{\forall}\bar{\mathsf{x}}\,\underset{\cdot}{\forall}\bar{\mathsf{y}}\big(\bar{\mathsf{x}} \underset{\cdot}{=} \bar{\mathsf{y}} \underset{\cdot}{\to} (\alpha \underset{\cdot}{\to} \alpha[\bar{\mathsf{y}}/\bar{\mathsf{x}}])\big).
\end{aligned}$$

Strictly speaking, la_4 and la_7 are only terms if the ternary substitution operation $x[y/z]$ introduced in proposition 10.51 is expressed by a term of $\mathcal{L}^*$. If the language does not contain a term corresponding to this operation, then uses of the terms la_4 and la_7 in what follows are to be treated as abbreviations for the corresponding Δ-formula. Theorem 10.34 confirms that it is safe to assume that $\mathcal{L}^*$ contains a function symbol for free substitution and that this function symbol can be utilized in the construction of other Σ- and Δ-formulæ. In the following, we assume that the ternary function symbol is available in $\mathcal{L}^*$.

Building on the terms la_1 to la_7, we introduce a formula expressing the logical axioms.

10.52 DEFINITION $\mathsf{LogAx}(\mathsf{x})$ is the formula

$$\begin{aligned}
&\exists\alpha\exists\beta\exists\gamma\big(\mathsf{x}=\mathsf{la}_1(\alpha,\beta) \vee \mathsf{x}=\mathsf{la}_2(\alpha,\beta,\gamma) \vee \mathsf{x}=\mathsf{la}_3(\alpha,\beta)\big) \vee\\
&\qquad \exists\alpha\exists v\exists s\big(\mathsf{Var}(v) \wedge \mathsf{FreeFor}(v,s,\alpha) \wedge \mathsf{x}=\mathsf{la}_4(\alpha,v,s)\big) \vee\\
&\qquad \exists\alpha\exists\beta\exists v\big(\mathsf{Var}(v) \wedge \neg\mathsf{FV}(\beta,v) \wedge \mathsf{x}=\mathsf{la}_5(\alpha,\beta,v)\big) \vee\\
&\qquad \mathsf{x}=\mathsf{la}_6 \vee \exists\alpha\big(\mathsf{FreeFor}(\bar{\mathsf{x}},\bar{\mathsf{y}},\alpha) \wedge \mathsf{x}=\mathsf{la}_7(\alpha)\big).
\end{aligned}$$

The six existential quantifiers explicitly presented in LogAx can all be replaced by bounded quantifiers as they refer only to subexpressions of the argument x. However, the formulæ $\mathsf{FreeFor}$ and FV both feature unbounded quantifiers, as will the subformulæ $\mathsf{x} = \mathsf{la}_4(\alpha, \nu, s)$ and $\mathsf{x} = \mathsf{la}_7(\alpha)$ if there is no term expressing substitution. As these are all Δ-formulæ, we obtain the following characterization:

10.53 PROPOSITION *The formula* LogAx *is* Δ *and strongly pointwise expresses the set of logical axioms in* $\mathsf{E}^*_{\min}$.

By the same method we give a formula expressing the axioms of the theory $\mathsf{E}^*_{\min}$. The basic axioms can simply be enumerated as they are not schema. Instances of induction are expressed by a single term subject to the mentioned caveat on variable occurrences:

10.54 DEFINITION $\mathsf{ax}_{\mathrm{ind}}(x) := \dot{\forall}\overline{\mathsf{x}}(\dot{\forall}\overline{\mathsf{y}}\dot{\subset}\overline{\mathsf{x}}\, x[\overline{\mathsf{y}}/\overline{\mathsf{x}}] \dot{\to} x) \dot{\to} \dot{\forall}\overline{\mathsf{x}} x.$

10.55 PROPOSITION *If* y *is free for* x *in* $\varphi(\mathsf{x})$, *then*

$$\mathsf{E}^*_{\min} \vdash \mathsf{ax}_{\mathrm{ind}}(\overline{\varphi}) = \overline{\forall \mathsf{x}(\forall \mathsf{y} \subset \mathsf{x}\, \varphi(\mathsf{y}) \to \varphi(\mathsf{x})) \to \forall \mathsf{x}\, \varphi(\mathsf{x})}.$$

The induction axiom of $\mathsf{E}^*_{\min}$ consists of the universal closures of each instance of the induction schema.

10.56 DEFINITION Let $\mathcal{A}^*$ be the finite set of basic axioms of $\mathsf{E}^*_{\min}$. The formulæ $\mathsf{Axiom}_{\mathrm{ind}}$ and $\mathsf{Axiom}_{\mathsf{E}^*_{\min}}$ are given as follows:

$$\mathsf{Axiom}_{\mathrm{ind}}(\mathsf{x}) := \exists \alpha \subset \mathsf{x}\big(\mathsf{FreeFor}(\overline{\mathsf{y}}, \overline{\mathsf{x}}, \alpha) \wedge \neg \mathsf{FV}(\overline{\mathsf{y}}, \alpha) \wedge \mathsf{x} = \mathsf{ucl}(\mathsf{ax}_{\mathrm{ind}}(\alpha))\big),$$
$$\mathsf{Axiom}_{\mathsf{E}^*_{\min}}(\mathsf{x}) := \mathsf{Axiom}_{\mathrm{ind}}(\mathsf{x}) \vee \bigvee_{\varphi \in \mathcal{A}^*} \mathsf{x} = \overline{\varphi}.$$

10.57 PROPOSITION *The set of axioms of* $\mathsf{E}^*_{\min}$ *is strongly pointwise expressed in* $\mathsf{E}^*_{\min}$ *by the* Δ*-formula* $\mathsf{Axiom}_{\mathsf{E}^*_{\min}}$.

Likewise, there are Δ-formulæ $\mathsf{Axiom}_{\mathsf{E}_{\min}}$ and $\mathsf{Axiom}_{\mathsf{PA}}$ that strongly pointwise express the axioms of the theories $\mathsf{E}_{\min}$ and PA, respectively. In fact, all the specific theories we have so far considered have this property.

To the logical and nonlogical axioms we now add rules of inference. The two inference rules of predicate logic are *modus ponens*: from φ and $\varphi \to \psi$ infer ψ; and *generalization*: from φ infer $\forall \mathsf{v}_i\, \varphi$. Let Γ be a set of sentences. A derivation from Γ is a finite sequence $\varphi_0, \ldots, \varphi_n$ of formulæ such that for every $k \leq n$, one of four conditions hold:

(i) φ_k is a logical axiom,

(ii) $\varphi_k \in \Gamma$,

(iii) there exist $i, j < k$ such that $\varphi_i \equiv (\varphi_j \rightarrow \varphi_k)$, or

(iv) there exists $i < k$ and a variable x such that $\varphi_k \equiv \forall x\, \varphi_i$.

We say that φ is (logically) derivable from Γ, written $\Gamma \vdash \varphi$, if φ is a sentence and there exists a derivation $\varphi_0, \ldots, \varphi_n$ from assumptions Γ such that $\varphi \equiv \varphi_k$ for some $k \leq n$. Recall, a theory is set of sentences closed under derivability. If S is a theory with an associated set of axioms Γ, we use the term 'proof in S' in place of 'derivation from Γ', and 'theorem of S' or 'provable in S' instead of 'derivable from Γ'.

Derivations are expressed in E^* using the same template as expressing terms and formulæ. Unlike those concepts, however, the order in which formulæ occur in a derivation is important. Let $d = (\varphi_i)_{i \leq n}$ be a derivation of $\varphi_n \equiv (\bot \rightarrow \bot)$ from the empty set. We can assume this derivation does not utilize generalization (the reader can confirm the existence of such a derivation). Now consider extending d by a single formula $\varphi_{n+1} \equiv \bot$. Call this list d'. If d' were a derivation, it would witness that $\bot$ is a logical validity, which is plainly false. So d' is not a derivation. Nonetheless, d' *almost* satisfies the conditions for being a derivation: every formula φ_i in d' is either a logical axiom or the result of an application of modus ponens to formulæ in d'. This holds for $i \leq n$ because d is a derivation; for $i = n + 1$ because d' contains $(\bot \rightarrow \bot)$ and $\bot$. The reason why d' is not a derivation is that in the application of modus ponens giving rise to φ_{n+1}, the formula plays the role of both *premise* and *conclusion*, violating the requirement in clauses (iii) and (iv) that the premise(s) of every applied rule *strictly precede* the conclusion in the derivation.

Suppose $\mathsf{Axiom}_{\mathsf{E}^*}$ expresses the axioms of E^*. Proofs in E^* are expressed by the formula $\mathsf{Der}_{\mathsf{E}^*}$ below. The subformula $\mathsf{Inf}(z, w)$ states that w can be inferred from elements of z by an application of one of the two rules of inference: modus ponens or generalization. Recall that $\mathsf{Init}(z, y)$ expresses that z is a proper initial segment of the list y, so $w \in y \wedge \mathsf{Init}(z ^\frown \underline{\mathsf{e}} ^\frown w, y)$ states that w is an element of y and z is the list of elements preceding w in y.

$$\begin{aligned}
\mathsf{Der}_{\mathsf{E}^*}(y) &:= \mathsf{List}(y) \wedge \forall z \subseteq y\, \forall w \in y \big(\mathsf{Init}(z ^\frown \underline{\mathsf{e}} ^\frown w, y) \rightarrow \\
&\qquad\qquad \mathsf{LogAx}(w) \vee \mathsf{Axiom}_{\mathsf{E}^*}(w) \vee \mathsf{Inf}(z, w)\big), \\
\mathsf{Inf}(z, w) &:= \exists x \in z \big(x \,\dot{\rightarrow}\, w \in z \vee \exists v (\mathsf{Var}(v) \wedge w = \dot{\forall} v\, x)\big).
\end{aligned}$$

Provability in E^* is expressed as the existence of a derivation containing the sentence in question:

$$\mathsf{Bew}_{\mathsf{E}^*}(\mathsf{x}) := \mathsf{Sent}(\mathsf{x}) \wedge \exists y\big(\mathsf{Der}_{\mathsf{E}^*}(y) \wedge \mathsf{x} \in y\big).$$

We refer to $\mathsf{Bew}_{\mathsf{E}^*}$ as the provability predicate for E^* associated to the axiomatization $\mathsf{Axiom}_{\mathsf{E}^*}$. Provability predicates depend not only on the logical calculus and the chosen axiomatization of the theory, but also on the specific formula that expresses the axioms of the theory. Often we only specify the set of axioms of E^* and leave the choice of $\mathsf{Axiom}_{\mathsf{E}^*}$ to be inferred. In these cases, we have in mind the formula defined in analogy to $\mathsf{Axiom}_{\mathsf{E}^*_{\mathrm{min}}}$: finite collections of axioms are enumerated in the style of the basic axioms, and axiom schemas are expressed via instantiation of 'templates'. If the desired axiomatization can be inferred from context, we omit mention of it altogether and talk of *the* provability predicate for E^*.

We leave the proof of the next proposition to the reader.

10.58 PROPOSITION *Suppose the axioms of* E^* *are strongly pointwise expressed by* $\mathsf{Axiom}_{\mathsf{E}^*}(\mathsf{x})$ *in* $\mathsf{E}^*_{\mathrm{min}}$. *Then the derivations from* E^* *are strongly pointwise expressed by the formula* $\mathsf{Der}_{\mathsf{E}^*}(\mathsf{x})$ *and provability from* E^* *is pointwise expressed by* $\mathsf{Bew}_{\mathsf{E}^*}(\mathsf{x})$. *In particular, if* $\mathsf{Axiom}_{\mathsf{E}^*}$ *is* Δ, *then* $\mathsf{Bew}_{\mathsf{E}^*}$ *is* Σ *and for every sentence* φ,

$$\mathsf{E}^* \vdash \varphi \textit{ if and only if } \mathsf{E}^*_{\mathrm{min}} \vdash \mathsf{Bew}_{\mathsf{E}^*}(\overline{\varphi}).$$

There are many other theories whose set of axioms and of derivations are strongly pointwise expressed in $\mathsf{E}^*_{\mathrm{min}}$. The reader can verify, for instance, that the specific extensions of $\mathsf{E}^*_{\mathrm{min}}$ encountered in the preceding chapters all fall under the scope of proposition 10.58.[8] This observation is significant, as many of the central results on provability predicates apply to theories whose set of theorems is expressed by a Σ-formula.

10.59 DEFINITION An axiomatization of a theory E^* is *simple* if the set of axioms is pointwise expressed by a Δ-formula. A simple theory is one that admits a simple axiomatization.

[8] By 'specific extension' we mean an extension of the minimal theory $\mathsf{E}^*_{\mathrm{min}}$ by an explicitly denumerated collection of axioms, such as by the denotation axioms DP1–DP3 or by axioms for specific function symbols, in contrast to an arbitrary extension E^*, whose set of axioms may not, in general, be pointwise expressed in $\mathsf{E}^*_{\mathrm{min}}$.

Sometimes we talk of the provability predicate for a simple theory E^* without explicitly specifying an axiomatization. In those cases we mean the provability predicate associated to some simple axiomatization of the theory.

Proposition 10.58 is all that we require to conclude the first incompleteness theorem for $\mathsf{E}^*_{\min}$. The argument replicates the proof of theorem 6.6, using the provability predicate in place of $\Box$. The diagonal lemma provides a sentence γ such that $\mathsf{E}^*_{\min} \vdash \gamma \leftrightarrow \neg\mathsf{Bew}_{\mathsf{E}^*_{\min}}(\overline{\gamma})$. The pointwise expressibility of provability and the consistency of $\mathsf{E}^*_{\min}$ imply that $\mathsf{E}^*_{\min} \nvdash \gamma$ and $\mathsf{E}^*_{\min} \nvdash \neg\gamma$.

To apply the same argument to a simple extension E^* of the minimal theory, we require that the set of theorems of E^* be pointwise expressed in E^*:

$$\mathsf{E}^* \vdash \varphi \text{ if and only if } \mathsf{E}^* \vdash \mathsf{Bew}_{\mathsf{E}^*}(\overline{\varphi}). \tag{10.7}$$

Proposition 10.58 provides one direction of (10.7):

10.60 LEMMA *Let E^* be simple. If $\mathsf{E}^* \vdash \varphi$, then $\mathsf{E}^* \vdash \mathsf{Bew}_{\mathsf{E}^*}(\overline{\varphi})$.*

The same proposition hows that the other direction of (10.7) is equivalent to the statement

$$\mathsf{E}^* \vdash \mathsf{Bew}_{\mathsf{E}^*}(\overline{e}) \text{ implies } \mathsf{E}^*_{\min} \vdash \mathsf{Bew}_{\mathsf{E}^*}(\overline{e}) \quad \text{for every expression } e. \tag{10.8}$$

If E^* is both simple and admits a standard model, then $\mathsf{E}^* \vdash \mathsf{Bew}_{\mathsf{E}^*}(\overline{e})$ implies that $\mathsf{Bew}_{\mathsf{E}^*}(\overline{e})$ is true, so (10.8) holds by Σ-completeness. The existence of a standard model is a strong assumption on a theory. A weaker assumption that still ensures (10.8) is that of ω-consistency which we saw in chapter 6. We will employ the following formulation of the property:

10.61 PROPOSITION *E^* is ω-inconsistent if and only if there exists a formula $\psi(x)$ with the properties*

(i) $\mathsf{E}^* \vdash \psi(\overline{e})$ *for all expressions e,*

(ii) $\mathsf{E}^* \vdash \neg\forall x\, \psi(x)$.

PROOF Assume that E^* is ω-inconsistent and let $\varphi(x)$ be the formula fulfilling definition 6.28. Let $\psi(x) = \varphi(x) \vee \neg\mathsf{Nat}^*(x)$. The reader can confirm that ψ satisfies the desired properties.

Now suppose that conditions (i) and (ii) hold. We define $\varphi(x) := \mathsf{Nat}^*(x) \wedge \forall y\big(|y| < x \rightarrow \psi(y)\big)$, where $|y| < x$ is the formula introduced in section 9.3 expressing that the length of y is smaller than x. As there are only finitely many expressions of length k, we see that $\varphi(\underline{k})$ is provably equivalent to a finite conjunction of instantiations of ψ and, therefore, $\mathsf{E}^* \vdash \varphi(\underline{k})$ for every k. Observing that $\mathsf{E}^* \vdash \forall n\, \varphi(n) \rightarrow \forall x\, \psi(x)$, we have $\mathsf{E}^* \vdash \neg\forall n\, \varphi(n)$. Hence, E^* is ω-inconsistent. ⊣

10.62 PROPOSITION *Suppose* E^* *is simple and* ω*-consistent. Then for every sentence* φ,

$$\mathsf{E}^* \vdash \varphi \text{ if and only if } \mathsf{E}^* \vdash \mathsf{Bew}_{\mathsf{E}^*}(\overline{\varphi}).$$

PROOF The left-to-right direction is lemma 10.60. To show the converse, suppose $\mathsf{E}^* \nvdash \varphi$, so no derivation of E^* contains the sentence φ. As E^* is simple, $\mathsf{E}^* \vdash \neg\big(\mathsf{Der}_{\mathsf{E}^*}(\overline{e}) \wedge \overline{\varphi} \in \overline{e}\big)$ for every expression e. By ω-consistency, $\mathsf{E}^* \nvdash \mathsf{Bew}_{\mathsf{E}^*}(\overline{\varphi})$. ⊣

Proposition 10.62 shows that provability in E^* is pointwise expressible in E^* if E^* is both simple and ω-consistent. As we have remarked, pointwise expressibility of provability is all that is required to obtain the first incompleteness theorem:

10.63 GÖDEL'S FIRST INCOMPLETENESS THEOREM *Let* E^* *be simple and* ω*-consistent. Then there exists a sentence such that neither it nor its negation is derivable in* E^*.

PROOF Apply proposition 10.62 and theorem 6.6 to the theory E^* and use the formula $\mathsf{Bew}_{\mathsf{E}^*}(x)$ instead of $\Box(x)$. As ω-consistency implies consistency, E^* must be incomplete. ⊣

The reader already familiar with the incompleteness theorems will notice some differences in the statement of theorem 10.63 compared to its usual treatment in logic textbooks. Let us briefly remark on them. First, the incompleteness theorems, particularly the first, apply also to theories strictly weaker than $\mathsf{E}^*_{\mathrm{min}}$. As the proof demonstrates, it is sufficient that the diagonal lemma is available and that provability in the theory is pointwise expressible. The reader can confirm, for instance, that the axioms of induction are not required for either result.

Theorem 10.63 places two restrictions on the theory E^*: ω-consistency and simplicity. As we will see, the former assumption can be weakened in favour of consistency. That result, however, requires an altogether different proof because it is ω-consistency, rather than consistency, which ensured that $\mathsf{Bew}_{\mathsf{E}^*}$ pointwise expresses provability in E^*. In other words, proposition 10.62 does not hold if 'consistent' is substituted for 'ω-consistent'. We prove the stronger result in theorem 10.65, following the proof of Rosser (1936).

In place of the second assumption, simplicity of E^*, statements of the incompleteness theorems usually impose that the set of theorems of E^*, under a given Gödel coding of expressions as natural numbers, is recursively enumerable. A set of natural numbers is recursively enumerable if it is the domain of a partial recursive function or, equivalently, if it is the set of inputs on which a Turing machine halts. Kleene's normal form theorem (see, e.g., Boolos, Burgess, and Jeffrey 2007, theorem 8.4) and the results at the start of this chapter demonstrate that for sets of $\mathcal{L}^*$-expressions, recursive enumerability is equivalent to definability by Σ_1-formulæ of $\mathcal{L}^*_{\text{syn}}$, i.e., Σ-definability. The next result, due to Craig (1953) in the context of theories encoded in arithmetic, shows that the set of theorems of E^* is recursively enumerable if and only if the theory is simple.

10.64 CRAIG'S THEOREM *Suppose the set of theorems of* E^* *is definable by a* Σ-*formula* $\mathsf{Bew}(\mathsf{x})$. *Then* E^* *can be given a simple axiomatization and the provability predicate associated with this axiomatization is provably equivalent to* $\mathsf{Bew}(\mathsf{x})$.

PROOF Let $\mathsf{Bew}(\mathsf{x})$ be as in the statement of the theorem. By theorem 10.13, there is a bounded formula $\psi(x,y)$ in the language $\mathcal{L}^*_{\text{syn}}$ such that

$$\mathsf{E}^*_{\text{min}} \vdash \forall x\big(\mathsf{Bew}(x) \leftrightarrow \exists y\, \psi(x,y)\big).$$

Using ψ, we present a simple axiomatization of E^*. Let F^* be the theory axiomatized by all sentences $\varphi \wedge \overline{a} = \overline{a}$ such that $\psi(\overline{\varphi}, \overline{a})$ is true. We have $\mathsf{F}^* \vdash \psi$ if and only if ψ is logically derivable from the theorems of E^*. So E^* and F^* are identical as theories.

It should be clear that the following Σ_1-formula defines the axioms of F^*:

$$\mathsf{Ax}(x) \;:=\; \exists y \sqsubset x\, \exists z \sqsubset x\Big(x = \big(y \mathbin{\dot\wedge} (z \mathbin{\dot=} z)\big) \wedge \exists w\big(z = \mathsf{q}w \wedge \psi(y,w)\big)\Big).$$

Moreover, the formula is Δ because $\exists w\big(z = \mathsf{q}w \wedge \psi(y,w)\big)$ is provably equivalent over $\mathsf{E}^*_{\text{min}}$ to $\forall w\big(z = \mathsf{q}w \rightarrow \psi(y,w)\big)$ by axiom D3. So, E^* admits an axiomatization that is simple. ⊣

The sentence given by the proof of the first incompleteness theorem 10.63 is the diagonalization of a formula expressing unprovability:

$$\mathsf{E}^*_{\text{min}} \vdash \gamma \leftrightarrow \neg\mathsf{Bew}_{\mathsf{E}^*}(\overline{\gamma}).$$

That is, γ is equivalent to the statement that γ is not a theorem of E^*. As γ is a sentence of the language $\mathcal{L}^*_{\text{syn}}$, the truth value of γ is the same in all standard models of $\mathcal{L}^*$. Therefore, one of γ and $\neg\gamma$ must be true. The fact that $\mathsf{E}^*_{\text{min}}$ is complete for Σ-sentences yet $\mathsf{E}^* \nvdash \neg\gamma$, implies that it is γ, a Π_1-sentence, which is true. Nevertheless, the theories $\mathsf{E}^* + \gamma$ and $\mathsf{E}^* + \neg\gamma$ are both consistent. This is a corollary of the incompleteness theorem, for if $\mathsf{S} + \varphi$ is inconsistent then $\mathsf{S} \vdash \neg\varphi$ by the deduction theorem. A second corollary of the theorem is that the provability predicate $\mathsf{Bew}_{\mathsf{E}^*}(x)$ cannot be Δ if E^* is ω-consistent: if $\mathsf{Bew}_{\mathsf{E}^*}(x)$ were Π, then $\mathsf{E}^* \vdash \gamma$ would follow from Σ-completeness.

The assumption of ω-consistency can be weakened to mere consistency by a trick due to Rosser (1936). Instead of analyzing a sentence equivalent to its own underivability, we consider a sentence ρ equivalent to the statement 'If there is a derivation of ρ there exists a shorter derivation of $\neg\rho$'. There are different ways to measure the length of a derivation *d*. We could count, for instance, the number of uses of axioms and applications of inference rules in the derivation or the total number of symbols occurring in *d*. For Rosser's proof, it is convenient to take as the length of a derivation $d = (\varphi_i)_{i \leq k}$ the length of the expression $[\varphi_0, \varphi_1, \ldots, \varphi_k]$.

10.65 GÖDEL–ROSSER THEOREM *Let* E^* *be consistent and simple. Then there exists a sentence* ρ *such that neither* ρ *nor* $\neg\rho$ *is derivable.*

Let $\mathsf{Der}'_{\mathsf{E}^*}(x, y)$ express that x is a derivation containing y:

$$\mathsf{Der}'_{\mathsf{E}^*}(x, y) \ :=\ \mathsf{Der}_{\mathsf{E}^*}(x) \wedge y \in x.$$

The standard provability predicate for E^* is logically equivalent to the formula $\exists y \big(\mathsf{Sent}(x) \wedge \mathsf{Der}'_{\mathsf{E}^*}(x, y)\big)$. Rosser provability expresses not only the existence of a derivation of the sentence in question but also the nonexistence of any shorter derivation of its negation. Using the length function from definition 9.40, Rosser provability is expressed by

$$\mathsf{RBew}_{\mathsf{E}^*}(x) \ :=\ \exists y \Big(\mathsf{Sent}(x) \wedge \mathsf{Der}'_{\mathsf{E}^*}(y, x) \wedge \forall z \big(\mathsf{Der}'_{\mathsf{E}^*}(z, \dot{\neg} x) \rightarrow |y| < |z|\big)\Big).$$

Before we proceed with the proof of theorem 10.65 we observe that Rosser provability, like the canonical provability predicate, is closed under necessitation:

10.66 PROPOSITION *For every sentence* φ, *if* $\mathsf{E}^* \vdash \varphi$ *then* $\mathsf{E}^*_{\text{min}} \vdash \mathsf{RBew}_{\mathsf{E}^*}(\overline{\varphi})$.

PROOF We may assume that E^* is consistent, as otherwise the result is trivial. Suppose $\mathsf{E}^* \vdash \varphi$ and let $d = (\varphi_i)_{i \leq k}$ be a witnessing derivation. In the following, we write $\overline{d}$ for the quotation of the list d, i.e.,

$$\overline{d} := \overline{[\varphi_0, \ldots, \varphi_k]}.$$

Therefore, $\mathsf{E}^*_{\min} \vdash \mathsf{Der}'_{\mathsf{E}^*}(\overline{d}, \overline{\varphi})$. As E^* is consistent, also $\mathsf{E}^* \nvdash \neg\varphi$. Let $D_{<d}$ be the set of derivations from E^* shorter than d. As there is no derivation of $\neg\varphi$ in $D_{<d}$ and $D_{<d}$ is finite, we deduce that

$$\mathsf{E}^*_{\min} \vdash \forall z \Big(\mathsf{Der}'_{\mathsf{E}^*}(z, \overline{\neg\varphi}) \to \bigwedge_{e \in D_{<d}} z \neq \overline{e} \Big),$$

$$\mathsf{E}^*_{\min} \vdash \forall z \Big(\bigwedge_{e \in D_{<d}} z \neq \overline{e} \to |\overline{d}| < |z| \Big).$$

Hence, $\mathsf{E}^*_{\min} \vdash \mathsf{RBew}_{\mathsf{E}^*}(\overline{\varphi})$. ⊣

PROOF OF THEOREM 10.65 By the diagonal lemma, fix a sentence ρ such that $\mathsf{E}^* \vdash \rho \leftrightarrow \neg\mathsf{RBew}_{\mathsf{E}^*}(\overline{\rho})$. We show that $\mathsf{E}^* \nvdash \rho$ and $\mathsf{E}^* \nvdash \neg\rho$. The first case is easy: as $\mathsf{E}^* \vdash \rho \to \neg\mathsf{RBew}_{\mathsf{E}^*}(\overline{\rho})$ and E^* is consistent, the previous proposition shows $\mathsf{E}^* \nvdash \rho$. To see the second case, assume that $\mathsf{E}^* \vdash \neg\rho$ and let d be a derivation of $\neg\rho$. As in the previous proof, we write $\overline{d}$ for the quotation of the list given by d. Because E^* is consistent, there is no derivation of ρ. In particular, none of the finitely many derivations that are no longer than d is a derivation of ρ:

$$\mathsf{E}^* \vdash \forall y \big(\mathsf{Der}'_{\mathsf{E}^*}(y, \overline{\rho}) \to |\overline{d}| < |y| \big).$$

Since $\mathsf{E}^* \vdash \mathsf{Der}'_{\mathsf{E}^*}(\overline{d}, \overline{\neg\rho})$, the following is then immediate:

$$\mathsf{E}^* \vdash \forall y \Big(|\overline{d}| < |y| \to \exists z \big(\mathsf{Der}'_{\mathsf{E}^*}(z, \overline{\neg\rho}) \wedge |z| < |y| \big) \Big).$$

Combining these two theorems of E^*,

$$\mathsf{E}^* \vdash \forall y \Big(\mathsf{Der}'_{\mathsf{E}^*}(y, \overline{\rho}) \to \exists z \big(\mathsf{Der}'_{\mathsf{E}^*}(z, \overline{\neg\rho}) \wedge |z| < |y| \big) \Big).$$

Finally, note that $\mathsf{E}^* \vdash \forall y \forall z \big(|z| < |y| \to \neg |y| < |z| \big)$, whereby

$$\mathsf{E}^* \vdash \forall y \Big(\mathsf{Der}'_{\mathsf{E}^*}(y, \overline{\rho}) \to \exists z \big(\mathsf{Der}'_{\mathsf{E}^*}(z, \overline{\neg\rho}) \wedge \neg |y| < |z| \big) \Big).$$

In other words, $\mathsf{E}^* \vdash \neg\mathsf{RBew}_{\mathsf{E}^*}(\overline{\rho})$. But then $\mathsf{E}^* \vdash \rho$, which contradicts the consistency of E^*. Hence, $\mathsf{E}^* \nvdash \neg\rho$. ⊣

The Gödel–Rosser theorem entails that no consistent simple extension of $\mathsf{E}^*_{\min}$ derives all true statements in the language $\mathcal{L}^*_{\text{syn}}$, because for any such theory there exists a sentence such that neither it nor its negation is provable. Unlike for Gödel provability, the consistency statement for Rosser provability does not provide an example of an independent sentence as it is provable in E^*:

10.67 PROPOSITION *The Rosser consistency statement,* $\neg\mathsf{RBew}_{\mathsf{E}^*}(\overline{\bot})$, *is provable in* E^*.

PROOF The argument is simple. The Rosser consistency statement is provably equivalent to the formula

$$\forall y\Big(\mathsf{Der}'_{\mathsf{E}^*}(y, \overline{\bot}) \to \exists z\big(\mathsf{Der}'_{\mathsf{E}^*}(z, \overline{\neg\bot}) \wedge |z| < |y|\big)\Big).$$

Let d be a proof of $\neg\bot$. So, employing the notation of the previous proof, $\mathsf{E}^* \vdash \mathsf{Der}'_{\mathsf{E}^*}(\overline{d}, \overline{\neg\bot})$. Clearly, no shorter derivation is a proof of $\bot$ and this fact can be readily confirmed in E^* as there are only finitely many proofs of a given length. Hence, $\mathsf{E}^* \vdash \neg\mathsf{RBew}_{\mathsf{E}^*}(\overline{\bot})$. ⊣

Contrasting proposition 10.67 with Gödel's second incompleteness theorem for $\mathsf{E}^*_{\min}$ (see theorem 10.78), it is clear that Rosser provability expresses a different notion of provability to our canonical provability predicate $\mathsf{Bew}_{\mathsf{E}^*_{\min}}$. Provability predicates in the style of Rosser-provability have been studied to better understand how provability can be formally expressed; see, for example, Guaspari and Solovay (1979), Arai (1990), and Kurahashi (2021).

In chapter 6 we proved a version of Gödel's second incompleteness theorem for the theory E, showing that $\mathsf{E} \nvdash \neg\Box\overline{\bot}$ if E is consistent and satisfies the Löb derivability conditions (theorem 6.13). These are the following rule of inference and two axiom schemas:

NEC If $\mathsf{E} \vdash \varphi$ then $\mathsf{E} \vdash \Box\overline{\varphi}$.

K $\Box\overline{\varphi \to \psi} \to \Box\overline{\varphi} \to \Box\overline{\psi}$

4 $\Box\overline{\varphi} \to \Box\overline{\Box\overline{\varphi}}$

We have already established that every simple theory E^* is closed under necessitation if the provability predicate for E^* is used in place of $\Box$. We will now show that analogous formulations of the axiom schemas K and 4 are provable in E^*:

NEC* If $\mathsf{E}^* \vdash \varphi$ then $\mathsf{E}^* \vdash \mathsf{Bew}_{\mathsf{E}^*}(\overline{\varphi})$.

K* $\forall\alpha\forall\beta\Big(\mathsf{Bew}_{\mathsf{E}^*}(\alpha \underset{\cdot}{\to} \beta) \to \big(\mathsf{Bew}_{\mathsf{E}^*}(\alpha) \to \mathsf{Bew}_{\mathsf{E}^*}(\beta)\big)\Big)$

4* $\forall\alpha\Big(\mathsf{Bew}_{\mathsf{E}^*}(\alpha) \to \mathsf{Bew}_{\mathsf{E}^*}\big(\overline{\mathsf{Bew}_{\mathsf{E}^*}(\underset{\cdot}{\alpha})}\big)\Big)$

In our translations of K and 4, we have expressed each infinite schema as a single, universally quantified sentence. The quantification is not required for the proof of the second incompleteness theorem, but these formulations of the conditions are provable in all simple theories. As in chapter 6, we refer to the rule NEC* and the axioms K* and 4* as the Löb derivability conditions.

We begin with K* and related closure properties of the provability predicate. In the final two clauses of the next proposition, $x \subseteq y^\circ$ abbreviates the formula $\exists z\big(\mathsf{Den}(y, z) \wedge x \subseteq z\big)$.

10.68 PROPOSITION *The following are provable in* $\mathsf{E}^*_{\mathrm{min}}$:

(i) $\forall y\big(\mathsf{Der}_{\mathsf{E}^*}(y) \to \forall x \in y\ \mathsf{Form}(x)\big)$,

(ii) $\forall\alpha\forall\beta\Big(\mathsf{Bew}_{\mathsf{E}^*}(\alpha \underset{\cdot}{\to} \beta) \to \big(\mathsf{Bew}_{\mathsf{E}^*}(\alpha) \to \mathsf{Bew}_{\mathsf{E}^*}(\beta)\big)\Big)$,

(iii) $\forall\alpha\forall\beta\big(\mathsf{Bew}_{\mathsf{E}^*}(\alpha \underset{\cdot}{\wedge} \beta) \leftrightarrow \mathsf{Bew}_{\mathsf{E}^*}(\alpha) \wedge \mathsf{Bew}_{\mathsf{E}^*}(\beta)\big)$,

(iv) $\forall\alpha\Big(\mathsf{Bew}_{\mathsf{E}^*}(\alpha) \to \forall\beta\big(\mathsf{Sent}(\beta) \to \mathsf{Bew}_{\mathsf{E}^*}(\alpha \underset{\cdot}{\vee} \beta) \wedge \mathsf{Bew}_{\mathsf{E}^*}(\beta \underset{\cdot}{\vee} \alpha)\big)\Big)$,

(v) $\forall\alpha\forall v\forall t\Big(\mathsf{CTerm}(t) \to \big(\mathsf{Bew}_{\mathsf{E}^*}(\underset{\cdot}{\forall} v\, \alpha) \to \mathsf{Bew}_{\mathsf{E}^*}(\alpha[t/v])\big)\Big)$,

(vi) $\forall\alpha\forall v\forall t\Big(\mathsf{CTerm}(t) \to \big(\mathsf{Bew}_{\mathsf{E}^*}(\alpha[t/v]) \to \mathsf{Bew}_{\mathsf{E}^*}(\underset{\cdot}{\exists} v \alpha)\big)\Big)$,

(vii) $\forall\alpha\forall t\Big(\mathsf{CTerm}(t) \to \big(\exists x \subseteq t^\circ\ \mathsf{Bew}_{\mathsf{E}^*}(\alpha[\mathsf{q}x/v]) \to \mathsf{Bew}_{\mathsf{E}^*}(\underset{\cdot}{\exists} v \underset{\cdot}{\subseteq} t\ \alpha)\big)\Big)$,

(viii) $\forall\alpha\forall t\Big(\mathsf{CTerm}(t) \to \big(\forall x \subseteq t^\circ\ \mathsf{Bew}_{\mathsf{E}^*}(\alpha[\mathsf{q}x/v]) \to \mathsf{Bew}_{\mathsf{E}^*}(\underset{\cdot}{\forall} v \underset{\cdot}{\subseteq} t\ \alpha)\big)\Big)$.

PROOF Parts (ii)–(vi) express standard properties of provability. Items (vii) and (viii) state versions of the relationship between bounded quantification and disjunction/conjunction used in theorem 10.6. ⊣

Axiom 4* is an instance of the schema

$$\forall x\big(\varphi(x) \to \mathsf{Bew}_{\mathsf{E}^*}(\overline{\varphi(\underset{\cdot}{x})})\big). \tag{10.9}$$

As a schema, (10.9) expresses a strong completeness property for E*: every instantiation of φ that holds is provable. It is not difficult to see that (10.9) is not provable in E* if E* is simple (consider the Gödel sentence). In fact, the schema (10.9) is equivalent to the statement that E* is inconsistent:

10.69 PROPOSITION *Let* F^* *be a theory extending* $\mathsf{E}^*_{\min}$. *We have* $\mathsf{F}^* \vdash \mathsf{Bew}_{\mathsf{E}^*}(\overline{\bot})$ *if and only if* $\mathsf{F}^* \vdash \varphi \to \mathsf{Bew}_{\mathsf{E}^*}(\overline{\varphi})$ *for every sentence* φ.

PROOF One direction is a consequence of $\mathsf{E}^*_{\min} \vdash \forall \alpha \big(\mathsf{Sent}(\alpha) \to \mathsf{Bew}_{\mathsf{E}^*}(\overline{\bot} \dot{\to} \alpha)\big)$. For the other direction, we instantiate (10.9) first with the Gödel sentence for the theory E^*, and then with its negation:

$\mathsf{F}^* \vdash \gamma \leftrightarrow \neg \mathsf{Bew}_{\mathsf{E}^*}(\overline{\gamma})$	diagonal lemma
$\mathsf{F}^* \vdash \gamma \to \mathsf{Bew}_{\mathsf{E}^*}(\overline{\gamma})$	
$\mathsf{F}^* \vdash \neg \gamma$	logic
$\mathsf{F}^* \vdash \neg \gamma \to \mathsf{Bew}_{\mathsf{E}^*}(\overline{\neg \gamma})$	
$\mathsf{F}^* \vdash \mathsf{Bew}_{\mathsf{E}^*}(\overline{\neg \gamma})$	fourth line
$\mathsf{F}^* \vdash \mathsf{Bew}_{\mathsf{E}^*}(\overline{\gamma})$	first and third line
$\mathsf{F}^* \vdash \mathsf{Bew}_{\mathsf{E}^*}(\overline{\bot})$	fifth and sixth line ⊣

The particular instance of (10.9) giving rise to 4* has $\varphi(x)$ replaced by the Σ_1-formula $\mathsf{Bew}_{\mathsf{E}^*}$. Restricted to Σ-formulæ, the schema is a formal expression of the Σ-completeness theorem that all true Σ-sentences are provable in E^* (theorem 10.22), and can be derived in E^* by mirroring the proof of the theorem within the theory E^*.

10.70 FORMALIZED Σ-COMPLETENESS THEOREM *Let* $\varphi(x_1, \ldots, x_n)$ *be a* Σ-*formula with at most the displayed variables occurring free. Then*

$$\mathsf{E}^* \vdash \forall x_1 \cdots \forall x_n \Big(\varphi(x_1, \ldots, x_n) \to \mathsf{Bew}_{\mathsf{E}^*}\big(\overline{\varphi(\dot{x}_1, \ldots, \dot{x}_n)}\big)\Big).$$

The proof of theorem 10.70 requires a number of auxiliary lemmas which we now present. As with the Σ-completeness section 10.1, we first prove the theorem for the case where φ is a Σ_1-formula of $\mathcal{L}^*_{\mathrm{syn}}$, and then generalize to the statement above. The proof proceeds by induction on the Σ_1-formula φ. In the base case, φ is an atomic formula of $\mathcal{L}^*_{\mathrm{syn}}$. There are two relation symbols in $\mathcal{L}^*_{\mathrm{syn}}$, equality and sym, and it is the former which provides the main challenge.

We rely on the capability of E^* to express the true equations between closed terms. In definition 9.25 we introduced the formula $\mathsf{Den}(x, y)$ expressing that x is a closed term denoting y. We proved that this formula pointwise expresses the semantic denotation function (proposition 9.26), namely,

(i) $\mathsf{E}^* \vdash \mathsf{Den}(\overline{s}, s)$ for every closed term s of $\mathcal{L}^*_\cdot$;

(ii) $\mathsf{E}^* \vdash \forall x(\mathsf{CTerm}(x) \to \exists y\, \mathsf{Den}(x,y))$;

(iii) $\mathsf{E}^* \vdash \forall x \forall y \forall z(\mathsf{Den}(x,y) \wedge \mathsf{Den}(x,z) \to y=z)$.

The following generalization of property (i) above will be useful:

10.71 LEMMA *Let s be a term and suppose the variables in s all occur among $x_0, \ldots, x_n$. Then* $\mathsf{E}^* \vdash \forall x_0 \cdots \forall x_n\, \mathsf{Den}(\overline{s(\dot{x}_0, \ldots, \dot{x}_n)}, s)$.

PROOF By induction on s. The argument is identical to the proof of (i) above, except for the base case where $s \equiv x_i$ is a variable. In that scenario we know that

$$\mathsf{E}^*_{\min} \vdash \overline{s(\dot{x}_0, \ldots, \dot{x}_n)} = \mathsf{q}x_i,$$

and since $\mathsf{E}^*_{\min} \vdash \forall x\, \mathsf{Den}(\mathsf{q}x, x)$, the desired result is obtained. ⊣

As we observed in section 9.2, the formal denotation function enables us to express the property of being a true equation between closed terms:

10.72 DEFINITION $\mathsf{Tr}_{\mathrm{eq}}(x) \;:=\; \exists s \exists t\big(x = s \mathbin{\dot{=}} t \wedge \exists z(\mathsf{Den}(s,z) \wedge \mathsf{Den}(t,z))\big)$.

Expressing the previous result in terms of $\mathsf{Tr}_{\mathrm{eq}}$, we have

10.73 LEMMA *Let $s(x_0, \ldots, x_n)$ and $t(x_0, \ldots, x_n)$ be terms containing at most the distinguished variables.*

$$\mathsf{E}^* \vdash \forall x_0 \cdots \forall x_n\Big(s = t \leftrightarrow \mathsf{Tr}_{\mathrm{eq}}\big(\overline{s(\dot{x}_0, \ldots, \dot{x}_n) = t(\dot{x}_0, \ldots, \dot{x}_n)}\big)\Big).$$

The base case of formalized Σ-completeness will be a consequence of the next two lemmas. Let $\mathsf{CTerm}_{\mathrm{syn}}(x)$ express that x is a closed term of $\mathcal{L}^*_{\mathrm{syn}}$.

10.74 LEMMA $\mathsf{E}^* \vdash \forall s \forall t\big(\mathsf{CTerm}_{\mathrm{syn}}(s \mathbin{\dot{\frown}} t) \wedge \mathsf{Tr}_{\mathrm{eq}}(s \mathbin{\dot{=}} t) \to \mathsf{Bew}_{\mathsf{E}^*}(s \mathbin{\dot{=}} t)\big)$.

10.75 LEMMA $\mathsf{E}^* \vdash \forall s \forall t\big(\mathsf{CTerm}_{\mathrm{syn}}(s \mathbin{\dot{\frown}} t) \wedge \neg\mathsf{Tr}_{\mathrm{eq}}(s \mathbin{\dot{=}} t) \to \mathsf{Bew}_{\mathsf{E}^*}(\dot{\neg} s \mathbin{\dot{=}} t)\big)$.

The proof of the two lemmas follow the argument given for the base case of the completeness theorem for bounded formulæ, theorem 10.6. We require a formalized version of proposition 10.10:

$$\mathsf{E}^* \vdash \forall s \forall x\big(\mathsf{CTerm}_{\mathrm{syn}}(s) \wedge \mathsf{Den}(s,x) \to \mathsf{Bew}_{\mathsf{E}^*}(s \mathbin{\dot{=}} \mathsf{q}x)\big).$$

This result is proved by formal induction on the closed term s in the same manner as in that proposition. Although not difficult, the argument requires formal accounts of a number of earlier results, most notably propositions 8.55, 8.66, and 8.72, which we will not present.

We are now in position to prove the formalized Σ-completeness theorem:

PROOF OF THEOREM 10.70 As outlined, we first establish the claim of the theorem for the case that φ is a Σ_1-formula of $\mathcal{L}^*_{\mathrm{syn}}$. More specifically, we prove the theorem for the case that φ is constructed from atomic and negated atomic equations via the defined connectives $\wedge$ and $\vee$, bounded universal quantifiers, and unbounded existential quantifiers. This collection of Σ_1-formulæ lacks the atomic formula sym (and its negated instances). Given that $\mathsf{sym}\,x$ is provably equivalent to the formula $x \neq \underline{0} \wedge \mathsf{Sing}(\mathsf{q}x)$ over the axioms of $\mathsf{E}^*_{\mathrm{min}}$ (proposition 8.65), every Σ_1-formula of $\mathcal{L}^*_{\mathrm{syn}}$ is provably equivalent to a formula of the above shape. In the second part of the proof, we show how the theorem extends to arbitrary Σ-formulæ.

If φ is an equation or negated equation, the combination of lemma 10.73 and either lemma 10.74 or lemma 10.75 yields the desired result. The case in which φ is a conjunction, a disjunction, or a bounded quantification follows from the induction hypothesis and proposition 10.68. In the case of disjunction, suppose $\varphi \equiv \psi \vee \chi$ contains only x free. We argue as follows:

$$\mathsf{E}^* \vdash \forall x\Big(\varphi(x) \to \mathsf{Bew}_{\mathsf{E}^*}\big(\overline{\psi(\dot{x})}\big) \vee \mathsf{Bew}_{\mathsf{E}^*}\big(\overline{\chi(\dot{x})}\big)\Big) \qquad \text{induction hypothesis}$$

$$\mathsf{E}^* \vdash \forall x\Big(\varphi(x) \to \mathsf{Bew}_{\mathsf{E}^*}\big(\overline{\varphi(\dot{x})}\big) \vee \mathsf{Bew}_{\mathsf{E}^*}\big(\overline{\varphi(\dot{x})}\big)\Big) \qquad \text{proposition 10.68}$$

$$\mathsf{E}^* \vdash \forall x\Big(\varphi(x) \to \mathsf{Bew}_{\mathsf{E}^*}\big(\overline{\varphi(\dot{x})}\big)\Big) \qquad \text{logic}$$

The other cases are similar.

Finally, we consider $\varphi \equiv \exists z\, \psi$. Let us restrict to the case where φ contains at most one variable free, say x, as the broader scenario is a straightforward generalization. The induction hypothesis provides

$$\mathsf{E}^* \vdash \forall x \forall z\Big(\psi(x, z) \to \mathsf{Bew}_{\mathsf{E}^*}\big(\overline{\psi(\dot{x}, \dot{z})}\big)\Big),$$

which leads to the following implications:

$$\mathsf{E}^* \vdash \forall x\Big(\varphi(x) \to \exists z\, \mathsf{Bew}_{\mathsf{E}^*}\big(\overline{\psi(\dot{x}, \dot{z})}\big)\Big) \qquad \text{logic}$$

$$\mathsf{E}^* \vdash \forall x\Big(\varphi(x) \to \mathsf{Bew}_{\mathsf{E}^*}\big(\overline{\exists z\, \psi(\dot{x}, z)}\big)\Big) \qquad \text{proposition 10.68(vii)}$$

$$\mathsf{E}^* \vdash \forall x\Big(\varphi(x) \to \mathsf{Bew}_{\mathsf{E}^*}\big(\overline{\varphi(\dot{x})}\big)\Big) \qquad \text{logic}$$

Having established the theorem for Σ_1-formulæ of $\mathcal{L}^*_{\text{syn}}$, we now generalize to arbitrary Σ-formulæ. Let φ be a Σ-formula. To simplify notation, we assume that φ contains at most one variable free, say x. Let ψ be the Σ_1-formula of $\mathcal{L}^*_{\text{syn}}$ such that $\mathsf{E}^* \vdash \forall x\big(\varphi(x) \leftrightarrow \psi(x)\big)$. Necessitation (lemma 10.60) for derivability gives

$$\mathsf{E}^* \vdash \mathsf{Bew}_{\mathsf{E}^*}\big(\overline{\forall x\big(\psi(x) \to \varphi(x)\big)}\big). \tag{10.10}$$

Therefore,

$\mathsf{E}^* \vdash \forall x\big(\varphi(x) \to \psi(x)\big)$	assumption
$\mathsf{E}^* \vdash \forall x\big(\varphi(x) \to \mathsf{Bew}_{\mathsf{E}^*}\big(\overline{\psi(\dot{x})}\big)\big)$	first part of proof
$\mathsf{E}^* \vdash \forall x\big(\varphi(x) \to \mathsf{Bew}_{\mathsf{E}^*}\big(\overline{\varphi(\dot{x})}\big)\big)$	(10.10) ⊣

Axiom 4^* is an application of the Σ-completeness theorem:

10.76 COROLLARY *If* E^* *is simple, then* $\mathsf{E}^* \vdash 4^*$.

If E^* contains K^* and 4^*, and is closed under necessitation for $\mathsf{Bew}_{\mathsf{E}^*}$, then Löb's theorem holds for E^*:

10.77 LÖB'S THEOREM *If* E^* *is simple, then*

$$\mathsf{E}^* \vdash \mathsf{Bew}_{\mathsf{E}^*}\big(\overline{\mathsf{Bew}_{\mathsf{E}^*}(\overline{\varphi}) \to \varphi}\big) \to \mathsf{Bew}_{\mathsf{E}^*}(\overline{\varphi}).$$

PROOF The same proof as theorem 6.11; a generalization of the theorem applicable to E^* is given in theorem 10.79 below. ⊣

As we saw in chapter 6, Gödel's second incompleteness theorem is a corollary of Löb's theorem:

10.78 GÖDEL'S SECOND INCOMPLETENESS THEOREM *Let* E^* *be consistent and simple. Then* $\mathsf{E}^* \nvdash \neg\mathsf{Bew}_{\mathsf{E}^*}(\overline{\bot})$.

PROOF We replicate the proof of theorem 6.6. Assume that $\mathsf{E}^* \vdash \mathsf{Bew}_{\mathsf{E}^*}(\overline{\bot}) \to \bot$. Then $\mathsf{E}^* \vdash \mathsf{Bew}_{\mathsf{E}^*}\big(\overline{\mathsf{Bew}_{\mathsf{E}^*}(\overline{\bot}) \to \bot}\big)$ by proposition 10.58 and simplicity of E^*. By Löb's theorem it follows that E^* is inconsistent. ⊣

The proof of Löb's theorem relies only on the schematic versions of K and 4. From the universally quantified forms of these axioms, a strengthening of Löb's theorem is provable:

10.79 GENERALIZED LÖB'S THEOREM *Let* E^* *be simple. Then*

$$\mathsf{E}^* \vdash \forall\alpha\big(\mathsf{Bew}_{\mathsf{E}^*}\big(\overline{\mathsf{Bew}_{\mathsf{E}^*}(\underset{\cdot}{\alpha})} \mathbin{\underset{\cdot}{\to}} \alpha\big) \to \mathsf{Bew}_{\mathsf{E}^*}(\alpha)\big).$$

PROOF We abbreviate $\mathsf{Bew}_{\mathsf{E}^*}(\mathsf{x})$ as $\Box\mathsf{x}$ in the proof. The parameterized diagonal lemma 6.17 provides a formula $\varphi(\mathsf{x})$ such that

$$\mathsf{E}^* \vdash \forall\alpha\big(\varphi(\alpha) \leftrightarrow \Box r(\alpha)\big), \quad \text{where } r(\mathsf{x}) := \mathsf{sub}(\overline{\varphi \to \mathsf{x}}, \bar{\mathsf{x}}, \mathsf{x}). \tag{10.11}$$

We may apply necessitation and proposition 10.68(v) to the left-to-right direction of (10.11) to deduce that

$$\mathsf{E}^* \vdash \forall\alpha\, \Box\overline{\varphi(\underset{\cdot}{\alpha}) \to \Box r(\underset{\cdot}{\alpha})}. \tag{10.12}$$

Likewise, working with the right-to-left direction of (10.11), and applying necessitation, proposition 10.68(v), and K^*, we obtain

$$\mathsf{E}^* \vdash \forall\alpha\big(\Box\overline{\Box r(\underset{\cdot}{\alpha})} \to \Box\overline{\varphi(\underset{\cdot}{\alpha})}\big). \tag{10.13}$$

Appealing to PL2 and proposition 10.68 yields

$$\mathsf{E}^* \vdash \forall\beta\forall\gamma\forall\delta\big(\Box(\beta \mathbin{\underset{\cdot}{\to}} \gamma) \wedge \Box(\gamma \mathbin{\underset{\cdot}{\to}} \delta) \to \Box(\beta \mathbin{\underset{\cdot}{\to}} \delta)\big). \tag{10.14}$$

Now we argue informally within E^*. Fix α and assume

$$\Box r(\alpha). \tag{10.15}$$

By 4^* we have $\Box\overline{\Box r(\underset{\cdot}{\alpha})}$, whence $\Box\overline{\varphi(\underset{\cdot}{\alpha})}$ by (10.13). Combining with (10.15) and K^* yields $\Box\alpha$. So

$$\mathsf{E}^* \vdash \forall\alpha\big(\Box r(\alpha) \to \Box\alpha\big). \tag{10.16}$$

An application of necessitation gives rise to

$$\mathsf{E}^* \vdash \forall\alpha\, \Box\overline{\Box r(\underset{\cdot}{\alpha}) \to \Box\underset{\cdot}{\alpha}}. \tag{10.17}$$

We argue within E^* again, assuming $\Box(\overline{\Box\underset{\cdot}{\alpha}} \mathbin{\underset{\cdot}{\to}} \alpha)$. Then

$\Box\big(\overline{\Box r(\underset{\cdot}{\alpha})} \mathbin{\underset{\cdot}{\to}} \alpha\big)$	(10.14) & (10.17) with $\beta = \overline{\Box r(\underset{\cdot}{\alpha})}$, $\gamma = \overline{\Box\underset{\cdot}{\alpha}}$, $\delta = \alpha$
$\Box r(\alpha)$	(10.14) & (10.12) with $\beta = \overline{\varphi(\underset{\cdot}{\alpha})}$, $\gamma = \overline{\Box r(\underset{\cdot}{\alpha})}$, $\delta = \alpha$
$\Box\alpha$	(10.16)

So $\mathsf{E}^* \vdash \forall\alpha\big(\Box(\overline{\Box\underset{\cdot}{\alpha}} \mathbin{\underset{\cdot}{\to}} \alpha) \to \Box\alpha\big)$. ⊣

11 Formal Truth

In this chapter we examine the capacity of theories of syntax to express truth. The undefinability of truth (theorem 6.2) reminds us that the T-schema, the collection of formulæ

$$\Box\overline{\psi} \leftrightarrow \psi \tag{11.1}$$

where ψ ranges over all sentences of $\mathcal{L}^*$, is inconsistent over $\mathsf{E}^*_{\mathrm{min}}$. In chapter 6 we established that even weakened forms of the T-schema, such as replacing one direction by a rule of inference, are, if not outright inconsistent, at least incompatible with reading $\Box\overline{\psi}$ as 'ψ is a true sentence in the language $\mathcal{L}^*$'. Nevertheless, there are consistent restrictions of (11.1), such as to the $\Box$-free sentences.[1]

We will examine two kinds of truth predicate, corresponding to *definable* and *axiomatizable* notions of truth respectively. In the first kind we assume that $\Box$ names a formula instead of a symbol of $\mathcal{L}^*$ and we identify natural classes of sentences for which the T-schema (11.1) is derivable in $\mathsf{E}^*_{\mathrm{min}}$ for ψ ranging over such a class. The proof of theorem 6.3 shows that to every finite set of sentences can be associated a truth predicate. We have already seen one, albeit simple, example of a truth predicate for an infinite set of sentences: the expressibility of the denotation function for $\mathcal{L}^*$ gave rise to a truth predicate for the set of closed equations. The formula $\mathsf{Tr}_{\mathrm{at}}(x)$ defined on page 221 is a truth predicate for the atomic sentences of $\mathcal{L}^*$. These constructions can easily be extended to yield definable truth predicates for the quantifier-free sentences of $\mathcal{L}^*$, using the method developed in the previous chapter for expressing inductively defined sets of expressions.

One of the main results of this chapter is that the formulæ of $\mathcal{L}^*$ can be separated into a hierarchy $\Sigma_1 \subseteq \Sigma_2 \subseteq \Sigma_3 \subseteq \cdots$ starting from the class Σ_1 of existential formulæ and having the property that each level of the hierarchy admits a definable truth predicate located at the same level. We will also show that these

[1] Theorem 6.3, which established the consistency of the $\Box$-free T-schema over $\mathsf{E}_{\mathrm{min}}$, does not apply directly to $\mathsf{E}^*_{\mathrm{min}}$ because, unlike $\mathsf{E}_{\mathrm{min}}$, the predicate symbol $\Box$ occurs in nonlogical axioms of $\mathsf{E}^*_{\mathrm{min}}$. The proof of theorem 6.3, however, still establishes the claimed result; cf. theorem 11.34 below.

definable truth predicates provably satisfy other desirable properties beyond the T-schema, including quantified claims such as that a conjunction of two arbitrary sentences is true if and only if both sentences are true.

In the second part of the chapter we examine theories with *axiomatized* truth predicates. These are theories of truth in the sense of chapter 6, where the predicate $\square$ expresses truth by means of new axioms added to the theory of expressions. Rather than focusing on consistent restrictions of the T-schema – which McGee's theorem 6.31 shows is problematic – our attention will be on axioms and rules of inference that individually express natural and consistent properties of truth. Many candidates arise from the Tarskian definition of truth in a model. As an example, the clause for negation,

$$\mathbb{E}^* \vDash \neg\alpha \text{ if and only if } \mathbb{E}^* \nvDash \alpha,$$

motivates the following formula as a potential axiom for truth:

$$\forall x\big(\mathsf{Sent}(x) \to (\square \underset{-}{\neg} x \leftrightarrow \neg\square x)\big).$$

Interesting theories arise when we consider axioms that introduce or eliminate occurrences of the truth predicate, such as $\forall x\big(\mathsf{Sent}(x) \to \big(\square(\underline{\square}\mathsf{q}x) \leftrightarrow \square x\big)\big)$ or the rule of necessitation and its converse, $\mathsf{E}^* \vdash \varphi$ if and only if $\mathsf{E}^* \vdash \square\overline{\varphi}$. As we observed in section 6.1, these principles of truth skirt the border of paradox. And compared to axioms arising directly from our established semantics, it is less clear how to find models for theories with these kinds of axioms or rules.

11.1 Partial Truth Predicates

Fix a language $\mathcal{L}^*$ fulfilling the basic requirements laid out in definition 8.33 and a theory E^* in this language containing at least the minimal set of axioms. We continue to utilize the syntactic abbreviations introduced in previous chapters, such as the defined terms $\underset{.}{\to}$, $\underset{.}{\forall}$, $\underset{.}{\subsetneq}$, and function symbols for Σ-expressible functions.

In the previous chapter, the formula classes Σ, Π, and Δ were introduced and studied. These sets of formulæ are all defined relative to the sublanguage $\mathcal{L}^*_{\text{syn}}$ which contains the syntactic constants present in $\mathcal{L}^*$ but no further symbols over $\mathcal{L}^*_{\text{min}}$. Unless $\mathcal{L}^*_{\text{min}}$ and $\mathcal{L}^*$ coincide, there will be $\mathcal{L}^*_{\text{syn}}$-symbols not in $\mathcal{L}^*_{\text{min}}$ and $\mathcal{L}^*$-symbols not in $\mathcal{L}^*_{\text{syn}}$. A formula is Σ if it is provably equivalent (over E^*) to a Σ_1-formula of $\mathcal{L}^*_{\text{syn}}$, it is Π if its negation is Σ, and it is Δ if it is both Σ and Π.

We observed that many properties, relations, and functions on expressions are defined by formulæ in these classes and are therefore pointwise expressed in $\mathsf{E}^*_{\text{min}}$. In the present chapter, there will be greater focus on the full language $\mathcal{L}^*$ than on $\mathcal{L}^*_{\text{syn}}$. As such, our notion of the complexity of formulæ will be founded on the classes Σ_1 and Π_1. A formula that has provably equivalent counterparts in in both classes will be called Δ_1. The Δ_1-formulæ include, by definition, all Δ-formulæ. Employing a similar argument as in proposition 10.18, it can be shown there exist Δ_1-formulæ which are not Δ.

11.1 DEFINITION A formula is Δ_1 if it is provably equivalent over E^* to both a Σ_1- and a Π_1-formula. That is, φ is Δ_1 if there exist formulæ ψ and χ which are Σ_1 and Π_1, respectively, such that $\mathsf{E}^* \vdash \varphi \leftrightarrow \psi$ and $\mathsf{E}^* \vdash \varphi \leftrightarrow \chi$.

In chapter 9 we proved that denotation for closed terms of $\mathcal{L}^*$ is pointwise expressed in $\mathsf{E}^*_{\text{min}}$ by a formula Den of $\mathcal{L}^*$. As we make extensive use of the formalized denotation function, we abbreviate its use via an introduced function symbol. Following the notation of the previous chapter, we write this function symbol as x°, which expresses the denotation of x under the assumption that x is a closed term of $\mathcal{L}^*$ (if x is not a closed term of $\mathcal{L}^*$ we assume that x° is undefined). This function symbol is not considered a symbol of $\mathcal{L}^*$ (cf. theorem 9.20) and so serves only as a metalinguistic abbreviation for a formula involving Den. Formally, the use of this function symbol is specified via one of two identifications, the choice depending on whether an existential or universal quantifier is desired. Our results from section 10.1 show that the two options for replacing occurrences of this function symbol are equivalent over $\mathsf{E}^*_{\text{min}}$:

$$\varphi(s^\circ) \equiv \mathsf{CTerm}(s) \wedge \exists y\big(\mathsf{Den}(s,y) \wedge \varphi(y)\big),$$
$$\varphi(s^\circ) \equiv \mathsf{CTerm}(s) \wedge \forall y\big(\mathsf{Den}(s,y) \rightarrow \varphi(y)\big).$$

In the following, we assume that Den is given as a Σ_1-formula, as outlined in section 9.2. If all the optional function symbols of $\mathcal{L}^*$ are pointwise expressed in E^* by Σ-formulæ – such as if all function symbols of $\mathcal{L}^*$ are in $\mathcal{L}^*_{\text{min}}$ – then Den is also Δ. In general, though, Den need not be Δ.

The next proposition restates proposition 9.26 on formal denotation using the introduced notation:

11.2 PROPOSITION

(i) *For every closed term s of* $\mathcal{L}^*_\circ$ $\mathsf{E}^* \vdash \overline{s}^\circ = s$.

(ii) $\mathsf{E}^* \vdash \forall x\ (\mathsf{q}x)^\circ = x$.

(iii) *For any two closed terms s and t of* $\mathcal{L}^*_\circ$ $\mathsf{E}^* \vdash s = t \leftrightarrow \overline{s}^\circ = \overline{t}^\circ$.

In section 9.2 we introduced a formula $\mathsf{Tr}_{\mathrm{at}}(x)$ expressing the true atomic sentences of $\mathcal{L}^*_\circ$. It will be convenient to assume an alternative, though provably equivalent, formulation:

11.3 DEFINITION Let $\mathcal{R}$ be the set of relation symbols of $\mathcal{L}^*_\circ$, including equality. The formula $\mathsf{Tr}_{\mathrm{at}}(x)$ is defined as follows, where a_{R} is the arity of the predicate symbol $\mathsf{R} \in \mathcal{R}$:

$$\mathsf{Tr}_{\mathrm{at}}(x) \ := \ \bigvee_{\mathsf{R}\in\mathcal{R}} \exists x_1 \cdots \exists x_{a_{\mathsf{R}}} \exists y_1 \cdots \exists y_{a_{\mathsf{R}}} \Big(x = \underset{\cdot}{\mathsf{R}} x_1 \cdots x_{a_{\mathsf{R}}} \wedge \mathsf{R} y_1 \cdots y_{a_{\mathsf{R}}} \wedge \bigwedge_{j=1}^{a_i} \mathsf{Den}(x_i, y_i) \Big).$$

11.4 PROPOSITION $\mathsf{Tr}_{\mathrm{at}}$ *is a truth predicate for atomic sentences. Moreover, for each* $k \in \mathbb{N}$ *and each predicate symbol* R *of* $\mathcal{L}^*$ *whose arity is k, the following sentence is provable in* E^*:

$$\forall s_1 \cdots \forall s_k \Big(\mathsf{CTerm}(s_1) \wedge \cdots \wedge \mathsf{CTerm}(s_k) \rightarrow \big(\mathsf{R} s_1^\circ \cdots s_k^\circ \leftrightarrow \mathsf{Tr}_{\mathrm{at}}(\underset{\cdot}{\mathsf{R}} s_1 \cdots s_k) \big) \Big).$$

PROOF Immediate, following the definition and established properties of $(\cdot)^\circ$. ⊣

The truth predicate for the atomic formulæ provides another example of a Σ_1-formula which is not Σ. Suppose $\mathcal{L}^*$ contains a function or predicate symbol beyond $\mathcal{L}^*_{\min}$. Proposition 10.18 presented a Σ_1-formula which is not Σ over $\mathsf{E}^*_{\min}$. Following the proof of the proposition, there is an atomic formula $\psi(\mathsf{v}_0, \ldots, \mathsf{v}_k)$ with only the variables marked occurring such that the formula

$$\varphi(\mathsf{x}) \ \equiv \ \exists \mathsf{v}_1 \cdots \exists \mathsf{v}_k \ \psi(\mathsf{x}, \mathsf{v}_1, \ldots, \mathsf{v}_k)$$

is not provably equivalent to a formula of $\mathcal{L}^*_{\mathrm{syn}}$ in $\mathsf{E}^*_{\min}$. The T-schema for atoms provides a provably equivalent form of φ using $\mathsf{Tr}_{\mathrm{at}}$:

$$\mathsf{E}^*_{\min} \vdash \forall \mathsf{x} \Big(\varphi(\mathsf{x}) \leftrightarrow \exists \mathsf{v}_1 \cdots \exists \mathsf{v}_k \ \mathsf{Tr}_{\mathrm{at}}\big(\overline{\psi(\underset{\cdot}{\mathsf{x}}, \underset{\cdot}{\mathsf{v}}_1, \ldots, \underset{\cdot}{\mathsf{v}}_k)} \big) \Big).$$

The term $\overline{\psi(\cdots)}$ is in the language $\mathcal{L}^*_{\text{syn}}$. Moreover, we know Σ-formulæ are closed under prefixing by existential quantifiers. Therefore, Tr_{at} is not Σ. Like the formula expressing denotation, the variant of Tr_{at} expressing the true atomic sentences of $\mathcal{L}^*_{\text{syn}}$ is a Σ-formula. This truth predicate can be defined as in definition 11.3, but with the two-element set $\{=, \mathsf{sym}\}$ replacing $\mathcal{R}$.

After atomic sentences, the next step is to extend the truth predicate Tr_{at} to the class of bounded formulæ. The truc bounded sentences can be determined by closing the true atoms and negated false atoms under the connectives $\wedge$ and $\vee$ and the bounded quantifiers $\forall v \subseteq t$ and $\exists v \subseteq t$ in a way that preserves truth. An implication $\alpha \to \beta$, for example, is deemed true only if either $\neg\alpha$ or β is, and a negated implication $\neg(\alpha \to \beta)$ only if both α and $\neg\beta$ are. A bounded universal quantification $\forall v \subseteq t\ \alpha$ is true if and only if $\alpha[\overline{a}/v]$ is true for every expression $a \subseteq t^\circ$; its negation $\neg\forall v \subseteq t\ \alpha$ iff $\neg\alpha[\overline{a}/v]$ is true for some $a \subseteq t^\circ$.

The set of bounded formulæ is often denoted Δ_0; for this reason we name the corresponding truth predicate Tr_{Δ_0}. The formula can be constructed using our general template for expressing syntactic properties as Σ-formulæ (though here the result will be a Σ_1-formula and not necessarily Σ). We begin with an auxiliary formula $\psi_{\Delta_0}(\alpha, z)$ expressing that α is true under the assumption that z is a list of true sentences:

$$\begin{aligned}
\psi_{\Delta_0}(\alpha, z) \ :=\ & \big(\mathsf{Atom}(\alpha) \wedge \mathsf{Tr}_{\text{at}}(\alpha)\big) \\
& \vee\ \exists\beta\big(\alpha = \dot{\neg}\beta \wedge \mathsf{Atom}(\beta) \wedge \neg\mathsf{Tr}_{\text{at}}(\beta)\big) \\
& \vee\ \exists\beta\big(\alpha = \dot{\neg}\dot{\neg}\beta \wedge \beta \in z\big) \\
& \vee\ \exists\beta\exists\gamma\big(\alpha = \beta \dot{\to} \gamma \wedge (\dot{\neg}\beta \in z \vee \gamma \in z)\big) \\
& \vee\ \exists\beta\exists\gamma\big(\alpha = \dot{\neg}(\beta \dot{\to} \gamma) \wedge \beta \in z \wedge \dot{\neg}\gamma \in z\big) \\
& \vee\ \exists\beta\exists v\exists s\big(\alpha = \dot{\forall} v \dot{\subseteq} s\, \beta \wedge \mathsf{CTerm}(s) \wedge \forall x \subseteq s^\circ\ \beta[\mathsf{q}x/v] \in z\big) \\
& \vee\ \exists\beta\exists v\exists s\big(\alpha = \dot{\neg}\dot{\forall} v \dot{\subseteq} s\, \beta \wedge \mathsf{CTerm}(s) \wedge \exists x \subseteq s^\circ\ \dot{\neg}\beta[\mathsf{q}x/v] \in z\big).
\end{aligned}$$

It should be clear that the existential quantifiers $\exists\beta$, $\exists\gamma$, $\exists v$, and $\exists s$ in the formula above can be replaced by bounded quantifiers. The two occurrences of Tr_{at} in ψ_{Δ_0}, however, feature unbounded quantifiers. Nevertheless, since Tr_{at} is Δ_1, so is ψ_{Δ_0}.

11.5 DEFINITION $\mathsf{Tr}_{\Delta_0}(x) \ :=\ \exists z\big(\mathsf{List}(z) \wedge x \in z \wedge \forall w \in z\ \psi_{\Delta_0}(w, z)\big)$.

We claim that Tr_{Δ_0} behaves as a truth predicate for bounded sentences, in the sense that the sentence $\varphi \leftrightarrow \mathsf{Tr}_{\Delta_0}(\overline{\varphi})$ is derivable in $\mathsf{E}^*_{\text{min}}$ whenever φ is a bounded sentence. This result is a consequence of the next proposition, which shows that our truth predicate for bounded sentences commutes with the connectives and quantifiers in the intended way:

11.6 PROPOSITION *The following are provable in* E^**:*

(i) $\forall\alpha\big(\mathsf{Tr}_{\Delta_0}(\underset{.}{\neg}\underset{.}{\neg}\alpha) \leftrightarrow \mathsf{Tr}_{\Delta_0}(\alpha)\big)$,

(ii) $\forall\alpha\forall\beta\big(\mathsf{Tr}_{\Delta_0}(\alpha\underset{.}{\rightarrow}\beta) \leftrightarrow \mathsf{Tr}_{\Delta_0}(\underset{.}{\neg}\alpha) \vee \mathsf{Tr}_{\Delta_0}(\beta)\big)$,

(iii) $\forall\alpha\forall\beta\big(\mathsf{Tr}_{\Delta_0}(\underset{.}{\neg}(\alpha\underset{.}{\rightarrow}\beta)) \leftrightarrow \mathsf{Tr}_{\Delta_0}(\alpha) \wedge \mathsf{Tr}_{\Delta_0}(\underset{.}{\neg}\beta)\big)$,

(iv) $\forall\alpha\forall s\forall v\big(\mathsf{Tr}_{\Delta_0}(\underset{.}{\forall} v \underset{.}{\subseteq} s\ \alpha) \leftrightarrow \forall x \subseteq s^\circ\ \mathsf{Tr}_{\Delta_0}(\alpha[\mathsf{q}x/v])\big)$,

(v) $\forall\alpha\forall s\forall v\big(\mathsf{Tr}_{\Delta_0}(\underset{.}{\neg}(\underset{.}{\forall} v \underset{.}{\subseteq} s\ \alpha)) \leftrightarrow \exists x \subseteq s^\circ\ \mathsf{Tr}_{\Delta_0}(\underset{.}{\neg}\alpha[\mathsf{q}x/v])\big)$.

PROOF The left-to-right implication of each clause is a consequence of the definition. Concerning the other direction, we first observe that, provably in E^*, if z and z' are lists of bounded sentences such that z' contains every element of z then $\psi(w,z) \rightarrow \psi(w,z')$. This observation covers all the clauses except (iv). To see (iv), assume, for suitable α, s, and v, that $\mathsf{Tr}_{\Delta_0}(\alpha[\mathsf{q}x/v])$ holds for every $x \subseteq s^\circ$. Let z_x be a list satisfying $\alpha[\mathsf{q}x/v] \in z_x$ and $\forall w \in z_x\ \psi_{\Delta_0}(w, z_x)$ (such a list exists by the assumption $\mathsf{Tr}_{\Delta_0}(\alpha[\mathsf{q}x/v])$). Let z be a list which has as an element every element of z_x for each $x \subseteq s^\circ$. Thus, z is such that $\psi_{\Delta_0}(\underset{.}{\forall} v \underset{.}{\subseteq} s\ \alpha, z)$ and $\forall w \in z\ \psi_{\Delta_0}(w,z)$. Appending to z the sentence $\underset{.}{\forall} v \underset{.}{\subseteq} s\ \alpha$ yields a list witnessing $\mathsf{Tr}_{\Delta_0}(\underset{.}{\forall} v \underset{.}{\subseteq} s\ \alpha)$. ⊣

The equivalences in the previous proposition yield a stronger statement than merely the T-schema for bounded sentences:

11.7 THEOREM *Let* $\varphi(x_1,\ldots,x_n)$ *be a bounded formula with at most the displayed variables free. Then the following sentence is provable in* E^**:*

$$\forall s_1 \cdots \forall s_n\Big(\bigwedge_{i=1}^{n}\mathsf{CTerm}(s_i) \rightarrow \big(\varphi(s_1^\circ,\ldots,s_n^\circ) \leftrightarrow \mathsf{Tr}_{\Delta_0}(\overline{\varphi}[s_1,\ldots,s_n])\big)\Big).$$

In particular, for every bounded sentence φ, $\mathsf{E}^*_{\min} \vdash \varphi \leftrightarrow \mathsf{Tr}_{\Delta_0}(\overline{\varphi})$.

PROOF By induction on the formula φ. If φ is atomic, apply the definition of Tr_{Δ_0} and proposition 11.4. If φ is an implication or bounded universally quantified formula, apply proposition 11.6 and the induction hypothesis. Otherwise, φ is the negation of a bounded formula, say $\varphi \equiv \neg\psi$, and we perform an analogous case distinction on ψ. For instance, if $\varphi \equiv \neg\forall x \subseteq s\ \psi_0(x)$ (and assuming for simplicity that φ is closed), we have

$$\begin{aligned}
\mathsf{E}^* \vdash \mathsf{Tr}_{\Delta_0}(\overline{\varphi}) &\leftrightarrow \exists x \subseteq \overline{s}^\circ\ \mathsf{Tr}_{\Delta_0}(\dot\neg\overline{\psi}[\mathsf{q}x/\overline{x}]) && \text{proposition 11.6}\\
&\leftrightarrow \exists x \subseteq s\ \mathsf{Tr}_{\Delta_0}(\dot\neg\overline{\psi}[\mathsf{q}x/\overline{x}]) && \text{since } \mathsf{E}^* \vdash s = \overline{s}^\circ\\
&\leftrightarrow \exists x \subseteq s\ \mathsf{Tr}_{\Delta_0}(\overline{\neg\psi(\dot x)}) && \text{assumption}\\
&\leftrightarrow \varphi && \text{induction hypothesis}
\end{aligned}$$

⊣

Missing from proposition 11.6 is the claim that a bounded sentence is true if and only if its negation is not true, which follows from the next lemma:

11.8 LEMMA *Let* $\mathsf{Sent}_{\Delta_0}(\mathsf{x})$ *be the* Δ*-formula derived from* Sent *expressing that* x *is a bounded sentence. Then the following hold:*

$$\mathsf{E}^* \vdash \forall\alpha\big(\mathsf{Sent}_{\Delta_0}(\alpha) \to \mathsf{Tr}_{\Delta_0}(\alpha) \vee \mathsf{Tr}_{\Delta_0}(\dot\neg\alpha)\big),$$
$$\mathsf{E}^* \vdash \forall\alpha\big(\mathsf{Sent}_{\Delta_0}(\alpha) \to \neg\mathsf{Tr}_{\Delta_0}(\alpha) \vee \neg\mathsf{Tr}_{\Delta_0}(\dot\neg\alpha)\big).$$

PROOF The two claims are established simultaneously by formal induction on the bounded formula α. We leave the argument as an exercise, though note that arguing by induction on sentences is not as straightforward as induction on formulæ, as we must consider arbitrary substitution instances of subformulæ and not simply subformulæ themselves. This can be handled by inducting over all instantiations of formulæ or on the number of logical connectives and quantifiers in α. ⊣

Combining this lemma with proposition 11.6, we deduce that Tr_{Δ_0} satisfies a number of further properties that may be expected of a truth predicate for bounded formulæ:

11.9 LEMMA *The following are provable in* E^*:

(i) $\forall\alpha\forall\beta\Big(\mathsf{Sent}_{\Delta_0}(\alpha \dot\wedge \beta) \to \big(\mathsf{Tr}_{\Delta_0}(\alpha \dot\to \beta) \leftrightarrow \big(\mathsf{Tr}_{\Delta_0}(\alpha) \to \mathsf{Tr}_{\Delta_0}(\beta)\big)\big)\Big)$,

(ii) $\forall\alpha\forall\beta\Big(\mathsf{Sent}_{\Delta_0}(\alpha \dot\wedge \beta) \to \big(\mathsf{Tr}_{\Delta_0}(\alpha \dot\wedge \beta) \leftrightarrow \mathsf{Tr}_{\Delta_0}(\alpha) \wedge \mathsf{Tr}_{\Delta_0}(\beta)\big)\Big)$,

(iii) $\forall\alpha\forall\beta\Big(\mathsf{Sent}_{\Delta_0}(\alpha \dot\wedge \beta) \to \big(\mathsf{Tr}_{\Delta_0}(\alpha \dot\vee \beta) \leftrightarrow \mathsf{Tr}_{\Delta_0}(\alpha) \vee \mathsf{Tr}_{\Delta_0}(\beta)\big)\Big)$,

(iv) $\forall\alpha\forall v\forall s\forall t\Big(\mathsf{CTerm}(s \dot\frown t) \wedge s^\circ = t^\circ \to \big(\mathsf{Tr}_{\Delta_0}(\alpha[s/v]) \leftrightarrow \mathsf{Tr}_{\Delta_0}(\alpha[t/v])\big)\Big)$,

(v) $\forall\alpha\forall s\forall v\Big(\mathsf{Tr}_{\Delta_0}(\dot\forall v \dot\subseteq s\ \alpha) \leftrightarrow \forall t\big(\mathsf{CTerm}(t) \wedge t^\circ \subseteq s^\circ \to \mathsf{Tr}_{\Delta_0}(\alpha[t/v])\big)\Big)$,

(vi) $\forall\alpha\forall s\forall v\big(\mathsf{Tr}_{\Delta_0}(\dot{\exists} v \dot{\subseteq} s\,\alpha) \leftrightarrow \exists t\big(\mathsf{CTerm}(t) \wedge t^\circ \subseteq s^\circ \wedge \mathsf{Tr}_{\Delta_0}(\alpha[t/v])\big)\big)$.

Recall that $\mathsf{E}^*_{\min} \vdash \forall s\forall t\big(\mathsf{CTerm}(s \dot{\frown} t) \leftrightarrow \mathsf{CTerm}(s) \wedge \mathsf{CTerm}(t)\big)$, so (iv) expresses that truth for bounded sentences is preserved by substitution of equal closed terms. Similarly, the clause $\mathsf{Sent}_{\Delta_0}(\alpha \dot{\wedge} \beta)$ in (i)–(iii) provides a shorthand for expressing that α and β are both bounded sentences.

PROOF Claims (i)–(iii) follow from previous results. For (iv) we must prove a more general statement, namely that for every bounded formula α and all closed terms $s_0, \ldots, s_k, t_0, \ldots, t_k$ satisfying $s_i^\circ = t_i^\circ$ for all $i \leq k$, if $\alpha[s_0/v_0]\cdots[s_k/v_k]$ is a true sentence, then so is $\alpha[t_0/v_0]\cdots[t_k/v_k]$. From (iv), the remaining two items are straightforward: Assuming $\mathsf{Tr}_{\Delta_0}(\dot{\forall} v \dot{\subseteq} s\,\alpha)$, we deduce $\mathsf{Tr}_{\Delta_0}\big(\alpha[\mathsf{q}x/v]\big)$ for every $x \subseteq s^\circ$ by proposition 11.6, whereby (iv) implies $\mathsf{Tr}_{\Delta_0}\big(\alpha[t/v]\big)$ for every closed term t satisfying $t^\circ \subseteq s^\circ$. Similarly for the right-to-left direction of (vi). ⊣

Attempting to apply the reasoning behind Tarski's theorem reveals certain constraints on Tr_{Δ_0} in particular and on definable truth predicates in general. Suppose S is a set of sentences and $\tau(x)$ is a formula for which all S-instances of the T-schema are provable in E^*:

$$\mathsf{E}^* \vdash \varphi \leftrightarrow \tau(\overline{\varphi}) \qquad \text{for every } \varphi \in S.$$

By diagonalization, there is a sentence γ such that $\mathsf{E}^* \vdash \gamma \leftrightarrow \neg\tau(\overline{\gamma})$. Moreover, the proof of diagonalization defines γ as the sentence $\neg\tau(t)$ for a particular term t. So, unless E^* is inconsistent, γ is not an element of S. Since the bounded sentences are closed under negation, it follows that Tr_{Δ_0} is not equivalent to a bounded formula.

11.10 THEOREM *Tr_{Δ_0} is a Δ_1-formula not equivalent to any bounded formula, unless E^* is inconsistent.*

PROOF As presented, Tr_{Δ_0} is neither Σ_1 nor Π_1, due to $\mathsf{Tr}_{\mathrm{at}}$ and $\neg\mathsf{Tr}_{\mathrm{at}}$ both occurring as subformulæ of ψ_{Δ_0}. However, as $\mathsf{Tr}_{\mathrm{at}}$ is Δ_1, it follows that Tr_{Δ_0} is equivalent to a Σ_1-formula. Moreover, lemma 11.9 implies

$$\mathsf{E}^* \vdash \forall x\big(\neg\mathsf{Tr}_{\Delta_0}(x) \leftrightarrow \neg\mathsf{Sent}_{\Delta_0}(x) \vee \mathsf{Tr}_{\Delta_0}(\dot{\neg} x)\big).$$

So Tr_{Δ_0} is also equivalent to a Π_1-formula and is therefore Δ_1. For the second part, assume, to the contrary, that $\tau(x)$ is a bounded formula and

$$\mathsf{E}^* \vdash \forall x\big(\tau(x) \leftrightarrow \mathsf{Tr}_{\Delta_0}(x)\big). \tag{11.2}$$

Consider the 'liar' sentence for $\tau(\mathsf{x})$, that is, the sentence γ given by diagonalizing $\neg\tau(\mathsf{x})$. As remarked, γ has the form $\neg\tau(t)$ for a closed term t, so is bounded. Theorem 11.7 implies that E^* is inconsistent:

$$\begin{array}{ll} \mathsf{E}^* \vdash \gamma \leftrightarrow \mathsf{Tr}_{\Delta_0}(\overline{\gamma}) & \gamma \text{ is bounded} \\ \mathsf{E}^* \vdash \gamma \leftrightarrow \tau(\overline{\gamma}) & (11.2) \\ \mathsf{E}^* \vdash \gamma \leftrightarrow \neg\gamma & \text{construction of } \gamma \qquad \dashv \end{array}$$

Building on Tr_{Δ_0} – which we henceforth assume is given in its Σ_1-form – truth predicates for sentences featuring limited unbounded quantification can be obtained. We begin with the Σ_1-sentences. The formula ψ_{Σ_1} below is structurally simpler than Tr_{Δ_0} and more similar in construction to the formulæ expressing terms, formulæ, and proofs. Given a Σ_1-formula α we stipulate the existence of a finite set Z of formulæ which contains α and is such that every $\beta \in Z$ is true under the assumption that Z contains all true immediate subformulæ of β.

$$\begin{aligned} \psi_{\Sigma_1}(\alpha, z) \; := \; & \big(\mathsf{Sent}_{\Delta_0}(\alpha) \wedge \mathsf{Tr}_{\Delta_0}(\alpha)\big) \\ & \vee \exists\beta\exists\gamma\big(\alpha = \beta \mathbin{\dot\wedge} \gamma \wedge \beta \in z \wedge \gamma \in z\big) \\ & \vee \exists\beta\exists\gamma\big(\alpha = \beta \mathbin{\dot\vee} \gamma \wedge (\beta \in z \vee \gamma \in z)\big) \\ & \vee \exists\beta\exists v\exists s\big(\alpha = \dot\forall v \mathbin{\dot\subseteq} s\, \beta \wedge \mathsf{CTerm}(s) \wedge \forall x \subseteq s^\circ\, \beta[\mathsf{q}x/v] \in z\big) \\ & \vee \exists\beta\exists v\big(\alpha = \dot\exists v \beta \wedge \exists x\, \beta[\mathsf{q}x/v] \in z\big). \end{aligned}$$

Since Tr_{Δ_0} is assumed to be in its Σ_1-form, ψ_{Σ_1} is a Σ_1-formula. Even though Sent_{Δ_0} and Tr_{Δ_0} are examples of Δ_1-formulæ, it does not follow that ψ_{Σ_1} is Δ_1 because of the unbounded existential quantifier '$\exists x$' in the final clause.

11.11 DEFINITION $\mathsf{Tr}_{\Sigma_1}(x) := \exists z\big(\mathsf{List}(z) \wedge x \in z \wedge \forall w \in z\; \psi_{\Sigma_1}(w, z)\big)$.

Observe that Tr_{Σ_1} is a Σ_1-formula. This definition can be shown to satisfy a number of properties in common with Tr_{Δ_0}:

11.12 PROPOSITION *Let* Sent_{Σ_1} *be the variant of* Sent *expressing the* Σ_1*-sentences of* $\mathcal{L}^*$*. The following are provable in* E^**:*

(i) $\forall x\big(\mathsf{Tr}_{\Sigma_1}(x) \rightarrow \mathsf{Sent}_{\Sigma_1}(x)\big)$,

(ii) $\forall\alpha\forall\beta\big(\mathsf{Tr}_{\Sigma_1}(\alpha \mathbin{\dot\wedge} \beta) \leftrightarrow \mathsf{Tr}_{\Sigma_1}(\alpha) \wedge \mathsf{Tr}_{\Sigma_1}(\beta)\big)$,

(iii) $\forall\alpha\forall\beta\big(\mathsf{Tr}_{\Sigma_1}(\alpha\underset{\cdot}{\vee}\beta) \leftrightarrow \mathsf{Tr}_{\Sigma_1}(\alpha) \vee \mathsf{Tr}_{\Sigma_1}(\beta)\big)$,

(iv) $\forall\alpha\forall s\forall v\big(\mathsf{Tr}_{\Sigma_1}(\underset{\cdot}{\forall} v\underset{\cdot}{\subseteq} s\,\alpha) \leftrightarrow \forall x\subseteq s^\circ\, \mathsf{Tr}_{\Sigma_1}(\alpha[\mathsf{q}x/v])\big)$,

(v) $\forall\alpha\forall s\forall v\big(\mathsf{Tr}_{\Sigma_1}(\underset{\cdot}{\exists} v\underset{\cdot}{\subseteq} s\,\alpha) \leftrightarrow \exists x\subseteq s^\circ\, \mathsf{Tr}_{\Sigma_1}(\alpha[\mathsf{q}x/v])\big)$,

(vi) $\forall\alpha\forall v\big(\mathsf{Tr}_{\Sigma_1}(\underset{\cdot}{\exists} v\alpha) \leftrightarrow \exists x\, \mathsf{Tr}_{\Sigma_1}(\alpha[\mathsf{q}x/v])\big)$,

(vii) $\forall\alpha\Big(\mathsf{Sent}_{\Delta_0}(\alpha) \to \big(\mathsf{Tr}_{\Sigma_1}(\alpha) \leftrightarrow \mathsf{Tr}_{\Delta_0}(\alpha)\big)\Big)$.

PROOF The choice of ψ_{Σ_1} ensures that $\forall x(\mathsf{Tr}_{\Sigma_1}(x) \to \mathsf{Sent}(x))$, and the strengthening of this result required to deduce (i) is straightforward. Claims (ii)–(v) follow the same arguments as proposition 11.6. Although not being a clause that holds for Tr_{Δ_0}, (vi) is likewise straightforward. Finally, (vii) is established by formal induction on α using (ii)–(v) and the analogous clauses from proposition 11.6. ⊣

A stronger form of the quantifier axioms is also derivable, where substitution acts on arbitrary closed terms, not only pure terms:

11.13 LEMMA *The following are provable in* E^**:*

(i) $\forall\alpha\exists v\exists s\exists t\Big(\mathsf{CTerm}(s \,\underset{\cdot}{\frown}\, t) \wedge s^\circ = t^\circ \to \big(\mathsf{Tr}_{\Sigma_1}(\alpha[s/v]) \leftrightarrow \mathsf{Tr}_{\Sigma_1}(\alpha[t/v])\big)\Big)$,

(ii) $\forall\alpha\exists s\exists v\Big(\mathsf{Tr}_{\Sigma_1}(\underset{\cdot}{\forall} v\underset{\cdot}{\subseteq} s\,\alpha) \leftrightarrow \forall t\big(\mathsf{CTerm}(t) \wedge t^\circ\subseteq s^\circ \to \mathsf{Tr}_{\Sigma_1}(\alpha[t/v])\big)\Big)$,

(iii) $\forall\alpha\exists v\big(\mathsf{Tr}_{\Sigma_1}(\underset{\cdot}{\exists} v\alpha) \leftrightarrow \exists s\, \mathsf{Tr}_{\Sigma_1}(\alpha[s/v])\big)$.

PROOF Analogous to lemma 11.9. ⊣

Combining these results, we deduce that Tr_{Σ_1} is a truth predicate for Σ_1-sentences:

11.14 THEOREM *Let $\varphi(x_1,\dots,x_k)$ be a Σ_1-formula with at most the displayed variables free. Then the following sentence is provable in* E^**:*

$$\forall s_1\cdots\forall s_n\Big(\bigwedge_{i=1}^{n}\mathsf{CTerm}(s_i) \to \big(\varphi(s_1^\circ,\dots,s_n^\circ) \leftrightarrow \mathsf{Tr}_{\Sigma_1}(\overline{\varphi}[s_1,\dots,s_n])\big)\Big).$$

In particular, $\mathsf{E} \vdash \varphi \leftrightarrow \mathsf{Tr}_{\Sigma_1}(\overline{\varphi})$ *if φ is a Σ_1-sentence.*

As Tr_{Σ_1} is a Σ_1-formula, it can be inserted for φ in theorem 11.14:

$$\mathsf{E}^*_{\min} \vdash \forall x\Big(\mathsf{Tr}_{\Sigma_1}(x) \leftrightarrow \mathsf{Tr}_{\Sigma_1}\big(\overline{\mathsf{Tr}_{\Sigma_1}(\underset{\cdot}{x})}\big)\Big). \tag{11.3}$$

Unlike the truth predicate Tr_{Δ_0}, which theorem 11.10 shows is not equivalent to any bounded formula, here we have a defined truth predicate for a collection of formulæ that contains the truth predicate itself. Property (11.3) does not contradict Tarski's theorem because Σ_1 – more precisely, the set of formulæ provably equivalent to Σ_1-formulæ – is not closed under negation. The 'liar' sentence for this Σ_1 truth predicate is constructed by diagonalizing on the formula $\neg\mathsf{Tr}_{\Sigma_1}$, which is not Σ_1. Just as there are Δ_1-formulæ not equivalent to any bounded formula, there are Σ_1-formulæ that are not equivalent to any Π_1-formula in a consistent theory E^*. In other words, Σ_1 and Π_1 both properly extend Δ_1.

11.15 THEOREM *There exists a Σ_1-formula which is not provably equivalent to a Π_1-formula in any consistent theory* E^*.

PROOF As remarked, we consider the Σ_1-formula Tr_{Σ_1}. Assume, on the contrary, that $\tau(x)$ is a Σ_1-formula such that $\mathsf{E}^* \vdash \forall x\big(\mathsf{Tr}_{\Sigma_1}(x) \leftrightarrow \neg\tau(x)\big)$. Diagonalization yields a term t such that

$$\mathsf{E}^*_{\min} \vdash t = \overline{\tau(t)}.$$

In particular, $\mathsf{E}^* \vdash \mathsf{Tr}_{\Sigma_1}(t) \leftrightarrow \tau(t)$, because $\tau \in \Sigma_1$. But also

$$\mathsf{E}^* \vdash \mathsf{Tr}_{\Sigma_1}(t) \leftrightarrow \neg\tau(t),$$

so E^* is inconsistent. ⊣

The Σ-completeness theorem 10.14 established that every true Σ_1-sentence of $\mathcal{L}^*_{\mathrm{syn}}$ is a theorem of $\mathsf{E}^*_{\min}$. The formalized Σ-completeness theorem 10.70 generalized this result by showing that the implication $\varphi \to \mathsf{Bew}_{\mathsf{E}^*_{\min}}(\overline{\varphi})$ is provable in $\mathsf{E}^*_{\min}$ whenever φ is a Σ-sentence (over $\mathsf{E}^*_{\min}$). A more literal formalization of the claim 'All true Σ-sentences are provable in $\mathsf{E}^*_{\min}$' can be given using defined truth predicates. Let $\mathsf{Sent}_{\mathrm{syn}}(x)$ be the natural variant of $\mathsf{Sent}(x)$ expressing that x is a sentence of $\mathcal{L}^*_{\mathrm{syn}}$. The true Σ-sentences over $\mathsf{E}^*_{\min}$ are expressed by the formula

$$\mathsf{Tr}_{\Sigma}(x) \;:=\; \exists\beta\big(\mathsf{Sent}_{\mathrm{syn}}(\beta) \wedge \mathsf{Tr}_{\Sigma_1}(\beta) \wedge \mathsf{Bew}_{\mathsf{E}^*_{\min}}(\beta \mathbin{\dot\leftrightarrow} x)\big).$$

A direct formalization of the Σ-completeness theorem in $\mathsf{E}^*_{\min}$ takes the following form:

11.16 THEOREM $\mathsf{E}^*_{\min} \vdash \forall\alpha\big(\mathsf{Tr}_{\Sigma}(\alpha) \to \mathsf{Bew}_{\mathsf{E}^*_{\min}}(\alpha)\big)$.

The proof applies the formalized Σ-completeness theorem to the derived truth predicate for Σ_1-sentences of $\mathcal{L}^*_{\text{syn}}$, namely the formula $\mathsf{Sent}_{\text{syn}}(x) \wedge \mathsf{Tr}_{\Sigma_1}(x)$. To be allowed to do this we must determine that the formula is actually Σ. As we observed with Tr_{at}, a truth predicate like Tr_{Σ_1} will not be Σ if $\mathcal{L}^*$ contains a function or predicate symbol not in $\mathcal{L}^*_{\text{min}}$. The reader can confirm, however, that restricting attention to the language $\mathcal{L}^*_{\text{syn}}$ is sufficient to obtain a Σ-formula.

PROOF As an instance of formalized Σ-completeness (theorem 10.70) we have

$$\mathsf{E}^*_{\text{min}} \vdash \forall x\Big(\mathsf{Sent}_{\text{syn}}(x) \wedge \mathsf{Tr}_{\Sigma_1}(x) \to \mathsf{Bew}_{\mathsf{E}^*_{\text{min}}}\big(\overline{\mathsf{Sent}_{\text{syn}}(\dot{x}) \wedge \mathsf{Tr}_{\Sigma_1}(\dot{x})}\big)\Big).$$

Theorem 11.14 established that $\mathsf{E}^*_{\text{min}} \vdash \mathsf{Tr}_{\Sigma_1}(\overline{\varphi}) \to \varphi$ for every Σ_1-sentence φ. The proof of the theorem can be carried out within the theory $\mathsf{E}^*_{\text{min}}$, yielding

$$\mathsf{E}^*_{\text{min}} \vdash \forall \alpha\Big(\mathsf{Sent}_{\Sigma_1}(\alpha) \to \mathsf{Bew}_{\mathsf{E}^*_{\text{min}}}\big(\overline{\mathsf{Tr}_{\Sigma_1}(\dot{\alpha})} \mathbin{\dot{\to}} \alpha\big)\Big).$$

Noting that $\mathsf{Tr}_{\Sigma_1}(x) \to \mathsf{Sent}_{\Sigma_1}(x)$ is provable in $\mathsf{E}^*_{\text{min}}$ (proposition 11.12), the observations above and proposition 10.68 entail that

$$\mathsf{E}^*_{\text{min}} \vdash \forall \alpha \forall x\big(\mathsf{Sent}_{\text{syn}}(x) \wedge \mathsf{Tr}_{\Sigma_1}(x) \wedge \mathsf{Bew}_{\mathsf{E}^*_{\text{min}}}(x \mathbin{\dot{\leftrightarrow}} \alpha) \to \mathsf{Bew}_{\mathsf{E}^*_{\text{min}}}(\alpha)\big).$$

By logic, we conclude $\mathsf{E}^*_{\text{min}} \vdash \forall \alpha\big(\mathsf{Tr}_{\Sigma}(\alpha) \to \mathsf{Bew}_{\mathsf{E}^*_{\text{min}}}(\alpha)\big)$. ⊣

Theorem 11.15 provides the latest in a string of negative consequences of diagonalization: we have the paradoxes of chapter 6, including Tarski's undefinability theorem and Gödel's incompleteness theorems, the denotation paradox of chapter 9, and the two separation results (theorems 11.10 and 11.15) of the present section.

Diagonalization is also a useful tool for constructing formulæ which have specific properties. The method of diagonalization provides for each formula $\varphi(x)$ a sentence α such that $\mathsf{E}^*_{\text{min}} \vdash \alpha \leftrightarrow \varphi(\overline{\alpha})$. In other words, given a property φ, we can find a formula α equivalent to the statement that φ holds of α. The next theorem demonstrates a different kind of diagonalization. It states that for certain formulæ ψ there exists a formula α such that

$$\mathsf{E}^*_{\text{min}} \vdash \alpha \leftrightarrow \psi(\alpha). \tag{11.4}$$

By writing $\psi(\alpha)$ instead of $\psi(\overline{\alpha})$ we mean that α has been inserted into the formula ψ and occurs as a *subformula* of $\psi(\alpha)$. We call α a fixed point of ψ if (11.4) holds. Rather than expressing a statement about the *expression* α, as the formula $\varphi(\overline{\alpha})$ does, $\psi(\alpha)$ expresses a property of the *extension* of α, namely, a statement about the collection of expressions that satisfy α.

Before we state the theorem properly, it is important to clarify the construction of $\psi(\alpha)$. Let P be a fresh n-ary relation symbol. We write $\psi(x_1,\ldots,x_k;\mathsf{P})$ to emphasize that $\psi(x_1,\ldots,x_k)$ is a formula of $\mathcal{L}^*\cup\{\mathsf{P}\}$, the language expanded to include P but not its associated syntactic constant. Given such a formula and a formula $\alpha(\mathsf{v}_1,\ldots,\mathsf{v}_n)$ with only the marked variables occurring free, we define $\psi(x_1,\ldots,x_k;\alpha)$ to be the formula which results from replacing every occurrence of P in ψ by α. This means that each atom of the form $\mathsf{P}t_1\cdots t_n$ in ψ for terms $t_1,\ldots,t_n$ becomes $\alpha(t_1,\ldots,t_n)$ in $\psi(x_1,\ldots,x_k;\alpha)$. For example, if $\psi(\mathsf{P})$ is

$$\forall x\exists y\big(\mathsf{P}xy\wedge\mathsf{P}x(y^\frown y)\big)$$

and $\alpha\equiv\mathsf{v}_1\subseteq\mathsf{v}_2$, then $\psi(x_1,\ldots,x_k;\alpha)\equiv\forall x\exists y(x\subseteq y\wedge x\subseteq y^\frown y.)$

Unlike the method of diagonalization, the fixed-point statement (11.4) does not have a solution for all choices of $\psi(\mathsf{P})$. In particular, there can be no solution in the case $\psi\equiv\neg\mathsf{P}$ (where the arity of P is 0). The first restriction we impose is thus to formulæ with only positive occurrences of P:

11.17 DEFINITION A formula ψ is P-positive provided one of the following conditions holds:

(i) ψ does not contain P, or $\psi\equiv\mathsf{P}t_1\cdots t_n$ for terms $t_1,\ldots,t_n$.

(ii) $\psi\equiv\psi_1\to\psi_2$ and $\neg\psi_1$ and ψ_2 are P-positive.

(iii) $\psi\equiv\neg(\psi_1\to\psi_2)$ and ψ_1 and $\neg\psi_2$ are P-positive.

(iv) $\psi\equiv\neg\neg\psi_1$ and ψ_1 is P-positive.

(v) $\psi\equiv\forall x\,\psi_1$ and ψ_1 is P-positive.

(vi) $\psi\equiv\neg\forall x\,\psi_1$ and $\neg\psi_1$ is P-positive.

In particular, if ψ is constructed from atomic formulæ $\mathsf{P}t_1\cdots t_n$ and formulæ not containing P via the defined connectives $\wedge,\vee$ and quantifiers $\forall$ and $\exists$, then ψ is P-positive.

11.18 Σ_1-FIXED-POINT THEOREM *Let $\psi(\mathsf{v}_1,\ldots,\mathsf{v}_n;\mathsf{P})$ be a P-positive Σ_1-formula with at most the marked variables occurring free, and let the arity of P be n. Then there exists a Σ_1-formula α of $\mathcal{L}^*$ such that*

$$\mathsf{E}^*\vdash\forall\mathsf{v}_0\cdots\forall\mathsf{v}_n\big(\alpha(\mathsf{v}_1,\ldots,\mathsf{v}_n)\leftrightarrow\psi(\mathsf{v}_1,\ldots,\mathsf{v}_n;\alpha)\big).$$

For some formulæ fixed points are easy to find. Every formula is a fixed point of $\mathsf{P}\mathsf{v}_1\cdots\mathsf{v}_n$. Moreover, we have shown that many of the Σ_1-formulæ we have introduced satisfy fixed-point equations of the kind in theorem 11.18 (for example propositions 10.45, 10.68, and 11.12). The proof of the theorem presents a uniform method for 'solving' any fixed-point equation $\mathsf{P}\mathsf{v}_1\cdots\mathsf{v}_n \leftrightarrow \psi(\mathsf{v}_1,\ldots,\mathsf{v}_n;\mathsf{P})$ where ψ is a P-positive Σ_1-formula.

PROOF Without loss of generality we may assume that v_0 is not free in ψ and none of the variables $\mathsf{v}_0, \ldots, \mathsf{v}_n$ occur bound in ψ. Recall, $\mathsf{x} \equiv \mathsf{v}_0$. We present the argument for the case that $n = 1$, so Px is an atomic formula and the only variable free in ψ is y. Let $\hat{\psi}$ be given by

$$\hat{\psi}(\mathsf{x},\mathsf{y}) := \psi\big(\mathsf{y}; \mathsf{Tr}_{\Sigma_1}\big(\mathsf{sub}(\mathsf{x},\bar{\mathsf{y}},\mathsf{qy})\big)\big),$$

which replaces each atom $\mathsf{P}t$ in ψ by the Σ_1-formula $\mathsf{Tr}_{\Sigma_1}\big(\mathsf{sub}(\mathsf{x},\bar{\mathsf{y}},\mathsf{q}t)\big)$ expressing that x is a true Σ_1-formula when the variable y is replaced by the quotation of t°. Since ψ is P-positive, $\hat{\psi}$ is a Σ_1-formula. The diagonal lemma 5.13 yields a Σ_1-formula $\alpha(\mathsf{y})$ such that

$$\begin{aligned}
\mathsf{E}^* &\vdash \forall\mathsf{y}\Big(\alpha(\mathsf{y}) \leftrightarrow \psi\big(\mathsf{y}; \mathsf{Tr}_{\Sigma_1}\big(\mathsf{sub}(\overline{\alpha},\bar{\mathsf{y}},\mathsf{qy})\big)\big)\Big),\\
\mathsf{E}^* &\vdash \forall\mathsf{y}\Big(\alpha(\mathsf{y}) \leftrightarrow \psi\big(\mathsf{y}; \mathsf{Tr}_{\Sigma_1}\big(\overline{\alpha(\underset{\cdot}{\mathsf{y}})}\big)\big)\Big),\\
\mathsf{E}^* &\vdash \forall\mathsf{y}\big(\alpha(\mathsf{y}) \leftrightarrow \psi(\mathsf{y};\alpha)\big).
\end{aligned}$$

The final equivalence is due to theorem 11.14 as α is Σ_1. ⊣

Rather than explicitly defining a Σ_1-formula and demonstrating that the property it expresses fulfils a desired fixed-point equation, theorem 11.18 allows us to stipulate upfront the conditions a property should satisfy and presents a formula whose extension fulfils these conditions. For instance, let P be binary and define

$$\begin{aligned}
\psi_{\mathsf{FV}}(\mathsf{y},\mathsf{z};\mathsf{P}) := {}& \big(\mathsf{Var}(\mathsf{y}) \wedge \mathsf{Atom}(\mathsf{z}) \wedge \mathsf{y}\subseteq\mathsf{z}\big) \vee \exists\mathsf{w}\subseteq\mathsf{z}\,(\mathsf{z} = \underset{\cdot}{\neg}\mathsf{w} \wedge \mathsf{Pyw}) \vee\\
&\vee \exists\mathsf{v}_3\subseteq\mathsf{z}\,\exists\mathsf{v}_4\subseteq\mathsf{z}\,\big(\mathsf{z} = \mathsf{v}_3 \underset{\cdot}{\rightarrow} \mathsf{v}_4 \wedge (\mathsf{Pyv}_3 \vee \mathsf{Pyv}_4)\big) \vee\\
&\vee \exists\mathsf{v}_3\subseteq\mathsf{z}\,\exists\mathsf{v}_4\subseteq\mathsf{z}\,\big(\mathsf{z} = \underset{\cdot}{\forall}\mathsf{v}_3\,\mathsf{v}_4 \wedge \mathsf{Var}(\mathsf{v}_3) \wedge \mathsf{y} \neq \mathsf{v}_3 \wedge \mathsf{Pyv}_4\big).
\end{aligned}$$

This formula expresses the inductive clauses of the relation 'has a free occurrence of a variable'. Inserting a formula $\alpha(y,z)$ for P in ψ_{FV} gives rise to

$$\begin{aligned}\psi_{FV}(y,z;\alpha) \equiv \big(\mathsf{Var}(y) \wedge \mathsf{Atom}(z) \wedge y \subseteq z\big) \vee \exists w \subseteq z\,(z = \dot{\neg} w \wedge \alpha(y,w)) \vee \\ \vee \exists v_3 \subseteq z\, \exists v_4 \subseteq z\,\big(z = v_3 \dot{\rightarrow} v_4 \wedge (\alpha(y,v_3) \vee \alpha(y,v_4))\big) \vee \\ \vee \exists v_3 \subseteq z\, \exists v_4 \subseteq z\,\big(z = \dot{\forall} v_3\, v_4 \wedge \mathsf{Var}(v_3) \wedge y \neq v_3 \wedge \alpha(y,v_4)\big).\end{aligned}$$

Selecting the formula $\mathsf{FV}(y,z)$ (defined on page 268) for α, we obtain the following as a consequence of proposition 10.49:

$$\mathsf{E}^* \vdash \forall y \forall z\big(\mathsf{FV}(y,z) \leftrightarrow \psi_{FV}(y,z;\mathsf{FV})\big). \tag{11.5}$$

Theorem 11.18 provides a formula, which we shall call FV', that satisfies the same equation:

$$\mathsf{E}^* \vdash \forall y \forall z\big(\mathsf{FV}'(y,z) \leftrightarrow \psi_{FV}(y,z;\mathsf{FV}')\big). \tag{11.6}$$

Like FV, FV' is Σ_1 by construction. Inspecting the proof of theorem 11.18, however, shows the two formulæ to be essentially different. FV' is defined 'indirectly' via diagonalization and a partial truth predicate, whereas FV supposedly directly formalizes the notion of free variable. The fixed-point property (11.6) is a consequence of general results about diagonalization and the defined truth predicate for Σ_1-sentences. In contrast, establishing (11.5) relies on the specific definition of FV and the proof uses the axiom of induction.

Despite the differences, it can be shown that these two 'definitions' of free variable coincide:

$$\mathsf{E}^* \vdash \forall \alpha \forall \nu\big(\mathsf{FV}(\nu,\alpha) \leftrightarrow \mathsf{FV}'(\nu,\alpha)\big).$$

In fact, the proof does not rely on the particular construction of FV' given in the proof of theorem 11.18, as the next lemma emphasizes:

11.19 LEMMA *Let $\psi_{FV}(\mathsf{P})$ be as above and suppose $\alpha(y,z)$ is such that*

$$\mathsf{E}^* \vdash \forall y \forall z\big(\alpha(y,z) \leftrightarrow \psi_{FV}(y,z;\alpha)\big).$$

Then $\mathsf{E}^* \vdash \forall y \forall z\big(\alpha(y,z) \leftrightarrow \mathsf{FV}(y,z)\big)$.

We omit the proof of this lemma as it is not important for our considerations.

Rephrasing lemma 11.19, all 'solutions' to the equation in theorem 11.18 for the case $\psi \equiv \psi_{\mathsf{FV}}$ are provably equivalent. On first impression, the lemma may not seem surprising. After all, $\psi_{\mathsf{FV}}(\mathsf{P})$ directly expresses the inductive part of the property of having a free occurrence of a variable. Many fixed-point equations do not have unique solutions, including the simplest where P is a 0-ary predicate symbol and ψ is P. The fixed point constructed by the proof of theorem 11.18 for this choice of ψ is a formula α such that

$$\mathsf{E}^* \vdash \alpha \leftrightarrow \mathsf{Tr}_{\Sigma_1}(\overline{\alpha}).$$

Even this condition does not uniquely determine α, as theorem 11.14 shows. Looking closer at the proof, we see that the chosen α is the specific formula $\mathsf{Tr}_{\Sigma_1}(t)$ for a term t satisfying

$$\mathsf{E}^* \vdash t = \overline{\mathsf{Tr}_{\Sigma_1}(t)}. \tag{11.7}$$

That is to say, for the simplest fixed-point equation, where $\psi \equiv \mathsf{P}$, theorem 11.18 chooses ψ to be the 'truth teller' for the Σ_1 truth predicate. As we will explore in the next chapter, even (11.7) does not uniquely determine t. Nevertheless, it does determine the truth value of ψ, a fact that will be shown in theorem 11.31.

Stepping away from the trivial cases, we consider provability. Let $\psi_{\mathsf{Bew}}(\mathsf{P})$ express the inductive equation for the definition of 'is provable in $\mathsf{E}^*_{\min}$':

$$\psi_{\mathsf{Bew}}(\mathsf{x};\mathsf{P}) := \mathsf{Form}(\mathsf{x}) \wedge \Big(\mathsf{Axiom}_{\mathsf{PL}}(\mathsf{x}) \vee \mathsf{Axiom}_{\mathsf{E}^*_{\min}}(\mathsf{x}) \vee \\ \exists\alpha\exists v\Big(\big(\mathsf{P}\alpha \wedge \mathsf{P}(\alpha \,\dot{\rightarrow}\, \mathsf{x})\big) \vee \big(\mathsf{P}\alpha \wedge \mathsf{Var}(v) \wedge \mathsf{x} = \dot{\forall} v \alpha\big)\Big)\Big).$$

This formula expresses nothing more than the one-step condition for provability in $\mathsf{E}^*_{\min}$ relative to the predicate P. We have already observed that $\psi_{\mathsf{Bew}}(\mathsf{x};\mathsf{P})$ admits a fixed point:

$$\mathsf{E}^* \vdash \forall x\big(\mathsf{Bew}_{\mathsf{E}^*_{\min}}(x) \leftrightarrow \psi_{\mathsf{Bew}}(x;\mathsf{Bew}_{\mathsf{E}^*_{\min}})\big). \tag{11.8}$$

Theorem 11.18 provides an alternative fixed point which is also Σ_1. But as with the previous example, there are other fixed points, such as

$$\mathsf{E}^* \vdash \forall x\big(\mathsf{Sent}(x) \leftrightarrow \psi_{\mathsf{Bew}}(x;\mathsf{Sent})\big).$$

The left-to-right direction follows from the trivial observation that if x is a sentence, then so is $x \dot{\rightarrow} x$. The other direction is equally straightforward.

Returning to truth predicates, a partial truth predicate for Π_1-formulæ can be defined by dualizing the construction of Tr_{Σ_1}. In a sense, we want to say that a Π_1-formula is true if and only if its negation is equivalent to a true Σ_1-sentence. However, the negation of a Π_1-formula is not in general a Σ_1-formula, but merely logically equivalent to one. The solution is to formulate Π_1-truth in terms of non-truth: a Π_1-sentence is *false* if there exists a finite set of instantiations of subformulæ consisting of false bounded sentences and closed under falsity-preserving constructions of the Π_1-formula class. The local condition of this construction is stipulated by the following formula:

$$\begin{aligned}
\psi_{\Pi_1}(\alpha, z) := \ & \big(\mathsf{Sent}_{\Delta_0}(\alpha) \wedge \neg\mathsf{Tr}_{\Delta_0}(\alpha)\big) \vee \\
& \vee \exists\beta\exists\gamma\big(\alpha = \beta \dot{\wedge} \gamma \wedge (\beta \in z \vee \gamma \in z)\big) \\
& \vee \exists\beta\exists\gamma\big(\alpha = \beta \dot{\vee} \gamma \wedge \beta \in z \wedge \gamma \in z\big) \\
& \vee \exists\beta\exists v\exists s\big(\alpha = \dot{\exists} v \dot{\subseteq} s\, \beta \wedge \mathsf{CTerm}(s) \wedge \forall x \subseteq s^{\circ}\, \beta[\mathsf{q}x/v] \in z\big) \\
& \vee \exists\beta\exists v\big(\alpha = \dot{\forall} v \beta \wedge \exists w\, \beta[\mathsf{q}w/v] \in z\big).
\end{aligned}$$

A Π_1-formula is then true if and only if it avoids every such set of Π_1-formulæ:

11.20 DEFINITION $\mathsf{Tr}_{\Pi_1}(x) := \forall z\big(\mathsf{List}(z) \wedge \forall w \in z\, \psi_{\Pi_1}(w, z) \rightarrow x \notin z\big)$.

This formula is not explicitly Π_1, but is logically equivalent to a Π_1-formula as the subformula ψ_{Π_1} is equivalent to a Σ_1-formula and occurs in a negative position in Tr_{Π_1}. We skip stating the versions of the compositional clauses for this predicate in the hope that they are clear from the definition and earlier work. As we should expect, the formula is a partial truth predicate for Π_1-sentences:

11.21 THEOREM *Let $\varphi(x_1, \ldots, x_k)$ be a Π_1-formula with at most the displayed variables free. Then the following holds:*

$$\mathsf{E}^* \vdash \forall x_1 \cdots \forall x_k\Big(\varphi(x_1, \ldots, x_k) \leftrightarrow \mathsf{Tr}_{\Pi_1}\big(\overline{\varphi(\dot{x}_1, \ldots, \dot{x}_k)}\big)\Big).$$

It is not difficult to extend the construction of partial truth predicates to larger classes of formulæ. For instance, we can take the definition of Tr_{Π_1} and replace reference to bounded formulæ – the predicates Sent_{Δ_0} and Tr_{Δ_0} in $\psi_{\Pi_1}(\alpha, z)$ – by Σ_1-sentences, using the Σ_1 truth predicate. The result is a partial truth predicate for formulæ obtained by closing Σ_1 under the connectives $\wedge$ and $\vee$, bounded quantifiers, and unbounded universal quantifiers. This class is denoted Π_2 and marks the second step in the *quantifier hierarchy*.

11.22 DEFINITION Let $\Sigma_0 = \Pi_0 = \Delta_0$ be the set of bounded formulæ of $\mathcal{L}^*$. For each $n \geq 0$, the class Σ_{n+1} is the smallest set of formulæ satisfying the following four clauses:

(i) $\Pi_n \cup \Sigma_n \subseteq \Sigma_{n+1}$.

(ii) If $\varphi, \psi \in \Sigma_{n+1}$, then $\varphi \vee \psi \in \Sigma_{n+1}$ and $\varphi \wedge \psi \in \Sigma_{n+1}$.

(iii) If $\varphi \in \Sigma_{n+1}$, v a variable, and t a term not containing v, then $\forall v \subseteq t\, \varphi \in \Sigma_{n+1}$ and $\exists v \subseteq t\, \varphi \in \Sigma_{n+1}$.

(iv) If $\varphi \in \Sigma_{n+1}$, then $\exists v \varphi \in \Sigma_{n+1}$.

The class Π_{n+1} is defined analogously by the same clauses but with the next rule in place of (iv):

(v) If $\varphi \in \Pi_{n+1}$, then $\forall v \varphi \in \Pi_{n+1}$.

A formula is Δ_n if it is provably equivalent to both a Σ_n- and a Π_n-formula.

The reader should verify that the definition agrees with definition 10.11 in the case $n = 0$. The following two lemmas are direct generalizations of our results regarding Σ_1-formulæ:

11.23 LEMMA *Every formula is logically equivalent to a Σ_n-formula for some n. Every Σ_n-formula is logically equivalent to the negation of a Π_n-formula.*

11.24 LEMMA *Let φ be a Σ_{n+1}-formula. Then there exists a Π_n-formula $\psi(y)$ such that $\mathsf{E}^*_{\min} \vdash \varphi \leftrightarrow \exists y\, \psi(y)$. Similarly, for every Π_{n+1}-formula φ there exists a Σ_n-formula $\psi(y)$ such that $\mathsf{E}^*_{\min} \vdash \varphi \leftrightarrow \forall y\, \psi(y)$.*

We leave to the reader the task of designing Δ-formulæ Form_{Σ_n}, Form_{Π_n}, Sent_{Σ_n}, and Sent_{Π_n} expressing formulæ and sentences from the classes Σ_n and Π_n. As mentioned in the introduction to the chapter, partial truth predicates can be obtained for each level in the quantifier hierarchy by generalizing the construction for the Σ_1/Π_1-level.

11.25 DEFINITION By recursion on $n \geq 1$, we define formulæ $\mathsf{Tr}_{\Sigma_{n+1}}$ and $\mathsf{Tr}_{\Pi_{n+1}}$:

$$\begin{aligned}
\psi_{\Sigma_{n+1}}(\alpha, z) &:= \big(\mathsf{Sent}_{\Pi_n}(\alpha) \wedge \mathsf{Tr}_{\Pi_n}(\alpha)\big)\\
&\quad \vee\ \exists\beta\exists\gamma\big(\alpha = \beta \underset{\cdot}{\wedge} \gamma \wedge \beta \in z \wedge \gamma \in z\big)\\
&\quad \vee\ \exists\beta\exists\gamma\big(\alpha = \beta \underset{\cdot}{\vee} \gamma \wedge (\beta \in z \vee \gamma \in z)\big)\\
&\quad \vee\ \exists\beta\exists v\exists s\big(\alpha = \underset{\cdot}{\forall} v \underset{\cdot}{\subseteq} s\, \beta \wedge \mathsf{CTerm}(s) \wedge \forall x \subseteq s^{\circ}\, \beta[\mathsf{q}x/v] \in z\big)\\
&\quad \vee\ \exists\beta\exists v\big(\alpha = \underset{\cdot}{\exists} v \beta \wedge \exists w\, \beta[\mathsf{q}w/v] \in z\big),\\
\mathsf{Tr}_{\Sigma_{n+1}}(x) &:= \exists z\big(\mathsf{List}(z) \wedge x \in z \wedge \forall w \in z\ \psi_{\Sigma_{n+1}}(w, z)\big),
\end{aligned}$$

$$\begin{aligned}
\psi_{\Pi_{n+1}}(\alpha, z) &:= \big(\mathsf{Sent}_{\Sigma_n}(\alpha) \wedge \neg\mathsf{Tr}_{\Sigma_n}(\alpha)\big)\\
&\quad \vee\ \exists\beta\exists\gamma\big(\alpha = \beta \underset{\cdot}{\wedge} \gamma \wedge (\beta \in z \vee \gamma \in z)\big)\\
&\quad \vee\ \exists\beta\exists\gamma\big(\alpha = \beta \underset{\cdot}{\vee} \gamma \wedge \beta \in z \wedge \gamma \in z\big)\\
&\quad \vee\ \exists\beta\exists v\exists s\big(\alpha = \underset{\cdot}{\exists} v \underset{\cdot}{\subseteq} s\, \beta \wedge \mathsf{CTerm}(s) \wedge \forall x \subseteq s^{\circ}\, \beta[\mathsf{q}x/v] \in z\big)\\
&\quad \vee\ \exists\beta\exists v\big(\alpha = \underset{\cdot}{\forall} v \beta \wedge \exists w\, \beta[\mathsf{q}w/v] \in z\big),\\
\mathsf{Tr}_{\Pi_{n+1}}(x) &:= \forall z\big(\mathsf{List}(z) \wedge \forall w \in z\ \psi_{\Pi_{n+1}}(w, z) \to x \notin z\big).
\end{aligned}$$

11.26 PROPOSITION *For each $n \geq 0$, $\mathsf{Tr}_{\Sigma_{n+1}}$ is provably equivalent to a Σ_{n+1}-formula over $\mathsf{E}^*_{\min}$ and $\mathsf{Tr}_{\Pi_{n+1}}$ is provably equivalent to a Π_{n+1}-formula over $\mathsf{E}^*_{\min}$.*

PROOF By induction on n. The case $n = 0$ has already been observed. Suppose $n \geq 1$. We consider the formula $\mathsf{Tr}_{\Sigma_{n+1}}$. By the induction hypothesis, Tr_{Π_n} is provably equivalent to a Π_n-formula. As Sent_{Π_n} is Δ, it follows that $\psi_{\Sigma_{n+1}}$ is provably equivalent to a formula $\chi \vee \rho$ where χ is Π_n and ρ is Σ_1. In particular, $\psi_{\Sigma_{n+1}}$ is provably equivalent to a Σ_{n+1}-formula and, therefore, so is $\mathsf{Tr}_{\Sigma_{n+1}}$.

The argument for $\mathsf{Tr}_{\Pi_{n+1}}$ is similar: $\psi_{\Pi_{n+1}}$ can be expressed as a disjunction between a Π_n-formula and a Σ_1-formula. Therefore, $\mathsf{Tr}_{\Pi_{n+1}}$ is provably equivalent to a formula of Π_{n+1}. ⊣

The Σ_{n+1} truth predicate provably satisfies the expected closure conditions, as the next proposition demonstrates:

11.27 PROPOSITION *The formulæ below are derivable in E^* for each $n \geq 0$:*

(i) $\forall x\big(\mathsf{Tr}_{\Sigma_n}(x) \to \mathsf{Sent}_{\Sigma_n}(x)\big)$,

(ii) $\forall\alpha\forall\beta\big(\mathsf{Tr}_{\Sigma_n}(\alpha \mathbin{\dot\wedge} \beta) \leftrightarrow \mathsf{Tr}_{\Sigma_n}(\alpha) \wedge \mathsf{Tr}_{\Sigma_n}(\beta)\big)$,

(iii) $\forall\alpha\forall\beta\big(\mathsf{Tr}_{\Sigma_n}(\alpha \mathbin{\dot\vee} \beta) \leftrightarrow \mathsf{Tr}_{\Sigma_n}(\alpha) \vee \mathsf{Tr}_{\Sigma_n}(\beta)\big)$,

(iv) $\forall\alpha\forall s\forall v\big(\mathsf{Tr}_{\Sigma_n}(\dot\forall v \mathbin{\dot\subseteq} s\ \alpha) \leftrightarrow \forall x \subseteq s^\circ\ \mathsf{Tr}_{\Sigma_n}(\alpha[\mathsf{q}x/v])\big)$,

(v) $\forall\alpha\forall s\forall v\big(\mathsf{Tr}_{\Sigma_1}(\dot\exists v \mathbin{\dot\subseteq} s\ \alpha) \leftrightarrow \exists x \subseteq s^\circ\ \mathsf{Tr}_{\Sigma_1}(\alpha[\mathsf{q}x/v])\big)$,

(vi) $\forall\alpha\forall v\big(\mathsf{Tr}_{\Sigma_n}(\dot\exists v\alpha) \leftrightarrow \exists x\ \mathsf{Tr}_{\Sigma_n}(\alpha[\mathsf{q}x/v])\big)$,

(vii) $\forall\alpha\Big(\mathsf{Sent}_{\Pi_n}(\alpha) \to \big(\mathsf{Tr}_{\Sigma_{n+1}}(\alpha) \leftrightarrow \mathsf{Tr}_{\Pi_n}(\alpha)\big)\Big)$.

Recall that $\Pi_0 = \Delta_0$, so in the final equation the formulæ Sent_{Π_n} and Tr_{Π_n} are Sent_{Δ_0} and Tr_{Δ_0}, respectively, if $n = 0$. Analogous properties hold of the Π_n truth predicate. We omit the proof of proposition 11.27 as it is almost identical to the case of the Σ_1 truth predicate.

11.28 THEOREM *For each $n > 0$, Tr_{Σ_n} is a truth predicate for Σ_n-formulæ. That is, for every Σ_n-formula $\varphi(x_1, \ldots, x_k)$ with only the displayed free variables, we have*

$$\mathsf{E}^* \vdash \forall x_1 \cdots \forall x_k\Big(\varphi(x_1, \ldots, x_k) \leftrightarrow \mathsf{Tr}_{\Sigma_n}\big(\overline{\varphi(\dot x_1, \ldots, \dot x_k)}\big)\Big).$$

Likewise, Tr_{Π_n} is a truth predicate for Π_n-formulæ in the sense above.

Just as the partial truth predicate for Σ_1-formulæ allowed us to deduce that there are Σ_1-formulæ which are not Δ_1, theorem 11.28 implies that each level of the quantifier hierarchy $\Sigma_0 \subseteq \Sigma_1 \subseteq \cdots$ is strictly more expressive than the previous levels. This is shown by the next result.

11.29 COROLLARY *The quantifier hierarchy is strict: for every $n > 0$ there exists a Σ_n-formula not equivalent to any Π_n-formula over any consistent extension of $\mathsf{E}^*_{\min}$.*

PROOF We use the same argument as for Σ_1. Fix $n > 0$ and suppose there is a Σ_n-formula $\sigma(x)$ such that $\mathsf{E}^* = \mathsf{E}^*_{\min} + \forall x\big(\sigma(x) \leftrightarrow \neg\mathsf{Tr}_{\Sigma_n}(x)\big)$ is a consistent theory. Consider the formula γ given by diagonalization on $\sigma(\mathsf{x})$. Then γ is a Σ_n-sentence such that $\mathsf{E}^* \vdash \gamma \leftrightarrow \neg\mathsf{Tr}_{\Sigma_n}(\overline{\gamma})$. As also $\mathsf{E}^*_{\min} \vdash \gamma \leftrightarrow \mathsf{Tr}_{\Sigma_n}(\overline{\gamma})$, we conclude that E^* is inconsistent. ⊣

The proof of corollary 11.29 examines the liar sentence for an assumed Π_n-definition of Σ_n-truth. If we consider the liar sentence for the Σ_n truth predicate itself, that is, the sentence γ constructed by diagonalizing on the formula $\neg\mathsf{Tr}_{\Sigma_n}(\mathsf{x})$ for the language $\mathcal{L}^*_{\text{syn}}$, we can ask, since this is a sentence of $\mathcal{L}^*_{\text{syn}}$, whether γ is true or false in the standard model of $\mathsf{E}^*_{\min}$.

11.30 PROPOSITION *Let $n > 0$. If γ is any sentence of $\mathcal{L}^*_{\text{syn}}$ such that* $\mathsf{E}^* \vdash \gamma \leftrightarrow \neg\mathsf{Tr}_{\Sigma_n}(\overline{\gamma})$, *then* $\mathsf{E}^* \vdash \gamma$.

PROOF We may assume that E^* is consistent, as otherwise the claim holds trivially. If γ is Σ_n, then $\mathsf{E}^*_{\text{min}} \vdash \gamma \leftrightarrow \mathsf{Tr}_{\Sigma_n}(\overline{\gamma})$ by theorem 11.28. As E^* is consistent, γ cannot therefore be Σ_n. But then $\mathsf{E}^* \vdash \neg\mathsf{Sent}_{\Sigma_n}(\overline{\gamma})$ and, by the definition of the Σ_n partial truth predicate, $\mathsf{E}^* \vdash \neg\mathsf{Tr}_{\Sigma_n}(\overline{\gamma})$. So $\mathsf{E}^* \vdash \gamma$. ⊣

We can ask the same question about sentences τ for which $\tau \leftrightarrow \mathsf{Tr}_{\Sigma_n}(\overline{\tau})$ is provable in E^*. However, all Σ_n-sentences have this property. Some are true in the standard model and some are not. But as with the liar sentence we can also consider the specific sentence constructed by diagonalization. We call such a formula a Σ_n-*truth teller*. It has the form

(11.9) $\quad \tau := \mathsf{Tr}_{\Sigma_n}(s), \quad$ where s is a closed term such that $\mathsf{E}^*_{\text{min}} \vdash s = \overline{\tau}$.

Perhaps surprisingly, the Σ_n–truth tellers are refutable in E^*.

11.31 THEOREM *Let τ be a Σ_n–truth teller for some $n > 0$. Then* $\mathsf{E}^* \vdash \neg\tau$.

The strategy of the proof is to assume, working in E^*, that τ is true. By the definition of Tr_{Σ_n}, this means there exists a list l of true Σ_n-sentences containing τ. The conditions imposed on l by the truth predicate imply that l also contains a witness to the existential quantifier in τ. Recall $\tau \equiv \mathsf{Tr}_{\Sigma_n}(s)$ where $s = \overline{\tau}$. Thus, this witness is a term $\overline{l_1}$ where l_1 is a list of true Σ_n-sentences containing τ. That is, $l_1 \lhd l$ where $e \lhd f$ means $\overline{e} \subseteq f$. Repeating the argument yields an infinite sequence of expressions

$$\cdots \lhd l_2 \lhd l_1 \lhd l.$$

Proposition 8.83, however, established that the relation $\lhd$ is well-founded, meaning that there cannot exist such a sequence of expressions. So τ is not true.

Formally, the proof utilizes the rank induction principle on expressions introduced in section 8.4. This is the statement

$$\forall x\Big(\forall y\big(y \lhd x \to \varphi(y)\big) \to \varphi\Big) \to \forall x\, \varphi,$$

where $y \lhd x \equiv \mathsf{q}y \subseteq x$. Proposition 9.47 established that this principle is provable in $\mathsf{E}^*_{\text{min}}$. Our particular application of rank induction will use its form as a statement about expressions of minimal rank:

$$\exists x\, \varphi(x) \to \exists x\Big(\varphi(x) \wedge \forall y\big(y \lhd x \to \neg\varphi(y)\big)\Big).$$

In the argument sketched above we could, by rank induction, assume that l was a witness of minimal rank. The consequence that a second witness exists of lower rank contradicts the minimality of l. So $\neg\tau$ holds.

PROOF OF THEOREM 11.31 Let $\tau \equiv \mathsf{Tr}_{\Sigma_n}(s)$ as in the statement of the theorem. The principal connective of τ is an existential quantifier: let $\varphi(x,y)$ be the immediate subformula:

$$\varphi(x,y) \;\equiv\; \mathsf{List}(x) \wedge y \in x \wedge \forall w \in x\; \psi_{\Sigma_n}(w,x).$$

So $\tau \equiv \exists x\, \varphi(x,s)$. We argue informally within $\mathsf{E}^*_{\mathrm{min}}$. Henceforth, we call a (Σ_n-) formula α 'true' if $\mathsf{Tr}_{\Sigma_n}(\alpha)$. In search of a contradiction, suppose τ is true. The definition of Σ_n-truth implies there is an l such that $\varphi(l,\overline{\tau})$. By rank induction, we may assume that l has minimal rank, that is, for no $f \lhd l$ is $\varphi(f,\overline{\tau})$ the case. In particular, from $\varphi(l,\overline{\tau})$ it follows that l has four properties:

(i) l is a list of Σ_n-sentences;

(ii) $\overline{\tau}$ is an element of l;

(iii) every element of l is true;

(iv) if an existential formula $\overline{\exists v\, \alpha}$ is an element of l then there exists an e such that $\overline{\alpha}(\overline{e})$ is an element of l.

From (ii) and (iv) we have $\overline{\varphi(e,s)} \in l$ for some e. In particular, $e \lhd l$. Clause (iii) implies that $\overline{\varphi(e,s)}$ is a true sentence, from which $\varphi(e,\overline{\tau})$ follows, contradicting the choice of l. Hence, τ is not true. As τ is Σ_n we conclude $\neg\tau$. ⊣

11.32 THEOREM *Let $n > 0$ and π be the truth teller for the partial truth predicate Tr_{Π_n}. Then $\mathsf{E}^* \vdash \pi$.*

The theorem can be proved by a symmetric argument. As π is a Π_n-formula it suffices to assume, in E^*, $\neg\mathsf{Tr}_{\Pi_n}(\overline{\pi})$ and to argue by analogy to the Σ_n–truth teller.

Had we considered formulations of theorems 11.31 and 11.32 for a theory of arithmetic in place of E^* and with the partial truth predicates given as arithmetical formulæ expressing properties of an encoding of syntax in arithmetic, the question would arise whether the provability or refutability of the partial truth tellers is an inherent property of these predicates or a phenomenon of coding. Perhaps some alternative encoding of syntax in arithmetic would cause the diagonal sentence of the Σ_1 truth predicate to be provable or independent rather than refutable. As a statement about coding syntax in arithmetic, the conclusion of theorem 11.31 holds for any coding that respects the axioms of $\mathsf{E}^*_{\mathrm{min}}$. A similar observation was made by Halbach and Visser (2014b), expressed as assumptions on numerical codes of expressions analogous to requiring that $\lhd$ is well-founded. It is possible to devise arithmetic codings of syntax which violate the assumptions underpinning theorem 11.31 and induce provable Σ_n–truth tellers. Examples are proposed by Halbach and Visser (2014b) and explored in detail by Grabmayr and Visser (2021). Theorem 11.31 demonstrates that such codings derive from a conception of syntax fundamentally different to the one motivating our theories of expressions. We return to these considerations in chapter 12.

11.2 The Language of Truth

The preceding section examined truth predicates which could be defined within the language $\mathcal{L}^*$ and the theory E^*. By Tarski's theorem there is no formula of $\mathcal{L}^*$ which behaves as a truth predicate for the entire language. Nevertheless, fragments of $\mathcal{L}^*$, notably the levels of the quantifier hierarchy, do admit truth predicates. In the remainder of this chapter we explore how close a language can come to admitting a truth predicate without resulting in inconsistency. The focus will be on consistent extensions of the theory E^* by axioms expressing that a unary predicate in $\mathcal{L}^*$ (in our case the distinguished predicate $\Box$) has the properties we associate with our intuitive understanding of truth. The first example of this kind was presented in theorem 6.3, where it was shown that the weak theory E can be consistently extended by the axiom schema

$$\text{(T-schema)} \qquad \varphi \leftrightarrow \mathsf{Tr}\overline{\varphi}$$

for a fresh unary predicate symbol Tr where φ ranges over sentences lacking this predicate symbol.

Our present study begins with the expressive analogue of this theory, namely the theory $\mathsf{E}^*_{\mathrm{min}}$ extended by the T-schema for sentences of $\mathcal{L}^*$ that lack $\Box$. At the other end of the spectrum are theories in which truth is axiomatized by quantified clauses, such as the distribution of truth over arbitrary implications, expressed by the statement $\forall\alpha\forall\beta\big(\Box(\alpha \mathbin{\dot\to} \beta) \leftrightarrow (\Box\alpha \to \Box\beta)\big)$, and axioms of self-application such as $\forall\alpha\,(\Box\alpha \leftrightarrow \Box\dot\Box\alpha)$. Concerning assumptions of this kind, chapter 6 already presents a number of limiting results: Montague's paradox of the predicate version of the modal logic T (theorem 6.5), McGee's paradox on ω-inconsistency (theorem 6.31), Löb's theorem (theorem 6.11), and McGee's theorem on consistent sets of instances of the T-schema (theorem 6.4).

We now operate under the assumption that $\mathcal{L}^*$ contains the unary predicate symbol $\Box$ in addition to any other symbols over the minimal language $\mathcal{L}^*_{\text{min}}$. A formula that does not feature the predicate symbol $\Box$ is called $\Box$-free or, on occasion, truth-free. If $\Box$ is the only basic symbol of $\mathcal{L}^*$ beyond $\mathcal{L}^*_{\text{min}}$, then the $\Box$-free formulæ are just the formulæ of $\mathcal{L}^*_{\text{syn}}$ which, in this case, is the language $\mathcal{L}^*_{\text{min}}$ with the constant $\underline{\Box}$ added. If, however, $\mathcal{L}^*$ contains further basic symbols, then there are $\Box$-free formulæ that are not in $\mathcal{L}^*_{\text{syn}}$. Given the prominence of $\mathcal{L}^*_{\text{syn}}$ in previous chapters, some results that follow are stated for formulæ in $\mathcal{L}^*_{\text{syn}}$ even though they also hold for the larger class of $\Box$-free formulæ.

Recall that a standard model of $\mathcal{L}^*$ is a pair $\langle \mathbb{E}^*, V \rangle$ where $\mathbb{E}^*$ is the standard model for $\mathcal{L}^*_{\text{syn}}$ and V is a function providing an interpretation for each function and predicate symbol in $\mathcal{L}^* \setminus \mathcal{L}^*_{\text{syn}}$. Given a set $S \subseteq \mathcal{E}^*$ of expressions, we write $\langle \mathbb{E}^*, V, S \rangle$ for the standard model which interprets $\Box$ as the set S and agrees with $\langle \mathbb{E}^*, V \rangle$ on the interpretation of all other function and predicate symbols.

Quantifiers $\forall \alpha\, \varphi(\alpha)$ and $\exists \alpha\, \varphi(\alpha)$ abbreviate quantification restricted to formulæ: $\forall x \big(\mathsf{Form}(x) \to \varphi(x)\big)$ and $\exists x \big(\mathsf{Form}(x) \wedge \varphi(x)\big)$, respectively. Likewise for terms, but now such quantifications will always be restricted to *closed* terms. That is, $\forall t\, \varphi(t)$ and $\exists t\, \varphi(t)$ will serve as abbreviations for $\forall x \big(\mathsf{CTerm}(x) \to \varphi(x)\big)$ and $\exists x \big(\mathsf{CTerm}(x) \wedge \varphi(x)\big)$, respectively.

Let an extension E^* of the minimal theory $\mathsf{E}^*_{\text{min}}$ and a standard model $\mathbb{E}^*$ of $\mathcal{L}^*$ be fixed. If $\langle \mathbb{E}^*, V, S \rangle \vDash \mathsf{E}^*$ for every set $S \subseteq \mathcal{E}^*$ we say E^* is '$\Box$-agnostic relative to $\mathbb{E}^*$'. A theory is '$\Box$-agnostic' if it is $\Box$-agnostic relative to some standard model. Being $\Box$-agnostic means the theory places no restriction on the interpretation of the predicate $\Box$ relative to the selected standard model $\mathbb{E}^*$. The minimal theory $\mathsf{E}^*_{\text{min}}$ is an example of a $\Box$-agnostic theory. So is any extension of $\mathsf{E}^*_{\text{min}}$ by axioms that are $\Box$-free and true in $\mathbb{E}^*$. In contrast, $\mathsf{E}^*_{\text{min}} + \Box \underline{\bot}$ is not $\Box$-agnostic because $\langle \mathbb{E}^*, V, \varnothing \rangle \nvDash \Box \underline{\bot}$ for all V. Another example of failure of $\Box$-agnosticity is $\mathsf{E}^*_{\text{min}} + \forall x (\Box x \leftrightarrow \mathsf{R} x)$ where R is any unary predicate symbol different from $\Box$. In this case every model of E^* must interpret $\Box$ and R as the same set of $*$-expressions. Although the choice of interpretation is arbitrary, once an interpretation of R is fixed there is only one interpretation of $\Box$ validating the axiom.

As a general theme, given a particular set TA of 'axioms' about the truth predicate $\Box$, we will prove that $\mathsf{E}^* + \text{TA}$ is a consistent theory if E^* is $\Box$-agnostic. Such a result will, in particular, imply that the extension of the minimal theory $\mathsf{E}^*_{\min}$ of expressions by adding the set TA of sentences as axioms yields a consistent theory of truth.

11.3 Typed Truth

In chapter 6 we saw that the weak theory $\mathsf{E}_{\min}$ can be consistently extended by a restricted T-schema, the axiom schema

$$\Box\overline{\varphi} \leftrightarrow \varphi \quad \text{for } \varphi \text{ a } \Box\text{-free sentence.} \tag{11.10}$$

A theory of truth is *typed* if the truth predicate is posited to apply only to sentences that do not themselves contain the truth predicate, such as the one axiomatized by (11.10). We open our overview of theories of truth with a focus on typed theories, beginning with the typed T-schema over E^*, introduced by Tarski (1935) and known also as the theory of Tarski biconditionals, TB. As usual, E^* denotes some extension of the minimal theory $\mathsf{E}^*_{\min}$.

11.33 THEOREM *Suppose* E^* *is* $\Box$*-agnostic. Then* TB *has a standard model.*

PROOF We construct a model of TB from the standard model $\langle \mathbb{E}^*, V\rangle \vDash \mathsf{E}^*$ that exists since E^* is $\Box$-agnostic. The interpretation of $\Box$ in the new model will be the set

$$S = \{\psi\colon \psi \text{ is a } \Box\text{-free sentence and } \langle \mathbb{E}^*, V\rangle \vDash \psi\}.$$

Recall that if φ is $\Box$-free then $\langle \mathbb{E}^*, V, S\rangle \vDash \varphi$ if and only if $\langle \mathbb{E}^*, V\rangle \vDash \varphi$. For any $\Box$-free ψ we therefore have

$$\langle \mathbb{E}^*, V, S\rangle \vDash \Box\overline{\psi} \quad \text{iff} \quad \psi \in S, \quad \text{iff} \quad \langle \mathbb{E}^*, V\rangle \vDash \psi, \quad \text{iff} \quad \langle \mathbb{E}^*, V, S\rangle \vDash \psi.$$

So all instances of the typed T-schema are true in $\langle \mathbb{E}^*, V, S\rangle$. All that remains is to observe that the starting theory E^* is also true in this model. But as it is $\Box$-agnostic this is clear. ⊣

Recall that theorem 6.3 established a similar result for extensions of the weak theory E. In a direct reformulation of that theorem adapted to the current framework we would assume that E^* was given in the sublanguage $\mathcal{L}^*_0$ of $\mathcal{L}^*$ completely lacking $\Box$, and then expanded to be a theory in $\mathcal{L}^*$ with all instances of the typed

T-schema as additional axioms (theorem 6.3 used a predicate symbol Tr in place of $\Box$ to emphasize the freshness). This expansion of E^* occurs in two steps: First, E^* is made into a theory in the larger language $\mathcal{L}^*_{\Box}$ which involves adding to E^* all missing instances of axioms and rules of predicate logic for formulæ in $\mathcal{L}^*$ but not extending the schema of induction or other axiom schema that $\mathbb{E}^*$ might have. Let us call this theory $\mathsf{E}^*_{\Box}$. The second step adds to $\mathsf{E}^*_{\Box}$ all instances of the T-schema for sentences of $\mathcal{L}^*_0$. If the standard model of $\mathcal{L}^*$ is a model of E^*, then $\mathsf{E}^*_{\Box}$ will be $\Box$-agnostic. By theorem 11.33, therefore, $\mathsf{E}^*_{\Box}$ plus the typed T-schema is a consistent theory (with a standard model). It is possible to generalize the notion of $\Box$-agnosticity so that theorem 11.33 applies also to theories lacking standard models, thereby covering all cases of theorem 6.3 in the expressive framework. However, there is little to be gained from such a generalization and some later model constructions do not apply as broadly as theorem 11.33.

For theories of expressions with standard models, theorem 11.33 generalizes theorem 6.3 in two respects. First, the theorem permits E^* to contain nonlogical axioms involving the symbols $\Box$ and $\underline{\Box}$, provided the theory remains $\Box$-agnostic. The axiom schema of induction and the basic axioms for symbols are example axioms involving either $\Box$ or $\underline{\Box}$ which are present in the $\Box$-agnostic theory $\mathsf{E}^*_{\mathrm{min}}$ but not included in the theories covered by theorem 6.3. Second, theorem 11.33 establishes the consistency of the T-schema for all $\Box$-free sentences rather than only the sentences that contain neither $\Box$ nor its syntactic constant. The sentence $\Box\overline{\exists x\, x = \underline{\Box}}$ is provable in TB from the T-schema, but does not follow from theorem 6.3.

Before proceeding to extensions of TB we make a final observation on the theory of the typed T-schema. The proof we gave of theorem 11.33 was of a different style to the corresponding theorem 6.3. We provided a semantic argument, constructing a model of TB from a standard model of the background theory E^*. In contrast, the proof of theorem 6.3 manipulated derivations: we showed that any derivation of inconsistency from the typed T-schema can be converted into a derivation with the same conclusion in the background theory. The different method of proof is necessitated by the semantic assumption of the $\Box$-agnosticity of E^*.

The same, syntactic, method of proof can be used to show the consistency of TB under different assumptions about E^*. A strengthening of the assumptions on E^* yields a stronger conclusion, which cannot be derived from theorem 11.33 directly. Instead of mere consistency we can prove that every $\Box$-free theorem of TB is already derivable in E^* (since $\bot$ is $\Box$-free, we get that TB is consistent if

E^* is). This result is an example of a conservativity theorem: given an extension F^* of E^* and a sublanguage $\mathcal{M}$ of $\mathcal{L}^*$, F^* is a conservative extension of E^* for formulæ of $\mathcal{M}$ if, whenever $\mathsf{F}^* \vdash \varphi$ and φ is a sentence of $\mathcal{M}$, then $\mathsf{E}^* \vdash \varphi$. In the case of TB, we take $\mathcal{M}$ to be the language $\mathcal{L}^*$ minus the symbol $\Box$, so the $\mathcal{M}$-sentences are exactly the $\Box$-free sentences.

11.34 THEOREM · CONSERVATIVITY OF THE TYPED T-SCHEMA *Suppose* E^* *is an extension of* $\mathsf{E}^*_{\min}$ *by* $\Box$*-free axioms. Then* TB *is a conservative extension of* E^* *for* $\Box$*-free formulas. That is, if* $\mathsf{TB} \vdash \varphi$ *and* φ *is* $\Box$*-free, then* $\mathsf{E}^* \vdash \varphi$.

PROOF As in the proof of theorem 6.3 we show that in every derivation from the axioms of TB, the predicate $\Box$ can be replaced by a $\Box$-free formula satisfying the same axioms as $\Box$. Given a finite set Γ of sentences, let $\textsc{tb}_\Gamma$ be the set of instances of the T-schema for Γ and define $\Box_\Gamma$ by

$$\textsc{tb}_\Gamma := \{\psi \leftrightarrow \Box\overline{\psi} \colon \psi \in \Gamma\},$$
$$\Box_\Gamma(x) := \bigvee_{\gamma\in\Gamma}(x = \overline{\gamma} \wedge \gamma).$$

We write φ^Γ for the result of replacing each atomic formula $\Box t$ in φ by the formula $\Box_\Gamma(t)$. By the assumptions on E^* it follows that if $\mathsf{E}^* \vdash \varphi$ then $\mathsf{E}^* \vdash \varphi^\Gamma$ regardless of the choice of Γ.

Now suppose $\mathsf{TB} \vdash \varphi$ and φ is $\Box$-free. Let Γ be the finite set of $\Box$-free sentences such that $\mathsf{E}^* + \textsc{tb}_\Gamma \vdash \varphi$. So

$$\mathsf{E}^* \vdash \bigwedge \textsc{tb}_\Gamma \rightarrow \varphi.$$

By the observation above, $\mathsf{E}^* \vdash (\bigwedge \textsc{tb}_\Gamma \rightarrow \varphi)^\Gamma$. As φ is $\Box$-free, this means

$$\mathsf{E}^* \vdash \bigwedge (\textsc{tb}_\Gamma)^\Gamma \rightarrow \varphi.$$

But $\mathsf{E}^* \vdash \gamma \leftrightarrow \Box_\Gamma\overline{\gamma}$ for every $\gamma \in \Gamma$, so $\mathsf{E}^* \vdash \varphi$. ⊣

Analyzing the proof of theorem 11.34, it is clear that the result also applies to certain subtheories of $\mathsf{E}^*_{\min}$ in addition to its extensions. For example, the proof does not appeal to the principle induction, nor the axioms of substitution. Indeed, it is sufficient for the proof that $\mathsf{E}^* \vdash \neg\overline{\varphi} = \overline{\psi}$ whenever φ and ψ are distinct sentences. If we try to drop these assumptions and replace E^* by predicate logic, conservativity no longer holds because $\overline{\varphi} \neq \overline{\neg\varphi}$ is a logical consequence of the T-schema, yet not provable from predicate logic alone.

The typed T-schema is expressively weak. It can be shown that TB does not derive over $\mathsf{E}^*_{\min}$ quantified versions of the schema such as

$$\forall s \forall t \big(s^\circ = t^\circ \leftrightarrow \Box (s \mathbin{\dot{=}} t) \big). \tag{11.11}$$

This observation follows almost immediately from the proof of theorem 11.34 above: if (11.11) is derivable from the typed T-schema then, by theorem 11.34,

$$\mathsf{E}^*_{\min} \vdash \forall s \forall t \big(s^\circ = t^\circ \leftrightarrow \Box_\Gamma (s \mathbin{\dot{=}} t) \big)$$

for some finite set Γ of $\Box$-free sentences. Let t be a closed term for which the equation $\bar{t} = \bar{t}$ is not among the formulæ in Γ. We have $\mathsf{E}^*_{\min} \vdash \bar{t}^\circ = \bar{t}^\circ$, yet also $\mathsf{E}^*_{\min} \vdash \neg \Box_\Gamma (\bar{t} \mathbin{\dot{=}} \bar{t})$.

The quantified form of the T-schema in (11.11) is known as the uniform T-schema (in contrast to the 'local' T-schema of TB). Formally, we define the uniform T-schema for a set Γ of formulæ is the collection of sentences

$$\forall t_0 \cdots \forall t_{k-1} \big(\psi (t_0^\circ, \ldots, t_{k-1}^\circ) \leftrightarrow \Box \overline{\psi} [t_0, \ldots, t_{k-1}] \big) \tag{UTB$_\Gamma$}$$

where $\psi \in \Gamma$ is a formula whose free variables are precisely $\mathsf{v}_0, \ldots, \mathsf{v}_{k-1}$ and none of these variables are bound in ψ. The theory of the uniform typed T-schema is the theory $\mathsf{UTB} := \mathsf{E}^* + \textsc{utb}_{\mathrm{Form}_0}$, where Form_0 is the set of $\Box$-free formulæ.

As we saw in section 11.1, the partial truth predicates satisfy the uniform T-schema for the appropriate quantifier classes. Thus, we have already shown that the uniform T-schema for typed formulæ can be consistently added to $\mathsf{E}^*_{\min}$:

11.35 THEOREM *Suppose* E^* *is an extension of* $\mathsf{E}^*_{\min}$ *by* $\Box$*-free axioms. If* $\mathsf{UTB} \vdash \varphi$ *and* φ *is* $\Box$*-free, then* $\mathsf{E}^* \vdash \varphi$*. In particular,* UTB *is consistent if* E^* *is.*

PROOF We proceed along the lines of theorem 11.34 but appeal to the partial truth predicates of the previous section to provide a translation of the truth predicate. Suppose φ is a theorem of UTB in the language $\mathcal{L}^*_{\mathrm{syn}}$. It follows that there is a proof d of φ from the axioms of E^* plus finitely many instances of the T-schema

$$\forall t_1 \cdots \forall t_k \big(\psi (t_1^\circ, \ldots, t_k^\circ) \leftrightarrow \Box \overline{\psi} [t_1, \ldots, t_k] \big).$$

Let $\psi_0, \ldots, \psi_n$ list the $\mathcal{L}^*_{\mathrm{syn}}$-formulæ for which the T-schema occurs in d. Let l be such that these are all Σ_l-formulas. We now consider the interpretation of $\mathcal{L}^*$ which replaces each atomic formula $\Box t$ by the formula $\mathrm{Tr}_{\Sigma_l}(t)$. Writing ψ^{Tr} for result of applying this translation to ψ, by induction through d we deduce $\mathsf{E}^* \vdash \psi^{\mathrm{Tr}}$ for each formula ψ in d. Hence, $\mathsf{E}^* \vdash \varphi^{\mathrm{Tr}}$. But φ does not contain $\Box$, so $\mathsf{E}^* \vdash \varphi$. ⊣

Given that sequencing is available in E^*, every formula can be shown to be equivalent to a formula with just one free variable which ranges over sequences of expressions of corresponding length. The next result provides a sufficient condition for the uniform T-schema to be derivable from the one-variable instances.

11.36 PROPOSITION *Let* $\mathsf{Sent}_0(x)$ *express the property of being a* $\Box$*-free sentence and suppose the following statement is derivable in* E^**:*

$$\forall\alpha\,\forall\beta\big(\mathsf{Bew}_{\mathsf{E}^*}(\alpha \dot{\rightarrow} \beta) \wedge \mathsf{Sent}_0(\alpha \dot{\rightarrow} \beta) \rightarrow (\Box\alpha \rightarrow \Box\beta)\big).$$

Then, over E^**, every instance of the uniform T-schema is equivalent to an instance for a formula with at most one free variable. Moreover, the new instance of the T-schema uses the same non-*$\mathcal{L}^*_{\mathrm{min}}$*-symbols as the original instance.*

PROOF We use the fact that sequencing is expressible in E^*. Let $\psi(\mathsf{v}_1,\ldots,\mathsf{v}_k)$ be any formula. Without loss of generality we assume that v_0 occurs neither free nor bound in ψ. Recall the sequencing term $\langle\mathsf{v}_1,\ldots,\mathsf{v}_k\rangle$ introduced in chapter 8. We require a 'quoted' version of this term which takes as arguments (quotations of) k-many closed terms $t_1, \ldots, t_k$ and produces a closed term whose denotation is the sequence of expressions $t_1^\circ, \ldots, t_k^\circ$, that is, a term $s(\mathsf{v}_1,\ldots,\mathsf{v}_k)$ in k-many variables such that

$$\mathsf{E}^* \vdash \forall t_1 \cdots \forall t_k\Big(\mathsf{CTerm}\big(s(t_1,\ldots,t_k)\big) \wedge s(t_1,\ldots,t_k)^\circ = \langle t_1^\circ,\ldots,t_k^\circ\rangle\Big).$$

Define a new formula $\varphi(\mathsf{v}_0)$ with only v_0 free by

$$\varphi(\mathsf{v}_0) := \forall\mathsf{v}_1\cdots\forall\mathsf{v}_k\big(\mathsf{v}_0 = \langle\mathsf{v}_1,\ldots,\mathsf{v}_k\rangle \rightarrow \psi(\mathsf{v}_1,\ldots,\mathsf{v}_k)\big).$$

So $\mathsf{E}^* \vdash \forall\mathsf{v}_1\cdots\forall\mathsf{v}_k\big(\varphi(\langle\mathsf{v}_1,\ldots,\mathsf{v}_k\rangle) \leftrightarrow \psi(\mathsf{v}_1,\ldots,\mathsf{v}_k)\big)$. By the rules of provability and the main assumption of the proposition we obtain

$$\mathsf{E}^* \vdash \forall t_1 \cdots \forall t_k\big(\Box\overline{\varphi}(s(t_1,\ldots,t_k)) \leftrightarrow \Box\overline{\psi}[t_1,\ldots,t_k]\big).$$

Combining the two equivalences, we conclude the following as consequences of $\forall t\big(\varphi(t^\circ) \leftrightarrow \Box\overline{\varphi}(t)\big)$ over E^*.

$$\forall t_1 \cdots \forall t_k\Big(\psi(t_1^\circ,\ldots,t_k^\circ) \leftrightarrow \varphi\big(s(t_1,\ldots,t_k)^\circ\big)\Big),$$

$$\forall t_1 \cdots \forall t_k\Big(\psi(t_1^\circ,\ldots,t_k^\circ) \leftrightarrow \Box\overline{\varphi}[s(t_1,\ldots,t_k)]\Big),$$

$$\forall t_1 \cdots \forall t_k\Big(\psi(t_1^\circ,\ldots,t_k^\circ) \leftrightarrow \Box\overline{\psi}[t_1,\ldots,t_k]\Big). \qquad \dashv$$

11.4 Compositional Truth

Theorem 11.35 established that over $\mathsf{E}^*_{\min}$ the uniform typed T-schema does not give rise to any new $\Box$-free theorems. As a consequence, the formal counterpart of the statement 'All theorems of $\mathsf{E}^*_{\min}$ are true', $\forall\alpha\big(\mathsf{Bew}_{\mathsf{E}^*_{\min}}(\alpha) \to \Box\alpha\big)$, is not derivable in UTB. For if it were, then by appealing to the typed T-schema for falsum and theorem 11.35, $\mathsf{E}^*_{\min} \vdash \neg\mathsf{Bew}_{\mathsf{E}^*_{\min}}(\overline{\bot})$, which contradicts Gödel's incompleteness theorem. For a theory S, the formula

$$(\textsc{grp}) \qquad \forall\alpha\big(\mathsf{Bew}_{\mathsf{S}}(\alpha) \to \Box\alpha\big)$$

is referred to as the global reflection principle for S.

11.37 PROPOSITION *Suppose* E^* *is a simple extension of* $\mathsf{E}^*_{\min}$ *by* $\Box$*-free axioms. If* E^* *is consistent, then the global reflection principle for* E^* *is not derivable in* UTB.

PROOF Let γ be the global reflection principle for E^* and assume that $\mathsf{UTB} \vdash \gamma$. By the T-schema we have $\mathsf{UTB} \vdash \neg\Box\overline{\bot}$, so $\mathsf{UTB} \vdash \neg\mathsf{Bew}_{\mathsf{E}^*}(\overline{\bot})$. Given that E^* satisfies the requirements of theorem 11.35 and $\mathsf{Bew}_{\mathsf{E}^*}(\overline{\bot})$ is $\Box$-free, we deduce $\mathsf{E}^* \vdash \neg\mathsf{Bew}_{\mathsf{E}^*}(\overline{\bot})$. But by Gödel's second incompleteness theorem this is impossible if E^* is consistent. ⊣

The global reflection principle for $\mathsf{E}^*_{\min}$ may not be derivable from the typed T-schema, but it can be consistently added to it. In fact, the standard model constructed in theorem 11.33 already validates the restriction of the global reflection principle to $\Box$-free sentences, and a model of the full axiom is not difficult to construct. Suppose that E^* is $\Box$-agnostic and $\mathbb{E}^* \vDash \mathsf{E}^*$ is a standard model. Define

$$S_\varnothing = \big\{\varphi\colon \langle\mathbb{E}^*, V, \varnothing\rangle \vDash \varphi\big\}.$$

If φ is $\Box$-free, then $\langle\mathbb{E}^*, V, \varnothing\rangle \vDash \varphi$ if and only if $\langle\mathbb{E}^*, V, S_\varnothing\rangle \vDash \varphi$. So $\langle\mathbb{E}^*, V, S_\varnothing\rangle$ is a model of UTB. But also, because $\mathbb{E}^*$ is a standard model of E^*,

$$\begin{aligned} \langle\mathbb{E}^*, V, S_\varnothing\rangle \vDash \mathsf{Bew}_{\mathsf{E}^*}(\overline{\varphi}) \quad &\text{implies} \quad \mathsf{E}^* \vdash \varphi \\ &\text{implies} \quad \langle\mathbb{E}^*, V, S\rangle \vDash \varphi \text{ for every } S \subseteq \mathcal{E}^* \\ &\text{implies} \quad \langle\mathbb{E}^*, V, S_\varnothing\rangle \vDash \Box\overline{\varphi}. \end{aligned}$$

So the global reflection principle for E^* is true in $\langle\mathbb{E}^*, V, S_\varnothing\rangle$.

Aside from the global reflection principle there are other statements of a truth-theoretic nature which are true in $\langle \mathbb{E}^*, V, S_\varnothing \rangle$, such as

$$\forall\alpha\,(\Box\underset{.}{\neg}\alpha \leftrightarrow \neg\Box\alpha) \quad \text{and} \quad \forall\alpha\,\forall\beta\big(\Box(\alpha\underset{.}{\rightarrow}\beta) \leftrightarrow (\Box\alpha \rightarrow \Box\beta)\big),$$

and a similar clause for the universal quantifier:

$$\forall\alpha\,\forall v\Big(\mathsf{Var}(v) \rightarrow \big(\Box\underset{.}{\forall} v\,\alpha \leftrightarrow \forall t\;\Box\alpha[t/v]\big)\Big).$$

Read as statements about truth, the first expresses that a negated formula is true just if the formula itself is not true, and the final one expresses that a universally quantified formula is true if and only if every instantiation of the quantified variable by a term is true. Taken together, the statements express that truth – by which we mean the extension of $\Box$ in any model of these axioms – is closed under the same compositional clauses as the model-theoretic notion of 'truth in a standard model'.

11.38 DEFINITION CT is the theory extending E^* by the following axioms:

- CT1 $\forall s_1 \cdots \forall s_k\big(\Box(\underset{.}{\mathsf{R}} s_1 \cdots s_k) \leftrightarrow \mathsf{R}(s_1^\circ, \ldots, s_k^\circ)\big)$ for each k and each predicate symbol $\mathsf{R} \in \mathcal{L}^*$ of arity k, excluding $\Box$,
- CT2 $\forall\alpha\big(\mathsf{Sent}(\alpha) \rightarrow (\Box\underset{.}{\neg}\alpha \leftrightarrow \neg\Box\alpha)\big)$,
- CT3 $\forall\alpha\,\forall\beta\Big(\mathsf{Sent}(\alpha\underset{.}{\rightarrow}\beta) \rightarrow \big(\Box(\alpha\underset{.}{\rightarrow}\beta) \leftrightarrow (\Box\alpha \rightarrow \Box\beta)\big)\Big)$,
- CT4 $\forall\alpha\,\forall v\Big(\mathsf{Sent}(\underset{.}{\forall} v\,\alpha) \wedge \mathsf{Var}(v) \rightarrow \big(\Box\underset{.}{\forall} v\,\alpha \leftrightarrow \forall s\;\Box\alpha[s/v]\big)\Big)$.

In contrast to the versions of the axioms discussed above, the quantifiers in CT2–CT4 are restricted to sentences of $\mathcal{L}^*$, as it is more common to talk of a sentence being true/not true rather than an open formula. Many authors prefer to denote by CT the theory of a 'typed' compositional truth predicate, given by relativizing the quantifiers in CT2–CT4 to $\Box$-free sentences and the addition of a further axiom, $\forall x\big(\Box x \rightarrow \mathsf{Sent}_0(x)\big)$, restricting the extension of the truth predicate to $\Box$-free sentences. In our presentation, formulæ containing $\Box$ can occur under the scope of the truth predicate, but there is no axiom which determines whether a formula of the form $\Box s$ is true or not. For instance, the formula $\Box\overline{\forall x(\Box x \rightarrow \Box x)}$ can be derived via axioms CT3 and CT4, yet the 'untyped' T-schema,

$$\forall\alpha\big(\mathsf{Sent}(\alpha) \rightarrow (\Box\overline{\underset{.}{\Box}\alpha} \leftrightarrow \Box\alpha)\big),$$

is not provable from the axioms, as its addition to CT is inconsistent (see proposition 11.40). Halbach (2014) uses the name FS_0 for the theory in definition 11.38 as it represents the base level of a hierarchy of theories which approximate the Friedman–Sheard theory of truth FS, to be presented in section 11.7. A fully 'typed' compositional truth predicate can be defined in CT by the formula $\Box \mathsf{x} \wedge \mathsf{Sent}_0(\mathsf{x})$.

The compositional clauses for defined connectives, $\wedge$, $\vee$, and $\exists$, are derivable in CT. These are the formulæ

$$\forall\alpha\forall\beta\Big(\mathsf{Sent}(\alpha \underset{\cdot}{\to} \beta) \to \big(\Box(\alpha \underset{\cdot}{\wedge} \beta) \leftrightarrow \Box\alpha \wedge \Box\beta\big)\Big),$$

$$\forall\alpha\forall\beta\Big(\mathsf{Sent}(\alpha \underset{\cdot}{\to} \beta) \to \big(\Box(\alpha \underset{\cdot}{\vee} \beta) \leftrightarrow \Box\alpha \vee \Box\beta\big)\Big),$$

$$\forall\alpha\forall v\Big(\mathsf{Sent}(\underset{\cdot}{\exists} v\, \alpha) \wedge \mathsf{Var}(v) \to \big(\Box\underset{\cdot}{\exists} v\, \alpha \leftrightarrow \exists s\, \Box\alpha[s/v]\big)\Big).$$

We leave the verification of this claim to the reader.

11.39 PROPOSITION UTB *is a subtheory of* CT.

PROOF We are required to show that for every $\Box$-free formula $\varphi(\mathsf{v}_0, \ldots, \mathsf{v}_k)$ with only the distinguished variables free,

$$\mathsf{CT} \vdash \forall s_0 \cdots \forall s_k\big(\varphi(\mathring{s}_0, \ldots, \mathring{s}_k) \leftrightarrow \Box\overline{\varphi}[s_0, \ldots, s_k]\big).$$

Given the axioms of CT, this is readily proved by induction on φ. ⊣

11.40 PROPOSITION *If* $\mathsf{CT} \vdash \forall\alpha\big(\mathsf{Sent}(\alpha) \to (\Box\overline{\Box}\underset{\cdot}{\alpha} \leftrightarrow \Box\alpha)\big)$, *then* CT *is inconsistent.*

PROOF Repeating the induction proof of proposition 11.39, from the assumption $\mathsf{CT} \vdash \forall\alpha\big(\mathsf{Sent}(\alpha) \to (\Box\overline{\Box}\underset{\cdot}{\alpha} \leftrightarrow \Box\alpha)\big)$ it follows that the unrestricted T-schema is derivable in CT. ⊣

We have already observed that the axioms of CT have a standard model. This was the $\mathcal{L}^*$-structure $\langle \mathbb{E}^*, V, S_\varnothing\rangle$, where $S_\varnothing$ is the set of sentences true in $\langle \mathbb{E}^*, V, \varnothing\rangle$. So if $\langle \mathbb{E}^*, V, S_\varnothing\rangle \vDash \mathsf{E}^*$, then CT is consistent. In particular,

11.41 THEOREM *Suppose* E^* *is* $\Box$*-agnostic relative to the standard model* $\mathbb{E}^*$*. The standard model* $\langle \mathbb{E}^*, V, S_{\mathbb{E}^*}\rangle$ *where* $S_{\mathbb{E}^*} = \{\,\varphi \colon \langle \mathbb{E}^*, V\rangle \vDash \varphi\,\}$ *is a model of* CT.

Arguably, the compositional axioms are more fundamental to the notion of truth than the global reflection principle, for they describe the general interaction of truth and logic, rather than soundness for some specific theory. Indeed, global reflection for $\mathsf{E}^*_{\mathrm{min}}$ is a consequence of the compositional axioms, whereas the converse does not hold. As such, the consistency statement for $\mathsf{E}^*_{\mathrm{min}}$ is provable in CT and so the conservativity result we established for UTB (theorem 11.35) does not extend to CT.

The derivation of global reflection from the compositional clauses formalizes the consistency proof for $\mathsf{E}^*_{\mathrm{min}}$ from chapter 9. The argument is broken into three steps. First, we prove within CT the statement expressing that all the logical axioms are true. Second, we observe that the extension of the CT-truth predicate is closed under the inference rules of predicate logic. As a consequence, the global reflection principle for predicate logic is provable in CT. All that remains is then to establish, within CT, that all axioms of $\mathsf{E}^*_{\mathrm{min}}$ are true. For this third part, the axiom schema of induction constitutes the most complex case.

In the deductive system for classical predicate logic which we formalized in the preceding chapter, logical axioms may contain free variables. When we say that a formula with free variables is 'true in a model' we are referring to the universal closure of the formula, the sentence obtained by prefixing the formula with universal quantifiers for each free variable. In a standard model, the universal closure of a formula is true if and only if every substitution of closed terms for the free variables is true. The statement that all axioms of predicate logic are true can be rendered in $\mathcal{L}^*$ in two ways, referring either to the universal closure of an axiom or to arbitrary closed instantiations:

$$\forall\alpha\forall\beta\big(\mathsf{Axiom}_{\mathsf{PL}}(\alpha)\wedge\mathsf{Ins}(\beta,\alpha)\rightarrow\Box\beta\big),$$
$$\forall\alpha\big(\mathsf{Axiom}_{\mathsf{PL}}(\alpha)\rightarrow\Box\,\mathsf{ucl}\,\alpha\big).$$

The formulæ $\mathsf{Ins}(\beta,\alpha)$ and $\beta=\mathsf{ucl}\,\alpha$ – introduced on page 272 – express respectively that β is an instantiation of α, and the universal closure of α.

It is not difficult to see that the two statements are equivalent over CT. Appealing to (formal) induction on formulæ, it can be shown that

$$\mathsf{CT}\vdash\forall\alpha\Big(\Box\,\mathsf{ucl}\,\alpha\leftrightarrow\forall\beta\big(\mathsf{Ins}(\beta,\alpha)\rightarrow\Box\beta\big)\Big).\tag{11.12}$$

For the global reflection principle in CT, however, the formulation in terms of instantiations is technically more convenient:

11.42 PROPOSITION $\mathsf{CT} \vdash \forall\alpha\forall\beta\big(\mathsf{Axiom_{PL}}(\alpha) \wedge \mathsf{Ins}(\beta, \alpha) \rightarrow \Box\beta\big)$.

PROOF We present two of seven axiom schemas of PL (cf. section 10.4); the remaining ones are left to the reader. Consider an arbitrary closed instantiation of axiom PL1, which takes the form $\varphi \rightarrow (\psi \rightarrow \varphi)$ for sentences φ and ψ. We are required to prove

$$\mathsf{CT} \vdash \forall\alpha\forall\beta\Big(\mathsf{Sent}(\alpha) \wedge \mathsf{Sent}(\beta) \rightarrow \Box\big(\alpha \dot{\rightarrow} (\beta \dot{\rightarrow} \alpha)\big)\Big).$$

As an instance of PL1, however, we have

$$\mathsf{PL} \vdash \forall x\forall y\big(\Box x \rightarrow (\Box y \rightarrow \Box x)\big),$$

from which we readily obtain

$$\mathsf{PL} \vdash \forall\alpha\forall\beta\Big(\mathsf{Sent}(\alpha) \wedge \mathsf{Sent}(\beta) \rightarrow \big(\Box\alpha \rightarrow (\Box\beta \rightarrow \Box\alpha)\big)\Big).$$

Two applications of the compositional axiom CT3 yield the desired result.

The second case we provide is axiom PL4: $\forall \mathsf{v}_i\,\varphi(\mathsf{v}_i) \rightarrow \varphi(t)$ for t free for v_i in φ. For the lemma, we are required to prove the statement that all sentential instances of this axiom schema are true. That is, we want to show

$$\mathsf{CT} \vdash \forall\alpha\forall v\forall t\Big(\mathsf{FreeFor}(t, v, \alpha) \wedge \mathsf{Sent}\big(\alpha[t/v]\big) \rightarrow \Box\big(\dot{\forall} v\,\alpha \dot{\rightarrow} \alpha[t/v]\big)\Big).$$

But this follows directly from the compositional axioms CT4 and CT3. ⊣

From the statement that all logical axioms are true, the global reflection principle for predicate logic can be established by a (formal) induction on the length of proofs:

11.43 PROPOSITION $\mathsf{CT} \vdash \forall\alpha\big(\mathsf{Bew_{PL}}(\alpha) \rightarrow \Box\alpha\big)$.

PROOF We begin by restating the global reflection principle in a form that more closely resembles the previous proposition, that is, to prove

$$\mathsf{CT} \vdash \forall y\Big(\mathsf{Der_{PL}}(y) \rightarrow \forall\alpha\forall\beta\big(\alpha \in y \wedge \mathsf{Ins}(\beta, \alpha) \rightarrow \Box\beta\big)\Big).$$

The proof is by induction on the derivation y. Let d be a derivation in PL and suppose the final formula of d is α. Let β be an arbitrary instantiation of α. There are three cases for α:

(i) α is a logical axiom;

(ii) a proper subderivation of d contains formulæ γ and $\gamma \dot{\rightarrow} \alpha$ for some γ;

(iii) $\alpha = \dot{\forall} v_i \gamma$ for some i and γ, and a proper subderivation of d concludes with the formula γ.

In the first case, $\Box\beta$ obtains by the previous proposition. For the second case, there will be an instantiation δ of γ such that $\delta \dot{\rightarrow} \beta$ is an instantiation of $\gamma \dot{\rightarrow} \alpha$. Two applications of the induction hypothesis yield $\Box(\delta \dot{\rightarrow} \beta)$ and $\Box\delta$, whence $\Box\beta$ follows by CT3. In the final case, we have $\beta = \dot{\forall} v\, \delta(v)$ for a formula δ with at most v free. Applying the induction hypothesis to the subderivation with conclusion γ, we deduce, in particular, $\Box\delta(s)$ for every closed term s, whence $\Box\beta$ results from CT4. ⊣

Extending the previous result to $\mathsf{E}^*_{\min}$ follows a similar argument. The first step is to establish that all the axioms of $\mathsf{E}^*_{\min}$ are true:

11.44 PROPOSITION $\mathsf{CT} \vdash \forall\alpha\big(\mathsf{Axiom}_{\mathsf{E}^*_{\min}}(\alpha) \to \Box\alpha\big)$.

PROOF The axioms of $\mathsf{E}^*_{\min}$ fall into two categories. In the first are the basic axioms governing the operations of concatenation, quotation, and substitution: axioms B1–E3. As these are finitely many and all sentences of $\mathcal{L}^*$, the conjunction of all these axioms is proven true in TB+CT2+CT3. The second category of axioms is the universal closures of instances of the schema of induction. Applying (11.12), it suffices to prove that every instantiation of an instance of the induction axiom is true:

$$\mathsf{CT} \vdash \forall\alpha\forall\beta\Big(\mathsf{Ins}\big(\beta, \mathsf{ax}_{\mathrm{ind}}(\alpha)\big) \to \Box\beta\Big).$$

Arguing within CT, let $\gamma(v)$ be any formula of $\mathcal{L}^*$ with at most the variable v free, and set $\delta = \dot{\forall} x\big(\dot{\forall} y \,\dot{\subseteq}\, x\; \gamma(y) \;\dot{\rightarrow}\; \gamma(x)\big)$, stating that γ is progressive. We want to show $\Box(\delta \dot{\rightarrow} \dot{\forall} v \gamma)$. The first goal is to prove

$$\Box\delta \to \forall s\, \Box\gamma[s/v].$$

Assume $\Box\delta$. Passing the truth predicate through the first quantifier and connective of δ by means of the CT-axioms, we deduce

$$\forall s\Big(\Box\big(\dot{\forall} y \,\dot{\subsetneq}\, s\; \gamma[y/v]\big) \to \Box\gamma[s/v]\Big).$$

Continuing further with the antecedent leads to

$$\forall s\big(\forall t\big(t^\circ \subseteq s^\circ \to \Box\gamma[t/v]\big) \to \Box\gamma[s/v]\big).$$

This final formula is equivalent to the statement that $\forall s\big(s^\circ = \mathsf{x} \to \Box\gamma[s/v]\big)$ is progressive. So, we have shown $\Box\delta \to \forall s\,\Box\gamma[s/v]$, whence the CT-axioms imply

$$\Box(\delta \mathbin{\dot\to} \dot\forall v\gamma).$$

As γ was arbitrary, we are done. ⊣

11.45 THEOREM *The global reflection principle for* $\mathsf{E}^*_{\min}$ *is derivable in* CT. *That is,*

$$\mathsf{CT} \vdash \forall\alpha\big(\mathsf{Bew}_{\mathsf{E}^*_{\min}}(\alpha) \to \Box\alpha\big).$$

PROOF Rather than repeating the argument of proposition 11.43, we observe that $\mathsf{E}^*_{\min} \vdash \varphi$ if and only if there is a list $\varphi_1, \ldots, \varphi_n$ of $\mathsf{E}^*_{\min}$-axioms such that $\mathsf{PL} \vdash \varphi_1 \wedge \cdots \wedge \varphi_n \to \varphi$. As the equivalence is provable within $\mathsf{E}^*_{\min}$, the previous two propositions show that the global reflection principle for $\mathsf{E}^*_{\min}$ is provable in CT. ⊣

11.46 COROLLARY *The consistency statement for* $\mathsf{E}^*_{\min}$ *is derivable in* CT. *That is,* $\mathsf{CT} \vdash \neg\mathsf{Bew}_{\mathsf{E}^*_{\min}}(\ulcorner\bot\urcorner)$. *In particular,* CT *is not a conservative extension of* E^* *for* $\mathcal{L}^*_{\min}$*-sentences.*

The reason theorem 11.45 refers to $\mathsf{E}^*_{\min}$ and not E^* is simply that without restrictions on the choice of E^* it is not given that the statement 'all axioms of E^* are true' is derivable in CT. However, a direct consequence of our proof of theorem 11.45 is the following:

11.47 COROLLARY *Suppose* S *is a theory containing* CT *and* T *is a theory such that*

$$\mathsf{S} \vdash \forall\alpha\big(\mathsf{Axiom}_{\mathsf{T}}(\alpha) \to \Box\alpha\big).$$

Then the global reflection principle for T *is provable in* S.

The global reflection principle for a theory S is a formal statement of the soundness of S. We have already looked at formal statements of completeness in the form of the (formalized) Σ-completeness theorems 10.22 and 10.70 and at a version of the statement using partial truth predicates, theorem 11.16. Combining the two groups of results, we deduce that, over CT, truth and provability coincide for Σ-formulæ:

11.48 COROLLARY *Suppose* $\mathsf{E}^* = \mathsf{E}^*_{\min}$. *Then*

$$\mathsf{CT} \vdash \forall\alpha\Big(\mathsf{Sent}_{\Sigma_1}(\alpha) \wedge \mathsf{Sent}_{\mathrm{syn}}(\alpha) \to \big(\Box\alpha \leftrightarrow \mathsf{Bew}_{\mathsf{E}^*}(\alpha)\big)\Big).$$

PROOF The right-to-left implication is theorem 11.45. For the converse direction, namely $\Box\alpha \to \mathsf{Bew}_{\mathsf{E}^*}(\alpha)$ where α is any $\Box$-free Σ_1-sentence, we appeal to theorem 11.16 and

$$\mathsf{CT} \vdash \forall\alpha\big(\mathsf{Sent}_{\Sigma_1}(\alpha) \wedge \mathsf{Sent}_{\mathrm{syn}}(\alpha) \wedge \Box\alpha \to \mathsf{Tr}_{\Sigma}(\alpha)\big),$$

which is provable by induction on α. ⊣

An important ingredient in the proof of theorem 11.45 is the axiom of induction for formulæ containing the truth predicate $\Box$. This occurred in two essential places: deriving global reflection for predicate logic and proving the truth of all instances of induction. It is known that this assumption cannot be dropped. If the axiom schema of induction in E^* is replaced by the version for formulæ without the predicate $\Box$, then adding the four axioms of compositional truth in definition 11.38 gives rise to a conservative extension of E^* for formulæ of $\mathcal{L}^*_{\mathrm{syn}}$. That is to say, this subtheory of CT, commonly denoted CT^-, has the property that if $\mathsf{CT}^- \vdash \varphi$ and φ is $\Box$-free then $\mathsf{E}^* \vdash \varphi$. The axioms of CT^- are sufficient to derive the typed T-schema (the proof of proposition 11.39 did not depend on the axioms of induction), so CT^- still extends UTB over the same base theory. The conservativity result referred to was established by Kotlarski, Krajewski, and Lachlan (1981) (using the arithmetical theory PA in place of our E^*). Their argument is of a very different nature than the conservativity proofs we have so far considered and appeals to results in the theory of nonstandard models of E^*. Alternative proofs of the conservativity theorem were recently given by Enayat and Visser (2015), Leigh (2015), and Cieśliński (2021). Given that CT^- is consistent, it follows from corollary 11.46 that the global reflection principle for E^* is not derivable in CT^-.

Conservativity of axiomatic theories of truth over their base theory has been strongly associated with the philosophical position of deflationism, which holds that the concept of truth is insubstantial. Partly for this reason, there is interest in understanding the relationship between the two compositional theories of truth: the theory CT and its subtheory CT^- with induction restricted to truth-free formulæ. Important formal questions include determining which truth-theoretic assumptions can be added to CT^- without losing conservativity, and which give rise to nonconservative extensions. For instance, it is known that adding to CT^- the statement 'All instances of induction are true' yields a conservative extension of E^* (Kotlarski, Krajewski, and Lachlan 1981), whereas our proof of theorem 11.45 shows that induction for Π_1-formulæ involving $\Box$ is sufficient to derive global reflection for the base theory.

We will not delve deeper into these questions here. The interested reader will find an extensive discussion of deflationism in formal truth, for example, in Cieśliński (2017), Horsten (2011), and Halbach (2014).

11.5 Existential Type-Free Truth

The axioms of the compositional theory of truth CT are intuitively correct statements about the interplay of truth and the connectives, quantifiers, and atomic predicates of our formal language. Our proof of consistency (theorem 11.41) supports this view, for there we showed that the compositional truth predicate of CT has a natural interpretation as the set of sentences true in any given standard model of $\mathsf{E}^*_{\mathrm{min}}$.

Given the naturalness of the CT-axioms and the inconsistency which arises when adding the corresponding 'axiom' for iterated truth:

$$\forall \alpha \big(\mathsf{Sent}(\alpha) \to (\Box \underset{\cdot}{\overline{\Box \alpha}} \leftrightarrow \Box \alpha)\big),$$

it is not unreasonable to surmise that self-applicable notions of truth lack intuitive and well-motivated axiomatic theories. Yet, in fact we have already seen an example of a consistent axiomatization of self-applicable truth, though it was not presented as such, namely the compositional clauses validated by partial truth predicates. For example, using $\Box$ in place of the Σ_1 partial truth predicate Tr_{Σ_1}, we have shown already that the following compositional 'axioms' are derivable in E^* (proposition 11.12 and lemma 11.13):

ET1 $\forall s_1 \cdots \forall s_k \big(\Box \underset{\cdot}{\mathsf{R}} s_1 \cdots s_k \leftrightarrow \mathsf{R}(s_1^\circ, \ldots, s_k^\circ)\big)$ for each k and each predicate symbol $\mathsf{R} \in \mathcal{L}^*_{\mathrm{syn}}$ of arity k,

ET2 $\forall s_1 \cdots \forall s_k \big(\Box (\underset{\cdot}{\neg} \underline{\mathsf{R}} s_1 \cdots s_k) \leftrightarrow \neg \mathsf{R}(s_1^\circ, \ldots, s_k^\circ)\big)$ for each k and each predicate symbol $\mathsf{R} \in \mathcal{L}^*_{\mathrm{syn}}$ of arity k,

ET3 $\forall \alpha \forall \beta \Big(\mathsf{Sent}(\alpha \underset{\cdot}{\to} \beta) \to \big(\Box(\alpha \underset{\cdot}{\land} \beta) \leftrightarrow (\Box \alpha \land \Box \beta)\big)\Big)$,

ET4 $\forall \alpha \forall \beta \Big(\mathsf{Sent}(\alpha \underset{\cdot}{\to} \beta) \to \big(\Box(\alpha \underset{\cdot}{\lor} \beta) \leftrightarrow (\Box \alpha \lor \Box \beta)\big)\Big)$,

ET5 $\forall\alpha\forall v\big(\mathsf{Sent}(\dot{\exists}v\,\alpha) \to (\Box\dot{\exists}v\,\alpha \leftrightarrow \exists x\,\Box\alpha[\mathsf{q}x/v])\big)$,

ET6 $\forall\alpha\forall s\forall v\big(\mathsf{Sent}(\dot{\forall}v\dot{\subseteq}s\;\alpha) \to (\Box\dot{\forall}v\dot{\subseteq}s\;\alpha \leftrightarrow \forall x\subseteq s^{\circ}\,\Box\alpha[\mathsf{q}x/v])\big)$,

ET7 $\forall\alpha\big(\mathsf{Sent}(\alpha) \to (\Box\overline{\dot{\Box}\alpha} \leftrightarrow \Box\alpha)\big)$.

The label ET stands for 'existential truth'. Let ET denote the theory extending $\mathsf{E}^{*}_{\min}$ by the axioms ET1–ET7.

The axioms of ET express the natural compositional clauses for atomic and negated atomic formulæ, the connectives conjunction and disjunction, existential and bounded universal quantifiers, and nested occurrences of the truth predicate. Natural candidates for compositional axioms that are missing from this list include, of course, axioms for the unbounded universal quantifier, for negation, and for implication all present in CT. The clause for the universal quantifier (but not the existential quantifier) is motivated by the Π_n partial truth predicates, but the only definable truth predicate we have considered which satisfies the corresponding clauses for negation and implication is the predicate Tr_{Δ_0} for Δ_0-formulæ. This latter predicate, however, does not satisfy the corresponding version of the axiom of self-application ET7, as the proof of theorem 11.10 demonstrated.

From our work on CT it should be clear that ET derives the T-schema for all formulæ without $\Box$ that can be constructed from atomic and negated atomic formulæ using the (defined) connectives $\wedge$ and $\vee$, the bounded universal and the unbounded existential quantifier. The final axiom, ET7, adds the atomic formula $\Box x$ to this collection, but not its negation. These formulæ are all examples of Σ_1-formulæ that are $\Box$-positive. Note, however, that there are formulæ, such as $\neg\neg\Box s$, which are $\Box$-positive and Σ_1 but not in the class described. Nonetheless, every Σ_1-formula is logically equivalent to a formula in the class. In the next section we consider an extension of ET in which truth adequately applies to all $\Box$-positive sentences. For the purposes of the present section, however, it is convenient to take the $\Box$-positive Σ_1-sentences as the sentences that can be constructed from atomic and negated $\Box$-free atomic formulæ and the atomic truth predicate $\Box$ by the 'positive' connectives $\wedge$ and $\vee$, the bounded universal quantifier, and the unbounded existential quantifier. The proof of the following proposition is left to the reader.

11.49 PROPOSITION *The uniform T-schema is derivable in* ET *for all $\Box$-positive Σ_1-formulæ.*

With the possible exception of generalizing principle ET6 to unbounded universal quantifiers, no other compositional 'axiom' that we have so far considered can be consistently added to the collection ET1–ET7. We saw already that axiom ET7 is inconsistent over CT, but that result can be strengthened to put blame specifically on the clauses for negation and implication which designate truth values to non-$\Box$-positive sentences.

11.50 LEMMA *Suppose* $\mathsf{E}^* \vdash \forall\alpha\big(\mathsf{Sent}(\alpha) \to (\Box\overline{\Box\dot{\alpha}} \leftrightarrow \Box\alpha)\big)$. *Then if either* $\mathsf{E}^* \vdash$ CT2 *or* $\mathsf{E}^* \vdash$ CT1 $\wedge$ CT3, *then* E^* *is inconsistent.*

PROOF Suppose $\mathsf{E}^* \vdash$ CT2 and let λ be the liar sentence. Recall $\lambda := \neg\Box t$ for a closed term t with $\mathsf{E}^* \vdash t = \overline{\neg\Box t}$ (cf. lemma 5.11). The following equivalences obtain:

$$
\begin{aligned}
\mathsf{E}^* \vdash \lambda &\leftrightarrow \neg\Box t \\
&\leftrightarrow \neg\Box\overline{\Box t} && \Box\overline{\Box t} \leftrightarrow \Box t \\
&\leftrightarrow \Box\overline{\neg\Box t} && \text{CT2} \\
&\leftrightarrow \Box t && t = \overline{\neg\Box t} \\
&\leftrightarrow \neg\lambda
\end{aligned}
$$

So E^* is inconsistent. An analogous argument holds if instead we assume $\mathsf{E}^* \vdash$ CT1 $\wedge$ CT3. In this case it is necessary to consider the variant of the liar sentence based on implication instead of negation: $\kappa \equiv \Box s \to \bot$ where $\bot \equiv \underline{\forall}\underline{=}\underline{\neg}$ and $\mathsf{E}^* \vdash s = \overline{\kappa}$:

$$
\begin{aligned}
\mathsf{E}^* \vdash \kappa &\leftrightarrow (\Box s \to \bot) \\
&\leftrightarrow (\Box\overline{\Box s} \to \Box\overline{\bot}) && \Box\overline{\Box s} \to \Box s \ \&\ \text{CT1} \\
&\leftrightarrow \Box\overline{\Box s \to \bot} && \text{CT3} \\
&\leftrightarrow \Box s && s = \overline{\kappa} \\
&\leftrightarrow \neg\kappa
\end{aligned}
$$

⊣

Returning to our original motivation behind the axioms of ET as abstracting the partial truth predicate for Σ_1-sentences, it is tempting to surmise that ET conservatively extends E^*. While this is indeed correct, it is not realized by the simple interpretation alluded to above which replaces the predicate symbol $\Box$ by the formula Tr_{Σ_1} (leaving all other symbols unchanged). The reason is the final axiom, where in order to obtain the corresponding statement about Σ_1-truth we require also to replace quotations of the kind $\overline{\Box \underset{\cdot}{\alpha}}$ by $\overline{\mathsf{Tr}_{\Sigma_1}(\underset{\cdot}{\alpha})}$. But this kind of interpretation of languages is not admissible as, for example, $\mathsf{Sing}(\overline{\Box})$ is derivable yet $\mathsf{Sing}(\overline{\mathsf{Tr}_{\Sigma_1}})$ is clearly false.

Rather, conservativity is proven by designing a new predicate, $\mathsf{Tr}^{\Box}_{\Sigma_1}$, which acts as compositional truth predicate for Σ_1-formulæ that contain $\Box$ and asserts the atomic formula $\Box s$ to be 'true' if (and only if) $\mathsf{Tr}^{\Box}_{\Sigma_1}(s^\circ)$. Such a formula can be constructed using the Σ_1 truth predicate by diagonalization as an instance of an implicit Σ_1-definition:

11.51 PROPOSITION ET *is a conservative extension of* $\mathsf{E}^*_{\min}$ *for* $\Box$*-free formulæ. In particular,* ET *is consistent.*

PROOF Let ET extend the minimal base theory $\mathsf{E}^*_{\min}$ by the seven axioms ET1–ET7. Recall the formula $\psi_{\Sigma_1}(\alpha, z)$ used in the definition of Tr_{Σ_1} which checks whether the Σ_1-formula α is true by reference to the immediate subformulæ of α using the assumption that z is a list of true formulæ (definition 11.11). From this formula define

$$\psi^{\mathsf{P}}_{\Sigma_1}(\alpha, z) := \psi_{\Sigma_1}(\alpha, z) \lor \exists s\big(\alpha = \underset{\cdot}{\Box} s \land \mathsf{P}(s^\circ)\big),$$
$$\mathsf{Tr}^{\mathsf{P}}_{\Sigma_1}(x) := \exists z\big(\mathsf{list}(z) \land x \in z \land \forall w \in z\ \psi^{\mathsf{P}}_{\Sigma_1}(w, z)\big),$$

where P is a fresh unary predicate symbol. The latter formula is a P-positive Σ_1-formula. Theorem 11.18 yields a (Σ_1-)formula $\mathsf{Tr}^{\Box}_{\Sigma_1}(x)$ such that the equivalence

$$\mathsf{Tr}^{\Box}_{\Sigma_1}(x) \leftrightarrow \exists z\Big(\mathsf{list}(z) \land x \in z \land \forall w \in z\big(\psi_{\Sigma_1}(w, z) \lor \exists s\big(\alpha = \underset{\cdot}{\Box} s \land \mathsf{Tr}^{\Box}_{\Sigma_1}(s^\circ)\big)\big)\Big)$$

is derivable in $\mathsf{E}^*_{\min}$. Given a formula φ of $\mathcal{L}^*$ let $\varphi^\Box$ be the result of replacing every atomic subformula $\Box t$ in φ by $\mathsf{Tr}^{\Box}_{\Sigma_1}(t)$. We leave it to the reader to prove, by induction on derivations, that $\mathsf{ET} \vdash \varphi$ implies $\mathsf{E}^*_{\min} \vdash \varphi^\Box$. As $\varphi \equiv \varphi^\Box$ for φ not containing $\Box$, the proof is complete. ⊣

We now turn to the issue of extending ET to a more expressive axiomatic theory of truth. We have seen that neither the compositional axiom for negated formulæ nor the one for implications can be consistently added to ET. With respect to the axioms we have encountered so far, an obvious question is whether the compositional clause for unbounded universal quantification,

$$\forall \alpha \forall v\Big(\mathsf{Sent}(\underset{\cdot}{\forall} v\, \alpha) \land \mathsf{Var}(v) \to \big(\Box \underset{\cdot}{\forall} v\, \alpha \leftrightarrow \forall s\, \Box \alpha[s/v]\big)\Big),$$

can be consistently added. A second issue is the apparent lack of expressiveness of a truth predicate restricted to positive formulæ. Consider the formal analogues of the following three statements:

- it is true that $\underline{\mathsf{v}} \mathbin{\underline{=}} \underline{\neg}$ is true: $\Box\overline{\Box\overline{\underline{\mathsf{v}} \mathbin{\underline{=}} \underline{\neg}}}$;
- it is not true that $\underline{\mathsf{v}} \mathbin{\underline{=}} \underline{\neg}$ is true: $\neg\Box\overline{\Box\overline{\underline{\mathsf{v}} \mathbin{\underline{=}} \underline{\neg}}}$;
- it is true that $\underline{\mathsf{v}} \mathbin{\underline{=}} \underline{\neg}$ is not true: $\Box\overline{\neg\Box\overline{\underline{\mathsf{v}} \mathbin{\underline{=}} \underline{\neg}}}$.

The first two statements are theorems of ET, but the third is not, as there is no way to derive a sentence $\Box\overline{\varphi}$ in ET (without assumptions) if φ is not $\Box$-positive. We see this from the interpretation of ET in $\mathsf{E}^*_{\min}$ given in the proof of proposition 11.51: letting $\mathsf{Sent}^\Box$ be the natural formula expressing that its only argument is the quotation of a $\Box$-positive sentence, we have

$$\mathsf{E}^*_{\min} \vdash \forall\alpha\big(\mathsf{Tr}^\Box_{\Sigma_1}(\alpha) \to \mathsf{Sent}^\Box(\alpha)\big),$$

which can be verified by formal induction on α. So, if $\mathsf{ET} \vdash \Box\overline{\varphi}$ then, by the proof of proposition 11.51, it follows that $\mathsf{E}^*_{\min} \vdash \mathsf{Sent}^\Box(\overline{\varphi})$.

Despite the problems with admitting negation under the scope of the truth predicate, there is nothing paradoxical about the third example. Sentences of this kind can be consistently added to ET, but to do this systematically requires care in the axiomatic treatment of negation and truth.

11.6 Kripke–Feferman Truth

The next axiomatic theory is an extension of ET in which we can reason about $\Box$-positive formulæ and their negations in full generality. The Kripke–Feferman theory of truth, denoted KF, was introduced by Feferman (1991) based on Kripke's (1975) semantic theory. We assume that $\mathcal{L}^*$ contains two distinct unary relation symbols, $\Box$ and $\boxdot$. Henceforth, a formula is 'truth-free' if it contains neither of these symbols (their syntactic constants are permitted). In the following definition we use $\mathcal{L}^*_0$ for the sublanguage of $\mathcal{L}^*$ with the predicate symbols $\Box$ and $\boxdot$ removed.

11.52 DEFINITION KF is the extension of E^* by the following axioms:

KF1 $\forall s_1 \cdots \forall s_k \big(\Box \underset{\cdot}{\mathsf{R}} s_1 \cdots s_k \leftrightarrow \mathsf{R} s_1^\circ \cdots s_k^\circ\big)$ for each k and each relation symbol R of $\mathcal{L}^*_0$ of arity k,

KF2 $\forall s_1 \cdots \forall s_k \big(\boxdot \underset{\cdot}{\mathsf{R}} s_1 \cdots s_k \leftrightarrow \neg \mathsf{R} s_1^{\circ} \cdots s_k^{\circ}\big)$ for each k and each relation symbol R of $\mathcal{L}_0^*$ of arity k,

KF3 $\forall \alpha \big(\mathsf{Sent}(\alpha) \rightarrow (\Box \underset{\cdot}{\neg} \alpha \leftrightarrow \boxdot \alpha)\big)$,

KF4 $\forall \alpha \big(\mathsf{Sent}(\alpha) \rightarrow (\boxdot \underset{\cdot}{\neg} \alpha \leftrightarrow \Box \alpha)\big)$,

KF5 $\forall \alpha \forall \beta \Big(\mathsf{Sent}(\alpha \underset{\cdot}{\rightarrow} \beta) \rightarrow \big(\Box(\alpha \underset{\cdot}{\rightarrow} \beta) \leftrightarrow (\boxdot \alpha \vee \Box \beta)\big)\Big)$,

KF6 $\forall \alpha \forall \beta \Big(\mathsf{Sent}(\alpha \underset{\cdot}{\rightarrow} \beta) \rightarrow \big(\boxdot(\alpha \underset{\cdot}{\rightarrow} \beta) \leftrightarrow (\Box \alpha \wedge \boxdot \beta)\big)\Big)$,

KF7 $\forall \alpha \forall v \big(\mathsf{Sent}(\underset{\cdot}{\forall} v\, \alpha) \rightarrow (\Box \underset{\cdot}{\forall} v\, \alpha \leftrightarrow \forall s\, \Box \alpha[s/v])\big)$,

KF8 $\forall \alpha \forall v \big(\mathsf{Sent}(\underset{\cdot}{\forall} v\, \alpha) \rightarrow (\boxdot \underset{\cdot}{\forall} v\, \alpha \leftrightarrow \exists s\, \boxdot \alpha[s/v])\big)$,

KF9 $\forall s \big(\Box \underset{\cdot}{\Box} s \leftrightarrow \Box s^{\circ}\big) \wedge \forall s \big(\Box \underset{\cdot}{\boxdot} s \leftrightarrow \boxdot s^{\circ}\big)$,

KF10 $\forall s \big(\boxdot \underset{\cdot}{\Box} s \leftrightarrow \boxdot s^{\circ}\big) \wedge \forall s \big(\boxdot \underset{\cdot}{\boxdot} s \leftrightarrow \Box s^{\circ}\big)$.

Reading $\Box x$ as 'x is true' and $\boxdot x$ as 'x is false', the axioms of KF express natural conditions of truth and falsity for $\mathcal{L}^*$-sentences. Axiom KF3, for instance, expresses that a negated sentence is true if and only if the sentence in question is false. Axiom KF6 expresses the analogous clause for implication, whereby an implication is true if and only if either the antecedent is false or the consequent is true. Note, this is not the same as the compositional axiom CT3, which is inconsistent with the axioms of KF. The final two axioms, KF9 and KF10, generalize axiom ET7 to two predicates: a sentence $\Box s$ is true if and only if s denotes a true sentence, $\boxdot s$ is true if and only if s denotes a false sentence, and so on.

We have reverted to giving compositional clauses for the primary connectives of the language $\mathcal{L}^*$, namely negation, implication, and universal quantification. This fixes the issue with the previous theory ET, where the T-schema is derivable only for a subset of the $\Box$-positive formulæ. For example, the T-schema instance $\Box \overline{\neg\neg\Box s} \leftrightarrow \neg\neg\Box s^{\circ}$ is derivable in KF by combining the axioms for negation and self-application. Before we examine the derivable T-schema instances more closely, our first task is to verify that, indeed, ET is extended by KF:

11.53 PROPOSITION *The following are derivable in* KF. *In particular,* ET *is a subtheory of* KF.

(i) $\forall \alpha \forall \beta \Big(\mathsf{Sent}(\alpha \underset{\cdot}{\rightarrow} \beta) \rightarrow \big(\Box(\alpha \underset{\cdot}{\wedge} \beta) \leftrightarrow (\Box \alpha \wedge \Box \beta)\big)\Big)$,

(ii) $\forall \alpha \forall \beta \Big(\mathsf{Sent}(\alpha \underset{\cdot}{\rightarrow} \beta) \rightarrow \big(\boxdot(\alpha \underset{\cdot}{\wedge} \beta) \leftrightarrow (\boxdot \alpha \vee \boxdot \beta)\big)\Big)$,

(iii) $\forall\alpha\forall\beta\Big(\mathsf{Sent}(\alpha\underset{\cdot}{\to}\beta)\to\big(\Box(\alpha\underset{\cdot}{\vee}\beta)\leftrightarrow(\Box\alpha\vee\Box\beta)\big)\Big)$,

(iv) $\forall\alpha\forall\beta\Big(\mathsf{Sent}(\alpha\underset{\cdot}{\to}\beta)\to\big(\boxdot(\alpha\underset{\cdot}{\vee}\beta)\leftrightarrow(\boxdot\alpha\wedge\boxdot\beta)\big)\Big)$,

(v) $\forall\alpha\big(\mathsf{Sent}(\alpha)\to(\Box\underset{\cdot}{\neg}\underset{\cdot}{\neg}\alpha\leftrightarrow\Box\alpha)\big)$,

(vi) $\forall\alpha\big(\mathsf{Sent}(\alpha)\to(\boxdot\underset{\cdot}{\neg}\underset{\cdot}{\neg}\alpha\leftrightarrow\boxdot\alpha)\big)$,

(vii) $\forall\alpha\forall v\big(\mathsf{Sent}(\underset{\cdot}{\forall}v\,\alpha)\to(\Box\underset{\cdot}{\exists}v\,\alpha\leftrightarrow\exists s\,\Box\alpha[s/v])\big)$,

(viii) $\forall\alpha\forall v\big(\mathsf{Sent}(\underset{\cdot}{\forall}v\,\alpha)\to(\boxdot\underset{\cdot}{\exists}v\,\alpha\leftrightarrow\forall s\,\boxdot\alpha[s/v])\big)$.

PROOF We consider (ii). Recall $\mathsf{E}^*_{\mathrm{min}}\vdash\forall\alpha\forall\beta\big(\alpha\underset{\cdot}{\wedge}\beta=\underset{\cdot}{\neg}(\alpha\underset{\cdot}{\to}\underset{\cdot}{\neg}\beta)\big)$. So

$$\begin{aligned}\mathsf{KF}\vdash\forall\alpha\forall\beta\Big(\mathsf{Sent}(\alpha\underset{\cdot}{\to}\beta)\to\big(\boxdot(\alpha\underset{\cdot}{\wedge}\beta)&\leftrightarrow\Box(\alpha\underset{\cdot}{\to}\underset{\cdot}{\neg}\beta)\big)\Big) && \text{KF4}\\ &\leftrightarrow\boxdot\alpha\vee\Box\underset{\cdot}{\neg}\beta && \text{KF5}\\ &\leftrightarrow\boxdot\alpha\vee\boxdot\beta && \text{KF3}\end{aligned}$$

The other cases are similar. ⊣

From proposition 11.53 it immediately follows that the uniform T-schema is derivable in KF for formulæ built from truth-free formulæ and the atomic formulæ $\Box s$ and $\boxdot s$ using the defined connectives $\wedge$ and $\vee$ and the two quantifiers $\forall$ and $\exists$. Working instead with the axioms of KF it is possible to derive a stronger result, the T-schema for all formulæ which are positive with respect to both $\Box$ and $\boxdot$. Henceforth, we call such a formula, i.e., one that is both $\Box$- and $\boxdot$-positive, merely 'positive'.

11.54 PROPOSITION *All instances of the uniform T-schema for positive formulæ are derivable in* KF.

PROOF By induction on the instances of the T-schema. Axioms KF1 and KF9 provide the T-schema for all atomic formulæ. The only positive negated atomic formulæ are truth-free, and KF2 implies all such instances of the T-schema. For non-atomic formulæ, KF derives

$$\Box(\alpha\underset{\cdot}{\to}\beta)\leftrightarrow\Box\underset{\cdot}{\neg}\alpha\vee\Box\beta\quad\text{and}\quad\Box\underset{\cdot}{\neg}(\alpha\underset{\cdot}{\to}\beta)\leftrightarrow\Box\alpha\wedge\Box\underset{\cdot}{\neg}\beta$$

under the assumption that α and β are sentences. Given that $\varphi\to\psi$ is positive if and only if $\neg\varphi$ and ψ are positive, and $\neg(\varphi\to\psi)$ is positive if and only if φ and $\neg\psi$ are positive, the induction hypothesis and the compositional clauses for the two quantifiers complete the argument. ⊣

A corresponding property can be formulated for the 'falsity' predicate $\boxdot$, but here it is helpful to restrict attention to formulæ built from the atomic and negated atomic formulæ using only the defined connectives $\wedge$ and $\vee$ and quantifiers $\forall$ and $\exists$. Given that φ is such a formula, the dual of φ is the formula $\varphi^{\perp}$ determined as follows: The dual of the atomic formula $\Box s$ is $\boxdot s$, and conversely, the dual of $\boxdot s$ is $\Box s$. The dual of any other atomic formula is the negation of that formula. The dual of a non-atomic formula is given by the equations

$$(\varphi\wedge\psi)^{\perp} \equiv \varphi^{\perp}\vee\psi^{\perp}, \qquad (\forall v\,\varphi)^{\perp} \equiv \exists v\,\varphi^{\perp}, \qquad (\neg\varphi)^{\perp} \equiv \neg\varphi^{\perp},$$
$$(\varphi\vee\psi)^{\perp} \equiv \varphi^{\perp}\wedge\psi^{\perp}, \qquad (\exists v\,\varphi)^{\perp} \equiv \forall v\,\varphi^{\perp},$$

where, in the case of negation, φ is restricted to atomic formulæ only. For instance, $\neg\neg \mathsf{x}=\mathsf{y} \wedge (\Box\mathsf{x} \vee \neg\boxdot\mathsf{y})$ is the dual of $\neg\mathsf{x}=\mathsf{y} \vee (\boxdot\mathsf{x} \wedge \neg\Box\mathsf{y})$. The definition can be extended to arbitrary formulæ (built from the connectives $\neg$ and $\rightarrow$) by first expressing the formula in the above form and then computing its dual. The F-schema for a positive sentence φ is the sentence

(F-schema) $$\boxdot\overline{\varphi} \leftrightarrow \varphi^{\perp}.$$

The uniform F-schema is the generalization of this schema in line with the uniform T-schema:

11.55 PROPOSITION *All instances of the uniform F-schema for positive formulæ are derivable in* KF.

PROOF Let φ be any positive formula. In the definition of $\varphi^{\perp}$ the first step is the conversion of φ into a formula using connectives $\wedge$ and $\vee$, quantifiers $\forall$ and $\exists$, and atomic and negated atomic formulæ. This can be achieved, for example, by the translation

$$(\varphi\rightarrow\psi)^{*} \equiv (\neg\varphi)^{*}\vee\psi^{*}, \qquad (\neg\neg\varphi)^{*} \equiv \varphi^{*},$$
$$\big(\neg(\varphi\rightarrow\psi)\big)^{*} \equiv \varphi^{*}\wedge(\neg\psi)^{*}, \qquad (\neg\forall v\,\varphi)^{*} \equiv \exists v(\neg\varphi)^{*},$$

with $\varphi^{*} \equiv \varphi$ in case φ is atomic or negated atomic. Now if $\psi \equiv \varphi^{*}$, clearly $\mathsf{E}^{*} \vdash \varphi^{\perp} \leftrightarrow \psi^{\perp}$. Since also

$$\mathsf{KF} \vdash (\varphi\leftrightarrow\varphi^{*}) \wedge (\Box\overline{\varphi} \leftrightarrow \Box\overline{\varphi^{*}}),$$

it remains only to show that the F-schema is derivable for positive formulæ φ^{*}. But this is a straightforward proof by induction on φ^{*}, using proposition 11.53 and the definition of $\varphi^{\perp}$. $\dashv$

The uniform T- and F-schemas together are as strong as KF itself in the sense that adding the T- and F-schemas to E^* (with induction expanded to the language with T and F) proves the same truth-free sentences as KF itself. However, there are theorems of KF such as KF3–KF8 that are not provable from the schemas. See Halbach (2014, sec. 19.5).

The motivation behind the definition of the dual $\varphi^\perp$ is that if falsity is lack of truth, and truth lack of falsity, then duality is negation:

$$\mathsf{E}^*+\forall x\,(\Box x \leftrightarrow \neg\boxdot x) \vdash \varphi^\perp \leftrightarrow \neg\varphi$$

for all formulæ φ. However, $\forall x\,(\Box x \leftrightarrow \neg\boxdot x)$ is inconsistent with the axioms of KF because it implies the CT-axiom for negation (CT2), which we know is inconsistent with ET. But under the truth predicate, dual and negation coincide in the sense that

$$\mathsf{KF} \vdash \forall\alpha\big(\mathsf{Sent}(\alpha) \to (\Box\alpha^\perp \leftrightarrow \boxdot\alpha)\big),$$

which we leave to the reader to verify.

As we have already observed, CT is not a subtheory of KF. Nevertheless, it is possible to define, within KF, a CT-style truth predicate. That is, there is a formula $\Box_0$ of one free variable such that the axioms of CT, formulated for $\Box_0$ in place of $\Box$, are derivable in KF. We require that $\mathcal{L}^*$ contain a unary predicate P distinct from $\Box$ and $\boxdot$. Given a formula φ, let φ^{P} be the result of substituting P for $\Box$ and $\neg\mathsf{P}$ for $\boxdot$ in φ. In particular, φ^{P} is always a truth-free formula, and if φ is truth-free then $\varphi^{\mathsf{P}} \equiv \varphi$. Let $f(x) := \mathsf{sub}\big(\mathsf{sub}(x,\overline{\Box},\overline{\mathsf{P}}),\overline{\boxdot},\overline{\neg\mathsf{P}}\big)$ be the term expressing this substitution. Define

$$\Box_0(\mathsf{x}) := \Box f(\mathsf{x}) \quad \text{and} \quad \boxdot_0(\mathsf{x}) := \boxdot f(\mathsf{x}),$$

Note, the equation $\overline{\varphi^{\mathsf{P}}} = f(\overline{\varphi})$ is a theorem of E^* for every φ.

11.56 PROPOSITION *The axioms of* CT, *formulated with* $\Box_0$ *in place of* $\Box$, *are derivable in* KF.

PROOF The axiom for negation, equivalent over CT to

$$\forall\alpha\big(\mathsf{Sent}(\alpha) \to (\boxdot_0\alpha \leftrightarrow \neg\Box_0\alpha)\big),$$

is key, so we begin by deriving this in KF. The proof proceeds by formal induction on the number of connectives and quantifiers in α. Let α be any sentence. We require to show

$$\boxdot f(\alpha) \leftrightarrow \neg\Box f(\alpha) \tag{11.13}$$

from the assumption that the equivalence holds for every sentence β of lower logical complexity than α. The case that α is atomic splits into two subcases, depending on whether α is truth-free or not. In the former case, $f(\alpha) = \alpha$ and (11.13) follows from axioms KF1 and KF2. In the latter case, α is either $\Box s$ or $\boxdot s$ for some closed term s. Here we again use the two axioms KF1 and KF2, but for the atomic formula Ps. Considering, for example, the case of $\boxdot s$,

$$\begin{aligned} \boxdot f(\boxdot s) &\leftrightarrow \Box \underline{\mathrm{P}}s && \text{definition, KF4} \\ &\leftrightarrow \neg \boxdot \underline{\mathrm{P}}s && \text{KF1, KF2} \\ &\leftrightarrow \neg \Box f(\boxdot s) && \text{KF3, definition} \end{aligned}$$

If $\alpha = \underset{\cdot}{\neg}\beta$, then the induction hypothesis yields $\boxdot\beta \leftrightarrow \neg\Box\beta$ and (11.13) is deduced as follows:

$$\begin{aligned} \boxdot\alpha &\leftrightarrow \Box\beta && \text{KF3, KF4} \\ &\leftrightarrow \neg\neg\Box\beta && \\ &\leftrightarrow \neg\Box\alpha && \text{induction hypothesis} \end{aligned}$$

If $\alpha = \beta \underset{\cdot}{\rightarrow} \gamma$, we deduce (11.13) as follows:

$$\begin{aligned} \boxdot\alpha &\leftrightarrow \Box\beta \wedge \boxdot\gamma && \text{KF6} \\ &\leftrightarrow \neg\boxdot\beta \wedge \neg\Box\gamma && \text{induction hypothesis} \\ &\leftrightarrow \neg(\boxdot\beta \vee \Box\gamma) && \\ &\leftrightarrow \neg\Box\alpha && \text{KF5} \end{aligned}$$

We omit the final case $\alpha = \underset{\cdot}{\forall} v \beta$. The equivalence in (11.13) allows us to also derive the CT-axiom for implication by combining it with the axiom for implication:

$$\begin{aligned} \mathsf{KF} \vdash \forall\alpha\forall\beta\Big(\mathsf{Sent}(\alpha \underset{\cdot}{\rightarrow} \beta) \rightarrow \big(\Box_0(\alpha \underset{\cdot}{\rightarrow} \beta) &\leftrightarrow \boxdot_0\alpha \vee \Box_0\beta\big)\Big) \\ &\leftrightarrow (\Box_0\alpha \rightarrow \Box_0\beta). \end{aligned}$$

The final axiom of CT to check is the compositional clause for the universal quantifier. This follows from axiom KF7 and the definition of f. ⊣

Proposition 11.56 gives the basis for embedding the theory CT into KF. Given φ, let $G(\varphi)$ be the formula determined by the following clauses:

- $G(\Box s) \equiv \Box_0 s$,

- $G(\Box s) \equiv \boxdot_0 s$,
- $G(\varphi) \equiv \varphi$ for φ any other atomic formula,
- $G(\varphi \to \psi) \equiv G(\varphi) \to G(\psi)$,
- $G(\neg\varphi) \equiv \neg G(\varphi)$,
- $G(\forall v \varphi) \equiv \forall v\, G(\varphi)$.

The result of applying the function G to each CT-axiom is, therefore, derivable in KF. Provided the same holds for the axioms of the base theory E^*, the compositional theory of truth CT is interpretable in KF:

11.57 THEOREM *Suppose* $\mathsf{KF} \vdash G(\varphi)$ *whenever* $\mathsf{E}^* \vdash \varphi$. *Then* $\mathsf{CT} \vdash \varphi$ *implies* $\mathsf{KF} \vdash G(\varphi)$. *In particular, if* $\mathsf{E}^* = \mathsf{E}^*_{\min}$, *then* $\mathsf{CT} \vdash \varphi$ *implies* $\mathsf{KF} \vdash G(\varphi)$.

PROOF From the assumption, we have that $\mathsf{KF} \vdash G(\varphi)$ if φ is an axiom of E^*. Clearly, $\mathsf{KF} \vdash G(\varphi)$ also holds if φ is an axiom of predicate logic. Each CT-axiom is likewise derivable in KF. An induction on derivations shows that $\mathsf{CT} \vdash \varphi$ implies $\mathsf{KF} \vdash G(\varphi)$. As $G(\varphi)$ is an axiom of $\mathsf{E}^*_{\min}$ whenever φ is, the second part of the theorem is a consequence of the first. ⊣

11.58 COROLLARY *The global reflection principle for* $\mathsf{E}^*_{\min}$, *restricted to sentences in* $\mathcal{L}^*_{\text{syn}}$, *is derivable in* KF. *That is,* $\mathsf{KF} \vdash \forall\alpha\big(\mathsf{Sent}_{\text{syn}}(\alpha) \wedge \mathsf{Bew}_{\mathsf{E}^*_{\min}}(\alpha) \to \Box\alpha\big)$. *In particular, the consistency statement for* $\mathsf{E}^*_{\min}$ *is derivable in* KF.

PROOF The global reflection principle for $\mathsf{E}^*_{\min}$ is derivable in CT (theorem 11.45). Theorem 11.57 therefore implies

$$\mathsf{KF} \vdash \forall\alpha\big(\mathsf{Sent}(\alpha) \wedge \mathsf{Bew}_{\mathsf{E}^*_{\min}}(\alpha) \to \Box_0\alpha\big).$$

The equivalence of $\Box_0$ and $\Box$ on truth-free formulæ is are provable in E^*:

$$\mathsf{E}^* \vdash \forall\alpha\big(\mathsf{Sent}_{\text{syn}}(\alpha) \to (\Box_0\alpha \leftrightarrow \Box\alpha)\big).$$

Hence, the first claim of the corollary is proven. The second part follows from the first by instantiating the quantifier $\forall\alpha$ with $\bot$. ⊣

The preceding analysis did not appeal to the axioms for nested truth. Considering now these axioms, we see that KF also captures truth (and falsity) over the typed predicate $\Box_0$:

$$\mathsf{KF} \vdash \forall\alpha\big(\mathsf{Sent}(\alpha) \to (\Box\overline{\Box_0 \underset{\cdot}{\alpha}} \leftrightarrow \Box_0\alpha)\big),$$
$$\mathsf{KF} \vdash \forall\alpha\big(\mathsf{Sent}(\alpha) \to (\boxdot\overline{\Box_0 \underset{\cdot}{\alpha}} \leftrightarrow \neg\Box_0\alpha)\big).$$

The first of these statements is just an instance of axiom KF9; the second relies on axiom KF10, which entails $\boxdot\overline{\Box_0 \underset{\cdot}{\alpha}} \leftrightarrow \boxdot_0\alpha$, and proposition 11.56.

As a consequence, KF derives the CT-axioms wherein the quantifiers are restricted to formulæ of $\mathcal{L}^*$ for which the predicates $\Box$ and $\boxdot$ occur in the contexts $\Box_0$ and $\boxdot_0$ only. We can reformulate this statement in the style of proposition 11.56 by considering a formula $\Box_1$ given by

$$\Box_1(x) := \Box g(x),$$

where g is the term expressing, within $\mathcal{L}^*$, the substitution determined by the function G.

11.59 PROPOSITION *The axioms of* CT, *formulated with* $\Box_1$ *in place of* $\Box$, *are derivable in* KF. *In addition,* KF *derives* $\forall s\,(\Box_1\underset{\cdot}{\Box}_0 s \leftrightarrow \Box_0 s^\circ)$, *where* $\underset{\cdot}{\Box}_0 s$ *denotes the term* $\mathsf{sub}(\overline{\Box_0}, \bar{\mathsf{x}}, s)$.

PROOF The proof of the main claim is analogous to that of proposition 11.56. For the second part we argue informally in KF. Let s be a closed term. The definitions of $\Box_1$ and g entail

$$\begin{aligned} \Box_1\underset{\cdot}{\Box}_0 s &\leftrightarrow \Box g\big(\mathsf{sub}(\overline{\Box_0}, \bar{\mathsf{x}}, s)\big) \\ &\leftrightarrow \Box\underline{\Box}\mathsf{sub}\big(\overline{f(f(\mathsf{x}))}, \bar{\mathsf{x}}, s\big). \end{aligned}$$

From the definition of f it is clear that the denotation of $\mathsf{sub}\big(\overline{f(f(\mathsf{x}))}, \bar{\mathsf{x}}, s\big)$ is $f\big(f(s^\circ)\big)$, namely the translation of s° under F twice. Given that $f\big(f(x)\big) = f(x)$ is provable by formal induction, KF9 implies

$$\Box_1\underset{\cdot}{\Box}_0 s \leftrightarrow \Box f\big(f(s^\circ)\big) \leftrightarrow \Box_0 s^\circ$$

and we are done. ⊣

Whereas proposition 11.56 shows that CT can be viewed as a subtheory of KF, proposition 11.59 goes one step further. It shows that KF includes the theory defined as CT, where $\Box$ is replaced by $\Box_1$ and E^* has been chosen to be the version of CT for $\Box_0$. It is worth stating this remark more precisely. Let $\mathcal{L}^*$ contain two unary predicate symbols, $\Box_0$ and $\Box_1$. Let RT_1 name the theory extending E^* by the CT-axioms formulated for the predicate $\Box_0$, where axiom CT1 applies only to relation symbols in $\mathcal{L}^*_{\mathrm{min}}$. Extending RT_1, we define a theory RT_2 by adding a second copy of the CT-axioms, this time formulated for the predicate $\Box_1$ with the predicate symbol $\Box_0$ admitted in CT1. Proposition 11.59 shows that the two truth predicates of RT_1 are definable from the single truth predicate of KF.

RT_1 and RT_2 are just the first two levels of a hierarchy of CT-like theories, called the 'ramified truth hierarchy', which we now define:

11.60 DEFINITION Let n be a positive integer and suppose $\mathcal{L}^*$ contains n distinct unary predicates $\Box_0, \dots, \Box_{n-1}$. The theory of ramified truth for n truth predicates, RT_n, is the extension of E^* by the following axioms for every $m < n$:

RT1 $\forall s_1 \cdots \forall s_k (\Box_m \underset{\cdot}{\mathsf{R}} s_1 \cdots s_k \leftrightarrow \mathsf{R} s_1^\circ \cdots s_k^\circ)$ for each k and each predicate symbol R of arity k excluding $\Box_0, \dots, \Box_{n-1}$,

RT2 $\forall s (\Box_m \underset{\cdot}{\Box_k} s \leftrightarrow \Box_k s^\circ)$ for each $k < m$,

RT3 $\forall \alpha \big(\mathsf{Sent}(\alpha) \to (\Box_m \underset{\cdot}{\neg} \alpha \leftrightarrow \neg \Box_m \alpha)\big)$,

RT4 $\forall \alpha \forall \beta \Big(\mathsf{Sent}(\alpha \underset{\cdot}{\to} \beta) \to \big(\Box_m(\alpha \underset{\cdot}{\to} \beta) \leftrightarrow (\Box_m \alpha \to \Box_m \beta)\big)\Big)$,

RT5 $\forall \alpha \forall v \big(\mathsf{Sent}(\underset{\cdot}{\forall} v\, \alpha) \to (\Box_m \underset{\cdot}{\forall} v\, \alpha \leftrightarrow \forall s\, \Box_m \alpha[s/v])\big)$.

RT_0 is nothing more than the theory E^*. For $n > 0$, RT_n is obtained from RT_{n-1} by the addition of the CT-axioms for a fresh predicate symbol $\Box_n$ with the language of RT_n permitted in CT1. Theorem 11.45 implies that each level of the ramified truth hierarchy is strictly stronger than the previous, for it implies that the global reflection principle for RT_n is derivable in RT_{n+1} and, as a consequence, that RT_n proves the consistency statement for both E^* and each RT_m with $m < n$. Given our construction of compositional truth predicates within KF, it is almost immediate that every (finite) level of the ramified truth hierarchy is definable from the single truth predicate of KF.

11.61 THEOREM *The theory* KF *defines the truth predicates of* RT_n *for every* n. *As a consequence, if* $\mathsf{RT}_n \vdash \varphi$ *for some* n *and* φ *is in the language* $\mathcal{L}^*_{\mathrm{syn}}$ *then* $\mathsf{KF} \vdash \varphi$.

Here we present only a sketch of the main result as the argument is technically involved and beyond the scope of this text. A detailed comparison of KF and the ramified hierarchy, including a generalization of theorem 11.61 to transfinite hierarchies of truth predicates, is given in Halbach (2014).

PROOF SKETCH We generalize the earlier formulæ $\Box_0(\mathsf{x})$ and $\Box_1(\mathsf{x})$ to higher levels of the hierarchy. Given that the formula $\Box_m(\mathsf{x})$ is defined, $\Box_{m+1}(\mathsf{x})$ is chosen to be a formula expressing that the result of replacing all occurrences of $\Box$ in x by $\Box_m$ is true. So $\Box_1(\mathsf{x})$ is the formula $\Box g(\mathsf{x})$ described above, and $\Box_2(\mathsf{x})$ is $\Box h(\mathsf{x})$ where h is a (Σ-definable) term expressing the substitution of $\Box_1$ for $\Box$ in the formula x. Building on propositions 11.56 and 11.59, it can be shown that KF proves that each formula $\Box_m(\mathsf{x})$ fulfils the corresponding axioms RT_n for $n \geq m$.

The second part of the theorem is a consequence of the fact that the translation between the languages of ramified truth and of Kripke–Feferman truth does not alter formulæ in the language $\mathcal{L}^*_{\mathsf{syn}}$. ⊣

Having briefly examined the expressive and deductive strength of a self-applicable truth predicate, we shall conclude our study of Kripke–Feferman truth by establishing the consistency of the axioms over a broad range of starting theories. A standard model of KF is determined by a standard model $\langle \mathbb{E}^*, V \rangle$ of $\mathsf{E}^*_{\mathsf{min}}$ and two sets of expressions $T, F \subseteq \mathcal{E}^*$ to interpret the predicates $\Box$ and $\boxdot$ respectively. We write such a model as $\langle \mathbb{E}^*, T, F \rangle$. Once one of the two sets is chosen the other is uniquely determined because, from $\langle \mathbb{E}^*, T, F \rangle \vDash \mathsf{KF}$, KF3 and KF4 yield

$$F = \{\, \varphi\colon \neg\varphi \in T \,\} \quad \text{and} \quad T = \{\, \varphi\colon \neg\varphi \in F \,\}.$$

Thus, to define a model of KF it suffices to specify an interpretation of one of the two predicates and let the interpretation of the other predicate be determined by the equations above. Axiomatically, this approach amounts to treating KF as a theory in a single predicate $\Box$ given by replacing the formula $\boxdot s$ with $\Box \underset{\cdot}{\neg} s$, and similarly for the syntactic constant $\underset{\cdot}{\boxdot}$. This reformulation trivializes the axiom KF3, rendering it as $\forall\alpha\,(\Box\underset{\cdot}{\neg}\alpha \leftrightarrow \Box\underset{\cdot}{\neg}\alpha)$, replaces KF4 by $\forall\alpha\,(\Box\underset{\cdot}{\neg}\underset{\cdot}{\neg}\alpha \leftrightarrow \Box\alpha)$, and affects the other axioms likewise. Halbach (2014) axiomatizes KF in this way with just a single predicate for truth. Our consistency proof will be for the theory with two-predicates. We will define an interpretation of $\Box$ that, when accompanied by the corresponding interpretation for $\boxdot$ given by the equation above, yields a model of KF. Because we are working with a theory axiomatizing two distinguished predicates, a generalization of $\Box$-agnosticity is necessary. We say that E^* is '$\{\Box, \boxdot\}$-agnostic' if there is a standard model $\mathbb{E}^*$ for the language $\mathcal{L}^*$ such that for every pair of sets $T, F \subseteq \mathcal{E}^*$ the structure $\langle \mathbb{E}^*, T, F \rangle$ is a model of E^*. Recall, for example, that $\mathsf{E}^*_{\min}$ is $\{\square, \boxdot\}$-agnostic. The consistency theorem is then stated as follows:

11.62 THEOREM *Suppose* E^* *is* $\{\square, \boxdot\}$*-agnostic. Then* KF *has a standard model.*

In the following, we suppose that E^* is $\{\square, \boxdot\}$-agnostic and that $\mathbb{E}^*$ is a standard model of E^* witnessing this fact. Models of KF are necessarily more complex than the models of CT we have considered thus far, due to the two axioms of self-application. The model construction we present is the semantic theory of truth introduced by Kripke (1975) and applied to KF by Feferman (1991). In the present context, the construction asks us to consider a certain operation on sets of expressions that, given an interpretation for $\square$ (and, by duality, an interpretation for $\boxdot$), returns an interpretation which is in a sense closer to validating the KF-axioms. The operation is given in detail below. In short, it takes an arbitrary interpretation of $\square$, say T, and adds to it any conjunction of two formulæ if both formulæ are already in T, any universally quantified formula if every instantiation of the formula is in T, and so on. We will observe that any fixed point of this operation, that is, any set of expressions which remains unchanged by the operation, induces a model of KF. A standard model of KF can thus be given by isolating some set of expressions which is a fixed point of the operation. Even so, it remains to prove that fixed points of the operation exist at all. This result relies on a fundamental result from order theory known as the Knaster–Tarski theorem.

We start with the definition of the operation on expressions. Let T be any set of sentences. A new set $\Gamma(T)$ of sentences is determined by setting $\varphi \in \Gamma(T)$ if and only if one of nine criteria is satisfied:

(i) φ is an atomic sentence of $\mathcal{L}^*_{\mathrm{syn}}$ and $\mathbb{E}^* \vDash \varphi$;

(ii) φ is a negated atomic sentence of $\mathcal{L}^*_{\mathrm{syn}}$ and $\mathbb{E}^* \vDash \varphi$;

(iii) $\varphi \equiv \neg\neg\psi$ for some ψ, and $\psi \in T$;

(iv) $\varphi \equiv \psi \to \chi$ for some ψ and χ, and T contains either $\neg\psi$ or χ;

(v) $\varphi \equiv \neg(\psi \to \chi)$ for some ψ and χ, and T contains both ψ and $\neg\chi$;

(vi) $\varphi \equiv \forall v\, \psi(v)$ for some ψ, and $\psi(s) \in T$ for every closed term s;

(vii) $\varphi \equiv \neg\forall v\, \varphi(v)$ for some ψ, and $\neg\psi(s) \in T$ for some closed term s;

(viii) $\varphi \equiv \Box s$ or $\varphi \equiv \neg\boxdot s$ for some ψ and some closed term s, and s denotes (in $\mathbb{E}^*$) an element of T;

(ix) $\varphi \equiv \neg\Box s$ or $\varphi \equiv \boxdot s$ for some ψ and some closed term s, and s denotes (in $\mathbb{E}^*$) an expression e such that $\neg e \in T$.

The first result we require is that fixed points of the function Γ determine models of KF:

11.63 PROPOSITION *Suppose $T \subseteq \mathcal{E}^*$ is a set of expressions such that $T = \Gamma(T)$. Let $F = \{\, e \in \mathcal{E}^* \colon \neg e \in T \,\}$. Then the structure $\langle \mathbb{E}^*, T, F \rangle$ is a model of* KF.

PROOF Because of our assumptions on E^* it suffices to show that the interpretation of $\Box$ as T and $\boxdot$ as F validate the ten axioms of KF. Concerning, for example, KF2, suppose $\mathsf{R}s_1 \cdots s_k$ is a truth-free atomic formula. Then

$$
\begin{array}{lll}
\langle \mathbb{E}^*, T, F \rangle \vDash \boxdot \underline{\mathsf{R}} s_1 \cdots s_k & \text{iff } \mathsf{R}s_1^\circ \cdots s_k^\circ \in F & \\
 & \text{iff } \neg\mathsf{R}s_1^\circ \cdots s_k^\circ \in T & \text{definition of } F \\
 & \text{iff } \neg\mathsf{R}s_1^\circ \cdots s_k^\circ \in \Gamma(T) & \text{as } \Gamma(T) = T \\
 & \text{iff } \mathbb{E}^* \vDash \neg\mathsf{R}s_1^\circ \cdots s_k^\circ & \text{definition of } \Gamma(T) \\
 & \text{iff } \langle \mathbb{E}^*, T, F \rangle \vDash \neg\mathsf{R}s_1^\circ \cdots s_k^\circ & \text{as } \mathsf{R} \in \mathcal{L}^*_{\text{syn}}
\end{array}
$$

So $\langle \mathbb{E}^*, T, F \rangle \vDash$ KF2. Axiom KF5 is validated by the following equivalence, which holds for all sentences α and β:

$$
\begin{array}{ll}
\langle \mathbb{E}^*, T, F \rangle \vDash \Box \overline{\alpha \to \beta} & \text{iff } \alpha \to \beta \in T \\
 & \text{iff } \alpha \to \beta \in \Gamma(T) \\
 & \text{iff } \neg\alpha \in T \text{ or } \beta \in T \\
 & \text{iff } \langle \mathbb{E}^*, T, F \rangle \vDash \boxdot \overline{\alpha} \vee \Box \overline{\beta}
\end{array}
$$

Concerning the axioms of self-application, KF9 and KF10, the latter is validated as follows:

$$
\begin{array}{ll}
\langle \mathbb{E}^*, T, F \rangle \vDash \boxdot \underline{\Box} s & \text{iff } \Box s \in F \\
 & \text{iff } \neg\Box s \in \Gamma(T) \\
 & \text{iff } \neg s^\circ \in T \\
 & \text{iff } \langle \mathbb{E}^*, T, F \rangle \vDash \boxdot s^\circ
\end{array}
$$

We leave the remaining cases to the reader. ⊣

Proposition 11.63 is an important part of the consistency proof. However, it still remains to be shown that there are $T \subseteq \mathcal{E}^*$ such that $T = \Gamma(T)$. We will not present this argument in full as it relies on a method of proof, namely transfinite induction, that is outside the scope of this text and presented in detail in most accounts on formal truth. The key observation which enables the existence of fixed points to be deduced is that the function Γ preserves the subset-relation between interpretations, the proof of which is by inspecting the various cases in the definition of $\Gamma(T)$.

11.64 LEMMA *If* $T_0 \subseteq T_1 \subseteq \mathcal{E}^*$, *then* $\Gamma(T_0) \subseteq \Gamma(T_1)$.

A function satisfying lemma 11.64 is said to be monotone. More generally, a function Γ on subsets of a set A is *monotone* if whenever $X \subseteq Y \subseteq A$, then $\Gamma(X) \subseteq \Gamma(Y)$.

The existence of fixed points of Γ and, thereby, of models of KF is a corollary of the

11.65 KNASTER–TARSKI THEOREM (KNASTER 1928, TARSKI 1955) *Let A be a non-empty set and Γ a monotone function on subsets of A. There exists a set $X \subseteq A$ which is a fixed point of Γ, i.e., $\Gamma(X) = X$. In particular, there exist both least and greatest fixed points of Γ, namely sets $X_{\min} = \Gamma(X_{\min})$ and $X_{\max} = \Gamma(X_{\max})$ such that for every fixed point Y of Γ, $X_{\min} \subseteq Y \subseteq X_{\max}$.*

We sketch the argument behind theorem 11.65 in the context of our specific choice of operation Γ. Starting with a trivial interpretation of truth, such as $T = \varnothing$ or $T =$ Sent, the operation Γ can be repeatedly applied to T, inducing a sequence $T = T_0$, $T_1 = \Gamma(T_0)$, $T_2 = \Gamma(T_1)$, … of interpretations, each improving on the previous in respect to validating instantiations of the KF-axioms. The previous lemma implies that $T_0 \subseteq T_1 \subseteq T_2 \subseteq \cdots$, if $T_0 = \varnothing$, and that $T_0 \supseteq T_1 \supseteq T_2 \supseteq \cdots$, if $T_0 =$ Sent. In the limit, this sequence uniquely determines a set of expressions T_ω by taking either the union of the finite iterations or the intersection, depending on the choice of T_0. But it can be shown that T_ω does not yet yield a model of KF and can be further refined by repeatedly applying the refining operation: $T_{\omega+1} = \Gamma(T_\omega)$, $T_{\omega+2} = \Gamma(T_{\omega+1})$, and so on. As before, $T_\omega \subseteq T_{\omega+1} \subseteq \cdots$ or $T_\omega \supseteq T_{\omega+1} \supseteq \cdots$, according to the choice of T_0. This sequence also isolates a limit set that, although still not a model of KF, can be refined further. Continuing to apply the function Γ and taking the limit of each subsequent sequence, it can be shown that this process must eventually isolate a set T_∞ which is a fixed point, i.e., $\Gamma(T_\infty) = T_\infty$. If T_0 was chosen to be empty, T_∞ will be the least fixed point of Γ in the sense of theorem 11.65, and the greatest fixed point if the initial set comprised all sentences. In either case, the previous proposition shows that T_∞ describes a model of KF.

The reason we draw attention to the existence of least and greatest fixed points of Γ is that these shed light on additional axioms that can be added to KF. First though, observe that because the formula

$$\forall\alpha\big(\mathsf{Sent}(\alpha) \to (\boxdot\alpha \leftrightarrow \neg\Box\alpha)\big), \tag{11.14}$$

is inconsistent with KF, the consistency proof for KF demonstrates that there is no set T which satisfies $\Gamma(T) = T$ and

$$\varphi \in F \text{ if and only if } \varphi \notin T.$$

If, however, we let T be the least fixed point of Γ, then it can be shown that

$$T \cap F = \varnothing.$$

Therefore, $\langle \mathbb{E}^*, T, F\rangle$, where F is defined as earlier, models the left-to-right direction of the equivalence in (11.14). That is, we have obtained a model satisfying

$$\langle \mathbb{E}^*, T, F\rangle \vDash \forall\alpha\big(\mathsf{Sent}(\alpha) \to \neg(\boxdot\alpha \wedge \Box\alpha)\big). \tag{11.15}$$

By a simple induction on formulæ, it even follows that $\langle \mathbb{E}^*, T, F\rangle$ validates one direction of the unrestricted T-schema:

$$\langle \mathbb{E}^*, T, F\rangle \vDash \Box\overline{\varphi} \to \varphi.$$

Dually, if T is the greatest fixed point of Γ, then

$$T \cup F = \mathrm{Sent}$$

and the other direction of both (11.14) and the unrestricted T-schema is validated:

$$\begin{aligned} &\langle \mathbb{E}^*, T, F\rangle \vDash \forall\alpha\big(\mathsf{Sent}(\alpha) \to (\Box\alpha \vee \boxdot\alpha)\big), \\ &\langle \mathbb{E}^*, T, F\rangle \vDash \varphi \to \Box\overline{\varphi}. \end{aligned} \tag{11.16}$$

The principle in (11.15) expresses that the extension of truth is *consistent:* no sentence is labelled as both true and false. The principle in (11.16) expresses that every sentence is either true or false, and is therefore known as the axiom of completeness. Either of the two statements can be consistently added to KF, but together they are inconsistent. In other words, every model of KF either admits truth-value gaps, sentences demarcated as neither true nor false, or truth-value gluts, sentences which are both true and false. To find concrete examples we need look no further than the liar sentence, $\lambda \leftrightarrow \neg\Box\overline{\lambda}$. Recall, $\lambda \equiv \neg\Box t$ for a term t such that $\mathsf{E}^* \vdash t = \overline{\lambda}$. If $\lambda \in T$, then, as $T = \Gamma(T)$, $\neg t^\circ \in T$, that is, $\neg\lambda \in T$. So $\lambda \in T$ implies $\lambda \in F$. Similarly, $\lambda \in F$ implies $\lambda \in T$. So, in any model of KF, the liar sentence is either labelled as neither true nor false, or as both.

As a consequence, the logic that applies under the truth predicate, KF's 'internal logic', is not classical logic. The law of excluded middle is not true: $\mathsf{KF} \nvdash \Box\overline{\lambda \vee \neg\lambda}$. Even the rule of modus ponens does not hold under the truth predicate: there are formulæ φ and ψ such that $\mathsf{KF} \nvdash \Box\overline{\varphi \to \psi} \to (\Box\overline{\varphi} \to \Box\overline{\psi})$ (choose, for example, $\varphi \equiv \lambda$ and $\psi \equiv \bot$ and consider the model of KF based on the greatest fixed point of Γ). Rather than classical logic, the logic under the Kripke–Feferman truth predicate can be characterized as a 3-valued logic, specifically, Kleene's (1952) 'strong' 3-valued logic.

11.7 Friedman–Sheard Truth

An alternative theory of truth can be obtained by adding to CT different means for deriving formulæ with nested occurrences of the truth predicate. The system introduced by Friedman and Sheard (1987) extends CT by two rules of inference: the rule of necessitation and its converse, co-necessitation.

11.66 DEFINITION FS is the theory which extends E^* by the following axioms and two rules of inference:

FS1 $\forall s_1 \cdots \forall s_k \big(\Box \underline{\mathsf{R}} s_1 \cdots s_k \leftrightarrow \mathsf{R}(s_1^\circ, \ldots, s_k^\circ)\big)$ for each k and each predicate symbol R of $\mathcal{L}^*_{\mathrm{syn}}$ of arity k;

FS2 $\forall\alpha\big(\mathsf{Sent}(\alpha) \to (\Box\underset{\cdot}{\neg}\alpha \leftrightarrow \neg\Box\alpha)\big)$;

FS3 $\forall\alpha\forall\beta\Big(\mathsf{Sent}(\alpha \underset{\cdot}{\to} \beta) \to \big(\Box(\alpha \underset{\cdot}{\to} \beta) \leftrightarrow (\Box\alpha \to \Box\beta)\big)\Big)$;

FS4 $\forall\alpha\forall v\big(\mathsf{Sent}(\underset{\cdot}{\forall} v\,\alpha) \to (\Box\underset{\cdot}{\forall} v\,\alpha \leftrightarrow \forall s\, \Box\alpha[s/v])\big)$;

FS5 NEC: if $\mathsf{FS} \vdash \varphi$ then $\mathsf{FS} \vdash \Box\overline{\varphi}$;

FS6 CoNEC: if $\mathsf{FS} \vdash \Box\overline{\varphi}$ then $\mathsf{FS} \vdash \varphi$.

In contrast to the Kripke–Feferman theory of truth, FS maintains the full compositional axiom for negation in CT. In particular, every model of FS has an interpretation of truth which is both consistent, $\forall\alpha\big(\mathsf{Sent}(\alpha) \to \neg(\Box\alpha \wedge \Box\dot{\neg}\alpha)\big)$, and complete, $\forall\alpha\big(\mathsf{Sent}(\alpha) \to \Box\alpha \vee \Box\dot{\neg}\alpha\big)$. The Friedman–Sheard truth predicate is therefore fully classical as, like in CT, all instances of the principle of excluded middle are provably true.

The consistency of FS, even in the case that $\mathsf{E}^* = \mathsf{E}^*_{\min}$, is far from obvious, though. The rule of necessitation features in many of the paradoxes in chapter 6. Moreover, we have seen inconsistencies arising from combining the compositional axioms with principles of nested truth. Nevertheless, in some respects the consistency argument is made simpler by (non-trivial) self-application arising only through rules of inference. It is, for instance, not necessary to construct a model of the whole theory FS to show it consistent. Rather, it suffices to provide a model for each subtheory of FS where the rules NEC and CoNEC can be applied at most a fixed number of times. These models need not validate further applications of the rules. Thus, and temporally ignoring the role of CoNEC, we will construct a sequence of standard models $\mathbb{E}^*_0, \mathbb{E}^*_1, \ldots$ such that for each $n \geq 0$, any formula which can be derived from the axioms of CT by the use of at most n applications of the rule NEC is true in $\mathbb{E}^*_n$. This can be achieved by ensuring that each $\mathbb{E}^*_n$ is a model of CT and that $\mathbb{E}^*_n \vDash \varphi$ implies $\mathbb{E}^*_{n+1} \vDash \Box\overline{\varphi}$ for all sentences φ (cf. lemma 11.68). Our study of standard models of CT readily shows how to construct such a hierarchy. Starting from a standard model $\mathbb{E}$ of E^*, define a sequence of interpretations for the truth predicate by recursion:

$$S_0 := \{\, \varphi \in \mathrm{Sent}\colon \mathbb{E}^* \vDash \varphi \,\},$$
$$S_{n+1} := \{\, \varphi \in \mathrm{Sent}\colon \langle \mathbb{E}^*, S_n \rangle \vDash \varphi \,\}.$$

Let $\mathbb{E}^*_n = \langle \mathbb{E}^*, S_n \rangle$. So $\mathbb{E}^*_0$ is the $\mathcal{L}^*$-structure based on $\mathbb{E}^*$ in which the truth predicate $\Box$ is interpreted as the set of sentences true in $\mathbb{E}^*$, and $\mathbb{E}^*_{n+1}$ is the same $\mathcal{L}^*$-structure but with $\Box$ interpreted as the set of sentences true in $\mathbb{E}^*_n$.

Using this hierarchy of structures, we can prove that FS without the rule CoNEC is consistent. Suppose E^* is $\Box$-agnostic relative to the standard model $\mathbb{E}^*$. The next two lemmas show that each structure in the hierarchy is a model of the compositional axioms and validates the appropriate number of applications of NEC:

11.67 LEMMA *For every $n \geq 0$, $\mathbb{E}^*_n \vDash \mathsf{CT}$.*

PROOF By induction on n. Theorem 11.41 implies $\mathbb{E}_0^* \models \mathsf{CT}$ and entails that $\mathbb{E}_{n+1}^* \models \mathsf{CT}$ if $\mathbb{E}_n^* \models \mathsf{CT}$. Hence, $\mathbb{E}_n^* \models \mathsf{CT}$ for every $n \geq 0$. ⊣

As discussed, we begin with the fragments of FS given by dropping the co-necessitation rule and restricting applications of the necessitation rule. Let $\mathsf{FS}_0 = \mathsf{CT}$ and for $n > 0$ let FS_n be the theory axiomatized by CT plus the sentence $\Box\overline{\varphi}$ for each sentence φ such that $\mathsf{FS}_{n-1} \vdash \varphi$. Clearly, if φ is a theorem of CT+NEC then $\mathsf{FS}_n \vdash \varphi$ for some $n \geq 0$. So CT+NEC is consistent if and only if every fragment FS_n has a model.

11.68 LEMMA *For every* $m \geq 0$, $\mathbb{E}_m^* \models \mathsf{FS}_m$.

PROOF The proof proceeds by induction on m. In the base case, $m = 0$, $\mathbb{E}_0^* \models \mathsf{FS}_0$ by lemma 11.67. For the induction case, suppose $\mathbb{E}_m^* \models \mathsf{FS}_m$. Then $\mathbb{E}_{m+1}^* \models \mathsf{CT}$ by lemma 11.67 and, also, $\mathbb{E}_{m+1}^* \models \Box\overline{\varphi}$ for every sentence φ such that $\mathbb{E}_m^* \models \varphi$. In particular, $\mathbb{E}_{m+1}^* \models \Box\overline{\varphi}$ for every sentence φ such that $\mathsf{FS}_m \vdash \varphi$. Every theorem of FS_{m+1} can be expressed as a derivation from the axioms of CT plus finitely many formulæ of the kind $\Box\overline{\varphi}$ where $\mathsf{FS}_m \vdash \varphi$. Hence, $\mathbb{E}_{m+1}^* \models \mathsf{FS}_{m+1}$. ⊣

Lemma 11.68 is sufficient to deduce that FS without the rule of co-necessitation is consistent:

11.69 PROPOSITION *Under the assumption that* E^* *is* $\Box$*-agnostic, the theory extending* E^* *by the* FS*-axioms* FS1–FS4 *and the rule of necessitation,* FS5*, is consistent.*

PROOF This theory is precisely CT + NEC. In search of a contradiction assume CT+NEC $\vdash \varphi \wedge \neg\varphi$ for some sentence φ. A derivation witnessing this fact can make use of only finitely many applications of the rule of necessitation, whence, for some $m \geq 0$, FS_m is inconsistent. But this contradicts lemma 11.68, so CT + NEC is consistent. ⊣

We can now incorporate the co-necessitation rule into the mix. As before, we will not attempt to define a model of FS but rather show that every theorem of FS is satisfied by the model $\mathbb{E}_n^*$ for some n. The central observation that makes this argument possible is the following generalization of lemma 11.68:

11.70 LEMMA *For all* m *and every* $n \geq m$, $\mathbb{E}_n^* \models \mathsf{FS}_m$.

PROOF Let $m \leq n$. Lemma 11.68 implies $\mathbb{E}_n^* \vDash \mathsf{FS}_n$. Since FS_m is a subtheory of FS_n, this yields $\mathbb{E}_n^* \vDash \mathsf{FS}_m$. ⊣

11.71 THEOREM *Let* E^* *be* $\Box$*-agnostic. Then* FS *is a consistent theory.*

PROOF Suppose E^* is $\Box$-agnostic with respect to the standard model $\mathbb{E}^*$ and let $\mathbb{E}_0^*, \mathbb{E}_1^*, \ldots$ be the sequence of $\mathcal{L}^*$-structures defined above. We prove that every theorem of FS is true in all but finitely many structures in this hierarchy. That is, if $\mathsf{FS} \vdash \varphi$, then there exists $m \geq 0$ such that

$$\mathbb{E}_n^* \vDash \varphi \quad \text{for all } n \geq m. \tag{11.17}$$

The argument builds upon the observation in lemma 11.70 by considering the set of sentences which are true in all but finitely many structures in this hierarchy:

$$\mathcal{S} = \left\{ \varphi \in \text{Sent: there is an } m \text{ such that for all } n \geq m\text{: } \mathbb{E}_n^* \vDash \varphi \right\}.$$

The first task is to show that if $\mathsf{FS} \vdash \varphi$, then $\varphi \in \mathcal{S}$. We have already observed that $\mathbb{E}_n^* \vDash \mathsf{CT}$ for every $n \geq 0$, and hence the axioms (and theorems) of CT are all contained in $\mathcal{S}$. In addition, given $\varphi \in \mathcal{S}$ and $\varphi \to \psi \in \mathcal{S}$, this means there exist numbers $m_0, m_1 \geq 0$ such that

$$\begin{aligned} &\text{for all } n \geq m_0, \ \mathbb{E}_n^* \vDash \varphi, \\ &\text{for all } n \geq m_1, \ \mathbb{E}_n^* \vDash \varphi \to \psi. \end{aligned}$$

Let $m = \max\{m_0, m_1\}$. Given any $n \geq m$, we observe that $\mathbb{E}_n^* \vDash \varphi \wedge (\varphi \to \psi)$, so $\mathbb{E}_n^* \vDash \psi$. Hence, $\psi \in \mathcal{S}$. So, $\mathcal{S}$ is closed under modus ponens.

Now, if $\varphi \in \mathcal{S}$, then $\Box\overline{\varphi} \in \mathcal{S}$ because $\mathbb{E}_n^* \vDash \varphi$ if and only if $\mathbb{E}_{n+1}^* \vDash \Box\overline{\varphi}$. Conversely, if $\mathbb{E}_n^* \vDash \Box\overline{\varphi}$ for all $n \geq m$, then also $\mathbb{E}_n^* \vDash \varphi$ for all $n \geq m$. So, $\mathcal{S}$ is closed under both rules NEC and CoNEC, from which it follows that $\mathcal{S}$ contains all theorems of FS.

All that remains is to show $\mathcal{S}$ is not inconsistent, that there is no formula φ such that both φ and $\neg\varphi$ are in $\mathcal{S}$. If, on the contrary, there existed such a φ, then by the definition of $\mathcal{S}$ there must be some $m \geq 0$ such that $\mathbb{E}_m^* \vDash \varphi \wedge \neg\varphi$, which is clearly impossible. ⊣

As FS (over a $\Box$-agnostic theory) is consistent, the completeness theorem implies that the theory has a model. That we did not attempt to construct a model of FS was not merely a matter of convenience: since FS extends CT by the rule of necessitation, McGee's paradox applies, with the consequence that there is no standard model:

11.72 THEOREM FS *is ω-inconsistent. That is, there exists a formula $\varphi(\mathsf{x})$ such that* FS $\vdash \exists \mathsf{x} \neg\varphi(\mathsf{x})$ *but also* FS $\vdash \varphi(\overline{e})$ *for every $e \in \mathcal{E}^*$. In particular, there is no standard model of* FS.

The theorem is an application of McGee's theorem 6.31. FS is closed under the rule of necessitation and, as it extends CT, proves all instances of the three schemas

(i) $\Box\overline{\varphi \to \psi} \to (\Box\overline{\varphi} \to \Box\overline{\psi})$,

(ii) $\Box\overline{\neg\varphi} \to \neg\Box\overline{\varphi}$,

(iii) $\forall \mathsf{x}\, \Box\overline{\chi(\dot{\mathsf{x}})} \to \Box\overline{\forall \mathsf{x}\, \chi}$.

Unlike the first and second schema above, the final schema is not simply an instantiation of the CT-axiom for the quantifier. The antecedent of the implication in (iii) claims that $\chi(s)$ is true for every pure term s, whereas to deduce the truth of $\forall x\, \chi$ from CT4 one appears to require the stronger assumption that χ is true for every closed term. However, formal induction allows us to deduce

$$\mathsf{CT} \vdash \forall \mathsf{x}\, \Box\overline{\chi(\dot{\mathsf{x}})} \to \forall s\, \Box\overline{\chi}[s/\overline{\mathsf{x}}].$$

We omit a proof of this claim as it is technically involved, but the argument is similar to the one used to derive proposition 11.44, using induction on the values of closed terms to deduce $\forall s\, \Box\overline{\chi}[s/\overline{\mathsf{x}}]$, given the antecedent as assumption.

McGee's theorem appeals to diagonalization to define a formula $\gamma(x)$ such that

(i) $\mathsf{E}^* \vdash \gamma(\underline{0}) \leftrightarrow \exists n \neg\Box\overline{\gamma(\dot{n})}$,

(ii) $\mathsf{E}^* \vdash \gamma(\underline{n+1}) \leftrightarrow \Box\overline{\gamma(\underline{n})}$ for each $n \geq 0$.

(The formula σ in the proof of theorem 6.31 will be equivalent to $\gamma(\underline{0})$.) Arguing on condition (i), using the compositional axiom and an instance of NEC, we deduce FS $\vdash \gamma(\underline{0})$. Repeated applications of NEC then yield FS $\vdash \gamma(\underline{n})$ for every $n \geq 0$. But by (i) also FS $\vdash \exists n \neg\gamma(n)$. Hence FS is ω-inconsistent.

We can gain some insight into this paradox by examining how the argument behaves in the sequence of models $\mathbb{E}^*_0, \mathbb{E}^*_1, \ldots$. For this purpose, it is convenient to assume that the initial structure $\mathbb{E}^*$ has a trivial interpretation of truth in which all sentences are assumed true, that is, $\mathbb{E}^* \vDash \forall x\, \Box x$. Then, trivially, $\mathbb{E}^* \vDash \neg\gamma(\underline{0})$ by the equivalence in (i). The structure $\mathbb{E}^*_0$ satisfies a sentence $\Box\overline{\varphi}$ if and only if

$\mathbb{E}^* \vDash \varphi$, so $\mathbb{E}_0^* \vDash \neg\Box\overline{\gamma(\underline{0})}$ and therefore $\mathbb{E}_0^* \vDash \gamma(\underline{0}) \wedge \neg\gamma(\underline{1})$, using the equivalence in (ii). Taking this further, the definition of $\mathbb{E}_1^*$ entails

$$\mathbb{E}_1^* \vDash \Box\overline{\gamma(\underline{0})} \wedge \neg\Box\overline{\gamma(\underline{1})},$$
$$\mathbb{E}_1^* \vDash \gamma(\underline{1}) \wedge \gamma(\underline{0}) \wedge \neg\gamma(\underline{2}).$$

Generalizing, for every $n \geq 0$,

$$\mathbb{E}_n^* \vDash \gamma(\underline{0}) \wedge \cdots \wedge \gamma(\underline{n}) \wedge \neg\gamma(\underline{n+1}).$$

In particular, for every $n \geq 0$ there exists some $m > 0$ such that $\mathbb{E}_n^* \vDash \neg\gamma(\underline{m})$. As a result, every structure validates $\exists n \neg\Box\overline{\gamma(\dot{n})}$. However, the witness m necessarily increases as n increases, so there is no single instantiation $\neg\gamma(\underline{m})$ that holds in all but finitely many of the structures. In sum, each formula $\gamma(\underline{m})$ is an element of the set S defined in the proof of theorem 11.71, as is the formula $\exists n \neg\gamma(n)$, but there is no m such that $\neg\gamma(\underline{m}) \in S$.

Although there is no standard model of FS, the fact that the consistency proof depends on varying the interpretation of the truth predicate on a single fixed standard model ensures there is no ω-inconsistency among only the $\Box$-free theorems of FS:

11.73 COROLLARY *Suppose* $\mathsf{E}^* = \mathsf{E}^*_{\min}$. *Then the* $\Box$*-free theorems of* FS *are true in any standard model of* $\mathsf{E}^*_{\min}$.

PROOF Suppose $\mathsf{E}^* = \mathsf{E}^*_{\min}$ and that $\mathbb{E}^*$ is a standard model of $\mathsf{E}^*_{\min}$. By the proof of theorem 11.62, if $\mathsf{FS} \vdash \varphi$, then there exists $m \geq 0$ such that $\mathbb{E}_m^* \vDash \varphi$. But $\mathbb{E}_m^*$ and $\mathbb{E}^*$ differ only in their interpretation of the predicate symbol $\Box$, so if φ is $\Box$-free, then $\mathbb{E}^* \vDash \varphi$. ⊣

At this point it is perhaps worth comparing the consistency proofs for FS and KF. Recall, the consistency of KF was established by isolating a model $\langle \mathbb{E}^*, T, F\rangle$ where the set T was a fixed point of a particular function Γ operating on sets of sentences. One method of obtaining such a model is to iteratively apply the function Γ, starting from a trivial interpretation of truth, for instance $S_0 = \varnothing$, giving rise to an increasing 'hierarchy' of interpretations $S_0 = \varnothing \subseteq \Gamma(S_0) \subseteq \Gamma(\Gamma(S_0)) \subseteq \cdots$. In the case of FS, the transition from $\mathbb{E}_n^*$ to $\mathbb{E}_{n+1}^*$ can likewise be as a series of iterations of a function on interpretations of truth. Given a set of sentences $S \subseteq \text{Sent}$, define $\Delta(S)$ as the set $\{\varphi \in \text{Sent} \colon \langle \mathbb{E}^*, V, S\rangle \vDash \varphi\}$. Starting from a standard model

$\mathbb{E}_0^* = \langle \mathbb{E}^*, V, S \rangle$, define $\mathbb{E}_{n+1}^*$ to be the $\mathcal{L}^*$-structure $\big\langle \mathbb{E}^*, V, \Delta^{n+1}(S) \big\rangle$ where $\Delta^k(T)$ denotes k-many applications of Δ to the set S. However, in contrast to Γ, Δ is not a function that admits fixed points:

11.74 PROPOSITION *For every set $S \subseteq \text{Sent}$, $\Delta(S) \neq S$.*

PROOF It suffices to consider the liar sentence λ. We have $\lambda \in S$ if and only if $\langle \mathbb{E}^*, V, S \rangle \vDash \Box\overline{\lambda}$, if and only if $\langle \mathbb{E}^*, V, S \rangle \nvDash \lambda$, if and only if $\lambda \notin \Delta(S)$. ⊣

Applying the proof of this proposition to the sequence of models $\mathbb{E}_0^*, \mathbb{E}_1^*, \ldots$, we see that the liar sentence alternates between being marked as true and as false: if, say, $\mathbb{E}_0^* \nvDash \lambda$ then $\mathbb{E}_1^* \vDash \lambda$, $\mathbb{E}_2^* \nvDash \lambda$, $\mathbb{E}_3^* \vDash \lambda$, and so on. In other words, regardless of the status of the liar sentence in the starting model, the set $\mathcal{S}$ defined in theorem 11.71 contains neither λ nor $\neg\lambda$.

With the consistency of FS established, let us conclude with some observations on the theorems of this system. As FS extends CT, we know that the global reflection principle for $\mathsf{E}_{\min}^*$ is derivable in FS. The complexity of the consistency proof for the theory suggests that the addition of necessitation and co-necessitation gives rise to a richer concept of truth than available in CT alone. The next two results confirm this to be the case:

11.75 THEOREM *Suppose E^* extends $\mathsf{E}_{\min}^*$ by finitely many axioms. Then* FS *proves the global reflection principle for* CT.

PROOF Including the axioms of the base theory E^*, CT is given by adding finitely many axioms to the axioms of $\mathsf{E}_{\min}^*$. Each of these additional axioms can be proved 'true' in FS by an application of NEC. Combining theorem 11.45 and corollary 11.47 therefore yields

$$\mathsf{FS} \vdash \forall\alpha\big(\mathsf{Bew}_{\mathsf{CT}}(\alpha) \rightarrow \Box\alpha\big).$$ ⊣

As the global reflection principle is itself a single formula, FS also proves that the formula is true, whereby the previous theorem can be iterated:

11.76 COROLLARY *Suppose $\mathsf{E}^* = \mathsf{E}_{\min}^*$. Let $\mathsf{G}_0 = \mathsf{CT}$ and for each n let G_{n+1} be the extension of* CT *by the global reflection principle for G_n. That is,*

$$\mathsf{G}_{n+1} \ := \ \mathsf{CT} + \forall\alpha\big(\mathsf{Bew}_{\mathsf{G}_n}(\alpha) \rightarrow \Box\alpha\big).$$

Then G_n is a subtheory of FS *for every n.*

PROOF Repeated applications of corollary 11.47 and necessitation. ⊣

The Friedman–Sheard theory of truth derives not only the soundness of CT, but the soundness of this soundness claim, and so on. In this sense FS is closely related to the ramified theory of truth introduced in the previous section. That theory extends E^* by the compositional axioms for a hierarchy of indexed truth predicates. In the ramified theory of truth the soundness statement for the theory CT, now formulated for a truth predicate $\Box_0$ and denoted RT_0, is expressed by a second truth predicate in the hierarchy, $\Box_1$, as the statement

$$\forall \alpha \big(\mathsf{Bew}_{\mathsf{RT}_0}(\alpha) \rightarrow \Box_1 \alpha\big).$$

The rules of necessitation and co-necessitation can be seen as collapsing the hierarchy of typed truth predicates into a single truth predicate. Just as we could mimic finite levels of the theory of ramified truth in KF, so too is this possible in FS. Indeed, the same realization of the ramified hierarchu applies to FS:

11.77 THEOREM *The theory* FS *defines the truth predicates of* RT_n *for every n. As a consequence, if* $\mathsf{RT}_n \vdash \varphi$ *for some n and* φ *is in the language* $\mathcal{L}^*_{\mathrm{syn}}$*, then* $\mathsf{FS} \vdash \varphi$.

11.8 Syntax and Semantics

In this chapter we have focused more than usual for books on the paradoxes and related topics on definable truth predicates, namely on the partial truth predicates. Often they are seen as auxiliary notions that facilitate many proofs, and they are very useful indeed. However, they also ought to receive more attention from philosophers. Partial truth predicates do not really fit into a picture of where syntactic and semantic notion are strictly separated. Philosophers often define semantic notions in the metalanguage where they are neatly kept apart from the object language. In truth theory, however, semantic notions are standardly treated as primitive notions in the object language. Paradoxes and related phenomena ought to depend on the availability of such primitive notions, or so many philosophers seem to think. We have shown that at least truth teller sentences can be obtained in pure syntax theory by using partial truth predicates.

As mentioned, such truth tellers have been investigated in an arithmetical setting. However, when looking at truth tellers and other similar sentences, the chosen coding impinges on the behaviour of such sentences as Grabmayr and

Visser (2021) have shown. If they are studied in syntax theory, the choice of the coding can have no influence on the results, because it is completely eliminated.

Of course, the truth predicates of the typed theories TB, UTB, CT and the untyped theories KF and FS are not definable in pure syntax theory without the primitive symbol □ by Tarski's theorem on the undefinability of truth. For theories of truth with a primitive truth predicate analogous to these theories with □ – and perhaps further primitive semantic predicates such as ⊡ – the choice of the coding is less likely to have any effect on results; but it may well have effects. A relevant example of an inconsistency result sensitive to the coding, which was devised originally by Heck (2007) and slightly modified by Schindler (2015), is analyzed in some detail by Grabmayr and Visser (2021). The result also depends on the availability of function symbols. Hence, even truth theories with a primitive truth predicate are not immune to the vagaries of coding. The choice of a syntax theory as base theory definitely excludes any such dependencies; and using a syntax theory, as we do, provides a much more direct axiomatization of the objects to which truth and other semantic notions are ascribed by avoiding any detours through coding.

Of course, most of the better known results on theories of truth carry over to versions with a syntax theory as base theory. In this chapter we have introduced some of the most important in order to demonstrate how these results can be presented in a theory of syntax. At this point we release the reader from our setting to the literature in which other base theories are employed. More truth theories and results on them can be found in Cantini (1996), Cieśliński (2017), Halbach (2014), and Horsten (2011). Field (2008) focuses more on nonclassical theories. For a more general introduction into formal theories of truth including semantic, see Beall, Glanzberg, and Ripley (2018) and McGee (1991). Kaye (1991) discusses partial truth predicates and provides more examples of their application. These books just provide starting points from which the reader may venture into the world of paradox and truth theories.

12 Generalizations and Intensionality

Whenever formalization is used as a tool in philosophy, questions about the adequacy of the formalization arise. We called certain sentences 'truth tellers' or 'consistency statements'; we said of certain sentences that they say of themselves that they are not provable; and so on. In this final chapter we ask whether these labels are appropriate.

The situation is more complicated than in many other areas of philosophy in which formalizations are employed. Elsewhere it is much clearer what the counterparts of formal sentences are in natural language. Mathematical logicians often try to dodge questions about what sentences in arithmetic or in a syntax theory really say; their proofs and results are mathematically precise and do not rely on informal readings. However, for the relevance of these results and for their philosophical significance it often does matter what they mean and whether a specific sentence really expresses the consistency of a theory.

In mathematical logic the question of what exactly sentences express usually arises when one tries to generalize results and prove, for instance, that no member of an infinite class of systems proves its own consistency. In such cases one would like to have criteria that, applied to a sentence, can be used to determine whether the sentence expresses a system's consistency or not.

In this chapter we look at some simple attempts to provide such criteria for certain limited cases and show that identifying general criteria is difficult. Some results are extremely robust, and formalizations can be varied to a great extent in certain dimensions without changing the results. In other cases, however, results are extremely sensitive to even small changes.

12.1 Intensionality

So far we have been proceeding in a 'naïve' way in most of our formalizations and in labelling them. We give some examples. In chapter 10 we constructed a formula $\mathsf{Bew}_{\mathsf{E}^*}(x)$ and called it a 'provability predicate' for E^*.[1] In corollary 11.46 we claimed that the truth theory CT proves the putative consistency statement $\neg\mathsf{Bew}_{\mathsf{E}^*_{\min}}(\overline{\bot})$ for the minimal theory $\mathsf{E}^*_{\min}$. In section 11.1 we investigated a Σ_1-sentence that was described as saying about itself that it is Σ_1-true. We did not provide explicit justifications for our claims that $\mathsf{Bew}_{\mathsf{E}^*}(x)$ expresses provability, $\neg\mathsf{Bew}_{\mathsf{E}^*_{\min}}(\overline{\bot})$ is a consistency statement, and the sentence from section 11.1 says about itself that it is Σ_1-true. The method of formalization is naïve, because we were hoping that the reader would agree at every step of the construction of the formula or sentence that this was a 'natural' way to proceed in the formalization of provability, consistency, Σ_1 truth, and so on.

In what follows we frequently call $\mathsf{Bew}_{\mathsf{E}^*_{\min}}(x)$ the *canonical* provability predicate for $\mathsf{E}^*_{\min}$. Similarly, we will call $\neg\mathsf{Bew}_{\mathsf{E}^*_{\min}}(\overline{\bot})$ the canonical consistency statement. That is, by 'canonical' we always mean the formula or construction we have employed. This does not mean that a canonical provability expresses provability in a more natural or 'more adequate' way than other formulæ; that remains to be seen.

In fact, we have not provided any criteria for the naturalness or adequacy of a formalization. One might hope that the adequacy of the canonical choices is obvious from the resemblance of the formalization to the metatheoretic counterpart. This is to some extent plausible in the case of the provability predicate $\mathsf{Bew}_{\mathsf{E}^*_{\min}}(x)$ of $\mathsf{E}^*_{\min}$ and in the more general case of $\mathsf{Bew}_{\mathsf{E}^*}(x)$, which is the provability predicate of E^*, that is, of some fixed simple extension of $\mathsf{E}^*_{\min}$ in the sense of definition 10.59. In section 10.4 we described a proof system in some detail and then formalized it in a direct way, so that the formal provability predicate resembled the metatheoretic notion of provability in E^* in many relevant aspects.

In other cases, however, naturalness as resemblance to the metatheoretic definition of the notion does not take us very far. For instance, our formulæ $\mathsf{Tr}_{\Sigma_n}(x)$ for Σ_n truth do not resemble straightforward metatheoretic definitions of Σ_n truth: In the metatheory we can define Σ_n truth as the truth of a Σ_n sentence in the standard model (we restrict ourselves to the minimal language $\mathcal{L}^*_{\min}$ for this definition). But obviously, there is no formula in $\mathcal{L}^*_{\min}$ resembling this truth definition, because truth in the standard model is expressed in set-theoretic terms and not expressible in $\mathcal{L}^*_{\min}$.

[1] This claim is somewhat simplified, because E^* is some simple extension of $\mathsf{E}^*_{\min}$ without an explicitly given list of axioms. This is already a generalization of the kind we are going to discuss in the present chapter.

Self-reference is another example for the insufficiency of the resemblance criterion for adequacy. Let us call a sentence that says about itself that it is provable a *Henkin sentence*, a sentence that says about itself that it is unprovable a *Gödel sentence*, and a sentence that says of itself that it is Σ_1-true a Σ_1*–truth teller*. In English we can produce self-referential sentences by using pronouns, demonstratives, and so on, and form sentences such as 'This sentence is not provable' or 'I am not provable'. In $\mathcal{L}^*$, pronouns or demonstratives are not available. To obtain self-referential sentences we have availed ourselves of the trick in the proof of the diagonal lemma. Therefore, our canonical Henkin, Gödel, and truth teller sentences in $\mathcal{L}^*$ do not directly resemble claims of the form 'I am not provable (true, etc.)'. Of course, we could have carried out the diagonal construction in English, and then these English sentences would structurally resemble their formal counterparts. However, we would still be left with the problem of explaining why a convoluted metatheoretic sentence in English ascribes the relevant property to itself; and we would still be left wondering why the sentence states its own unprovability, Σ_1-truth, and so on.

Despite all the worries, we do not think that, for instance, calling $\mathsf{Bew}_{\mathsf{E}^*}(x)$ a provability predicate is especially problematic. The difficulties are those often encountered in conceptual analyses. This is not to say that there are no problems; but they are not worse than those found in many other parts of philosophy. That our analyses produce formal predicates and sentences does not make them less adequate than others that stay in the realm of natural language. Here we do not attempt to say anything about the general problems of conceptual analysis.

Nevertheless, in the cases mentioned, there are particular reasons to replace resemblance with more robust criteria for the adequacy of formalizations. In contrast to many conceptual analyses in analytic philosophy, it may be necessary to generalize our analyses; and if we try to generalize results it may be impossible to rely on resemblance. For instance, if we generalize the second incompleteness theorem, we may be tempted to say that no theory or at least no simple theory extending $\mathsf{E}^*_{\mathrm{min}}$ proves its own consistency. For each of the infinitely many extensions we need at least some associated consistency statement, or even *the* consistency statement. The resemblance criterion is difficult to apply to expressing consistency when we are not explicitly given the system whose consistency we are trying to express.

Even when we talk only about a specific theory such as $\mathsf{E}^*_{\mathrm{min}}$, we may want to generalize. The resemblance criterion may fail to determine a unique formalization of the consistency statement. Thus, we might aim to prove that all sentence that can reasonably be considered to express the consistency of $\mathsf{E}^*_{\min}$ are not provable in $\mathsf{E}^*_{\min}$.

This does not mean that we need to specify precise criteria satisfied exactly by those sentences expressing the consistency of the relevant system. If we can prove the unprovability of all sentences satisfying some necessary criterion for expressing consistency, then we are justified in claiming that all consistency statements are unprovable. Generally, we may attempt to make observations from previous chapters more robust by replacing our 'naïve' formalizations with a necessary criterion for a formal sentence or formula to express a claim or property and then show the result for all sentences and formulæ satisfying that criterion.

The theorems of previous chapters are not dependent on such criteria. We proved precise mathematical statements and showed that specific sentences of $\mathcal{L}^*$ are provable, refutable, true in the standard model, and so on. However, the significance of most of these results depends on what these sentences express. In some few cases it does not matter. For instance, if we are only interested in showing that a theory is incomplete, it does not matter what the sentence shown to be independent expresses. If the sentence does not state its own unprovability, the result is still significant. The description of the Gödel sentence as stating its own unprovability may be seen as a heuristic for the proof that becomes irrelevant once the result established. In contrast, if the sentence shown to be unprovable in the second incompleteness theorem does not express consistency, the result does not yield any insight beyond that provided by the first incompleteness theorem. Similarly, we showed of specific sentences that they are refutable. Only when we describe them as truth teller sentences does their refutability assume significance.

In many cases logicians have tried to generalize only one particular step of the construction of a sentence. For instance, in the case of the second incompleteness theorem for $\mathsf{E}^*_{\min}$, we may generalize only over the provability predicate. That is, we may for instance try to demonstrate the unprovability of $\neg\mathsf{Bew}'_{\mathsf{E}^*_{\min}}(\overline{\bot})$ for arbitrary provability predicates $\mathsf{Bew}'_{\mathsf{E}^*_{\min}}(x)$, while keeping the way we construct the consistency statement from these provability predicates fixed. That is, we understand inconsistency as the provability of the fixed contradiction $\bot$, which is by definition $\neg\,\underline{\forall} = \underline{\forall}$; and we do not understand it as the provability of another contradiction or as the provability of all sentences or as the provability of some sentence together with its negation. We return to this point below.[2]

We may also focus, not on the entire provability predicate, but exclusively on the formula $\mathsf{Axiom}_{\mathsf{E}^*_{\mathrm{min}}}(x)$ which expresses that x is an axiom of $\mathsf{E}^*_{\mathrm{min}}$, and keep the construction of the provability predicate from this formula fixed. In fact, we have already proved such a generalization: Gödel's second incompleteness theorem 10.78 was demonstrated for E^*, which is an arbitrary simple extension of $\mathsf{E}^*_{\mathrm{min}}$. Expressing that x is one of finitely many formulæ $\varphi_1, \dots, \varphi_n$ is straightforward, because we can use the expression $x = \overline{\varphi_1} \vee \cdots \vee x = \overline{\varphi_n}$ for this purpose. This is exactly what we did in the construction of $\mathsf{Axiom}_{\mathsf{E}^*}(x)$ in definition 10.56.

Generalizations in metamathematics thus often take the following form: A result is established about a specific sentence, whose construction relies on a subexpression e. Then generality is achieved by proving that the result still obtains if the subexpression e is replaced with an 'extensionally' equivalent expression. The relevant notion of extensional equivalence varies from case to case. We provide examples below.

Given a notion of extensional equivalence, results can be classified as extensional or intensional. As an example we consider again the second incompleteness theorem for $\mathsf{E}^*_{\mathrm{min}}$, that is, the unprovability of $\neg\mathsf{Bew}_{\mathsf{E}^*_{\mathrm{min}}}(\overline{\bot})$ in $\mathsf{E}^*_{\mathrm{min}}$. We can ask whether this result is extensional with respect to the provability predicate $\mathsf{Bew}_{\mathsf{E}^*_{\mathrm{min}}}(x)$, or in other words, whether the result still obtains when $\mathsf{Bew}_{\mathsf{E}^*_{\mathrm{min}}}(x)$ is replaced with an extensionally equivalent formula.

With the usual understanding of extensionality in mind, it may be natural to expect that any formula $\varphi(x)$ that has the same extension as $\mathsf{Bew}_{\mathsf{E}^*_{\mathrm{min}}}(x)$ in the standard model qualifies as extensionally equivalent. But this understanding of extensional equivalence is not very useful here. First, some fixed model or, more generally, some kind of semantics is required, because otherwise we do not have any extensions in the usual sense. In case we have additional vocabulary in $\mathcal{L}^*$ we lack an intended model and E^* may fail to prove anything about the additional vocabulary. Therefore, we focus on the minimal language $\mathcal{L}^*_{\mathrm{min}}$. For this language, we do have a standard model $\mathbb{E}^*$. However, extensional equivalence

[2] Which contradiction is used does not matter as long as the canonical provability predicate is used and the contradiction can be seen to be a contradiction in $\mathsf{E}^*_{\mathrm{min}}$. However, it can be crucial if the provability predicate does not satisfy K. For such provability predicates a version of the second incompleteness theorem can be still be provable, as Jeroslow (1973) showed; but it can also fail. Consequently, if the provability predicate does not satisfy K, the choice of the contradiction is another source of intensionality. It will not be discussed here. See also (Kurahashi 2020).

as sameness of extension in $\mathbb{E}^*$ is not sufficiently restrictive for our present purposes. This can be seen as follows: The formula $\mathsf{Bew}_{\mathsf{E}^*_{\min}}(x) \wedge \neg\mathsf{Bew}_{\mathsf{E}^*_{\min}}(\overline{\bot})$ has the same extension in $\mathbb{E}^*$ as $\mathsf{Bew}_{\mathsf{E}^*_{\min}}(x)$. If the canonical provability predicate in the consistency statement $\neg\mathsf{Bew}_{\mathsf{E}^*_{\min}}(\overline{\bot})$ is replaced by the provability predicate $\mathsf{Bew}_{\mathsf{E}^*_{\min}}(x) \wedge \neg\mathsf{Bew}_{\mathsf{E}^*_{\min}}(\overline{\bot})$ with the same extension, we obtain the new consistency statement

$$\neg\big(\mathsf{Bew}_{\mathsf{E}^*_{\min}}(\overline{\bot}) \wedge \neg\mathsf{Bew}_{\mathsf{E}^*_{\min}}(\overline{\bot})\big).$$

This consistency statement, however, is a tautology and therefore provable. Of course, this is a silly counterexample to the second incompleteness theorem: we cannot prove even for a single sentence that it is provable in the sense of this 'provability predicate'; no instance $\mathsf{Bew}_{\mathsf{E}^*_{\min}}(\overline{\varphi}) \wedge \neg\mathsf{Bew}_{\mathsf{E}^*_{\min}}(\overline{\bot})$ is provable in $\mathsf{E}^*_{\min}$. We conclude that the formula $\mathsf{Bew}_{\mathsf{E}^*_{\min}}(x) \wedge \neg\mathsf{Bew}_{\mathsf{E}^*_{\min}}(\overline{\bot})$ fails to qualify as a provability predicate, even though it has the same extension as the canonical provability predicate $\mathsf{Bew}_{\mathsf{E}^*_{\min}}(x)$. We need to employ a stricter notion of extensional equivalence.

We say that $\varphi(x)$ and $\psi(x)$ are 'pointwise equivalent' in E^* iff, for all expressions e, the following equivalence is satisfied:

$$\mathsf{E}^* \vdash \varphi(\overline{e}) \quad \text{iff} \quad \mathsf{E}^* \vdash \psi(\overline{e}).$$

Returning to the special case of the minimal theory $\mathsf{E}^*_{\min}$, we can now declare all formulæ pointwise equivalent to $\mathsf{Bew}_{\mathsf{E}^*_{\min}}(x)$ 'extensionally correct provability predicates'. Now, proposition 10.62 implies, for all sentences φ,

$$\mathsf{E}^*_{\min} \vdash \varphi \quad \text{iff} \quad \mathsf{E}^*_{\min} \vdash \mathsf{Bew}_{\mathsf{E}^*_{\min}}(\overline{\varphi}).$$

Moreover, it follows from proposition 10.58 that $\mathsf{E}^*_{\min} \nvdash \mathsf{Bew}_{\mathsf{E}^*}(\overline{e})$ if e is not a sentence. Thus, a formula $\beta(x)$ is an extensionally correct provability predicate iff, for all expressions e, the following equivalence obtains:

$$\mathsf{E}^*_{\min} \vdash \beta(\overline{e}) \quad \text{iff} \quad e \text{ is a sentence } \varphi \text{ with } \mathsf{E}^*_{\min} \vdash \varphi. \tag{12.1}$$

In an arithmetical context this would mean that β 'weakly represents' or 'numerates' provability.

Condition (12.1) provides a definition of extensional correctness that is independent of the canonical provability predicate. In most discussions, this definition is chosen.

Any two extensionally correct provability predicates have the same extension in the standard model; but some formulæ with the same extension are not extensionally correct. For instance, the formula $\mathsf{Bew}_{\mathsf{E}^*_{\min}}(x) \wedge \neg\mathsf{Bew}_{\mathsf{E}^*_{\min}}(\overline{\bot})$ discussed above has the same extension as $\mathsf{Bew}_{\mathsf{E}^*_{\min}}(x)$, but is not extensionally correct in the sense of (12.1).

Pointwise equivalence is one way to understand extensional equivalence for provability predicates. For the moment, we understand extensional equivalence in this way; and with this notion of extensional equivalence we can classify results involving $\mathsf{Bew}_{\mathsf{E}^*_{\min}}(x)$ into intensional and extensional results.

We look again at the second incompleteness theorem for $\mathsf{E}^*_{\min}$, which says that the sentence $\neg\mathsf{Bew}_{\mathsf{E}^*_{\min}}(\overline{\bot})$ is not provable in $\mathsf{E}^*_{\min}$. The theorem is extensional iff $\neg\beta(\overline{\bot})$ is not provable in $\mathsf{E}^*_{\min}$ for each formula $\beta(x)$ which is extensionally, that is, pointwise, equivalent to $\mathsf{Bew}_{\mathsf{E}^*_{\min}}(x)$. But there are extensionally correct provability predicates $\beta(x)$, and thus formulæ extensionally equivalent to $\mathsf{Bew}_{\mathsf{E}^*_{\min}}(x)$, such that $\mathsf{E}^*_{\min} \vdash \neg\beta(\overline{\bot})$. The Rosser provability predicate is, by proposition 10.67, an example. Consequently, the second incompleteness theorem for $\mathsf{E}^*_{\min}$ is intensional.

Other results are extensional. The Gödel sentence we constructed for the proof of the first incompleteness theorem for $\mathsf{E}^*_{\min}$ is of the form $\neg\mathsf{Bew}_{\mathsf{E}^*_{\min}}(t)$, where the term t is obtained by the usual diagonal construction. The pure first incompleteness theorem for $\mathsf{E}^*_{\min}$ merely states that $\mathsf{E}^*_{\min}$ is incomplete, and thus, as mentioned above, the problem of extensionality does not arise. However, we can ask specifically about the provability of the Gödel sentence $\neg\mathsf{Bew}_{\mathsf{E}^*_{\min}}(t)$. By the proof of theorem 10.63, it is independent of $\mathsf{E}^*_{\min}$. The additional assumption in the theorem that E^* is ω-consistent is not needed here, because we focus on the ω-consistent minimal system $\mathsf{E}^*_{\min}$. The only property of $\mathsf{Bew}_{\mathsf{E}^*_{\min}}(x)$ required for the proof is proposition 10.62, that is, the observation that $\mathsf{Bew}_{\mathsf{E}^*_{\min}}(x)$ is an extensionally correct provability predicate. Therefore, the independence of the Gödel sentence is an extensional result.

The notion of extensionality just outlined is inspired by Feferman (1960, p. 35):

> In broad terms, the applications of the method [of arithmetization] can be classified as being *extensional* if essentially only numerically correct definitions are needed, or *intensional* if the definitions must more fully *express* the notions involved, so that various of the general properties of these notions can be formally derived.

We do not claim that our distinction between intensional and extensional results involving the provability predicate coincides with Feferman's. For a start, Feferman's setting is arithmetical, in contrast to our syntax-theoretic language. While most of Feferman's examples concern provability, he also lists Tarski's theorem on the undefinability of truth as an extensional result, which is obviously not covered by our characterization. We surmise that his notion of numerical correctness is closely related to our notion of extensional correctness.

Our definition of the extensional equivalence of provability predicates as pointwise equivalence may strike the reader as a misapplication of the term 'extensional'. Extensional equivalence should be merely defined as having the same extension under the intended interpretation, or so one might argue. The objection may be justified from the modern use of the notion of extensionality; but there are older uses that vary significantly from the standard modern use. We refer the reader to (Carnap 1934, section 71), for an attempt to clarify older uses of the term. We do not pretend that our notion of extensionality has more in common with these notions than a superficial similarity.

The conception of extensional equivalence is sensible for provability predicates. For other predicates, other notions of extensional equivalence may be more suitable, as we argue below.

The distinction between extensional and intensional results can be extended beyond extensionality with respect to a formula. As mentioned above, given a formula expressing provability, we may form a consistency statement in different ways. Instead of $\neg \underline{\forall} = \underline{\forall}$ as $\bot$ in the consistency statement $\neg \mathsf{Bew}_{E^*}(\overline{\bot})$, we could have used some other contradiction. Of course, $\bot$ is not a subformula of $\neg \mathsf{Bew}_{E^*}(\overline{\bot})$, because it is mentioned, not used. Hence, extensionality with respect to $\bot$ cannot be understood as the substitutability of a certain subformula. Moreover, as mentioned above, we could also form a consistency statement by defining it, not as the provability of a single contradiction, but as the provability of *all* sentences. In this case we would not vary the formula expressing provability but rather the construction of the consistency statement *from* this formula.

Another dimension of intensionality concerns self-reference. When we ask about the provability of a sentence that ascribes some property to itself, we may try prove a result for all diagonal sentences. If this is possible, the result would qualify as extensional with respect to self-reference. If a uniform result cannot be established for all diagonal sentences, we can still try to prove a result for other constructions that deviate from that in our proof of the diagonal lemma and not only those obtained through the construction in lemma 5.10.

Of course, the different dimensions of intensionality are not independent. A result may be extensional with respect to self-reference when the property in question is expressed by a certain formula, but become intensional when expressed by another formula.

12.2 Sources of Intensionality

In an arithmetical setting, Halbach and Visser (2014a) distinguish three sources of intensionality that arise in the construction of sentences that are usually described as self-referential, such as Gödel sentences. This is because there are three main steps involved in the construction of such statements. Of course, our present interests differ from those in (Halbach and Visser 2014a): here, not only self-referential statements are considered and, above all, our syntax theory requires no coding in arithmetic. However, we think that it is still interesting to look at each of the three sources and to compare our syntax-theoretic approach with the usual arithmetized.

The three sources of intensionality are intensionality from coding, from the expression of properties, and from self-reference. They are still all relevant to our approach. Of course, we do not code syntax in arithmetic, but we may be unable to escape intensionality from coding completely. Above, we have already discussed intensionality from the expression of the property of provability. Below, we will generalize this discussion. Even though self-reference has played such a central role in the discussion of paradoxes, little attention has been paid to intensionality arising from it in the literature.

Intensionality from Coding

In arithmetized metamathematics, expressions of the language of arithmetic are assigned numbers as codes. We can then use the language of arithmetic to talk, indirectly via their codes or numbers, about its own expressions. Assigning numbers to symbols and then to complex expressions of the language is the first step in the construction of Gödel sentences, consistency statements, truth tellers, and so on. We can now ask whether a result is extensional with respect to the coding. That is, we can ask whether a given result holds, not only for a chosen coding, but for all 'extensionally equivalent' codings. In order to ask the question, we thus require a sensible conception of the extensional equivalence of codings.

In most logic textbooks some coding is fixed, and then results such as Gödel's second incompleteness theorem are proved for that specific coding schema. It would be very worrying if different extensionally equivalent coding schemas gave different results concerning the provability or unprovability of a formula. When logicians claim that a theory such as Peano arithmetic does not prove its own consistency statement, they commonly do not mention a specific coding schema; rather, they fix a specific coding schema and prove the second incompleteness theorem based on that coding. If, under another reasonable coding schema, the consistency statement became provable – while all other steps in the construction of the consistency statement are kept fixed – the second incompleteness theorem would lose much of its philosophical significance.

One could try to overcome the worry by proving that the second incompleteness theorem is extensional with respect to the coding schema, or more technically expressed, that it is invariant under changes in the coding. What strikes us as the most promising approach is to start with some fixed coding that is clearly reasonable and then prove for all extensionally equivalent codings that the proof still goes through. We could also simply show that the proof obtains for all reasonable coding schemas. This, of course, requires at least a necessary condition that all reasonable coding schemas satisfy.

Clearly, not just any assignment of numbers to expressions yields a reasonable coding schema; there must be restrictions. For instance, the assignment of numbers to expressions will have to be 'efficient'. A general criterion is difficult to come by, though (see Grabmayr and Visser 2021). What a reasonable coding is will depend on the underlying theory. When we go to a weaker theory – for instance, when we think about the second incompleteness theorem for weak theories – we will need a coding schema that permits even the weak theory to prove certain basic syntactic facts. If a theory cannot prove a consistency statement because the encoding of syntax is not sufficiently efficient, that will not count as a proof of the second incompleteness theorem.

Although a suitable notion of extensional equivalence of codings is still missing, as far as we know, we suggest that it can be understood along the following lines: Extensional equivalence for coding schemas is provable intertranslatability of coding schemas. At least, we must be able to define, in the theory, a provably computable injective function f that assigns to any code n of an expression in the first coding schema the code $f(n)$ of the same expression in the second.[3] Further conditions will have to be imposed on the translations f between codings. In particular, we will need to translate the operations of concatenation, substitution, and so on, from one coding to the other.

The topic of intensionality from coding is not well explored, and much work remains to be done. Here, we will not go any deeper into the problems of arithmetical codings and appropriate notions of extensional equivalence between them, because our approach is based on a theory of syntax instead of arithmetic. Our proofs of the second incompleteness theorem 10.78 and other results do not require any coding, because we can formalize consistency statements directly without the detour via some coding schema. Therefore, it seems we can dodge one source of intensionality: syntax theory makes coding in arithmetic superfluous.

However, this does not mean that with our syntax theory types of intensionality similar to that from coding can be avoided completely. Although we do not employ any coding in the strict sense, there may be other decisions that can cause similar issues. For instance, in E^* we settled on an understanding of variables as expressions of the form $(\mathsf{v}\cdots\mathsf{v})$ (definition 8.34). Of course, we could also have understood variables in a different way, for instance, as v followed by Arabic numerals or strings of negation symbols. Obviously, all proofs would still go through *mutatis mutandis.*

Saying that other ways of representing variables would not affect the results is merely the syntactic version of proving invariance of results under a change of the coding scheme with respect to the variables. Hence, using syntax theory does not fully block intensionality from coding.

We could insist that there is actually no decision involved in the way we think of variables and that they just are expressions of the form $(\mathsf{v}\cdots\mathsf{v})$. But *stipulating* that expressions of the form $(\mathsf{v}\cdots\mathsf{v})$ are the variables is equivalent to the stipulation, in an arithmetical setting, that the variables *are* certain numbers, which is often expressed by saying that expressions and their codes are 'identified'. Both still look like somewhat arbitrary decisions that evoke the feeling that they could have been taken in a different way.

The way we deal with variables was only a relatively trivial example for intensionality from coding-like phenomena in syntax theory. Lurking in the background are much bigger decisions. In our formal syntax theories, expressions are

[3] Balthasar Grabmayr, Volker Halbach, Beau Mount, and Albert Visser have worked on the elaboration of such an approach.

obtained by concatenating symbols; that is, we describe a linear notation (even though, metalinguistically, we used overlining, and thus a nonlinear notation, for our simple theory E). Others might prefer to understand formulæ as syntactic trees and, therefore, as essentially two-dimensional objects. Proponents of such an approach will think of our linear expressions as codes for trees and view our theory E^* in the same way as we see arithmetic, namely as an indirect way of talking about expressions. At any rate, it will be difficult to conceive syntactic trees as mere notations of our linear language $\mathcal{L}^*$ in the sense of section 5.1. For us, the expressions of $\mathcal{L}^*$ are linear strings of symbols, not trees or something else. $\mathcal{L}^*$ may have notations written from left to right or from right to left, or in still another direction; therefore, the direction of the notation may not be integral to our syntax theory, in contrast to its linearity.

We claim that our theory is a direct axiomatization of the theory of these linear expressions, while arithmetic is not.[4] In arithmetic we have operations such as successor, addition, and multiplication that do not directly describe any operations on expressions of $\mathcal{L}^*$ (although arithmetic may describe a linear theory of a language with exactly one symbol). We claim that a proper syntax theory is superior to doing syntax theory indirectly in arithmetic: it eliminates the need to encode operations and thus intensionality at least to some extent.

A fundamental difference between coded syntax theory and direct syntax theory is that coding adds additional properties or 'structure': when expressions are coded, we can ask whether (the code of) an expression has certain arithmetical properties, whether it is even or odd, or whether it is numerically smaller than (the code of) another expression. In syntax theory these additional properties are absent, and therefore the intensionality from these coding choices is removed.

For instance, the status of the arithmetical sentence saying about itself that it (or rather its code) is even is highly sensitive to the coding, and any result will be intensional. That sentence does not have a counterpart in syntax theory. These kinds of silly examples of intensionality are thus avoided.

In sum, we do not claim that there are no other valuable ways of doing syntax theory. Intensionality may even arise from the way one does syntax theory. However, by adopting syntax theory instead of arithmetized metamathematics

[4]The justification of this claim requires a thorough discussion, which we do not give here. There are interesting and difficult metaphysical issues that we prefer to avoid here – after several abandoned attempts at tackling them.

we can at least avoid many artificial choices that have to be made when syntax is coded in arithmetic.

Intensionality from the Expression of Properties and Relations

There are different ways to express properties and relations in E^*, if they are expressible at all. This is the most thoroughly studied source of intensionality. It came into focus when logicians tried to generalize the second incompleteness theorem. These generalizations, as well as sensible conceptions of extensional equivalence and correctness, were discussed above. In particular, we argued that it does not suffice to focus on the extension of a formula of $\mathcal{L}^*_{\mathrm{min}}$ in the standard model $\mathbb{E}^*$. Even if a formula $\varphi(x)$ applies exactly to the $\mathsf{E}^*_{\mathrm{min}}$-provable formulæ in $\mathbb{E}^*$ it should not count as 'extensionally correct' for the purpose of generalizations, nor as a provability predicate. For $\varphi(x)$ to be a provability predicate, we need to be able to prove certain facts about provability in $\mathsf{E}^*_{\mathrm{min}}$ in the sense of $\varphi(x)$.

In (12.1) we understood extensional correctness for provability predicates as pointwise expressibility. That is, we said that a formula $\beta(x)$ is an extensionally correct provability predicate iff, for all expressions e the following equivalence obtains:

$$\mathsf{E}^*_{\mathrm{min}} \vdash \beta(\overline{e}) \quad \text{iff} \quad e \text{ is a sentence } \varphi \text{ with } \mathsf{E}^*_{\mathrm{min}} \vdash \varphi. \tag{12.1}$$

Halbach and Visser (2014a) called (12.1) 'Kreisel's condition' for expressing provability, because Kreisel (1953, p. 405) was the first to suggest that a formula expresses provability iff it satisfies the above condition. Of course, we have adapted Kreisel's condition to our syntax theory. Kreisel himself formulated it in an arithmetical setting and for 'standard formal system[s] adequate for recursive number theory'.

We have used (12.1) to distinguish between extensional and intensional results. Since (12.1) cannot distinguish between the canonical provability predicate $\mathsf{Bew}_{\mathsf{E}^*_{\mathrm{min}}}(x)$ and the Rosser provability predicate $\mathsf{RBew}_{\mathsf{E}^*_{\mathrm{min}}}(x)$, both express provability in $\mathsf{E}^*_{\mathrm{min}}$ pointwise, that is, in accordance with Kreisel's condition. In other words, both express provability pointwise, they are pointwise equivalent, and in this sense extensionally equivalent. Nevertheless, the second incompleteness theorem fails for Rosser provability, because E^* proves $\neg\mathsf{RBew}_{\mathsf{E}^*}(\overline{\bot})$ by proposition 10.67, as we noted above. Thus, the second incompleteness theorem is intensional with respect to the provability predicate, if extensional equivalence is understood as pointwise equivalence.

It may now be asked why pointwise equivalence or correctness has been used for the distinction between extensional and intensional results. There are other notions of equivalence and correctness that could have been employed, and some of them will be discussed below. Our choice of pointwise correctness is motivated by what we think is the traditional notion of extensionality in metamathematics. Results that are extensional in this sense are robust and can easily be generalized. In particular, if the theorems of a theory are recursively enumerable (or semi-computable), then a general theorem tells us that there is a formula that is a pointwise correct provability predicate (cf. the discussion after theorem 10.63). We do not go into details here, but they are standard in the literature on the incompleteness theorems. Thus, extensional results can easily be generalized to recursively enumerable extensions of our theory $\mathsf{E}^*_{\min}$, or to certain arithmetical theories in an arithmetized setting, although often some additional assumption such as ω-consistency is required (see again the comments following theorem 10.63). Intensional results cannot be generalized so easily. Hence, there are good reasons to distinguish between extensional and intensional results in the sense outlined above.

The intensionality of the second incompleteness theorem in the sense above prompts the question whether there are stricter criteria for extensional equivalence and correctness such that the second incompleteness theorem is provable for all formulæ extensionally equivalent (in this narrower sense) to the canonical provability predicate, that is, for all extensionally correct formulæ. One might try to strengthen, say, the criterion of pointwise expressibility. For instance, one could use *strong* pointwise expressibility instead. A property P is strongly pointwise expressed by the formula $\varphi(x)$ iff the following two conditions are satisfied by all expressions e:

$$\begin{aligned} \mathsf{E}^*_{\min} &\vdash \varphi(\overline{e}) && \text{iff} \quad e \text{ has property } P, \\ \mathsf{E}^*_{\min} &\vdash \neg\varphi(\overline{e}) && \text{iff} \quad e \text{ does not have property } P. \end{aligned}$$

In proposition 10.37 we showed that the property of being a term can be strongly pointwise expressed. For provability, however, the criterion is useless.

12.1 PROPOSITION *Assume that there is a formula $\beta(x)$ such that, for all expressions e, the following two conditions hold:*

$$\mathsf{E}^* \vdash \beta(\overline{e}) \quad \textit{iff} \quad e \textit{ is a sentence } \varphi \textit{ with } \mathsf{E}^* \vdash \varphi,$$
$$\mathsf{E}^* \vdash \neg\beta(\overline{e}) \quad \textit{iff} \quad e \textit{ is not a sentence } \varphi \textit{ with } \mathsf{E}^* \vdash \varphi.$$

Then E^* is inconsistent. Therefore, there is no such formula for the minimal theory $\mathsf{E}^*_{\mathrm{min}}$, because this theory is consistent.

PROOF Assume that E^* is consistent. By the diagonal lemma there is a sentence γ with

$$\mathsf{E}^* \vdash \gamma \leftrightarrow \neg\beta(\overline{\gamma}).$$

As in the proof of the first incompleteness theorem, that is, theorem 10.63, we show $\mathsf{E}^* \nvdash \gamma$. Therefore, by consistency and the assumption, $\mathsf{E}^* \vdash \neg\beta(\overline{\gamma})$ and, by the diagonal property of γ, also $\mathsf{E}^* \vdash \gamma$. This is a contradiction. Hence, E^* must be inconsistent. ⊣

Thus, strong pointwise expressibility may provide us with a sensible criterion for deciding whether a formula expresses the property of being a term, but certainly not for deciding whether it expresses the property of being provable, unless we say that provability is not expressible in a consistent E^* at all. For other properties, pointwise expressibility – both in its 'weak' normal form and its strong form – fails as a useful criterion. For instance, Σ_n-truth for $n > 1$ and Π_n-truth for $n \geq 1$ cannot be expressed in E^* in the sense of weak or strong pointwise expressibility at all, unless E^* is inconsistent. We do not prove this here.

Weak and strong pointwise expressibility are hardly suitable as general criteria for the expression of arbitrary properties. Historically, they arose from the proofs of the first incompleteness theorem and similar results, where we can generalize over all formulæ pointwise expressing the property, because these properties are sufficiently simple. This illustrates that a given analysis of extensional equivalence can be suitable for some property but useless for others.

We can still try to specify notions of 'extensional equivalence' and 'extensional correctness' that provide us with a criterion for the expression of provability such that the second incompleteness theorem holds for all extensionally correct formulæ or all formulæ extensionally equivalent to the canonical provability predicate. These notions of equivalence and correctness may no longer qualify as extensional in a straightforward sense. At any rate, the conditions of correctness we are going to discuss now are usually seen as intensional.

We can try to formulate another necessary criterion for correctness or for expressing provability by looking at our proof of the second incompleteness theorem. In it we proved first the Löb derivability conditions NEC*, K*, and 4* for $\mathsf{Bew}_{\mathsf{E}^*}(x)$ in a universally quantified form on page 283 and then proved the second incompleteness theorem from them. We could say that any formula satisfying these conditions instead of $\mathsf{Bew}_{\mathsf{E}^*}(x)$ is a provability predicate. More generally, we could state:

MEANING-POSTULATE CONDITION *A formula $\varphi(x)$ expresses a property P of expressions (or is correct for P) iff* E* *proves all meaning postulates for the property P for $\varphi(x)$.*

Unlike pointwise expressibility, this criterion can be applied also to more complex properties. For instance, we may say that a formula $\tau(x)$ expresses Σ_n-truth iff E* proves

$$\varphi \leftrightarrow \tau(\overline{\varphi})$$

for all Σ_n-sentences. Our theorem 11.28 then shows that our formulæ $\mathsf{Tr}_{\Sigma_n}(x)$ actually do express Σ_n-truth.

Of course, the meaning-postulate condition suffers from the problem that it is unclear what the meaning postulates for a given property P are. The worries here are not as deep as Quine's (1964) about meaning postulates and analyticity; we do not have to understand meaning postulates in the sense of Carnap. The worry is much more basic: Löb (1955) arrived at his derivability conditions by proving them for a natural provability predicate. They are by no means obvious. In other words, we have a provability predicate, for instance our canonical provability predicate, and isolate some of its properties that enable us to prove the second incompleteness theorem, Löb's theorem, and so on. Then we declare these properties to be meaning postulates for provability and claim that whatever satisfies these conditions is a provability predicate. Nevertheless, we must have recognized the initial formula as a provability predicate without any meaning postulates available. Therefore it is at least strange to say that whatever formula satisfies these principles expresses provability. If we had proceeded in a purely naïve way, we might have chosen $\Box\overline{\varphi} \to \varphi$ as a meaning postulate for provability, but we would hardly have chosen the elaborate Löb derivability conditions.

It is also not clear why one should choose exactly the conditions NEC*, K*, and 4*. In other exposition schematic forms of K* and 4* are used, analogous to NEC and contains K and 4 in the proof of theorem 6.11. Kurahashi (2020) lists various sets of derivability conditions and shows that they can have very different properties. Which set is used also depends on which version of the second incompleteness theorem we aim to prove. Thus, there is no single set of meaning postulates that can be extracted from the literature.

This is not to say that these 'meaning postulates' are of no interest. In fact, it can be shown that they are not as arbitrary as it may seem. If we include Löb's theorem 10.77 as a further postulate, we even have a completeness theorem of a kind, namely Solovay's (1976) completeness theorem.[5] But they just isolate very important properties of the provability predicate. By themselves they are insufficient to characterize provability: as a sufficient criterion for provability the Löb derivability conditions are completely hopeless, because they are satisfied even by the trivial formula $x = x$.

Therefore we consider another strategy by looking at how we (or rather Löb) arrived at the meaning postulates for provability. We think that $\mathsf{Bew}_{\mathsf{E}^*}(x)$ expresses provability in E*, while Rosser provability does not, or that $\mathsf{Bew}_{\mathsf{E}^*}(x)$ expresses provability 'more adequately' than the Rosser provability predicate, because $\mathsf{Bew}_{\mathsf{E}^*}(x)$ is defined to resemble our metatheoretic definition of provability in E*.[6]

RESEMBLANCE CONDITION *A formula $\varphi(x)$ expresses a property P of expressions (or is correct for P) iff $\varphi(x)$ resembles the definition of P in the relevant way.*

In this condition we talk about properties, not only sets, because a set can be described in very different ways, while we assume that there is a preferred definition for a property. It requires, of course, that the definition of the property is somehow given. In contrast to the criteria discussed so far the resemblance criterion can hardly be made philosophically precise.

In the case of provability, the canonical provability predicate $\mathsf{Bew}_{\mathsf{E}^*}(x)$ resembles the metatheoretic definition of provability in E*. Thus we can say that a formula $\varphi(x)$ expresses provability in E* iff $\varphi(x)$ resembles $\mathsf{Bew}_{\mathsf{E}^*}(x)$.

---

[5]Boolos (1993) and Smoryński (1985) discuss this and other results in detail. Here we cannot provide a serious discussion of provability logic.

[6]We apologize for forming the comparative of 'adequate'. We are not quite sure how to make sense of 'expressing adequately' as a comparative notion.

The application of the resemblance criterion to $\mathsf{Bew}_{\mathsf{E}^*}(x)$ and $\mathsf{RBew}_{\mathsf{E}^*}(x)$ should be obvious: Rosser provability in theorem 10.65 contains an extra condition that is not in the usual metatheoretic definition of provability. Therefore, $\mathsf{RBew}_{\mathsf{E}^*}(x)$ does not resemble $\mathsf{Bew}_{\mathsf{E}^*}(x)$.

With other properties it is even less clear how to apply the resemblance criterion. In particular, we are wondering how to apply the criterion to partial truth predicates such as our predicates $\mathsf{Tr}_{\Sigma_n}(x)$. It seems rather implausible to say that our partial truth predicates $\mathsf{Tr}_{\Sigma_n}(x)$ resemble the metatheoretic definition of Σ_n-truth, because our metatheoretic definition of Σ_n-truth is very different from the construction of $\mathsf{Tr}_{\Sigma_n}(x)$. For partial truth predicates, the meaning-postulate approach seems more suited.

Of course, resemblance is a highly vague notion. It is, presumably, a comparative notion: a formula can resemble the metatheoretic definition of a property more or less strongly. Making the required notion of resemblance explicit is very difficult. The metatheory does not really come *in* a fixed language that could be readily translated into our object language.

It was one of our objectives to provide a theory of syntax that can be seen as a fully formalized and regimented metatheory. If we were really to adopt E^* as our metatheory, we could apply the resemblance condition in a straightforward way by understanding resemblance as syntactic identity.

Intensionality from Self-Reference

The third source of intensionality arises only for claims about (genuinely or putatively) self-referential sentences. It is not relevant for the second incompleteness theorem, for instance. However, when we ask about the status of the Gödel sentence, which states its own unprovability, the Henkin sentence, which states its own provability, the truth teller, which states its own Σ_n-truth, or similar sentences, then this source of intensionality can be crucial. Of course, logicians are ready to admit that there is not only one Gödel, Henkin, or Σ_n–truth teller sentence. However, the singular may be justified by showing that all sentences which can be seen as attributing to themselves a certain property are provably equivalent in some theory, or are equivalent in some other way; but without further evidence there is no reason to assume that, for instance, all Henkin sentences are equivalent. For instance, there may be two distinct sentences saying about themselves that they are provable, and one of them is indeed provable while the other is refutable.

Whether the different sentences which say about themselves that they have a certain property behave in different ways may depend on how that property is expressed. That is, the two sources of intensionality may interact. We will give examples of this in the next section, where we discuss self-reference and the interaction of different sources of intensionality more broadly.

12.3 Self-Reference

In this section we discuss the meanings of claims of the following kind, where S is some sentence:

> S says about itself that it has property P.
> S ascribes/attributes to itself property P.

We take all these sentences to be mere equivalents. As we have done already in the foregoing, we simply call sentences self-referential rather than using the more complicated phrases above. Thus, when a sentence is described as 'self-referential', this is always with respect to a certain property, even if that property is not explicitly mentioned.

If the property P is given by some predicate in English, for instance, by 'is provable', then we also treat these claims as equivalent with the following claims:

> S says (about itself) that it is provable.
> S claims its own provability.
> S states (of itself) that it is provable.

Outside logic, in less artificial contexts, self-reference is usually associated with the indexical 'I'. However, there are two fundamental differences to putative self-reference in formal languages, if such pronouns are used. First, an agent claiming 'I am Bond' says about himself or herself that he or she is Bond. In logic, in contrast, self-reference is ascribed, not to people, but to sentences or, perhaps, propositions. Secondly, in the languages we are interested in, such as $\mathcal{L}$, $\mathcal{L}^*$, or the language of arithmetic, there is no equivalent to the pronoun 'I' that rigidly refers to the speaker, the utterance, or the sentence in which it occurs.[7] In our formal

[7] This is not to say that there have been no attempts to add such pronouns to formal languages. I merely claim that they are not found in our syntax theory or arithmetic.

languages self-reference can only be established via descriptions, if at all. Therefore, looking at the vast literature on indexicals, rigid designators, and centred worlds will be of limited help.

The sentences in natural language that may be to some degree analogous to potentially self-referential sentences in logic will contain definite descriptions or names. They will still normally refer to people, not sentences, but may be give us some guidance for the notion of self-reference in formal languages. For instance, if the older author of *The Road to Paradox* says 'The older author of *The Road to Paradox* wrote the first chapter', he would make a claim about himself, and his utterance and belief would be about himself and therefore self-referential. Of course, the older author might not even realize that he is the older author and that the utterance is self-referential; but let us say that does not prevent self-reference in the sense in which we are interested. Sentences that are not obviously or *a priori* self-referential may nonetheless be self-referential. Even a sentence such as 'Everything is self-identical', uttered by the older author, should qualify as self-referential, because it is about everything – including the older author.

Gödel (1931, p. 175) said about his eponymous sentence that was obtained via diagonalization: 'We thus have a sentence before us that states its own unprovability.'[8] However, declarations of this kind often do not serve more than didactical or heuristic purposes. Gödel may have arrived at the proof of the incompleteness theorems by thinking about self-reference and the liar sentence, but the notion of self-reference can be completely dispensed with in the actual proofs. This is not to say that diagonalization can be dispensed with; but whether diagonalization generates self-reference, and how the two are related, is irrelevant to the proof.

What is needed for the proof of the first incompleteness theorem or the liar paradox is a diagonal sentence for the predicate $\mathsf{Bew}_{E^*}(\mathsf{x})$ in the first incompleteness theorem 10.63 and $\neg\Box\mathsf{x}$ in the liar paradox theorem 6.1. Generally, we say that γ is a diagonal sentence for $\psi(x)$ relative to a system S iff $\gamma \leftrightarrow \psi(\overline{\gamma})$ is provable in S. For the proofs of the liar paradox and thus of Tarski's theorem of the undefinability of truth (theorem 6.2), for the proof of the first incompleteness theorem 10.63, including the Rosser variant (theorem 10.65), and the inconsistency results in chapter 6, any diagonal sentence is sufficient, whether it is obtained by the diagonal lemma or not. The diagonal lemma 5.12 yields a diagonal sentence

[8] The German original reads: 'Wir haben also einen Satz vor uns, der seine eigene Unbeweisbarkeit behauptet.'

for any given $\psi(x)$, but there will always be further diagonal sentences.[9]

Being a diagonal sentence is at best a necessary condition for being self-referential, but certainly not sufficient. As an example against the sufficiency of the condition, consider the formula $\mathsf{x}=\mathsf{x}$. Every provable sentence φ is a diagonal sentence of $\mathsf{x}=\mathsf{x}$:

$$\mathsf{E}^* \vdash \varphi \quad \text{implies} \quad \mathsf{E}^* \vdash \varphi \leftrightarrow \overline{\varphi}=\overline{\varphi}.$$

Consequently, $\forall y\; y=y$ and $\overline{\land}=\overline{\land}$ are diagonal sentences of $\mathsf{x}=\mathsf{x}$. But they are hardly self-referential. Thus, being a diagonal sentence of $\mathsf{x}=\mathsf{x}$ is not sufficient for ascribing to oneself the property of being self-identical.

This leaves one wondering why often in the literature a very close connection is assumed between self-reference and being a diagonal sentence. We speculate that many logicians have focused on diagonal sentences of the negated canonical unprovability predicate $\neg\mathsf{Bew}_{\mathsf{E}^*}(\mathsf{x})$ (and, perhaps, also of the unnegated provability predicate). For this formula there is an erroneous argument that might be thought to provide justification for the claim that all its diagonal sentences state their own unprovability.

First, we assume that the canonical method in lemma 5.10 for establishing the strong diagonal lemma, that is, lemma 5.11, and from this the usual diagonal lemma 5.12, yields a sentence γ that states its own unprovability. Then we can show that all diagonal sentences of $\neg\mathsf{Bew}_{\mathsf{E}^*}(\mathsf{x})$ are provably equivalent. That is, up to provable equivalence there is only one Gödel sentence. If we now further assume that, if a sentence γ states its own unprovability, then all sentences provably equivalent to γ state their own unprovability, then indeed *all* diagonal sentences of the canonical provability predicate $\neg\mathsf{Bew}_{\mathsf{E}^*}(\mathsf{x})$ would state their own unprovability. Since the canonical Gödel sentence γ does state its own unprovability, all diagonal sentences of $\neg\mathsf{Bew}_{\mathsf{E}^*}(\mathsf{x})$ do. More succinctly, up to provable equivalence there is only one diagonal sentence of $\neg\mathsf{Bew}_{\mathsf{E}^*}(\mathsf{x})$ and thus only one Gödel sentence, and that sentence is self-referential and states its own unprovability.

Before we show what is wrong with this argument, we establish the claim that all diagonal sentences of the canonical provability predicate are indeed provably equivalent:

12.2 PROPOSITION *If* $\mathsf{E}^* \vdash \gamma \leftrightarrow \neg\mathsf{Bew}_{\mathsf{E}^*}(\overline{\gamma})$ *and* $\mathsf{E}^* \vdash \delta \leftrightarrow \neg\mathsf{Bew}_{\mathsf{E}^*}(\overline{\delta})$ *obtain, then* $\mathsf{E}^* \vdash \gamma \leftrightarrow \delta$ *holds.*

[9] The set of diagonal sentences for any given formula is as complex as it can be. For a precise formulation of this claim and proofs, see observations 2.1 and 2.2 in (Halbach and Visser 2014a).

PROOF We prove only $\mathsf{E}^* \vdash \delta \to \gamma$. The other direction is proved alike. Using the Löb derivability conditions we reason in E^* as follows:

	$\neg\gamma \leftrightarrow \mathsf{Bew}_{\mathsf{E}^*}(\overline{\gamma})$	assumption
(12.2)	$\mathsf{Bew}_{\mathsf{E}^*}(\overline{\neg\gamma}) \leftrightarrow \mathsf{Bew}_{\mathsf{E}^*}\big(\overline{\mathsf{Bew}_{\mathsf{E}^*}(\overline{\gamma})}\big)$	NEC* and K*
(12.3)	$\mathsf{Bew}_{\mathsf{E}^*}(\overline{\gamma}) \to \mathsf{Bew}_{\mathsf{E}^*}\big(\overline{\mathsf{Bew}_{\mathsf{E}^*}(\overline{\gamma})}\big)$	4*
(12.4)	$\neg\gamma \to \mathsf{Bew}_{\mathsf{E}^*}(\overline{\gamma}) \wedge \mathsf{Bew}_{\mathsf{E}^*}(\overline{\neg\gamma})$	(12.2) and (12.3)
	$\gamma \wedge \neg\gamma \to \delta$	taut.
	$\mathsf{Bew}_{\mathsf{E}^*}(\overline{\gamma}) \wedge \mathsf{Bew}_{\mathsf{E}^*}(\overline{\neg\gamma}) \to \mathsf{Bew}_{\mathsf{E}^*}(\overline{\delta})$	NEC* and K*
	$\neg\gamma \to \mathsf{Bew}_{\mathsf{E}^*}(\overline{\delta})$	(12.4)
	$\neg\gamma \to \neg\delta$	assumption
(12.5)	$\delta \to \gamma$	⊣

It is clear that we have used very specific assumptions about the canonical unprovability predicate, which allowed us to establish the provable equivalence of all diagonal sentences. Other formulæ have diagonal sentences that are not all equivalent. The point of partial truth predicates is that all sentences in the range of application are diagonal sentences. Consider a trivial quantifier-free tautology such as $\overline{\neg}=\overline{\neg}$ and a contradiction $\neg\overline{\neg}=\overline{\neg}$. Both are diagonal sentences of Σ_1-truth, that is, we have by theorem 11.14:

$$\mathsf{E}^* \vdash \overline{\neg}=\overline{\neg} \leftrightarrow \mathsf{Tr}_{\Sigma_1}(\overline{\overline{\neg}=\overline{\neg}}), \tag{12.6}$$

$$\mathsf{E}^* \vdash \neg\overline{\neg}=\overline{\neg} \leftrightarrow \mathsf{Tr}_{\Sigma_1}(\overline{\neg\overline{\neg}=\overline{\neg}}). \tag{12.7}$$

Now, does proposition 12.2 show that all diagonal sentences of the negated canonical provability predicate state their own unprovability? As mentioned above, the outlined argument is erroneous. The problem with it is the assumption that, if γ is self-referential, then all sentences provably equivalent to γ are also self-referential. There is no justification for this assumption. If it is applied to properties different from unprovability, it is clearly false. By Löb's theorem, all diagonal sentences of the canonical provability $\mathsf{Bew}_{\mathsf{E}^*}(x)$ are provably equivalent, because the diagonal sentences are exactly the provable sentences (cf. theorem 10.77 and corollary 6.12). The canonical diagonal sentence of $\mathsf{Bew}_{\mathsf{E}^*}(x)$, obtained in the style of lemma 5.10, is presumably self-referential. But it is provably equivalent to $\overline{\neg}=\overline{\neg}$ because both sentences are provable, and the latter is clearly not self-referential.

Generally, we have to reject the claim that if a sentence γ is self-referential, then all sentences provably equivalent to it are also self-referential. In fact, this is trivial: the diagonal sentences of the formula $\mathsf{x}=\mathsf{x}$ above are exactly the provable sentences, just as for the canonical provability predicate; and, just as in the case of the canonical provability predicate, while $\mathsf{x}=\mathsf{x}$ does have self-referential diagonal sentences, it also has many that fail to be self-referential.

Of course, there is a difference between the diagonal sentences of $\mathsf{x} = \mathsf{x}$ or $\mathsf{Bew}_{\mathsf{E}^*}(\mathsf{x})$ on the one hand, and those of $\neg\mathsf{Bew}_{\mathsf{E}^*}(\mathsf{x})$ on the other: the diagonal sentences of the former are all provable, while those of $\neg\mathsf{Bew}_{\mathsf{E}^*}(\mathsf{x})$ are independent, as long as E^* is ω-consistent. But this difference cannot justify the assumption that all diagonal sentences of $\neg\mathsf{Bew}_{\mathsf{E}^*}(\mathsf{x})$ are self-referential; they are just harder to come by.

At any rate, we cannot see a good argument for the claim that a sentence γ ascribes to itself the property P just because γ is a diagonal sentence of a formula $\varphi(\mathsf{x})$ expressing the property P. This applies also to cases where all diagonal sentences of $\varphi(\mathsf{x})$ are provably equivalent.

The diagonal property, however, is still important, because it is precisely defined – in contrast to the nebulous property of self-reference. It permits stating and proving robust results in the way pointwise expressibility allows us to prove robust general results about provability. Directly proving something about all sentences that ascribe to themselves the property P via $\varphi(\mathsf{x})$ is difficult, because we do not have a mathematically precise characterization of these sentences. But if we prove something about all diagonal sentences of $\varphi(\mathsf{x})$ then that is a precise claim; and we have thereby proved it also for all sentences ascribing to themselves the property P, because being a diagonal sentence of $\varphi(\mathsf{x})$ is a necessary condition for ascribing the property P to oneself.

The diagonal property can be used to distinguish between intensional and extensional results with respect to self-reference, as already mentioned on page 362: a result is extensional with respect to self-reference iff it holds for all diagonal sentences. We have proved various results by using the canonical diagonal construction, but in many cases it does not matter how the diagonal sentence is obtained.

There are some results that are obviously extensional with respect to self-reference. For instance, as a variant of the liar paradox we may prove that, in a consistent theory, we cannot have the T-sentence for the sentence that states its own untruth. Of course, we can prove this for all diagonal sentences of $\neg\Box\mathsf{x}$.

If provability is expressed by the canonical provability predicate, many results become extensional with respect to self-reference. The canonical diagonal sentence of $\neg\mathsf{Bew}_{\mathsf{E}^*}(\mathsf{x})$, which could be called *the* Gödel sentence, is not provable, assuming that the theory is ω-consistent. This result is extensional; by proposition 12.2, it holds for all diagonal sentences of unprovability.

Löb's solution to Henkin's problem shows that the following result is also extensional with respect to self-reference:

12.3 PROPOSITION *The canonical diagonal sentence of* $\mathsf{Bew}_{\mathsf{E}^*}(\mathsf{x})$ *is provable in* E^*.

By Löb's theorem, proposition 12.3 holds for all diagonal sentences, not only the canonical ones. Thus it is extensional with respect to self-reference, even though it is intensional with respect to the expression of provability, as it fails, for instance, for Rosser provability.

The extensionality of Löb's theorem and, of results generally, about the canonical provability predicate more generally open the way to an elegant analysis of provability in modal logic (see, e.g., Boolos 1993 or Verbrugge 2017). Without extensionality with respect to self-reference this would not be possible in the same way.

Moreover, this kind of extensionality allowed logicians to largely dispense with the cumbersome notion of self-reference in the study of provability and to replace it with the notion of a diagonal sentence (see Smoryński 1991). However, although we may be able to kick away self-reference as the ladder that led us to Löb's theorem in the study of canonical provability, we cannot do so for other modal predicates. It is often not much appreciated that extensionality with respect to self-reference is very specific to the canonical provability predicate. We will now look at predicates and results that are intensional with respect to self-reference.

12.4 Henkin Sentences and Intensionality

In this and the next section, we look at some examples of intensionality from self-reference. Since obtaining self-reference is the last step in the construction of a Henkin, truth teller, or Gödel sentence, after coding (in the case of arithmetic) and expression of a property through a formula, all three potential sources of intensionality come into play for such sentences. Thus, in the case of provability our examples need to be constructed from a non-canonical provability predicate, because results based on the canonical provability predicate are extensional with respect to self-reference, as explained in the last section.

Historically, the intricacies of self-reference emerged with Henkin's problem. Formulating the problem is not completely straightforward. Roughly speaking, the problem is about the status of Henkin sentences, that is, commonly described as sentences stating their own provability; but so far we do not have a precise definition of what a Henkin sentence is. Henkin (1952) and Kreisel (1953) did not just arbitrarily fix a provability predicate and a diagonal sentence of the predicate, but rather specified conditions on the provability predicate and on the diagonal sentence built from it. Here we do not attempt to outline the historical development, and refer the reader to (Halbach and Visser 2014a) and (Halbach and Visser 2014c). We merely report some results from this paper.

With respect to the provability predicate, we require that the formula pointwise express provability.[10]

The condition of self-reference is more intricate. We consider only self-reference via a closed term, not via quantification. A formula $\varphi(t)$ is self-referential with respect to (the property expressed by) $\varphi(x)$ if t refers to φ.[11] This formulation uses the semantic notion of reference, which could be explained with the semantics for the language $\mathcal{L}^*$ outlined in section 9.1. Halbach and Visser (2014a) call this the 'Kreisel–Henkin criterion for self-reference.' In our setting and in arithmetic we can avoid the appeal to semantics, because we have a canonical term $\overline{\varphi}$ for every sentence φ. It seems this is the usual way to apply the Kreisel–Henkin criterion:

PROOF-THEORETIC KREISEL–HENKIN CRITERION *Assume that the formula $\varphi(x)$ with only x free expresses the property P and t is a closed term. Then the sentence $\varphi(t)$* says of itself (via t) that it has property P *iff* $\mathsf{E}^* \vdash t = \overline{\varphi(t)}$.

The relativization to a closed term t is required, because $\varphi(t)$ could be self-referential through another closed term or through quantification. Usually we suppress the reference to the specific term.

Theorem 10.6 shows that $t = \overline{\varphi(t)}$ is decidable in E^*. In particular, $t = \overline{\varphi(t)}$ is provable whenever it is true; and it is refutable whenever it is false. Therefore,

[10] As far as we know, Kreisel (1953) was the first to formulate the condition of (weak) representability in arithmetic, which is the arithmetical counterpart of our notion of pointwise expressibility.

[11] This kind of self-reference has been studied by Picollo (2018), who considered the general notion of reference via a closed term in arithmetic, calling it *m-reference* for 'reference by mention'.

it does not make a difference whether we say '$\mathsf{E}^* \vdash t = \overline{\varphi(t)}$' or 'The value of t is $\varphi(t)$' in the formulation of the Kreisel–Henkin criterion. For other languages and theories this need not be the case, because the theory may not prove the relevant true identities.

As mentioned above, the Kreisel–Henkin criterion is at best a sufficient criterion for self-reference. The language of set theory usually does not feature any closed terms and, hence, the Kreisel–Henkin criterion is not applicable. However, we would still say that there is self-reference in such languages; but it has to be established by quantification, not closed terms. Also in $\mathcal{L}^*$there are ways to obtain apparently self-referential statements via quantification instead of closed terms. Explicating self-reference by quantification is not straightforward. We will not deal with it here and refer the reader to (Picollo 2018).

Being a diagonal sentence is a necessary condition for being self-referential, while satisfying the Kreisel–Henkin criterion is a sufficient condition for self-reference via a closed term. If this is correct, then the former condition should be implied by the latter. This is the content of the following trivial observation:

12.4 PROPOSITION *If $\varphi(t)$ says of itself that it has property P (expressed by $\varphi(\mathsf{x})$) according to the proof-theoretic Kreisel–Henkin criterion, then $\varphi(t)$ is a diagonal sentence of $\varphi(\mathsf{x})$.*

PROOF By assumption we have $\mathsf{E}^* \vdash t = \overline{\varphi(t)}$. By the laws of identity this implies $\mathsf{E}^* \vdash \varphi(t) \leftrightarrow \varphi(\overline{\varphi(t)})$. ⊣

After discussing self-reference, we return to the main topic of this section, the construction of provable and refutable Henkin sentences. We have imposed two constraints on the construction of a Henkin sentence: First, provability predicates $\varphi(x)$ must pointwise express provability. Secondly, a Henkin sentence $\varphi(t)$ constructed from such a $\varphi(x)$ must say of itself that it is provable by the proof-theoretic Kreisel–Henkin criterion.

Within these constraints a refutable Henkin sentence can be produced. The following result is an adaption of a construction by Henkin mentioned in Kreisel's paper 1953:

12.5 PROPOSITION *There is a formula $\mathsf{Bew}'_{\mathsf{E}^*}(\mathsf{x})$ and a term t_1 with the following properties:*

(i) $\mathsf{Bew}'_{\mathsf{E}^*}(\mathsf{x})$ *pointwise expresses provability in* E^*,

(ii) $\mathsf{Bew}'_{\mathsf{E}^*}(t_1)$ *says about itself that it is provable in* E^**, according to the Kreisel–Henkin criterion, and*

(iii) $\mathsf{E}^* \vdash \neg\mathsf{Bew}'_{\mathsf{E}^*}(t_1)$.

Thus, we have a refutable Henkin sentence. The proof of the claim is surprising, because the Henkin sentence is *not* obtained by applying the diagonal lemma to the formula expressing provability.

PROOF The strong diagonal lemma is applied to the formula $\mathsf{x} \neq \mathsf{x} \wedge \mathsf{Bew}_{\mathsf{E}^*}(\mathsf{x})$, which yields a term t_1 with the following property:

(12.8) $$\mathsf{E}^* \vdash t_1 = \overline{t_1 \neq t_1 \wedge \mathsf{Bew}_{\mathsf{E}^*}(t_1)}.$$

Now we set

$$\mathsf{Bew}'_{\mathsf{E}^*}(\mathsf{x}) \equiv \mathsf{x} \neq t_1 \wedge \mathsf{Bew}_{\mathsf{E}^*}(\mathsf{x}).$$

We show that $\mathsf{Bew}'_{\mathsf{E}^*}(\mathsf{x})$ expresses E^*-provability pointwise. Because we can prove $\neg\mathsf{Bew}_{\mathsf{E}^*}(\overline{e})$ for all expressions e that are not formulæ, it suffices to establish the following equivalence for all formulæ:

(12.9) $$\mathsf{E}^* \vdash \varphi \quad \text{iff} \quad \mathsf{E}^* \vdash \mathsf{Bew}'_{\mathsf{E}^*}(\overline{\varphi}).$$

If φ is not the sentence $\mathsf{Bew}'_{\mathsf{E}^*}(t_1)$, then $\overline{\varphi} \neq t_1$ is provable and $\mathsf{Bew}'_{\mathsf{E}^*}(t_1)$ and $\mathsf{Bew}_{\mathsf{E}^*}(t_1)$ are provably equivalent, and thus (12.9) is satisfied for such φ, because the canonical provability predicate $\mathsf{Bew}_{\mathsf{E}^*}(\mathsf{x})$ expresses provability pointwise.

If φ *is* the sentence $\mathsf{Bew}'_{\mathsf{E}^*}(t_1)$, then, trivially,

$$\mathsf{E}^* \vdash \neg\big(t_1 \neq t_1 \wedge \mathsf{Bew}_{\mathsf{E}^*}(t_1)\big)$$

and

$$\mathsf{E}^* \vdash \neg\Big(\overline{\mathsf{Bew}'_{\mathsf{E}^*}(t_1)} \neq t_1 \wedge \mathsf{Bew}_{\mathsf{E}^*}\big(\overline{\mathsf{Bew}'_{\mathsf{E}^*}(t_1)}\big)\Big),$$

because in both formulæ the first conjunct is refutable. It follows that $\mathsf{Bew}'_{\mathsf{E}^*}(\mathsf{x})$ expresses provability pointwise also for $\mathsf{Bew}'_{\mathsf{E}^*}(t_1)$ as φ, assuming that E^* is consistent, as both sides of the equivalence hold:

(12.10) $$\mathsf{E}^* \vdash \neg\mathsf{Bew}'_{\mathsf{E}^*}(t_1)$$

and

$$\mathsf{E}^* \vdash \neg\mathsf{Bew}'_{\mathsf{E}^*}\big(\overline{\mathsf{Bew}'_{\mathsf{E}^*}(t_1)}\big).$$

Of course, if E^* is inconsistent, (12.9) is trivially satisfied, and thus (i) is established.

For (ii), we need to prove $t_1 = \overline{\mathsf{Bew}'_{\mathsf{E}^*}(t_1)}$ in E^*, which is just (12.8). It is important that we do *not* obtain the term t_1 by applying the strong diagonal lemma to $\mathsf{Bew}_{\mathsf{E}^*}(\mathsf{x})$. We comment on this below.

Claim (iii) has been proved above as (12.10). ⊣

Proposition 12.3 yields a provable and proposition 12.5 a refutable Henkin sentence. The two examples differ not only in the provability predicate, but also in the way the Henkin sentence is obtained from the respective provability predicate: in the provable Henkin sentence from proposition 12.3, provability is expressed in the canonical way and the diagonal sentence can be obtained canonically. In the refutable Henkin sentence in proposition 12.5, provability is expressed in a non-canonical way and the construction of the diagonal sentence is non-canonical, too. That is, to obtain a refutable Henkin sentence, two sources of intensionality are exploited in the proof above. Kreisel (1953) emphasized that the answer to Henkin's problem depends on how provability is expressed, but did not comment on the way self-reference is obtained.

We now ask whether we can improve on proposition 12.3 and use only one source of intensionality. We already know from Löb's theorem that we have to use a non-canonical provability predicate, because all diagonal sentences of the canonical provability predicate are provable.

(i) Can we obtain both a refutable and a provable Henkin sentence by varying only the way the Henkin sentence is obtained from a fixed provability predicate?

(ii) Can we obtain a refutable and a provable Henkin sentence by varying only the provability predicate, but using in both cases the canonical diagonal construction?

Proposition 12.5 and the lemma below provide a positive answer to the first question. In the following lemma we apply the canonical construction from the diagonal lemma to $\mathsf{Bew}'_{\mathsf{E}^*}(\mathsf{x})$ to obtain a provable Henkin sentence:

12.6 LEMMA *Let t_1 be the term from* (12.8). *Then for any term t_2 such that*

(i) $\mathsf{E}^* \vdash t_2 \neq t_1$ *and*

(ii) $\mathsf{E}^* \vdash t_2 = \overline{\mathsf{Bew}'_{\mathsf{E}^*}(t_2)}$,

we have $\mathsf{E}^* \vdash \mathsf{Bew}'_{\mathsf{E}^*}(t_2)$. *In particular, the sentence obtained from applying the strong diagonal lemma to* $\mathsf{Bew}'_{\mathsf{E}^*}(\mathsf{x})$ *is a provable Henkin sentence.*

PROOF We reason as follows:

$$
\begin{aligned}
\mathsf{E}^* \vdash \mathsf{Bew}'_{\mathsf{E}^*}(t_2) &\leftrightarrow t_2 \neq t_1 \wedge \mathsf{Bew}_{\mathsf{E}^*}(t_2) && \text{def. } \mathsf{Bew}'_{\mathsf{E}^*}(\mathsf{x})\\
&\leftrightarrow \mathsf{Bew}_{\mathsf{E}^*}(t_2) && \text{assumption (i)}\\
&\leftrightarrow \mathsf{Bew}_{\mathsf{E}^*}\big(\overline{\mathsf{Bew}'_{\mathsf{E}^*}(t_2)}\big) && \text{assumption (ii)}
\end{aligned}
$$

That is, $\mathsf{Bew}'_{\mathsf{E}^*}(t_2)$ is a diagonal sentence of the canonical provability predicate $\mathsf{Bew}_{\mathsf{E}^*}(\mathsf{x})$ and thus provable by Löb's theorem. It is easy to see that by applying the canonical diagonal construction to $\mathsf{Bew}'_{\mathsf{E}^*}(\mathsf{x})$ a term different from t_1 is obtained.⊣

Thus, we can obtain a provable and a refutable Henkin sentence from the same provability predicate, which answers question (i) above. For a positive answer to question (ii), we have to specify two provability predicates such that the canonical diagonal sentence of the one predicate is provable while that of the other is refutable. For the provable Henkin sentence, we can use the canonical provability predicate, of course. The provability predicate for the refutable Henkin sentence is constructed in the proof of the next proposition. The Henkin sentence resulting from this provability predicate shows that it was not necessary to use a non-canonical diagonal sentence for proving proposition 12.5. A generalization of the result was proved by Visser in (Halbach and Visser 2014a, theorem 5.1).

12.7 PROPOSITION *There is a formula* $\mathsf{Bew}^V_{\mathsf{E}^*}(\mathsf{x})$ *pointwise expressing* E^**-provability such that applying the usual construction for proving the strong diagonal lemma to* $\mathsf{Bew}^V_{\mathsf{E}^*}(\mathsf{x})$ *yields a refutable Henkin sentence.*

PROOF By the 'usual' construction we mean the construction in lemma 5.10 and the strong diagonalization lemma 5.11 that yields, applied to a formula $\varphi(\mathsf{x})$ without bound occurrences of x, a diagonal sentence. The function that yields, applied to $\varphi(\mathsf{x})$, this diagonal sentence can be defined in syntax theory in the following way:

$$
\mathsf{d}(y) := \mathsf{sub}\Big(y, \overline{\mathsf{x}}, \mathsf{sub}\big(\overline{\mathsf{dia}(\mathsf{x})}, \overline{\mathsf{x}}, \mathsf{q}\,\mathsf{sub}(y, \overline{\mathsf{x}}, \overline{\mathsf{dia}(\mathsf{x})})\big)\Big).
$$

With this definition, the following can be established for any $\varphi(\mathsf{x})$:

$$
\mathsf{E}^* \vdash \mathsf{d}\big(\overline{\varphi(\mathsf{x})}\big) = \overline{\varphi\big(\mathsf{dia}\big(\overline{\varphi(\mathsf{dia}(\mathsf{x}))}\big)\big)}. \tag{12.11}
$$

We are now ready to define the provability predicate $\mathsf{Bew}^V_{E^*}(x)$. It is obtained by taking a diagonal formula of the formula $y \neq d(x) \wedge \mathsf{Bew}_{E^*}(y)$ with respect to x. Here it does not matter in which way the diagonal formula is obtained: $\mathsf{Bew}_{E^*}(x)$ is the canonical provability predicate, but any formula expressing provability pointwise will suffice. The following claim is the diagonal property with the free variable y renamed as x:

$$(12.12)\qquad E^* \vdash \mathsf{Bew}^V_{E^*}(x) \leftrightarrow x \neq d(\overline{\mathsf{Bew}^V_{E^*}(x)}) \wedge \mathsf{Bew}_{E^*}(x).$$

Applying the standard diagonalization procedure to $\mathsf{Bew}^V_{E^*}(x)$ produces the diagonal sentence $\mathsf{Bew}^V_{E^*}(\mathrm{dia}(\overline{\mathsf{Bew}^V_{E^*}(\mathrm{dia}(x))}))$. This claim can be proved in E^* as an instance of (12.11):

$$(12.13)\qquad E^* \vdash d(\overline{\mathsf{Bew}^V_{E^*}(x)}) = \overline{\mathsf{Bew}^V_{E^*}(\mathrm{dia}(\overline{\mathsf{Bew}^V_{E^*}(\mathrm{dia}(x))}))}.$$

Abbreviating the diagonal sentence $\mathsf{Bew}^V_{E^*}(\mathrm{dia}(\overline{\mathsf{Bew}^V_{E^*}(\mathrm{dia}(x))}))$ as γ, we have:

$$\begin{aligned} E^* \vdash \gamma &\leftrightarrow \mathsf{Bew}^V_{E^*}(\overline{\gamma}) && \text{diagonal prop.}\\ &\leftrightarrow \overline{\gamma} \neq d(\overline{\mathsf{Bew}^V_{E^*}(x)}) \wedge \mathsf{Bew}_{E^*}(\overline{\gamma}) && (12.12)\\ &\leftrightarrow d(\overline{\mathsf{Bew}^V_{E^*}(x)}) \neq d(\overline{\mathsf{Bew}^V_{E^*}(x)}) && \text{def. } \gamma \text{ and } (12.13) \end{aligned}$$

Because the sentence in the last line is a contradiction, $E^* \vdash \neg\gamma$ has been established; and we have produced a refutable Henkin sentence by applying the usual construction to the predicate $\mathsf{Bew}^V_{E^*}(x)$.

We still need to show that $\mathsf{Bew}^V_{E^*}(x)$ expresses provability pointwise. By (12.12) it is sufficient to prove the following:

$$E^* \vdash \varphi \quad \text{iff} \quad E^* \vdash \overline{\varphi} \neq d(\overline{\mathsf{Bew}^V_{E^*}(x)}) \wedge \mathsf{Bew}_{E^*}(\overline{\varphi}).$$

This is trivial for all φ different from γ, because the canonical provability predicate expresses provability pointwise. For γ, the equivalence holds because both sides are refutable: we have already shown that γ is refutable, and the right-hand side is refutable because of (12.13). $\dashv$

12.5 Truth Tellers and Intensionality

As long as provability is expressed by the canonical predicate $\mathsf{Bew}_{E^*}(x)$, intensionality from self-reference can hardly arise. All diagonal sentences of the canonical provability predicate are provably equivalent, as are all diagonal sentences of its negation. Presumably, this is the reason why intensionality from self-reference has not played a significant rôle in the development of metamathematics.

Provability is special in this respect. Other notions are not as well-behaved. They may lack a canonical predicate expressing them; and even if they have one, diagonal sentences of these predicates may exhibit a very diverse behaviour.

In this section we look at the notion of truth for a restricted class of sentences. The T-schema should hold for many instances for a truth predicate. For disquotationalists, the truth predicate's diagonal sentences are its *raison d'être*. Of course, Tarski's theorem and the liar paradox impose limits on the permitted instances of the T-schema; but we have seen various ways to obtain truth predicates for comprehensive classes of sentences already.

In this section we focus on Σ_1-sentences as the relevant instances of the T-schema. In many ways they form an interesting class of sentences. Very roughly, it is obtained from the full language by removing the universal quantifier. It cannot be closed under negation, because otherwise we could define the universal quantifier. If a Σ_1-sentence is true, it is true in a finite submodel of $\mathbb{E}^*$ obtained from $\mathbb{E}^*$ by removing all expressions beyond a certain length. Once a Σ_1-sentence is true within such a submodel, it cannot become false by the addition of longer expressions. This is in contrast to Π_1-sentences, which may have arbitrarily large counterexamples. Very roughly, this is the reason why all true Σ_1-sentences are provable, as we showed in theorem 10.22. This is in contrast to Π_1 and all other sentence classes with universal quantifiers.

These properties of the class of Σ_1-sentences allow us to define or axiomatize the set of true Σ_1-sentences in our formal language, which makes it interesting as a case study for intensionality arising from different ways to express Σ_1-truth. We will look at the analogues of Henkin sentences for truth instead of provability. These sentences are of course truth tellers, that is, sentences which say about themselves that they are true.

We focus mainly on the language of syntax $\mathcal{L}^*_{\text{syn}}$, which does not contain any optional vocabulary or $\Box$ except for syntactic constants, and the minimal theory $\mathsf{E}^*_{\text{min}}$. If we admit arbitrary additional vocabulary, some of the mentioned properties of Σ_1-sentences can get lost (see section 10.1). For instance, if we admitted an additional predicate symbol without any specific axioms for it, Σ_1-completeness would be lost. We would even lack a notion of truth for such sentences unless a specific interpretation for this predicate is specified. We also exclude all optional axioms for E^*, because E^* may be unsound or even inconsistent, which would block or complicate certain moves below. For $\mathcal{L}^*_{\text{syn}}$ we have the standard model $\mathbb{E}^*$ which interprets the vocabulary in the intended sense. However, we will consider a specific expansion of $\mathcal{L}^*_{\text{syn}}$ by the unary predicate $\Box$, axiomatized by the theory CT of typed compositional truth, as in definition 11.38.

We consider three different ways to express the property of being a true Σ_1-sentence of $\mathcal{L}^*_{\text{syn}}$. We care only how these predicates behave on Σ_1-sentences of $\mathcal{L}^*_{\text{syn}}$, but not on more complex sentences. In a sense to be explained, the following three formulæ all express Σ_1:

(i) the partial truth predicate $\mathsf{Tr}_{\Sigma_1}(x)$ as defined in definition 11.11,

(ii) the canonical provability predicate $\mathsf{Bew}_{\mathsf{E}^*_{\min}}(x)$,

(iii) the truth predicate $\Box x$ of CT.

We will look at truth tellers generated from these three formulæ, which all behave in different ways. We do not know whether one of them deserves the label 'canonical'. None of the predicates resembles the metatheoretic definition of Σ_1-truth, which is provably the truth of a Σ_1-sentence in the standard model. However, none of the three truth predicates is as contrived as the provability predicate $\mathsf{Bew}'_{\mathsf{E}^*}(x)$ which was used to obtain a refutable Henkin sentence.

The notion of being a Σ_1-sentence of $\mathcal{L}^*_{\text{syn}}$ is expressible in $\mathcal{L}^*_{\text{syn}}$. In section 11.1 we hinted at the definition of a formula $\mathsf{Sent}_{\Sigma_1}(x)$ expressing that x is a Σ_1-sentence, and that of a formula $\mathsf{Sent}_{\text{syn}}(x)$ expressing that x is a sentence of $\mathcal{L}^*_{\text{syn}}$.[12] Then $\mathsf{Sent}_{\Sigma_1}(x) \wedge \mathsf{Sent}_{\text{syn}}(x)$ picks out exactly the sentences we are interested in, namely the Σ_1-sentences of $\mathcal{L}^*_{\text{syn}}$.

On the set of sentences we are interested in, that is, the set of Σ_1-sentences of $\mathcal{L}^*_{\text{syn}}$, all three formulæ provably coincide:

12.8 PROPOSITION

$$\mathsf{CT} \vdash \forall x\Big(\mathsf{Sent}_{\Sigma_1}(x) \wedge \mathsf{Sent}_{\text{syn}}(x) \to \big(\mathsf{Tr}_{\Sigma_1}(x) \leftrightarrow \mathsf{Bew}_{\mathsf{E}^*_{\min}}(x)\big)\Big),$$

$$\mathsf{CT} \vdash \forall x\Big(\mathsf{Sent}_{\Sigma_1}(x) \wedge \mathsf{Sent}_{\text{syn}}(x) \to \big(\Box x \leftrightarrow \mathsf{Bew}_{\mathsf{E}^*_{\min}}(x)\big)\Big).$$

[12] Of course, there are different ways to define these formulæ, which gives rise to more intensionality phenomena. Here we stick to two formulæ that have the expected properties, and do not open another can of worms by considering variations of these formulæ.

On the set of sentences that are not Σ_1-sentences, the three predicates behave differently, of course. In order to make them coincide on all objects, we could obviously replace

$$\mathsf{Bew}_{\mathsf{E}^*_{\min}}(x) \quad \text{with} \quad \mathsf{Bew}_{\mathsf{E}^*_{\min}}(x) \wedge \mathsf{Sent}_{\Sigma_1}(x) \wedge \mathsf{Sent}_{\mathrm{syn}}(x) \tag{12.14}$$

and

$$\Box x \quad \text{with} \quad \Box x \wedge \mathsf{Sent}_{\Sigma_1}(x) \wedge \mathsf{Sent}_{\mathrm{syn}}(x). \tag{12.15}$$

We do not add these conjuncts, which would generate predicates that provably apply only to Σ_1-sentences of $\mathcal{L}^*_{\mathrm{syn}}$. However, much of what we say below holds of these variants, too.

For $\mathsf{Tr}_{\Sigma_1}(x)$ a restriction is superfluous, as it is already built into the definition. In proposition 11.12 we showed

$$\forall x\big(\mathsf{Tr}_{\Sigma_1}(x) \rightarrow \mathsf{Sent}_{\Sigma_1}(x)\big). \tag{12.16}$$

We now turn to the proof of the proposition above:

PROOF Theorem 11.16 gives the left-to-right direction of the equivalence in the first line:

$$\mathsf{CT} \vdash \forall x\Big(\mathsf{Sent}_{\Sigma_1}(x) \wedge \mathsf{Sent}_{\mathrm{syn}}(x) \rightarrow \big(\mathsf{Tr}_{\Sigma_1}(x) \rightarrow \mathsf{Bew}_{\mathsf{E}^*_{\min}}(x)\big)\Big).$$

The second line is corollary 11.48. In the proof of that corollary we also mentioned

$$\mathsf{CT} \vdash \forall \alpha\big(\mathsf{Sent}_{\Sigma_1}(\alpha) \wedge \Box\alpha \rightarrow \mathsf{Tr}_{\Sigma_1}(\alpha)\big),$$

which yields the missing direction of the first line. ⊣

Why should the three formulæ count as truth predicates for Σ_1-sentences of the language $\mathcal{L}^*_{\mathrm{syn}}$? Using the above proposition, we can show that all three formulæ pointwise express the property of being a true Σ_1-sentence of the language $\mathcal{L}^*_{\mathrm{syn}}$, if only Σ_1-sentences of $\mathcal{L}^*_{\mathrm{syn}}$ are considered. That is, for each of the three formulæ as $\tau(x)$, the following equivalence holds for all Σ_1-sentences φ of $\mathcal{L}^*_{\mathrm{syn}}$:

$$\mathbb{E}^* \models \varphi \quad \text{iff} \quad \mathsf{E}^*_{\min} \vdash \tau(\overline{\varphi}). \tag{12.17}$$

The claim for the canonical provability predicate follows from theorem 10.22, lemma 10.60, and the soundness of $\mathsf{E}^*_{\min}$. The preceding proposition implies that the claim holds also for the two other formulæ.

If we used the restricted variants (12.14) and (12.15) above, this would hold for all expressions of $\mathcal{L}^*_{\mathrm{syn}}$ and these variants would express Σ_1-truth pointwise.

Applied to truth predicates in general, pointwise expressibility does not seem to provide a sufficient or necessary condition for expressing truth restricted to some not trivially small class of sentences. It is not sufficient, because the truth predicate does not have to satisfy the T-schema for the sentences in this class, nor does it have to satisfy the compositional axioms for truth, which one might expect to hold if $\tau(x)$ is a truth predicate. Pointwise expressibility is also not a necessary condition for being a truth predicate, if $\mathsf{Tr}_{\Pi_1}(x)$ is a truth predicate for Π_1-sentences, because (12.17) fails for Π_1-sentences and $\mathsf{Tr}_{\Pi_1}(x)$ as $\tau(x)$.

Thus we need some additional evidence for the claim that all three formulæ are reasonable truth predicates for Σ_1-sentences. The meaning postulate approach seem better suited than pointwise expression. All three formulæ are truth predicates in the sense of the meaning postulate condition. In theorem 11.14 we showed that the schema for $\mathsf{Tr}_{\Sigma_1}(x)$ is provable for all Σ_1-sentences φ:

$$\text{(12.18)} \qquad \mathsf{E}^*_{\mathrm{min}} \vdash \mathsf{Tr}_{\Sigma_1}(\overline{\varphi}) \leftrightarrow \varphi.$$

The compositional principles for truth, restricted to Σ_1-sentences of $\mathcal{L}^*_{\mathrm{syn}}$, are also provable in $\mathsf{E}^*_{\mathrm{min}}$, as was shown in proposition 11.12. The theory ET on page 328 is based on this truth predicate $\mathsf{Tr}_{\Sigma_1}(x)$. By proposition 12.8, also $\mathsf{Bew}_{\mathsf{E}^*_{\mathrm{min}}}(x)$ and $\Box x$ satisfy these meaning postulates in CT. In this sense all three are well-behaved truth predicates for Σ_1-sentences of $\mathcal{L}^*_{\mathrm{min}}$.

In order to obtain truth tellers, we need to construct self-referential sentences that ascribe to themselves the property of being true Σ_1-sentences of the language $\mathsf{E}^*_{\mathrm{min}}$. All Σ_1-sentences of $\mathcal{L}^*_{\mathrm{syn}}$ are diagonal sentences of the three truth predicates. Clearly, not all qualify as self-referential, as was shown with the examples (12.6) and (12.7).

12.9 PROPOSITION

(i) $\mathsf{CT} \vdash \neg\gamma_1$, *if* γ_1 *is the canonical diagonal sentence of* $\mathsf{Tr}_{\Sigma_1}(\mathsf{x})$.

(ii) $\mathsf{CT} \vdash \gamma_2$, *if* γ_2 *is a diagonal sentence of* $\mathsf{Bew}_{\mathsf{E}^*_{\mathrm{min}}}(\mathsf{x})$.

(iii) *The canonical diagonal sentence of* $\Box\mathsf{x}$ *is independent of* CT.

Therefore, we have a refutable, a provable, and an independent Σ_1–truth teller sentence, all obtained by the canonical diagonal construction.

PROOF Claim (i) is theorem 11.31. Claim (ii) follows from Löb's theorem. For (iii) we observe that CT does not decide the truth of any sentence of the form $\Box t$. This can be shown by an easy model construction. The canonical diagonal sentence of $\Box$x is of this form, of course. ⊣

The claim (ii) holds also if $\mathsf{Bew}_{\mathsf{E}^*_{\mathrm{min}}}(x)$ is replaced with its variant $\mathsf{Bew}_{\mathsf{E}^*_{\mathrm{min}}}(x) \wedge \mathsf{Sent}_{\Sigma_1}(x) \wedge \mathsf{Sent}_{\mathrm{syn}}(x)$, while (iii) fails if $\Box x$ is replaced with $\Box x \wedge \mathsf{Sent}_{\Sigma_1}(x) \wedge \mathsf{Sent}_{\mathrm{syn}}(x)$: sentences containing $\Box$ are then refutable. Generally, $\Box$x does not yield interesting truth tellers, because it is a typed truth predicate, and diagonalizing $\Box$x leads one outside the range of application of that truth predicate. The truth tellers in (i) and (ii) fall in the range of application of the respective predicates.

12.6 Uniqueness

The examples in this chapter show that it is not straightforward to generalize results. There is no simple general criterion that can be used to determine whether a formula expresses a certain property or relation or whether a sentence expresses a certain claim. For different properties, various necessary conditions can be used to prove generalizations, but that does not bring us closer to a general criterion.

In the literature, the problems of intensionality in metamathematics have been discussed in detail for provability. But provability is a serendipitous case. If we assume that provability satisfies Löb's conditions, as the canonical provability predicate does, diagonal sentences behave uniformly and many intensionality phenomena are blocked. All diagonal sentences of the provability predicate are provable and thus provably equivalent. Also, all diagonal sentences of the *negation* of the provability predicate are provably equivalent. Talking about *the* Henkin sentence and *the* Gödel sentence is thus unlikely to cause problems. But logicians like Henkin and Kreisel certainly did not expect provability to be so well-behaved. Löb's theorem came as a lucky surprise.

Properties other than provability are less tame. In the previous section, we considered three different ways to express Σ_1-truth. All three formulæ are well-behaved in provably satisfying all the usual postulates one might expect from a formula expressing Σ_1-truth. The three formulæ are CT-provably equivalent. Thus, one might assume that if one of them correctly expresses Σ_1-truth then all of them do. Yet, if we ask Henkin's question for Σ_1-truth, that is, if we construct sentences ascribing to themselves the property of being Σ_1-true via the three respective formulæ, we obtain refutable, provable, and independent truth teller sentences. Therefore, if we ask about the status of self-referential sentences in general, we cannot even assume that provably equivalent formulæ yield the same result with the canonical diagonal construction.

Self-reference remains elusive. As mentioned, the talk about self-reference in Gödel, Henkin, and truth teller sentences may be only metaphorical. In this chapter we have often treated the canonical diagonalization method introduced in chapter 5 as the gold standard of self-reference in our syntax theory. However, we lack an argument why diagonal sentences obtained with this method should be in any way 'more self-referential' than other diagonal sentences satisfying the Kreisel–Henkin criterion for self-reference. After all, the usual diagonalization method was introduced by Gödel as a trick to mimic self-reference in natural languages without devices such as indexicals or demonstratives. To claim retrospectively that Gödel's method is a preferred method for obtaining self-reference puts that methodology on its head. This is not to say that self-reference via Gödel's diagonal method produces a sentence that is not 'as self-referential' as simpler constructions in natural language with indexicals or the like. We just doubt that any of the methods of obtaining a sentence that is self-referential in the Kreisel–Henkin sense is superior to others; they all yield equally self-referential sentences.

The observations in this chapter raise doubts about the characterization of a specific sentence as *the* Σ_1–truth teller sentence of $\mathsf{E}^*_{\mathrm{min}}$. There is no unique such sentence. Similarly, there are provable and refutable sentences which, by proposition 12.5 and lemma 12.6, say about themselves that they are provable in the sense of $\mathsf{Bew}'_{\mathsf{E}^*}(\mathsf{x})$.

Thus, once one looks beyond the canonical provability predicate, many results are less stable than one might think. We should abandon the expectation that there are definite answers to questions such as whether the truth teller sentence is true, or whether the liar sentence lacks a truth value, and so on. There is more than one such sentence. To find answers to these questions, and solutions to the paradoxes, we may have to ask more precise questions.

Bibliography

Arai, Toshiyasu (1990), 'Derivability conditions on Rosser's provability predicates', *Notre Dame Journal of Formal Logic* 31(4), 487–497

Asher, Nicholas and Hans Kamp (1989), 'Self-reference, attitudes, and paradox', *in* G. Chierchia, B. H. Partee, and R. Turner, eds, *Properties, Types and Meaning*, vol. 1, Dordrecht, Kluwer, pp. 85–158

Barrett, Thomas William and Hans Halvorson (2017), 'Quine's conjecture on many-sorted logic', *Synthese* 194, 3563–3582

Bealer, George (1982), *Quality and Concept*, Clarendon Press

– (1993), 'Universals', *Journal of Philosophy* 90, 5–32

Beall, JC, Michael Glanzberg, and David Ripley (2018), *Formal Theories of Truth*, Oxford University Press

– (2020), 'Liar paradox', *in* E. N. Zalta, ed, *The Stanford Encyclopedia of Philosophy*, fall 2020 edition, Metaphysics Research Lab, Stanford University

Belnap, Nuel and Anil Gupta (1993), *The Revision Theory of Truth*, Cambridge, Massachusetts, MIT Press

Blau, Ulrich (2008), *Die Logik der Unbestimmtheiten und Paradoxien*, Heidelberg, Synchron

Boolos, George S. (1993), *The Logic of Provability*, Cambridge University Press

Boolos, George S., John P. Burgess, and Richard C. Jeffrey (2007), *Computability and Logic*, fifth edition, Cambridge, Cambridge University Press

Bull, R. A. (1969), 'On modal logic with propositional quantifiers', *Journal of Symbolic Logic* 34, 257–263

Cantini, Andrea (1996), *Logical Frameworks for Truth and Abstraction: An Axiomatic Study*, Studies in Logic and the Foundations of Mathematics 135, Amsterdam et al., Elsevier

Cappelen, Herman and Ernest Lepore (2007), *Language Turned on Itself: The Semantics and Pragmatics of Metalinguistic Discourse*, Oxford University Press

Carnap, Rudolf (1934), *Logische Syntax der Sprache*, Wien, Springer

Chagrov, Alexander and Michael Zakharyaschev (1997), *Modal Logic*, Oxford Logic Guides, Oxford University Press

Chellas, Brian F. (1980), *Modal Logic: An Introduction*, Cambridge, Massachusetts, Cambridge University Press

Chisholm, Roderick M. (1957), *Perceiving*, London, Routledge & Kegan Paul

Church, Alonzo (1950), 'On Carnap's analysis of statements of assertion and belief', *Analysis* 10, 97–99

Cieśliński, Cezary (2017), *The Epistemic Lightness of Truth: Deflationism and its Logic*, Cambridge University Press

– (2021), 'Interpreting the compositional truth predicate in models of arithmetic', *Archive for Mathematical Logic* 60(6), 749–770

Cook, Roy (2014), *The Yablo Paradox: An Essay on Circularity*, Oxford University Press

Copeland, B. Jack (2002), 'The genesis of possible worlds semantics', *Journal of Philosophical Logic* 31, 99–137

Corcoran, John, William Frank, and Michael Maloney (1974), 'String theory', *Journal of Symbolic Logic* 39(4), 625–37

Craig, William (1953), 'On axiomatizability within a system', *Journal of Symbolic Logic* 18(1), 30–32

Curry, Haskell B. (1942), 'The inconsistency of certain formal logics', *Journal of Symbolic Logic* 7, 115–117

Ehrenfeucht, Andrzej and Solomon Feferman (1960), 'Representability of recursively enumerable sets in formal theories', *Archiv für Mathematische Logik und Grundlagenforschung* 5, 37–41

Enayat, Ali and Albert Visser (2015), 'New constructions of satisfaction classes', *in* T. Achourioti, H. Galinon, K. Fujimoto, and J. Martinez-Fernandez, eds, *Unifying the Philosophy of Truth*, Springer, pp. 321–335

Feferman, Solomon (1960), 'Arithmetization of metamathematics in a general setting', *Fundamenta Mathematicae* 49, 35–91

– (1991), 'Reflecting on incompleteness', *Journal of Symbolic Logic* 56, 1–49

Felappi, Giulia (2014), 'In defence of sententialism', *Dialectica* 68, 581–603

Field, Hartry (1994), 'Disquotational truth and factually defective discourse', *The Philosophical Review* 103, 405–452

– (2008), *Saving Truth from Paradox*, Oxford University Press

Fine, Kit (1970), 'Propositional quantifiers in modal logic', *Theoria* 36, 336–346

– (1980), 'First-order modal theories', *Studia Logica* 39, 159–202

Frege, Gottlob (1893), *Grundgesetze der Arithmetik*, vol. I, Verlag Hermann Pohle

Friedman, Harvey and Michael Sheard (1987), 'An axiomatic approach to self-referential truth', *Annals of Pure and Applied Logic* 33, 1–21

Fujimoto, Kentaro (2012), 'Classes and truths in set theory', *Annals of Pure and Applied Logic* 163, 1484–1523

Gödel, Kurt (1931), 'Über formal unentscheidbare Sätze der Principia Mathematica und verwandter Systeme I', *Monatshefte für Mathematik* 38, 173–198

Goodman, Nelson and Willard Van Orman Quine (1947), 'Steps toward a constructive nominalism', *Journal of Symbolic Logic* 12, 105–122

Grabmayr, Balthasar and Albert Visser (2021), 'Self-reference upfront: A study of self-referential Gödel numberings', *Review of Symbolic Logic*, 1–40

Grzegorczyk, Andrzej (2005), 'Undecidability without arithmetization', *Studia Logica* 79, 305–313

Guaspari, David and Robert M. Solovay (1979), 'Rosser sentences', *Annals of Mathematical Logic* 16(1), 81–99

Halbach, Volker (1995), 'Tarski-hierarchies', *Erkenntnis* 43, 339–367

– (2001), 'How innocent is deflationism?', *Synthese* 126, 167–194

– (2006), 'How not to state the T-sentences', *Analysis* 66, 276–280, correction of printing error in vol. 67, 268

– (2008), 'On a side effect of solving Fitch's paradox by typing knowledge', *Analysis* 68, 114–120

– (2010), *The Logic Manual*, Oxford University Press

– (2014), *Axiomatic Theories of Truth*, revised edition (first edition 2011), Cambridge, Cambridge University Press

Halbach, Volker (2016), 'The root of evil: A self-referential play in one act', *in* J. van Eijck, R. Iemhoff, and J. J. Joosten, eds, *Liber Amicorum Alberti: A Tribute to Albert Visser*, London, College Publications, pp. 155–163

– (2021), 'The fourth grade of modal involvement', *in* C. Nicolai and J. Stern, eds, *Modes of Truth: The Unified Approach to Modality, Truth, and Paradox*, New York, Routledge, pp. 331–356

Halbach, Volker and Leon Horsten (2006), 'Axiomatizing Kripke's theory of truth', *Journal of Symbolic Logic* 71, 677–712

Halbach, Volker, Hannes Leitgeb, and Philip Welch (2003), 'Possible-worlds semantics for modal notions conceived as predicates', *Journal of Philosophical Logic* 32, 179–223

Halbach, Volker and Carlo Nicolai (2018), 'On the costs of nonclassical logic', *Journal of Philosophical Logic* 47, 227–257

Halbach, Volker and Holger Sturm (2004), 'Bealers Masterargument: Ein Lehrstück zum Verhältnis von Metaphysik und Semantik', *Facta Philosophica* 6, 97–110

Halbach, Volker and Albert Visser (2014a), 'Self-reference in arithmetic I', *Review of Symbolic Logic* 7, 671–691

– (2014b), 'Self-reference in arithmetic II', *Review of Symbolic Logic* 7, 692–712

– (2014c), 'The Henkin sentence', *in* M. Manzano, I. Sain, and E. Alonso, eds, *The Life and Work of Leon Henkin*, Studies in Universal Logic, Basel, Birkhäuser, pp. 249–264

Halbach, Volker and Philip Welch (2009), 'Necessities and necessary truths: A prolegomenon to the metaphysics of modality', *Mind* 118, 71–100

Halbach, Volker and Shuoying Zhang (2016), 'Yablo without Gödel', *Analysis* 76, 53–59

Hamilton, A. G. (1988), *Logic for Mathematicians*, revised edition, Cambridge University Press

Heck Jr, R. K. (2007), 'Self-reference and the languages of arithmetic', *Philosophia Mathematica* 15(1), 1–29, originally published under the name "Richard G. Heck, Jr"

Henkin, Leon (1952), 'A problem concerning provability', *Journal of Symbolic Logic* 17, 160

Herzberger, Hans G. (1982), 'Notes on naive semantics', *Journal of Philosophical Logic* 11, 61–102

Hilbert, David and Paul Bernays (1939), *Grundlagen der Mathematik*, vol. II, Berlin, Springer

Horsten, Leon (2011), *The Tarskian Turn: Deflationism and Axiomatic Truth*, Cambridge, Massachusetts, MIT Press

Horsten, Leon and Hannes Leitgeb (2001), 'No future', *Journal of Philosophical Logic* 30, 259–265

Horwich, Paul (1998), *Truth*, second edition, Oxford University Press, first edition 1990

Hsiung, Ming (2021), 'Unwinding modal paradoxes on digraphs', *Journal of Philosophical Logic* 50, 319–362

Hughes, George E. and Max J. Cresswell (1996), *A New Introduction to Modal Logic*, London and New York, Routledge

Jeroslow, Robert (1973), 'Redundancies in the Hilbert–Bernays derivability conditions for Gödel's second incompleteness theorem', *Journal of Symbolic Logic* 38, 359–367

Kaplan, David (1970), 'S5 with quantifiable propositional variables', *Journal of Symbolic Logic* 35, abstract, 355

Kaye, Richard (1991), *Models of Peano Arithmetic*, Oxford Logic Guides, Oxford University Press

Ketland, Jeffrey (2005), 'Deflationism and Gödel phenomena – reply to Tennant', *Mind* 114, 75–88

Kleene, Stephen (1952), 'Finite axiomatizability of theories in the predicate calculus using additional predicate symbols', *in Memoirs of the American Mathematical Society no. 10*, Providence, Rhode Island, American Mathematical Society, pp. 27–68

Knaster, Bronisław (1928), 'Un théorème sur les fonctions d'ensembles', *Annales de la Société Polonaise de Mathématique* 6, 133–134

Kotlarski, Henryk, Stanisław Krajewski, and Alistair Lachlan (1981), 'Construction of satisfaction classes for nonstandard models', *Canadian Mathematical Bulletin* 24, 283–293

Kreisel, Georg (1953), 'On a problem of Henkin's', *Indagationes Mathematicae* 15, 405–406

Kripke, Saul (1959), 'A completeness theorem in modal logic', *Journal of Symbolic Logic* 24, 1–14

– (1972), 'Naming and necessity', *in* D. Davidson and G. Harman, eds, *The Semantics of Natural Languages*, Dordrecht, Reidel, pp. 253–355

– (1975), 'Outline of a theory of truth', *Journal of Philosophy* 72, 690–716, Reprinted in Martin 1984

– (1976), 'Is there a problem about substitutional quantification?', *in* G. Evans and J. McDowell, eds, *Truth and Meaning: Essays in Semantics*, Oxford, Clarendon Press, pp. 325–419

– (1979), 'A puzzle about belief', *in* A. Margalit, ed, *Meaning and Use*, Dordrecht, Reidel, pp. 239–83

– (1980), *Naming and Necessity*, Harvard University Press

– (2019), 'Ungroundedness in Tarskian languages', *Journal of Philosophical Logic* 48, 603–609

Kurahashi, Taishi (2020), 'A note on derivability conditions', *The Journal of Symbolic Logic* 85, 1224–1253

– (2021), 'Rosser provability and the second incompleteness theorem', *in* T. Arai, M. Kikuchi, S. Kuroda, M. Okada, and T. Yorioka, eds, *Advances in Mathematical Logic*, Springer Nature, pp. 77–97

Leeds, Stephen (1979), 'Church's translation argument', *Canadian Journal of Philosophy* 9, 43–51

Leigh, Graham E. (2015), 'Conservativity for theories of compositional truth via cut elimination', *Journal of Symbolic Logic* 80, 825–865

Leitgeb, Hannes (2001), 'Theories of truth which have no standard models', *Studia Logica* 21, 69–87

Lewis, Clarence I. and Cooper H. Langford (1932), *Symbolic Logic*, second edition 1959, New York: Dover, London, Century

Lewis, David K. (1968), 'Counterpart theory and quantified modal logic', *Journal of Philosophy* 65, 113–126

– (1986), *On the Plurality of Worlds*, Malden, Massachusetts, Blackwell Publishers

Lewis, David K. and Stephanie Lewis (1970), 'Holes', *Australasian Journal of Philosophy* 48, 206–212

Lewy, Casimir (1947), 'Truth and significance', *Analysis* 8, 24–27

Löb, Martin H. (1955), 'Solution of a problem of Leon Henkin', *Journal of Symbolic Logic* 20, 115–118

Martin, Robert L., ed (1984), *Recent Essays on Truth and the Liar Paradox*, Oxford and New York, Clarendon Press and Oxford University Press

McCarthy, Timothy (1988), 'Ungroundedness in classical languages', *Journal of Philosophical Logic* 17, 61–74

McGee, Vann (1985), 'How truthlike can a predicate be? A negative result', *Journal of Philosophical Logic* 14, 399–410

– (1991), *Truth, Vagueness, and Paradox: An Essay on the Logic of Truth*, Indianapolis and Cambridge, Hackett Publishing

– (1992), 'Maximal consistent sets of instances of Tarski's schema (T)', *Journal of Philosophical Logic* 21, 235–241

McLarty, Colin (2010), 'What does it take to prove Fermat's last theorem? Grothendieck and the logic of number theory', *Bulletin of Symbolic Logic* 16(3), 359–377

Moltmann, Friederike (2003), 'Propositional attitudes without propositions', *Synthese* 135, 77–118

– (2018), 'Truth predicates, truth bearers, and their variants', *Synthese*

Montague, Richard (1963), 'Syntactical treatments of modality, with corollaries on reflexion principles and finite axiomatizability', *Acta Philosophica Fennica* 16, reprinted in Montague 1974, pp. 286–302, 153–67

– (1974), *Formal Philosophy: Selected Papers of Richard Montague*, edited and with an introduction by Richmond H. Thomason, New Haven and London, Yale University Press

Moore, George Edward (1966), 'Selections from a course of lectures given in 1925–26', *in* C. Lewy, ed, *Lectures on Philosophy*, London, George Allen & Unwin, pp. 107–149

Mount, Beau Madison (2019), 'Type-free Ramseyan truth theories: A preliminary report', unpublished draft

Nicolai, Carlo and Johannes Stern, eds (2021), *Modes of Truth: The Unified Approach to Modality, Truth, and Paradox*, New York, Routledge

Paseau, Alexander (2008), 'Fitch's argument and typing knowledge', *Notre Dame Journal of Formal Logic* 49, 153–176

– (2009), 'How to type: reply to Halbach', *Analysis* 69, 280–286

Perlis, Donald (1988), 'Languages with self-reference II: knowledge, belief, and modality', *Artificial Intelligence* 34, 179–212

Picollo, Lavinia (2018), 'Reference in arithmetic', *Review of Symbolic Logic* 11, 573–603

Priest, Graham (1997), 'Yablo's paradox', *Analysis* 57, 236–242

Prior, Arthur (1971), *Objects of Thought*, Oxford, Clarendon Press

Quine, Willard Van Orman (1940), *Mathematical Logic*, New York, Norton, various reprints

– (1943), 'Notes on existence and necessity', *Journal of Philosophy* 40, 113–127

– (1960), *Word and Object*, Cambridge, Massachusetts, MIT Press

– (1964), 'Two dogmas of empiricism', *in From a Logical Point of View*, second edition, Cambridge, Massachusetts, Harvard University Press, pp. 20–46

– (1970), *Philosophy of Logic*, Cambridge, Massachusetts, Harvard University Press

– (1976a), 'Quantifiers and propositional attitudes', *in The Ways of Paradox*, revised and enlarged edition, Cambridge, Massachusetts, Harvard University Press, pp. 185–196

– (1976b), 'The ways of paradox', *in The Ways of Paradox*, revised and enlarged edition, Cambridge, Massachusetts, Harvard University Press, pp. 1–18

Ramsey, Frank Plumpton (1926), 'The foundations of mathematics', *Proceedings of the London Mathematical Society (Series 2)* 5, 338–384

Rosser, John B. (1936), 'Extensions of some theorems of Gödel and Church', *Journal of Symbolic Logic* 1, 87–91

Sackris, David (2016), 'Salmon's translation argument', *Southwest Philosophy Review* 32, 163–182

Salmon, Nathan (2001), 'The very possibility of language: A sermon on the consequences of missing Church', *in* C. A. Anderson and M. Zelëny, eds, *Logic, Meaning, and Computation: Essays in Memory of Alonzo Church*, Kluwer, pp. 573–595

Schindler, Thomas (2015), 'A disquotational theory of truth as strong as Z_2^-', *Journal of Philosophical Logic* 44, 395–410

Shoenfield, Joseph (1967), *Mathematical Logic*, Reading, Massachusetts, Addison-Wesley

Sider, Theodore (2010), *Logic for Philosophy*, Oxford University Press

Smoryński, Craig (1981), 'Fifty years of self-reference in arithmetic', *Notre Dame Journal of Formal Logic* 22, 357–374

– (1985), *Self-Reference and Modal Logic*, Universitext, New York et al., Springer

– (1991), 'The development of self-reference: Löb's theorem', *in* T. Drucker, ed, *Perspectives on the History of Mathematical Logic*, Boston, Birkhäuser, pp. 110–133

Smullyan, Raymond M. (1957), 'Languages in which self reference is possible', *Journal of Symbolic Logic* 22, 55–67

Solovay, Robert M. (1976), 'Provability interpretations of modal logic', *Israel Journal of Mathematics* 25, 287–304

Stern, Johannes (2016), *Toward Predicate Approaches to Modality*, Trends in Logic 44, Cham, Springer

Stern, Johannes and Martin Fischer (2015), 'Paradoxes of interaction?', *Journal of Philosophical Logic* 44, 287–308

Tarski, Alfred (1935), 'Der Wahrheitsbegriff in den formalisierten Sprachen', *Studia Philosophica Commentarii Societatis Philosophicae Polonorum* 1, 261–405, translated as 'The Concept of Truth in Formalized Languages' in Tarski 1956, pp. 152–278; page references are given for the translation

– (1955), 'A lattice-theoretical fixpoint theorem and its applications', *Pacific Journal of Mathematics* 5(2), 285–309

– (1956), *Logic, Semantics, Metamathematics: Papers from 1923 to 1938*, Oxford, Clarendon Press

Thomason, Richmond H. (1980), 'A note on syntactical treatments of modality', *Synthese* 44, 391–396

Troelstra, Anne S. and Dirk van Dalen (1988), *Constructivism in Mathematics: An Introduction,* 2 vols, Studies in Logic and the Foundations of Mathematics 121 and 123, Amsterdam et al., North-Holland

Troelstra, Anne S. and Helmut Schwichtenberg (2000), *Basic Proof Theory*, second edition, Cambridge tracts in theoretical computer science 43, Cambridge University Press

Tye, Michael (1989), *The Metaphysics of Mind*, Cambridge University Press

Verbrugge, Rineke (L.C.) (2017), 'Provability logic', *in* E. N. Zalta, ed, *The Stanford Encyclopedia of Philosophy*, fall 2017 edition, Metaphysics Research Lab, Stanford University

Visser, Albert (1989), 'Semantics and the liar paradox', *in* D. Gabbay and F. Guenthner, eds, *Handbook of Philosophical Logic*, vol. 4, Dordrecht, Reidel, pp. 617–706

– (2009), 'Growing commas: A study of sequentiality and concatenation', *Notre Dame Journal of Formal Logic* 50, 61–85

Wiles, Andrew (1995), 'Modular elliptic curves and Fermat's Last Theorem', *Annals of Mathematics. Second Series* 141(3), 443–551

Yablo, Stephen (1993), 'Paradox without self-reference', *Analysis* 53, 251–252

Index

Printed in the United States
by Baker & Taylor Publisher Services